A PLUME BOOK

THE NATURAL CAT

ANITRA FRAZIER is executive director of Anitra's Natural Cat, a house call service providing holistic health care and grooming to the "furry-purrys" of New York City, as well as worldwide telephone consultations. She also heads Fluff City, New York's feline health spa and hospice. Anitra's clients have included hundreds of brilliant and influential cats, some of whom share their lives with luminaries from the worlds of film, theater, fashion, and classical music. She is the author of *The Natural Cat* and *It's a Cat's Life*. Her current projects include a novel, a short story collection, and *Jailin and Beek Beek,* a children's book. Anitra teaches intermediate yoga at Integral Yoga Institute's uptown center and rides a Raleigh three-speed bike.

NORMA ECKROATE has coauthored numerous books since she and Anitra Frazier teamed up for the first edition of *The Natural Cat.* Her current titles include *The Dog Whisperer* (with Paul Owens), *The Puppy Whisperer* (with Paul Owens and Terence Cranendonk), *Complete Holistic Care and Healing for Horses* (with Mary Brennan, DVM), and *Switched-On Living* (with Jerry Teplitz, PhD). Norma also produced the DVDs *The Dog Whisperer, Vol. 1: Beginning and Intermediate Dog Training* and *The Dog Whisperer, Vol. 2: Solving Common Behavior Problems for Puppies and Dogs.* She loves writing about the benefits of holistic health for both animals and people, as well as the importance of "positive-only" animal training.

NEWLY REVISED AND EXPANDED

The

Natural Cat

THE COMPREHENSIVE GUIDE
TO OPTIMUM CARE

Anitra Frazier
with Norma Eckroate

Foreword by Richard H. Pitcairn, DVM, PhD
Illustrated by Glenna Hartwell

A PLUME BOOK

This book is not a veterinary reference book. The advice it contains is general, not specific, and neither the authors nor the publishers can be held responsible for any adverse reactions to the recipes, formulas, recommendations, or instructions contained herein. Do not try to diagnose or treat a feline health problem without consulting a qualified veterinarian, preferably one with a holistic practice. The recommendations in this book should not be instituted without seeking professional advice for your cat's specific needs.

PLUME
Published by the Penguin Group
Penguin Group (USA) Inc., 375 Hudson Street, New York, New York 10014, U.S.A. • Penguin Group (Canada), 90 Eglinton Avenue East, Suite 700, Toronto, Ontario, Canada M4P 2Y3 (a division of Pearson Penguin Canada Inc.) • Penguin Books Ltd., 80 Strand, London WC2R ORL, England • Penguin Ireland, 25 St. Stephen's Green, Dublin 2, Ireland (a division of Penguin Books Ltd.) • Penguin Group (Australia), 250 Camberwell Road, Camberwell, Victoria 3124, Australia (a division of Pearson Australia Group Pty. Ltd.) • Penguin Books India Pvt. Ltd., 11 Community Centre, Panchsheel Park, New Delhi – 110 017, India • Penguin Group (NZ), 67 Apollo Drive, Rosedale, North Shore 0632, New Zealand (a division of Pearson New Zealand Ltd) • Penguin Books (South Africa) (Pty.) Ltd., 24 Sturdee Avenue, Rosebank, Johannesburg 2196, South Africa

Penguin Books Ltd., Registered Offices: 80 Strand, London WC2R ORL, England

First published by Plume, a member of Penguin Group (USA) Inc.

First Printing, December 2008
10   9   8   7   6   5   4   3

 REGISTERED TRADEMARK—MARCA REGISTRADA

LIBRARY OF CONGRESS CATALOGING-IN-PUBLICATION DATA

Frazier, Anitra, 1936–
    The natural cat : the comprehensive guide to optimum care / by Anitra Frazier and Norma Eckroate.
        p. cm.
    "A Plume Book."
    Includes bibliographical references and index.
    ISBN 978-0-452-28975-8
    1. Cats. 2. Cats—Health. I. Eckroate, Norma. II. Frazier, Anitra, 1936– New natural cat. III. Title.
    SF447.F7 2008
    636.8'0893—dc22   2008028660

Printed in the United States of America
Set in Palatino
Designed by Eve L. Kirch

BOOKS ARE AVAILABLE AT QUANTITY DISCOUNTS WHEN USED TO PROMOTE PRODUCTS OR SERVICES. FOR INFORMATION PLEASE WRITE TO PREMIUM MARKETING DIVISION, PENGUIN GROUP (USA) INC., 375 HUDSON STREET, NEW YORK, NEW YORK 10014.

Dedicated to
the owners who asked
and the cats who taught

ACKNOWLEDGMENTS

Special thanks go to Dr. Richard H. Pitcairn for his encouragement and guidance through the years, his generous contribution of recipes and information, and his astute editing of the veterinary medical material in Chapters 11 and 12.

Our heartfelt thanks for their contributions to this book also go to:

Phyllis Levy, our guiding light

Doctors, healers, and teachers: Dr. Paul Rowan, Dr. Gerald Johnson, Dr. Edwina Ho, and Dr. Amrita McLanahan

Sources of information and inspiration: Integral Yoga Institute and Association for Research and Enlightenment

And the many supporters who cheered us on, especially: Alicia Perez, Matt Sartwell, Sandra Martin, Margaret Blackstone, Andrew Lewis, Sharon and Steve Sherman, Lucy and Dan Kaplan, Olga Aparicio, Lynne and Gus Gustavson, Ursula Jahoda, Swami Gurucharanananda, Phyllis Embleton, Mark MacCauley, and J. David Stites

For this revised edition, there are more individuals and cats to thank than space in this book allows. However, a few people have lent extraordinary support:

Michael Dym, VMD, for his very generous contributions of research material and his technical advice

Alberto Gil, DVM, whose support is invaluable and whose insights are both inspirational and practical

Acknowledgments

Megan Bamford, DVM, for her generous input

Bryan Kortis, CEO and founder of Neighborhood Cats, Inc., for his insightful contributions to the feral cat chapter

Emma Cobb, who gave me hands-on experience with the wild ones

Emigdea Vinces, my helper and friend, who does everything to perfection

Sande Shurin at the Transformational Acting Studio and the actors in the Breakthrough Class for their inspiration

Our wonderful agent, Lisa Hagan, who constantly cheers us on, and our kind and supportive editors at Plume, Cherise Davis Fisher, Jennifer Risser, and Allison Dickens

My patient friends and family who had the understanding to give me the space I needed to complete this revised edition

And, finally, Norma would like to thank Anitra. When we started writing the first edition of this book in 1980, who knew that it would soon be considered a seminal work. I am grateful for the opportunity to assist you in helping so many cats by sharing the holistic nature of life, health, and healing with their humans. As the Universe must have planned all along, coauthoring this book also led to a lifelong second career as others also entrusted me to assist in wordsmithing their lives' work. In the process, my life is immeasurably richer. So blessings to you, dear friend, for entrusting me with this important undertaking. It's been a fun ride!

CONTENTS

Foreword by Richard H. Pitcairn, DVM, PhD xv

Introduction to the Revised Edition 1

Introduction 3

Chapter

1

Desirable Behavior in Cats and Their Guardians 9

9   Communicating with Your Cat
13 Emotions and Well-Being
16 Behavior Patterns and Communication
24 If You're Bitten
26 Dealing with Abused or Neglected Animals
27 The Proper Way to Pick Up a Cat
29 Collars and Identification
31 The Carry Case
34 Communicating "Good-bye" and "I'll Be Back"
37 Introducing a New Cat into the Household
42 Dangers in the Home
48 Game Time and Encouraging Exercise

Chapter

2

Diet 55

56 The Primary Feeding Rule: Remove Food Between
      Meals
59 The No-Nos: Foods to Avoid
66 The High-Quality Diet: Fluff City in Thirty Days

Contents

70 The I'll-Do-Anything-for-My-Cat Diet
76 Supplements
78 Delicious Treats and Crunchies
80 Additional Acceptable Foods
82 How Much to Feed?
82 Changing over to the New Diet
85 Other Beneficial Side Effects of a High-Quality Diet
86 Feeding Kittens
89 Feeding the Aging Cat

Chapter

3

The Litter Box   91

91 The Litter Box Problem
93 The Requirements for a Litter Box
94 What Litter Is Best?
99 An Easy, Convenient, and Effective System
101 Cleaning the Litter Box
102 Keeping Watch over the "Output"
104 Training Kittens to Use the Litter Box
106 Soiling Outside the Box
110 Special Litter Box Considerations for the Older or Ailing Cat

Chapter

4

The Scratching Post and Scratching Problems   111

111 The Scratching Post They Love
114 Where to Put the Scratching Post
114 Encouraging Use of the Scratching Post
115 The Physical and Emotional Effects of Declawing

Chapter

5

The Cat and the Human Family   119

119 The New Baby
121 Young Children
122 Visitors in the Home
123 Allergic to Cats?
126 Taking the Cat Along: Vacations, Visits, and Moving
129 Visiting a New Place
131 While You're Away

Chapter

6

"Neuter and Spay, It's the Kindest Way"   135

135   Undesirable Behavior of the Unneutered Male Cat
136   Undesirable Behavior of the Unspayed Female Cat
137   The Nightmare of Unwanted Kittens
138   The Proper Time to Get Your Cat Neutered or Spayed
141   The Neutering Procedure

Chapter

7

Ferals—The Wild Ones   143

144   The Difference between Strays and Ferals
146   The Feral Colony
147   Trap-Neuter-Return (TNR): The Win-Win Solution

Chapter

8

Grooming   155

156   High-Quality Diet = High-Quality Coat
158   Finding a Groomer
159   Grooming Considerations
162   The Grooming Tools
164   The Grooming Procedure
189   The Bath
197   Grooming for Seasonal and Stress Situations

Chapter

9

Interspecies Communication   205

Chapter

10

Selecting Methods of Treatment and Seeking Professional Help   211

211   Homeopathy
214   Acupuncture and Traditional Chinese Medicine
215   Chiropractic
215   Bach Flower Remedies
216   Herbs
217   Affirmation and Visualization

Contents

219 When Do You Need the Veterinarian?
228 The Therapeutic Environment in the Veterinary Clinic
231 Choosing a Veterinarian
234 Visiting Rights
235 The Second Opinion
236 Holistic Professionals
240 A Holistic Perspective on Conventional Veterinary Treatments
247 Hospitalization
248 Euthanasia

Chapter

11

Home Nursing and Health Care   253

253 The Immune System
255 Stress: A Cat's Natural Enemy
260 Administering Medications
262 Therapeutic Communication
263 Wrapping the Cat for Medication
266 Giving Pills
268 Giving Liquid Medication
268 Giving Paste or Gel Medications (The Pâté Method)
269 Cleaning Around the Eyes
270 Administering Eyedrops and Irrigating Tear Ducts
275 Applying Salve to the Eyes
276 Giving Nose Drops
277 Giving Ear Medication
278 Ear Cleaning and Treatment
282 Soaking Feet and Cleaning Cuticles
286 Fasting
286 Force Feeding/Finger Feeding or Dropper Feeding
290 Taking the Temperature
292 Giving Enemas
296 Compresses
297 Subcutaneous Hydration
304 Recipes, Formulas, and Extras for Home Nursing
309 Using Homeopathic Remedies
313 Using Bach Flower Remedies

314 Using Herbs
324 Shopping List of Home Nursing Items

Chapter

12

A Guide to Common Feline Health Problems   327

328 Allergies
332 Arthritis
336 Blindness
338 Body Odors
340 Cancer
342 Cardiomyopathy
344 Claw and Cuticle Problems
347 Constipation
351 Dandruff
353 Deafness
354 Diabetes
358 Diarrhea
361 Dry Coat
363 Ear Problems
368 Eye Problems
374 Feline Acne
376 Feline Infectious Peritonitis (FIP)
380 Feline Leukemia and Feline AIDS
384 Feline Urologic Syndrome (FUS)
390 Fleas
397 Hair Balls
399 Hyperthyroidism
403 Hypoglycemia
406 Hypothyroidism
408 Injuries
420 Irritable Bowel Syndrome (IBS)
423 Kidney and Bladder Stones
426 Kidney Disease
432 Liver Disease and Liver Damage
435 Mange Mites
438 Matting Fur
441 Nervousness, Hiding, and Ill Temper
444 Obesity

Contents

449 Oily Coat
451 Pancreatitis
454 Parasites
460 Respiratory Infections
462 Ringworm
466 Skin Problems
470 Starvation
474 Stud Tail
477 Teeth and Gums
481 Vomiting
482 Weight Loss

489 **Appendix**
489   **Product Recommendations**
492   **Recommended Books and Periodicals**
492   **Holistic Veterinarians**
495 **Bibliography**
497 **Index**

FOREWORD

This is a very special book. It is written by a woman who was willing to put aside a mass of opinion and ignorance and find out for herself the truth about cats.

What strikes me as her greatest contribution (besides a wealth of practical and useful information) is her approach toward understanding. Rather than letting herself be captivated by ideas and images passed on by many sources, she determined to find out firsthand how to care for cats—by asking the animals themselves.

I am reminded of a conversation that took place some years ago between the author J. Allen Boone and Mojave Dan, a desert hermit who had close communion with animals. As he wrote in his fascinating book *Kinship with All Life,* Boone had been struggling to find out the real truth about the nature of a remarkable dog who was his companion. So he put the issue to his friend Dan. After a long silence, Dan's cogent reply was "There's facts about dogs, and there's opinions about them. The dogs have the facts, and the humans have the opinions. . . . If you want facts about a dog, always get them straight from the dog. If you want opinions, get them from the human."

Much of what Anitra Frazier has learned about cats has come in just such a way, and she has reaped a wealth of information about them. Her book invites you to travel the same road. As you read it, you can see how she evolved the process of watching cats without a screen of preconceptions. This kind of learning does not end.

There is another hidden value in all of this. Many people have learned through relating to animals what it is to care for and accept responsibility for another being. All the basic elements of a relationship are there—the same elements found in a relationship with a friend, husband or wife, child, or even a plant. If one can discover how to relate fully to an animal, without exploitation, with real care and concern for its welfare and continued physical and psychological well-being, then one can relate to anyone. The skills involved are universal.

Many people have found in themselves a compassion they did not know existed by relating to an animal in their life. This potential is meant to be extended to all relationships. Some, however, focus their affections on only one or two animals and, in so doing, become withdrawn into themselves. Later, when the animal dies, as it inevitably will, such people may suffer terrible anguish. I bring this up here because I see it so often. Reading Anitra's book reminded me again of the potential that can be realized through relationships with a cat or any animal. Not stopping at this point—extending that potential to ever wider circles of both people and animals—can allow for a continuous learning that is immensely rewarding.

The Natural Cat is also extremely practical and covers common and mundane problems in a unique way—holistically. That is, the author considers all aspects of the animal's life and environment, both psychological and physical.

I want to emphasize Anitra's sections on declawing and overpopulation. As a veterinarian, I have seen firsthand the incredible suffering of cats who have an amputation of what is to them their fingers. And my work in an SPCA clinic (Society for the Prevention of Cruelty to Animals) brings me face to face daily with the suffering and neglect of unwanted animals. It is a blight on our society that such conditions should exist.

I heartily recommend this book to you. Use it as a learning tool and as a source of practical information. May both you and your animal friends profit!

Richard H. Pitcairn, DVM, PhD

INTRODUCTION TO THE REVISED EDITION

Everything happens for a reason. It has been eighteen years since the last revision of this book. While eighteen years is much too long to wait, it does allow for a crystal clear view of the contrast between the state of holistic animal health then and now.

Some will say the most important changes are the increased availability of homeopathic remedies, Bach flower remedies, herbal tinctures and formulas, and the fast-growing number of veterinarians who now include one or more of the holistic modalities in their practice. All of these things have certainly made life a lot better for us and the animals we love. You, the animal guardians, have helped to make this happen by stepping up to take the reins into your own hands.

Kidney disease patients are living longer and more comfortably because of you. *The Natural Cat* taught you to give fluids subcutaneously at home. Such a thing was almost unheard of at the time. But you—the loving and determined guardians—went to your vets, asked for the fluids, and asked for instruction in the technique. If your vets discouraged you from doing it, you went out and found ones who were helpful and supportive. Now vets all over the country are suggesting this at-home therapy as a matter of course. Cats you will never meet are benefitting from your determination. Congratulations!

Control over what happens to the animals we love has shifted further into the hands of their guardians, where it belongs. Keep learning, keep insisting, and enjoy what you have accomplished. The holistic health movement is thriving, and we who love the animals are more influential than ever before.

INTRODUCTION

C ats?"

"Yes. Holistic health care—for cats."

People find it hard to believe that such a career exists. "However did you get started doing *that*!?" they usually ask.

When I was little I had two alternative goals of what I wanted to do when I grew up. One was to work somehow with animals; the other was to perform on the stage.

I attended Lebanon Valley College, a Pennsylvania Dutch institution that had a top-notch conservatory of music, and I lucked out in finding a great voice teacher. Thanks to him I ended up in show business. I landed my first job with a professional summer stock theater three days after graduation, and my first career was launched. I was never famous, but then I didn't want to be. "Stars don't get to work as often," actress Barbara Barrie pointed out to me.

I enjoyed my career to the hilt, from the exciting Broadway openings to the television commercials and the national tours. It was during this period that two new elements entered my life that were to have profound effects in the not-too-distant future: I became a student at Integral Yoga Institute, and somebody gave me a cat. She was my first, a huge female Siamese named Eurydice. It was she who began my cat education.

I'd probably still be cavorting around on Broadway if I hadn't taken a working vacation with Club Med. I went to teach yoga in Yugoslavia, and there I picked up hepatitis. I nearly died. When I recovered enough strength to work again, I still looked too awful to think of appearing onstage or before a camera. So I started looking for something else.

The job that came my way was working for Dr. Paul Rowan, who was a cat specialist in Greenwich Village at that time. I learned a lot about cats working with Dr. Rowan and his staff, but I learned even more about what people don't know about cats. Dr. Rowan had specialized in cats because cats were "treated like second-class citizens or 'difficult' dogs." Paul Rowan found better ways of doing a lot of things where cats were concerned, and he and his staff were constantly revising and improving their standard operating procedures.

The day they decided to send me out to groom cats in their own homes, my life changed completely. A white hatbox marked "grooming kit" was shoved into my hands along with a ragged piece of tablet paper listing the names and addresses of five cats that needed grooming. I knew next to nothing about grooming cats in their own homes, or anywhere else for that matter, and there was nowhere I could go to learn. "Nobody's ever done it before," they said. "Why don't you just give it a try."

Although I didn't know it at the time, when I accepted that white hatbox one door clicked shut behind me and another opened and I stepped through. Suddenly the actress who put on costumes and makeup and sang and danced onstage seemed only like an acquaintance I had once known. It was as if I had been reincarnated into a new life without dying in between.

When I was "thrown to the cats," so to speak, the cats caught me. They taught me everything I needed to know from then on. I *had* to learn from the cats—there was no one else to teach me. I was the slowest student in all creation at first as I learned anatomy, skin tensions, fur texture, and scissor angles. The pussycats persevered with me, and I also learned patience and concentration. I watched the cats, I felt the cats, I listened to the cats, and I loved the cats. The love between us opened the doors of communication, and the cats gave me lessons in all the things a cat thinks are most important. Cat lessons are there for everybody; you only have to love and ask—ask not what you want to know but what it is that they would like you to know. My first cat lessons were on how to groom them and how to keep every part of their external bodies just the way they most like them to be.

Because I visited them in their home environment, I was soon made aware of problems and unanswered questions that caregivers all over New York City had in common—about random wetting, how to train to the scratching post, persistent health problems, and special home nursing care—things that were outside the realm of grooming.

Of course, my first move was to refer all problems to the veterinarians, assuming that they would have the answers. In this I found I was mistaken. Many of these problems were not in their field. In fact, before long I had a whole collection of problems that did not seem to be in anybody's field. So I looked for the answers. I asked. I read. But in the end it was the cats themselves that came through for me once again. "Stick as close as you can to nature," Dr. Rowan used to say, "and you'll never go very far wrong." So I researched how cats handle some of these problems in the wild. What is the purpose of their behavior? As possible answers began to emerge they all seemed to fall under that old heading, "Nobody's ever done it that way before; why don't you just try it?"

Many answers came from the sick cats and the castoffs—cats so old or sick, so smelly or ugly, that no one wanted them. When I invited them to spend whatever time they had left with me, I never dreamed that they would pay for their keep in the solid gold coin of knowledge gained. You don't learn much from a cat that is young and strong, healthy and well-adjusted. These castoff cats taught me with their bodies, their patience, and their love. Home care of the sick cat I learned from sick cats. My recommendations concerning proper diet and feeding habits are largely a distillation of what is found in nature. I didn't create any of this information. I only asked the questions, and, by the grace of the cat goddess, the answers came.

By the time I met Norma Eckroate and her big red Maine coon cat, Clarence, I had seven years of experience behind me. I could handle just about any cat, keep him calm, and convince him to let me do whatever was needed.

Norma, like so many of us, had been doing everything she was told to do for the cat she loved, but still his health was sliding downhill and she was in fear of losing him. "One more attack of feline urologic syndrome," the veterinarian had said, "and we'll have to do a urethrostomy or put him to sleep." Norma and Clarence were at their wits' end.

I took one look at greasy, sick, matted, flea-ridden Clarence and I totally flipped out. I became so upset that I lost what little tact I had ever possessed. I cut the commercial flea collar off his neck and flung it into the wastebasket. All through the grooming and bath I lectured poor Norma on the horrors and futility of most commercial flea products. Then I went on and on about the food she was feeding Clarence and how it could contribute to his disease. Clarence's brush was *wrong*; his diet was *wrong*; the litter box was *wrong*—I didn't have one good word to say to that poor, distraught, concerned lady.

Norma did not become discouraged; she did not become angry—far from it, she seemed immensely relieved and buoyed by the new information, which she believed would turn the tide in Clarence's favor. "Everything you're saying makes perfect sense," she exclaimed. "You really must write it all down in a book!"

By that time Clarence was looking and feeling much more comfortable and I was calmer. So I just laughed. "I can't type," I replied, "and I can't spell, and I'm not organized."

"Oh, I can do all that," she said, smiling. "I'll help you." And so she did.

While we were writing the book we were warned by levelheaded friends that such a work would probably never be published. We would be sued, they said, for suggesting that grocery store cat foods were far from perfect. As for encouraging people to start telling their veterinarians how to reduce stress while their cats were hospitalized, well, it just wasn't done! Sympathetic friends described the book as being "too far in the vanguard and ahead of its time." Others, less sympathetic, declared us to be out on the lunatic fringe.

Nevertheless, I did have a lot of new information, and I did feel responsible for its perpetuation. All those new facts and techniques could not be left in one person's head. After all, what if something were to happen to me? Bop! Information disappears!

There turned out to be an awful lot of people out there whose main concern was "What is the best for my cat?" Our little *Natural Cat* didn't land us in jail after all.

The Natural Cat is no longer "far in the vanguard" or "out on the lunatic fringe." Instead, we find ourselves smack-dab in the middle of the establishment and that won't do at all. An updated and vastly expanded edition was clearly called for. After all, much progress had been made in the world of natural and holistic health care.

You, the caregivers, haven't stopped asking questions. Far from it; *The Natural Cat* opened your minds to new possibilities and seemed to generate as many questions as it gave answers. Now more and more people want to know about visualization, Bach flower remedies, interspecies communication, and all manner of new and expanded home nursing techniques that can bolster the health of those wonderful cats who cherish us.

The cats have continued to teach me. They have entrusted me with their bodies and honored me by opening their minds, and they have made of themselves a bridge to link me with other humans who have shared with me their knowledge and their own wonderful questions.

So, you see, this book isn't really by me. The information is coming through me but not from me. Knowledge is like the air; it's there for you to use and pass along but not to possess.

New knowledge seems to evolve out of the old. It is my hope that the knowledge contained in this book will generate further new knowledge in the mind of each reader. After all, each cat is unique, just as each one of us is unique. I know that with this in mind you will not make the mistake of thinking of anything in this book as "the last word." There is always the possibility of finding an even better way. Perhaps it will be your cat, giving cat lessons to you, who will reveal this even better way. All you have to do is keep your mind open, and love, and ask.

Desirable Behavior in Cats and Their Guardians 1

ommunication and understanding are the two most important links between cats and their human companions. It is obvious to sensitive and caring people that their cats are aware when they are unhappy or under the weather. Likewise, the cats respond with joy when their guardians are happy.

By understanding the cat's psyche, you are better able to open the pathways to a rewarding and fulfilling relationship—for you and for your feline friend. All you have to do is look at any situation from your cat's point of view.

Communicating with Your Cat

The golden rule for a cat's guardian is "Don't limit yourself." In your relationship with any cat, you will discover new dimensions of sensitivity. A cat's senses of hearing and smell are literally hundreds of times more acute than ours. When new guardians discover petting, they first learn the pleasures of medium and firm stroking. This then evolves naturally into a luxurious massage of the back of the neck, the sides of the spine, or the muscles of the thighs, depending upon the preferences of the cat you're with. All you need is a desire to learn. Cats are excellent teachers.

There is also another dimension of stroking in which you deliberately hold yourself back. Because cats are much more sensitive than we are, both physically and emotionally, they are fascinated by the very light touch. Actually, if you want to experiment, you can try what I call the "feather" touch and the "almost" touch. For the "feather" touch your hand touches only the very tips of the hair throughout the entire stroking motion. Your cat will probably respond by arching his back up against your hand and purring encouragement for you to proceed on to a medium and then firm stroke.

To describe the "almost" touch, which is the most tantalizing of all, I'll share with you a charming scene I witnessed during a retreat at the Integral Yoga Ashram in Virginia. One afternoon, while walking down a woodland path, I came upon one of the swamis surrounded by a little group of kindergarten children. She had apparently been conducting a nature walk when I happened upon them. One little fellow was crouched down on all fours in the middle of the path, nose to nose with a big monarch butterfly. Of course, the child reached out to touch the beautiful creature, and as he did, the swami said softly, "Just pet his aura, Michael, that's the way to pet a butterfly."

"Just pet the aura" is a good description of the "almost" touch. All during the stroke keep your hand from ½ to 1 inch away from the cat's fur, and you may be very surprised at the response.

Both of these techniques are especially good for cats who are frightened, ill, or arthritic. They also work magic on cats who have been abused in the past or are half wild or feral. It demonstrates that you are gentle and harmless and that your territory is a safe place. Speak in a low murmur while you stroke.

The very best lesson in the soft approach can be learned from your cat. First, put your hands behind your back and, bending over, reach out to your cat with just your nose. Then stop about six inches away, be still, and wait—and your cat will reach forward and demonstrate to you how very softly it is possible to touch somebody. This approach to a cat—this overture with the nose—demonstrates great trust and friendliness, because you are exposing your eyes and face without having any defense in reserve. It conveys the message "I love you and trust you" very nicely. I use it often when greeting a cat client with whom I am already acquainted. However, I never use this approach on a strange cat until I have first ascertained that she is fairly calm—although this action does serve to calm some nervous cats. Nor would I use the nose overture with ferals because, to a wild cat, a stare is a prelude to an attack.

Another dimension in interacting with your cat is throwing a "cat kiss" from across the room. A cat kiss is a long, slow blink with your gaze and attention fixed on the cat's eyes before, during, and after the blink. When throwing a cat kiss, I always think the phrase "I love you" ("I" before, "love" during, and "you" after the blink).

Cats don't communicate only with sound—in fact, they seldom communicate that way. I notice that cats use the slow eye blink communication when they are feeling relaxed, contented, and secure. I started practicing every time I could get a cat's eye attention and found that I received a return blink from the cat by the second try. Delighted with my break in the language barrier, I began throwing these cat kisses to any and all cats with whom I came in eye contact.

If you'd like to perfect the technique, you need to be aware that you are really doing two things at the same time: the physical focus and blink plus the mental message, "I love you." Practice them separately; then put them together. Think the "I love you" with emotional warmth, but do not get so enthusiastic that you screw up your face or squeeze your eyes shut. That only clouds the issue. The blink is slow and gentle; the mental message is warm and strong.

The supreme test came for me when I began throwing cat kisses to strange felines on the other side of closed windows as I walked down the street. After my technique was perfected, I was thrilled to discover that these strangers would automatically throw back a leisurely reply. They seemed to take it in stride that a human walking by would casually throw them a kiss. Only twice have I had the experience of a cat doing a sort of double take afterward. Looking rather surprised, they seemed to be thinking, "Hey, she speaks Cat!"

Keep in mind that, because cats are so much more sensitive than we are, they will always enjoy the kiss or loving word thrown from afar. Also remember that cats, being so small, feel very much at our mercy. A cat's hiss is not aggressive; it is a defensive act to try to make the large and threatening human back off just enough so the cat can slip away unharmed. A hissing cat is a frightened cat. Whenever you deal with a cat who is nervous, frightened, or just standoffish, you must become totally permissive. If the cat doesn't want to be touched, don't touch; if he wants to leave, let him go. You must take great pains to be polite—polite in the cat sense. In this way, you will leave the door open for your relationship to progress at a later date.

A really top-notch-caregiver will always be polite with any cat, as a matter of course. Never walk up to a cat and scoop him or her up without first announcing your presence and your intent and asking permission. If you have more than one cat, you can see a demonstration of this sort of politeness by watching a performance of the cats' "I want to sit next to you" ritual. The ritual usually goes like this: Marbles is sleeping on a chair, and Roger jumps up next to her. Roger begins licking the sleeping Marbles, thereby announcing his presence and begging leave to stay. Marbles either (1) returns the grooming with a casual lick or two, indicating acceptance; (2) ignores Roger, indicating basic neutrality with "You better not disturb me" undertones; or (3) she lifts her head and growls a rejection, indicating that Roger had better jump down. A cat never just plops down next to another cat. Those tentative licks are their equivalent for saying, "May I?" Impolite cats are simply not acceptable to other cats. Cats are willing to make all sorts of allowances for the humans they love, but isn't it much nicer to slip gracefully into their society by being polite on their terms?

Because cats seldom express themselves with sound (except for the Siamese), people sometimes think that they are uncommunicative. In reality, cats have a vast and rich vocabulary of body postures, poses, mental pictures, emotions, and actions with which they communicate among themselves—or with anyone else who knows the language.

The carriage of the tail is often a clue to how your cat is feeling. A tail held high is jaunty, enthusiastic, or playful. A tail between the legs or wrapped very tightly around the ankles indicates fear. A tail carried in a low graceful arc is casual as is a tail loosely wrapped around a reclining cat. A cat uses his tail for balance when he leaps. He can also use it to control nervousness and excitement by swinging or lashing the tail as an outlet for tension or to drain off excess energy.

The human mind is better equipped than the cat's for learning other languages. Therefore, it makes more sense for us to make the effort to learn and practice cat communication and etiquette than to expect a cat to act like a person.

However, when a close and loving relationship exists between a cat and a human, do not be surprised if, under certain circumstances, the cat begins to express himself in a very human way. Meowing or calling to get your attention is probably the most common example. Cats seldom communicate vocally with each other except when mating, fighting, or rounding up kittens. Modern science has now verified mental communication between cats. But your cat may have noticed that we humans gain each other's attention by making noise (how crude!) and so he decides to give it a try. Lo and behold, it works—so your cat has trained you to come when called.

The cat performs many of our hand skills with his mouth, such as picking up and carrying things and showing affection. Instead of petting, licking and grooming are used to demonstrate affection. However, many years ago when I used to hold my first cat, Eurydice, in my arms, she would reach up and tap my cheek or chin several times with her paw. I cannot think of any other explanation except that, out of her deep love for me, she was trying to express affection in a way that I would understand. She was copying my way of showing love. Eurydice was my first cat, and at that time, I assumed that her behavior was altogether unique. She was my darling, and I was quite convinced that I was living with the most intelligent, most loving, and most wonderful cat in the world. Be that as it may, I have, over the years, seen this same loving communication displayed between many cats and their guardians. I'm sure anyone who has enjoyed close relationships with cats could say the same. Mind you, I'm not saying that my Eurydice was not the most wonderful cat in the world; but I am admitting that in this one thing she was not unique.

Years later, Priscilla, my tiny blue point Siamese, would express affection to those with whom she was intimate by giving "hugs" with her teeth. I would always pick Priscilla up in my arms and hug her as soon as I arrived home. Priscilla knew that what humans do with the hands, cats do with the mouth, so she would reach up and take my chin between her teeth and "hug" it. I have since met several affectionate felines who express their love in this way "hugging" their human's arm or hand or ear. The cat's teeth close firmly but gently, denting but never breaking the skin. It is really an enormous compliment to that person and shows a great depth of understanding between cat and human, for—without that deep and loving rapport—a human might react with surprise, and if one should pull away quickly, one could scratch oneself on the cat's eyeteeth. Sometimes, when I stayed out too long, Priscilla would be so overcome with happiness and relief that I was safely back that she would "hug" a bit too hard. I never told her for fear she might misconstrue my protest and stop altogether, thinking that all "hugging with mouth" was unpleasant to me.

Please consult the new chapter on interspecies communication for more information and suggestions for communicating better with your cat (see page 205).

Emotions and Well-Being

It's often said that dogs resemble their humans in one way or another. I've observed that cats too can resemble their humans in temperament and emotional tendencies.

Recent studies have shown that cats "pick up" their guardian's thoughts just as they have always picked up the thoughts of their cat friends. You may walk into the kitchen twenty times a day, but the cat seems to know when it's her meal you're thinking about preparing, and then she comes running, even if you don't stick to a regular time schedule every day. It's also possible that they pick up mental images. For example, your thought of feeding Muffy is tied to an image in your own mind of getting a can of food out of the cupboard and opening it, and your cat "sees" that image.

In the same way, cats react to their guardians' attitudes, emotions, and physical condition. Deborah, a client of mine whose invalid mother lived in another state, noticed that time after time she would return from a family visit after her mother had taken a turn for the worse to find her cat, Dizzy, in the beginning stages of feline urologic syndrome (FUS), a stress-triggered disease. Knowing that FUS can be fatal if not caught in the very early stages, she was very concerned. After this occurred several times, she also noticed that the cat was always healthy when she returned from routine business trips. Dizzy was used to being left alone since Deborah frequently made business trips, and in every case, the same kindly neighbor was coming in to feed Dizzy the same high-quality food with the same special vitamins and supplements for FUS-prone cats.

I suspected that Dizzy was picking up Deborah's own emotional distress at her mother's condition and that Dizzy's sympathetic stress was creating a chemical imbalance within his body, making him more susceptible to the disease. FUS is usually triggered by negative emotions.

So we tried a little experiment. First, whenever she went away, Deborah would leave a cardboard carton on the floor for Dizzy to lounge about and play in. She lined the bottom with pajamas she had worn so that Dizzy would have the comfort of her scent while she was gone, thus providing both a new distraction and more security. Since Dizzy seemed to be picking up Deborah's thoughts and emotions anyway, I asked her to try consciously sending him some thoughts—thoughts about sensual pleasures or loving emotions that would make him feel the way she wanted him to feel: calm and happy.

It has been scientifically proven that thoughts can be transferred in picture form. "Sending love" is wonderful but only part of the picture. So two or three times a day Deborah would sit quietly and picture Dizzy lounging happily in his cardboard box just the way she hoped he would. She would also remind herself (and Dizzy) how pleasant and clean a cardboard box can smell, how quiet the world is when sounds are muffled by the walls of the box, and how soft and comforting the pajamas in the bottom were. She pictured herself sitting close by the box and feeling happy as she looked at Dizzy and loved him.

It worked. The FUS attacks stopped, and Dizzy greeted her with the same joyous excitement no matter where she was returning from. And there was an extra bonus as well. Those three-minute mental visits with Dizzy seemed to calm Deborah's mind as well. They were like little minivacations in the midst of a difficult situation. She found she could handle the problems better and return home less fatigued.

Sometimes when we're going through a stressful time, we may actually be more stressed or sad than we realize. We try to hide our stress because we think there's nothing we can do about it anyway and we don't want to upset the cat we love. *Don't try to hide your stress from your cat.* It's impossible anyway. Cats are different from us in many ways; this is one of them. They pick up our emotions as if we were broadcasting them. In fact, to a cat, we *are* broadcasting them. They have no idea that we are not picking up theirs as easily as they pick up ours. Humans interested in improving that score a bit can do so with study and practice.

Cats *always* know when something's wrong. If you don't share your emotions with them honestly, they'll assume that either (1) it's their fault or (2) you're both about to be attacked by predators. Cats' minds are very simple and direct: "Anxiety means danger."

Fate has brought the two of you together for a reason. Cats and humans do many different kinds of things for each other. One thing all cats do is help their human companions in times of stress. They work both physically and emotionally. Some cats focus mainly on one aspect or the other; some do both.

The most sensible approach is to openly admit to your feline partner exactly how you feel about what is troubling you. Then immediately follow up by expressing how glad you are that your cat is there to help you through the rough patches. Tell him how much it means to you that he is there to greet you when you come in the door. Tell him how it makes you feel when he purrs you to sleep at night or purrs you awake in the morning. "I'm so glad I have you" would sum it up nicely.

Pretty Linda, a slim gray tabby, spends most of her time on top of the high chest near the kitchen. When I arrive home, she greets me in her unique way by opening her eyes and turning her face toward me. One day it dawned on me that she had absolutely no idea that I was not picking up her gladness as easily as she was picking up mine. She knew that her greeting was positively exuberant, more than equal to the more obvious demonstrations of Princess, Kathy, and Cosmo, who danced, purred, and rubbed their joyful greeting.

I realized that our Linda didn't just turn her head. Humans turn their head. Linda was turning her eyes and ears and nose. She saw me, she heard my steps, my voice, my very breath. I saw her lovely white whiskers quivering beside her nostrils, and it became apparent that she was drinking in my aroma: the bike tires, my outdoor clothes, all the scents from all the cats I had visited that day, my skin, my breath, and surely my mental state. She never knew that I didn't understand this at first—that I was not as attuned as her and the rest of the cats. To her it was simply a normal part of greeting somebody.

Cats will comfort you and surround you with love in their own manner whether you're aware of it or not. Their methods go far beyond the merely physical, but they do treasure our conscious acknowledgment of their effort.

Behavior Patterns and Communication

One of the cat's greatest fears is fear of the unknown. Conversely, familiarity breeds contentment. Cats love familiar smells, patterns, places, and sounds. The very fact that a thing is well-known and familiar makes it dear to the heart of a cat. We can use this love of sameness as a tool to direct the cat's behavior patterns. If we make certain ground familiar, that is the path the cat will want to take. And to engineer a situation so that the cat wants to do what we want him to do is really the only way to control a cat's behavior patterns.

You can't train a cat the way you would train a dog or a child. A dog positively enjoys learning to do anything that will please you. And if you're training children you can explain reasons and advantages for behavior patterns you wish them to adopt.

There is, however, one golden rule in all three cases. In training a cat, a dog, or a young child, it is most important that you be consistent. If there is something that you don't want the cat to do, such as jumping on a table when there is food on it, then don't *ever* invite the cat up onto the table. *Never*. Not for any reason; not even if there is no food there. If you see the cat on the table, shove him or her unceremoniously off with a word of disappointment. You must keep it simple—not confusing.

It is difficult to train a cat not to jump up on the table or riffle through the wastebasket, because these are negative lessons. It is much easier to train the cat *to* do something. For example, if you want a cat *not* to scratch the couch and *to* scratch the scratching post, just forget about the couch, which is the "no-no," and concentrate on building fascinating rituals around the scratching post, which is the "yes-yes." (See the section in Chapter 4, "Encouraging Use of the Scratching Post.")

Velvet Paws for Human Flesh; Claws for Toys and Scratching Post

The need for consistency also applies when you're teaching a cat not to use teeth or claws on human flesh or clothing. Don't ever let anyone play with the cat using their hands or flesh or any part of their own bodies. That means *never*. The cat cannot make the distinction between being allowed to roughhouse with the man of the house and not being allowed to play rough with Great-Aunt Ethel when she extends a delicately veined hand to stroke behind the ear. And heaven forbid you should have young children come to visit who want to hug and pet a pussycat who has been taught that the use of teeth and claws on human flesh is okay.

My Big Purr was almost a year old when he was left at my door. He was a big Lynx point Siamese mix, a bit tense but very playful and soooo beautiful. He had evidently been encouraged to play roughly by someone in his past. About a week after he arrived, we were lying on the floor together and I was stroking him. He was all purrs and stretches. His purrs got louder and louder. Then suddenly, without warning, his body contracted, he trapped my arm in his front claws, pulled my hand into his teeth, and pressed his hind claws into the soft flesh of my inner arm, preparing to rake the claws down my skin. I froze, afraid to move.

I didn't know what to do. Purr was not angry with me; he was just so overcome by happiness and love that his emotions overflowed and expressed themselves in this very wild and primitive way. Many cats bite softly to express affection. But Purr's former guardian must have made the mistake of playing roughly with him, using hands instead of a toy. This naturally taught Purr that using claws and teeth on skin was okay.

Play Biting and Scratching

To a cat, biting, scratching, and raking with the back claws are not only perfectly normal but a very necessary part of learning to be a cat. They are a major reason why cats have survived over the millennia. It is natural for all kittens to begin practicing these skills when they are about two-and-a-half or three weeks old.

To a cat, all forms of play are a means of strengthening and improving survival traits, and all games fall into one of two categories: (1) "catch and kill" games that prepare them to feed themselves and survive and (2) "fight and win" games that prepare them to defend themselves and survive. At about three weeks of age, a litter of kittens begins play biting and scratching with each other and with their mother. (Watch how she flicks her tail to tempt them.) By the time they are eight or ten weeks old, all should have learned how to play safely without really hurting each other. This makes perfect sense when you realize that healthy well-adjusted adult cats continue to enjoy these games all their lives. It would run counter to the law of preservation of the species if the prohibition against doing harm during play were not built in by nature during those early weeks with the mother.

If a kitten plays too roughly, the mother will discipline the kitten by holding him down with a paw and growling. If he again becomes too rough, she may take his scruff in her mouth and hold his head and shoulder down while holding his body down with a paw. Do not attempt to duplicate the mother cat's response to rough play by lifting a cat up by the scruff. The hindquarters are too heavy and it puts too much strain on the neck.

If, later on, a guardian uses his hands and fingers to play roughly with the kitten or cat, he teaches the cat that it is okay to play rough with teeth and claws— the exact opposite of what his mother was so careful to instill in him. Moreover, the cat will learn that it's okay to do this on human skin. This mistake is usually made by a younger kitten who can't yet do much harm. But as the cat grows up, what was amusing in a kitten becomes downright dangerous in a larger animal.

Few people know how to break this pattern once they have inadvertently established it. Some begin by hitting the cat, which only reinforces the feeling of roughness and brutality. Some even go so far as to mutilate their cat with a declawing operation. In this case, the cat usually becomes a biter. In both cases, the situation becomes progressively worse instead of better. The cat adores the guardian and reaches out for physical closeness and play in the very way the guardian has taught him as a kitten. The cat and the guardian both end up sad and lonely. They miss the closeness and fun but don't know how to get it back without the guardian getting scratched and the cat getting yelled at.

Of course, the easiest way out is never to start the pattern in the first place.

Never play with a cat or kitten with your bare hands. Use a toy, a sash, or ball—never your hand (and, incidentally, never use a grooming tool as a toy). In short, if you don't want the cat to scratch something, don't even begin to suggest it. Never let the cat start in the first place.

Use your hands for stroking, petting, grooming, transporting, sometimes medicating, but never for play. To cats, play means teeth and claws—catch and kill. If they are not scratching, pouncing, and biting, it's not really play; it's love and cuddle. Show them from the start that hands and skin are for love and cuddle; toys are for play.

If you are dealing with a kitten who gets carried away and carelessly uses claws on the skin, just stop dead and relax *toward* him and disengage the claws, unhooking them by pushing the paw *forward,* never pull away. Then immediately put the offending kitten gently but firmly away from you with words of deep disappointment. Do not become excited in any way or raise your voice; you want to put a big damper on all exuberance or emotion. Then ignore the kitten for at least three minutes—don't even allow eye contact. Thus you are demonstrating that claws on skin are socially unacceptable—and cats are very social animals. Do the same thing in exactly the same way every time the kitten uses claws on skin. A kitten learns faster if your reaction does not vary. Another variation would be to place the offender in a room alone for a little while ("time out"). This works well as long as you are sure to leave a couple of toys in the room so you are stopping the undesirable pattern and giving an acceptable outlet for his energy at the same time. Include a stuffed toy of about his own size for him to wrestle with.

If the pattern continues you can imitate the mother's reaction. After you disengage the claws, grasp the scruff in one hand and gently but firmly hold his head and shoulders down on the floor. Your other hand can control the haunches. Hold for thirty seconds. This is "time out" big time.

At the same time that you are reshaping your cat's behavior patterns, be sure to offer plenty of fascinating alternatives to help drain off the energy. Play catch and kill games two or three times a day using a ball, a toy mouse, or a sash. Get creative, and use your imagination to devise ways to refocus his energy. (See "Game Time and Encouraging Exercise" on page 48 for suggestions.)

Fear Biting

Fear biting is defensive. It is sometimes but not always preceded by a hiss of warning. It happens when a cat wants to get away but can't. She may want to get away from being held or some other physical restraint, or from a threat, a pain, a noise or smell that is so strong it's painful, or a scary unknown. (To most cats, anything new or unknown is scary.) In such circumstances, a cat needs to feel free to run away at any time. We humans can anticipate many of these situations, and if they can't be avoided, we can do our best to introduce them in a gentle, non-threatening manner and cushion the stress. (See "Stress: A Cat's Natural Enemy," on page 255.) We are usually forewarned and take care to protect ourselves from harm.

The most challenging fear biting situation arises from what is often called "overstimulation biting." Before I heard the term, I called it "hypersensitivity to stimuli" because part of the cause of overstimulation biting is, of course, the fact that cats are so much more sensitive than we are. But equally important is the cat's tolerance level—his sensitivity threshold. It works the same as an individual's pain threshold. If you stimulate the cat beyond what he can tolerate (his threshold), you cause a sort of short-circuit in his mind. His conscious control clicks off and automatic instinct takes over. It doesn't matter whether the stimulus is pain or pleasure, all that matters is that it is too much—more than he can handle. If you pet some cats too long, the pleasure may build up past his sensitivity threshold; then instinct takes over and "stop it, stop it, stop it!" becomes his whole world. One minute he is lying in your lap purring, the next he is viciously attacking your hand. This is often called the Jekyll and Hyde reaction.

What is overstimulation to one cat may be very pleasant to another. My blue Persian, Princess, likes nothing better than to lie in my arms, belly up, while I stroke her inner thighs. She relaxes into a semicomatose heap of warm fur, eyes squinting in pleasure, purr buzzing softly, while I call her my furry bundle and hug the tip of her right ear with my lips. But Princess is a most unusual cat. She is a master of relaxation and tranquility. With most cats, even a cat with an average threshold of tolerance, stroking the belly even once or twice is a sure way to experience a firsthand demonstration of overstimulation biting. Be very careful if you try it.

Big Purr, my very first Cat-in-Chief, was a perfect example of Jekyll and Hyde biting. When he and I were lying on the floor, and he suddenly trapped my hand in his teeth, I was at a loss. At this early stage of my career, I had never even heard of Jekyll and Hyde biting.

Fortunately, the instinct that made me freeze was correct. Purr froze too. My wrist was still held by his front claws, my hand clamped in his teeth. Those miniature scimitars in the back were still denting my arm, ready to rake it open. But it was as if time had stopped and several things had begun to happen in that one moment. I had no past experience to help me; no bit of forgotten lore came bubbling up to the surface out of all the book learning stored in the depths of my memory.

I like to think that the compassionate Cat Goddess, She who had seen fit to put Purr and me together in the first place, saw that we two had stumbled into dangerous territory. Perhaps it was She who nudged my instincts in the right direction. Suddenly fear dissolved and all I could feel was my love for Purr and my heart breaking because he was hurting me. I started to cry (a clear, honest, nonthreatening emotion), and as I said his name, I leaned in closer toward the teeth and into the claws of the cat I loved. Purr unhooked himself instantly! The look on his face was one of total confusion.

Purr provided many learning experiences over the years. Most were filled with laughter and fun, but some, like this one, were complex. I'm not sure to this day if I've extracted all I was supposed to learn from that experience. The first thing I realized almost immediately afterward was that *prey pulls away. Always!* When I leaned in *against* his teeth and claws, I broke the expected chain of events. I confused his instinct and he couldn't go on. His mind clicked back to conscious thinking mode, and there I was crying and broadcasting love with my mind at the same time. Now he was the one who didn't know what to do, but I did!

When in doubt, use distraction. Cats live very much in the present. I wanted Purr to forget the bad reaction and enjoy a good one. Easy! I grabbed his crocheted mouse by the tail and dangled it past his nose. Purr shook himself and poised for the "Mouse Game." He loved the Mouse Game! I threw the mouse in a high arc. Purr launched himself into the air, batted the mouse into the kitchen, chased it down, and captured it. That mouse never had a chance.

As I continued to study the biting phenomenon, I learned that there are warning signals that anyone can see if they know what to look for. Like any behavior, biting or scratching is the last link in a chain of events, and what you need to do is distract the cat while he's still several links away from that final link. Before Purr reached his threshold of stimulation, he would swivel his ears out to the side, and pull them closer to his head. His pupils would dilate and his tail would begin to whip tensely from side to side. If I saw these signs, then I knew to stop petting him and casually direct his attention to something else. I would gently knock a cushion onto the floor or playfully toss a toy or even a magazine to the other side of the room.

I tell my clients with similar problems to carry small toys around with them in case the need arises. As soon as you toss it, change your thoughts to something like, "Was that a pigeon I heard at the window?" or perhaps, "I'm hungry; are you hungry? Let's go to the kitchen and find a crunchy."

Anger Biting

Anger biting is the least likely cause of a bite or scratch. I am not talking about those times when a cat gets mad at us and bops (as opposed to rakes) with his claws out or grabs with his teeth and even breaks the outer layer of skin. These acts are under the cat's conscious control. Cats don't speak English; they speak cat, and hitting with claws out yet not hurting is a *strong statement*! It has happened to me many times over the years. I take it as a great compliment when I'm dematting a cat and the cat is totally in my power and cannot escape but still trusts me enough to make a *strong statement*. He's saying, "Stop, Anitra!"

I always do as they say. How else can one learn from a cat? I tell him he's absolutely right, and I go and work on a different area of his body or I comb his neck just to make him feel good. Because he has honored me with a clear communication, I now understand that, to finish removing the mats from the problem area, I must first give it a rest, then (1) come at it from a different angle, and (2) work on it in much shorter segments of time.

True anger biting is deadly serious. As in Jekyll and Hyde biting, the cat's mind clicks into instinctual mode. However, instead of fear-escape, here the engulfing drive is rage-kill (or eliminate). In anger biting, there is an underlying willingness to die in the attempt to kill. There is no mistaking this when a wild intact male screams a challenge at an interloper or a mother cat protecting her kittens routs a starving coyote. In both of these cases, that pervasive, raw message—"I will kill or die trying"—is clearly broadcast to every animal in the vicinity. Defending against predators or defending possession of food can also cause anger biting.

Since there are very few unspayed females or intact males in most households, and since there is usually adequate food and shelter for the cats, anger biting is rare. The only possible provocation left might be jealousy over a guardian or territory.

Preventing Biting

- Leave kittens with their mother for ten weeks; eight weeks at a minimum.
- Provide a cat companion if possible.
- Never play with a cat or kitten with your hands. Throw a toy or pull a sash. Keep your hands at least two feet away from a playing cat.
- Keep claws nicely blunted. (See "Clipping the Claws," page 176.)
- Carry small toys and balls with you and throw them across the floor to distract the cat if you see flattening ears or a slashing tail.
- Provide loose toys, interactive toys, and mechanical toys. (See "Game Time and Encouraging Exercise" page 48.)
- Provide one large stuffed toy about the cat's size or slightly smaller for wrestling.
- Provide a scratching post.
- Eliminate all foods containing colorings, preservatives, salt, or sugar. These ingredients can abrade the nerve endings, causing tension and lowering the cat's tolerance threshold.
- A cat is more likely to bite when he is tense—and more likely to be relaxed after a meal—so do grooming or introduce a new friend an hour or so after mealtime.
- Never allow declawing. Besides damaging physical and mental health, declawing turns scratchers into biters.
- Vaccines, especially the rabies vaccine, can cause a cat to become hypersensitive to stimuli. Don't allow any vaccine not required by law. A classical homeopath can help rid the body of the effects of past vaccines.
- If biting and/or scratching and/or tension persists, let your vet examine the cat and take blood tests, including the special test for hyperthyroidism. Illness can be a root cause for many problems.
- Use Bach flower remedies (see directions for use on page 313):

  Elm—promotes optimism
  Larch—promotes confidence
  Mimulus—calms fear of known threats (noise; riding in car)
  Aspen—calms vague fears and general anxiety

If You're Bitten

A really serious bite is usually an anger bite or, rarely, a fear bite. For whatever reason, the cat's mind clicks into instinctive mode and leaves rational thinking behind. Sometimes the cat bites and holds on with his claws and won't let go. Bites are very painful. If you are bitten, you may want to scream and hit the cat—anything to make him let go. That will be *your* instinct kicking in, and unfortunately, such actions will only build the hysteria, augment the frenzy, and drive the cat to bite even harder. Force and violence only make things worse. (Incidentally, squirting the cat with water, which some people recommend for dealing with biting, has very mixed success.)

Dealing with the Cat

If you are bitten, your best move is to do something so weird—something so utterly peculiar and shocking to the cat's mind—that it will surprise him right out of that instinctive mode and back into conscious control and reality. Whether the cat bites a human or another animal, the victim always tries to pull away from the cat's mouth. So surprise him; don't pull away. Press in toward the cat. Sometimes this is enough to confuse the cat and make him stop. If not, grab his head from behind, place your index finger and thumb on both cheeks, and press the cheeks in between his teeth as you continue to press toward the cat. An equally good alternative would be to grab something like a toy, a wad of tissue, or the end of a scarf and stuff it into the side of his mouth and push it back toward the throat. This will definitely confuse him. Not only is his prey not trying to pull free, it's actually burrowing down into his throat! These tactics work very well. The cat will want to pull away and spit out the stuff in his mouth. Biting is no longer important to him.

About ten years ago, a veterinarian shared yet another technique with me. I'm *not* recommending that anyone else try this. I had been working with cats for twenty years when I heard about it. I've only needed to do it three or four times, but it works like a charm. I slide my index finger into the cat's mouth and wiggled the fingertip a tiny bit as I slide it back toward the throat. Talk about a weird feeling! The cat *can't wait* to disengage and get away from that THING trying to crawl down his throat. Force and strength have nothing to do with it. What works is the direction and the movement. Once the cat has disengaged, try to herd him into another room and close the door.

Dealing with the Bite

Once the biting is over and the cat has been sequestered, immediately focus on the wound. It's always better if the wound bleeds. If it's already bleeding, good. Make it bleed more. If it's hardly bleeding at all, do your best to make it bleed at least a little more. Blood is slightly antiseptic; it contains healing antibodies, and it can wash away germs and debris. Encourage bleeding by running very warm water over the wound and massaging toward the wound. As soon as possible, soak the bite in very warm Epsom salt solution. Epsom salts draw out poisons, germs, and debris. I always keep some on hand. If you have none, use a very strong salt solution. It doesn't work as well, but it's better than nothing. Don't use alcohol. Strong antiseptics kill germs but they also injure tissue and destroy the healing antibodies. I use hydrogen peroxide after the Epsom salt soak. It kills germs, foams out debris, and leaves the tissue and healing antibodies intact.

While you're bleeding and soaking the wound, take stock of the situation. If the cat who attacked you is a stranger, you need to consider the possibility of rabies infection. Your veterinarian will help you decide whether the cat was rabid and may advise you to see your doctor. Also, try to find anyone who might know something about the cat. Rabies is rare, but you need to make certain that you're safe and even if you know the cat is healthy, you still must guard against infection—even if the wound bled copiously. If you see a red line running from the wound toward the heart, the wound is infected. You should then consult your doctor, who will likely prescribe a course of antibiotics to treat the infection. I have found that a bite is more likely to become septic and need further treatment if (1) it's your first bite, (2) your body is already weakened by stress or an infection, (3) you don't encourage the bleeding and soak the wound right away, or (4) the cat who bit you has dirty teeth.

Back in the 1970s when I was first learning nursing procedures and grooming, I was handling all sorts of cats all over town. I used to get bitten two or three times a year. I'd run to the sink, turn on the hot water, bleed the wound as best I could, and ask the cat's guardian to please pass the salt and give me a mug. I'd soak the bite in the mug of salty water—as hot as I could stand it—and that would hold me until I could get home and call my homeopath. There would be swelling and some pain, and before the wound was healed, there would often be pus. But I only saw the dreaded red lines running toward my heart after the first bite. My body seemed to handle the bites better and better over the years. Nowadays I seldom get bitten. Maybe once every three or four years I receive a glancing chomp. I think of it as a sort of booster bite. It's reassuring to watch it heal up quickly and to know that my immune system retains its ability to handle bites efficiently.

Dealing with Abused or Neglected Animals

Just as you would feed a starving animal frequent small meals but never a large meal, give the emotionally deprived cat frequent casual contact for very short periods. In some cases it may be necessary to start by pulling yourself back all the way to just eye and voice contact. Then, when you add petting, move slowly, use the light touch, and *keep it short*—less than thirty seconds. Always stop soon enough to leave him wanting more. The object is to repeat the desirable pattern: love and petting make love and purring, over and over again. Never ever allow your actions to go on so long that you trigger the undesirable response of biting, scratching, or hiding in fear. Be alert for that signal in the chain of events that is a link or two *before* the unwanted behavior.

Patience is all-important; it's better to go too slow than too fast. When I start repatterning a cat who has been abused or locked in a cage for a long time, I know before I start that I can expect to work with the patient for several weeks before he begins to relax and enjoy a normal relationship.

From time to time I come upon a guardian who is unwittingly initiating the scratch and bite response by overstimulating a hypersensitive cat. When some cats are petted they will first react with a typical purring, stretching, and kneading response. However, if the petting becomes too vigorous or is simply carried on too long, cats are sometimes stimulated beyond the point where they can control themselves. Then, in a reaction similar to fear biting (see page 20), the emotions engulf the cat, being out of control frightens him, and, just as in classic fear biting, he will instinctively lash out at the cause of this emotional tidal wave: you. I see this reaction most often in cats who have come out of a situation where there was very little demonstration of love. They are taken into a new home starving for affection and physical closeness, and when they get it they experience a kind of emotional indigestion. When this happens, keep calm. The cat will be as frightened of his sudden and unexpected reaction as you are. Gently withdraw and try to remember how long you were petting your friend before this reaction occurred. Next time, you must stop earlier. Remember, until he settles down, it's better to stop too soon than too late. *Always leave him wanting more.*

The Proper Way to Pick Up a Cat

When I go into someone's home to groom, I always ask the guardian to pick up the cat and place her on the grooming area. This is because I want to demonstrate to the cat that her beloved, trusted guardian approves of the proceedings. I was amazed to see how many guardians did not know how to pick up a cat comfortably. I saw cats dangling by their midriffs, gasping for breath over their guardian's arm, and, even more frequently, cats clasped under the armpits, leaving their heavy hindquarters swinging in the air, their shoulders hunched up to their cheeks, and a look of long-suffering patience on their little faces. In such cases, I always delay the grooming session a moment to give a few pointers on how a cat prefers to be picked up.

Here are a few rules to remember before you begin:

1. Before you pick up the cat, announce your intent to do so. Extend your hands, rub your fingers and thumb together.
2. Before you pick up the cat, *face the cat away from you.*
3. Hindquarters must be supported comfortably. They are the heaviest part of the cat's body.
4. Leave the legs as free as possible to give the cat a feeling of freedom and safety. Cats hate to have their forelegs or paws held.
5. Don't squeeze or grasp too hard.
6. Never breathe into the cat's ears, eyes, or nose—it tickles.

Now you're ready to begin. Once the cat is facing away from you, all you have to do is slip one hand under the cat's chest and the other hand under a thigh *from behind*. In both picking up and putting down, move the head slightly ahead of the hindlegs. When picking him up, this raises the cat's head up, tilting the cat's weight onto the hand that supports the rear, so the cat is sitting on your palm. When putting the cat down, it tilts the cat's head down allowing the cat to see where he is going. Because the legs are always left free and pointing toward the floor, the cat feels very safe and secure during both the lifting and the lowering.

My Big Purr wanted no part of being picked up when I first got him. I had no wish to impose my will on an affectionate and exciting animal, but for the sake of practicality, I knew that I had to be able to pick Purr up to place him in the carry case for the annual trip to the veterinarian, and there were bound to be other times when I would need to pick him up. So, using cats' love of ritual, I invented a wonderful new game that we called "Pick up/ Put down."

An action becomes ritual when it is repeated frequently. So, for a few weeks, we played Pick up/Put down two or three times a day. I would come up behind Purr, announce my intention by rubbing my thumb against my other fingers, which made a "shushing" sound near his ear, and repeat the ritual phrase "Do you want to come?" His natural reaction was usually to jump up with glee and face me, with an expectant look on his face. I would then turn him around to face away from me, stroke my hands around and underneath his chest and hindquarters, and lift him up a bit, just barely disengaging his feet from the ground. During this action, I always repeated the second ritual phrase, "There's my good boy." The trick is, while cats are learning, you must put their feet back down again *before* they begin to get nervous and wiggle. Design calmness into the pattern, and *leave them wanting more*. Always follow this ritual with stroking and lavish praise and approval.

For the first few days, the whole procedure took less than ten seconds. By the third day, I was lifting him up about three feet, always keeping my face close to the back of his neck to help him feel secure. Because I was bent over, I was able to nuzzle my nose and my mouth against his ruff and murmur loving words. The ritual still lasted less than ten seconds. In two weeks, I could lift him up, straighten up myself, and tuck his hindquarters between my arm and body at the side of my waist. His front feet were still left dangling floorward, while my right hand supported his chest—so he still had a feeling of security. I learned from Purr that a cat doesn't wiggle as much if you move about while you're carrying him. So it's easier if you have a definite place to go or a reason for picking him up. If you stand still, keep yourself in control by putting the cat down before he starts wiggling to jump down.

Collars and Identification

In the past, I never said much about collars and identification tags and chips because I'm really not comfortable with allowing a cat to be outside the house where a sudden sound like an ambulance rushing by or a sudden threat like a dog on the loose could startle her. Frightened cats have been known to run until they drop and then not be able to find their way home. There is also the problem of bears and coyotes who are crowded out of their territory by home construction. They are wandering closer to suburban areas, and they do hunt down and kill cats for food. There are bears all over suburban New Jersey these days, and last year a coyote was seen in New York City's Central Park. I recommend building secure covered runs and play areas outdoors and fully screened sun porches.

However, as my friend and coauthor Norma pointed out to me, Hurricane Katrina left many animal refugees in its wake. Since then we have all been more aware of our pets' vulnerability to natural disasters. Our cats need to wear identification. Norma feared that if her home in Los Angeles was damaged in an earthquake and her cats got out, she might very well lose them if they had no identification.

I recommend a good "break-away" collar with an attached identification tag, giving your cat's name and your name and telephone number. It's a good idea to include additional numbers, such as your cell phone number or your vet's office, in the event that your phone service is disrupted. You don't need to label each phone number; if the tag has the cat's name and your name, that's sufficient information for a caring person to track you down.

The collar should be made of strong, high-quality nylon because it's lighter than leather, lasts longer, and can be easily washed. The collar must be the "break-away" kind that opens automatically if it snags or hooks onto something. This feature could save your cat's life. The tag needs to be small and light, with deeply etched words and numbers. This is not the time to look for a bargain; an illegible tag is worse than no tag at all. The collar and tag are like the scratching post—you're going to have them for years, so buy a good one that will please you both.

Now high-tech identification tags are also available. As of this writing, KoogaTAG, a very small, thin USB computer drive that hangs on your cat's collar, offers the most features. It's very lightweight and is waterproof, about an inch long and a half-inch wide, and as thin as a quarter. Your personal information is securely stored but it is not printed on the tag, so your privacy is protected. If your animal is lost, you can call the KoogaTAG lost pet center any time of day or night and they will immediately notify all of the shelters and veterinarians in your area. Once you log into the KoogaTAG website (or access the saved files on your own computer), you can also print a lost pet poster with your cat's photo and information. And anyone who finds your cat simply calls the toll free number on the tag and gives the ID number found on it to get Muffy back in your arms as quickly as possible. The KoogaTAG also stores medical records, which is a great benefit if you end up at an emergency clinic since they can pop the device into a computer and review the records stored on it.

The only downside to this identification tag is that if the collar is lost, the tag is lost too. However, even then, there is a greater chance for a quick reunion with Muffy since the KoogaTAG lost pet center will have sent an alert with a photo and description of her to all of the local shelters and veterinarians. If someone calls KoogaTAG with a description of a collarless cat who matches Muffy's description, they will let you know so you can follow up on it. I think the added security is worth the nominal cost of the KoogaTAG. It can be purchased at www.Kooga-Pet.com or by calling 800-351-1312.

If your cat or dog is lost, in addition to posting flyers, you might also want to utilize a service called Find Toto. This internet-based company provides a type of Amber Alert for missing animals by calling your neighbors and leaving a recorded message that describes your animal and gives other relevant information, including your phone number and the company's web address, www.FindToto.com. This website also allows you to post your animal's photo.

What about those new microchips that are surgically implanted under the skin for identification? If your cat gets lost and is found, the chip can be read electronically by an animal shelter or veterinarian's office, and your cat will be returned to you. However, there are several different scanner-microchip systems, so an identification can only be made if your cat's microchip matches with the scanner used by that facility. Furthermore, many vets warn against using them. There are reports that the chips—when used on cats—migrate away from their original site under the skin, causing physical problems. More important, cases of soft tissue tumors surrounding the chips have been reported. I cannot recommend them. Why take a chance?

The Carry Case

When you choose the carry case, remember above all that you and your feline companion are going to depend upon that case for the next twenty years or more. You'll be using it for the yearly trip to the veterinarian and for any other trips, such as moving or vacations. But, even more important, the proper case is like an insurance policy. Come fire or flood, come sickness or accident, come hell or high water, you and your beloved cat can pick up and *go* in security and comfort.

Keeping in mind the number of years you're going to be using the case, you should not choose a case because it is on sale or because it matches your luggage; you should choose a case because:

1. *It fits your cat.* Don't choose a case that is too large. The passenger should be able to stand up, turn around, and sit down, but it should not be so large that the cat will slide around. That would be frightening. Cats like to be able to brace themselves against the sides. It gives them a feeling of control over what's happening to their bodies. Size small is fine for a kitten, but your cat will soon outgrow it. My solution is to get a size medium and put a smaller cardboard box inside, nicely braced with newspapers or towels, until the kitten grows into the medium size case. I have met a few very large males, like Clarence, my Maine coon friend, who do require a size large case.

2. *It feels safe and comfortable to your cat.* Choose a hard-sided case. Those soft collapsible cases are very frightening to cats. Every time you put the thing down, the sides and top start collapsing inward, sagging down on top of the poor little pussycat trapped inside. Avoid the soft-sided collapsible cases.

3. *It's simple and easy to put your cat in and take her out.* Choose a case that hinges open from the top and allows you to lower your cat in from above, not the kind where you're expected to push and cram the cat in through a little door in the end.

4. *It is designed with your cat's comfort and pleasure in mind.* The case must have several large ventilation holes in *both* ends. To avoid motion sickness, choose a case with a transparent lid so your passenger can see out and enjoy his trip, and potential admirers can see in. If you ever choose to do so, you can always make such a case opaque by simply draping a scarf across the top.

5. *It is well built and safe.* Examine all hinges, clasps, and handles to be sure

all are secure and strong enough to support easily at least twice your cat's actual weight. Open it and close it and swing it around with some books in it before you buy it.

6. *It feels good to your hand and is comfortable to carry.* This is just as important as any of the above criteria. After all, you, the guardian, are an equal partner in using the case.

Warning: *Do not get a case large enough for two cats!* You'll hate it for the next twenty years and so will your cats. A two-cat case, even if there's only one cat inside, is heavy, awkward, and unmanageable. As for the two cats inside, how would you like it if you were traveling in very cramped quarters and your companion "had a little accident" all over the floor?

If you need a case to tide you over until you find the right one, I suggest the disposable cardboard type. They have no see-through top, but otherwise they work well as a temporary case. They're light, comfortable for cat and owner, and quite strong as long as you put them together *exactly* as directed.

Once in a great while I have found myself in some dire situation where I must transport a cat and the only case available is obviously on its last legs. To ensure that the thing won't fall open once we're out on the street, I loop a belt or a couple of those stretchy bungee cords around the case.

Once you acquire a carry case you feel good about, the next step is to introduce your fuzzy friend to all the positive aspects of his "private module." Leave it out and open one or two days a week for him to play or nap in. Some cases are a bit top-heavy. If so, be sure it's braced securely so that it doesn't tip over and make a bad impression. Serve a treat or some catnip in the case every week or so to build positive associations. If your cat is the timid type, once a week put him in the case and take him for a little jaunt around the living room, followed by a play session and a treat.

There is yet another nice advantage to owning the ideal carry case: you can make it cool in the summer and turn it into a snug little heated compartment in winter. You should be able to weatherproof your cat's carry case easily. This is difficult if you have the type with a lot of screen or grillwork suitable only for warm climates.

Let's assume for the sake of illustration that (heaven forbid) your cat falls ill in the middle of a snowstorm. Prepare the carry case in the following way. First, fold two kitchen towels (or paper towels) to fit over the air holes in both ends of the case and tape the towel in place with masking tape. Also tape closed any additional holes in the case with masking tape. That way, air can filter in through the towel but the case will be windproof.

Now you need a plastic bottle. Save an empty shampoo bottle or, if you have none, empty your shampoo into a mixing bowl and fill your shampoo bottle with water as hot as you can handle. The hotter, the better. Screw on the lid and drop the bottle into a thick wool sock, preferably one that you've recently worn. Thus you are providing both heat and the comfortable, familiar scent of your beloved foot. Fold a towel into the bottom of the case—preferably a towel of a becoming color so it will subliminally affect the mind of the veterinarian or whomever you are going to see. Slip the sock-covered hot water bottle under the towel in the bottom of the carry case.

Grab a large brown paper bag and container of your cat's high-quality food in case the cat must stay overnight at the hospital.

If you must transport your cat during a heat wave, leave all the ventilation holes wide open and use ice water in the shampoo bottle—or, better yet, use a "dry ice pillow." Available in drugstores, this is a heavy plastic pillow filled with a liquid that freezes easily and is kept in the freezer for use on swellings or headaches—or to air-condition pussycat carry cases. Be sure to wrap the ice bag or cold water bottle in a sock or towel so it doesn't come into direct contact with the cat.

Putting the Cat into the Case

If you find yourself in the middle of some emergency such as illness or an accident, before even looking at the cat, take three slow, deep breaths, inhaling and exhaling through the nose. The three breaths will calm your mind. Just as your cat comforts you when you are upset or ill, you must now control your fears and nervousness sufficiently to provide truly honest reassurance. You can do this by focusing on the many positive aspects of the trip. Let your mind dwell on the help and relief in store for your feline friend and how good it will be to have him diagnosed and be able to do something about the problem. Just before picking up the cat, put your hand into the box so that you feel how nice and warm (or cool) it is in there. As you pick your cat up and put him in, talk about that warmth. Say how you wish *you* were in a nice, warm box instead of having to walk out into that cold weather.

The proper way to put the cat in the carry case is basically the same way you always put a cat down—front feet first. If you've been playing Pick up/Put down (page 28) you should have no problems. The second the cat's front feet touch the bottom of the box, quickly close the lid *on your own hand*. This accomplishes two things: speed and safety. You will be able to shut it rapidly and successfully because you will be secure in the knowledge that there is not the slightest chance of pinching the cat's tail. Your hand gives that protection. Now gently extricate your finger as you tuck the tail, ear, or what-have-you inside. Grab the paper bag, the cans of food, and the patient's veterinary records, and off you go.

Communicating "Good-bye" and "I'll Be Back"

Many of the caregivers I know have wished fervently again and again that they could somehow communicate to their cat the reassurance that they will return home before the day is over. But most people don't think the cat can understand these things. They say, "He gets so upset when I leave, if only I could made him understand that it's all right; that I'll be back soon." Cheer up, you *can* make your cat understand. I had exactly the same thoughts and the same problem. I simply made my leave-taking into a ritual. This dovetailed nicely, incidentally, with my desire to shape Big Purr's behavior along more adventurous lines—he was inclined to experience undue alarm any time he was outside the apartment door.

On a normal working day, when I'm going to be home again to feed the cats dinner sometime before midnight, our ritual is this: I throw my purse and grooming kit into the basket of my bike and wheel it into position facing the door. Because Purr now knows that he has the leading role in this good-bye ritual, he comes prancing along and leaps up onto the bike seat. "Are you going to walk me to the elevator?" I ask. I always use the same words and say them in the same tone as I lift him off the seat and place him in the bike basket on top of my backpack. I wait for him to settle himself comfortably, then open the door and wheel him on the bike out of the apartment and down the hall to the elevator, where I park. Then, while assuring him that he is the most courageous and adventurous cat I have ever met, I pick him up and carry him back to the apartment, giving lots of kisses and nuzzlings and thanking him profusely for his protection. We have never had a problem with lions or tigers or bears in our hall since Big Purr arrived on the job. I put him down inside, and then the most important part of the ritual begins: communicating that I am coming back.

Communicating clearly with your cats is mostly a matter of simplifying your own thinking and looking at the situation from the cat's point of view. It will be helpful for you also to read the sections "Therapeutic Communication" (page 262) and "Affirmation and Visualization" (page 217). Cats perceive our thoughts in terms of mental pictures, sense memories (sight, hearing, taste, touch, and smell), and accompanying emotions. This last is the most important. Cats are very emotionally oriented.

My simple "Good-bye, I'll be back tonight" communication is transmitted with accompanying thoughts that go something like this: "We'll see-touch each other with gladness when it's black dark night outside the window." I picture and feel myself seeing and touching Purr. Then I add the emotion of gladness and picture the dark window in the background to give a time reference.

Later that night when it all comes true, it is always a sort of déjà vu in its most pleasurable form as I mentally watch while Purr and I live out the picture I promised him that morning.

The more I practiced what I came to think of as assurance of my homecoming, the easier it became for me to feel it and perceive it from the cat's point of view. Cats are very sense-oriented, so I kept adding sensory details until my assurance of homecoming went something like this:

See: Window, black, dark
Hear: Sound of elevator door, footsteps, bicycle, key in lock
See: Front door opens, Anitra and bike come in
Smell: Cold on boots and bicycle tires (or heat in summer)
Feel: Gladness
Touch: Nuzzle, cold gloves, warm neck of Anitra
Hear: Voice, purrs

Then we go to the kitchen and make a delicious dinner.

I started out speaking these words out loud each time I left, trying my best to visualize the scene and recall the appropriate senses and emotions. As we repeated the ritual day after day, I found that the sense memories were sharpening and the pictures were becoming more complete and clearer. Big Purr was coaching me in interspecies communication. I felt no pressure or anxiety about succeeding; I practiced with him because it was fun. I knew he loved me whether I could speak "Cat" or not.

At first I practiced the technique with little faith in myself. "I know he'll pick up some of what I'm trying to send," I told myself, "and it certainly can't do any harm to try." It wasn't until weeks later when I was doing the ritual one morning that I felt my sense memories suddenly clearing and sharpening beyond anything that I had ever experienced in my whole life. I realized with a feeling of total awe that I was *receiving* impressions from Big Purr. There he sat, blue eyes alight, smiling up at me. He had been joyfully joining in the ritual for all those weeks, sending me his communication, until finally, at long last, my rusty human mind opened up and I became consciously aware of his participation and of the wonder that was taking place between us. The emotion that engulfed me then was very similar to a feeling I had had only one time before—it was years ago in college, the very first time I ever sang with a full orchestra accompaniment.

If I'm going away for the weekend or off on vacation, I must communicate that more time will pass before I come home. I do this by picturing day and then night, day and then night, several times outside the window and visualizing who it is that will be coming in to feed and care for them in my stead.

I have observed that my "good-bye for a long time" ritual is almost super-fluous. The appearance of my suitcase tells them all they need to know. In fact, when the suitcase comes out the first thing Purr does is leap inside it and refuse to budge, perhaps hoping that if he can prevent the suitcase from going anywhere, then I'll stay too. Then, when I try to make my exit, instead of sitting quietly on the floor, looking up at me soulfully and tapping me politely with his mitten, Purr imposes his body between me and the door, grabs my pants with his claws, and rolls about on his back. He refuses to let go, trying to convince me that now is the time for play. Nevertheless, here again I push on with the communication, and right before I pick up the suitcase, I use the ritual phrase "Okay, Purr, I'm leaving you in charge." Then I grab the suitcase, slip through the door, throw him a last blink, and lock up.

It is clear from his behavior that he knows full well I'm not coming home that night. Purr, being the dominant male, will communicate this information to the other cats by his attitude when my usual coming-home time rolls around. And anyway, I remind myself as I descend in the elevator, my assistant will be in to feed them. She has her own special games with the cats that they all enjoy.

Introducing a New Cat into the Household

Cats who live with a cat friend (or friends) live longer and healthier lives. When choosing a second cat, aim for one that will complement your first cat's personality and will not threaten his position as first in your heart and master (or mistress) of the territory.

If your cat is	*Look for a cat who is*
A floor cat who perches on chairs or stools or under things	A high jumper who perches on upper shelves
A snuggler who loves to be with people	A playful clown who focuses on other cats more than people: a cat's cat
Elderly or sick	A cat's cat; mature and calm; loving to other cats—no rambunctious kittens, please
Healthy but overweight	Rambunctious but respectful; a kitten of two months or more would do very nicely here
Too energetic and running you ragged; demanding of your time and attention	Young and playful and jolly; a kitten could work but it should be more than five months old; a youngster of up to three years who would take your friend in paw and direct her energy would be ideal
The cat you adore, but you are worried that she is left alone too much	A cat's cat who enjoys the company of cats as much as, if not more than, the company of people

Often there is no question of a choice. The new cat is suddenly there, presented by fate, and the kindly human makes the decision to accept, protect, nurture, and do whatever else is needed for this gift from the cat goddess.

Whether you choose a second cat or have one thrust upon you, your first move is the same: *don't* take the new cat home; take her to your own trusted veterinarian and have her examined for parasites and tested for feline leukemia. You owe it to yourself as well as your trusting feline friend at home not to bring in anything contagious with the new cat friend. Besides, this will give you some very necessary time to prepare your beloved feline at home.

Before the New Cat Arrives

Demonstrate to your first cat how much you love him and need him. If possible, for at least a week before the new cat arrives, give him extra attention. Lavish him with affection, giving physical and eye and voice contact. If you make a bit of a pest of yourself, that's all the better; it will help him to feel even more secure.

Communicate the advantages of having a cat friend. During that week and again the day before the new cat arrives, explain to him that many cats have a cat friend to sleep with and to play with and to generally help take care of the household. Picture these things and communicate the emotions as you did when you communicated "Good-bye" and "I'll be back." Remind him how nice it was back in the old days when, as a tiny kitten, he used to snuggle down with his littermates and romp with them and get into trouble together. "Remember when . . ." is a very good phrase to use.

When the big day arrives *do not bring the new cat into the house yourself!* Find someone who is not well-known to your cat who will bring the new cat into the house for the first time and play the part of the new cat's person. Have that person pet the new cat all over to get his scent on the cat and the cat's scent all over him. The ideal person is someone your cat has never met, but who would enjoy participating in the charade that follows. Cats are naturally territorial, and you and your family are the most cherished components of your first cat's territory. The entire introduction procedure that follows has been formulated to demonstrate clearly to your cat that he is your cherished family member. He is your first love; he is yours and you are his, and you have no interest whatsoever in any other animal.

Remember, we already know that you and the family will accept the new cat. The introduction is designed to ensure that *your cat* will accept him as well so that the newcomer can slide smoothly into everyone's life without experiencing undue trauma. Convey this concept clearly to each person in the household. If you want to make life easy for the newcomer, you'll have to ignore him at first.

Last, but definitely not least, to ensure a lethargic attitude, make sure both cats have had a delicious meal about one hour before the introduction begins and be sure all claws are clipped.

Steps for Introducing a New Cat[1]

1. Have the person your cat doesn't know, the "visitor," arrive with the new cat in a carry case that has plenty of air holes so your cat can easily smell that the visitor has a cat with him. There should be torn strips of newspaper in the bottom of the carrier for later use (which I'll get to in step 4).

2. All family members should be *completely oblivious* to the new cat in the carry case. Let the visitor sit with the carry case on his lap for ten or twenty minutes to establish his sole ownership of and interest in the new cat. During this time indulge in a casual conversation about other matters: the weather, vacation plans, or your favorite restaurant—in short, anything *except* cats. Your attitude toward that carry case and its contents should be exactly the same as it would be if your visitor had walked in with an umbrella or an attaché case.

3. After twenty minutes or so the visitor should shift the carry case to the floor next to his feet, making it convenient for your cat to get a better sniff. Continue your pleasant and interesting conversation about sports, end-of-season sales, and so on. If your cat comes over and sniffs the case and then walks away, ignore him, continue chatting and proceed to step 5. If your cat stays away from the case, include step 4.

4. To help your cat become more familiar with the new cat's scent, the visitor should open the carrier a crack and take a handful of the torn newspaper strips from the bottom, which are of course impregnated with the new cat's odor. The visitor should then make a trip to the bathroom carrying the strips with him and just happen to accidentally drop several of the paper strips along the way, giving your cat the opportunity to become familiar with the newcomer's scent from a safe distance. Continue your fascinating discussion, projecting feelings of calm contentment.

5. Let the visitor continue to sit and talk for a while longer, the carry case at his feet. When your cat sits calmly in the room without staring continually at the carry case, you may safely proceed to step 6.

1. Parts of this procedure were first introduced in *The Inner Cat* by Carole C. Wilbourn. See Bibliography, p. 495.

6. Invite your cat out to the kitchen for a snack. Have all family members join you, leaving the visitor and "his" cat alone. During this time the visitor should open the carry case and let the new cat out. This accomplishes two things: (1) as you're all together in the kitchen, your cat won't blame any of the family for allowing a new cat out in his territory; and (2) this gives the new cat a few minutes to explore the strange territory alone so he won't be quite so tense and frightened.

7. When your cat finishes his snack and decides to go back to keep an eye on events in the living room, *the family should stay in the kitchen*. Demonstrate your lack of concern by discussing the feasibility of a trip to Venezuela next year.

8. The minute your cat enters the living room, the visiting person should announce clearly his intent to join you in the kitchen and do so, adding his vibes of blissful lack of concern to yours.

9. At no time should anyone offer any expressions of encouragement to the cats. You must all maintain your position of disinterested detachment. The minute you express any interest at all, your cat will become possessive and react with hostility toward the intruder. If you cannot resist an impulse to "peek," one person may do so but only if she can give the impression that she is really doing something else. For example, someone might stroll casually into the living room to collect a magazine or to change the channel on the television and then return to the kitchen.

Hissing is perfectly normal. Hissing is not aggressive; it is defensive, one cat asking another to back off and give him more time to adjust. Disgruntled muttering is less desirable but still should be ignored. As long as there are no humans around to be claimed as territory and defended, the relationship should develop slowly and peacefully.

However, loud growling or screaming is a sure sign that serious trouble is about to develop. To distract the cats in the living room from their focus on each other, accidentally drop a metal pan and two lids onto the kitchen floor. If the loud growling and screaming resumes, you may need to separate the cats. This is almost always a sign that one of the previous steps was not carried out properly.

10. When the two cats reach the stage where they are not pacing around but are sitting down in the same room, either watching each other or not, it is time for the humans to demonstrate further their attitude of blissful unconcern by going out for a walk. Leave the cats alone for thirty minutes or so. Be sure to continue to talk about unrelated subjects. Scientific studies have confirmed that cats can pick up your emotions even at long distances.

11. When you return, greet your cat in a loving but casual manner; then settle into the living room for another ten-minute conversation. If there is still nothing worse than hissing going on, the visitor can leave at any time. He will just happen accidentally to forget his cat.

12. The final stages of the introduction will continue at the cats' own pace over the next few days or weeks. *The slower the better.* You and your family must continue to ignore the new cat. Place food on the floor for him, but don't call him or talk to him. Try not to get caught looking at him, and for heaven's sakes, don't touch him if you can avoid it. The cats will explore what it's like to be together in each room of your home. Territories will be identified and claimed.

If hissing or chasing occurs, such interaction is normal in cat society and is best ignored by humans, who seldom understand fully the complexities of cat relationships anyway. In truth, chasing can be a good sign, especially if the chaser and the chasee reverse roles periodically. Another sign of progress is sitting in the same room, no matter how far apart, and *not* staring at each other. When that happens, you're almost home—but not quite. You still mustn't touch the new cat or talk to him or give any sign that you care a hoot about him. Refer to the new cat as the visitor's cat and project no more emotional involvement with him than you would if your visitor had left behind an umbrella. If the new cat jumps up on your lap, put him gently on the floor and say something like "I wish George would come back and take his cat out of our way" and request your own cat's help in dealing with this "problem." At the same time leave them alone together as much as possible and encourage togetherness by providing new experiences that the two cats can share while you're not around. Leave the stepladder up in the middle of the floor while you're gone one day; another time you can bring home two cardboard boxes and leave them side-by-side in the corner of the living room.

When you have the urge to love and nurture the new cat, stay your hand! Be strong for his sake. The success of the relationship between the two cats depends on it. Don't think you can sneak in a stroke or a snuggle when your first cat is not around. He'll smell your scent on the newcomer, and the cats' relationship will take a violent and giant step backward. The better you play your part, the quicker friendship will flower between the two cats. A really skillful guardian can engineer the situation so the first cat will ask to have the new cat included in games, and then in petting and other activities. You should appear to grant these requests with a tiny bit of reluctance at first, giving in at last only because your first cat is so adorable you can refuse him nothing. Now that you have "agreed" to let the new cat stay, this is the time to assure your first cat that the new cat belongs to him, rather than to you. When you arrive home, call for your first cat first. Pet him first, even if the new cat is waiting at the door and clamoring for your attention. For the next few weeks continue to pet your first cat first and play with him more than the new cat, making it very clear that your first cat is the one you prefer above all others.

The goal of the loving guardian is a strong bond of affection and communion between the two cats. When that bond first begins to form and strengthen, the cats often go through a stage of intense interaction that seems almost to exclude the human members of the family. Don't worry. Watch the drama unfold; enjoy the spectacle and be proud of your success, secure in the knowledge that very soon you will have not one but two furry-purries to greet you at the door, supervise your household activities, and snuggle you to sleep at night.

Dangers in the Home

Cats who belong to a loving guardian just naturally assume that their human will never hurt them. They will stick their noses into the oven, not realizing you are about to light it; they will leave their tails trailing behind in the door, not realizing you are about to slam it. Our feline friends are not frightened, and so they are not cautious. If we try a little bit to think like a cat, we have a better chance of protecting them.

For us, the sense of sight is Number One; to a cat, *smell* and *hearing* are much more important. Think of the times that you have seen a cat looking in the mirror at himself. You probably wondered why he seemed disinterested. Didn't his eyes tell him that another cat was there? Yes, they *did*. But his nose and ears told him that he was alone, and his nose and ears are what he believes.

Cats go places that we wouldn't think of going because their noses tell them these are nice places—they're interesting and smell wonderful. Cats have been locked in refrigerators because their human guardian turned away and, without looking, slammed the door closed. The guardian would never think of crawling into a refrigerator, so it does not occur to him that a cat might find it fascinating. Insulation muffles the cat's cries, and by the time the cat is missed it is often too late. With a cat loose in the house, you can never again open or close any door or drawer with automatic mindlessness. For the rest of your life with a cat, you must always *look as you close*.

We all tend to forget that for cats the home is not a natural environment. We have taken the cats out of their natural environment for our own pleasure, so it behooves us to protect them from dangers that they do not automatically recognize. Most cats are curious. Don't ever leave your window or the door to the balcony open; the scents that blow in are absolutely fascinating. Almost all cats find cooking odors from other homes and body odors from other people's animals and birds positively irresistible. Sooner or later your cat will explore them. Chances are she will explore them repeatedly day after day, returning again and again to the open window or balcony. Sooner or later a little stray piece of fluff will blow by or a tiny insect on the edge will capture her attention. As she lunges to capture that elusive object, one second is all it takes for her to fall. I have come to dread the springtime in New York City because it ushers in the season of death and mutilation from such falls. The late Dr. Camuti, the famous cat specialist, said that of all the cases he saw in New York, the most frequent calls were for cats falling out of windows and off balconies.

In all my years as a cat groomer in New York, I have observed that all the cats who fall have one thing in common—each one is a cat to whom "it could not possibly happen." This group of cats is divided into two categories—either "He's been sitting there for eight years, he's certainly not going to fall out now" or "She's terrified of the balcony—how is she going to fall if she never goes out there?" These cats are crippled or die because they are not protected. The cats who are likely to fall out, the ones who are lively and who would obviously leap to the rail of the balcony if allowed to do so, are the ones who are protected because their danger is obvious. So they never fall.

I have twice heard of cats falling from a window that was open "only an inch." In one of these cases, I know for a fact that the owner spoke the truth— but if cats want to explore the outside world they begin by thrusting their noses through even the smallest opening. They work and pry until the whole head gets through. Then pressing their shoulder under is easiest of all, and there they are— trapped on a narrow ledge.

Females in heat and unneutered males are especially prone to this maneuver. They know that there is no mate inside the apartment or home, and if they get the merest whiff of one from outdoors it's all over. Declawed cats, of course, have notoriously poor balance.

Even if you could swear that your cats are fully aware of the dangerous distance between the ledge and the street, you must remember that pussycats' minds are different from ours. They will not always perceive distance in the same way we do. Sure, you held Samantha up to the railing yesterday, and she looked over, and she was scared. But that doesn't mean that tomorrow she won't forget and assume that the floor height on this side of the railing must be the same on the other side too.

Cats perceive the world differently. They live almost exclusively in the present, with a very limited and hazy memory of the past and almost no concept of the future. Their concept of space and depth differs from ours too. Remember also that cats frequently fall out of windows that are open from the top. Window screens are not expensive.

Once you've screened the windows, the average home is still booby-trapped with objects harmful to a pussycat. For example, many simple cleaning compounds such as Lysol, as well as dishwashing compounds, are fatal if the cat gets even one lick of them. That is why I wash the litter box with plain chlorine-based cleanser or a cleaning solution I make myself (see page 102). Because anything cats step in is going to go into their mouths, I always rinse like crazy. Cats are always licking their paws, especially if they smell something disagreeable on them. So think twice about anything you use to clean surfaces in the home or any spray, like room deodorizer. That spray eventually settles on the floor where your cat walks. Any product containing phenol is particularly deadly. If I use any compound about which I am in doubt, and I must admit I'm in doubt about most of them, I just rinse like crazy. Of course, you must store any cleaning fluids or medicines in a safe catproof place.

The fumes from mothballs destroy the cat's liver cells. A cat accidentally locked in a closet (or sleeping by choice in a closet) where moth crystals or balls are used can inhale enough fumes in a few hours to destroy the liver beyond repair. Such cats with irreversible liver damage are usually put to sleep by the veterinarian in order to avoid a slow, lingering death. A delightful alternative to moth crystals is cedar. Remember your grandmother's cedar chest? You can turn any drawer into a cedar chest by placing three or four small cedar blocks in among your sweaters. They're available from several mail-order companies including L. L. Bean.

If your cat lies on a towel, give him one without fabric softener. Fabric softener coats the fibers (making them almost waterproof), and some of this chemical will adhere to your skin and the cat's fur and be licked off later. Incidentally, commercial room deodorizers are made of volatile chemicals. I don't pretend to understand why anyone would pay money to add more chemicals to the air we breathe. Most of these products are downright painful to the cat's sensitive nose.

You should never have occasion to use mouse and rat poisons—for obvious reasons. But city people, like it or not, must be prepared to face the cockroach problem. Roach sprays and powders are deadly to small animals and extremely debilitating and dangerous to us big ones. My own alternative is roach traps. Although I have found their effectiveness to be far below satisfactory when used as directed, I have added a refinement of my own that renders them diabolically successful. Every morning and every evening when I feed the cats, I simply take a tiny dot of cat food and place it in the middle of a sticky roach trap. The roaches can't resist it. This trap baiting must be done twice a day, and I find it's best to use only one trap at a time so as not to confuse the little horrors.

A staggering number of plants are poisonous. The Animal Poison Control Center, which is run by the American Society for the Prevention of Cruelty to Animals, lists numerous plants that are toxic to animals, causing "systemic effects and/or intense effects on the gastrointestinal tract." Here is a partial list:

Aloe	Deadly nightshade
Amaryllis	Dieffenbachia (or dumb cane)
Asparagus fern	Dracaena
Autumn crocus	Dumb cane (or dieffenbachia)
Avocado plant	Elephant ears
Azalea	Fern (most varieties)
Bird-of-paradise	Flamingo plant
Bittersweet (American and	Florida beauty
European)	Foxglove
Buddhist pine	Gladiolus
Castor bean	Golden pothos
Chinaberry tree	Heavenly bamboo
Chinese evergreen	Holly
Christmas rose	Hyacinth
Clematis	Hydrangea
Cyclamen	Iris
Daffodil	Ivy (most varieties)

Kalanchoe

Lilies

Marijuana

Mistletoe

Morning glory

Narcissus

Oleander

Panda

Philodendron

Rhododendron

Rhubarb leaves

Sago palm

Schefflera

Taro vine

Tomato plant

Tulip

Yew

Yucca

Other plants, such as yard grass and poinsettia, are less toxic, although they can sometimes cause vomiting, depression, or diarrhea. These symptoms are generally mild and self-limiting and often do not require any treatment. (See "Vomiting," page 481.) For more specific information about potential dangers, consult the Animal Poison Control Center at www.aspca.org/apcc or call their hotline at 888-426-4435.

Even if you decide to play it safe and have only hanging plants of the most innocent variety, there are still plant-related dangers at Christmastime. Angel hair cuts and can be lethal if swallowed or if a tiny piece is inhaled into the cat's lungs. Tinsel is just as dangerous as any string or rubber band. Cats should not be allowed to chew the needles of the Christmas tree or drink the water that it stands in. Needles can damage mouth tissue and irritate the stomach, and the water can be toxic, especially if a preservative has been used. So be sure to cover the Christmas tree stand with a tree skirt so even the most determined pussycats could never get their tongues into the water.

Certain foods can also be toxic. Remember that the cat's system is different from ours. Some foods that we routinely ingest are very toxic to cats. They include:

Alcoholic beverages

Apricot and peach pits

Avocado

Cherry (fruit, bar, stones, and leaves)

Chocolate (all forms)

Coffee (all forms)

Macadamia nuts

Moldy or spoiled foods
Mushrooms
Onions, onion powder
Products sweetened with xylitol
Raisins and grapes
Salt
Uncooked potatoes
Yeast dough

In the garage, be careful to clean up any spilled antifreeze. Most cats adore its sweet taste and even a few drops can cause irreversible kidney damage if swallowed. In the winter be careful to check under the hood and fender of your car before you start it. Outdoor cats will seek the warmth of the recently used engine and then fall asleep there.

Many uncommonly used cat toys are quite dangerous. Strings, yarn, and rubber bands have caused many cat deaths. Cats' tongues are constructed so that it is almost impossible for them to spit anything out. The stereotyped picture of kittens playing with a ball of yarn can easily become a horror story. Once they start to swallow a string, they can't stop—they can only swallow more. Strangulation can occur from yarns and string. In addition, yarns, string, and rubber bands can become wrapped around the intestine. Surgery can sometimes save such an animal, but all too often the string has cut through the intestines, allowing the fecal matter to contaminate the abdominal cavity. Peritonitis results. Let your cat chase a sash instead of yarn or string. Be safe.

It's the same with tinfoil balls, corks, and cellophane balls. These articles make stimulating cat toys that crackle and skitter across the floor, tempting even the most lethargic or overweight felines to have a go at the game. But when game time is over, store such toys in an inaccessible container. A piece of cork can cause choking; a piece of aluminum foil is not digestible and can block the intestine. Cellophane cigarette wrappers turn "glassy" when they come into contact with the digestive juices in the cat's stomach. Death by internal hemorrhage follows cuts from such cellophane.

Many toys sold in pet shops and supermarkets are actually quite dangerous because the decorations and trim are only glued on, and when they fall off they are easily swallowed by the cat. Choose toys that are crocheted or sewn together. Don't allow the cat to play with any object that could possibly be swallowed.

Incidentally, a ping-pong ball makes a great cat toy and an absolutely safe one. Another winner is the plastic lid from bottled water, the cap from a ballpoint pen, or the leaves at the top of a celery stalk.

The Tree House Animal Foundation hits the nail on the head with their slogan, "Remember, your cat cannot judge safety for himself, he needs your help."

Game Time and Encouraging Exercise

Now that you're thinking like a cat to keep your cat safe, let's think like a cat to encourage exercise and have some fun. All cats need exercise. Be aware of how much time your cats spend in active play. It will help their circulation greatly if you can get them to join you in some high-energy sport at least once a day. If your cats do not seem to exercise much, you'll have to figure out ways to make them want to without letting them know that you want them to. The secret is to structure situations that will tempt them to chase or jump or run.

Cats are very imaginative, creative, and curious. The "plank game" is especially helpful if you have a rambunctious and energetic cat or kitten that demands more of your time than you can give. It combines the benefits of variety and interest, the possibility of multiple cat participants, and easy storage behind any open door—and it's a godsend for busy guardians. During the rambunctious months, you can use the plank to occupy the kitten while you get some work done. The plank can also help when introducing a new cat to the household or in any situation where there is a lack of trust between cats. The plank game allows you to devise situations where the two (or more) cats will share a common new experience and turn them into a team.

Buy a wood plank from the lumber store. It should be six feet long and at least four inches wide, safe but still exciting. Some hardy souls use a seven-foot plank, which allows for even more game options. Once a day, position the plank in a different spot in your home, such as:

- Between two chairs or between the couch and a chair, to form a bridge
- Wedged against the wall, with the bottom on the floor and the top on a chair
- Tilted with the bottom on a chair and the top on a slightly higher bookshelf

Be creative—but always check that both ends of the plank are firmly planted and secure. The cardinal rule is stability. If you set the plank at an angle, like a ramp, start with a very gentle angle, then gradually explore your cat's abilities. Be creative, but don't allow your feline friends to tempt you to give up stability in favor of excitement and adventure. Insist upon a win-win situation. Store the plank upright behind an open door between uses.

In the hands of a skillful guardian, simple objects such as a ball or crumpled paper can also inspire satisfyingly boisterous play. Cats really make themselves believe that the object is some living creature that they are actually going to catch and kill. They endow that toy with all sorts of wonderful qualities such as juiciness, delectable smell, and wiliness; they unsheathe their claws, slash with their fangs, growl, and sometimes even salivate. It therefore behooves us, their partners in play, if we wish to come up to their highly imaginative standards, to throw ourselves enthusiastically into the job of creating the startled, fluttering bird, the terrified chipmunk, or the innocent, tender field mouse.

There is one time in nature when activity is a necessity—before meals. If cats living in the wild are going to eat, they must first "catch and kill." Because cats love ritual, a good before-meal ritual could involve a "catch and kill" game.

What should you use to tempt them? Different cats have different tastes in toys. What frightens one cat will fascinate another. There are several elements to consider: size, weight, texture, sound, and smell. An interesting crinkly sound or a scratchy-scrapy sound when something is dragged across the floor is fascinating to a cat. Crumpled paper thrown across a bare floor or a tissue paper or wax paper ball might do the trick, because cats usually prefer lightweight toys. Just remember—things a cat catches and kills in the wild are all lightweight. Have you ever held a bird or a mouse? They weigh practically nothing.

Texture is another interesting aspect to consider. Cats are much more aware of texture than we are. Big Purr's favorite toy, which he brings to me to have me throw for him, is a large-size pipe cleaner twisted into the outline of a butterfly. This particular kind of pipe cleaner has little sharp prickly things twisted into the usual chenille. I should think they would prick his sensitive lips and nose, but I've tried other pipe cleaners and he always goes looking for his old favorite, the worn old prickly one.

If you want the cat to chase a ball or sash or pipe cleaner, you're going to have to do your best to make the toy behave as much like "prey" as possible. For example, don't throw the ball *to* the cat—the mouse doesn't run into the cat's arms. The mouse runs *away* from the cat or scampers innocently by as the cat lies crouched and waiting. Draw the string *across* in front of the cat, preferably almost out of reach, and make the motion jumpy and erratic, like a living creature scurrying along unaware of the fierce and lurking predator. Throw the ball from *behind* the cat so that it rolls past him and away like a little creature who has been alarmed and is streaking for its hole.

When Purr and I play with his pipe cleaner, I throw it up in an arc in front of him so that the apex is three or four feet above the ground. His part is to take one or two steps and then leap, capturing the helpless pipe cleaner in midair. Obviously the pipe cleaner is a little bird who has been frightened by Purr's presence—and I assume that I'm the bush where the bird has been sitting. He also has a variation where, instead of "capturing" it, he bats it viciously into the bedroom, runs after it, and pounces. I always wish at these times that a photographer were standing by to capture forever that lithe body stretched out in midair, head back, fangs bared, and the look of fierce concentration in the eyes. He looks so ferocious and becomes so emotionally involved in the game that I'm sure he salivates, preparatory to eating what he catches. For that reason, I try to play this game right before meals. After each catch, I always praise him effusively. It took me longer to learn how to throw the pipe cleaners correctly than it took Purr to learn to catch them. He was a natural—I wasn't.

Success is an important part of game playing. Remember that a game, to be a game, must be fun—and failure is no fun. So don't roll the ball so fast that the scurrying creature that it represents makes it safely to its hole every time. Your cat will soon begin to feel that it's hopeless to try and will just give up. Instead, endow the field mouse with a thorn in its toe so that it cannot scurry fast enough to escape the fierce predator. Make the startled bird a fledgling whose little feathers cannot lift it high enough to escape your cat's sharp claws. Then, when your cat achieves success, enjoy it with him. Express delight, give praise, and pet him.

Even though Purr is a large cat, he prefers his ultralightweight, small, delicate toy. Once a month or so I dip it in catnip powder to enhance the dimension of smell and taste. He enjoys that a lot, I can tell you.

Little Karunaji, who is a half-grown kitten, doesn't care a rap for Purr's favorite toy. Karunaji stole the metal replica of the Eiffel Tower with a tiny thermometer set into it that sat on my bedroom windowsill. Because it is three inches long, and made of solid brass, it appears too large and heavy for a cat's taste. The texture of cold metal would seem unappealing to a cat. But Karunaji loves it. It makes a satisfying clatter when she bats it across the bare floorboards. Karunaji also loves a long, heavy seashell and a clattery walnut shell.

A crumpled-up paper tied to the end of a long string is very hard to resist. Many cats respond better to something that seems to leap up—for example, something tied to a string can be made to leap up suddenly. A Toughie Mouse from the Felix Katnip Tree Company (which can be ordered by mail—see "Product Recommendations," in the Appendix) is smaller and heavier, while a sheet of tablet paper crumpled into a ball is larger and lighter, with the added advantage of going "klittery-scrape" as you drag it along the floor.

Supersuccessful Cat Toys

Ping-pong ball

Peacock feather: used by cat show judges to draw a response from blasé show types (available from florist suppliers)

Pipe cleaner

Crumpled paper, tissue paper, or waxed paper

Super Ball (children's toy)

Small seashell

Green bean

Toilet paper cylinder

Cap from a pen or water bottle

Cat Dancer: a big winner and a favorite here at Fluff City

Toughie Mouse from Felix Katnip Tree Company

Feline Flyer: fishing pole with feathers on the end of a string

Kitty Go Crazy Interactive Cat Toy: If your cat likes this motorized toy as much as others do, the toy may need repair after a particularly boisterous session. If so, get your duct tape out and improvise. There's an optional, alternate ball for the smaller, doughnut-shaped track on this toy that "talks"; you may regret it if you insert it in the track. However, you might want to use it as a separate cat toy.

Dangling Toy: Attaches to any door frame with a spring mechanism, as a cat toy dangling from a bungee-like cord.

Doughnut-shaped track with a plastic ball that flies around inside; if at all possible, replace the original ball with a real, authentic ping-pong ball. You will be very surprised at the difference. For one thing, it gives the cat an opportunity to "win" by freeing the ball. Have several ping-pong balls handy as they will end up under furniture and behind radiators.

Dangerous Toys to Avoid

Crinkly foil balls (made specifically as cat toys and sold in pet stores)
Aluminum foil crushed into a ball
Cellophane crushed into a ball
Anything with "eyes" or decorations that might be pulled off and swallowed

I divide cats into two categories—the mousers and the bird catchers. The mousers like my Princess love to chase things along the floor and pounce on them; the bird catchers like my Big Purr execute breath-taking leaps into the air to trap flying pipe cleaners. Try it both ways to find out which hunting method your cat prefers.

There is a great advantage to having a favorite game in which the *same* toy is always used in pretty much the *same* way, in the *same* area of the home, and always at the *same* time of day, because this sameness constitutes a ritual—and you know how cats love rituals. When you go away, this ritual can easily be taught to the cat sitter and will make the sitter seem more like a member of the family to your cat.

Catnip is a powerful tool that can be used for positive reinforcement. Catnip is a stimulant—a mild aphrodisiac. When powdered, it has a snufflike effect that elicits a good sneeze. And it's just a heck of a lot of fun. Guardians really should keep a supply on hand. Sometimes it's packaged poorly. Treat catnip like any herb; after you open it store it in a tightly covered jar. My cats' favorite brands are Felix Fine Ground Catnip and PetGuard organic catnip, which comes packaged in an attractive air tight container (see "Product Recommendations" in the Appendix).

One word of advice: you must keep control of the catnip source because cats will open things you thought they couldn't open and will go places you thought they couldn't get to in order to get at the catnip. One day you'll come home to find your cats rolling drunkenly on the rug, catnip littered all about. I'm not saying there is anything really wrong with this—the catnip won't hurt them if it's not used too often, and one good binge a year will brighten any cat's life. But cats become immune to the effect of catnip if it is used too frequently. Also, because catnip is a medicinal herb, it will antidote homeopathic remedies.

Dr. Rowan, the cat specialist for whom I worked, used to give catnip to every cat on the examining table. It was a wonderful way to distract the cats and help them to enjoy his gentle and thorough examination. Then he'd also throw a little catnip into the cat's carrying case so that the whole experience of going to the veterinarian, being examined, and having the teeth cleaned was sort of enveloped in a heavenly cloud of catnip. Out of the whole experience, that fabulous catnip is what the cats remembered—especially those cats whose guardians never bothered to have catnip at home. Boy, did they love going to see Dr. Rowan!

The office cats, however, were quite another story. There were always two or three of these cats in residence running around. They were strays found injured in the street, cats whose guardians brought them in and then deserted them, or cats with terminal illnesses being kept alive with carefully regulated doses of powerful medication because they were not suffering and they had indicated that they didn't want to pass on just yet. They worked their way—acting as hostesses and nurse's aides, calming the patients and their guardians. These office cats were constantly exposed to catnip. It was wafted in the air, bits and pieces fell to the floor several times a day—they could have it whenever they chose. I was surprised to learn soon after I started to work there that of all the resident cats there wasn't one who cared a rap about catnip. They were all overexposed. That really saddened me—all the others were having such a lot of fun. So ever since then I've always been very careful to give my cats catnip in any form only once a week. Then we have a party. I lay both Karate Cat scratching posts on their sides and sprinkle them with catnip. I also sprinkle catnip on the floor around the posts. All my cats sniff and sneeze, roll and lick and growl, and thrash around to their hearts' content. After an hour, I vacuum the whole mess up because by that time the entire group is stretched out sleeping the sleep of the sated. What a bash! Of course, when I'm going away I make sure that they have not had a catnip party for at least two weeks before I leave so that that happy ritual can then be performed by the sitter as a nice distraction.

Diet 2

Diet is a tool that any cat guardian can use to build health, long life, resistance to disease, and joyous and even temperament. It is a tool so powerful that it is almost a magic wand. *What* you feed your cats and, of equal importance, *how often* you feed them is something you, the caregiver, and no one else, can control. The magic wand is yours alone.

When I started grooming, I was still working part-time for Dr. Paul Rowan. Because I was spending a full hour with each caregiver during the grooming session, I realized that I had a unique opportunity to reinforce details of home care. So I asked Dr. Rowan if there was any information that he wanted me to pass along during the groomings. He thought for a split second and replied that I should try to get all of them to remove food between meals and add yeast and bran to the food. He explained that leaving the food available for only a half hour or so is more natural, because wild animals don't smell food and nibble all day long. And, he said, the added yeast and bran would raise the protein quality of the whole meal and keep the cat's resistance to disease high. So I dutifully passed these two bits of information along to every client I saw.

When I returned to my clients the next month for the usual grooming session, I found that these simple dietary changes had caused startling improvements in the cats' coats. In fact, the changes were incredible. Persians who always had some matting now had almost none. Oily coats were less oily. Dull, harsh coats began to feel silky and look fluffier and brighter. Of course, I should have expected these results: "You are what you eat." What the cat's guardian puts in the food dish is the raw material out of which the cat's body makes every tissue and cell. Good quality food results in good-quality fur, blood, organs, and

55

temperament—it improves everything. It only makes sense that better-quality food will result in better overall health. It's obvious now, as I look back. But at that time it was a new realization for me. That was the beginning.

Then I began to notice that cats whose health was below par did not show as dramatic a change in coat quality as young, healthy cats did. I reasoned that coat quality was a barometer of the internal health of the cat, so I began nutritional research into helping the cat's body overcome various physical ailments. I had seen the promise in those improved coats, so I knew that I could use improved nutrition to help the cat's body overcome any health problem and that the shiny, plushy coat would just naturally follow, like the night follows the day. Thirty-five years and thousands of cats later, I can honestly say that I was right.

The Primary Feeding Rule: Remove Food Between Meals

Dr. Rowan's advice, "Stick as close as you can to nature and you can never go very far wrong," has helped me out many a time. Let us examine how Mother Nature takes care of her children and arranges to keep them happy, healthy, and strong.

Cats in the wild eat once a day—*if* they are young and strong and lucky. For a wild cat, two servings of food a day would be a luxury bordering on decadence. In the wild, fasting periods occur naturally because of scarcity of prey or inclement weather, or because the animal is feeling sick and chooses to fast. A day or two or even three or four may go by before the cat takes a meal. Nature provides these fasting times for a very good reason. During a fast, the blood and energy that are usually used for digestion and assimilation are now available for use in other parts of the body. Healing and repair are accelerated during a fast. Waste disposal becomes more complete, and the body is able to deep-clean itself. If there are backed-up wastes in the system, they putrefy. Germs breed in putrefaction. So Mother Nature keeps her children free from disease by providing periodic fasts during which the organs of excretion—the intestines, kidneys, lungs, and skin—can get a good housecleaning. The short fast we provide for our animals between their two regular daily meals is precious little time for the cat's body to process food and accomplish the necessary waste disposal. Let us not take away even this little time by leaving food in the dish between meals.

Another reason for removing food between meals is that the *smell* of food (not the taste) triggers the cat's brain to prepare the body for digestion. The olfactory center in the brain sends out the message to slow down the metabolism so the body can concentrate on digesting food. Saliva and digestive juices begin to flow while blood flow and waste disposal slow down. All the organs except the stomach are undersupplied with blood during this process. While all this is a perfect setup for digesting food efficiently, it is not a state of affairs we would want to continue twenty-four hours a day. Moreover, if cats are constantly smelling food, the trigger mechanism in the brain that starts the whole digestive process will soon wear out and fail to respond. A cat's sense of smell is seven hundred times sharper than ours. Even the odor from a dirty food bowl or a bag of dry food stored in the cupboard can trigger this mechanism and keep the cat's body in constant preparation for digesting food. The resulting undersupply of blood to all organs (except the stomach) causes such cats to age faster than those whose food areas are kept scrupulously clean.

A third reason not to leave food available between meals will be of interest to all those guardians who have ever worried about feline urologic syndrome (FUS). Veterinarians usually prescribe acidifier pills for FUS patients to ensure that the urine stays nicely acidic. FUS germs thrive in an alkaline urine. Recent studies have revealed that every time a cat smells food his urine becomes more alkaline. Cats who fall ill with urinary blockage almost always come from homes where food of some kind is left available all day long. You can feed extra meals during the day if necessary, but just don't leave the leftovers down on the floor. Wash the dirty food dish and put it away, and store any dry food or treats in airtight jars. I keep a nice collection of screw-top jars for just this purpose. If you don't have an airtight jar, keep the dry treats in the refrigerator where no one can smell them.

Leaving food available all day is also the primary cause of the finicky eater syndrome. Slowed metabolism is a cause of several health problems—among them dandruff, obesity, and skinniness. If a cat has a poor appetite, the answer is not to leave more food available for longer periods but just the opposite—remove all food after one-half hour to give that trigger response a chance to rest.

You will be in harmony with nature's rhythms if you remember that your domestic cat's food equals the wild cat's mouse. The mice do not lounge around all day under the cat's nose waiting to be eaten. Meals are an important, but separate, part of the animal's day.

By all means, feed your cats twice a day or more often for special health problems or for kittens. But be sure to leave the food available for only a half hour—certainly no longer than forty-five minutes. Then remove it and wash everything nice and clean so that no smell remains. Leave fresh water for them to drink at all times.

Although I am not a psychologist, I have observed that leaving food available is with some people a deep psychological need. Removing the food is indeed a very real sacrifice on some people's part that they make out of deep love. I know in advance that these people may cheat a little, and if they do and if the cat is hooked on the old low-quality food, I'm not surprised when they call and say, "She's not eating the new food—she has eaten nothing in five days." I will tell you now what I always tell them: if you leave any food around between meals I cannot help you because the cat will not be hungry at mealtime. "But I'm away all day," they exclaim. Nevermind—go back and read the very beginning of this chapter and, if you still want to leave food around while you're gone, you're defeated before you start.

Some people feel they must leave food available because of their own erratic schedules, which may mean being out from early morning to late in the evening on occasion. My answer to them is to feed the second meal *whenever* they arrive home. The cat will not starve if dinner is a few hours later than usual. And, again, remember that in the wild a cat's mealtimes are highly irregular. To those who still can't bear the idea that Muffy will go unfed for a few hours, I remind them that we humans don't always eat our meals at the same time either.

To the guardians who confess their weakness and vow to turn over a new leaf, I give the following advice (and every one of the veterinarians with whom I've worked agree on this): no one has ever heard of a cat who starved to death while something edible was available twice a day. Some cats will hold out for five days before taking a nibble. They may cry and complain. A few creative types that I've known walk over to the dish, very obviously sniff it, then turn around and proceed to scratch the floor as if they were trying to cover excrement. Such behavior may be hard to resist if you do not have the thought firmly in your mind that you love your animals dearly and want them to stay alive and well for as many years as possible.

To make the change of not allowing the cat to smell food between meals more gradual and gentle, you can try feeding smaller meals more often. I tell my clients that I don't mind if they feed their cats six meals a day as long as they don't *leave* food lying out. Gradually you should reduce the number of meals to the norm of two or three a day.

Treats are fun and useful for reinforcing desirable behavior patterns and for hiding medicine in, but they shouldn't become a daily habit—otherwise, they are no longer treats, but become old hat.

The No-Nos: Foods to Avoid

Early in my search for a high-quality food—one with no preservatives, colorings, or other nonfood ingredients—it became obvious to me that most cat food stocked on grocery shelves did not fulfill the primary purpose of building health. Most simply sustain life, at least for a moderate amount of time, before endangering the cat's health with chemical additives, imbalances, nondigestibility, and general low quality.

Ingredients such as tuna, salt, sugar, and artificial flavors and scents tend to attract the cats and "hook" them. Artificial colors are there to attract people (cats don't care about the color of their food). Artificial flavors and colors are not food but chemicals that undermine health.

In researching the foods available, I was surprised to find that every manufacturer of every single cat food available in the grocery store could present the results of one or more "scientific tests" proving beyond all doubt that their food was absolutely wonderful for cats—the very best. Also, I viewed an "unbiased" report on pet foods on the television news, and it too stated that in effect everything on the shelf was perfectly fine because government regulations were so strict. But after the ethoxyquin scandal, the taurine scandal, and, in 2007, the melamine scandal, I can say, without reservation, balderdash!

Ethoxyquin is still used in many pet foods as a preservative. It was originally developed by Monsanto, the rubber corporation, as a rubber stabilizer for tires (to improve their resistance to cracking). Proving effective, it was soon adopted for other uses. Ethoxyquin is now used as a weed killer and to preserve fat. Because it was found to cause cancer, it was not approved for use in human food. But it was approved for use in pet food.

Breeders began finding more deformed puppies and kittens than ever before in their litters. Veterinarians found increased incidence of cancers of the throat, stomach, intestines, and rectum. They appealed to the government to ban ethoxyquin in pet food, but they were unsuccessful. They wrote articles in magazines and professional journals to alert the public. The public responded by carefully reading product labels, and soon sales of pet products containing ethoxyquin fell.

The government has since changed the wording in the labeling laws so that pet food companies are now only required to list ethoxyquin on their labels when directly placing it in their product. If they buy fat that is already preserved with ethoxyquin they do not have to list it on the label because they were not the ones who put the ethoxyquin in the fat. Several major pet food manufacturers have taken advantage of this loophole.

Another big recall of pet foods occurred when an alarming number of dogs and cats were brought to veterinarians with an array of symptoms that included blindness. Tests revealed a taurine deficiency in every case. The affected animals had not all been eating the same food. The pet foods that were implicated included major brands sold in supermarkets as well as two brands commonly sold by conventional veterinarians. I was puzzled by the problem because taurine is an amino acid, a protein found in meat, fish, eggs, and poultry, the main ingredients in most cat foods. How could a product containing meat, fish, or poultry be deficient in taurine?

I called Dr. Pitcairn, my veterinary homeopath and teacher, who specializes in small animal nutrition. "Could it be," I asked, "that most pet foods are so highly processed and cooked at such high temperatures for such a long time that the taurine molecules are being altered? Perhaps the animals' bodies aren't able to recognize them anymore, so they are passed off as waste instead of being assimilated?" Dr. Pitcairn's answer was, "Yes." That was what he had been thinking too.

The pet food companies did not respond by changing their processing methods; they simply added more taurine to the mix. The indigestible taurine and other altered proteins still have to be processed and then disposed of by the bodies of the animals who eat this food, and the burden falls squarely on the cats' kidneys. Kidney disease used to be found mainly in elderly cats; it has become more prevalent in younger cats now.

The big 2007 pet food recall was caused by the presence of melamine, a poison, in wheat gluten and rice protein that many pet food manufacturers had obtained from China. Melamine is used worldwide in the manufacture of plastics. It is also used in fertilizers, but only in Asia. In the United States it is not allowed in human or pet foods. However, over the last two decades, enforcement of the government's standards has slipped. Add to this the fact that at least six government inspection facilities have been closed since the war in Iraq began. At any rate, the melamine-tainted pet food ingredients were imported into the country and widely used, again by many popular brands.

I remember saying a quick prayer of thanksgiving because I knew that I and most of my clients would be perfectly safe. We were all feeding a combination of homemade raw food and PetGuard canned food to our cats. However, I was called upon by several new clients to help undo the damage. One of my worst memories is of hearing a soft tap on my door and finding the building janitor's twelve-year-old son standing there with tears running down his cheeks and the limp body of his little white poodle mix cradled in his arms. In the end, she did survive, but that unfortunate family is still struggling to pay off the vet bill.

Evidently my standards are quite a bit different from those of the government. Preservatives such as BHA, BHT, propyl gallate, nitrates, benzoate of soda (sodium benzoate), and ethoxyquin, and other additives such as colorings, artificial flavorings, and scents are not food. They are chemicals that, in sufficient amounts, are deadly poisons to cats. In lesser amounts, they produce illness—but in really minute quantities any damage builds up so slowly that it is hard to measure. These smaller amounts have been declared "safe" despite the fact that several of these substances cannot be excreted. They are stored in the fat and build up over the weeks and months as they are continually ingested. My feeling is simply that, if you do not have to include these nonfood chemical substances in your cat's diet, then don't. If a substance in a package marked "cat food" can be considered harmful in any way—in whatever quantity—I avoid that cat food completely. In most cases, research has never been done to discover the dangers encountered when different chemicals, some from one product and some from another, combine within the cat's body. Some of these chemicals are so dangerous that they are not permitted in human food. Several have been prohibited in England and other countries. I won't take a chance. I prefer safety and only the highest-quality nutrition.

If you pick up any canned cat food in your supermarket and read the tiny print under the heading "ingredients," you will undoubtedly see the words *meat by-products* or *beef by-products*. Dr. P. F. McGargle, a veterinarian who has also been a federal meat inspector, says by-products "can include moldy, rancid or spoiled processed meats as well as tissue too severely riddled with cancer to be eaten by people."[1] Dr. Alfred J. Plechner gives a more comprehensive list: "Diseased tissue, pus, hair, assorted slaughterhouse rejects, and carcasses in varying stages of decomposition are sterilized with chemicals, heat and pressure procedures."[2]

1. Pitcairn, Richard H., DVM, PhD, and Susan Hubble Pitcairn. *Dr. Pitcairn's Complete Guide to Natural Health for Dogs and Cats*. Emmaus, PA: Rodale Press, 1982, 13.
2. Plechner, Alfred J., DVM, and Martin Zucker. *Pet Allergies: Remedies for an Epidemic*. Inglewood, CA: Very Healthy Enterprises, 1986, 13.

Many by-products come from so-called "4-D" animals—dead, dying, diseased, and disabled—which the federal government does allow in pet food. The theory is that all harmful bacteria and viruses are destroyed by heat processing at high temperatures, which "sterilizes" the meat by-products. How would you feel if you knew that the food you ate every day was composed of diseased meat? Even if the government is right and all the bacteria and viruses have been killed by the processing, would you consider the resulting "food" to be *good* for you?

Be sure to read the ingredients even when you buy in the health food store or from your veterinarian. There is a well-known health food brand available all over the country that contains lots of tuna and by-products. In addition, many conventional veterinarians that I know routinely endorse a brand of food that contains both by-products and ethoxyquin. Remember, most veterinarians are not nutritionists; that's not their field.

In addition to the by-products and additives in commercial pet foods, there are some additional problems. From the standpoint of the careful caregiver who seeks to bolster the health of a cat through a natural approach, we need to consider the quality of the proteins and their assimilability (can they be easily used by the cat's body?).

The protein *quality* in most commercial cat foods is very low. Protein is made up of amino acids. They occur in different ratios in different types of meat tissue. Some amino acids are found more in muscle meat, some predominate in the organs, while others are dominant in meat parts such as blood vessels and intestines. Feet, eyes, feathers, and tumors are also made up of protein. Muscle meat and most organs are called "high quality protein" because the ratio in which the amino acids occur in these meats is the best ratio for maintaining a normal standard of health in cats. When a cat kills an animal or bird for food in the wild, Mother Nature provides a nice balance: mostly muscle meat, about one-sixth organ meats, and some intestines and blood vessels.

Lungs, intestines, and other meat by-products such as tumors which have been removed from those parts of the meat sold for human consumption are cheaper for cat food manufacturers to buy. The government regulates how much protein must be present in each can of food; however, the type of protein (the quality and balance of amino acids) is only loosely defined.

The second problem, that of *assimilability*, is affected by the processing of the food. As a rule, the lower the quality of the protein, the more processing it will need before it will pass government standards. Tumors and partially decayed meats (which are permitted by the federal government as well as many state governments) are processed not only with high heat but, in some cases, also with chemical sprays.

A cat's body is designed to assimilate raw food. It cannot sustain itself efficiently on lungs, tumors, intestines, and decayed matter processed with chemicals and extreme heat.

Dry Cat Food

Dry food is a prime suspect in causing feline urologic syndrome (FUS) and bladder stones. Dry food is always processed more than canned food, and the protein quality in most dry food is low. Both highly processed food and low-quality protein cause the urine to be *alkaline*, whereas a cat fed on high-quality, raw protein tends to have an *acidic* urine. An acidic urine prevents the growth of germs that cause FUS and also helps dissolve bladder stones and gravel.

One brand of dry cat food carries the slogan "Lowest in ash of all dry food." A clever piece of advertising: it is perfectly true. However, this is like saying that grapefruit is the lowest in acid of all citrus fruits. This statement is also perfectly true, but grapefruit, after all, is still a very acidic fruit compared to those outside the citrus family—just as all dry food is still more processed than canned food.

All the veterinarians I've worked with caution against a dry food diet and expressly forbid it if FUS has been diagnosed. Conversely, dry food manufacturers can present test results proving that a connection between dry food and FUS is, if not actually nonexistent, then at least inconclusive. Recent research has shown that the cat's urine alkalizes every time he smells or eats anything at all. Since caregivers who feed dry food are the ones most likely to leave food available all day long, this is yet another reason why dry food cats tend to suffer from FUS and bladder stones.

Dry food does not clean the teeth. It never has and it never will. No one claims that—not even the dry food manufacturers. I have met numerous cats formerly on an all-dry-food diet with the worst tartar in the world. There are three or four "health food" pet food companies that have carefully developed some very high-quality dry foods to go with their canned food lines. Because dry food is processed more than canned food, I do not feed these products as a meal. I use PetGuard dry food as high-quality treats. I tell my clients, "Don't call dry food 'food'; call it 'cookies' or 'treats' to remind yourself not to feed more than four or five 'cookies' a day." For acceptable crunchies and treats, see "Delicious Treats and Crunchies" later in this chapter.

Semimoist Food in Packets

Almost every brand of semimoist cat food has the words *complete nutrition* on the package. Keep in mind that the words *complete nutrition* mean only that the *minimum* daily requirement of all known vitamins and minerals are in there. It does not mean that these nutrients are necessarily present in a form that your cat can digest or assimilate. There's no guarantee of that. And, while we're on the subject, why don't we just take a look at the label and see what else is contained in that convenient little package of "complete nutrition"?

If a manufacturer wants to make a lot of money on a food product for human or animal consumption, a major criterion is to make something with the longest possible shelf life. The amount of preservatives used in semimoist food is so great that its shelf life approaches infinity. In his book *Pet Allergies: Remedies for an Epidemic*, Dr. Alfred J. Plechner writes: "Semi-moist [food] is a horror story . . . tinted, flavored and processed with a genuine Hollywood flair for special effects. They use artificial colors and flavors, emulsifiers, preservatives, salt, sugar and whatever else most humans avoid who are interested in good health. In my opinion, semi-moist should be placed in a time capsule to serve as a record of modern food technology gone mad."[3]

If you still have any doubt why I would not use semimoist food, I suggest you look at the stool deposited by a cat or dog fed on these substances. The stool looks like Technicolor plastic.

Fish

The word "fish" on a cat food label can mean any part of the fish. Almost all commercial cat foods use mostly the cheaper parts of the fish—heads, tails, scales, and bones, which are very high in insoluble mineral salts (ash) that can form stones and gravel in the bladder and urinary tract. Very few pet food manufacturers use the filets or whole fish, which are much more expensive and generally only sold for human consumption. PetGuard is the only company I know of that

---

3. Plechner and Zucker, p. 31.

uses only filets and whole fish in their recipe. They do not use tuna which has its own set of problems.

Many popular brands of cat food contain tuna. "Tuna junkie" is an expression used by veterinarians to describe a cat "hooked" on tuna. The flavor is so strong that cats who eat a lot of tuna come to believe that tuna is the only thing that constitutes food—nothing else fits into that category for them. Tuna is used precisely because of its strong addictive properties.

Canned tuna in the cat's diet has two drawbacks. First, the vegetable oil it is packed in tends to rob the cat's body of vitamin E. When the stored vitamin E is sufficiently depleted, a condition called "steatitis" results. Steatitis—or "yellow fat disease"—causes the cat first to become extremely nervous and then to become supersensitive in all the nerve endings in the skin; it is very painful for such a cat to be touched in any way. If an autopsy is done on these cats, the fat is buttercup yellow instead of white. The disease can be cured by giving megadoses of vitamin E under the careful supervision of a veterinarian and, of course, by discontinuing any food containing vegetable oil or mineral oil because this will deplete the body's stores of vitamin E even more.

Upon mentioning to one veterinarian that I had noticed some cat food companies were adding vitamin E to the tuna fish, the doctor replied that its effectiveness would be like putting a little chemotherapy pill into each pack of cigarettes. Besides the fact that the oil used with tuna depletes the system of vitamin E, tuna, as well as swordfish, salmon, and other carnivorous fish, are at the top of the food chain and therefore contain larger amounts of mercury. Bottom feeders like cod, scrod, haddock, halibut, flounder, and sole contain much less mercury.

In addition, one recent study at Cornell University showed that tuna cat food had unusually high levels of the toxic metal methylmercury. The Cornell researchers pointed out that the tuna used in cat food comes from the red meat part of the fish, which apparently contains more toxins than the white meat tuna sold for human consumption. The white tuna meat contains less, but mercury is still present there too.

Ham and Pork

Compared to us humans, cats are very small animals. Ham and pork contain fat globules so large that they clog the cat's blood vessels. Just think of your own tiniest capillary and then think what those globules must do in the capillaries and veins of a cat fifteen times smaller than yourself. The preservatives and colorings used in bacon, hot dogs, sausages, and lunch meats are, frankly, lethal in sufficient quantity—even for us big animals. Also, I don't believe in polluting a cat's system with the nitrates and nitrites that are used to preserve most of these meats.

The High-Quality Diet: Fluff City in Thirty Days

Canned foods, although not the best choice, can be a nice, easy, middle-of-the-road diet if you beef them up with supplements and if you choose from the pure-food varieties made without by-products and preservatives. These are now available from pet food distributors and your health food store. Freeze-dried and frozen cat foods are also available from natural pet food companies. See "Product Recommendations," in the Appendix, for brands. Try several to see what your cat likes. Then try to settle on at least three or four flavors; variety in the diet is best.

Surprisingly, the price of the "health food brands" without preservatives or by-products is about the same as the price of the so-called prescription canned foods sometimes sold by veterinarians and the "gourmet" canned foods in supermarkets. One reason the pure-food brands can give better quality at about the same price is that they don't do major advertising. They put the money into the food and let the results of feeding their higher-quality food speak for itself. As long as we're talking about expense, consider also how much a careful caregiver saves on veterinary bills.

I prefer to save money by buying by the case from a wholesale pet food distributor. Be sure that organ meat constitutes no more than one-sixth of the weekly diet because, if a cat killed an animal in the wild for dinner, only one-sixth of the prey would be organs. If you can't find any health food brands in your area (check with both pet food suppliers and health food stores) check the Appendix for ethical companies that will ship directly to you.

Baby food meat and vegetable mixes such as Junior High Meat Dinner (vegetables and lamb, turkey and rice, and so on) are also acceptable but incomplete. You need to add fat, calcium, and fiber to make them suitable for a cat (see page 68). The baby food recipe on page 89 can be used to wean kittens or to feed sick cats with mouth problems. In all cases, high-quality canned food is better and homemade raw food is best.

Not even the best canned food from the health food store is perfect, because every canned food is processed by heat, and many vitamins and enzymes are destroyed by heat. Even the newer frozen and freeze-dried natural cat foods don't have all the virtues of fresh food. Cats who hunt and kill in the wild consume the whole mouse, right down to the whiskers. They will eat some hair and probably get a little dirt off the ground in the process. Nature has a purpose in letting the cat ingest these little extras. Hair is roughage, minerals, and protein. Dust is full of minerals. The mouse's stomach contains predigested grains full of B vitamins and enzymes. And the mouse was alive a moment before, so the meat is still pulsing with life. (I wonder how long the meat inside of that can has been dead.) How shall we supply the missing elements? Let's think of building a mouse!

To supply the contents of the mouse's stomach, we will use wheat bran. To supply the minerals and roughage of the mouse's hair, we will use bran, again, and either kelp or a mixed trace mineral powder. To supply something living, something still alive when your cat eats it: yeast. The yeast will also raise the quality of the protein in the entire meal and replace some of the amino acids and many of those B vitamins that were destroyed by heat during the canning process, those same B vitamins that the wild cat gets from the contents of the mouse's stomach.

I add lecithin granules because they emulsify fatty wastes, help do away with dandruff, and make the coat texture absolutely gorgeous. For longhaired cats, lecithin granules are a must. Because cats' requirements for vitamin E are very high and because vitamin E in food is extremely perishable, I keep a bottle of 400-unit vitamin E capsules available in the refrigerator. Once a week, I puncture one for each of the cats and squeeze its contents into their food. An alternate method is to wipe it onto the cat's wrist and let him lick it off, or squeeze the oil onto your finger and then wipe it off on the cat's eyetooth. Once a week I also give each cat the contents of a low-potency capsule, which contains 10,000 units vitamin A and 400 units vitamin D. An even better and easier alternative is to include a good multivitamin in your cat's food every day. I recommend Nu-Cats or Tabby Tabs (see "Product Recommendations" in the Appendix).

At first you may think that you need a full-fledged chemist or a master chef to implement the plan. Take heart. In working with hundreds of very busy New Yorkers, I soon realized that if I wanted all of my cat friends to have the very best it was absolutely necessary to devise a way that was fast and simple for the guardians. If your cat is healthy and you simply want to keep him that way:

- Feed a raw food diet
- Give a good multivitamin as directed, and
- Add ½ to 1 tsp of Anitra's Vita-Mineral Mix to each meal
- Anitra's Vita-Mineral Mix is available now from the PetGuard Company. Find it in health food and pet supply stores. If you'd like to make it yourself, all the ingredients are available in health food stores.

Anitra's Vita-Mineral Mix

1½ cups yeast powder (any food yeast: brewer's, tarula, or nutritional)
¼ cup kelp powder *or* ¼ cup mixed trace mineral powder
1 cup lecithin granules
2 cups wheat bran
2 cups bonemeal, calcium lactate, or calcium gluconate

- Mix together and store in a covered container. Be sure to *refrigerate* (everything but the lecithin and minerals perishes at room temperature).
- Add ½–1 teaspoonful of Anitra's Vita-Mineral Mix to each cat's meal (1–2 teaspoonfuls per cat per day).
- Once a week give each cat 400 units vitamin E (alpha tocopherol, not mixed tocopherols) and the contents of a vitamin A and D capsule (10,000 units vitamin A and 400 units vitamin D). If your cat dislikes the taste of these supplements in his food, just puncture the capsule with a pin and squirt it into the cat's cheek pouch or diagonally across the tongue. (Never squirt a liquid down the center of the throat. If the cat is inhaling, he could choke.) Or just give a good multivitamin for cats every day as directed.

This way you can add all these supplements without having to take five different jars out of the refrigerator twice a day. Store the leftover food in a covered glass or plastic container and refrigerate. *Do not store in the can.* Cans are usually made of aluminum and the can's seam is sealed closed with lead. Once you open the can and break the vacuum, oxygen and moisture are free to mix with the lead and aluminum. Molecules from these toxic metals can then get into the food. Avoid lead and aluminum contamination by removing the food from the can as soon as you open it. I use a glass container to store the leftover food because glass conducts the cold in the refrigerator. Colder food stays fresher longer. A peanut butter jar is good; a pickled artichoke jar is perfect. Some imported jams come in jars that are especially pleasing to the eye and hand. Here's a perfect excuse to splurge on one you always wanted to try and then keep that attractive and practical jar as your permanent cat food storage jar for the refrigerator.

After using Anitra's Vita-Mineral Mix for one month, approximately 85 percent of my clients noticed the following changes: dandruff gone; oiliness diminishing and disappearing; matting diminishing and disappearing; shine appearing; texture becoming thick, rich, and plushy. Of the other 15 percent, most noticed the changes after two, three, or six months because the cats were older and had slower metabolisms, or because the guardians were slower to remove all food between meals. For example, some guardians, instead of removing the food after a half hour, would leave the food for as much as an hour and a half for the first couple of weeks. Others, whose cats were "hooked" on one of the really low-quality foods, spent the first couple of weeks mixing the old food with the new food, gradually diminishing the former low-quality food until the cat was eating only the high-quality food. Remember that speed is unimportant as long as you and your cat are going in the right direction.

Many of my clients, on seeing the spectacular results in their cats' furs, decided to include the ingredients in Anitra's Vita-Mineral Mix in their own diets— as I myself do. If you're one of those people who wash your hair not because it's dirty but because it's lank or oily or if you use some sort of conditioner or styling gel to give it shine or body, I suggest you give these supplements a try. You will also appreciate the effect on your fingernails and the whites of your eyes.

Many cats who have canine friends are sharing their Anitra's Vita-Mineral Mix. After all, why shouldn't the whole family look stunning. A high-quality diet will benefit any animal. However, it's good to keep in mind that the dog's basic requirements differ slightly from the cat's. Dogs are a bit more like us humans in that they can be vegetarians if all their essential amino acids are supplied; also, they need less fat than cats. The better cat food companies listed in the Appendix also sell dog food and one even offers a vegetarian variety for dogs and a hypoallergenic variety for both dogs and cats.

With any animal, it's very important to remove food after a half hour, leaving only water available between meals. This way the internal organs will all be well supplied with blood and the metabolism will be youthful. Removing food between meals keeps your cat spry. My Priscilla, at fifteen, was still the champion soccer player with our dented ping-pong ball. Her haunches were so shapely they drove Big Purr crazy. He'd try to nibble her neck and lick her ears at every opportunity. Priscilla, being a lady, would respond by giving him a swat on the nose. Priscilla weighs only four and a half pounds, to Purr's twelve.

The I'll-Do-Anything-for-My-Cat Diet

The caregiver who prepares his or her own cat food from scratch really has a firm grip on that health-bestowing magic wand. It's simple to do; the very minimal time you spend making up food will be saved later because your cats will be healthier on their tailor-made diet, and you will be required to spend less time on nursing care, pilling, and ferrying to the veterinarian in later years. And—surprise!—the cost is the same or even less than the cost of canned cat food. I suggest you first try it for a month, because that gives you time to get it down to a quick, easy routine, and it gives your cats time to show evidence of this best-of-all-diets with improved coat, temperament, and general health.

Because you are making up your own formula, you can tailor the texture as well as the taste and nutritional content to your cats' taste and individual needs. It's wise to blend or mash most of it well at first in order to mix the vegetables with the meat; otherwise some cats will pick out the meat pieces and leave the rest. Most cats enjoy a smooth, creamy consistency like baby food. You can always hold a few chunks of meat and baked carrot to mix in at mealtime if your cats find chomping on lumps exciting. You'll have to ask their opinion on that.

If you can manage to get all organically grown products, that, of course, is best. Commercial pesticides used on vegetables are poisonous, and chemical fertilizers lower vitamin content considerably. The hormones and antibiotics injected as a matter of course into all the meat and poultry available on the open market are better left right where they are—on the open market, not in your cat's stomach, or your family's either for that matter. If you can't always get organic foods, by all means use whatever foods you're buying for the rest of the household. The vegetables will still be fresh and the meat will be raw. That is the most important part of the recipe. However, if the meat is not organic, stick to beef. Chicken, turkey, and eggs, unless they are organic, contain a lot more hormones and antibiotics than beef.

Remember, you won't be paying more for the food because you will be serving quality instead of quantity. The proteins you will use are so nicely balanced that your cats will need to eat less. This careful protein balance yields the added dividend of saving the cats' kidneys and keeping them functioning efficiently into old age.

Raw-Food Diet

Before I give the recipe, I'll let you in on a few facts about feeding a raw food diet. There are many benefits to be gained by serving raw meat and vegetables. It is, of course, the most natural diet of all. Cats in the wild don't build a campfire and toast their mice like marshmallows. When food is cooked, both vitamins and enzymes are destroyed. Also, the fat and protein molecules can be altered by the heating process, making it more difficult for the cat's system to digest and use them.

Between the years 1932 and 1942 extensive and long-range testing was done on animals by Dr. Francis M. Pottenger. The results showed that animals fed only cooked food, even though the diet was perfectly balanced, showed markedly reduced immune response. As the study progressed, heart lesions, allergies, arthritis, hepatitis, irritable bowel syndrome, feline urologic syndrome, and other illnesses became more and more common in the cats who were fed cooked food. It took only three generations to reduce the immune response to virtually zero. I am reminded of the heartbroken caregivers I meet every day whose cats are bravely fighting feline leukemia and the other numerous immune deficiency diseases we are hearing so much about in recent years. Dr. Pottenger's experiments went on to show that the health of these unfortunate animals could be improved simply by returning them to a raw food diet. Because the raw food diet is homemade, it also eliminates your cat's exposure to dangerous preservatives and other chemicals that are often present in common pet foods.

Whenever I suggest feeding a raw food diet, which includes raw meat, the concerned guardian inevitably asks, "Aren't you concerned about germs and parasites?" My answer is, "Yes, I am. So I take extra precautions with the meat portion." I buy only a small supply that will be eaten up in two days. I buy fresh ground beef from a store that I know has a rapid turnover of merchandise. Organic meats are more resistant to parasites because the food animals have not been treated with steroids or antibiotics. I stretch the meat by adding one organic egg to each ½ lb. of meat. I store the meat in a covered glass jar in the refrigerator. Glass conducts the cold and keeps it fresher longer. I take it out only long enough to remove the portion I need. I don't let it sit at room temperature for even sixty seconds. Then I put the rest right back in the refrigerator. The food is left available for thirty minutes or less; then, if there are leftovers, I put them out for the street cats to enjoy.

Many of my clients are now incorporating a large percentage of raw food into their cats' diets. Some lucky cats are receiving the all-raw-food diet. In every case improvement is obvious. Even cats who are already blooming with health and beauty achieve still higher levels of robust good health within one month.

Since I started feeding my raw food recipe, I've seen enormous health benefits in my clients' cats as well as my own. Now I would never consider feeding anything else. Because the cat's enjoyment is a very important element in the meal, I mix in a half-teaspoon of PetGuard canned food and a little water as a gravy. I also keep a nice variety of PetGuard canned food on the shelf to tide me over in case the raw meat meals run out and a last minute substitute is needed.

If you decide that you want your feline companion to have all the benefits of a raw food diet, bravo! Most cats dive right in and lap it up like little vacuum cleaners. But sometimes you have to be patient. If your cat is sensitive to change, start by feeding part raw and part cooked foods and work into it slowly, or mix in some canned food at first until your fuzzy gourmet gets accustomed to the finest. Once she's eating a totally raw food diet with the added supplements you can sit back and enjoy your rewards. You'll see improvement in not only the fur, but also the cat's muscle tone, play patterns, and responsiveness. People who have never met a raw food cat before will ask if your cat is some wonderful new breed. Raw food cats are very classy animals.

Please be patient with yourself as well as with your cats. The cats may need time to make the changeover, but they aren't the only ones; you definitely will too. You'll need to learn new ways of "fixing" the cat's food. You'll be grating vegetables, and mixing calcium powder into the meat. These are simple skills, but nowadays there are many adults who have never practiced them. Before you say "It takes too long" or "I can't," give yourself a week or so to practice. It takes less than twenty seconds to grate zucchini, and you'll be pleased to see how quickly you pick up speed. And remember, a new skill is more precious than gold. Don't worry if you can't do everything you'd like to do right at first. Speed doesn't matter. Speed will come. If you know what you really want for your cats, they'll have it eventually because you've already got what it takes: the patience and perseverance that come with love.

Ground Rules for the Raw Meat Diet to Ensure Optimum Health and Safety

1. *Choosing the meat.* If possible, buy high-fat meat (15 percent or more fat). Cats require much more animal fat than we do. (Note: If you buy low-fat meat, I'll give you directions below for adding butter to increase the fat content. However, be aware that vegetable oil *cannot* be substituted for the butter.)

Choose from:

- Raw ground round, chuck, or sirloin
- Organic ground chicken or turkey

2. *Adding calcium to the meat—and more fat in the form of butter if necessary.* Because meat is high in phosphorus, it is very important to balance the phosphorus by adding one teaspoon of powdered calcium to each pound of ground meat. Commercial pet food companies are prohibited from selling a pet food unless the calcium and phosphorus are in balance. An imbalance, over time, can cause serious heart and lung problems. Fortunately, maintaining the balance is very simple.

Unless your meat is at least 15 percent fat, you'll also want to add 2 teaspoons of butter per pound of meat.

The easiest plan is just to mix the calcium (and butter, if needed) with the meat as soon as you get home. Here's how:

- Put the ground meat on the table
- Flatten it out like pizza dough
- Sprinkle on the proper amount of calcium powder (1 teaspoon for each pound of meat)
- Add the butter (if needed) by cutting it into tiny bits and sprinkling it over the meat (or use very soft butter)
- Roll it all up like a jelly roll
- Press it flat again and roll it up from a different angle

Now the meat is ready to use in the recipe below. The calcium powder can be put away until the next time you buy meat.

3. *Vegetables.* Choose according to your cat's preferences or health needs. Cooked vegetables are fine; it's the meat that should be raw.

4. *Texture.* Texture is important to a cat. If you're grating carrots or zucchini, use the holes on the grater that look like tiny teardrops. If you're cooking a vegetable, cook it more than you would for yourself—until it's soft enough to mash and blend in easily with the ground meat.

5. *Temperature.* Never feed chilled food. Cats vomit easily. Heat a coffee mug by rinsing it under hot water. Put the portion you are feeding into the hot mug and press it against the warm inside wall of the mug. Then stand the mug in a bowl of warm water. (Don't use hot water; you don't want to cook your nice raw meat.) *Never use a microwave oven.* Microwaving destroys *all* enzymes and most vitamins.

6. *Storing the food.* Always store food in the refrigerator in a glass container to keep it fresher. After you have settled on two or three recipes that your cats always enjoy, you can prepare larger amounts and freeze them if you like. Self-seal plastic bags are fine for freezing, but not for refrigerator storage. Food that has never been frozen is best, but frozen raw meals are still a hundred times better than canned food. If you are going away or your baby is due in three weeks or if a sitter will be feeding the cats, just put one meal or one day's servings into a self-seal plastic bag. If you press it flat before freezing it, it will thaw more quickly than if you simply leave it in a ball. Thaw as needed by moving the bag of frozen meals from the freezer to the refrigerator the day before. If you forget, you can quickly thaw the meals by dropping the plastic bag of food into a bowl of warm-ish water. (Once the food is thawed, don't store leftovers in the plastic bag; transfer them to a glass container to store in the refrigerator.)

Raw Meat Recipe

Note: To allow you to make any quantity of food that you need, I'm giving the measurements in parts rather than specific measures. Use the same size measuring spoon or cup for all ingredients, whether it is a tablespoon, quarter-cup, one-cup, or two-cup size. For example, in the recipe below, if you use a quarter-cup measure for 3 parts of meat, use the same quarter-cup measure for 1 part of vegetables.

4 parts meat with the calcium already mixed in
1 part vegetable—choosing from any of the following:

- Steamed broccoli or asparagus
- Finely grated carrot or zucchini

- Finely cut alfalfa or clover sprouts
- Baked carrot or winter squash
- Frozen winter squash (thaw and use)
- Organic canned pumpkin
- Organic canned tomato sauce

Organic raw egg (optional). Use one egg per pound of meat. The egg will count toward your meat, so subtract an equivalent amount from the meat/calcium mixture.

- Add enough spring or filtered water so you can mix well to a soft consistency.
- Store in a glass jar in the refrigerator or freeze as directed above. Before serving, warm in a mug as directed on page 74.
- At mealtime, add the following to each cat's portion:

1 good multivitamin (I use Nu-Cat or Tabby Tabs)
½ to 1 teaspoon Anitra's Vita-Mineral Mix (see page 68)
Other supplements according to your cat's health needs

Since raw foods do not have as strong a taste as cooked foods, you may need to mix them half-and-half with canned food at first or you can enhance the flavor with what I call a "bribe food." Bribe foods are strong-smelling, strong-tasting treats that can be mixed in easily to flavor the entire meal or sprinkled on top as an enticement.

Bribe Foods

- 1 teaspoon PetGuard "Savory Seafood" or any flavor your cats love
- ½ slightly cooked chicken liver
- 1 inch piece of sardine in tomato sauce or canned mackerel
- Anitra's Natural Cat Treat, crushed
- 3 to 4 drops tamari soy sauce
- ¼ teaspoon brewer or nutritional yeast sprinkled on top or PetGuard yeast and garlic powder

- 1 teaspoon baby food lamb smeared all over the top
- Halo "Dinner Party Powder" sprinkled on top
- Kitty Kaviar Shaved Bonito Flakes

Supplements

First let's clarify the difference between the words *vitamin* and *supplement*. A supplement simply means "something added." A nutritional supplement can be a vitamin or a mineral, like vitamin E or calcium, but more often it is a special food substance that has a very high content of one or more vitamins or minerals, such as cod liver oil with its high vitamin A and D content or kelp or Green Magma powder or parsley tea with high mineral content. Whenever possible I prefer to recommend a food supplement as opposed to a vitamin, because nature includes many of the elements needed by the body to process and use the vitamins present in that supplement. For example, it is easier for the body to extract, process, and use the B vitamins when they are given as yeast (a food high in B vitamins) than when they are given in a B complex pill. Sometimes, however, it may be better to give a vitamin pill—if, for example, the cat needs very large amounts of that particular vitamin, or if there is a possibility that the patient might react adversely to the supplement source. For example, yeast should not be given to cats who are suffering from an attack of feline urologic syndrome. It is to be hoped that the food supplement can be used at a later time after the cat's health has returned to normal. A third reason for giving the isolated vitamins is simply that it's often easier for the caregiver. It's better for the cats to receive one multivitamin a day than for him to be left with nothing but processed food.

Supplements are needed for several reasons. At least two or three reasons will apply to any companion cat living today:

1. Cats who have been eating mostly cooked food do not have the normal complement of enzymes in their digestive juices and will not be able to extract the vitamins from the food they eat as well as a wild cat who is killing and eating raw prey.

2. Cats who are ill will not have the standard amounts of enzymes either (see number 1 above).

3. In modern farming methods the use of chemical fertilizers and sprays greatly reduces the nutritional content of foods and throws the vitamin and mineral content of foods out of balance, in some cases creating deficiencies.

4. The use of steroids and antibiotics is ubiquitous in commercial meat and poultry, and when these products are eaten, they greatly increase the need for certain nutrients to help the body process the toxic substances. (This is one of the reasons organically grown meat and poultry are far superior.)

5. Certain diseases such as irritable bowel syndrome and kidney disease reduce the cat's ability to absorb enough nutrients.

6. Certain nutrients, such as vitamins C, E, and the B complex, are used up quickly amidst the stresses of normal modern life. They are used up even faster when unusual stress is present, such as stress due to travel, sickness, X rays, loneliness, lack of direct sunlight, or loud music or noise.

7. No two cats are alike. Genes can predispose *any* animal to have an unusually high requirement for one nutrient or another.

One simple rule will make life easier for the caregiver determined to do everything possible to keep his furry friend in the best of health. It is this: there are *oil-soluble* nutrients and *water-soluble* nutrients. The oil solubles are vitamins A, D, and E. All the rest, both vitamins and minerals, are water soluble. Oil-soluble vitamins (A, D, and E) can be stored by the body and need be given only once a week. All the water-soluble nutrients should be replenished at every meal because they are continually lost in the urine. This is why the various feeding suggestions allow you to give the vitamins A, D, and E only once a week.

If you ever sneak between-meal snacks to your cats, for heaven's sake stop during illness. To fight an infection or infestation, the body needs that time between meals to cleanse itself of the poisons as much as it needs that supernutritious food you are giving at mealtime. This might be a good time to add an extra vitamin-rich meal. Supplements are always given with or after a meal, when the stomach is full. Get a multivitamin especially for cats from the health food store or from the veterinarian and make sure they are pills or liquid. There is a kind of vitamin that comes in a tube and is suspended in mineral oil. It has a high sugar content and resembles brown petroleum jelly. This is not good because mineral oil washes vitamins A, D, and E right out of the system. Also, most of these products contain the preservative sodium benzoate, which is dangerous, particularly to cats. (There are also feline laxatives that contain the same drawbacks. Mineral oil should be used very, very rarely and only under specific instructions from the veterinarian; benzoate of soda should never be given to a cat.)

My cats adore their vitamin tablets. Natural pet vitamin tablets can be purchased at most health food stores or from your holistic vet. They're about as big as a dime and, although they smell perfectly horrible to me, I have to be careful how I present them, because if I place the tablets too close together on the floor my sweet and gregarious cats are not above hissing and swatting each other to try to get a bigger share. They find them truly delicious. It's also acceptable to crush the pills and mix them into the food if your cat indicates this preference.

Delicious Treats and Crunchies

If you would like to give your cat treats and be sure that all the side effects are beneficial, try two or three yeast tablets or one desiccated liver tablet, or tear up a sheet of nori seaweed. Nutritious treats for cats are also available in health food stores and from some pet food suppliers. I recommend "Anitra's Natural Cat Treat," "Purrlicious," and "Yeast and Garlic Wafers" from PetGuard; "Liv-a-Littles" (chicken, salmon, or cod) and "Dinner Party" from Halo; and Kitty Kaviar. I don't recommend using dry food for meals; however, I do use PetGuard dry food as an occasional treat, five or six pieces at a time. These high-quality treats contain no chemical preservatives, so store them in a tightly closed screw-top container and in a cool place. (See "Product Recommendations," page 489.)

A tray of kitty grass or wheat grass is a wonderful and healthy treat. Some cats adore the fresh, tender blades of grass; some cats don't. Some cats like to eat it and lie on it too. Some sniff only; others devour the whole thing within a half hour. Some cats eat it and then vomit. Although this is not dangerous, it is unsightly. If vomiting occurs, you might want to remove the grass for a few days and then try again at a later time.

Buy a mature plot of kitty grass at the farmer's market or health food store. You can also buy a kit of unsprouted kitty grass at the pet store and simply follow instructions. The other choice is to grow your own.

Growing Your Own Kitty Grass

At a gardening store, buy two small pots with drain holes in the bottom and built-in saucers and a good-quality, organic potting soil (for vegetables and fruit). You need two pots because the kitty grass matures and then begins to wither within a week to ten days. So you'll want to start a second pot while the first is being enjoyed by your cats. Then, at the health food store, buy wheat berries. They can usually be found in the cereal section. Then:

1. Fill one of the pots with potting soil to about one and a half inches from the top.
2. Sprinkle enough wheat berries to make one layer on the top of the soil.
3. Cover the wheat berries with just enough soil so that they are completely covered. About ⅛ to ¼ inch of additional soil should do it.
4. Put the pot in the kitchen sink and add water to completely moisten all of the soil. You'll know it's well-moistened when water comes out of the drain holes. Carefully tip the pot to empty the built-in saucer of additional water.
5. Keep the pot on a counter near the sink and lightly sprinkle with water once or twice a day. When the sprouts are about a half-inch long, move the pot to a bright sunny window. The grass will take five or six days to grow to 3 or 4 inches. If your cat is allowed on the counter, cheating is permitted if he wants to munch on the grass before it's officially full-grown.
6. When the pot is ready to serve, put it in one of your cat's favorite places. Then, in a couple of days, start a second pot.

Once you start rotating the pots, you don't have to start over with all new potting soil. Just pull out the withered grass, top off the container with fresh potting soil, and start a new batch. Since the soil will eventually become depleted of its nutrients, every now and then you'll want to use totally fresh potting soil.

*　　　*　　　*

To help clean teeth and provide a super source of calcium, Dr. Rowan recommends broiled chicken neck vertebrae served as a treat. The vertebrae are the *only* cooked poultry bones that are allowed, because they do not splinter, they crumble. Do not feed any other cooked poultry bones to your cat except the neck vertebrae. Most cats prefer their chicken neck broiled or roasted as opposed to boiled in water. Dr. Pitcairn and I prefer serving the necks raw because heat destroys the valuable enzymes but some cats insist that they be cooked. Raw birds are closer to the cat's natural diet. If the bird is raw you can feed other bones as well. In fact, Dr. Pitcairn once suggested I serve each cat half of a Rock Cornish game hen. I respectfully declined, explaining that while a half a bird might be devoured in short order by the country cats in his neck of the woods, it would seem a bit overwhelming to our apartment kitties here in New York City, many of whom weigh very little more than the game hen does. At the time I was thinking particularly of Marfie Lund, a dainty little shaded silver Persian who tips the scales at four and a half pounds.

Whether you cook the necks or serve them raw, I suggest presenting the first serving in the bathroom on the tiles, or better yet, in the tub, because the vast majority of cats become extremely excited upon sniffing the poultry and tend to revert to primitive behavior—drooling, growling, and muttering, and dragging the piece away from the rest of the group even if there is no group present, pretending to kill it over and over again. It's fun to watch, and you may see a side of your cat that hasn't come out before.

One word of caution: too much chicken neck tends to make the stool hard, so I never give an entire meal of neck vertebrae. Give one or two vertebrae before or after half of a normal meal to which you have added an extra half-teaspoonful of bran and a teaspoonful of water. This will condition the stool and overcome the hardening effects of the chicken neck. Give only one or two vertebrae per cat one or two times a week.

Additional Acceptable Foods

Guardians frequently ask about variety in the cat's diet. Cats in the wild eat sprouting grass and grains; they steal eggs from a nest; they eat a variety of different birds, frogs, lizards, rodents, and who knows what sorts of vegetables and fruits. There are many similar foods you can add to your cat's meal or give as a side dish:

- A teaspoonful of finely chopped alfalfa sprouts (high in nutrients and still full of life when cats eat them)
- Buttered whole wheat toast
- Steamed broccoli tops or Chinese broccoli in garlic sauce

- Peas, corn, squash, or other steamed vegetables
- Baked carrots or winter squash (see recipe below)
- A soft-boiled egg, or egg scrambled in butter with or without a sprinkle of cheddar cheese
- Raw organic egg yolk served in a quarter-cup of half-and-half
- Cooked meat or poultry (remember: no ham, pork, or poultry bones—and be sure there is some vegetable and whole grain in the same meal)
- An olive
- A cantaloupe ball
- A small chunk of cheese (cheddar helps dissolve tartar)
- A sliver of pizza
- One to three strings of spaghetti dripping with tomato sauce and cheese (only one, unless it is whole grain)
- A slice of sautéed tofu (bean curd) sprinkled with soy sauce
- A torn up sheet of nori seaweed

Note: Never feed chocolate or cocoa.

Baked Carrot or Winter Squash Recipe

- Cut thoroughly washed organic carrots in half lengthwise or cut a squash in two and take out the seeds.
- Line the carrots up head to tail or place the squash cut-side down on a buttered cookie sheet.
- Bake at 450 degrees until a fork slides easily through the carrot or the squash is soft to the touch. The vegetable should be soft enough to mash.

Be sure to make enough or there may be none left for the cats.

Ask your cats, even about the most unlikely foods. If they crave something containing sugar, white flour, and so on, this is a symptom of a system out of balance. Upgrade the diet in general. Rare treats can be useful for hiding medication if, heaven forbid, your cat should become ill and have to take a pill (see "Giving Pills," page 266).

As I write this I am enjoying one of my "kitchen sink soups": broccoli, daikon, and aramanth in a thickened broth of tamari, lemon, and garlic. Big black Bartholomew inserts an exploratory paw, pulls out a small broccoli flower, and sends it, plop, onto my manuscript. He sniffs it, then wolfs it down before I can scold him, licking up the soupy residue and leaving the manuscript cleaner than it was before Bartie used it for a plate. I'll leave him a nice little puddle in the bottom of my bowl. After all, it's all good stuff in there.

I mix chopped alfalfa sprouts in with the meal fairly often. I'm told that alfalfa sprouts tend to satisfy the most incorrigible house-plant nibbler.

How Much to Feed?

When asked about how much to feed, I tell the guardian I have to know the cat. Most people overfeed their cats. A cat's stomach, before it expands, is the size of a quarter or a fifty-cent piece. A 7 lb. cat who eats two tablespoonfuls of food at each meal is doing fine. An easy way to regulate the amount is to think of time rather than quantity. In other words, if your cat is healthy and of normal size, and doesn't have a psychological gorging problem, and he's neither too fat nor too thin, then the sky's the limit for a half hour or so—twice a day. Also, your cat will not be eating exactly the same amount every day of the year. Appetites vary with temperature, activity, stress, and so on. It's easy for me to see the patterns because I see so many cats every day.

People who previously fed low-quality foods are often alarmed because their cats eat less of the new food. I explain to them that the cats have been overeating because their systems have been reaching for missing nutrients. The poor cats eat and eat the same low-quality food, from which they can never get the nutrients they crave. That is why feeding low-quality food makes for obese cats. The new high-quality food is nutritionally complete and digestible, so the cats are satisfied. They are getting *quality* as opposed to *quantity*. Flabby cats tend to firm up—they don't necessarily lose a lot of weight—they just get slimmer, more muscular, and more active.

Changing over to the New Diet

One sacrifice that is the hallmark of the concerned and loving guardian is that he takes responsibility and acknowledges the fact that he knows more about nutrition than the cat. I have discussed the various reasons cats can be hooked on an undesirable diet. Just the fact that "Familiarity breeds contentment in a cat" is enough to hook them on almost anything—simply because it is familiar.

When I see new clients and give instructions for an optimum diet, I always take care to explain that these "health food" cat foods do not contain any sugar, salt, or artificial flavors. Their very purity may make them seem uninteresting to a cat if his palate has been jaded by the stimulating artificial flavors of grocery store cat foods. Moreover, if food has always been left available in the past, the guardian's job is going to be even more difficult when he tries to make the changeover to a high-quality diet. One thing that will smooth the path is to add about three drops of tamari soy sauce or one of the other bribe foods given on page 75 to each serving. This works to perk up the flavor a bit just at first. Even if you use soy sauce you won't be using as much sodium as most commercial food manufacturers do, and you can gradually do away with it as your cats get used to the taste of normal food. (If your cat is a heart or arthritis patient, he needs a low-sodium diet. You can use potassium chloride [salt substitute] or low-sodium tamari.)

The cat sitters I recommend to people who travel are frequently faced with the assignment of making the dietary changeover while the cat's human is gone. They have a thorough grounding in the nutritional aspects of cat care, along with everything else. And, because their love is a love of all cats, they're in a good position to remain emotionally detached so they can do what is best for the cat without catering to any psychological needs of their own. Here's the method I have them use.

First, present the new food—the ideal diet. Keep in your conscious mind the thought of the nutritional soundness of the meal and how delicious it is. (Most cats adore yeast and kelp.) Your own emotions of approval will be communicated to your cats. If you're really handling your conscious thoughts properly, you yourself will be salivating when you put the plate on the floor. Do what is natural then—smack your lips, swallow, say you wish you had a delicious dinner like this; then leave the cats alone. Start your own dinner, wash the dishes, or go read a book. If the cats refuse the food, first of all ascertain whether they have eaten anything. Half a teaspoonful per cat is an acceptable amount. Don't put so much food on the plates that you won't be able to tell how much anyone has eaten. Give them only a tablespoon at first; you can always give seconds if they want it. They'll eat more next time—because they won't be eating between meals.

But let's say the cats eat nothing. Not one morsel passes their lips. After forty-five minutes, cheerfully clean away the food and casually forget the whole incident. If they ask for food between meals, give them extra love, cuddling, and play instead. Active play is especially good because it will work up an appetite. Repeat this procedure for a minimum of four meals; after all, that's only two days. A fast of two days is extremely beneficial because many old wastes and toxins will be excreted by the body quickly. That's what a fast is—it cleans the body fast! (*Note:* If your cat is seriously ill, check with your veterinarian. No fasting at all is allowed for kittens or for cats with diabetes, cancer, or hyperthyroidism unless carefully supervised by the veterinarian. See "Fasting," page 286.)

Some cats, especially those who are used to having food left available all day, will take a nibble of their meal and walk away. Caregivers of this type are often distressed by the thought of Muffy "going hungry all day." Take heart; there is a compromise. You may feed three or even four meals a day at first as long as you don't break the cardinal rule: always remove all food after a half hour.

A guardian of a positively obese cat will sometimes ask me in a tremulous voice, "But what if she skips a meal—what if she doesn't eat anything at all—what shall I do?" I look at the huge animal sprawled at our feet and then back at the guardian, and I reply, very solemnly, "Applaud." The person usually laughs and relaxes.

After you've done your duty for four meals, you deserve a pat on the back. Ninety-eight percent of the cats will have made the changeover by this time. (Eighty percent of the cats welcome the new food the moment it is set on the floor—they dive into it. This section is only for the benefit of those poor creatures who have no appetite because their food was left available between meals or they were hooked on some undesirable product.)

If your cats are in that small percentage that has not eaten the new food after two days, they will now be hungry—and they will jump at any compromise you offer. So, fine—we'll compromise. I'm not made of stone. Let's try the old "special treats ploy." The technique here is to add something that is utterly delicious, something that you would not feed every day, something that is not in itself complete nutrition. For example, something from the list of bribe foods on page 75. The next step is to start gradually decreasing the percentage of the bribe food and increasing the percentage of the new food.

- *First two days.* Three parts special treat food to one part ideal diet. Feed extremely small meals—about half the size of your cat's usual meals. If he wants more, give him only the ideal diet food as a second serving.
- *Next three days.* Fifty-fifty ratio. Again keep the meals very small, as before.
- *Next three days.* One part special treat food to three parts ideal diet.

- *From then on.* Only the ideal diet. Your cat can finally have as much as he likes twice a day.

Then you're home free. *Caution:* do not use as the treat food the same food your cat is addicted to. I have seen this method of mixing the old diet with the new ultimately work after fasting a cat two days, but the number of days allowed before making each ratio change must be doubled, and even then there are sometimes setbacks. Try your best not to use any really undesirable food as a bribe. If you're going to use fish, make sure it's not tuna, which has been found to contain higher levels of mercury and magnesium than other fish. To avoid getting your cats hooked on anything ever again, do your best to feed a variety of flavors.

Nature moves slowly. After your cat is nicely accustomed to the new regimen, you will not perceive at first the change that is occurring within the cat—the improved condition of the walls of the veins; the new chemical balance of the blood that feeds every organ, including the brain and the nerves. Then, the resulting youthfulness, the mellowing of the disposition, will creep in like the unfolding of a rose, which can be seen clearly in speeded-up photography but cannot be perceived when you simply stand and look at it. Intellectually, you know the rose is blooming because you've already seen the results many times before. You can assure anyone who has not seen a full-blown rose that yes, truly, that bud will become, in time, a ravishing bloom. It will be like that with the high-quality diet once you see the results for the first time in your own cats. You'll be able to pass it on to others for the benefit of other cats. In fact, the more trouble you have, the more pitfalls you overcome, the better equipped you will be to help others through the rough patches. So enjoy your trials and laugh at your errors. Remember, patience and perseverance, like love, always win in the end.

Other Beneficial Side Effects of a High-Quality Diet

One thing I did not expect was the way the diet influenced temperament. The minerals and B vitamins have a favorable effect on the nerves. "She came right out into the living room when company was there" is the sort of comment I hear after a couple of months on the new diet. "He's starting to play again," "She doesn't hiss at the children any more"—in other words, the temperament seems to move toward the golden mean. Nervous cats calm down; lazy cats perk up. Well, why not? Metabolism is speeded up; old waste products are being eliminated; the body is cleaner inside; irritating toxins are disappearing day by day; and health-building nutrients are in plentiful supply. The body of such a cat has a high resistance to both disease and stress.

Another lovely side effect is the aroma exuded by the furs of a healthy cat. To the joys of softness, luster, warmth, and shininess, add also a delightful and subtle perfume.

Feeding Kittens

If you are so rash as to adopt a young kitten, you must realize that kittens eat much more frequently than do grown cats. Their little stomachs are minute, and their metabolism is super fast. The smaller the animal, the more rapid the metabolism. Birds, for example, spend practically every waking hour finding food to fuel their bodies. A kitten between six and ten weeks old requires six to eight meals a day. From ten weeks to four months, five or six meals are required; four meals until six or seven months; then three meals a day up to the age of nine months. Sometime before they're a year old, try to get them down to two meals a day.

Kittens should not be taken from the mother before they are six weeks old. Eight or ten weeks is wiser and kinder. Otherwise, they get oral fixations and spend their lives sucking buttons and earlobes. Although this may seem cute to some people, it saddens anyone who knows that it is a symptom of maladjustment caused by too-early weaning. Add to this other neurotic behavior due to lack of parental patterning. Very young kittens must have an adult cat to teach them cat etiquette, grooming, and good litter box habits. A human, no matter how loving and patient, is not enough. I was fortunate that Big Purr was a marvelous uncle. He positively doted on kittens. I have noticed that many large neutered males enjoy the role of uncle.

A kitten, once weaned, can eat the same food formula you feed any healthy cat, as discussed earlier in this chapter. A growing kitten needs a high-protein diet, and that's what this is. You might like to add an extra quarter-teaspoonful of butter once a day because kittens can use more fat. Now is the time to get them used to a variety of food textures. And this is definitely the time for an extra multivitamin supplement. Kittens need more of every nutrient to help their bodies manufacture strong muscles and bones.

If, through no fault of yours or the kitten's, you should suddenly find yourself with a kitten of less than six weeks on your hands, then you've got special problems. Many years ago, when I was still performing on Broadway, the employees of a printing office called me to say they had discovered a sodden shoebox in the gutter out front with four newborn kittens in it. They had already called the ASPCA (the American Society for the Prevention of Cruelty to Animals) and a couple of other humane shelters. Each time, they received the same advice: "Kill the kittens quickly and painlessly—kittens that young cannot survive." Then somebody said they knew a lady who liked cats and maybe she would help. At that time I knew next to nothing about feline nutrition. "Fools rush in"—I hopped a subway down there and accepted the four kittens. Three of them were making sounds. The fourth was dead when I arrived. They really were newborn—I doubt they had ever nursed at all.

I called a vet, who gave me the same advice that the animal shelters had given the office workers. When I insisted that I wanted to try to save them, he referred me to a very large pet store that sold powdered queen's milk. (A queen is a female cat.) My friend Mark came over and assisted in keeping the kittens warm. We held them under our sweaters next to our skin. We couldn't find a doll baby bottle so we used a rubber ear syringe made for a baby's ears. We lost two more kittens in twenty-four hours despite feeding every two hours and stroking a warm washcloth over their genitals to get them to pass wastes.

At that time I had two female cats, both neutered. And, although I wasn't sure whether they would accept a kitten or kill it, I was desperate and decided to take a chance. I put the remaining little black male on the carpet in front of Lee-la and Pixie, my two Siamese. That's what I should have done in the first place. Lee-la curled her body around him, and she and Pixie both went to work with those rough Siamese tongues. Lee-la licked and massaged the kitten's lower abdomen with grim determination until, in less than one minute, the little fellow had passed a stool. If it's going in one end and it's coming out the other, that's a favorable sign. Pixie cleaned his eyes and his ears to her satisfaction, despite the little one's feeble protests. And, as she began licking his back, the little black male fell asleep. At that point I felt safe in giving him a name, because it looked like the odds in his favor had just risen a good bit. Being newly into yoga, I decided to call him Jai, which means "victory" in Sanskrit. Sanskrit words impart their vibrations to anyone who hears them, and I figured that "Jai" was just what this little squirt needed.

Jai continued to get queen's milk for three weeks. He also continued to get bathed and cuddled and thoroughly mothered by my two prim Siamese ladies.

At three weeks of age, I began mixing the baby food mixture given below with the milk. I got him to lick out of a plate by putting some of this food on my finger and dirtying his nose with it. I put just a drop on the tip of his nose, and his little tongue would automatically come out to lick it off. It tasted good. He looked for more and found it on my finger. I kept dipping my finger into the dish and offering it to him. Each time I made him reach closer and closer to the dish by moving my finger down toward it. Being bright, he soon figured out that my finger was a middleman he could do away with by going straight to the source. At five weeks, I had intended to gradually introduce grown-up cat food. However, Jai found it for himself and attacked his foster mothers' plates with such gusto that my problem became one of preventing his overeating.

If you can't get powdered queen's milk, here is my recipe for nursing kittens:

Mock Nursing Formula

2 cups whole milk—goat's milk is best
2 raw organic egg yolks—or 1 yolk and 1 teaspoon warm coconut oil
2 tablespoons protein powder
6 drops liquid vitamins for children or Nu-Cat liquid vitamins
1 teaspoon mixed intestinal flora (see "Product Recommendations" in the
    Appendix)

Beat with a fork or whisk. Warm the formula first to bath temperature (101 degrees) by standing feeder in a bowl of hot water. Feed kittens with a doll bottle or pet nurser (sold in any large pet supply store).

Use the following chart to determine a feeding schedule:

Kitten's weight	How much	How often
Under 4 ounces	About ½ teaspoon per feeding	Every 2 hours
4–8 ounces	2–4 tablespoons per day	Every 3 hours
8–24 ounces	6–10 tablespoons per day	Every 4 hours

Then begin weaning, mixing queen's milk or the formula with the weaning recipe:

Weaning Recipe

1 jar baby food meat (lamb, beef, or chicken)
3 teaspoons baby food carrot or squash
1 raw organic egg yolk *or* **½ teaspoon butter**
3 drops children's liquid vitamins *or* **NuCat liquid vitamins**
½ teaspoon food yeast
⅛ teaspoon calcium lactate or calcium gluconate
Spring or distilled water to desired consistency

Until Jai was six weeks old, I must have fed him six to eight meals a day. Jai remained petite up through six months. He had a mature conformation, but his size was that of an eight-week-old kitten. He looked like a miniature cat. Soon afterward he was adopted by a nice young couple who moved to California. There he had a yard, sunshine, and air—and, before long, a girlfriend (both cats were neutered). I was informed through mutual friends that my tiny Jai was tiny no more. He grew and filled out to become a big, strapping male, the terror of chipmunks.

Feeding the Aging Cat

In the aging cat, the assimilation of nutrients is not as efficient as in younger cats. Attack the problem in three ways:

1. *Feed smaller meals more frequently, as a kitten is fed.* My Priscilla, who is seventeen and a half, gets three or four meals a day depending on my work schedule. I don't make the mistake of giving large meals in hopes of putting more weight on her. The object is to have the stomach less than three-quarters full, because its muscular action is not as strong as it was. And, because digestive juices and enzymes are not as plentifully supplied by her system as before, a small meal will be more efficiently mixed with the digestive juices that are available. Once a week, as usual, I give 400 units of vitamin E (alpha tocopherol), 10,000 units of vitamin A, and 400 units of vitamin D.

2. *Supply some additional enzymes and bile.* I give Priscilla one-quarter teaspoon of feline digestive enzymes or one half of a digestive enzyme tablet from the health food store either in her meal or, more frequently, after the meal crushed up in her favorite dessert of half-and-half and egg yolk. She gets about two teaspoonfuls of this dessert with the half tablet plus one-sixteenth teaspoon of vitamin C crystals. I also mix in four drops of cod liver oil and 10 milligrams of vitamin B complex. The enzyme tablet contains bile and enzymes to augment those produced by her own body. (See "Product Recommendations," page 489.)

3. *Make sure that the diet is supplied with a much larger amount of vitamins, because the cat won't assimilate them all anyway.* Use more of the high-powered foods such as cod liver oil, alfalfa sprouts, organic raw egg yolk, Green Magma, and Anitra's Vita-Mineral Mix, and give a multivitamin for cats every day. Cats are naturally heavy meat eaters, and because meat is not a perfectly balanced protein it is not unusual to find that cats over fifteen years old have some percentage of kidney failure (see "Diet for the Cat with Kidney Problems," page 431).

The aging cat needs less protein. He's not growing and he's less active. Because too much protein is hard on the kidneys, you will notice the formula below is lower in protein than the basic diet for a cat in his prime:

3 parts protein
1 or 2 parts vegetable

Slightly increase the cat's favorite vegetable and emphasize *raw* meat with its easily digested and better-balanced proteins.

If you're feeding one of the canned foods, you can alter it for the older cat in this way:

1 6 oz. can food
2 tablespoons vegetable
¼ teaspoon feline digestive enzymes
All of the daily and weekly supplements listed on page 76

I have completely eliminated all junk food from Pricilla's diet. A young body can process out and dispose of the sugar in half a teaspoonful of vanilla ice cream. Now that Priscilla is seventeen and a half, half-and-half or light cream is nicer, and much more chic.

The Litter Box 3

I have been caring for cats for about thirty-five years. Very early on, my apartment evolved into what it is today, a feline health spa. My sister called it "Fluff City" and the name stuck. Human visitors always look around, trying to spot all the cats. Two will usually be peering from atop the climber; the rest will be scattered about, sleeping on the radiator or inside the snug retreats, lounging on the windowsill or the cable TV box, or prancing at our feet, rubbing against our legs.

"How many cats do you *have* here?" amazed visitors ask.

I answer, "We're always somewhere between seven and twelve."

"But there's no smell!" they exclaim.

"Well, of course there's no smell," I laugh. "If I don't know how to keep a litter box by now, I think I'd better quit!"

There's nothing difficult about keeping a perfect litter box. It's only a matter of knowing what to do. Time and again guardians call me for help when a cat is wetting or dirtying outside the box. No matter what I suspect about the reason for this behavior, I always begin by examining the litter box setup and making sure it is a perfect as possible. Fortunately, correcting the litter box setup *almost always* corrects the problem. If not, I address other possible reasons, which are discussed later in this chapter.

The Litter Box Problem

I have seen litter box setups that must have cost a small fortune. Pet shops have a formidable array—some with plastic domes, plastic liners, and built-in sieves. Some have mechanical strainers. For litter, you can choose from a myriad of clumpable and nonclumping materials, including clay, silica gel, recycled newspaper, pine or cedar sawdust, and sand. New eco-friendly litters are also common these days, including those made of corn, corncobs, cornhusks, wheat by-products, wheat grass, beet pulp, oat hulls, and green tea leaves. Litter boxes are moved about from the kitchen to the bathroom to behind the bed to under the coffee table. There are usually one to ten in a household. Because of the random wetting problem, cats are thrown out, given back, given away, or killed. The litter box can be a headache for both the cats and their guardians—unless you know how to simplify the system and give the cats what they need.

At the very beginning of my career, I knew that I absolutely had to devise a litter box setup that was comfortable in every way for both cats and guardians. I thought back to what Dr. Rowan had once told me, "Stick as close as you can to nature, and you'll never go too far wrong." He was discussing food and feeding at the time, but I felt that the same concept would apply to the litter box problem. So, how does a wild cat behave in this respect?

The cat's urine is very concentrated, and the smell is very strong. Because this smell could attract predators to the nest, cats in the wild always urinate far away from their habitat or any place of activity. They do not urinate where they sleep, eat, hunt, or play. Young kittens are frequently and thoroughly cleaned by the mother, who then swallows any waste matter, passing it through her own system to be neatly disposed of later with her own body wastes. With this kind of training in cleanliness from birth, is it any wonder that cats are fastidious about where they urinate?

Many a random wetting problem begins when the litter box is placed near the food dish or a favorite resting place. That litter box looks great, but the cats would have to be insane to soil near an area where they rest or eat. So the cat simply begins to search for a more acceptable place to use. (See "Feline Urologic Syndrome (FUS)," page 384.)

Cats hide their urine. They are not comfortable when forced to stand on old, half-wet litter to void again. Cats, in fact, have a universally accepted reputation for neatness. That's one of the attributes we find so endearing about them.

You might even say they are very much like us. Imagine if you walked into a bathroom and found that the toilet had already been used—but not flushed. What would you automatically do? And even if you couldn't flush the toilet before you used it, would you have to stand inside the dirty toilet to use it? And, even if you did, do you have long, silky bloomers that dangle down into that smelly mess? Ugh!

Cats cannot flush their toilet; you have to do it for them. Put the litter pan in the bathroom, and when you flush for yourself flush for them too. Persian cats have especially long, fluffy bloomers, and they are notoriously fastidious about keeping their fur clean.

Surprisingly, I have found that the people with the smelliest apartments are most often those who own the largest, most complicated, and most expensive litter box setups. It is apparent that the bigger the box and the deeper the bed of litter, the less likely the owner is to clean the box regularly; therefore, the smell worsens and there is a greater probability of random wetting.

The Requirements for a Litter Box

Now let us list the requirements for the litter box, for both cats and guardians:

Cat	*Guardian*
Clean	Clean
Odorless	Odorless
Convenient	Convenient
Out of the way	Out of the way
	Inexpensive
	Simple and quick
	Sanitary

You'll notice that the cats' requirements are the same as ours, though we also require reasonable cost, simplicity, and efficiency (because we must maintain the facility) as well as cleanliness (because that is our responsibility; pussycats don't know about germs).

I began my research by simply trying to satisfy the cats' requirements, regardless of time or expense. Surprise! I discovered that this method also turned out to fulfill all of my requirements as well. Here was a case where the very best method for the cats also turned out to be the easiest, cheapest, and most sanitary for their humans.

What Litter Is Best?

Back in the old days, clay litter was all we had. When the new clumping litter first came out in the 1990s, I strongly advised my clients against using it for a number of reasons, which I'll detail below. Since then, thank goodness, new types of clumping litter have appeared on the market that do not have the problems of the original type.

Clay litter is still by far the cheapest, and it is an acceptable choice. But my favorite is a corn-based clumping litter, World's Best Cat Litter. It's a bit more expensive, but it lasts a long time and saves a lot of time, and for me, it is definitely worth a few dollars more per month.

The original clumping litter—and still the most commonly used—contains sodium bentonite and diatomaceous silica. Although these are natural ingredients, the same clumping properties that make them so advantageous as a cat litter also make them a cause for concern. These clumping properties cause the litter to swell to about 15 times its original volume when it touches moisture and to become very hard, resulting in a cement-like clump that can be conveniently scooped out with a slotted litter scoop and thrown in the garbage. Less litter is used because once the clumps and solids are scooped out, only a small amount of fresh litter is needed to restore the litter to its usual level.

Most brands of this type indicate on the package that the clumps should not be flushed down the toilet. Clearly, this is because once that clump is formed, it is well neigh impossible to break up, and it could wreak havoc on your plumbing. The bits that make up this clump are very fine; they *always* adhere to the cat's pads and the tufts between his toes. Because cats *always* lick off and swallow anything that adheres to any part of themselves, one wonders exactly what this material that is so dangerous to household plumbing may do once it gets inside our cats' intestines. The answer is not pretty.

When clumping litters first came out, busy cat lovers were delighted at the prospect of saving precious time. However, within a few months after the product's release, trouble was already brewing. Breeders and veterinarians noticed an alarming increase in incidences of irritable bowel syndrome and other intestinal problems. Kittens were especially vulnerable, many dying mysteriously shortly after they first learned to use the litter box. Autopsies on some of these cats and kittens revealed a cement-like coating on the intestinal walls. Some of the kittens' intestines were entirely filled with the stuff.

As we already know, bits of whatever litter you use adhere to the paw tufts and are swallowed by the cats. The inside of the intestines is very moist, so any ingested bit of clumping litter that contains sodium bentonite or silica ends up clinging to the walls of the intestines. Another concern is that cats and kittens inhale the litter into their lungs when they kick the litter around.

Young kittens have yet another area of vulnerability. If you've ever watched kittens being trained to use the litter box, you know it is always a comical sight. Having only recently learned to walk on solid floors or rugs, they lose their balance in the shifting sands of the litter box, fall over, and end up with specks of litter clinging to their noses, which they instinctively lick off and swallow. If a kitten ingests a harmless type of litter, such as the corn-based clumping litter that I use, it will eventually come out at the other end. But clumping litter containing sodium bentonite or silica will form a cement-like coating on the intestinal walls and will never come out.

Once it collects on the intestinal walls, this substance continues to attract moisture. These clumps can also collect and hold old fecal matter in the lower digestive tract, inhibiting proper digestion of food and causing toxicity. All of this puts an enormous stress on the immune system, making the cat more susceptible to any infection that comes along such as viruses, bacteria, parasites, and yeast infections.[1]

Dogs are not immune from this problem either. Despite our best efforts to keep them from the litter box, some dogs just can't resist eating litter-covered cat excrement as a between-meal snack. I'm also concerned about potential health hazards for the human family. The clays used in these litters are also used to make absorbents for oil spills in garages and for industrial cleanup. These products include warnings that their dust could cause respiratory or cancer hazards to people and caution that workers should wear masks when using them. Of course, when we pour the litter into the box, when the cats kick it around, and when we remove it, we create a little dust. Even if one argues that the quantity of dust is insignificant as a cause for human health concerns, our cats' health is a concern because they are standing right in it and their tiny lungs put them at greater risk.

As the medical concerns about clumping litter became apparent, breeders and veterinarians called manufacturers to alert them to the problem and asked them to recall the product. They were met with indignation and denial. One vet

1. Syufy, Franny. *Cat Litter—To Scoop or Not to Scoop: The Rise and Fall of Clumping Clay Litter* (About.com; referenced June 19, 2007).

told me that the company's response was, "Well, they're not supposed to eat it, for heaven's sake!" They then went on to explain how the laws that govern pet food safety do not apply to litter—therefore, they were not liable and they saw no reason to stop selling it.

After veterinarians' warnings appeared in magazines and professional journals all around the country, new types of clumping litter were developed out of natural ingredients with no health hazards attached. They do not contain sodium bentonite and silica. I prefer the type that is made from the corn plant. It will not clog up anybody's plumbing—not your toilet's or that of your cats. Like the bad clumping litter, it forms clumps that are good and firm but that break up and liquefy when thrown into water. You can flush it away—even if your home has a septic tank. However, in some areas of the country environmental guidelines suggest that all litter be disposed of in the trash.[2] If you decide to dispose of litter in the toilet, start the flush before you dump and then dump slowly to eliminate the slightest chance of clogging.

The most popular corn-based brand of litter—and the one I always use—is World's Best Cat Litter. It is more expensive than the old-fashioned clay litter, but I find that the time I save makes it well worth the difference in price. There is one other tiny little thing I should tell you about corn-based clumping litter. Once or twice I have noticed the presence of small moths flitting about after opening a new bag of litter. Don't worry if this happens. These are *not* the kind of moths that eat sweaters, and they soon disappear. They are Indianmeal moths; the same type that can be found in any milled cereal product that's been hanging around in your cupboard too long, particularly during hot summer months. Actually the moths can be an added bonus for the short time before they disappear. My cats find them intriguing and they are guaranteed to promote vigorous exercise.

I always recommend that my clients purchase a litter with no added perfumes or deodorizers. There is a clumping litter available that is scented with lavender, which is supposed to attract cats. Whether it does or not, I don't know. It's harmless enough if you want to try it, but there are many reasons why a cat refuses to use the litter box. It's always better to eliminate the cause of the problem rather than trying to override the cat's instincts and possibly mask an important symptom.

If you prefer, regular clay litter is also a fine choice, and it is less expensive.

2. Most cat litter sold in California now includes the following notice, which is either posted above the product or pasted on the label: "The State of California encourages the disposal of cat feces in trash and discourages flushing cat feces in toilets or disposing of them in drains."

Any commercial nonclumping clay litter is fine as long as it doesn't contain extra chemicals such as those green and blue deodorizing pellets. When the cats step on the pellets, they release a deodorizing chemical. Of course, the chemical also gets on their feet and they have to lick it off. If the deodorizer is baking soda, the cats will be licking and ingesting sodium (salt). This is no better than the chemical deodorizers because sodium alkalizes the urine, which should be acid to prevent the formation of crystals. (See "Feline Urologic Syndrome (FUS)," page 384.)

You and your cat can work out your preferences as long as the litter is safe for the whole family. However, I have met one or two finicky Persians who prefer a litter made of newspaper because it doesn't cling to their silky bloomers. In this case you'd simply dispose of the litter in the trash.

POPULAR LITTERS

Here's a brief overview of some of the more popular litters that are available today. I have attempted to list the pros and cons of each type; however, please note that some litters contain ingredients from more than one category, such as a wood-based product that contains some clay. As manufacturers seek to find new eco-friendly types of litter, no doubt there will be additional options in the future.

Corn-Based Litter
Several brands available.

- Good clumping
- High cost
- Deodorizes
- Scatters but has very little dust
- Flushable (if flushing is acceptable in your area)

Wheat-Based Litter
Several brands available.

- Fair clumping; clumps are poorer and more gooey than corn-based litter
- Moderate price
- Poor deodorizing
- Scatters but has very little dust
- Flushable (if flushing is acceptable in your area)

Nonclumping Clay

Numerous companies manufacture clay litters. Be sure to avoid any litter that has chemical deodorizers.

- Doesn't clump
- Cheapest
- Deodorizes if properly used

- Scatters and has dust
- Cannot flush

Clumping Clay Litters (Made with Sodium Bentonite Clay and/or Silica Clay)

- Not acceptable due to health issues—harmful when ingested or inhaled (which all cats will do)

Green Tea Litter

Uses recycled green tea leaves from the bottled drink industry, as well as sawdust.

- Doesn't clump
- Very expensive
- Deodorizes beautifully

- Some scatter, no dust
- Flushable (if flushing is acceptable in your area)

Wood-Based Litter

Uses cedar, pine, etc. Some are made of by-products from the lumber industry; others are made from virgin wood pulp.

- Questions about whether natural oils present in the wood could be harmful to cats and whether the aromas (pine) will antidote homeopathic remedies
- Moderate price

- Masks odor but not for long
- Doesn't scatter
- Most indicate on the package that they are flushable in moderate amounts

Newspaper-Based Litter (Made of Recycled Newspapers)

- Comes in two basic forms: fluffy and pellets

- Very reasonably priced

- Odor can be quite offensive if not cleaned *at once*
- No dust, but tends to be messy

- Can be flushed but depends on plumbing type and local laws

Silica Gel Litter

- Looks like crystals
- You can rinse them every couple of days and reuse them

- Supposedly they deodorize, but I have seen them in use and the smell is always quite offensive

An Easy, Convenient, and Effective System

Put the litter box near the toilet. This provides privacy for the cat and is convenient for you. The cat doesn't eat or sleep near the toilet, and you can easily clean it every time you go into the bathroom. Many guardians put the box in the tub because it's easier to brush up any litter that is kicked out.

If you have a small bathroom, use a square plastic dishpan as your cat's litter box. It's plenty large enough for most cats, and it has the added advantages of being super-light and easy to lift up and clean. You can find them with sides that are four or six inches high; if you choose six inches, less litter will be kicked out onto the floor. Don't buy one of those expensive, covered litter boxes—it's not convenient for you or your cat. The dome prevents you from seeing whether it needs cleaning, and you have to struggle with the dome every time you want to check the box and clean it. It also makes it very difficult to monitor your cat's stool, a must if you want to reassure yourself of your furry friend's continuing good health (more about that later). Also, because cats squat upright, a low roof can cause hunching and impaired movement of the bowels and bladder.

And don't line your nice, smooth plastic pan with anything. Newspaper does not deodorize; it smells. And those messy plastic liners always form little wrinkles where wet litter hides to smell and breed germs. Fifty percent of the time the cat's claw puts a hole in it anyway, and the urine drains through and sits there in a puddle underneath the liner where there is no litter to absorb it or the odor.

For nonclumping clay litter or any other nonclumping litter

1. Use only plain, nondeodorizing litter.

2. Put 1–1½ inches of litter in the box; *no more*. Don't make the mistake of putting too much clay litter in the box. You want the wet to hit the bottom and clump, not spread and seep through the other litter to contaminate it and make it smell. In my travels visiting feline clients, I have come across great, huge litter pans with ten to fifteen pounds of clay litter in them. These pans are always the smelliest, because the urine doesn't hit the bottom and clump but continues to permeate the whole ten pounds of litter like a miasmic fog. If you're using non-clumping litter, the rule is, "If the litter smells, use less and clean more often."

3. If you're going to be gone eight hours or more and you have more than a couple of cats, get one pan for every two cats and clean them on arising, before leaving, when you return, and before bed. It takes about fifteen seconds per pan for each cleaning.

4. When cleaning clay or other nonclumping litter, use a large kitchen serving spoon instead of a commercial "litter scoop" full of holes and slits. If you try to remove the wet nonclumping litter with a commercial litter scoop full of holes and slits, you'll have some mess on your hands. Half the wet bits of litter will filter merrily down onto the floor, the toilet seat, or back into the clean litter to contaminate it and make it smell. Supposedly the slitted scoops are to be used to lift out "the solid matter." Well, if you just stop to think about it, the solid matter is not the problem. The stool will smell bad for about three minutes, but then it's dry. The cats can easily step around that. It's the wetness that really smells; it's the wet parts that breed germs; and it's the wet parts that make it impossible for a cat to use the box without stepping on old urine.

5. Get a metal serving spoon—one that's shaped like a giant tablespoon, with no holes or slits in it—and keep it on a hook or in a glass or mug near the box. Whenever you pass the bathroom, take a quick look at the box. If you see a covered mound or a little wet circle, which is like the tip of an iceberg, pick the litter box up and gently shake or scrape all the dry litter to a clean corner, exposing the wet clump or clumps. Then take your serving spoon and remove every bit of the wet clump and dispose of it. The remaining litter is left clean and uncontaminated, so shake it evenly across the pan again, rinse the spoon, and replace the spoon on its hook.

6. With my method, you need to change and wash the whole pan only once or twice a week. When they do the complete cleaning, meticulous caregivers will

feel as if they are cleaning an already clean litter box. Because they have scooped out the wet clumps so often, there is absolutely no odor about the plastic box. At the most, there might be a little dot of dry stool clinging to the side. (See "Cleaning the Litter Box" below.)

Note for the "Super-Finicky" Caregiver: I might add that there are some people who, instead of scooping out the wet with a spoon, prefer to dump the whole thing twice a day. They put even less litter in the box—say three-quarters of an inch—and rinse the box out with water each time. I call these people "super-finicky," and their cats are absolutely ecstatic about this system.

With this new litter box system for clay litter, get ready to buy a lot less litter. You will be amazed at how little you will be using.

For clumping litter:

1. Use a natural, plant-based clumping litter.
2. Use a deeper bed of litter. Put three or four inches of litter in the box. Unlike clay litter, you want the urine to form a clump *before* it hits the bottom. You'll get a nice, hard little clump that is easy to scoop away.
3. Use a commercial slotted litter scoop to remove feces and clumps. (I recommend the plastic Van Ness Giant LS2.) Unlike with clay litter, all the urine will be totally within the clump. No half-wet pieces of dirty litter will remain. All the loose, clean pieces of litter you pick up with the clump can be shaken back into the box through the slits in the scoop.
4. Unless local regulations prohibit it, flush the clump away in the toilet.
5. Clean monthly using the protocol below. The corn clumping litter stays so clean that I need to wash the box only once a month.

Cleaning the Litter Box

After dumping what little litter remains in the box, I rinse it out with water, dump that out, sprinkle in a little cleanser (see "Litter Box Cleaner" below), and scrub the box inside and out with a vegetable brush that I keep on a hook next to the litter spoon. I always used to use a plain chlorine-based cleanser to clean the box until I got an idea from something my vet was using to disinfect the examining table in between patients (plain chlorine bleach and water). A 20 to 1 ratio of water to chlorine bleach kills germs, viruses, and fungus. It's cheap, easy, effective, and safe.

Litter Box Cleaner

- Mark off a large spray bottle into twenty-one parts.
- Fill it with nineteen parts water, one part chlorine bleach, and one part Dr. Bronner's Liquid Soap, available in most health food stores. (Don't use detergent. Liquid soap works great, but when detergent is combined with chlorine, a toxic chlorine gas is released.)

After I scrub, I rinse like crazy. If you think I'm finicky about food, I become absolutely rabid about any chemicals a cat might get on his paws or fur and lick off. No residue of soap or cleaner must be left in the box.

There is just no need for those deodorant sprays made especially for "kitty's box." Three of my pussycat clients in one household came down with a stubborn case of foot fungus, the cause of which was finally traced to an aerosol spray for the box. I explained to that caregiver that if you smell an odor from the box, there is something about your routine you need to correct. Usually people use too much litter and are not cleaning frequently enough. Using deodorant spray on a dirty box is like spraying perfume on a dirty body. Careful caregivers have no need of such products.

Keeping Watch over the "Output"

If you have more than one cat, it's an advantage if you can identify each cat's stool in order to be sure that each cat puts out a stool once or twice a day. There are many instances when knowing what's going in one end and what's coming out the other is worth its weight in gold and it gives the caregiver peace of mind.

Whenever I am helping a client care for a sick cat, I always ask about the condition and frequency of the stool. It tells me as much about the patient's needs as his temperature; maybe more.

"But I have three cats," the client will explain, "and I work all day. How am I going to be able to tell which stool is which when I finally get home at night and clean the box?"

"It's easy," I reply. "Once you know the tricks."

DETERMINING WHOSE STOOL IS WHOSE IN THE MULTI-CAT HOME

Here is how you, too, can learn to become a veritable Sherlock Holmes of the litter box:

1. While you're learning, keep the box extra clean. If you see one of the cats leaving the box and you check and find a stool or a wet spot, you'll immediately know whose it is.
2. Each cat will have slightly (or very) different toilet habits. If you hear someone in the box, go and quietly check who it is. When he leaves you'll have a golden opportunity to learn how to identify that cat's stool. Here's what to look for:

    A. The stool's location: Front? Back? Left? Right? (Each cat tends to use his own special area.)
    B. Does he cover—or not?
    C. When does he pass a stool? In the morning? After dinner? During the night?
    D. Appearance of the stool: A long cigar? Two? Small, hard balls? (I hope not.) A lumpy, brown puddle? (Again, I hope not.)

If you notice a change in the consistency of a cat's stools, immediately try to figure out what caused the change. Did the cat eat a milk product that made the stool runny? Did the cat eat more than her share of chicken neck vertebrae, which turned the stool into a series of hard little balls? If you don't know the cause of the change, then watch the cat closely for the appearance of any other adverse symptoms such as copious water drinking, loss of appetite, lethargy, and so on. (Also see "Diarrhea," page 358; "Constipation," page 347; and "Irritable Bowel Syndrome (IBS)," page 420.) Hopefully the stool will return to normal tomorrow, and you can breathe easy again.

Training Kittens to Use the Litter Box

The mother cat always toilet trains the kittens herself, so you never have to worry—well, hardly ever. On occasion, I receive calls for help from people with a litter of kittens who are wetting and dirtying outside the box. Because "everyone knows" that you don't have to housebreak a cat, the amazed caregivers wonder if these accidents are happening because the kittens are still too young. The answer is, *No!* Under normal circumstances, a kitten does not dirty or wet outside the box. Abnormal circumstances include being taken from the mother before she completes their training, inaccessibility of a litter box, sides that are too high for tiny legs to climb over, unsanitary conditions in the litter box, use of a strong-smelling chemical or deodorizer around the litter box, or placing the litter box near the food or water bowl. Some kittens that are adopted from shelters and rescue organizations have been kept in a small confined space like a kennel, where they were allowed to soil anywhere. They haven't had the opportunity to learn about litter boxes, so you have to start from scratch and be ready for a gradual learning curve. Luckily, most of them learn very quickly. For more on how to handle these situations, see "Soiling outside the Box," page 106.

Years ago I encountered yet another reason for this problem—Triple Champion Purr-du's Lee-la of Mar Wal was lacking some basic instinctual programming. She was a lovely chocolate point Siamese. To see her was to lose your heart. She was all purrs and cuddling and posing and sweetness—the darling of all who beheld her. Lee-la knew she was a winner, and because the world had always treated her royally, she had come to expect the very best at all times. She had never been frightened, so she did not know fear. Lee-la was not the brightest cat I ever met, but with all that charm and beauty, who cared?—until her kittens began to use the rugs for a toilet. The family was shocked; Lee-la was unconcerned. Because Lee-la didn't know what fear was, she lacked that basic instinct to protect her young from danger by teaching them to bury their wastes away from the nest, so that the smell would never draw predators near. Her six kittens were happy, healthy, and absolutely beautiful, but Lee-la's laissez-faire policy was driving the family to distraction.

The solution to this, as in so many situations, is found on a very primitive level. First let's examine exactly how, in nature, this automatic kitten training actually does occur; then, if necessity arises, a human can duplicate it.

After nursing, newborn kittens pass wastes while lying on their backs when they feel the mother's tongue stroking down their belly and out along the tail. The tiny amount of waste is simply cleaned away by the sweep of the mother's tongue and swallowed by the mother. The procedure is a study in efficiency, cleanliness, and safety. The mother disposes of the wastes a safe distance from the nest, passing them out of her body with her own stool.

When the kittens are old enough to walk a little distance and squat without falling over, the mother will lead them to a preferred place (the litter box, for domestic cats) and as they stand in the litter she begins to lick the genital area from behind, thus triggering the response of urinating and passing stool.

When the tiny stools and thimblefuls of urine are all deposited in the litter the mother then rallies her kittens to a jolly group effort of covering up the wastes. The kittens dutifully scratch and sniff and circle around with such vigor that the litter usually flies in all directions, showering the rug and floor for several feet around. Then the proud parent chases them all out of the box and the group runs pell-mell away, putting a safe distance between themselves and the area where any lingering smell could attract predators.

So, if some crucial part of the training is missing, the solution is obvious. Someone must supply the missing element—in the case of Lee-la, the mother's tongue, which triggers the response to deposit wastes in the litter.

Here's how it's done. After each meal, which is the usual time for the kittens to pass wastes, carry the kitten or kittens into the litter box. Dip a small piece of washcloth into a cup of hot water, wring it out, and wrap it around your finger so it will feel as much as possible like a warm, rough cat's tongue. Then, with the kitten standing in the litter, place the finger between the kitten's hind legs so that the tip of your finger rests against the stomach. Stroke the warm, cloth-covered finger backward against the kitten's tummy and up across the genitals and anus once or twice. Dip the washcloth in the hot water again and repeat, or go on to the next kitten. When a kitten begins to squat and pass wastes, gently stroke its forehead as a sign of encouragement and approval. At the end of the exercise, cover the wastes with your fingertip, lift the kittens out of the box, and lure them away with a toy.

Lee-la used to love to watch the performance from her queenly perch up on the bathroom sink. She would purr loudly the whole time. Indeed, I had the feeling that by the time those kittens were finally litter trained, Triple Champion Purr-du's Lee-la of Mar Wal was just as proud of me as she was of them. (The complete story of Lee-La is found in Chapter 1 of our book *It's a Cat's Life*. Her name in the story was changed to Su-shi to protect her privacy.)

Caution: While you or the mother cat are carrying on litter box training, you must be sure to keep the box scrupulously clean and use less litter than usual (even if you are using the new corn clumping litter). The kittens' feet are so tiny they sink into the litter. Their little legs are so short that if the litter is too deep, you'll have them falling over and swimming through it. Use only one-quarter-inch depth until the babies are eight weeks old, and I'll say it again—never use clumping litter unless it is made of corn or wheat. (See "Product Recommendations," page 489.)

If your kitten is already three months old or older, watch him like a hawk and as soon as he looks like he might urinate or pass a stool, gently scoop him up and place him in the litter box. If you miss the opportunity, all is not lost. Simply use paper towels to pick up or soak up any waste from the carpet or floor. Then place the stool or the urine-soaked paper towel in the litter box. Then bring the cat or kitten over to the box and place her gently in it. The odor from the waste will tell her that this is the correct place for this activity.

Do not in any way express displeasure if your cat wets or passes stool outside the box; that would only confuse her, and it won't assist in the process one iota. In fact, act happy as you transport her to the litter box. You want her to know that elimination is not a bad thing while you reinforce the correct place for it. During times when you cannot be there to watch the kitten, confine her to a small area with the litter box. Be sure it's pleasant. Give her a snug retreat to recline in (page 304) and a dish of water. This must not seem like a punishment.

Because your cat may well be attracted to the odor on the floor or carpet, she may want to use the same place to eliminate wastes again, so be sure to thoroughly clean the area where she soiled as soon as possible. Remember, even if you can't smell the odor, your cat can. (See "Removing Cat Urine Odor" on page 109.)

For more on kittens and the litter box, see Chapter 2 of our book *It's a Cat's Life*.

Soiling Outside the Box

Spraying, marking, or any soiling outside the litter box is a symptom of a problem, something gone wrong. *And 90 percent of all problems have more than one cause.* To eliminate any problem you need to find out the cause or causes and eliminate them. Here is a list of questions that will help:

1. *Is your cat older or ailing?* Medical problems in the intestine or urinary tract can cause constipation, diarrhea, bladder stones, or feline urologic syndrome (FUS). These medical conditions interfere with the usual "go to the box" signal and result in "accidents."

2. *Does your cat have arthritis?* If so, perhaps he can't step over the side to get into the litter box. (See "Arthritis," page 332.) Review the next section, "Special Litter Box Considerations for the Older or Ailing Cat."

3. *Is the litter box clean?* Did you wash it but not rinse out the cleanser well enough? (Review "Cleaning the Litter Box" on page 101.)

4. *Location! Location! Location!* Did you move the box recently? Is it in a busy, noisy, or exposed area? It should be in a quiet place where a cat can have her privacy and won't feel exposed. Is it too close to the area where you serve Fluffy's dinner? Cats don't want to soil anywhere near their dining area. Is it too far away for a cat who is sick or old? If you answer yes to any of these questions, move the litter box to a more appropriate place or add additional litter boxes for an ailing or elderly feline.

5. *Do you have enough litter boxes, considering the size of your home or the number of cats in your household?* Cleanliness and proximity are important for our fastidious friends. Get a second or even a third litter box if necessary and be sure to clean them all on a regular schedule.

6. *Is the litter box new?* It may smell wrong or be otherwise inhospitable due to a low cover or moving parts. Get a nice, simple litter box. Before using it, scrub it all over with cleanser and rinse it well.

7. *Did you change to a perfumed or deodorized litter that smells wrong to your cat or one that feels terrible underfoot?* Either go back to the litter your cat found acceptable or try other available litters. I recommend the corn-based litter for numerous reasons (see "What Litter Is Best?" page 94).

8. *Is another cat or a dog keeping your cat from using the litter box?* Make more than one box available. Place them far apart and put one in an area that is protected, where only the one cat can access it.

9. *Are stray or feral cats coming near your cat's territory?* This could be especially problematic if an unneutered male is roaming near your house and marking the territory or if an unspayed female is in heat. The win-win solution is to trap, neuter, and return the unneutered cats. This will benefit all concerned—you, your cats, and especially the unneutered wild or stray cats outside. (See "Ferals—The Wild Ones," page 143.)

10. *Is your cat stressed by a change in the home or some routine?* Do you have a new job, a new family member, a new baby, houseguests, or even new furniture? Did someone move away or did your work or school schedule change? The organs of excretion are sometimes the target of the cat's stress. Review Chapter 5, "The Cat and the Human Family" (page 119); "Nervousness, Hiding, and Ill Temper" (page 441); "While You're Away" (page 131); "Antistress Supplements" (page 305); and "Feline Urologic Syndrome (FUS)" (page 384).

11. *Did your cat accidentally get locked away from the litter box by a closed door?* Instruct guests, cleaning people, or handymen to leave interior doors open when possible for your cat's comfort needs. This is especially important for people who live in small apartments and must use the bathroom as a location for the litter box.

12. *Did your cat or kitten learn how to use the litter box?* If he was not trained properly as a tiny kitten by his mother, you'll have to help him out. Review "Training Kittens to Use the Litter Box," page 104.

13. *Did you change the box itself or the brand or type of litter?* Is the litter deodorized or perfumed? Did your cat develop an aversion to the texture of the litter you've been using? In all of these cases, keep the litter setup simple. Try using two or three simple litter boxes, each with a different type of the many acceptable litters given above. Use litters with different textures. Also, carefully examine your cat's claws and pads for possible problems.

14. *Are you using a harsh cleaning product with an odor that repels the cat or kitten?* Review "Cleaning the Litter Box," page 101.

I'll say a word here about temporary solutions to make life easier while you're getting the problem solved. I have been asked about repellant sprays that are supposed to keep the cat away from an area. They seldom work; the cat will simply go elsewhere to soil. In addition, they have proven to be toxic to some cats and have caused headaches and nausea in some humans.

There is, however, a product called Feliway that contains artificial olfactory pheromones that appease anxiety. It comes in a spray or plug-in diffuser. Because nearly all soiling is caused by some problem that has upset the cat, Feliway works by calming him to the point where he doesn't soil anymore. I have received good reports about 80 percent of the time. Here is a harmless stopgap measure that can save your carpet (and your sanity) while you are tracking down the cause.

REMOVING CAT URINE ODOR

If your cat or kitten urinates anywhere other than the litter box, remove any hint of the odor as soon as possible so her natural instincts won't draw her back to that area again. If the wet area is on carpet, you'll have to act before it soaks all the way into the carpet padding. If the urine is already dried on the carpet, you'll still want to act fast so the urine odor will not continue to attract your cat. If necessary, use a black light. When you turn out all the lights in the room, the black light will identify soiled areas. You can then lightly outline the areas with chalk. To properly clean the soiled areas:

1. *Soak up as much urine as possible.* First place a thick layer of paper towels on the wet area and then cover that with a layer of newspaper. Then stand on it for a minute or so. Your weight will help the soaking process. Remove the padding and repeat until the area is barely damp.

2. *Rinse the area by wetting it with water and repeating the process above.* This second step will allow you to remove as much urine as possible before using the cleaner. Your goal is also to remove any cleaners or chemicals that were previously used on the carpet because they can interfere with the effectiveness of the enzymatic cleaner you will use next. If you have a carpet shampooer, use it to get the area as dry as possible.

3. *Use an enzymatic cleaner from a pet store.* These cleaners are nontoxic. They contain enzymes that combine with the urine and actually change the urine molecules into a new substance that has no odor. Because the proteins in animal urine are extremely strong, it is vital that you remove the stain thoroughly—so really soak the area. Regular carpet shampoos and other cleaning products will not successfully remove the odor. Be sure to follow the instructions on the bottle. Usually you have to *soak* the area, not rinse or dry it; just let the carpet dry on its own.

Note: Do not use ammonia or vinegar to clean urine-soaked carpet. They don't effectively eliminate or cover the urine odor. Rather, they mask the odor temporarily and can permanently set the proteins in the urine into the carpet fibers. If this happens, your cat will be able to detect them and will be tempted to use this same area over and over again. If this happens, there may be no other solution except taking up the carpet and padding and throwing them out.

Special Litter Box Considerations for the Older or Ailing Cat

My Suzi is twenty years old. When she was nineteen, she began "making mistakes" from time to time, urinating in the kitchen. My veterinarian found no evidence of bladder infection; we reasoned that she was just a little confused. Sometimes she'd wake up and have to urinate, but she'd forget which sleeping area she had been using and in which direction she should proceed to get to the bathroom, so she'd end up in the kitchen and then not be able to hold her urine any longer.

I decided it was time to add an extra litter box in the living room for her convenience. It was a plastic dishpan with two pages of newspaper folded flat in the bottom and three paper towels on top for extra quick absorbency so she wouldn't be troubled by getting moisture on her paws. I didn't use litter because I don't want anyone kicking litter on my living room floor. I put it near the kitchen door and the problem was solved. (Today I'd use a "wee-wee pad" from the pet store instead of the newspaper and towel.)

When your feline friend becomes a senior citizen, he or she needs special consideration. If your veterinarian finds no urinary infection, there are several other possible causes for wetting outside the box. Elderly or sick cats may become too weak to walk all the way to the box, or a weakened bladder may release the urine before they can make it. Arthritis may slow them down, make it painful to step over the high sides into the box, or prevent them from squatting properly.

Once a cat passes the age of fourteen, there should be a litter box on every floor of the house. If she can't step over the side, find a new litter box with lower sides, use a brick or a book to form a low step next to the box, or cut an opening in the side of the box, leaving only two or three inches on the bottom to keep the litter from tumbling out. If she can't squat properly and the urine sprays outside the box, put newspaper and paper towel on the floor and masking-tape it to the bathroom wall next to the box.

The deep love that exists between you and your old friend will inspire you to devise ingenious methods of solving her problem without her ever suspecting that she has one.

The Scratching Post and Scratching Problems 4

I t is a sad fact that many poorly informed guardians have had their cats declawed simply because they thought it was the only way to keep them from scratching furniture, carpeting, or even people. Fortunately, this is not the case. A normal adult cat does not use his claws inappropriately. I hope the declawing operation will become obsolete as guardians learn to meet their cats' needs by supplying scratching posts that the cats find irresistible.

The Scratching Post They Love

Cats should be encouraged to scratch because all the musculature, from the claws through the legs and shoulders and down the back, are exercised and toned when the cat scratches to clean and sharpen his claws. A cat who doesn't scratch has underdeveloped muscles. All wild cats love a good claw at a nice rough tree. This tells us that the scratching post should be rough, too.

Unfortunately, most posts in pet shops are made to attract humans instead of cats because it's the humans who walk in with the money to buy the post. Ninety-nine percent of all humans are attracted by a soft-looking, fluffy-wuffy scratching post. The *cat* should be fluffy-wuffy—the *post* should be rough and coarse. We may not find it practical to bring a tree trunk into the house or a small apartment, but there are other alternatives. Cats are attracted to something rough, like the back of a good rug or, heaven forbid, Great-Grandmother's needlepoint footstool. What the cat needs is a post so wonderfully rough and scratchy that Great-Grandmother's needlepoint becomes second-rate by comparison.

Luckily, such posts are available from pet shops. You will undoubtedly find the ubiquitous fluffy-wuffy variety covered with various colors and textures of carpet. But, if you search just a bit further, you will strike gold and come upon one that is covered with rope or, even better, a nice big, strong, stable post covered with rough scratchy sisal, a harsh, scratchy hemp product. If it's impregnated with catnip, all the better. If not, not to worry. Choose your cat's post for texture and stability; you can buy a container of the very finest catnip and rub it all over the post yourself. I recommend the Karate Kat Ultimate Scratching Post, Felix Katnip Tree, Bizzy-Kitty Scratching Pad, or Smart Cat's Ultimate Scratching Post.

I have seen my Big Purr take a flying leap off the table to land on the top of the post. Balancing nicely, he extends the claws of all four feet and blissfully digs in. A far-off look of ecstasy suffuses his countenance as he sways. It is a subtle and sensual dance. As the clawing goes deeper and the dance steps become more pronounced, Purr's post trembles with the violence of his digging and pulling. But it never tips over, because Big Purr's post has a very firm base.

Many cats are declawed because of *fluffy* scratching posts. Fluffy scratching posts do not fulfill their purpose from the cats' point of view, so your cats go to your furniture in desperation. Then the cat's guardians complain, "I tried a post, and he refuses to use it." It's not the cat's fault—it's the fault of the post. Either it is too fluffy, or too rickety, or too small. The trick is to give your cats a post they can't resist.

If you want to make your own scratching post, use a rug with a rough backing and put the backing side out. Also, make sure the whole thing is secure and won't wobble or fall over. If you meet these two criteria, you're home free. Don't, for heaven's sake, buy one of those ridiculous things you're supposed to hang from a doorknob. Tree trunks do not dangle and sway back and forth. And even the backside of a piece of carpet laid on the floor is better than a fluffy-wuffy post. If you've already been taken in by the fluffy-wuffy variety, why not recover it with carpet turned backside out? This will work fine as long as you have a large, firm base.

As a stopgap measure, the disposable corrugated cardboard scratching boards can also work well and some cats will use the cork variety, but both must be firmly braced so they don't slide around. My Julia, who is semiferal, prefers the disposable scratching board above all else. I think it's because it's supposed to get destroyed. Every cat enjoys destroying something with their claws once in a while. Therein lies the attraction.

Now there is one more thing you can do to ensure that your cats will really go for that new scratching post: wrap it up. You know how cats are; they like to feel they're getting away with something, like it's their own idea. So anytime you want a cat to do something, try to set up the situation so he'll have to work for it a little bit. After you rub fresh catnip all over the post, pop a big brown bag over the top and wrap it up with some tissue paper or wrapping paper. Then lay the package on the floor, walk away as if you have no further interest in it, and sit down to watch the fun.

Here's what usually happens next: if you just leave the package lying on the floor inside the door, your cats will soon trot over to have a good sniff. The odor of catnip wafting from that parcel is absolutely irresistible. They may begin to attack it with violence, ripping and tearing at it with their teeth and claws. By now, some of the very potent catnip will have fallen out. The catnip may propel your cats onto cloud nine, rolling about on their backs from side to side and rubbing their cheeks against the wonderful package in ecstasy. It is not unusual to see cats grab the post with front claws, hugging it to them, while raking it viciously with the hind claws. Their excitement can be felt like the temperature in the room. The catnip may not do much for you, but your cats' wild abandon will tell its own story.

In order to stretch out your cats' pleasure and anticipation of this new toy, leave the post wrapped as it is for an hour or even a day and just let them enjoy ripping at the paper and tape and getting mini-scratches at whatever bit of the post they expose. As a matter of fact, anytime you want your cats to do something, your best bet is to engineer the circumstances so that you keep the cats in the position of asking for it or reaching for it rather than presenting it to them on a silver platter, or even worse, thrusting it at them.

Perhaps the next day, when your cats begin to attack the parcel, you can go ahead and get down on the rug and help them as they rip and tear the wrapping paper away, exposing completely that irresistible scratchiness—the naked post covered with powdered catnip. Once the post is completely exposed, the cats will probably press the whole length of their bodies close against its primitive roughness and begin rubbing their cheeks against the sisal fabric and chewing on it. Go ahead—join the party. Scratch it yourself. What an intriguing sound for a pussycat's ears! Then scratch the cats. Really get into it, with your nails and your hands. You'll send them into fresh throes of sensual delight. Cloud nine will be left far below. Their eyes may glaze over slightly, and they may utter low guttural sounds from deep in their throats. Do not be alarmed, it's normal when cats are totally focused on hitherto-undreamed-of pleasure.

In ten or fifteen minutes, the cats, thoroughly sated, will tumble into a heap somewhere to sleep it off. Now is a good time to stand the post erect and set it in its permanent place.

Where to Put the Scratching Post

There are several advantageous places to position the post:

- In a corner, with the base touching two right-angle walls so it won't slide around.
- Next to Great-Grandmother's needlepoint footstool, so that when the cats go for the footstool they will see the post and, naturally, prefer the post.
- On its side, like a tilt-board, to make it seem less threatening because many highly bred or nervous cats can be extremely suspicious of anything new or strange.

Once you and your cats decide on the best placement for the post, you can make it even more secure by putting double-face carpet tape on the bottom all around the edge.

If your cats do not immediately leap on the post and begin scratching like mad, you can (1) scratch the post yourself and tell them how much you enjoy the sensation or (2) lay the post on its side, pick the cats up, and stand them on the tilting post. Never grab cats' legs or feet and force them onto the post. Cats hate that, and it will have a very negative effect—just the opposite of what you're trying to achieve. Just stroke firmly down their necks and backs so that you urge their bodies backward. Most cats dig their claws into the post as an expression of ecstasy. Alternate between scratching the post with your finger nails in front of them with the firm, stroking, pulling gesture down their backs. In other words, you are creating a situation where they feel ecstasy, and at the same time you are showing them how to express it.

Encouraging Use of the Scratching Post

To reinforce the association of happiness with the post, include the use of the post in other situations that are normally happy occasions, for example, your arrival home, before and after feeding, or before and after play time. When I'm caring for cats who are up for adoption, I make sure they are dedicated scratching post users so there is no danger of their ever being declawed by a misinformed future guardian.

Every time I come home, the cats are happy and excited. But I don't pet them right away. First I run to the scratching post and begin scratching the top of the post with my nails and tell the cats how glad I am to be back and how much I missed them. In response, they all crowd in and begin clawing the post. As soon as they start clawing the post, I stop scratching it and start scratching them, continuing my verbal assurances of love, interspersed with comments about how strong, lithe, and graceful they look while scratching the post. Because cats adore ritual and sameness, I further reinforce the pleasure of the situation by beginning with a ritual phrase. I always say, "Let's greet, let's greet" while I run from the door to the post.

Because "catch and kill" with the use of claws precedes eating in nature, you can also scratch the post before you prepare the cat's food, perhaps using a ritualistic phrase such as "Are you hungry?" "Is it time?" or something worked out by you and your cat. After eating, the phrase might be "Was it good?" The same principle can be used before and after play time.

Don't freshen the catnip on the post more than once a week, because otherwise the cats will become immune to its effects and will not react as strongly. Don't use catnip at all if your cats are being treated homeopathically. (See "Homeopathy," page 211.)

Once you have provided a heavenly scratching opportunity, your cat will probably focus all of his efforts on that. But if he still has an unfortunate tendency to scratch on old familiar places like the ottoman or the drapes, you might try a product called Sticky Paws. These transparent medical-grade adhesive strips are double-sided. Positioned on the forbidden scratching area, they will deter Muffy because cats hate to put their paws on sticky surfaces.

The Physical and Emotional Effects of Declawing

Many veterinarians do not explain to the cat's guardian the true seriousness, both physically and emotionally, of the declawing operation. Realistically, it is ten amputations. Moreover, it is ten difficult and complex amputations. The cat must remain under an anesthetic quite a long time. Anesthetizing a cat for even a short time is, as everyone knows, chancy. People sometimes compare declawing to removing the first joint of all ten fingers, but the claw is harder to remove because humans do not retract their fingertips. Your fingertip is not set into the joint below in a complex fashion. A cat's claw involves tendons and muscles that we don't have. Someone once described declawing to me as "cutting pieces out of animals' bodies for convenience." I was absolutely horrified by the starkness of the way she faced this reality. People prefer not to discuss this so graphically in polite company. I apologize to those who already know the reality for reminding you of it and for bringing into your conscious mind again something so painful. But I have met too many loving guardians who were never told, or who had the operation misrepresented to them only to find out, perhaps years after it was done, the truth about what they had allowed to happen to the animal they loved. There are many veterinarians in the United States and England who refuse to do the operation and are happy to explain why. In many countries, declawing is illegal or considered inhumane. In the United States, it is opposed by the Humane Association of the United States, the American Society for the Prevention of Cruelty to Animals, and many other animal rights groups. As of this writing, it is illegal to declaw a cat in West Hollywood, California. Other jurisdictions are considering similar legislation.

The physical effect of declawing is a gradual weakening of the muscles of the legs, shoulders, and back. Balance is impaired. The cat is 75 percent defenseless—cats don't defend themselves with their teeth, they defend themselves with their claws.

The long-range effects are both physical and emotional. A declawed cat is, in reality, a clubfooted animal. He cannot walk normally but must forever after move with his weight back on the rear of his pads. Oh yes, he will probably adjust and look quite normal to anyone who doesn't know how a cat is really supposed to move and stand, but the posture of a declawed cat is irrevocably altered, and gone is the easeful grace that is his birthright. The carriage of the spine is also subtly altered. Important nerves exit between each vertebrae, connecting the brain with each organ. Therefore every organ in the body is affected too. Because they are defenseless, declawed cats live in a constant state of stress. This is very draining, and because of the constant stress, these cats are more prone to disease. (See "Stress: A Cat's Natural Enemy," page 255.)

Declawed cats bite sooner and more often than cats that have their claws, both because they are more tense and nervous and because they no longer have their claws to use as a warning. The claws are their first line of defense. With that gone, they must resort to desperate measures—the use of their teeth. They don't *want* to bite, but in the absence of their claws it's an automatic response. For that reason, a declawed cat is not one you would want to have around young children.

Newborn kittens until the age of three weeks or so have not yet learned to retract their claws. But once cats begin to have control of their claws they can be trained to use them on toys and the post but not on human flesh. (Review "Velvet Paws for Human Flesh; Claws for Toys and Scratching Post" on page 17.)

I call the first eight months or so of a cat's life the rambunctious months. During this time kittens are learning to use that wonderful body nature has given them. All cats have to learn how to use their claws. Just as a little human baby uses his teeth on everything in sight when he is teething, a kitten will try his claws on drapes, furniture, and everything within reach during the rambunctious months. Many cats are mutilated with a declawing operation at this time because their guardians don't realize that just as human babies eventually outgrow the desire to chew on buttons and fingers, kittens grow out of their desire to claw everything and are easily satisfied with a workout on their scratching post.

Declawed cats are much harder for a groomer or veterinarian to handle because of their nervous state and their proclivity for using teeth. Cats use claws as a mode of expression. We humans have sounds and words and laughter, but cats say, "Mmmm, this feels good" by gently kneading their claws. When I'm grooming, a cat will sometimes say to me, "Hey, stop that, wait a minute" by hitting me with their claws when their patience is running out. They do not scratch or harm me in any way. They are simply making a strong statement. I know that "claws out," in this case, means that I have not listened when they tried to warn me with a meow, a wiggle, or a bop with a paw, claws in. Cats are polite; they give a warning before they hurt you. If you declaw cats, you have taken away this means of being polite and giving warning first. In a way it could be likened to removing a person's larynx. Even if you promise that that person would always be protected, certainly never have to cry for help, even if you promise that that person would always have anything and everything that he might desire (and in real life you can never be sure you can fulfill such promises), still, the larynx is gone. The choice of communicating in the normal way is no longer that person's choice.

Many times I have encountered guardians who, after realizing what a declawing operation really means, vow never again to allow a cat of theirs to be declawed. Then, when they begin living with a normal cat, they are amazed and enchanted by the difference and by their new feline friend's athletic prowess and grace, and they point out to me how very unusual their cat is in this respect. I have to explain to them that their cat is not unusual; he's simply normal. All cats leap and bound like super ballet dancers if their feet have not been mutilated.

If you would like more information about claws and declawing, see "Claw and Cuticle Problems" on page 344 and the section "Foot and Claw Problems" in *Dr. Pitcairn's Complete Guide to Natural Health for Dogs and Cats.*

The Cat and the Human Family 5

Because my job entails going into people's homes to take care of their cats, I have a unique opportunity to observe firsthand that delightful and complex interaction that takes place between the human family and its cats. I know so many of these families, and our relationship has extended now over so many years, that many common problems have been brought to my attention time and time again, which I will discuss in this chapter.

The New Baby

Whenever a family is expecting a baby, concerns about safety and hygiene naturally arise. The available information about cats and babies seems to be composed of a mixture of facts, half-truths, and out-and-out fiction.

Many people have asked me if it's true that cleaning the litter box can cause a miscarriage. It sounds silly at first, doesn't it? But, oddly enough, there *can* be a connection. Toxoplasmosis is the disease to which these people are referring. The dried, microscopic cysts sometimes blow around, mixed with dust. Most people and animals have at some point inhaled some of it and contracted a mild case of toxoplasmosis without realizing it and have developed an immunity. Another common way to catch toxoplasmosis is by eating contaminated raw meat or by touching raw meat and then touching vegetables that will remain raw. The contamination is killed when you cook the meat, but it will remain on the raw foods. For cats to carry the disease they must first have eaten a rat or mouse who has the disease or eaten contaminated raw meat at home. If you have a concern, there's a simple test that will tell you if your cat is carrying the disease or is immune to it. There is also a blood test for humans to determine if you already have an immunity to toxoplasmosis. If neither you nor your cat has developed an immunity, then you should be very careful. If your cat does indeed contract the disease, there will be microscopic cysts in the stool. Herein lies the potential danger. In order to pass toxoplasmosis on to a human, the human must in turn ingest these cysts. Because they are in the cat's stool, you might think that this is impossible. But wait—what if, while cleaning the litter box, someone touches some stool on the side of the box? If that person does not wash the hand carefully before picking up and eating a piece of food, that food could be inadvertently contaminated. Contamination could also occur after grooming cats or cleaning the genital area. Unlikely as it sounds, pregnant women have been known to contract toxoplasmosis, and this disease *can* cause birth defects or miscarriage. My advice has always been "Why worry? If the possibility is preying on your mind, simply drop your cat's fresh stool sample off at your veterinarian and he will test it for you and tell you whether or not your cat is carrying toxoplasmosis. You can also get your own blood and urine tested. You may very well have a natural immunity to toxoplasmosis; most of us do. And in the meantime, review the litter box chapter (page 91) and remember to wash your hands after touching raw meat or cleaning the litter box."

An old wives' tale that I've encountered more than once has two variations, the most primitive being that cats like to suck the breath out of babies. The second variation is that the cat will smother the baby. Every time I hear of this slander, I think of little Matthew who was born into a household that boasted four large cats. The cats ranged in temperament from lethargic to skittish, from friendly to withdrawn, and from playful to solitary. Both males and females were represented in this group and all were of normal intelligence.

From the time Matthew came home from the hospital, all of the cats loved to sleep with him in the crib. At first, three of the four cats were larger than Matthew. Just imagine what it must feel like to be small enough to snuggle your whole body against a cat's chest and be completely enveloped in that warm, soft fur. Imagine being surrounded by the sound of a cat's purr. I don't know if the cats had anything to do with it, but Matthew was a very mellow and sunny baby, always grinning and gurgling.

When Matthew started to crawl, he would sometimes reach for the cats and try to grab hold of them. It was a simple matter for them to slip away from his grasp when they had had enough, and they still continued to sleep with him.

During the crawling stage, Matthew and the cats really had a great time because at this point Matthew was almost as smart as the cats. The cats could understand him and play with him safely because Matthew had not yet reached the stage where he was strong enough or coordinated enough to grab and hold a cat. He couldn't yet prevent the cats from leaving when they wanted to.

Matthew's mother knew that the toddler stage begins a time of transition for both Matthew and the cats and that the cats had to be protected. The time was approaching when Matthew would be strong enough to inadvertently harm a cat. A toddler may pick up a heavy toy and swing it about and accidentally hit the loving animal sitting close by. Toddlers are not yet capable of understanding that they now have enough strength to harm their feline playmate. More adult supervision was needed now until Matthew learned the rules involved in dealing with an animal friend.

The very first rule that will keep them safe for the rest of their lives is this: never try to hold a cat if the cat wants to go. If you always let cats go, they will always come back to you. Especially when dealing with strange cats (or dogs), never touch them with more than one hand at a time. That way it's clear to the animals that they are free to leave if they want to, and they won't feel threatened. As long as cats can leave if they want to, they will never have reason to scratch. Cats scratch only as a last resort if they are extremely upset and frightened and can not get away.

Young Children

Declawed cats are not good to have around children. They are less secure in their own abilities to escape and will be more likely to bite. Cats with all their claws intact are by far the gentlest and safest companions for young children. As children grow up, they will probably find the feeding and litter cleaning fascinating. Many children like to help with these activities, and I know several bright young people who have taken them over completely and have even included grooming in their list of accomplishments. This is one of the lovely contributions that your cats make to your children's education and personal growth. Just by their mere presence in the family, cats introduce the youngsters to a sense of responsibility.

Of course, the wise parent and loving guardian would never actually use a helpless animal as a tool to teach children responsibility. Children may help with pet care, but the adult is still in charge and overseeing. There may come a time when the children are given full responsibility and think they are totally in charge, but the responsible guardian will keep a constant, if surreptitious, check to see that each mealtime, each cleanup, each grooming session, and the condition of the litter box continue on the same high standards that prevailed before the younger family members took over. In other words, children are sometimes careless or forgetful. We all know it's true. It's both normal and usual for children. They'll understand the consequences of their lapses when they get older, but not now. You, the parent, must maintain an ever-watchful eye during those years while they're learning.

A word to the wise—little children frequently hurt animals simply because they do not realize what constitutes pain or distress to an animal. Many children love cymbals and drums and cap pistols—however, such things could cause physical pain to a cat's sensitive ears and could permanently damage the hearing. Cats are different from people, and it takes quite a while before children are old enough to understand that. (I might add—I've met many adults who still haven't achieved that understanding.)

Children raised in a loving household with animal friends will usually grow up to love animals. When remembering their own childhoods, what a pity it is if they have painful memories of their own cruelty to animals through ignorance or parental indulgence. The memories children will have when they grow up are being made now. Protect your children from painful memories by protecting the cat until the children are old enough to fully understand.

Visitors in the Home

Not everyone understands cats. Many a tragedy has struck because well-meaning friends or relatives or occasional workers come into a home and innocently open a window. If you expect workers to arrive while you are away, lock the cat in one room with litter and water and put a sign on the door that clearly states not to open the door or let the cat out. Many cats are afraid of workers, and a surprisingly large number of workers are afraid of or do not like cats. When friends and relatives come to visit, you can make sure that they know that care must be taken when opening or closing doors or drawers. You can also explain the danger of windows and make sure they know they should not play roughly with the cat with their hands.

Allergic to Cats?

I have frequently had the experience of people coming to visit who didn't know I had cats. Several times those people have told me that they were always allergic to cats and cannot understand why they were not having a reaction to mine. It's nice to be able to help such people understand the reasons by explaining how diet and feeding patterns cut down cat allergens, which are the substances they are allergic to. (See Chapter 2, "Diet.")

I remember Marcie and Lou Gustavson, a nice young couple who moved in down the hall. Lou was highly allergic to cats and a number of other things. Marcie had always lived with cats and missed them terribly, so one evening they came over to visit me and my cats. I had eleven cats in residence at the time: my own three, a couple of convalescents boarding for nursing care, and six adoptables. Both Marcie and Lou had a great time petting and hugging and playing with all the cats. Lou reasoned that he could always leave if his eyes started to itch or if he had trouble breathing. When Lou had no allergic response, Marcie immediately began to wonder if perhaps all was not lost as far as Lou and cats being able to live together. She asked hopefully if I thought they could try adopting a couple of cats if she kept the cats strictly to the diet I suggested and removed the food between meals. I felt a bit hesitant about committing myself. I'd never tried to solve this particular problem before, and I certainly didn't want to disappoint Marcie. But, because I had so many cats up for adoption, I decided that we should give it the old college try.

I told them that we'd have a much better chance of success if we not only controlled the amount of dander on the cat but also tried to increase Lou's tolerance to allergens. They were all for that, of course. Because allergies are evidence of a faulty immune response, I have found that housecleaning a clogged intestinal tract goes a long way toward alleviating the condition. I wanted to give us a wider margin within which to work.

After explaining this, I asked Lou if he would make some changes in his own diet. Drawing from my experience with yoga and macrobiotics, I told him to eliminate eggs, pork, white sugar, fruit juices (they contain more sugar than a Coke), and caffeine from his diet. I also asked him to eat fish instead of red meats and cut down on butter and other dairy products. I asked him to add two tablespoons of bran and a tablespoonful of lecithin granules to his diet each day and to eat as much raw food as possible: salads, sushi, carrots, seasonal fruit.

He was game to try. When I asked them if they had any special cats in mind, they just looked at each other and smiled. Lou said, "I think we'd like to take 'the married couple.' " I couldn't believe my luck. "The married couple"—Sally and Victor—were two short-haired black cats who had been waiting for adoption for several months.

When I got her, Sally was the smallest cat I ever saw in my life. She was nine years old, and she did not even tip the scale at four pounds. She had arrived when her owner left her with me, supposedly for boarding, and was never heard from again. I soon found out why. Sally immediately began defecating all over the apartment. She was in sad shape. She had been declawed and was a veritable walking snowdrift of dandruff. She crouched morosely inside an empty cat food carton in my back room, hurling threats at any cat who came too close. None of the other cats liked her. So she just sat there frowning, all hunched up in a ball. I wondered how in the world I was ever going to get rid of this one. Who in their right mind would want to adopt an angry pile of dandruff who defecated all over the place?

The veterinarian diagnosed her as having Irritable Bowel Syndrome and I started adjusting her diet until she was eating my basic raw food diet with Anitra's Vita-Mineral Mix; a multivitamin; and, for her intestines, ¼ teaspoon mixed intestinal flora, $\frac{1}{32}$ teaspoon Green Magma, and ⅛ teaspoon fine bran. It took a month and a half to heal her irritated intestines and condition her stool so she didn't have to either strain or suddenly let go wherever she was. Of course, this high-quality diet, which was specifically adjusted for her particular intestinal needs, immediately had its effect on the dandruff. Teeny tiny little Sally developed a plushy coat in two months flat. But she still huddled morosely in her box most of the time.

Four-year-old Victor came strolling onto the scene in the company of two other cats, all of whom had been left homeless when an elderly client had been taken to the hospital with a heart attack and never returned. Victor was as big as Sally was tiny. He was the very picture of shiny black health and vigor. His former guardian had had the cats on a high-quality diet for over two years. Victor spotted Sally from the doorway when he went to explore the back room. He just strolled over, jaunty and jolly. "Hi, good looking," he seemed to be saying as he stretched himself out next to Sally's carton. Sally cowered back, muttering swear noises, but I noticed she didn't show her fangs and I saw her blink a couple of times, a sure sign that her heart was not entirely made of ice. I think Victor was a gift from the compassionate cat goddess to Sally. He was so mellow and sweet that nobody could resist him—human or animal.

By the second day, Sally and Victor were an item. Victor moved into Sally's carton, and there was a great deal of mutual licking and close cuddling. After Victor's arrival, Sally was seen more and more at large in the room. Victor was the leader, but Sally did follow and leave her cloistered bower. As I watched the romance unfolding, the question was never far from my mind as to how in the world I would ever get them adopted together. It's hard enough to find a home for one cat—opportunities for placing two together are almost nonexistent. I had been steeling myself for the day when I would have to break up Sally and Victor. I doubted that I could do it and still go on living with myself.

Then into my life walked this nice young couple who announced they'd like to take the two of them. On top of that, from the looks on their faces, I could see that they were already falling in love with my Sally and Victor. Obviously the Gustavsons were a second gift from the cat goddess.

At the end of the month, Marcie called to report that Lou had found his tendency to allergic reactions in general to have lessened. They were anxious to come over and pick up the cats, both of them feeling very positive that all would go well. Lou had lost five pounds during that first month on the new diet and, incidentally, a year later he still declares that he feels better than he has for a long time. Sally does too. There's no longer any evidence that she ever had Irritable Bowel Syndrome. And Lou's allergy to cats seems to be completely controlled. And Apartment 5J down the hall now boasts not one but two married couples. (See "Allergies," page 328, and "Dandruff," page 351.)

Taking the Cat Along:
Vacations, Visits, and Moving

Because cats are such territorial animals, loving sameness the way they do, uprooting them and moving them around can be a traumatic event. However, if uprooting them means that they can then be with you, their beloved human, that is often better than leaving them temporarily behind. The thing to do is try it a few times and find out what works best for you and your cats. For the best chance of success and a smooth transition, start preparing in advance. Tell the cats about the trip you are planning, how happy it will make you to have them with you, and what the trip will be like in every detail from their point of view. Leave the carry case out for at least a few hours a day so they can sniff it and get used to it. Many cats will nap in the carrier. It is a nice size and shape for napping. Throw the weekly catnip party inside the carrier. If your cat has a favorite treat such as olives, cantaloupe, or sweet corn, feed him that particular tidbit inside the carrier once or twice. This way you're creating all sorts of happy associations connected with the carrier.

Review how to choose the case and how to place the cat in the carrier by reviewing the pertinent section in Chapter 1.

When the day of the journey arrives, withhold all food and water after midnight of the night before. Skipping breakfast is not one-quarter as traumatic as it would be if the cat dirtied inside the carrier. Whatever your mode or modes of transportation, your safest bet is to leave the carrier closed the whole time, although if traveling by plane they'll probably ask you to open it at the inspection point before you get on the plane. Ask the inspector to allow you to open it inside a room where you can shut the door. No one wants a terrified cat escaping and running loose in the departure lounge.

Once comfortably seated in your conveyance, you may consider opening the case but keeping your furry friend inside so he can stretch a little, look around, and get a little more reassurance from you. This sometimes works very well. Again, the only way to find out is to try it. The thing to keep in mind is not to open the case all the way until you have a firm grip on the cat. Make sure you keep your hold on the cat in such a way that at any moment you can easily close the case again. In other words, do not allow the cat to put paws up on the edge of the case. Let the cat sit on your lap *inside* the open case, and you can put your arms into the case and wrap them around him. This is known as "The Open Case Hug."

As always, when introducing any new activity to the cat, your attitude and mental vibrations are all-important. If you are nervous about putting the cat into the case, your cat will be nervous about getting into the case. If you are nervous about flying, your cat will feel apprehensive about flying. Keep your mind centered on the positive aspects and the comforts and pleasures of your cat's situation—how secure the case is and how pleasant it is to be in a case and be carried. Put a nice soft towel in the bottom of the case plus a small piece of your clothing such as a sock or glove to provide additional comfort. Don't allow anyone to rap on the case or call to your cat. When cats are confined in a case and cannot run away, it is in the worst possible taste to expose them to strangers.

I think the watchword is casualness. Try to keep your feelings casual about everything. If you get all upset because your flight is delayed, cats will pick up your emotions, and, because they don't know about schedules, they will assume that you are upset because some danger threatens you.

What about traveling with your cat on public transportation? As of this writing, in the United States service animals are the only four-footed creatures allowed on Amtrak and Greyhound. You'll have to check on the rules for other train and bus carriers. As for airline travel, I don't recommend sending your cat in the luggage compartment. I have never done it because no one can guarantee the animal's safety. Frankly, I am afraid. I know people who have done it with no ill effects to their animals but, on the other hand, I have also heard of animals arriving dead or near death. They were frozen to death from the high altitudes or brain damaged from a lack of oxygen. More than once, heavy baggage has crashed against the carrier, springing it open and releasing hysterical animals to run loose among the baggage until the guardian could be summoned to help capture them.

If you know you're going to travel by plane, first check to see if your preferred airline allows animals in the passenger cabin. Some airlines prohibit all but service animals on board. Others vary in terms of the number of animals allowed per flight. The easiest way that several of my clients have found is to buy a seat for your cat. Granted, this is quite expensive. So, if you want to avoid this expense, make your reservations very early and secure "pet permission" when you do. Make sure the pet permission is clearly indicated on your written confirmation.

Once you get pet permission, the airline may then insist that you buy a special carrier that fits underneath the seat. I cannot caution you strongly enough to get that carrier well in advance. There are many carriers available that are designed to fit under the airline seat. You'll want to look them over and choose one that does not collapse in on top of your cat and that allows your cat to move and stretch a bit. It is important to let him try it out and get used to reclining in it well in advance. Remember, cats don't like surprises.

My friend and coauthor Norma had to fly with her cat Clarence when she was returning to New York after a season of winter stock at a theater in Florida. She tried gently putting Clarence into the case just to see if he would fit because it looked so small. She admits that she was having serious doubts and that her mind was not tranquil about it. Clarence became totally hysterical, yowling and ripping at the case, so she let him out at once. Norma then considered sending him in the plane's luggage compartment, but Clarence had been ailing and just the thought of his riding there upset her. Various friends gave conflicting advice, and because Norma had had no direct experience before, she resolved in desperation to ask Clarence one more time. So, the next day, she sat down with him and opened the case on the bed. Very slowly, very clearly, and in great detail, she explained to Clarence the pros and cons of the two alternatives. Then she told him how she felt and how much nicer it would be for her to have him close to her on the trip.

Then she looked into Clarence's eyes and told him very clearly that she wanted to try it just one more time. She picked him up, laid him on his side inside the carrier, and firmly closed the lid. This time Clarence didn't say a word but just lay there waiting for Norma to make the next move, whatever that might be. She opened the case, and Clarence sat up, stretched, and stepped out in a dignified manner. He succeeded in reassuring Norma that the carry case would be okay.

Before the day of the flight, friends who saw the case, squat and tiny as it was, and saw Clarence, large and sprawling as he was, gave the opinion that shutting a monster like Clarence in "that little thing" was tantamount to cruelty. Norma had fresh misgivings, vacillating in her mind between the tiny airline carry case and the great unknown luggage compartment. But in the end she stuck by Clarence's decision, as she had promised him she would.

When travel day arrived, sure enough Clarence kept his side of the bargain. As Norma chatted about the positive aspects of the trip, Clarence curled himself down in that cheap little plastic monstrosity and said not a word when the lid was closed. Norma continued to talk about how nice it would be to be home, mentioning Clarence's favorite sunny windowsill where he had his own special view of New York City's pigeons. On the way to the airport, Norma was sharing a cab with her friend Jennie, and guilt feelings kept creeping into her mind about

Clarence's cramped accommodations. Jennie, a cat lover herself, said she thought Clarence looked quite snug and content. "You know how cats like to crawl into tight little places," she said. "It makes them feel safe." Of course, Jennie was perfectly right, and a great load of guilt and apprehension lifted from Norma's mind. Norma and Clarence were free to enjoy the fun parts of the trip. About 98 percent of the time, with about 98 percent of the cats, if you feel happy and secure and satisfied about the way your animal friends are traveling, they will too.

Some cats travel just fine without giving them anything to help calm them. If your cat is the nervous type, Bach flower remedies or herbs may be all he needs. One of my vets, Dr. Dym, prescribes a combination of Bach flower remedies, based upon the individual patient's needs. The herb valerian has also been used with success to calm nervousness. Sprinkle a little in the carry case.

Pharmaceutical tranquilizers weaken the cat's immune system—they are just not very good for cats. They lower resistance to disease. However, in certain circumstances, for certain types of cats, a tranquilizer might be needed. If you decide you must use one, ask your cat's veterinarian to prescribe whatever would be best for him and allow enough time to try out the dosage at least once before the actual travel day arrives. Give it to him on an empty stomach, just as you would when you travel. Food in the stomach changes your cat's body chemistry and alters the way the dosage works. Every cat is different, and if the dosage is not just right a cat may have a hyperreaction: the tranquilizer, instead of calming the cat, can render him quite hysterical. So you must work out the dosage in advance.

To cushion the stress of travel and of tranquilizers, add the antistress supplements to meals for one week before and one week after the trip (see "Antistress Supplements," (page 305).

Visiting a New Place

When you arrive, remember how territorially conscious cats are and how uneasy they are with new people and places. You can cushion an otherwise stressful situation by limiting the number of new things they must deal with. First of all, confine the cats to a small space such as the bedroom and bathroom. Even if you're visiting your great grandmother in her three-story farmhouse, don't let them explore until they have spent at least one night in the restricted territory and have become familiar with it. When you first arrive, set up the old, familiar litter box and their own food and water dish so they will see that their personal necessities are there for them. Now is a purrfect time to give your furry companions a "snug retreat" (see page 304). A cardboard box like a wine carton, turned on its side and set in an open closet or behind a chair will calm their nerves and brighten their outlook. Line it with a T-shirt or some other soft clothing you have worn. You may discover that you're never allowed to take it away again; not even after they're very much at home in their new territory. Visit them every two or three hours during that first and second day. Also leave some of your personal belongings with your smell on them lying about before you leave them. In this way, you reassure them that you're coming back. Hopefully you will have brought their favorite toys, and before you leave you can reassure them even further if you run through their favorite games a couple of times, just as you always do at home.

So, after you have given them their own familiar things, strewn a few of your own familiar possessions about the room, and played their old, familiar games, you can leave with a light heart, knowing that they will probably spend a fascinating hour exploring the new territory and then fall asleep.

The next day, if you decide to let them increase their territory, make sure that you explore it first for dangers such as unscreened windows and poisonous plants or chemicals. Then you may wish to increase the territory gradually, a few rooms at a time. Be sure that everyone who enters and leaves the house knows that your cats are running around loose and that people must be careful about closet doors, drawers, and certainly the door to the outside. You and your host may well decide on certain areas to which they will not be admitted, such as a damp cellar, a dusty attic, or certainly an unscreened balcony.

If you stay in a hotel, you must put a sign on the door cautioning all who enter not to let the cats out. It's always good to speak to your maid personally, making sure that she understands the situation clearly and that she's not afraid of cats. In some instances, it's wiser to arrange to pick up your own clean linens at the desk rather than chance a maid or bellman unthinkingly opening a window or door.

If you're moving into a new home, the thing to do to keep stress to a minimum is to surround the cats with familiarity and keep them away from the area of upheaval as much as possible. In other words, on the last couple of days before the move, when packing and bustle reaches its height and when you are the busiest, confine them to your bedroom and have the packing boxes in the living room and the kitchen. Leave a few pieces of clothing that you have worn lying around in there so that they have the comfort of your scent even while you're busy elsewhere. If the premoving bustle outside the bedroom becomes noisy, turn on the radio and tune to a classical station and let it play softly. Put in a short appearance every hour or so, letting them feel that you are calm and satisfied and pleased that they are there in the bedroom.

On the actual moving day, the best plan is to confine the cats to some room that the movers will not enter. This may be a bathroom. Give them their litter and water, their favorite toys, a piece of your clothing, and a cardboard box or brown paper bag to hide in or play in as a special treat. Put a sign on the bathroom door and have it locked, if possible, or stretch a piece of masking tape across the knob to remind everyone of your instructions. Here again, keep your attitude casual. Emphasize to them the fun they'll have playing in the paper bag. Don't think about the fact that they're closed off in the bathroom. Tell them how lucky they are to be able to rest quietly here while you deal with those noisy movers.

The cats should arrive at the new home only after you have at least one room pretty well settled where you can confine them. They'll see the old, familiar furniture and feel reassured. Just as when you are visiting someone else's house, let them get used to one or two rooms first and then add a couple of rooms to their territory each day. Don't forget to check your new home carefully before you let the cats explore it. Be sure that it is just as safe and cat-proof as their old home was.

While You're Away

Sara and Dan were going to be away for two weeks. They were worried about what to do with their beloved Midnight while they were gone—hire a daily sitter; take him to stay with Norma, who already had a cat; ask Aunt Dot, who doesn't have a cat, to keep him; or board him with a veterinarian or at a pet motel? I heard nothing about it until two days before they were scheduled to leave.

I said, right off, that boarding was not a good idea. Even if they board Midnight at a facility that lets the cats out for a walk twice a day up and down the halls, it's still a small cage. And Midnight would still be exposed to new viruses and germs. If the boarding facility is also a pet hospital, there would also be the additional stress of being around cats who are in trouble, in pain, and frightened.

Aunt Dot might be okay because she has no other animals, especially if she already knows and loves Midnight. You'd have to be certain, though, that her windows were screened and that she wouldn't let him out. And you'd have to be sure to supply her with the correct food and Anitra's Vita-Mineral Mix. Then you wouldn't have to give a lecture on feline nutrition but only a five-minute talk on the evils of leaving food available between meals.

The absence of the beloved humans is the first stress factor. And being placed in a new environment is Stress Number Two. Therefore, Sara and Dan should give Midnight 10 milligrams of vitamin B complex and add $\frac{1}{16}$ teaspoon ascorbic acid crystals (250 units of vitamin C) twice daily for two days before leaving. If Aunt Dot is amenable, she can also mix $\frac{1}{16}$ teaspoon ascorbic acid crystals into the food twice a day. It would be helpful for him to have the vitamin C for the first five days of his stay. There are new germs at Aunt Dot's that he didn't have in his own environment. And the stress will lower his resistance; the Vita-Mineral Mix, the B complex, and vitamin C will help bolster it a little.

Norma's cat, Clarence, is an old sweetie pie. I personally would love to spend two weeks with Clarence. But Midnight will not be aware that Clarence is a old sweetie pie. To him, Clarence will simply constitute a great big Stress Number Three—a strange cat. Midnight will feel he is invading "strange cat's" territory. Moreover, instead of the strange new germs he would encounter in a no-cat household, he will encounter a different balance of cat germs at Clarence's house.

Of course, if Midnight is a physically strong robust cat, the pros could outweigh the cons as far as leaving him with Norma and Clarence. Norma is a cat care expert, and Midnight would have the comfort of her companionship as opposed to being left alone. Then, too, Midnight and Clarence might just form such a warm and wonderful friendship that his stay might very well be like sending a child to summer camp. There are always a lot of unknown variables to deal with when working with living creatures.

The safest and most common way to deal with the situation is to hire a sitter. The only sitters I trust are my own, but it can become expensive if you have to hire a professional cat sitter for an extended length of time. By hiring a sitter, you've avoided Stress Number Three (strange new territory) but introduced Stress Number Four—and that's the growing loneliness. I feel very sorry for single cats. Every time a cat is left alone, after a certain amount of time, he begins to expect you. If you usually come home at 5:00 P.M., then at 5:30 your cat begins to worry. By 6:00, your cat will assume that you have been killed and eaten by predators and will begin to mourn. It is quite a strain for a pussycat to be left alone for two weeks with a sitter appearing only once or twice a day. (See "Communicating 'Goodbye' and 'I'll Be Back,' " page 34.)

If only Midnight had a friend, he would never again have to face the horror of being alone. Cats are group animals. They live in colonies or in prides. When they are together, the worst of terrors are lessened. "Our humans may have met with an accident, but together we'll work it out—we'll muddle through somehow, together"; "At least we'll be warm, together"; "Together we can play." Hopefully, by the second day they will begin to expect the sitter, who cleans the litter, supplies the food, and spends the remainder of the hour cuddling, grooming, and playing.

So if Midnight is to be left alone in the apartment, extra care must be taken to give him reassurance and to distract and entertain him. The first two days, the sitter should come twice a day instead of once. This will hasten Midnight's acceptance of the sitter and quickly build the new pattern of sitter, food, and fun. Dan and Sara should arrange for the sitter to come twice on two or three other days if he or she deems it advisable. They should be sure to leave the carry case out, with all the old medical records and any test results tucked inside just in case, and leave a good supply of the raw food in the freezer and some canned food as well. Then leave the can opener in plain sight, and a note listing:

- The telephone number where they are staying
- The telephone number of a close friend or relative in the immediate neighborhood who also has a key
- The veterinarian's phone number
- Instructions for feeding
- Any instructions for medication
- Where to find toys, grooming tools, and catnip

They should also leave a snug retreat for Midnight to lounge in and line it with soft pieces of clothing worn by both Dan and Sara.

Midnight must be distracted from his loneliness. A toy left lying around all the time is no longer exciting. Catnip, if given every day, becomes a bore. So Sara and Dan should not give catnip for two weeks before they leave. And they should gather up all the toys the day before they go, leaving only one toy on the floor.

Dan and Sara should instruct the sitter to rotate the toys, giving Midnight a different one each day so that each toy is taken away from him before it becomes boring. They should leave one large brown paper bag for each week they will be gone. Then one day a week, instead of the toy, the brown paper bag can be opened and thrown on the floor for Midnight to play with. The next day can be catnip day, putting the catnip inside of or on top of the brown paper bag—excitement upon excitement. The following day the sitter can take it away and rotate a different toy.

To give Midnight the feeling that the apartment is not deserted, the sitter should leave a different light on each night and alternate days with the radio on and the radio off (this also discourages burglars). A small pile of dirty laundry can be left in the corner of the bedroom, and Midnight should be able to get into the bedroom closet and sit on the shoes.

I have several thoughtful clients who leave special food treats for their cats, to assuage their own guilt about leaving for vacation or business trips. Constance leaves barbecued chicken. Caroline leaves sliced turkey; Mrs. Aparicio, miniature shrimp. If I were leaving any of my cats all alone, I'd leave a couple of broiled chicken thighs and, for Priscilla, some baby food oatmeal and half-and-half.

All these things can be fed along with the other food, not exclusively. You don't want to throw the nutrition out of balance along with all the other stress factors.

I have several clients who like to call once a week to assure themselves that all is going well. Usually there is some little thing you want to check on. Is he having a stool every day? If not, the ground psyllium husks are in the cabinet. Is he eating? If not, there's baby food in the small cabinet over the refrigerator.

Remember, there are much worse things that can happen to a cat than your going away for two weeks. Granted, it's hard, but at least he has shelter and food.

But what if you could cut the stress factor by 50 percent? What if you could really relax, secure in the knowledge that your Midnight is having a ball? It's easy. Get him a friend. Someone he can train in his own pawprints. Someone to get into trouble with when your back is turned. Even if you work at home and you're home twenty-four hours a day, and you adore your cat, and your cat adores you, think of it this way: what if you were living with two of the most wonderful elephants in the world? You love them dearly, and they dote on your every move. They give you the very best food, they give you everything that you want plus a few extra things you never even thought of to surprise and delight you. In short, they give you everything your heart could possibly desire except . . . another human. . . . Need I say more?

"Neuter and Spay, It's the Kindest Way" 6

Neuter and spay, it's the kindest way", could be the slogan of any of our humane animal organizations. It is the kindest and the easiest path to take for the cats, their guardians, and for society at large. I've heard many myths about the disadvantages of neutering and spaying. People think their cats will become fat or lethargic, or will miss having a sexual life, or the female will miss mothering kittens. None of these things need be true. Cats become obese and lethargic because of faulty feeding or because they were neutered too early. Cats live in the present—in the absolute "now"—and they become sexually stimulated and crave a mate only if their glands tell them to. Sexual thoughts or the need to mother never occur to a neutered cat. However, there *are* drawbacks for both the male and the female (a) if they are *not* neutered or (b) if they are neutered too early.

Undesirable Behavior of the Unneutered Male Cat

Unaltered males are not generally kept as housecats. Catteries who maintain an unaltered tom to sire kittens keep him confined to a space where it will be easy to clean up the urine he will spray about. The cattery will have anywhere from six to twenty females for him to service plus a book of outside females who come to him regularly for stud service. A male who is not used for stud regularly can become very tense, nervous, and out of sorts, because he is uncomfortable.

Unaltered males spray. Testosterone causes their urine to smell very strong and quite different from the urine of a neutered male. A full tom will spray in various places all around his territory to mark it as his own. This is as natural as sneezing and not something he can be trained away from. Once you've smelled the urine or spray of an unaltered tom, it's not something you'll easily forget. I can tell the minute I walk into a home if somebody is keeping an unaltered tom. No litter can absorb that smell.

If a tom is allowed to wander about the neighborhood, wander is just what he does, ranging far and wide searching for a female in heat. And when he finds one there are bound to be other toms on the spot waiting to contest his right to mate with her. There are always fights before mating. And these fights are brutal and deadly serious. A fight to the death is common, and serious infections from puncture wounds unavoidable. The unaltered tom, allowed to roam free, leads a short and violent life. And if there are no females in season available for a couple of weeks, his aggression will be easily triggered at home. If he becomes unaccountably rough in play, the lack of a female is usually the reason.

Undesirable Behavior of the Unspayed Female Cat

A female in heat seldom sprays—she calls. You can tell if a female is in season even if she doesn't call very much by stroking down her back. She will push her hindquarters up into the air with her tail looped over to the side in the invitation to mate position. Unspayed female cats generally become high-strung, nervous, and jumpy. They are usually thin and debilitated. Going through heat after heat drains their body. They easily fall victim to any disease germ that happens to be around—their resistance will be low.

The female's ovaries manufacture eggs with each heat. Unlike humans, these eggs are not released and passed out of the body, but remain in the ovary unless she is fertilized. If the female goes through heat after heat and is not fertilized, these unused eggs are encysted. Cystic ovaries are a sign of a female who has gone through several heats before she's spayed. If a cat comes into heat more than twice a year, you can be pretty sure she has cystic ovaries. Unspayed female cats almost always develop cancerous tumors. Oddly enough, these tumors usually form on the mammary glands rather than on the cystic ovaries and the uterus.

I've met a few people who've bought male and female cats, planning to breed them. Besides all the potential problems that can be encountered in the course of the mating and birth process, having kittens is a lot of work and costs a lot of money. The mother needs special food and extra vitamins at frequent intervals. And the kittens need constant supervision and feedings six times a day from four weeks on. Both the mother and the kittens can fall prey to a number of diseases along the way. I have warned several people who had this idea in mind that a female can have her neck broken during mating—it is a rough and violent ritual. Also, if the mother is at all small, you could easily lose her during the birth of the kittens. Veterinarians are finding that the need for cesarean section births is becoming more and more frequent. This is especially true with Persians and American shorthairs, who are bred with small hips and large heads. But even a seemingly robust domestic shorthaired cat can have a problem giving birth. I clearly remember my shock on seeing not one but three females in a single clinic one day, all cesarean cases. They would have died if their guardians hadn't acted quickly and brought them in. And they were all supposedly healthy domestic shorthairs.

Another potential problem after the birth is that during the nursing weeks the mother may experience calcium-deficiency convulsions. She needs four to six meals of calcium-rich foods. In addition, her body needs vitamin D to assimilate the calcium and plenty of fats and high-quality protein.

The Nightmare of Unwanted Kittens

The wandering tom is capable of siring hundreds of kittens every year. The horror of the situation in New York City alone is something that I would rather not bring into my conscious mind. But here again, like the true facts about declawing, I think this is something that responsible people must be made aware of to enable them to make an intelligent decision concerning neutering, spaying, and allowing cats to have kittens.

Every single day in New York City, hundreds of cats are euthanized (killed). The overpopulation makes cats into trash—refuse. Cats for laboratory use are in such plentiful supply that the going rate is $5 a head. There are too many kittens. Sometimes I hear, "Oh, I have homes already for my cat's kittens, even if she had ten kittens there are people just waiting to take them." I explain to these people that this means there are ten homes that could have saved the lives of ten other kittens who are already alive and otherwise will probably die horribly. Or I hear, "I just want her to have one litter." Well, let's suppose one litter results in five kittens. And let's suppose that each kitten lives an average of even fifteen years.

137

Because you have made the decision to allow your cat to have these little mites, it behooves you to realize that each little mite represents not only six weeks of cuteness romping around your kitchen but fifteen or twenty years of life for which you are responsible.

You may blithely state that you already have five homes—five people panting to sweep a kitten up in their arms and cherish it forever. I assure you that you cannot take for granted that "forever" really *means* forever or that the new guardian won't feed a poor-quality diet or leave a window open or allow the cats to run outside unsupervised. Can you be sure the cats will have a yearly exam? Will their teeth be kept clean for fifteen years? And suppose, just suppose, that even one of those five kittens is not neutered and brings forth five more kittens. You must share that responsibility too, you know. If not for your original litter, the second litter would never have been born. And how would you feel if one day you found out that one of those little kittens of yours had been cruelly mutilated by a declawing operation?

Neuter and spay, it's the kindest way. Suggest to your friends who want kittens that they save a cat from possible death at one of the shelters.

The Proper Time to Get Your Cat Neutered or Spayed

The very best time to have the cat neutered is, for a female, after she goes through her first heat; for a male, when the urine changes odor and becomes very pungent. These are the signs in the male and female that the sexual center has transferred from the organs to the base of the brain. You can then remove the organs and yet not disturb the basic sexuality of the cat. Insist that your cat pass through these physical changes before the operation is done. Take it from me—*it matters!* A little care and patience now will pay off in a higher standard of health for the next fifteen or twenty years. The age range for sexual maturity can vary. I've known females who go into heat as early as five months, and I've met Persians who have shown no sign of maturity until a year and a half. The age is somewhere within that range for males also.

A few years ago, after the advent of microscopic surgery, a practice called "juvenile neutering"—also referred to as "early neuter/spay"—began gaining popularity, especially among humane workers. Now, the pendulum has swung so wildly toward the practice that nearly all humane organizations are requiring that all puppies and kittens be neutered before they can be adopted, even if the animal in question is a ten-week-old kitten. Some parts of the country are even trying to pass laws to mandate this practice.

In discussing this with many humane workers, I found that the prevalent belief is that early neutering will result in fewer animals being given to shelters and, consequently, fewer euthanasias. Existing statistics do not seem to bear this out. One explanation given is that the people who are adopting these early neutered kittens and puppies are the same people who would have had them neutered at the proper time anyway.

Studies have been done on several species to verify the long-term effects of early neutering. There is a wealth of material available on dogs, some on mice, and some on humans, but so far there is little research available on cats. However, some of the findings pertain to all species.

At the time the individual reaches maturity, several different sex hormones begin to circulate throughout the body. These hormones play a vital role in the normal development of many body parts and functions, most of them having nothing whatsoever to do with reproduction. For example, without these initial sex hormones during the formative months, bone growth cannot be completed normally. This can lead to joint and disc problems later in life. Sex hormones also play a role in the body's ability to mount an immune response to vaccination. Animals who are neutered too early suffer more frequent adverse vaccine reactions, ranging from hives to personality disorders to cardiac arrest. In addition, the anesthetic alone, when used on such young kittens, can cause upper respiratory complications that, all too often, prove fatal.

Urological disorders and autoimmune diseases seem also to occur more frequently in animals neutered before maturity, especially males. The earlier the neutering is done, the greater the adverse effect on the health of the animal, especially later in life. The conclusion is that neutering after full maturity produces the best outcome.

Veterinarians seem to be divided on this issue. Many have come out strongly against juvenile neutering. Those who are in favor of it say that "It is safe" and "It does no harm." In considering the two opinions, I can only assume that those in favor of the procedure must be referring to the fact that most of the puppies and kittens *do* live through the operation and *do* recover from the surgery. I assume they are not addressing the long-term effects.

Discussing the current trend with one of my own vets, Dr. Michael Dym, I expressed my concern and the hope that although the current trend did represent a frightening swing toward excess, it was bound to reverse itself and, like a pendulum, would swing back in the opposite direction until sanity would be restored. Dr. Dym's reply was so perceptive that I asked for permission to quote him here.

Dr. Dym said, "The current standard practice of neutering and spaying cats before sexual maturity will be looked upon in the not-too-distant future as being just as detrimental to their future health as multiple and overvaccination or over-processed, artificially preserved foods. Both of these we now know to be major factors in premature chronic disease and cancer. Moreover, we are finding this in younger and younger animals. As the retrospective epidemiological studies and the prospective research studies are published, the evidence is certainly mounting to show strong association between early sexual sterilization and chronic ill health and certain cancers later in life."

Dr. Dym went on to point out that the same group of veterinarians who used to repeat vaccinations every year with "booster shots" are now warning against it. Veterinarians who used to give up to eight or ten different vaccines at the same time are now counseling that, "the fewer, the better" is a good rule.

Commercial pet foods were also once accepted without much scrutiny. "The government regulations are very strict," we were told, "so we don't have to worry." There have been major recalls of pet foods not once but three times in recent years—because animals were made sick and, in many cases, died after ingesting government approved foods. New, organic pet foods, homemade foods, frozen raw pet foods, and raw homemade foods are gaining in popularity by leaps and bounds. Dr. Dym estimated that it would take about five more years before the adverse effects of early neutering became obvious enough to reverse the trend.

Certainly, we are all working toward the same things—fewer animals left in shelters and a healthy, long life for all animals.

In the past, many shelters ensured the neutering of all adoptees by requiring the new guardian to pay for the neutering operation at the time of adoption. A certificate was then issued and was redeemed at the point when the animal reached maturity and was ready for neutering or spaying. If the guardian later elected to have the neutering done by his own veterinarian, a letter of proof from the vet would entitle the guardian to a refund of the fee at that time. In many cases the guardian sent the veterinarian's letter with an accompanying note saying that the fee should not be refunded but left with the shelter in gratitude for the wonderful work they were doing.

If you are planning to adopt a kitten, I suggest that you check on the policies of the shelters and rescue organizations in your area. Because of her concern about juvenile neutering, my coauthor Norma adopted her Sweet William from a rescue organization that did not require it, rather than from any of the local shelters, all of which did.

I always like to leave the door open for a win-win resolution. Cats and dogs are different from humans in many ways, but one of the ways we are entirely alike is that individuals attain maturity at different times. Yes, I want the animals neutered, but I also want to be sure they will not suffer in any way from that neutering—either at the time of the surgery or in the years that follow. This is easy to achieve if they are neutered after a female goes through one heat or after a male cat's urine becomes strongly pungent.

Requiring people who adopt from shelters (a win) to prepay for neutering allows each family to ensure that the animal they love will be neutered at the time that is right for that particular animal (another win).

Neuter and spay—but after maturity. That is, indeed, the kindest way.

Neutering a cat is a simple surgery. Because it's one of the most frequently done operations, almost any veterinarian is competent to perform it. Since anesthetic is used, you'll want to bolster your feline friend's resistance with the appropriate supplements. Holistic veterinarians warn against the use of vaccines or medications for fleas, worms, or ear mites close to the time when the cat will be anesthetized and undergo surgery.

The Neutering Procedure

The female stays overnight in the hospital, and when you pick her up the next day, you will be told to keep her quiet for a day or two. However, I remember when I was working for Dr. Rowan we frequently had guardians telephoning, all upset because their cat didn't *want* to be quiet—she didn't realize that she'd just had an operation. She felt perfectly fine and was leaping off the top of the bookcase and bounding from sofas to chairs as usual. When this operation is done by any competent veterinarian, it's a piece of cake.

Neutering a male is even simpler. They usually don't even stay overnight. When Big Purr was neutered, I took him in one morning and picked him up that evening. He didn't look any different at all, because most vets remove the testes but leave the scrotum. He certainly didn't act any different, either—except, thank heavens, he was no longer interested in spraying the drapes. I remember at one point I scooped him up in my arms for some reason and suddenly realized that I had lifted him with my hand under his scrotum. All his weight was sitting on that recent surgery. But Purr did not have the slightest reaction; he hadn't even thought about it. I was all upset over nothing.

Purr still enjoys sexual play. Once I was boarding a kitten who came into season while her owner was gone. She had a torrid affair with Purr day and night for a week. Purr wasn't too sure at first what he was supposed to do but after a day of experimentation, trial, and error, the two of them worked it out very nicely. By the time her owner returned she was out of heat and her owner took her in to her veterinarian to be spayed. My friend Phyllis's cats Barnaby and Tulip, both neutered, are a completely devoted couple and enjoy sexual play on a regular basis.

Cats neutered at the proper time do not suffer the enormous stress of unneutered cats. Their resistance to disease is higher; they're mellower and happier because life is easier. They indulge in sex play because they want to, not because they are driven by their glands. According to statistics, neutered cats live longer, healthier lives than unneutered cats.

In the case of feral kittens, we come up against a problem that remains unsolved. I freely admit that I have not yet discovered a win-win solution here. When a mass trapping of a feral colony is done, the trappers often have only one chance to neuter them all. If some kittens are young and malleable enough to be fostered, socialized, and adopted, then those can wait to be neutered at the proper time. But what about the kittens that are too wild to be adopted—and so must be released back into their home territory? What about neutering them? Should you do it now while you have the chance and hope for the best? Should you release them unneutered and let them mature normally and hope you can trap them again when they become mature? Can anyone really judge when that might be for each feral? How can we ever be sure each cat will be trapped again? Maybe one or two might wander away and will never be neutered.

My friends, as far as feral cats are concerned, we have a dilemma. I believe that as feral colony managers deal with this situation again and again, trying different tactics, this problem—like all problems—surely will be solved by people whose minds are open and whose intentions are positive. I, for one, intend to study and observe and try to share my thoughts and findings with my friends in the feral cat movement until, together, we find that win-win solution.

Ferals: The Wild Ones 7

There was a time, not too many years ago, when I knew next to nothing about wild cats. I didn't even know that "feral" was the correct term for a wild cat who had never had a human guardian. I didn't know they lived in colonies or how those colonies could be managed so the cats could live healthier, more comfortable lives.

Thanks to Neighborhood Cats and their many affiliate organizations who are facilitating the TNR (Trap-Neuter-Return) movement, we now know how to manage the hundreds of thousands of feral cat colonies all over the United States. The Humane Society of the United States and the American Society for the Prevention of Cruelty to Animals, as well as hundreds of local organizations, are working with Neighborhood Cats. Excellent handbooks, websites, workshops, and hands-on help such as low cost spay/neuter programs and cage and trap rental are available. Petco Foundation and PetSmart Charities, affiliates of national pet store chains, and PetGuard, a natural pet products company, all support the TNR movement with generous donations of money and food.

In this chapter, I will give an overview and some suggestions regarding feral cats, but most important, I will refer you to clear and comprehensive sources of information. The feral cat movement has grown so quickly that the information now available is far too much for a single chapter. An entire book could be devoted to feral kittens alone.

The Difference between Strays and Ferals

A stray cat is one who has lived with and been cared for by humans and was later abandoned or lost. The stray is trying to survive on his own. Some strays gradually revert to a feral nature but most do not. They would welcome the opportunity to once again live with a human guardian.

Ferals are cats living wild; most were born wild. Unlike strays, ferals are wary of humans and try to avoid all human contact. They may trust somewhat a person who feeds them regularly, but even then only one or two cats in a colony would allow even a brief touch. Ferals are wild animals; they do *not* want to be adopted any more than a badger or an eagle wants to be "given a good home." They already have a home with a circle of friends and family we humans refer to as "the colony."

To understand the nature of a feral, you must realize that they think of themselves first and foremost as prey and secondly as predators. This governs all their actions. This is not true of your feline friends who live with you. A feral cat may look the same, but a feral is a totally different animal.

It was Bryan Kortis, CEO of Neighborhood Cats, who introduced me to the fascinating world of feral cats. I met him several years ago when he brought his newly acquired cat, Chelsea, to me for grooming. Chelsea, a middle-aged tortoise shell Persian, had been wandering homeless for so many years that she was half feral and so seriously matted that she could hardly walk. As happens in so many situations, however, Chelsea's terrible plight turned out to work to the benefit of everyone, for it brought her to the attention of Bryan and then brought Bryan to me.

There is nothing I find more satisfying than grooming a really filthy, matted cat and making her feel all clean and comfortable again; but it does take quite a long time and, while I worked, we talked. Back then, there were no feral cat organizations in New York City. Bryan was just one of many kind and generous souls doing whatever they could to help the strays and ferals.

At that time, my knowledge of ferals was limited to the glimpses I caught of them whenever I traveled home after dark. I'd sometimes see one or two scurrying along the side of an alley or darting under the parked cars. They were pitiful, thin creatures with runny eyes and unhealed wounds. Most were sick or lame; all were scarred. My heart went out to them, and time after time I'd approach them in the gentlest possible way—always to no avail.

"How can anyone help if the cats won't even let us get close," I asked. "My heart breaks every time I see them."

"It doesn't have to be like that," said Bryan. He was caring for a feral colony in our neighborhood and invited me, again and again over the following weeks, to come and see the results of what he called a "a managed colony." I kept putting him off. I had learned long ago not to expose myself to suffering and sadness when there was nothing I could do about it. Nevertheless, Bryan persisted in his quiet way, and finally, late one winter afternoon, I agreed to go with him for the evening feeding. The temperature had been hovering around the zero degree mark for over a week. That evening it was down to five above zero when we started out and getting colder by the minute. There was ice underfoot and a cutting breeze that promised more snow before morning. Bryan led me though a maze of Upper West Side alleys and courtyards, around rows of garbage cans and under rusty fire escapes. We were walking on a layer of ice. My fingers inside my mittens were feeling colder by the minute and I was steeling my mind for the pitiful sight I knew I was about to witness.

We rounded the corner of another building and Bryan stopped and put a finger to his lips. "Shhh," he whispered, "we have to be absolutely quiet if you want to see them at all. They're just around the corner."

"What do you mean?" By now I was shivering and my toes were completely numb. I sure didn't fancy coming all this way and then not seeing any cats at all.

"They're going to run for their lives the minute they sense our presence," he whispered. "Remember, these cats are completely wild so don't make a sound. Just watch and you'll have about ten seconds to see them."

Mystified, I did as he asked and we crept over the ice and rounded the last corner. It was another small courtyard. The building extended ahead of us on our right. Against the building, I saw four white Styrofoam boxes about twice the size of a wine carton. Each was held up off the ice by bricks at each corner and each had a round opening cut in the side. About twelve feet away on the opposite side of the courtyard there was a little three-foot wall of brick and cement topped by a six-foot-chain-link fence.

The second we came tiptoeing around the corner, there was an explosion of cats out of the round doors in the boxes. Cats of all colors and sizes, three or four to a box, rocketed out the doors; hit the icy ground running; flew up that nine-foot barrier, barely touching it; went soaring out away from the top; hit the ice on the other side; and streaked away into the gloom of the alleys beyond. In the five or six seconds that they were visible, I had seen bright, clear eyes, rippling muscles, and furs thick and rich enough to put a polar bear to shame. To top it off, I had witnessed a feat of athletic prowess far beyond anything I would have thought possible for a cat. They were not just healthy; they were supercats! My heart leaped for joy and I realized I had been holding my breath.

"They're beautiful," I cried. "They're healthy and clean and strong!"

Bryan had been watching my reaction with a wide grin. "This," he spread his arms to encompass the boxes and the vanished cats, "is a managed colony. Come over here." He led me to the Styrofoam boxes. "Put your hand inside."

I hesitated.

"All the cats are gone," he assured me. "They won't be back till long after we leave."

I pulled off my mitten and slowly thrust my icy fingers through the round door. Inside, the box was like a warm oven!

"Styrofoam is an insulator," he explained and began gathering up the paper plates I hadn't noticed until then. Lined up along the building, they had held the morning meal. "Their own body heat keeps them nice and warm when they sleep in there."

From that first colony, Neighborhood Cats has grown into a nationwide Trap-Neuter-Return (TNR) organization. Our recent National Feral Cat Summit in San Francisco hosted representatives from over twenty states and three countries. TNR is an idea whose time has come, and that icy winter evening was my own introduction to the concept and to the fascinating world of feral cats.

The Feral Colony

There are hundreds of thousands of feral cat colonies all over the country. All too often, neighbors first discover the existence of a colony when the nuisance level becomes intolerable due to loud and vicious cat fights, the smell of urine, and the sight of injured and sick cats. Feral colonies are made up almost entirely of unneutered cats.

Bryan explained to me that a large part of the nuisance quotient is eliminated if the cats are neutered. Not only does neutering stop the birth of unwanted kittens, it also solves the problem of their odor. The urine of an unneutered male cat has a particularly pungent smell. The males spray their urine in various places to

(a) attract females and (b) announce their presence to other males and warn them that this territory has already been claimed. The females announce their readiness to be fertilized by "calling" loud and long, adding the nuisance of noise. Naturally, the other males don't all stay away. Part of the mating ritual includes loud and vicious fighting over the female—creating even more noise. The fighting also results in serious wounds. Both the wounds and the mating itself provide opportunity for the spread of feline leukemia and other communicable diseases.

Inevitably the noise, the stench, and the horrible condition of the cats causes neighbors to complain to the authorities, who used to respond by trapping as many cats as possible and hauling them off to the public shelter. Because the feral cats are wild, and therefore unadoptable, and because many of them are sick, all of the ferals were usually euthanized. This method of control is known as "trap and kill." It is a horrible experience for all involved: the cats, the neighbors, and the shelter workers. Moreover, it doesn't work; the problem will reemerge in only a few months.

Trap-Neuter-Return (TNR): The Win-Win Solution

If you stop for a moment and calmly think about the situation, you will realize, as I did, that no one is objecting to the wild pussycats. What they *are* objecting to is the noise, the smell, the unwanted kittens, and the unhappiness and pity one feels every time one sees a sick or starving animal. TNR is the one approach that will successfully eliminate all these negatives in a way that's beneficial for all involved.

Why Trap-Neuter-Return Works

1. *All of the cats in the colony are fixed; therefore:*

    - No more kittens; the colony's population gradually decreases
    - No more noise; no females calling, no males fighting
    - No wounds from fighting or mating; no spread of disease
    - No more testosterone in the urine; the urine has a milder smell
    - Neutered cats roam less and are less visible

2. *Presence of caretaker, food, and shelter; therefore:*

   - Healthier cats, fewer parasites, less disease
   - Sick, wounded, or newly neutered cats are promptly trapped, vetted, and returned or placed in homes if adoptable.
   - No more pity/sadness factor; healthy cats continue to deter the presence of rodents and are a source of pride for the community.

3. *Problems do not recur.*

   - Presence of neutered cats tends to prevent new, unneutered cats from moving in.

4. *Local shelters benefit.*

   - Fewer ferals and kittens are brought into shelters, freeing up shelter space and homes for adoptable housecats who would have otherwise been euthanized, because there are *always* more cats than there are humans who want them.

5. *Improved public relations*

   - When animal control changes from trap and kill to Trap-Neuter-Return, their image changes from killer to savior. Volunteers are attracted, more people choose to adopt at shelters, and fund-raising dramatically improves. San Francisco provides a typical example. During the ten years after TNR was introduced, euthanasia rates dropped by 70 percent, saving the county hundreds of thousands of dollars.

The Steps to Successful Trap-Neuter-Return

None of the steps necessary for a successful TNR effort are particularly difficult. However, it is vital to know what they are and in what order they should be done. If something is forgotten or steps are done out of order, it will delay success and result in a needless cost of extra money and time.

Below is a very condensed overview of the steps needed to accomplish the TNR of one colony. This is *not* meant as a complete guide to a TNR effort. That would require a lot more space. Luckily, a clear and detailed handbook, an exciting video, workshops, and sources of local help are all available on the Internet at www.NeighborhoodCats.org or by calling 212-662-5761.

- *Step 1: Build good community relations.* The long-term security of the colony will depend on the understanding and support of the people living and working nearby. Their concerns need to be heard and addressed.
- *Step 2: Set up feeding stations and shelters.* Establish a feeding schedule. Build up the cats' health before they are subjected to the stress of trapping, anesthesia, and surgery. (See "Surgery," page 246, and "Stress: A Cat's Natural Enemy," page 255.) A regular feeding time allows you to count and evaluate the cats. Besides, trapping is so much easier if the cats come to you at a set time and place and you don't have to search them out.
- *Step 3: Secure a holding space.* Depending on the weather, how many cats you have, who is doing the surgery, and other factors, the time the cats will need to be confined is usually three to six days. The holding space must be warm, dry, and secure (safe from predators, both animal and human). Cats remain in their traps except during the actual surgery.
- *Step 4: Schedule the spay/neuter and secure equipment.* You need to know the number of cats, the cost, where to borrow traps, the size of the holding space, any time limitations for the vet and volunteers, and the availability of traps. Also, you need to arrange transportation for the cats.
- *Step 5: Trap.* Allow at least two and preferably three days for trapping in case of inclement weather or other unexpected conditions. *Do not feed* for one full day before trapping so the cats will be hungry and go into the traps for food. Once a cat is captured and confined in a trap, clean the traps twice a day.
- *Step 6: Spay and neuter day. Give no food or water on the night before surgery— or on the morning of surgery.* Standard treatment includes spay/neuter, rabies vaccination, and ear-tipping to identify the cat as a spayed/neutered cat who is a member in good standing of a managed colony. I do not recommend early neutering of kittens (see Chapter 6, page 135). However, if someone makes that choice, be sure to consult a vet about when to stop feeding before the surgery. Kittens must continue to be fed closer to the time of surgery, but not too close, depending on age. I do not recommend giving multiple vaccines nor treating for fleas, worms, or ear mites at the same time as neutering. Too many chemicals at one time can cause sickness or death.

- *Step 7: Recovery.* Allow at least forty-eight hours for recovery. Feed and clean traps twice a day. Again, include stress and surgery supplements given on pages 305 and 246. Arrange longer-term care for any cat who becomes ill.
- *Step 8: Release.* This is the happiest day for everyone. Be sure there is adequate shelter in wintertime, especially for females with shaved bellies, and get your cameras ready!
- *Step 9: Continuing colony management.* A designated caretaker must feed the cats regularly, trap any unneutered newcomers or cats who are injured or ill, inspect the shelters, and act as intermediary with the community.

What Doesn't Work

Several previous methods of dealing with feral cats, which were tried by various organizations and municipalities, have failed because they all involved removing the cats from their territory, creating what is known as the "vacuum effect." The number of cats in a colony is determined naturally by how many cats the available food and shelter in the area can support (the "carrying factor").[1] The specific cats living in the colony may change over the years, but the total number of cats remains approximately the same. Each cat occupies what I think of as a "cat slot." Cats that are trapped and permanently removed leave empty slots that will soon be filled by (a) kittens of the two or three cats who escaped trapping and were left behind; (b) young cats from neighboring colonies who can't find any empty slots where they are; or (c) cats from the constant flow of lost or abandoned pets who are desperately looking for open slots in any colony. All of the old cats will be replaced by new ones, nearly all of whom will be unneutered.

What about Feral Kittens?

Can't the kittens be brought in and adopted? That depends on several factors. If the kitten is less than eight weeks old, if most of his recent ancestors were domestic housecats, if he has had loving contact with a colony manager or other human during the first four weeks while he is still nursing, and if he just has a naturally social personality, then he can probably be socialized.

1. Tabor, Rogert. *The Wild Life of the Domestic Cat.* London: Arrow Books, 1983, 182–83.

Socializing Ferals?

Most communities are forced to euthanize already friendly domestic cats who can't find homes. Unfortunately, a policy of socializing feral cats could mean even fewer spots for friendly cats already in the system. Unless the colony's territory has become untenable or unless the cat in question has become aged or handicapped, it's best to leave the feral in his home with the colony he knows.[2]

Diana has been with me for nine years. She came to me (pregnant) from a mountainside where gangs of local teenagers were shooting anything that moved. Julie, a city feral, lives with me because her colony's territory was covered over by a high-rise building. Both came as mature adult ferals and both cats are socialized enough to live at ease here. They have made cat friends, enjoy the food, have favorite perches—but neither will allow touching. Both would be happier if they could go back to their old life.

One day you may find yourself in a very difficult situation and want to help out by fostering or adopting feral kittens (but hopefully never a feral adult). Do consult the resources, websites, and handbooks listed in the back of this book.

Here are just a few guidelines to help you stay on the right track until you can get your hands on resources that explain in detail why the following suggestions are important and how they work. Each kitten is different and each of the steps below may take anywhere from five minutes to two weeks. Be guided by your kitten's responses and don't rush it.

Socializing Feral Kittens

- Vet the kittens *before* bringing them home. Be certain there are no fleas or parasites and that they are feline leukemia and AIDS negative. *Do not allow early neutering or any vaccines yet.*
- If there are fleas, it's better to bathe the kitten, even if tranquilizers must be used, rather than use chemical drops, powder, or spray. (See "Grooming and Bathing" in the Flea section on page 395.)
- Ferals think of themselves as part of a group. Keep kittens together. If two are not available, be sure they can smell and hear, and, if possible,

2. Kortis, Bryan. *The Neighborhood Cat's TNR Handbook: A Guide to Trap-Neuter-Return for the Feral Cat Caretaker.* New York: Neighborhood Cats, Inc., 2004, 95.

see another cat or cats. Perhaps install a hook and eye on the door of their room that leaves the door open a crack.

- If you can't get to them, you can't socialize them. Ferals are agoraphobic. They like a small room with hiding places. Put them in a bathroom. Be sure there are no holes in the wall under the sink and that there is no place they can wedge themselves into where no one can get them. The best place of all is a medium to large cage in a quiet room. Drape it on three sides and put a small carrier or snug retreat inside for them to hide in. Give them a litter box, water, and three to six meals a day.

- *Don't stare.* Their mother has taught them that humans are predators. A stare is a menace and a prelude to an attack. Let your gaze slide across them, and blink a lot.

- Calm them by talking. Keep your voice low, slow, and casual. No big emotions. Many short visits are better than one or two long ones.

- After they begin to come out of hiding while you're there, begin to play through the bars with them, using a cat dancer or a toy on a wand or string, such as a feline flyer. Don't thrust the toy at them; let them reach out for the toy. Then allow your fingers to touch their necks or backs while they play; only a little at first. Keep talking and never let them play with your hand or any body part.

- When they will eat in your presence, let your hand linger on the food dish while they eat. After this is accepted for a day or two, you can casually allow your hand to brush against their cheek fur as you remove it and leave the dish.

- After they start to love their play sessions, pet them more and more. Then begin playing Pick-up/Put-down (see page 28).

- Introduce additional territory gradually, one room at a time. Make sure each new room is secure and safe, with no holes where a cat could get inside the wall and no low furniture that only they can squeeze under.

I was asked to foster my first feral kittens after others had tried and had left out several of the steps above. Butch and Spike were little gray tabbies, litter mates about twelve weeks old, which is too late to begin socializing. To begin with, they had been separated (wrong!) and each was fostered with a kind and well-meaning guardian.

Butch was released into a three-room apartment (too large a territory) and immediately burrowed himself behind the stove where he remained for three days. He urinated all over himself when they tried to force him out with a broom. Neighborhood Cats was called in to help. They arranged for the building super-intendent to move the stove so they could trap Butch.

Spike fared no better. His new guardian lived in a terrifyingly big loft. He disappeared for two-and-a-half days. An expert from Neighborhood Cats finally located him in the guest alcove, inside the mattress that he had accessed through a hole in the bottom.

I estimate that it took me about four times longer to calm and socialize them than it would have if those first nice guardians had known what steps to follow in the first place. The two were finally adopted—together, of course—and now live in a delightfully small second floor duplex in Queens with a talented actress whom they adore.

Grooming 8

Grooming is not only a necessity for our loving feline friends but it's also very healthy for you, their human companion. Scientific studies have proven that stroking a cat lowers blood pressure. I am acquainted with several households where a person first adopted a cat because their doctor prescribed it for a heart or nervous problem. Grooming also establishes a wonderful and lasting bond between you and your cat. In addition to serving an important function, it is your way of expressing affection—and the purrs that greet your ears will confirm your cat's delight. If your cat has short hair, the two of you can enjoy finger grooming, the claw exam, and slicker brushing two or three times a week—or more, just for the pleasure. After all, grooming is love. Long haired cats will require more frequent attention.

Among cats, mutual grooming is a form of communication; it expresses love and acceptance and companionship. Grooming is a very natural thing to the cat and something they readily understand if properly approached and properly carried out.

Grooming is also a necessary part of cat care. Dry, artificial heat in winter causes cats to shed excessively. Cats also shed naturally in the spring and, to a lesser degree, again in the autumn.

Cats also shed during the slightest stress situation. If you're away for a while, if you take cats to the vet, if you take them visiting, if workers come to the house, if the cats fall ill—all these are stress situations that will produce excess shedding. If the cats are not groomed regularly, with a bit of special attention during shedding seasons and times of stress, they will attempt to groom themselves, with the result that they will swallow a great deal of hair. Living in the wild, they would be eating all raw food and they would not have had to deal with many of those stress situations or with the unnatural heat. The spring and autumn sheds would be the only difficult times for them.

Swallowing a lot of excess hair can affect cats in two ways—either they will form hair balls, which they will then vomit (like miniature wet hot dogs on the carpet), or they will try to pass the hair through the intestines. Because the latter method of disposal is not the most efficient, these hair masses are frequently not passed out at all, lodging instead in curves and bends of the intestinal tract and causing blockage. Cats with this problem then stop eating—or sometimes vomit an innocuous foamy substance instead of the hair they are trying to get rid of because the hair has passed beyond the stomach into the intestines and can no longer be vomited up. A veterinarian sometimes gives a strong laxative, in the hope of dislodging these lower-intestinal hair masses. If that doesn't work, the doctor can try an enema and, in extreme cases, surgery. What a pity this is, when just sixty seconds of grooming a day will do away with the necessity for even the laxative.

High-Quality Diet = High-Quality Coat

If you remember why we remove food between meals (see Chapter 2, "Diet"), you'll recall that leaving it available slows down the metabolism so that wastes build up and back up. The body will then try to deal with the situation by pushing some of these waste products out through the pores of the skin, resulting in oiliness and dandruff. On a low-quality diet, the cat will have more waste products to deal with. Also, the hair vitamins, mostly found in the vitamin B family, have either been destroyed in the heat processing of the cat food or are simply missing because they tend to be the more expensive ones. These coat quality and texture vitamins are the very ones that you are now supplying by adding Anitra's Vita-Mineral Mix (see page 68).

Old, dead hair slips out of the coat easily when the hair is healthy. Dead hair is retained in the coat for two reasons: (1) excessive oiliness and (2) a rough, poor-quality coat. Oiliness is caused by a diet too high in organ meats or other rich food or simply by not removing all food between meals. The lecithin in Anitra's Vita-Mineral Mix emulsifies the oil and fat and turns it into a water-soluble substance that the blood can carry off and dispose of in the urine. Oiliness turns your cats into little walking dust mops, attracting and holding not only their own hair but any dust and debris from the floor. Unwholesome hair texture works in exactly the same way. Each hair has many microscopic hairs growing out from it. On good-quality hair, these microscopic secondary hairs all grow down, pointing toward the tip of the hair and allowing dust, oil, water, and dead hair to slip right off. On poor-quality hair, they protrude out and up and every which way so they hold the dust and dead hair in the coat. You can imagine how a cat with a good-quality coat would be much easier to groom, because dust would not cling and old dead hair would come right out and not stay behind to build up into a mat in the cat's coat. The yeast and kelp or trace mineral powder in Anitra's Vita-Mineral Mix are specifically for the improvement of the quality of the hair follicle.

The first two or three years that I was grooming, I made it a point once a year to go to a cat show. I didn't look only at the cats. Because I was eager to learn anything I could from any source available, I took note of what kind of carry cases were used, what grooming tools, and what was in the bottles and boxes lined up on the shelf near each cat's cage. The first thing I noticed was that about 90 percent of the owners showing cats were using exactly the same bottles and boxes. And what was in them? They were marked "Hair thickener," "Baldness preventative," "Texturizing lotion," and "Whitening powder" (or "Darkening powder"). Next to these preparations, I always saw a supply of dry or semimoist cat food.

There must have been hundreds of guardians there, and it amazes me to this day that evidently none of them ever made a connection between what they were feeding the cats and the need for all of those artificial cosmetics to cover up the faults and the less-than-perfect coats that this low-quality food was producing. I have never used any sort of cosmetic powder or spray on a cat to change the existing texture of the natural coat. These products coat the hair and always make the coat more prone to picking up dirt, and therefore the cat needs bathing all the more frequently. Besides, all of these preparations contain chemicals, perfumes, and the like. I will not put such preparations on the cat when I know the cat is going to lick them off and ingest them. Virgin hair stays clean the longest. Even if the texture and thickness has not yet reached the optimum, you can't improve on nature. Hair in its natural, virgin state is uncoated, unconditioned, uncolored, and untreated. It provides the best insulation against both heat and cold. And nothing is easier for the cat's guardian to groom than virgin hair. Improve the texture, thickness, and quality of the hair by feeding the diet discussed in Chapter 2, not by spraying or smearing something over the surface. The cat manufactures the hair out of the raw material you provide in the food bowl: good-quality food produces a good-quality coat. Isn't it nice to know you have that option!

Finding a Groomer

New clients frequently tell me how they searched for months trying to find someone reputable and gentle to groom their cat. I must say I had the same problem, searching in vain for someone whom I could recommend to take my overload during the busy season. Even in a major metropolis like New York, I have not been able to find anyone whom I would trust to groom a cat except myself and the people I train. I've looked everywhere—in pet shops, dog-grooming salons (even the most expensive), kennels, and several veterinarians' offices. What I found was that in all of these places people with the highest standards were unwilling to groom cats because they did not feel at home doing it. They were comfortable with dogs but not with cats. People with lower standards would give it a try but were both slipshod and rough. Veterinarians would rather spend their time curing disease than grooming, and the good ones are generally already overbooked with more serious problems. They want to get the mats out as quickly as possible, so they use a shaver. Shavers pull and scrape and hurt, so most veterinarians use anesthetic or tranquilizers before grooming. Because anesthetics and tranquilizers constitute a serious stress, I found without exception that reputable veterinarians try to avoid anesthetizing and shaving a cat whenever they can. Several veterinarians I know refer all grooming problems to me.

Whoever agrees to groom your cat, I strongly advise that you arrange to be present the entire time for at least the first few visits. It is illegal for anyone but a veterinarian to dispense tranquilizers to an animal, yet I know of several groomers who slip them to cats. I have also heard all too frequently of how cats are "subdued" by dog groomers—by trusses, straps, and harnesses, or "It took three of us to hold her down." Cats can die of shock or heart attack under such brutal handling. You must be sure that anyone who grooms your cat is working *with* the cat, not against him.

If there's a problem finding someone to groom a badly matted cat or a cat with fleas or what-have-you here in the middle of New York City, I can well imagine the plight of someone living in a small town or rural area where even a dog groomer is not to be found and the only veterinarians available are those specializing in dairy herds. I decided to write this chapter in as much detail as possible for those guardians who have no choice but to try their best by themselves. It is much easier if you have someone to assist you. Your assistant can distract the cat with pleasurable sensations such as throat stroking, back scratching, and murmured praise. I use the cat's guardian for this, but you can get your cat's second most favorite person to help you.

I will try to give you all the help I can. Just remember that patience is the watchword. I was the slowest groomer on God's green earth when I started, but I was also the most careful.

Please be aware that just because I am telling you *how* to handle these problems does *not* mean that I am *advising* you to do so. If there's no one else, then you can give it a try. But there are many instances where I would strongly advise having the veterinarian anesthetize the cat and shave the mats out just one time. Then you can take over and maintain the coat so that it never gets matted again. Using scissors to cut through mats is dangerous business. The cat's skin texture is like the finest silk. The fact that it is loose, coupled with the bone structure and intricate musculature of the body, makes it very difficult for an untutored person to clip mats safely. And, yes, they must be clipped. Using a comb on a mat is worse than hopeless. It doesn't do any good at all, and it does do a lot of harm because you'll hurt the cat and teach him to hate being groomed.

If you elect to have the veterinarian shave the mats out, the perfect time would be when the teeth are cleaned. In fact, any time the cat has to be anesthetized for any reason be sure to check for tartar on the teeth and matting in the furs so these two things can get a free ride, as it were, and be taken care of then. Ear flushing is also a good thing to slip in at the time if the cat has a lot of wax in the ears. You can help your cat's body to process out the anesthetic more easily by adding the antistress supplements to the food for one week before and after the tranquilizer or anesthetic is used (see page 305).

Grooming Considerations

Once the cat is in good shape, you can do a complete grooming in sixty seconds. It should be done daily if you live with a longhaired cat and you want to keep a couple of jumps ahead of the mats so that your cat will never again have to be anesthetized and shaved.

Grooming should be a pleasure for all concerned. Because you know how much cats like ritual and sameness, make grooming into a ritual. Use the same place, the same tools, and groom the cat's body parts in the same order. If possible, do the grooming at the same hour of the day. Invite the cat to the grooming area with the same signal, and always follow grooming with the same treat.

First we'll cover the grooming area. You know how sensitive your cats are to your thoughts and emotions. They sympathize when you're sick or upset. They sense your calmness when they are upset, and thus they can be calmed. Likewise, they will sense your pleasure in grooming them. So you must choose a grooming area that is pleasing to you as well as to the cat.

I'm rather tall, so when I go into someone's home to groom their cat I always work on the kitchen counter. Also, kitchens are usually well lit, and that's important for the grooming area. Some of my shorter clients prefer to use something like a card table, which is a lot lower than the kitchen counter.

I do not spread a towel or anything else under the cat, because the hair sticks to towels and usually ends up back on the cat's coat and you end up grooming off the same hair two or three times. A towel is messy and it wrinkles the minute the cat moves around, creating an uncomfortable, lumpy surface for the cat to stand on—and we want the cat to be comfortable. The surface should be clean—no sense in getting jelly on the cat's tail. After washing the surface with a sponge, be sure to dry it thoroughly with a paper towel. Standing on a damp, cold surface is not your cat's idea of comfort.

Lay out all the grooming tools. (Grooming tools will be covered later in this chapter.) When everything is set up to your satisfactions, invite your cat to the grooming.

Now, in the beginning you will be lifting the cat onto the grooming area. As time goes on and the ritual is repeated, a surprisingly large number of cats will jump the gun and leap spontaneously onto the table themselves. I've had this experience with cat clients that I see regularly once a month. Especially in multiple-cat households, I frequently have to deal with a "me first" problem.

It's very important, though, that you be the one to put the cat back on the floor when you're finished. Never, never let the cat jump down. You must establish as an integral part of this ritual that you are the one who says when it is over. Telling him, "Okay, you're done" and letting him jump down is simply not clear enough. You must physically pick him up and place him on the floor yourself, with words of praise and admiration.

If you are just beginning to condition the cat to the joy and comfort of being groomed, you may find it best to spend the first four or five sessions going no further than the first step or two in the grooming procedure. If all you do is establish in his mind that being up on that table brings pleasure, you've already done a great deal. In fact, without this you will find it nearly impossible to do anything else. In the beginning, keep the sessions short. One minute is enough. Remember, sixty seconds a day accomplishes much more than a half-hour on Saturday. If at all possible, be sure that you put the cat down on the floor *before* he wants to go down. Try to leave him wanting more. If you must cut out a difficult mat or clean soil off the bloomers or perform some other tasks that is not altogether pleasurable, always finish the grooming with some type of combing that he does like, such as going back and recombing the head and neck or the cheeks and throat. Your cat will teach you about his special, favorite places. Groomings always begin and end with your cat's special favorite places.

As soon as I get to know a cat—sometimes after five minutes, sometimes after five months—I use my face and mouth a lot while grooming. Because cats groom with their mouths, they seem to understand and enjoy having me kiss them on top of their heads and murmur; take their ears between my lips and, as it were, "hug them with my lips"; and breathe warm air against the skin at the back of the neck or the shoulders. With a nervous cat, putting your face close to the cat's head or body gives him confidence, because subconsciously he knows that your face and eyes are vulnerable and that you would not expose them if there were any reason to get upset. The cat thinks that everything must be all right.

A word of caution: be careful not to puff air into the ears, eyes, nose, or onto the bare genital area. Cats won't like that a bit. And, instead of the calming effect you're trying for, they'll struggle to get away from that unpleasant sensation. Also, it is very important to make your kisses silent. Do not accompany them with a loud kissing sound, especially near the cat's ear. This sound is extremely piercing, even for a human. And for a cat, a kissing sound at the ear opening is quite painful.

You can use classical music while you groom for its calming influence. A CD or your computer's music player is better than a radio, because you have control over what is being played. The music should be played rather softly and be either soothing or happy. The main requirement is that you personally enjoy it. Steer clear of jazz, rock, pop, or rap music. The latest scientific experiments indicate that plants and animals respond best to classical or religious music, with Bach and Mozart played on guitar, mandolin, or harpsichord having the most positive effect.

When you use a shaver, the cat must be anesthetized because a shaver can be painful. There are several other grooming tools for sale to the professional groomer that make one think of a medieval torture chamber. One is called "the mat splitter." Having a mat splitter sounded like such a terrific idea that I ordered one. When the thing came, I was absolutely aghast at its design. It was something like a rake with curved teeth sharpened like little razors. I assume one is expected to drag it though the mats, incorporating some sort of sawing motion in the process. I could see at once that it was totally impractical and so badly designed as to be dangerous. I tried very gently running it through the silky fur of a freshly groomed cat. Even those lovely unmatted hairs were caught and pulled on the curved blades. I didn't even finish the stroke but threw the sadistic tool into the wastebasket. Over the years, I've run into many strange grooming tools. Clients pull them out of drawers to show me what they have been using to groom their cats. Any time a guardian tells me his or her cat "hates being groomed," I always ask to see the grooming tool. There's one sure way to make it clear to someone that a tool hurts: I hand them the tool and ask them to run it through their own hair.

The Grooming Tools

You will have to be the judge of what tool a cat's coat needs. Here is a list of the tools I carry around with me and their purpose (See Figure 1 on page 163):

- Large toenail clipper (the best kind are human toenail clippers), to clip the claws.
- Cotton swabs, for cleaning ears
- Vitamin E capsules (100-unit) or olive oil for oiling cotton swabs
- Metal combs—fine, medium, and most important of all, coarse (wide tooth)
- Shedding comb for short hair—used on longhaired cats after the coarse comb
- British fine and superfine comb (a largish flea comb) for "crew-cut" on Persians or all over for some shorthaired cats
- Blunt-nosed surgical scissors (I use a Miltex, available from any surgical supply house), for splitting and cutting away mats
- Slicker brush (size small) *for shorthaired cats only*
- Mini slicker brush for between the ears and on cheeks, chin, and throat
- 7½" or 8" Filipino straight scissors (not curved) for Teddy clip

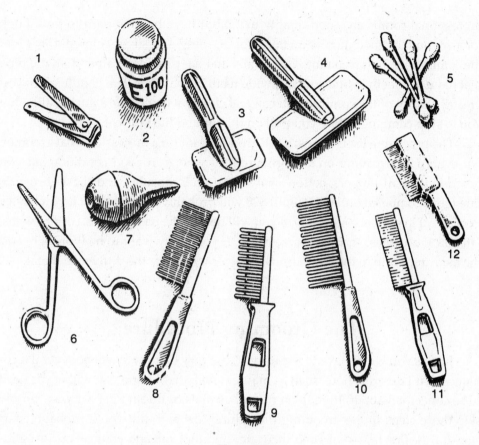

FIGURE 1
Grooming Tools

1. Large toenail clippers (a drugstore item)
2. Vitamin E capsules (100 units)
3. Slicker brush (mini)
4. Slicker brush (small)
5. Cotton swabs
6. 8" round nose scissors

7. Rubber ear syringe
8. Resco comb (medium)
9. British shorthair shedding comb
10. Resco comb (coarse)
11. British comb (fine)
12. British superfine flea comb

Most combs available in pet shops look like a human comb with a thicker tooth at each end made out of metal. They don't work well because those wide end teeth catch and pull the cat's fur. They are also usually made of poor-quality metal, which again causes the teeth of the comb to catch in the fur. The Resco professional combs are good-quality metal but have become hard to find. Look for any comb of good quality metal: smooth, shiny, and silver-colored. *Don't* buy the combs with Teflon coating. Get combs that have handles rather than the type that have fine teeth at one end and wide teeth at the other. The handle gives you greater control of the comb so you can feel clearly when it hits a tangle, allowing you to stop combing before you pull on the fur and hurt the cat.

The preceding list is almost a full grooming kit for a professional cat groomer. For everyday grooming on a shorthaired cat who is in good condition, all you need are the nail clippers, cotton swabs, vitamin E capsules, and slicker brush or fine-tooth comb. An outlay of about $20 will probably cover the lot. If you have a Persian cat in perfect condition, all you will need is the nail clippers, cotton swabs, vitamin E capsules, and the coarse comb. If you really want to be thorough, add the medium comb to the list. A finicky owner will enjoy the difference it makes.

The Grooming Procedure

Just as you won't have to use every tool every day, there will be several techniques that I describe here, such as mat removal, that I hope you will never need to be concerned about. If your cat never has mats or doesn't get ear wax, simply skip those steps in the grooming procedure. Just as I did, you'll probably start slow for the first few weeks and then later find that you and your cat are just gliding through the steps. You and your cats together will decide which techniques you want to spend extra time on because either they adore it or you judge that their particular coats need it.

Step 1: Finger Grooming

No matter what you're going to do in the grooming session, always begin every grooming with your hands. Your hands tell you what you will need to do; they tell your cat what to expect. The more your cat and you know in advance, the easier your session will be. *Cats hate surprises.* After you place the cat on the grooming table, facing away from you, stroke his head, neck, throat, chest, back, outer thighs, stomach, inner thighs, and bloomers. The reason for this "finger grooming" is that you are communicating to the cat what it is you are about to do and also what a pleasant, wonderful feeling it is going to be. As you stroke, either say or think, "I'm going to make you feel good here, and I'm going to make your furs nice there. I'm going to clean out that nasty loose hair." Think of massaging the cat's muscles with your fingertips, stimulating circulation ever so lightly. (See Figure 2 below.)

The second purpose for the "finger grooming" is to familiarize yourself with the condition of your cat's body and coat for today. Any little mats? How's the texture? Any soil on the bloomers? Has anything been dribbled onto that lovely ruff? You don't want the comb to catch in something and pull and hurt. Long before you finish your "finger grooming," you should be rewarded with a resonant purr.

Then, when you introduce the grooming tool, it will simply be an extension of what you've already done. The grooming tool will help you express the love more efficiently. Properly used, it should make your cat feel even better than your fingers did. His purr may increase in volume or be augmented by kneading with front paws.

FIGURE 2
Ruff, knickers, skirts, and bloomers

Step 2: Light Combing

If your cat is shorthaired, step 2 applies *only* if there is a buildup of loose hair in the coat as found during the shedding seasons. Usually for a shorthaired cat you can skip this step and simply use the slicker brush, or fine comb, described later.

If you're working with a longhaired cat and at some point on the body you encounter resistance indicating tangles or mats, go no further on that particular body area. Mats and tangles are dealt with later in step 4, after clipping the nails.

If cats are matted, they know it, and they also know just where the mats are. They will be afraid to have you comb through the mats because they know that such combing hurts. So don't even try to comb a resistant area; instead, follow the directions given in step 4 of the grooming procedure. On most days of the year, the whole combing procedure will be a "light combing" because you will not encounter resistance at any point—no mats and no tangles.

The first time that you decide to groom your cat seriously, by far the best plan is to begin with a comb that you think is sure to be too coarse (wide-toothed) and begin by using a stroke that you think is sure to be too light. You don't want to pull or make the cat uncomfortable in any way. If the comb goes sailing through without bringing very much hair with it, you can always graduate to the medium comb, then the fine. If you begin with a fine-toothed comb, you could end up pulling the hairs, which will certainly hurt and teach your cat to fear grooming. Or, as frequently happens, because the teeth of the comb are so close together, the comb may go slipping across the tops of the hairs, grooming them only about a quarter of the way down and leaving all the old, loose hair still lodged untouched near the roots to form mats.

Each time you begin grooming, remember to think of using the comb as a method of exploration. Don't automatically assume that the tips of the teeth are going to reach the cat's skin on the first stroke. Mentally divide the length of the cat's hair into quarters. On the first round over the cat's body, let the comb lightly explore the top quarter—the tips of the hair. If all is smooth sailing, go back over the cat again and include the next layer down, combing the outer *half* of the hairs. If you begin to encounter any resistance as the comb goes through, *stop* and comb that particular area *even more lightly* at first so that you *gradually* work the old hair out. Do the same on the third round, when you are combing through the outer three-quarters of the hairs, and on the fourth round, which ends with nice, firm strokes and the teeth scratching the skin.

You need two hands to comb a cat. Your comb hand grips the comb right up by the teeth, with your thumb actually resting against one side of the teeth, near the shank. You can see how this would not be possible if your comb had no handle and had teeth all the way across. You must use slow strokes while you're learning because your thumb must learn to be a sensory organ. It is through your thumb that you first get the message if there is any matting or resistance to the stroke. In others words, the sensitivity of your thumb keeps your cat safe from pulling.

Your other hand is used to smooth the skin flat ahead of the comb stroke or to press the skin away behind the comb, keeping it taut and free from rumples. A healthy cat's skin is quite loose and can form rolls or rumples under the fur. So this second hand is the "stroking hand." The reason for using the stroking hand will be easier to understand if you realize that, although we want to comb all the cat's fur, some of that fur is located over protruding bones such as those found by the armpit, down the center of the back, or around the hips.

As I said before, a healthy cat has loose skin. So the stroking hand is also used to shift that loose skin about so that you can move the fur you want to work on away from the bone or hollow and slide it over a muscle instead, then comb through it easily—and let it go back in place. Never comb over a bone or over the center of the throat. That would make your cat cough. (Try it lightly on yourself; you'll see what I mean.) You will probably find it helpful to practice sliding your cat's skin around. It's easy to make this feel awfully good, like any massage, and it can be incorporated into your usual petting and fondling routine.

Explain to the cat what you are doing as you work and be very clear about the reasons for each move you make. "This will get rid of the nasty dirt on your beautiful ruff." Or, "You'll feel so much better when all that old, loose hair is gone." (See "Therapeutic Communication," page 262.)

If, during the course of the grooming your cat makes a complaint or gives an alarm, *don't ignore it! Stop.* Nothing makes a cat more nervous than to think that he has no control over a situation. If he tells you to stop, stop. Acknowledge that you have heard. Try to find out what the problem is. Carefully solve the problem, explaining all the while how you intend to do it carefully and comfortably. Then continue on. Remember that the whole grooming is one big expression of affection.

The cat should be seated facing away from you. Here is the order in which you do the combing:

First, start with the back of the neck—they all love that.

Second, go on to the throat and chest. Reach the comb hand around one side of him and the stroking hand around the other side. Tip the cat's head back slightly and, starting at the top, on the cheeks, stroke the comb downward (see figure 3 below), using slow and short strokes. Work your way down gradually. No stroke should be longer than three or four inches. Remember, you're still exploring. Overlap your strokes so that each stroke is *begun* in an area that has already been combed and ends by stroking through uncombed hair. Work your way down from the cheeks through the sides of the throat, down the upper chest and lower chest, finally reaching between the legs. Your "finger grooming" will have revealed to you the bone structure under that chest fur so that you can avoid bumping the hard comb teeth against any protruding bones.

Third, comb the neck and throat again—not because it needs it, but because cats love it and you want to reinforce the feeling of pleasure at being groomed. For this reason, you'll be going back to the neck and throat after finishing each section of the cat's body.

FIGURE 3
To comb the ruff, tip the cat's head back slightly.

Fourth, do the back. Remember the little bumpy bones you found in the chest area? Well, you now have a whole long spine of bones running down the back. A good way to keep an area safe from the comb is to put your finger over the area. So put a finger over the upper spine and think of your cat's back as being shaped like the roof of a house with the spine on top. Use your stroking hand to slide the skin of the back to the right or left. Comb one side and then the other, stroking parallel to the spine but never allowing the comb to go bumping down the vertebrae. The back is where you will learn how to use the stroking hand. There are three ways to use the stroking hand, depending upon which area you are working on and the texture of your cat's hair and skin. The first method is to move the stroking hand ahead of the comb, pulling the skin forward and making sure there are no protruding bones or skin rumples for the comb to hit against (Figure 4, page 170). The second method is to use the stroking hand to hold the skin taut *behind* the comb, using the thumb to press the skin backward and away from you (see Figure 5 on page 171). A variation of this is using the thumb of the stroking hand to press or pull the skin to one side or the other in order to move it off a protruding bone or inaccessible depression in the cat's body. If all this sounds complicated, just remember the purpose of the stroking hand, which is to keep the comb or brush from hitting the cat's sensitive bones and to smooth out skin rumples.

When combing the back, as in combing the throat, use short strokes. Once you've become thoroughly familiar with your cat's body structure, you will know how many bumps and depressions lurk between the neck and the tail. Comb the back hair a little at a time, and use the same overlap technique that you used on the neck. Also, remember that the stroking hand is being used to control the tautness of the skin, and you will soon discover that that control cannot extend for more than three or four inches away from the hand's position.

A word about the comb angle: the comb should be held with the teeth pointing straight down at the cat's body or lagging a bit behind the stroke. By the time you comb down to the bottom layer, the points of the comb teeth should be directed against the skin. For the final comb through, don't think of combing hair, think of scratching skin.

In training a new client to comb his or her cat between groomings, I find that the most frequent mistake is to angle the teeth of the comb forward so that you are pushing the pointy teeth through the hair. This way your thumb cannot feel any sudden tangling, nor are you getting the teeth down to the skin. The second most frequent mistake, and by far the worst, is what I call the "eggbeater technique."

Figure 4

First stroking hand method: the skin is stretched by applying pressure and
pulling the skin toward you *ahead* of the direction of the comb.

Here, not only is the comb angled with the teeth pointing forward but the wrist is
flipped at the end of each stroke causing the comb to lift or pull the hair out away
from the body. Instead of starting at the tip of the hair and working down to the
root layer by layer, eggbeater aficionados dig in as close to the root as possible
and attempt to lift or pull *all* the loose hair off the cat at once. The thought in their
minds seems to be either that they are being thorough or that they are trying to
both comb and fluff the cat at the same time. They usually compound the error by
using quick, flipping strokes, which reminds me of someone beating an egg with
a fork—hence my label, "eggbeater technique." (Obviously, this mistake is almost
never made by guardians of shorthair cats.) I explain to them that no one can fluff
the cats' coats better than the cats themselves, when they shake vigorously after

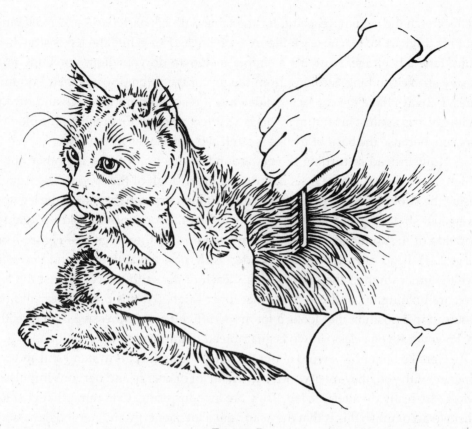

FIGURE 5

Second stroking hand method: the thumb holds the skin taut *behind* the comb.

the grooming is over. And the very best way to ensure that your cats will want to have a good shake is to slick their hair down as flat as possible, then put them down on the floor. They can't wait to shake it out!

Fifth, do the thighs. By now it has become obvious that skin that is stretched taut is easiest to comb over. You've used the stroking hand to accomplish this on the back. For the thigh, there is a third stroking hand technique you can use. Slide your stroking hand in from behind and between the cat's hind legs and reach forward until your hand is between the front legs with your palm under the cat's chest and your forearm under the belly. Now slowly begin lifting your forearm up a little. (This can also work if you lift with the hand, disengaging the front feet from the table.) Watch the thigh, leg, and foot. As you lift, the cat will automatically stretch the leg out, reaching for the table with his back paws and stretching out his thigh as he reaches (see Figure 6 on page 173). While the leg is stretched thus, take advantage. Now it's a simple matter to do your light, medium, and heavy stroke combing, stroking from the top of the thigh down. When I do this area, I always have the cat facing sideways. I reach in from the back and lift up with my arm against his tummy. This is a perfect position for combing the bloomers, too, because the back of the leg is stretched out as well as the side.

Now, instead of turning the cat around at this point to do the other outer thigh, leave the cat where he is and do the inner thigh of the *opposite leg*. Again, using the stroking hand, this time slip the hand underneath the foot of the leg you were just stretching and gently press up so that the foot and leg fold up against the side of the abdomen. The cat is now standing on three legs (see Figure 7 on page 174). Bend over the cat, look underneath, past the abdomen, and you will see the inner thigh of the opposite leg. Reach under with the comb past the leg you are holding up, and comb out that inner thigh. (At this point, you will find yourself in a position that looks a lot more difficult and impressive than it really is; however, a yoga class or two is guaranteed to improve your technique.)

Here I'd better say a word about the tail. In order for cats to stand still and co-operate with you, they must control an awful lot of energy and nervous impulses. Most cats really do a terrific job. They are awe-inspiring. One thing that enables them to accomplish this is that they can vent a lot of energy and nervousness with their tails: they can flick them, lash them from side to side, and generally express all the feelings they would otherwise have to bottle up. Groomers frequently have the impulse to confine the tail or hold it still while working on bloomers, the anal area, inner thigh, and so on. I tried the same thing in the beginning while I was learning. The cats soon made it very clear that if their tails are held still, then the movement will have to come out somewhere else. So, if you don't want dancing feet, you should as much as possible leave the tail free and try to work around it.

Now turn the cat around facing the opposite direction to do the other thigh. Once again, lift up on the tummy to do that outer thigh and bloomers. This time, slip the arm and hand under the cat from the front; then fold up the leg and reach under the leg to do the other inner thigh.

Sixth, the long, silky hair that forms the border between the sides of the cat and the belly is what I refer to as the "skirts." The skirts near the front of the thigh and near the armpit are areas where frequent matting occurs. Bloomers, skirts, and chest are the three areas that must be done every day.

FIGURE 6

Lift up the cat's abdomen with your arm to stretch the outer thigh for combing.

To groom the skirts, you use a technique similar to what you did on the outer thigh. Stretch out the area by lifting the cat. Face the cat away from you, open the stroking hand, and slip it under the cat's armpits and chest so that one armpit is resting on your middle finger and the other armpit is resting on your thumb. The index finger is against the cat's chest pointed up, toward his chin. Once again you are going to lift the cat, but don't lift the cat to a perpendicular position. This would make him afraid of falling backward, and he will probably start scrabbling with his back feet. Instead—and this is a subtle move—lift up just enough to disengage the front feet from the table by about two or three inches. The cat will be on a gentle diagonal, the chest resting heavily on your hand (see Figure 8 on page

FIGURE 7

To comb the inner thigh, slip the stroking hand under the outside foot and gently lift up. *Don't lift too high*, because your cat must balance on three legs.

175). Now, instead of lifting any farther, stretch the cat a tiny bit more forward, away from you, so that the skin under the skirts is nicely stretched out and you can do light, medium, and heavy combing of the skirts. Do the chest and abdomen at the same time as you reach under the cat and around to the skirts on the other side. You can even do fronts of thighs in this position, and that very tricky place where skirts join fronts of thighs.

In the beginning, before you and your cat get used to this little piece of choreography, you will almost certainly have to repeatedly put the cat down, reposition your grip, and lift again for a few more strokes. You may find it helpful to go back and comb the neck a few times between tries to reinforce positive feelings, especially when you're first learning this manuever, and don't hesitate to put your friend on the floor for a rest period of a couple of hours or even a day.

FIGURE 8

To comb the skirts, place one hand under the chest between the legs and lift up,
stretching the cat slightly forward.

Seventh, the chest between the front legs is mostly done by what I call the
braille method—you can't see what you're doing. Stand the cat facing away from
you on all fours and bring the stroking hand in from one side, the comb in from
the other. Reaching from back to front, up between the front legs as high up on
the chest as you can, stroke with one hand and follow with the comb. Coming at it

from the other angle, tilt the cat's chin up and comb down on the upper chest, try-ing to overlap with what you did on the lower chest by reaching down between the legs from front to back.

Eighth, grooming the tail is left for the final comb-out. Remember to finish by going back and combing the pleasure area again and again—neck, throat, or lower spine. A special word about the tail—use only the coarse comb on the tail no matter how sparse you think your cat's coat is. You didn't allow the comb to bump against the spinal vertebrae, and you apply the same principle here. The tail is an extension of the spine and very sensitive. Comb it in sections, just as you did the body of the cat. Don't try to cover the entire tail, base to tip, in one stroke. Work down in layers as you did with the combing of the body, and be supercare-ful not to pull and not to dig in. Tails are delicate. Don't hesitate to reach for the scissors and do some mat splitting if necessary before going on. (See step 4: "Get-ting Rid of the Mats," page 178.)

Step 3: Clipping the Claws

Claw clipping can be made very easy if the guardian remembers always to include stroking the paws every time he pets the cat. Make it a practice to gently stroke and massage the cat's pads and toes, massage the claws out and in, out and in, as a part of your everyday ritual of affection. That way, when it comes to claw clipping time, the cat will not find it in any way odd or alarming that you are picking up a paw and extruding the claws. Moreover, you must be familiar with the anatomy of your cat's claws before you try cutting them. This everyday fondling of the paws and claws gives you the opportunity you need to examine just how the claw slides in and out of the sheath. You will notice the circular downward curve of the claw as well as two other important features—the claw is flat (not round like a dog's claw), and there is a little pink membrane inside the claw reaching about halfway down the curve (see figure 9 on page 178).

During your examination, you may have noticed some waxy brown dirt around the cuticle area. You will need to clean it away in order to prevent irrita-tion, swelling, and infection. This is done right after claw clipping.

When I first started grooming, I experimented with every type of pet claw clipper I could get my hands on. I came to the conclusion that every single one I tried was designed for a small dog with a round claw. My pussycats did not have round claws; their claws are flat like my nail but turned on the side and thicker. A human toenail clipper was the answer. A great big clipper for flat nails. It works, and of all the clippers it's the easiest of all to use because when you squeeze the clipper shut your fingers are right up close to the claw you're working on.

The most dangerous types of clippers I've found are those where the fingers must grasp the end of a handle two or three inches distant from the claw. With a human toenail clipper, you're really working in close. Brace the little finger of your clipper hand against your other hand for steadiness when you clip. I also like to brace my elbows against the sides of my body. You will never clip too much if you don't think of cutting it short but rather of blunting the tip. Locate that pink nerve inside the claw, and notice the distance between the tip of the nerve and the tip of the claw. If you cut off only half of that distance or less, you'll always be safe. Never cut anywhere near the pink part because that's the nerve; that would hurt and teach the cat that claw clipping is painful. Incidentally, it is polite to clip your cat's claws before going to the veterinarian or groomer. This is also the best plan because more than once I have seen claws clipped by a veterinarian that were clipped far too short, right into the nerve. With such cats, it takes five or six sessions of careful and patient conditioning before I can convince them that Anitra does not hurt when she clips claws.

In order to maintain a clear memory of easy and pleasant claw clippings, it's nice if the guardian does it every two weeks. Don't expect to clip every claw every time. Some will certainly not need it. When you come to a claw that is already short enough, extrude it from the sheath as usual but just touch it gently with the metal clipper so that the cat has the impression that you have done something to each claw.

A word about extruding the claws: on the first try, most people try to squeeze the claw out. This will work, but it is not efficient and certainly doesn't make the cat feel good. Instead, put your finger on the pad under the claw, press up, and watch the claw come out automatically. Use your thumb above the claw just to hold the hair out of the way and keep the claw from sliding back into its sheath. Look at the curve of the claw, and as you position your clipper, think of making the clip so that the flattened end of the claw will end up parallel to the ground when the cat steps on it—not up and down and parallel to the wall in front of the cat.

Before you actually squeeze the clipper shut, make sure of two things. First and foremost, there must be no chance of catching a part of the pad in the clipper; second, hold the clipper still as you squeeze it—don't move it from side to side, or change position in any way during the clip, and don't pull (see figure 9 on page 178).

If, after clipping the claw, any dirt is left around the cuticles, now is the time

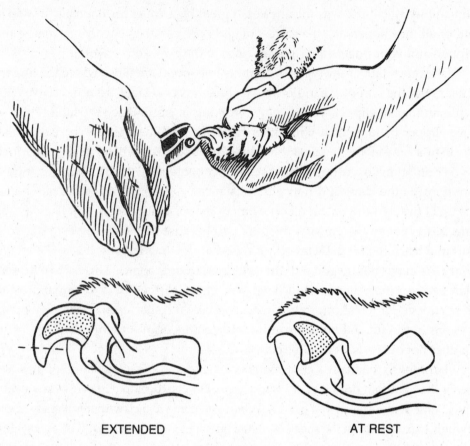

EXTENDED   AT REST

FIGURE 9
Clip the claw parallel to the ground. Clip only the area below the dotted line.

to clean the cuticles. You may be able to gently scrape it off with your thumbnail. If not, see "Soaking Feet and Cleaning Cuticles," page 282.

After you've finished grooming, the cat will probably run to the scratching post and start scratching like crazy to get his claws back in shape again the way he likes them.

Step 4: Getting Rid of the Mats

I feel a tremendous amount of hesitation in including instructions on the use of scissors for cutting out mats. It's such a dangerous business. And it's so hard to describe to someone secondhand, without having them actually present with the cat and the scissors.

I found that the very hardest cats to cut mats out of were elderly cats, because the skin is loose and flaccid as opposed to being loose and elastic; and black cats with dark skins, because it's hard to see where the hair ends and the skin begins. I remember the first matted cat I ever had to groom. It was quite an initiation. The cat was so matted that he was crippled. Any place a cat could get mats, he had them. The mats around the anus were mixed with excrement. He even had little minimats formed in the crew-cut between his ears. The rest of the body looked as if it were in a plaster cast between an inch and two inches thick. My first impulse when I saw him was to cry. I had never seen a cat in such a pitiful condition in all my life. I don't remember now what the owner's excuse was for allowing the cat to get like that, but I do remember that the first grooming of my entire life lasted five hours. I didn't know enough then to insist on stopping after two hours and coming back another day to give the cat a rest. I know I worked slowly—I remember the owner complained about how slowly it was going. She also complained about my fee, which was, at that time, $5.00 per hour or $25.00 for a five-hour grooming. But my feelings about a human being who could allow a cat to get into that condition were such that I didn't gave a damn about what that person thought about anything. My sole concern was to help the cat.

Here are a few tried-and-true general rules that will smooth your path:

1. For mat removal, use *only* scissors with a rounded tip. *No points.*
2. *Don't bathe the cat while mats are still in the coat* or you'll have some mess on your hands. The mats will seem to be glued to the skin. If this mistake has been made, *don't* try to groom the cat yourself. Let the vet anesthetize and shave the cat.
3. Before you cut and as you cut, be very sure that the whole time you can see where the skin is and where the hair is. If you lose sight of the skin, don't cut—stop.
4. With every single cut you do, cut slowly. Be aware of every single millimeter of the cutting motion.
5. You don't have to finish an area before going on to the next area. Work a little here, a little there. It's easier on the cat's nerves to go back again and again to a difficult spot, doing it a little at a time.
6. When working on one mat, don't hesitate to switch angles of approach—

working at it from the right, from the left, from the bottom, from all angles.

7. Give frequent rest breaks. Especially when removing mats, you must remember to put the cat down off the table *before* he starts wiggling and demanding it. If you're working with scissors, the cat must be still, not wiggly. You can spread out the mat removal process over days and weeks, doing a few mats a day. Simply say to yourself that the coat is no longer getting worse and worse—it is now improving, however slowly. Safety comes first.

8. Whenever you are working near any delicate area where you are afraid of cutting something such as a nipple or penis, just remember—if you know where it is, you won't cut it. So cover such areas with your finger while you're working nearby.

9. If the cat is moving, don't cut. Stop.

Splitting the Mats: Mats pull the skin terribly, especially on areas of articulation such as knees, thighs, and armpits—they hurt. Don't pet your cat on the mats. The less you touch them or move them around, the better. As I said, they hurt.

The very first thing I do for a matted cat is to split each mat apart into smaller pieces. This accomplishes three things. First and foremost, it gives the cat relief from the constant terrible pulling. Second, it demonstrates to the cat just what it is you are about to do to make him or her feel better. Third, it lets you see where the skin is. A mat is easier to remove in pieces than left whole. When I first began training assistants to remove mats, I advised them that if they split the mat into enough segments there would be very little else left to do.

To split a mat, insert the rounded nose of the lower blade of the scissors between the skin and the mat so that the blunt side of the blade is against the skin, and the sharp cutting edge is pushing up against the mat (Figure 10, page 181). *Caution*—do not use the scissors blade to pull the mat up or away from the skin. You want the skin to stay flat and smooth, moving it as little as possible. So leave the blunt side of the blade resting firmly on the skin and begin *slowly* to cut the mat in half.

Notice how, when the cutting in half is complete, the two halves of the mat spring apart. This is evidence that you have just released a great deal of tension from the skin.

FIGURE 10

To split a mat, hold the scissors at a right angle to the skin.

Split the same mat again and again. Try inserting the scissors between skin and mat from various angles. Use the angles that give less resistance. You will notice that with each mat certain angles are fairly easy, while other angles of entry are all but impossible. You'll only hurt the cat if you insist on fighting the lay of the hair. This splitting procedure so far is fairly safe as long as you never pull the mat up away from the body. Simply keep the cutting edge facing up away from the cat and cut through the mat. In other words, you are not removing the mat, you are splitting it into many small pieces. Do this with several, if not all, of the mats wherever they occur. Split them up to give the cat relief.

Some mats do not lend themselves well to this type of splitting. With armpit mats, where the anatomy is so convoluted, it is extremely difficult to slip the scissors between skin and mat. Also, mats around the anus and the bloomers are sometimes cement hard because they have been repeatedly soiled and wet.

Cutting Out the Pieces of the Mat: Just as you slipped the scissors between skin and mat and tilted the cutting edge up away from the cat to split the mat, to cut out pieces of the mat you must slip the blade in between the cat and the mat and tilt the blade a little to the side before cutting.

Choose a piece of mat. Note where the mat is, where the skin is, and the little bit of straight hair holding the mat to the skin. Slip the scissors blade between the mat and skin *close to the edge of the mat*. In other words, instead of inserting the blade near the middle of the mat to split it, insert the blade as *close as possible* to the edge of the mat. Begin tilting the cutting edge of the blade up, away from the cat, just as you did when you were going to split the mat. This time, however, don't tilt it all the way up. Bring it almost all the way so that the flat side of the blade is on an angle. Then again slowly cut through the hair between mat and skin at that angle, cutting the few hairs at the edge of the piece of mat. Then insert the blade again, close to the edge of the part of the mat that remains. Tilt the cutting edge of the blade up away from the cat (but not to a full ninety degrees) and cut through a few more hairs, separating even more of the piece of mat from the cat. Repeat this process until you have severed all the hairs that are holding the piece of mat to the body. This technique is also used on mats that are too thick or hard to split or mats that are in difficult anatomical areas where it would be dangerous to try to split them (armpits, elbows, ankles, and anus).

I cannot say it often enough—go slowly. The slower you go in the beginning, the better a groomer you will be in the end. The cat must be standing still, for his or her own safety, so here's a prime place to use an assistant to help keep the cat from wiggling around. A general suggestion: when you are inserting the scissors blade near the edge of the mat, the closer to the edge the better. In other words, the fewer hairs you try to snip through at one time, the safer you will be. Once again, it's a question of patience on your part. If the matting is extensive, it's far better to have the cat anesthetized and shaved that one time as long as you can trust the veterinarian.

Breaking Up Soft Mats: A soft mat is a mat that is not really a mat yet. Think of a cotton ball. It's nice and soft; it's not a bit lumpy—yet you could not comb through a cotton ball. If, during the light combing, you encounter any areas on the cat's coat where the comb will not go through but you can't feel a lump, treat it as a soft mat. If you do nothing about it, it will soon become a classic hard mat. Treat the soft mat exactly the same as when splitting a mat, except that in this case, to save as much hair as possible, you should slip in your scissors parallel to the lay of the hair. Don't cut across the lay, thus cutting off a lot of hair. Only cut through the tangles and debris that crisscross back and forth across the growing hair. The effect will be as if you were thinning. Cut parallel to the lay of the hair again and again and again, always keeping the cutting edge facing up away from the cat, just as you did in splitting the mat. Then take the coarse (wide-toothed) comb and begin with a very light touch. Gradually work deeper and deeper toward the skin, removing the hair debris you have freed. If the comb encounters resistance, go back and split some more. The more you split, the easier the combing will be and the better your cat will like it.

Step 5A: For Longhaired Cats: The Final Comb-Out

This step is simply a repetition of step 2—light combing. It is always done after removing mats or splitting soft mats. This step ends when you're combing through the entire cat with the points of the comb tines stroking directly against the skin of the cat and when you are encountering no resistance whatsoever in any part of the cat's fur.

Use a wide-tooth comb for this step. Then, if your cat's fur is not very thick, you can repeat with the medium comb and maybe even the shorthair shedding comb. For a longhair cat, the fine comb is used only on crew-cut, cheeks, chin, and sometimes the front knickers—shorthair places where it doesn't pull at all. The work with the medium and fine combs is for the pleasure of meticulous guardians and their fortunate cats. The purr crescendos to fortissimo during this step.

Step 5B: For Shorthaired Cats: The Slicker Brush

The slicker brush is a delightful tool that shorthaired cats become very fond of. Because it only reaches from one-half to one inch down the hair follicle, it is unsuitable for longhaired cats. If your cat has long hair, a slicker brush would groom only the tips of the hair. The slicker brush must be used properly, because it can prick and scratch if carelessly handled. Use the slicker brush only on the back, the sides, outer thighs, throat, and chest. Do not use it on the stomach—it could scratch the nipples. (Even for a shorthair cat, if the coat is in very poor condition you may need to begin by first combing with a coarse or medium comb as in step 2.)

Hold the slicker brush very loosely by the handle and stroke it ever so lightly down the cat's coat. The cats often press up against the slicker brush, urging you on to a firmer stroke. Don't initiate a firmer stroke yourself; let your cat guide you. In order to avoid pricking the cat with those sharp little needles of metal, be sure that you always *keep the handle low and close to the cat's body*. When learning to use a slicker brush, beginners always make the same two mistakes: they try to stroke too rapidly and, worse, they flick their wrist at the end of the stroke, thus raising the handle up and digging the little pointy wires into the cat's skin. The first two or three days that you try it, make each stroke an individual activity (see Figure 11 below). Curved slicker brushes have come on the market in recent years. Some groomers find them easier to use. (Not me.) Try them out carefully. Some short hair cats don't like the slicker brush at all. They prefer a fine tooth comb. As always, let your cat guide you in choosing the flat slicker, curved slicker, or fine tooth comb.

It's helpful to stroke the slicker brush a couple of times down your own fore-arm. Try it very lightly—a feather touch. Then add a little steady pressure. This will go a long way toward helping you to know your tool. Now try this: stroking

FIGURE 11

Use a slicker brush for shorthaired cats only. Stroke down the back parallel to (but not on) the spine, keeping the handle low and close to the body.

in slow motion, begin to raise the handle up away from your arm at the end of the stroke. Do it slowly, because you will feel how those little prickles dig in to your skin. A good way to keep the wire bristles at the correct angle is to think of keeping the knuckles of the brushing hand down on the fur, especially at the end of the stroke.

Some groomers hesitate to recommend the slicker brush for fear the client will use it carelessly and condition the cat to dislike being groomed because of the pain experienced from tipping the brush at an improper angle at the end of the stroke. But nothing works as well as a small slicker brush for shorthaired cats. Nothing removes the loose hair quite so efficiently and in such great volumes. Nothing scratches and stimulates the cat's skin in quite so delightful a fashion. Cats have told me with their purrs and by pressing their bodies up against the brush that they adore the slicker brush when it's used right.

If your cat has a coarse coat the Twinco slicker brush, size small or mini, will probably do the best job. For a finer textured coat, I use either a Warners or the Evergentle, again size small or mini. The Warners mini slicker fits exactly between a cat's ears to groom the forehead and also does a nice stroking down cheeks and throat.

Because you can't use the slicker brush on the abdomen or any bony place, such as the forelegs or tail, use the fine-toothed comb for those areas. Never press hard against the bones or the tail. Remember, the tail is an extension of the spine.

Step 6: Cleaning the Eyes

If your cat's eyes are bright and shiny and clean, skip this step. This step is only for those cats who have runny eyes or who tend to build up dirt in the corner of the eyes. (*Please note:* The eyes should also be cleaned before you administer medicinal eyedrops or salve.) First, you will want to clean around the eyes to remove any crustiness or discoloration. Because this exudation is caused by debris and discharge from the tear ducts, it is important to always irrigate the tear ducts at the same time that you clean around the eyes. The irrigation will clean and disinfect the tear ducts, so they work more efficiently and there will be less discharge (or hopefully none at all). When done properly, the cats love it because it gets rid of the itchy feeling caused by the unsightly discharge. I have elected to put the very easy instructions for cleaning around the eyes and tear duct irrigation in the home nursing care chapter. Please refer to "Cleaning around the Eyes," page 269, and "Administering Eyedrops and Irrigating Tear Ducts," page 270.

Step 7: Examining Teeth and Gums

Just as you should be aware of the condition of the cat's stool and urine for your own peace of mind, you will want to keep abreast of the condition of the teeth and gums. Tartar builds up on the teeth of most cats sooner or later, and it must be removed before it compromises the health of the gums, then the upper respiratory system, and finally the entire body. If you notice that the gums have a line of bright red near the teeth, this indicates that something is amiss with the cat's immune system. If you're not already feeding a diet based on raw meat, do it now. At the very least, add a raw organic egg yolk to each can of commercial food. Also, be sure the teeth are clean.

So, how are you going to look at the cat's gums? Take the pill-giving and ear- and eye-medicating position: kneel on the floor with your knees apart and feet together behind you, and then back the cat in toward you and have him sit. With your left hand, bring your thumb and forefinger under the cat's cheekbones and lift the head up, tilting it back as if to give a pill. With the right hand, lift the upper lip enough to peek at the gums and see if there's any tartar on the teeth. Then pull the lower lip down to check out the lower teeth. Also, insert the nail of your middle finger between the upper and lower front teeth and pull the lower jaw down so you can get a better look at the molars and the inside wall of the upper and lower teeth.

On your first examination, become consciously aware of the difference in color between teeth and tartar. It's easiest to learn to examine teeth before tartar builds up because the cat's mouth will be more comfortable and not overly sensitive. Also, if there is a lot of tartar on the teeth, it will be harder to distinguish between tartar and teeth. If a tooth is entirely covered with tartar you may mistake it for a clean tooth because you can no longer see the contrast between tartar and tooth. If I find anything amiss with a cat's teeth or gums, I always show the cat's guardian. I have found that most people can easily see the line of red on the gums near the teeth but most are not able to distinguish between tooth and tartar because tartar can be light yellow as well as dark tan.

So, in the beginning, examine the cat's teeth as a part of each grooming just so you can learn what the tartar looks like. Then, after it becomes obvious to you, you need only examine the teeth once a week. If you become aware that there's an awful lot of tartar buildup, plus inflamed gums, let the veterinarian clean the teeth. (See Chapter 10, "Selecting Methods of Treatment and Seeking Professional Help.") The gums will probably not improve until you clean the filthy tartar away from them. Incidentally, an unpleasant smell to the cat's fur often indicates a tartar problem because the cat will be washing himself with saliva that is loaded with smelly germs from the tartar.

Because teeth cleaning sometimes involves the use of anesthetic, it is to be hoped that this will not have to be done more than once a year at the most. Priscilla needs to have her teeth done every year, while Big Purr is eight years old and his teeth have never needed cleaning. If you see tartar forming in between cleanings, you can sometimes flick it off with a fingernail. This is easily done if you let the tartar build up to a good-sized chunk first (a layer or two is too hard to deal with). Then one day while you're examining, instead of simply pulling the lip back and looking, insert your right thumbnail between the tartar and the gum. Place your right index finger on the point of that tooth and attempt to scrape that tartar down with the thumbnail, toward the waiting index finger. This procedure is easier to practice on some cats than on others because of the cat's temperament, the caregivers' skill, and the density of the tartar. My Priscilla's tartar resembles granite, and the veterinarian advised me that my efforts with a thumbnail were worse than hopeless. However, I frequently use this method on cats that I'm grooming. The best approach is not to force the issue. Make a gentle attempt, each time you examine the teeth, to flick off some tartar. If the cat protests, respond politely with "Okay, never mind, we'll try it again next time." The cat will soon begin to smooth out your technique if you persist with patience.

However, don't try flicking tartar off the teeth if the gums are too inflamed. Inflamed gums hurt. Let the veterinarian take care of it under anesthetic. After dentistry has been completed, you can help discourage tartar by rubbing a paste made of mild cheddar cheese and water all over the teeth and gums once or twice a week. The enzyme that turns milk into cheddar tends to dissolve dental plaque. Also, the saltiness of cheddar will soothe and shrink swollen gum tissue. Try brushing your own teeth with it in the morning; you'll see how good it feels.

Step 8: Cleaning the Ears

I like to do the ears last. Many cats find ear cleaning itchy and tickly, because there are many little hairs in the ear that get moved around by the cotton swab. Many cats' ears are just not dirty, and in such cases I skip the ear cleaning. But, if you see a couple of black specks of wax, just take the cotton swab and clean *any part of the ear that you can actually see.* Don't try cleaning down into the ear canal, because you need a refined technique for that. It's not uncommon for a well-meaning person to inadvertently tamp the wax down farther into the ear canal and against the ear drum.

It's nice to put oil on the cotton swab. Bits of wax and debris will cling to the swab if it's a bit oily. Mineral oil is not acceptable, because the cat is going to wash the oil off and swallow it as soon as you put him down. I prefer to use the contents of a 100-unit vitamin E capsule. Don't buy vitamin E oil in a bottle. It begins to oxidize and go rancid the minute you break the seal. Even in the refrigerator it is usable for only two weeks. The capsule keeps the oil fresher. Also, I find that the capsules are easy to carry around with me as I go grooming from house to house. I just puncture a capsule, squeeze the contents onto a saucer, and roll the end of the cotton swab in it. That way I feel secure in the knowledge that the oil is sterile, and when the cats wash their ears they will get a tiny but beneficial amount of vitamin E instead of the mineral oil, which washes vitamins E, A, and D out of the system. In a pinch, olive oil will work just fine.

Remember, anything you put onto the cat's body will eventually be licked off and swallowed. And oils will also be absorbed through the skin. So, if you're ever in doubt about using some substance on or around a cat, just ask yourself if you would mind if he lapped up half a teaspoonful of it. That's sure to awaken your good instincts.

Step 9: The Catnip Party and Admiration

At the end of every grooming, even the daily sixty-second grooming, you must make every effort to convince your cats that in being groomed they have performed the cleverest of feats. Assure them that the grooming has revealed anew all their natural beauty, their wealth of symmetry and grace. Stroke their favorite spots to end the grooming on a high level of sensual pleasure.

You cannot give catnip every day, or the cats will lose their taste for it. You should not use catnip at all if *any* of your cats are being treated homeopathically because catnip is a medicinal herb and can antidote the homeopathic remedy. But, if all the cats are healthy you can have a catnip party once a week, perhaps after grooming. Alternate treats can be any of those given on page 78. The all-out favorite with every cat and guardian I know is PetGuard Purrlicious.

The Bath

Whenever anybody asks, "Can you give a cat a bath?" they always ask it in hushed tones, as if it were almost unthinkable. The bath is easy. Bathing a cat is really quite simple if you know how to go about it. A bath is luxurious and pleasant—warm, gentle, and sweet-smelling. Cats love to be clean, to be massaged, to be crooned over. A bath is all these things. A bath can be a wonderful demonstration of love, physical affection, and sensual pleasure.

Many cats never need a bath. If they're on the proper diet, they may never need one their whole life long. However, there are special circumstances where I would definitely recommend that the cat be bathed: at the beginning and end of a flea treatment, if the cat has soiled himself with diarrhea, if the cat urinates on himself in the carrier or while he's in the cage at the veterinarian's, if the cat gets into something, or if something is spilled on him.

It doesn't hurt a cat to be bathed any more than it hurts you to have your hair washed. But it's much better if the cat's general health is on such a plane of perfection that bathing becomes superfluous. A cat who *needs* to be bathed every month because he's greasy has a health problem. A cat with kidney failure will benefit from frequent bathing; a cat with pancreas malfunction will also have a greasy coat. The bath doesn't solve the health problem—it just gets rid of the symptoms for a few days.

When new clients present me with a cat that has an oily coat and ask me to give a bath, I always inform them that if I bathe the cat now, before the diet has been upgraded, he will look great for about a week and a half, then he'll start getting greasy and dandruffy again. However, after he has been on the proper diet for about one month, he'll continue to look terrific for months or even forever. (Of course, if the cat is soiled in any way, I bathe him at once.) If I'm going to ask a cat to stand still for bathing and for drying and comb out, I feel that he deserves to stay looking clean and terrific for at least a couple of months after the bath. If his coat is greasy and full of dandruff, I suspect that food has been left available twenty-four hours a day, causing a slow metabolism and that a low-quality diet has been fed. The cat will continue to exude old wastes through the pores in the form of oil and dandruff for at least two weeks after beginning the high-quality diet. By then the backlog of wastes is gone. So I tell the caregiver to put the cat on the proper diet, remove food between meals, increase activity, and then in a month I'll come back and bathe the cat. When I do come back, often the guardian will say, "I'm so sorry, Anitra, but he looks so good. I don't think he needs a bath anymore." "Don't be sorry," I reply, "This is called success." I love to be able to say that, and the cat's humans are always so proud. Young cats respond fast to the dietary change—some old cats do too. You never know until you try.

But if the cat's oily coat has resulted in the dust mop effect, a bath may be just the thing he needs.

What do you need to give a bath? A cotton ball, some plain eye salve or petroleum jelly, two bath towels and two hand towels (you may not need them all), a wide-toothed comb (even for short hair—no slicker brushes are used here), a hand-held hair dryer, a cat shampoo or Dr. Bronner's liquid castile soap (see "Product Recommendations," in the Appendix), and a hose that will connect to the faucet of either the kitchen sink or the bathtub. The hose should be the type used in barber shops and beauty parlors for rinsing hair. For cat bathing, you must cut off the spray end so the water comes out of the hose in a stream—a wide spray is just what you *don't* want.

In giving the bath, you are aiming for clean, virgin hair because virgin hair sheds dust and dirt. Do not use any shampoos with additives such as conditioners, lanolin, and so on. Most pet store shampoos have these additives. They are undesirable because they coat the hair follicle and give you the dust mop effect all over again, which is just what you're trying to get rid of. Don't use a baby shampoo because it is too mild (you wash your hair once a week or more, but the cat gets a bath once or twice a year). If you can't find a pure castile veterinary shampoo without undesirable additives, look for a pure castile people shampoo. I prefer Dr. Bronner's liquid castile soap from the health food store. Usually a formula for oily hair will be stronger. Try the cosmetic section in a health food store. Most health food stores include a pet section. Several natural pet products companies make good shampoos (see "Product Recommendations," in the Appendix).

To prepare for the bath, first groom the cat to a fare-thee-well. *Never wet the cat's coat while there are mats or even loose hair present.* The very best plan is to groom the cat in the morning and bathe him in the afternoon. That way you're not asking the cat to hold still for such a long period at one time. Do a one-minute combing right before the bath.

Next, set up the dryer, the comb, and three or four towels in a comfortable place away from the bath where you can dry him. Adjust the dryer setting so that you have a good, strong stream of air but *not too much heat.* The temperature should be warm, never hot or cold. When it's properly set to your satisfaction, turn the dryer off until you need it.

Then mix a solution of half shampoo and half warm water into a dish or, better yet, an empty squeeze bottle. Shampoo must be warm and soothing, not cold and shocking. Attach the hose to the spigot and warm the tub or sink that you're going to use by swishing hot water around in it. The cat must be standing on pleasant warmth. Regulate the water temperature so that the stream of water coming through the hose is a bit warmer than baby bath temperature, more like adult bath temperature. The cat's body temperature is normally higher than ours. Test the temperature against the inside of your forearm. If you love it, your cat will love it. Let the water continue to run from now until the end of the bath.

While you're letting the water run a bit, put about a quarter of a cotton ball into each of the cat's ears. You don't have to stuff it down, just make sure it is secure. The cotton will absorb any stray droplet that might splash that way. A drop of water in the ear wouldn't hurt, but there's a chance the cat might be startled.

Then take the eye salve or petroleum jelly and apply a drop to the inside of the lower lid of each eye. (See "Cleaning Around the Eyes," page 268.) This will provide a film of oiliness over the eye, protecting the eyes from any stray drops of water or shampoo.

Don't begin to wet the cat until you're sure that the water temperature is going to remain constant throughout the bath. Put one large towel within easy reach of the bath area to receive the cat afterward. In the wintertime, many sensitive caregivers like to heat the towel on a radiator or in front of the oven.

Now the sink or tub is warm, the shampoo is warm, the water is warm, and the towel is warming. As you prepare each of these things, think of it as a gift you are going to give your cat. Consciously realize how much you yourself would enjoy each of these facets of the bath. Recent scientific research has established that cats "pick up" our mental attitudes and sensory impressions.

Back in the first year that I was grooming, before I had developed my techniques, my biggest concern was that the cats should stay calm and relaxed. In my zeal to reassure them, I myself would lie in the tub with the cat on top of me, attempting to demonstrate that it must be perfectly safe, or I would surely be drowned even before they were. Although this did work pretty well as far as calming the cat, I found it was rather difficult to give a thorough shampooing while lying supine with the cat standing on my stomach. Also, it didn't give the impression of professionalism I was striving to achieve.

Now, after thirty-five years of experience, and with my technique developed to a fine art, I still get wet. Oh, it's not that there is ever any wild splashing or thrashing about; the bath is still calm and luxurious. But there is just no substitute for the assurance that close physical proximity can give. You will want to nestle your cat close not only to your face but with your arms as well. I wear a sleeveless cotton smock that dries in a jiffy. I prefer to work in the kitchen sink, but if I have to use the tub I wear shorts because I will be kneeling in the wet.

Now arrange the hose on the floor of the tub or sink so the water is calmly running down the drain. No splashes or gushes, please. Pick up the cat and say that you're going to make him feel good. Explain that you're going to stand his paw pads in the "warm wet." Then go ahead and stand him in the nice warm sink or tub. *If you're using the sink,* start by placing his hind paws in the sink and his front paws on the drainboard. Hold the cat close to you—do a lot of nuzzling with your face near his head and neck. Having your face close to his in a new and unfamiliar situation is very reassuring. *If you're using the tub,* it's best if you get into the tub carrying your cat. Take the kneeling position as if to pill the cat (see Chapter 11) by backing the cat in toward you. In both these cases, you are playing down the water aspect. The cat hasn't really seen or felt much water yet.

If the cat reacts as if trying to tell you, "Hey, watch out, there's water here— I'm getting all wet!" don't lie! It never works anyway. Just put your face up next to his and reply calmly that you know about the water. Tell him that it's going to feel good, it's warm, and it will make him nice and clean. You must explain everything you are doing, because the cat will be reading your tone, and your words will carry the desired emotional reassurance. Continuing to talk and nuzzle, pick up the hose so the end where the water comes out is nestled in your palm. The cat still hasn't seen it. Before you introduce the sight of the hose, introduce the pleasant feeling of it by allowing the gentle, warm water from the hose to run against his haunch. As you nuzzle him and describe in detail how much you love nice warm water, wet his thighs, lower back, sides, inner thighs, upper back, shoulders, and chest in that order.

Throughout all this, you must tenaciously hang on to the truth of the situation—the water feels fabulous. If the water temperature should change, you'll know it even before he does because you'll feel it against your palm. By this time, he may be standing in a quarter inch or so of water sloshing about in the bottom of the tub or sink. He may find this alarming and assume that you are not aware of this shocking development. Continuing the nuzzling, you must make crystal clear to him that you are fully aware of his concern and the reason for it and that he is perfectly safe. (Never ask a cat to stand in water that is deeper than a half inch.) Remember that, in this case, if a cat is upset, he's upset because of fear of the *unknown*, not because of any kind of discomfort or *actual* danger. I call it suffering from an attack of the "what ifs." It's easy to understand—we humans do it all the time.

Now touch the hose to the bottom of the tub in front of him and let him see the water running down the drain. Still nuzzling, go back and redo his thighs, back, and so forth. This will prevent any chill. But this time continue on to include the throat and the back of the neck. Do not bathe the cat's face, forehead, or ears except when specifically soiled or when treating for fungus or fleas. Cats do pretty well in those areas by themselves. You can always wipe those areas off later with a damp cloth.

Now the cat's coat is thoroughly saturated with water. If the coat is greasy, you may have to go over it several times before it will hold the water. Before you apply the shampoo, lay the hose out of the way on the bottom of the sink or tub with the stream of water pouring down the drain so the cat feels he can safely forget about it. If you are working in the tub, you can push the tip of the hose a little way down the drain or hold the hose in place with your foot or knee. Now you are going to focus the cat's attention on one of the biggest pleasures of the bath. Apply the fragrant, warm shampoo solution to the neck, throat, shoulders, chest, armpits, upper back, lower back, tail, tummy, and inner thigh—in that order. If there's a problem area, such as lower back or tail greasiness or a soil or stain anywhere, apply the shampoo full strength in that area first. Massage the cat's body, working up a nice foamy lather all over. This step really makes the cat feel fabulous. During this step briefly reapply warm water every thirty seconds so the cat doesn't feel chilled.

If you're working with a really greasy coat and lots of dandruff and you fail to get a good lather on the first shampooing, don't worry. Rinse the cat off and do one soaping with one part liquid dishwashing detergent and four parts water. Use this only up to the shoulders; don't get it anywhere near the head. You always do two, or sometimes three, soapings anyway, so you can save the really fabulous massage for the second soaping when the shampoo is good and foamy. A guardian never has a better opportunity than during the bath to explore the incredible musculature of the cat. Keep up a running commentary to your cat exclaiming about the quality of his muscles and the delicacy of each bone your fingers encounter. As your fingers explore the cat's symmetry and grace, express delight in soft exclamations of appreciation. In trusting you so far as to submit to such a very odd ritual, your cat is, in effect, giving you a tremendous gift—his confidence and love.

To rinse, be careful to hold the hose with the tip nestled in your palm. *Never let the cat see water flying at him.* Rinse in the same order that you applied the shampoo, starting high on the neck so that the dirty shampoo runs down and off the legs. Rinse it off the back, off the sides, and so on, leaving the legs, paws, and tail until last.

Be thorough with the rinse. This is the most important part of the bath. Soap left in the coat is sticky and produces the dust mop effect. It is also itchy and causes matting in Persians. You can get away with a little mistake in any other step, but this one *must* be perfect. To be *sure* the coat is soap-free, press as much water as possible out of the coat, then you can finish with a lemon or vinegar rinse (see page 323). Then rinse again. Give attention to rinsing the tail, skirts, outer thighs, inner thighs, shoulders, and lower chest: in other words, all those places where the hair is thickest and matting tends to occur. During the rinsing, continue to nuzzle your face close to the cat's head as much as possible and call attention to the way the water is making him nice and warm again and how the nasty oiliness and dirt are being washed away down the drain.

When the coat is squeaky clean and free of soap, get rid of some of the water by pressing the coat against the skin and very lightly squeezing his legs, paws, and tail. Remove the cotton from the ears, grab the warm towel from the radiator or stove, and bundle the cat up in it, telling him that this warm towel and the forthcoming warm dryer are the rewards for the heroic patience he has displayed. Carry him out to the drying area. Fold another towel in half for him to stand or sit on and wrap him in another dry towel (the first towel is probably wet by now). The more towels you use, the faster he'll get dry. As you want the towel to absorb water, always use 100 percent cotton, and never use a towel that has been treated with fabric softener. It coats the fibers with a chemical and renders the towel nearly waterproof. Also, that chemical will transfer to the fur.

To introduce the dryer, use the same principle you used when introducing the water. Break the dryer up into its component parts—sound, sensation, and sight. As you're toweling the neck, nuzzling the cat's cheek, and telling him how delicious he smells, hold the dryer far away with your other hand, well out of his sight, and pointing *away* from the cat. Continue talking to him and casually turn the dryer on *low*, ignoring it completely and continuing to focus on the delicious-smelling cat.

Proceeding to the feel of the dryer (making sure he cannot see it yet), holding it at least one foot away slowly introduce the stream of comfortably warm air against the thigh or lower back. Try to always have your hand or finger on his body *included* in the path of that warm stream of air, so that you can judge the temperature. Don't allow the dryer to get too close. *The dryer must always be kept slowly moving.* If you hold it still, it will burn. Remember that the cat's skin is much more delicate and sensitive than ours. Think of the mucous membrane lining the inside of your lower lip. If you treat all the cat's body as if it were that sensitive, you'll always keep him safe.

The cat will probably move and want to get up. Turn the dryer off when this happens, readjust his position, and perhaps take a fresh towel. Drying is much more difficult to do alone. It goes three times faster if you can find someone to stroke the cat and distract him while you apply the dryer in one hand and the towel in the other. Allow the cat to see the dryer at a time when it has already been turned on and directed against the body for a minute or so. (Remember to keep the dryer moving.)

After the hair is more than half dry all over, begin combing very lightly with a wide-toothed comb as you dry. An assistant is invaluable here, because combing and blow-drying simultaneously speeds the drying about 300 percent. If you're alone, you have to go from one to the other. The comb is in the right hand, and the dryer is in the left hand. Comb ever so lightly, and again be sure to keep the dryer moving. Combing separates the hair so the stream of air can dry it even faster.

When drying the neck or throat, cup one hand or drape a small towel over the cat's ears, eyes, and nose so that the stream of air from the dryer never intrudes there. The cat can take care of drying those areas himself with his paw and tongue. It's also very easy for him to dry feet and ankles. Although the tail is easy enough for him to reach, the hair there is usually longer and thicker, so it's nice to give him a good headstart by using the dryer on the tail.

You don't have to get him absolutely dry, especially during the summer or in a well-heated apartment. However, the cat must be dry enough so you can easily run the comb through the hair all over the body. Otherwise longhaired cats may mat. Even if you try your best to get a cat completely dry, it's almost impossible. Anyway, cats reach their peak of fluffy beauty the day after a bath. When you decide to call it quits and put the cat down, go all out with positive reinforcement. If you have a brass band available, strike it up now. Tell your cat that he or she is not only the bravest and the most patient but also the softest and most gloriously beautiful creature with the most delectable scent on God's green earth. Repeat your rhapsodic performance at intervals all during the rest of that day and the next. It won't be difficult to do. You'll understand what I mean the first time you experience a freshly bathed cat. Chances are you won't be able to keep your hands off those lovely furs. After the first bath, I always remind every client that after the cat has been on the high-quality diet for a while this is the way the cat will always look and feel.

Two or three times a year, I run into cats who are afraid of the dryer. If you follow all the prescribed steps in introducing the dryer and yet the cat has a reaction verging on hysteria when you turn it on, don't persist. Just turn up the heat in the room, turn on the oven, and towel dry like crazy, using about eight or nine towels, and follow that with about fifty paper towels. Paper towels are also great for quick drying kittens or a sick cat before using the dryer. Another option is to use microfiber towels. They absorb moisture very quickly and are useful at this stage of the drying process. (They don't work as well when the cat first comes out of the bath because they are thin and often small and, therefore, not suitable for wrapping a cat for warmth.) Keep at it until you can successfully run the comb through all the hair. Your cat will still look beautiful tomorrow, just like a cat that has been blown dry.

I had this problem when I was caring for a big gray male named Apollo who was convalescing from a mouth tumor. The veterinarian wanted him bathed once a week to clean away the discharge from his mouth, which soiled his chest and front legs. Apollo is enormous, gentle, and intelligent; but the sound of that dryer threw him into such a state of helpless terror that he was not responsible for his actions.

I had to dry him quickly because I couldn't allow him to become chilled; it was early spring and the radiators were off. I solved the problem this way: every week after Apollo's bath I would dry him as well as I could with several terry cloth towels, then carry him in to the office where I had pulled out the bottom drawer of the desk and attached two clip-on reflector lamps with 100-watt bulbs. They were focused on a dry bathmat on the floor and were only about two feet away. Apollo would lounge there for an hour or so, turning himself like a sunbather and licking himself dry all over. I would pass by every fifteen minutes or so and hurry his process along by combing through whatever portion His Nibs was then exposing to the two hundred watts of warmth.

If you are bathing cats because they have fleas, refer to "Fleas" in Chapter 12. It is to be hoped that your cat does not have fleas. If not, you have the option of applying the "ounce of prevention" principle. If you think there is the slightest chance of a single flea rearing its ugly head anywhere near your cat, you may want to add an herbal flea repellent or oil of eucalyptus to the second soaping or finish off with a spray of Natural Animal Coat Enhancer; see Appendix, "Product Recommendations."

One word about dry shampoo—forget it. It coats the hair, and it just doesn't work well. The tiny bit of oil it absorbs could be done away with much more efficiently by using simple cornstarch or fine cornmeal. So don't waste your money, and don't put harmful perfumes and chemicals on your cat's coat.

Grooming for Seasonal and Stress Situations

Let's face it; there may come a time when you have to be away during the spring shed. We already know that a cat will shed during a time of stress and your being away will always be stressful for your furriest friends. So if you have to be away during a shed, have your sitter add the antistress supplement to Muffy's food (see page 305). And review the suggestions in the "While You're Away" section (page 131). Groom her to a fare-thee-well right before you leave and consider the benefits of the Cape Cod Clip or the Teddy.

Most of my new clients come to me either in the middle of the summer, after the big spring shed, or after they have been away, come back, and found their Persian full of mats. The format is almost always the same. The worried guardians call me and tell me they returned after a few weeks away to find the cat totally matted: "It's never happened before, and the cat won't let me comb him—can you help?" I always reassure them that I can put the cat back in shape again. But I ask them not to touch the mats until I get there. "Pretend to the cat that you've forgotten about the mats," I say. I don't want the cat to have a fresh memory of being hurt by someone fooling around with the mats.

Almost always the cats are grateful for my help the moment they catch on to what I'm doing. It happens again and again, and yet I'm always awed by how much a cat can understand. I get the guardian to talk to the cat about interesting things that happen in the cat's life, and this helps the cat to focus on his beloved human's voice rather than on the nerve-racking process of Anitra cutting out the mats. The poor guardians are always contrite, assuring me over and over again that this could not possibly have happened if they'd been home and it had certainly never happened before.

It doesn't ever have to happen again even if you do go away or some other stress situation occurs such as moving, sickness in the family, or anything that might be stressful to the cat and might keep you from the necessary daily grooming. All you have to do to prevent it is to plan in advance and take "a stitch in time." Half the battle is keeping the nutrition at a high level and doubling the amount of lecithin in the Anitra's Vita-Mineral Mix during times of stress. This makes the hair easier to groom. If you know already that your cat has a tendency toward either diarrhea or constipation when under stress, double the bran as well. If it is a Persian, trim more widely around the anus and inner thigh. My own Persians are always clipped down in those places as a matter of course.

Be very specific about the feeding instructions you give to whomever is going to take care of the cat. Now is certainly not the time to be lax. I am always surprised when guardians do not give detailed instructions for feeding to the person taking care of the cat in their absence. Even if they're paying the person, they seem to feel that it's enough to ask someone to care for Muffy and they don't want to ask the sitter to fuss with any sort of special dietary requirements. I tell these people that they are dead wrong.

First of all, sitters in general are very nice people. Just put yourself in the place of the sitter. What most nice sitters want more than anything else is to be given as *much* information as possible about how best to keep your pet in top physical shape until you get back. Taking care of someone else's cat is a heavy responsibility, even if it is also a great delight, so help them out; tell them everything. There is nothing more distressing to the sitter than to have to call you long-distance because Muffy had diarrhea and soiled her bloomers.

Even if your sitter declares that he or she will enjoy combing the cat, it's safest to clip the hair short, at least in the armpits, around the anus, and along the inner thigh. How far you extend the clipping depends on whether your cat's coat is easy to groom or long, thick, and difficult to groom. The principle is to clip down to an inch any and all hair that might present a problem to the neophyte groomer. Remember when you began grooming the cat, and recall which areas of the cat's fur tend to mat up first. You will definitely want to clip those areas shorter.

Clarence Eckroate's coat is sparse and silky. It's supereasy to groom, and Clarence's personality falls under the heading of "old sweetie pie." Normally we don't even clip his armpits. However, if Norma were to take a business trip in the middle of the shedding season, I would advise a modest trim in the armpits and around the anus just to be on the safe side.

Pandy Kaufman's coat is quite thick. Besides, she is a high-strung cat who has never learned to enjoy her groomings. Her guardian, Diane, and I have decided that it's wise to keep a jump ahead of the mats by clipping Pandy's armpits, leg creases, anus, and inner thighs every single month. Pandy is nervous enough during her grooming, which she barely puts up with. If a mat forms anywhere in the furs, Pandy knows it, focuses on it, and imagines all sorts of dire consequences that could befall her during that mat's removal. With Pandy, it's much wiser and kinder to clip too much rather than too little.

When Diane goes away, we go all out—stopping just short of the "Teddy Clip" (see "Method 1," page 201, and "Method 2," page 202). We trim down to less than a quarter inch all the hair on Pandy's abdomen, inner thighs, armpits, and chest. I extend the clipping line of the armpits and leg creases right up Pandy's sides toward the shoulder blades and hip bones respectively. When we're finished and place Pandy on the floor, she gives an irate shake, and as she stalks off we can see that she has so much fluffiness left that no one would ever be able to detect our sneaky clipping without turning Pandy upside down. Knowing Pandy, I can't see how that's likely to happen.

Sammy Levy's coat is the longest and thickest that I've ever seen. Sammy is a fabulous brown tabby Persian. His ruff hairs measure about four-and-half inches from root to tip. Sammy is a darling, but his health is rather delicate, and there have been a couple of times over the years when Sammy's coat became greasy and full of dandruff as a result of a breakdown in his physical health. He enjoys grooming to a certain extent but is supersensitive, and when he falls ill that sensitivity increases.

During his first illness, his guardian and I agreed that Sammy's comfort came first. We sacrificed the beautiful, thick, soft hair of his inner thighs, abdomen, chest, and so on. I gave him the same sort of clip I used on Pandy. With Sammy, I also took off part of the skirts and the fronts of the thighs. The clipping was so extensive that one could easily see the difference in Sammy's shape as he walked about. But Sammy loved it; on hot summer days, he'd lay his abdomen against the cool bathroom tiles and sleep with a contented smile on his face. Because the worst areas of potential matting were now eliminated, Sammy could again relax and enjoy the luxury of his biweekly grooming during his convalescence.

One thing I do every month when I see my regular longhaired clients is clip off all the fur in the armpits and about a half-inch of fur around the anus in a circle because these are the prime areas for matting. If the bloomers are full and fluffy, I also clip a "free-fall area" underneath the anus by clipping short some of the hair of the bloomers on the back of the inner thighs. More than one vet has told me he always knows when a Persian has Anitra as his groomer. They all have that neat little trim around the genitals.

When I clip armpits and the anal area, I cut the hair down to less than a sixteenth of an inch. No one but you and the pussycat will know that beneath that fluffy exterior the armpits are bare—unless, of course, your cat does a lot of waving.

To satisfy public demand, I have had to devise what I call the "Cape Cod Clip." This is for guardians who are taking their cats on summer vacation to woodsy, weedy, sandy, buggy areas full of briars and brambles. I had to think of a way to protect the cat from the sun above, leave most of the ruff and tail, satisfy the cat psychologically, and get rid of most of the cat's hair because no one wanted to bother with it in the wilderness. At the same time, my professional eye insisted that I end up with a cat who was still aesthetically pleasing.

I dubbed it the "Cape Cod Clip" in honor of the first cat I tried it on. Mimi was, as you may have guessed, bound for Cape Cod. She was an elderly tabby Persian with a medium-thick coat. I did the extensive clipping in the armpits, extending the clipping halfway up on both sides of the chest, and then clipped the chest fur down to a half inch. Beginning with the lower part of the ruff, I left the hair above longer and longer to blend the short chest hair in with her medium-length ruff. When working on a cat with a very long ruff of three or four inches, I usually trim the ruff hair down so it is no longer than two inches. I trim the leg creases, inner thighs, abdomen, and backs of inner thighs down to an eighth of an inch or less. If the cat has long, silky ankle feathers, I trim them right down, leaving the remaining inner leg fur about a quarter inch long. I trim the outer thighs down to a quarter or half inch, and about halfway up the thigh I allow the length of hair to increase so that, for about four inches on both sides of the spine, the hair is left at normal length to protect the cat from the sun. That area is very easy to groom, anyway.

From the long hair around the top of the cat's back to the very short hair on the abdomen, I simply taper gradually. For aesthetic reasons, you may want to cut off as much as a half inch from the underside of the tail, but *only near the anus* in order to taper the tail into the anal clip. Caution: don't cut the hair on the tail unless it's matted or badly soiled. Tail hair takes many months to grow in again.

On returning from Cape Cod, Mimi's guardian informed me that she was frequently asked what kind of a cat she had. People thought her cat was quite lovely and wondered where they could get one like her. She had a hard time convincing them that Mimi was a classic tabby Persian sporting her Cape Cod Clip.

When the first edition of this book was published in 1981, I'd never considered an all-over clip. Whenever I groomed, I always tried to save as much hair as possible. I thought that's what a cat would want. But my own cats corrected that assumption. It was they who taught me the many uses of the Teddy, and it was on them that I learned the technique and perfected the necessary skills. I and hundreds of other cats are grateful for their generosity and patience.

The Teddy begins like a Cape Cod Clip, clipping down the undersides and genital area to one-quarter inch or less. All the rest of the coat is clipped down evenly to between three-quarters of an inch and one-and-a-half inches. It's a very youthful look. When Persian kittens are born, their fur is all the same length, without the long fur on the ruff, cheeks, or bloomers; that comes later. So a Teddy makes a Persian look like the biggest kitten in the world.

Method 1

To achieve a nice, even one- to one-and-a-half-inch length, first thoroughly groom the coat. No mats or tangles, please. Then, use the scissors to separate a very thin line of hair. Tilt the scissors so the flats of both blades are lying against the skin. *Do not close the scissors.* You never cut the hair this close to the skin with the scissors positioned at this angle. Instead of cutting, lift the scissors slowly away from the body and stop at the length you want the hair to be. Then cut, never changing the angle of the scissors. To achieve a nice smooth finish, (a) clip a very thin line of hair each time, and (b) always include a bit of the already clipped hair along with the unclipped hair. Lift the scissors out and away from the body, and when you reach the ends of the clipped hair, you know that's where to cut the unclipped hair so that it all ends up the same length.

There are going to be some little irregularities, of course. This is, after all, a hand-clipped Teddy, so much classier than a shaved clip! So when does your cat need a new haircut? I find the Teddy reaches its peak of adorableness somewhere between one and three months, but you must judge for yourself.

Method 2

This method gives a slightly rougher appearance than method 1, like a shorn lamb, which has its own charms. It's very easy and very reassuring to the groomer because it is so safe. As with method 1, separate thin lines of hair to be clipped, but do it with the index and middle fingers of the stroking hand. Keep your fingers in a "nails up, palm down" position, and stop with the fingers resting lightly against the cat's body and the line of hair protruding up between the fingers. As above, hold the scissors with the flat sides of the blades facing the cat's body (against your fingers) and cut off the protruding line of hair right above your fingers. The resulting Teddy will be as long as the diameter of your fingers.

Often, I'll do a Teddy for some specific reason: the guardian doesn't want the coat to mat up while he's out of town, or we decide to clip the coat down for the summer. Then the cat shows us how much he enjoys it so we end up doing it more and more frequently.

My client Sara has four beautiful longhairs. One of them, Boo, is a very large black smoke Persian with a white moustache that makes him look like he ought to be cast in one of those "Got milk?" commercials. His undercoat is thick enough to see any cat comfortably through an arctic winter, but Boo believes firmly that twenty minutes is long enough for any cat to stand on a kitchen counter and put up with Anitra fussing with his furs. After that, my friendly, good-natured Boo hisses, wiggles, growls, and hits my comb hand with claws unsheathed. Mind you, he never actually hurts me, but he does make himself quite clear, "Your twenty minutes are up!"

The Teddy was our only way to achieve a perfectly groomed coat within Boo's time limit. Boo found it to be such a good idea that he now allows me an extra five minutes. Sara is delighted too. The Teddy shows off Boo's perfect, muscular physique, and his black smoke undercoat is now revealed in all its splendor. Boo was always attractive; now he's the handsomest cat in the tristate area.

My own little blue Persian, Princess, doesn't *need* a Teddy. Her furs are like the finest silk; they never mat, and she's groomed every morning before breakfast anyway. But she's loved the Teddy ever since I first clipped her down years ago before leaving on vacation. She begins badgering me at the first hint of warm weather. Not only that, she tries to wheedle me into it the minute our building's heat turns on in the winter. She loves being able to stroke her tongue right down to the skin on the first lick, and she adores the feel of the cool air on her skin when she lounges against the window screen. Besides, under all that blue Persian fur is a figure that could stop traffic.

Princess is my hostess, Fluff City's official greeter. There are always a lot of "oooohs" and "ahhhhs" from visitors when Princess comes to greet them, but I've noticed their voices go up an octave when she trots up to them in the Teddy clip. They can't keep their hands off her, and they tend to chuckle a lot when they touch her. That's just fine with Princess. Her mission in life is to tranquilize humanity with her furs. The Teddy is just one of her tools of the trade.

Interspecies Communication 9

All animals, and I am happy to say that includes you and me, communicate without words. Most humans are simply not aware of what they're sending and receiving. We humans rely on spoken language, so over the centuries we stopped focusing on other forms of communication. It's not that we lost the ability; we just didn't practice them anymore. Cats and other animals normally communicate through what we humans describe as "extra sensory perception," or ESP. To the cats it's not "extra," it's just as natural and ordinary as being able to smell when their guardian opens a can of sardines.

Every one of us, cats and humans alike, sends and receives impressions and communications in three modes: thought pictures (visual), sensory impressions (kinesthetic), and emotions and feelings (emotional). We humans are very visual; cats tend to be kinesthetic. They focus on odors, flavors, and textures more than we do.

We humans are communicating with our animals at all times. Most of us are not consciously aware of this. A professional interspecies communicator is someone who has learned to be aware and to consciously practice this skill. There are gifted and accomplished communicators available all around the country. Many offer classes and workshops. Each communicator is usually skilled in several areas, such as understanding physical sensations (where it hurts), finding lost animals, working out emotional problems, environmental problems, and group dynamic problems. Each communicator usually discovers his unique specialty.

When I first became aware of the possibility of developing this skill, I was hesitant. The concept was new to me, and I was wary of being like the sorcerer's apprentice who caused a lot of damage because he didn't understand how to use the knowledge he had. At the same time, I couldn't resist the opportunity to learn something that could help me to understand the animals better. I finally realized that just because I acquire information or a skill, it doesn't mean that I'm obliged to use it. It would be perfectly all right to hold the skill in reserve, verifying it by other means (asking others for their impressions or asking the vet to run tests), and acting upon it only if I was sure that such actions could do no harm.

If you have skipped ahead in this book and tried "Therapeutic Communication" (page 262) or "Affirmation and Visualization" (page 217), you have already taken a step or two in this direction. Here are a few suggestions for proceeding further:

- First, acknowledge that you really do want to explore further and know more.
- Acknowledge that you can go forward without any expectation of benefit or success and that the exploration itself will be satisfaction enough for you.
- Be respectful. Always ask the animal's permission to start communicating. Ask her to help you understand. If she says no, then accept her decision.
- Open your mind to any possibility. Accept whatever you pick up—an emotion, a picture, a kinesthetic (sense) impression, a phrase, or even nothing.
- If you want to convey a message, you must always remember that animals don't understand negatives. "I won't *(negative)* hurt you." The animal picks up "you" and "him" and "harm." Danger! What you really want to convey is something like "You're safe here." If you convey, "Don't *(negative)* scratch the sofa," the cat will pick up your thought picture as "sofa," "cat," and "scratching"—*without understanding the negative*. He may even run right over and do what you seem to be suggesting. What you really want him to pick up is, "Scratch on the post." So that's what you need to send him.
- Cats are kinesthetic (sensual), therefore emphasize sensory impressions when you can: "Dig your claws into that post! Feel the rough fabric under your pads. Ummmmm, nice!"
- Always include the appropriate emotion in your communication. Without emotion, the animal won't receive it. Samantha Khury, a very skilled and

sensitive interspecies communicator, teaches that "emotion is like the stamp that makes the letter go." You can write the greatest letter in the world, but if you forget to put the stamp on the envelope, no one will receive it. "Stretch up there and rip and tear and pull! Oh, what a strong cat!"

• Always remember that if a cat communicates with you clearly, that does not necessarily make him "right." Cats, like us, can sometimes be mistaken or limited and reach mistaken or limited conclusions. By the same token, humans are perfectly capable of misinterpretation.

The last suggestion brings to mind an elderly, green-eyed white Siamese mix named Ralph-O who presented me with just such a situation.

Ralph-O was supposed to receive subcutaneous hydration therapy as part of his treatment for kidney disease. Walt, his guardian, called to tell me that Ralph-O was wiggling so much that he couldn't give him the fluids he needed.

I had coached Walt on his fluid-giving technique, and he seemed to have it down pretty well. He had called once before to report that all was not going smoothly, and I had suggested that he ask his local vet if one of the technicians could check out his procedure. Still, the problems persisted. I wondered what it was about the procedure that was upsetting Ralph-O.

A professional interspecies communicator who I knew and respected was in town, so I suggested we take Ralph-O to see him. The session lasted a half hour. We left Ralph-O with the communicator and returned later. Besides information on how to make the fluid therapy more to Ralph-O's liking, Walt had also asked if there was anything else that his beloved Ralph-O would like him to do, or change, or give him.

Ralph-O made several requests. We were told that he missed the piano.

"Oh, yes," said Walt. "It used to be by the door when he was a kitten. Ralph-O always stood on top of the piano whenever anyone came in the door." Walt decided then and there to move a bookcase to that spot so Ralph-O could again greet guests from a lofty perch.

"There is one other thing," the communicator said, "but I don't know what it is. He keeps showing me something—a picture of something you used to give him to eat but . . . it looks like green mashed potatoes."

I was complete mystified. "What in the world . . ." I turned to Walt.

"Oh, wow," Walt shook his head, "that's the baby food peas. I remember; he used to like them a lot." Walt was amazed at the skill of the communicator.

Then we got the bad news. "Ralph-O hates the hydration," our communicator told us, sadly. "He says it hurts and he would rather die than continue to be hydrated."

I was in shock. Walt whispered, "You mean put him to sleep?"

The communicator nodded. "I can only tell you what he said."

I knew the communicator to be excellent and of the highest standards and I was the one responsible for sending Walt and Ralph-O to him. I felt like I was the one responsible for killing Ralph-O! That was ridiculous, I told myself as we headed home in the cab.

Ralph-O rode inside his case on Walt's lap. "I guess this is what is called a rock and a hard place," Walt murmured. "He feels terrible when he's not hydrated and terrible when he is. So," Walt sighed, "I guess I have to put him to sleep."

I have never been comfortable with rushing into things. "Let's not make any decisions until we think it through," I said. "He's all right for now; why don't you pick up some baby food peas and let him enjoy that tonight and we'll talk tomorrow."

Before dinner, I took the subway down to Integral Yoga and took a class. After supper, I sat down to think. I began by acknowledging that I really did want to find out what the correct action would be even if I didn't like it. After going over the whole situation in my mind, several facts became clear.

First and foremost, I realized, we were all so impressed with the fact that Ralph-O really communicated that all of us, including the communicator, had forgotten that Ralph-O was a cat—a normal cat with a normal cat's mind. He was not omniscient; in fact, his experience was quite limited. He had said that hydration hurt and he would rather die than experience further hydration because he thought that what Walt was doing was the only way it could be done. Apparently, when I was over there in the apartment teaching Walt and giving Ralph-O the fluids myself, he had felt next to nothing. So later when Walt gave him the fluids unsupervised, he didn't associate it with what I had done. It felt "different"; it hurt. In Ralph-O's mind, what Walt had done was "hydration" and what I had done was "nothing." He didn't know that hydration wasn't supposed to hurt. In fact, it never hurts if it's done properly. It's not unusual for cats to come running when they know the fluids are being heated up for them. I realized with a flood of relief that the problem was the way Walt was giving him the fluids. Walt was not known for his manual dexterity.

A win-win situation was possible. Ralph-O was adverse to the subcutaneous hydration only because "it hurt." The next day, I called Walt and suggested we try just one more thing. Walt arranged for the nice vet technician who had helped to teach him how to give the fluids to come over and give Ralph-O his hydration. When the tech finished, Ralph-O was still waiting for him to begin.

Ralph-O receives his hydration three times a week now. He and the vet tech have become good buddies, and Ralph-O actually seems to enjoy his hydration sessions. I think that the tablespoonful of baby food peas afterward might have something to do with it.

Selecting Methods of Treatment and Seeking Professional Help 10

The veterinarians I work with are open to and frequently encourage therapies such as homeopathy, acupuncture, chiropractic, flower essences, herbs, nutrition, behavior modification, stress reduction techniques, interspecies communication, nutraceuticals, and healing touch modalities such as reiki and Tellington TTouch. In this section, I will give an overview of some of these modalities. (Interspecies communication is discussed in a chapter of its own; see chapter 9.)

Homeopathy

Homeopathy is the medical science that cures by using the law of similars to stimulate the body's immune response. It was developed in Vienna during the late 1700s by Dr. Samuel Hahnemann. He found that giving the patient a substance that would produce the same symptoms as the disease he was suffering from would stimulate the patient's own immune system to fight the disease. Not only would the patient be cured, but he would also end up more resistant to the disease than he was before he got it.

If a patient has a cold with a runny nose and red irritated eyes, the homeopath might prescribe allium cepa, which is made from the juice of red onion. We all know how a red onion can make the nose run and the eyes feel irritated. In homeopathic form, this would prompt the body to deal with the runny, irritated eyes and nose.

Dr. Hahnemann taught that symptoms of illness are the body's normal, constructive response to an intolerable situation. Homeopathy supports and enhances that response. Giving a homeopathic remedy is like sending a message loud and clear to the body's immune system saying, "Here's what's wrong; now wake up and *do* something!" More than 1,500 remedies exist.

Dr. Hahnemann made another major discovery: the principle of the minimum dose. He diluted his remedies by 1 part to 1,000, 1 part to 1 million, 1 part to 1 billion, and even more, and then he shook them vigorously hundreds or thousands of times. His research revealed that the more a substance was diluted and shaken, the more potent it became. Diluting and shaking release and enhance the intrinsic curative energy in the basic molecules of the substance. It can even be diluted so much that no actual molecules remain and only the energy is present. The more dilute it becomes, the stronger it will be. (Less is more.)

Homeopathic remedies often cause a slight increase of symptoms at first. Then the immune system kicks in and overcomes the disease. If drugs have been used in the past, the homeopath may first have to prescribe a remedy to undo their adverse effects and help the body expel the residue before he can begin to treat the disease.

All of my veterinarians—Dr. Pitcairn, Dr. Gil, and Dr. Dym—are classical homeopaths. They all live far away, so my local veterinarian and I consult them by phone. I have never found any disease or behavior problem that did not respond favorably to homeopathy. Tumors, skin rashes, wetting outside the box, attacking people, diabetes, kidney disease, leukemia—I've seen them all turn into a dim unpleasant memory after a classical homeopathic veterinarian was consulted as part of a comprehensive program of natural treatment. I always designate the homeopath as the one in charge.

When the first edition of this book was published in 1981, I knew one homeopathic veterinarian and learned there were a few more scattered around the country. In those days, a veterinary homeopath was looked upon like a sorcerer in some states. They were both persecuted and prosecuted by the conventional medical powers. I personally know of a vet who lost his license for "using untried methods." Never mind that homeopathy has been in use since the 1700s and antibiotics were not invented until World War II—or the fact that the English royal family has had a personal homeopathic physician for many generations.

Now, in the twenty-first century, things are quite different. The public is clamoring for alternative treatments, and a veterinary clinic will attract many more clients if at least one of the vets is a homeopath. Problems arise when conventional, allopathic veterinarians try to use homeopathic remedies in an allopathic manner. Homeopathy is not just the remedies—but *how* they are used.

As mentioned above, the veterinary homeopaths that I work with are all classical. Classical homeopathy is a very long and involved study that can last a lifetime. Many students become impatient and drop out after a certain amount of time—looking for ways to speed up the results. Their methods may include injecting homeopathic remedies into acupuncture points and using a pendulum to aid in choosing a remedy. I don't say these methods are wrong; they may yield valuable new information at some future time. However, I do point out that they are not part of a classical homeopathic approach.

Guidelines to Finding a Veterinary Homeopath

Below are some guidelines that will help you determine whether the homeopath you have found practices classical homeopathy.

1. The classical homeopath will ask questions, many of which will seem unrelated to your cat's problem. The homeopathic prescription (the choice of remedy) is based on *all* of the symptoms present, regardless of whether they seem to be related to the main symptom. This includes the cat's preferences, habits, and emotional state. The conventional name of the disease has little influence upon a classical homeopath's prescription, although it is helpful in determining the prognosis and in selecting which symptoms are most important.

2. Remedies are given orally, not injected.

3. History of past illnesses is very useful to a classical homeopath.

4. Remedies are given only one at a time, never together or alternating. Each remedy is given plenty of time to work and will be evaluated before a different one is prescribed.

5. Food herbs such as psyllium or slippery elm may be used at the same time as homeopathic remedies. However, allopathic drugs and vaccines, medicinal herbs, Chinese herbs, and acupuncture are never used in conjunction with classical homeopathy because they will interfere with the curative response of the patient to the remedy.

6. Surgery is almost never recommended during homeopathic treatment. As Dr. Pitcairn has often said, "If you cut it out, you can't cure it." Also,

213

surgical removal of a tumor, wart, or other lesion makes it much more difficult for the patient to respond to the remedy.

7. If the animal already has a history of medication with allopathic drugs, a classical prescriber will work with the guardian to gradually eliminate these drugs. Even if the disease is incurable, using the best selected remedy or series of remedies plus good nutrition will give your companion the longest and best quality life.

Acupuncture and Traditional Chinese Medicine

Veterinary acupuncturists are trained in Traditional Chinese Medicine (TCM). In other words, acupuncture is a part of TCM. According to TCM, all illness is due to energy imbalances within the body and stimulation of specific points will correct those imbalances. The points treated are on the meridian lines, which are energy pathways that travel below the skin's surface. These energy pathways form a network that connects all parts of the body, including the circulatory, lymphatic, muscular, and nervous systems. Stimulation of the acupuncture points can be done with acupuncture needles; moxibustion (burning the herb mugwort near the point); electrical stimulation; or acupressure (also called shiatsu), a technique in which pressure is put on the points with the fingers. Acupressure or shiatsu can be used at the same time as homeopathy; acupuncture cannot.

Cats and other animals don't seem to find the insertion of the very fine acupuncture needles at all disturbing or painful, and in fact, they seem to like the treatments. That's probably due to the body's release of chemicals called endorphins during acupuncture. Endorphins have been referred to as "natural opiates" because they act on the same nerve cells as morphine and other opiate drugs, helping muscles relax and dulling pain.

Acupuncture is used to treat many different types of illness and injury, including musculoskeletal problems; skin diseases and allergic dermatitis; and respiratory, gastrointestinal, and cardiac problems. However, veterinarians use it mostly to relieve chronic pain, with arthritis among the most commonly treated conditions. TCM incorporates the use of herbs and nutrition along with acupuncture in a complementary fashion.

Chiropractic

Chiropractic is based on the concept that the skeletal system of the body, especially the spine, must be in correct alignment and that a misalignment can cause disturbances in neurological function and negatively affect the organs and other systems of the body. It involves manually adjusting misalignments, which are referred to as subluxations. A cat who has a sudden change in personality or disposition may be in discomfort. Veterinary chiropractic has successfully treated back, neck, leg, or tail pain; degenerative arthritis; disc problems; head tilt; injuries resulting from slips and falls; difficulty chewing; pain syndromes; and sciatic neuralgia. No matter what the problem is, the body will find it easier to solve that problem if it is properly aligned.

Bach Flower Remedies

Dr. Edward Bach lived in England between 1886 and 1936. In his practice of homeopathic medicine, he observed that his patients' physical ills were always preceded by mood changes. He reasoned that these emotional changes were a part of the disease and that a good doctor would be aided in his diagnosis by recognizing the moods and attitudes that usually accompany each malady. He believed that treating the emotional problem was a necessary part of treating the disease and, furthermore, that treating the emotional problem before the physical symptoms began to appear could actually prevent the disease from ever developing further.

Dr. Bach developed thirty-eight remedies to treat emotions, moods, and mental tendencies. They are all made from flowers; they are dilute, natural, gentle, and perfectly harmless. If you use the wrong remedy, the worst that will happen is nothing—zero results.

When working with an animal, you can mentally put yourself in his place and try to recognize what emotions are prompting his attitude or actions. Because cats as a species are emotionally closer to the primitive, wild state than other domestic animals, their survival mechanism is more active. Nearly all negative emotions—anger, jealousy, hatred, and so forth—are based on some type of fear.

For example, if you are introducing a new cat into a household where the old cat is very attached to his owners and possessive of his territory, you would look up fear and possessiveness in the Bach flower book. You might settle on mimulus (fear of losing home and protection, fear of future) and holly (jealousy, suspicion, envy). You might give the newcomer rock rose if she is terrified, star of Bethlehem if she has just been separated from her mother, gorse if she seems uncertain and hopeless, or heather if she is overly demanding and needy.

The most well-known and commonly used Bach flower remedy is a mixture of impatiens, star of Bethlehem, cherry plum, rock rose, and clematis; it is called Rescue Remedy. Most health food stores carry it. It is used for all forms of shock, both physical and emotional. It can be given every five minutes in severe cases.

Most health food stores carry the remedies and books explaining how to use them. Two of my favorites are *Bach Flower Therapy* by Mechthild Scheffer and *Bach Flower Remedies* by Dr. Edward Bach. I would suggest that you buy a book first; then buy the specific Bach flower remedies as you need them. It's best to use only two or three at a time. You'll gradually build up a nice little collection.

Herbs

Herbs are one of the oldest sources of healing in the world. Thousands of years ago when history was first recorded, herbs were already in use, established, and respected. How long they were in use before that, no one can be sure. In 300 BC herbal medicine was taught and practiced in the famous medical school in the cultural center of Alexandria. In AD 77 Pliny the Elder completed his *Historia Naturalis* of over one thousand herbs. During the Dark Ages monks and herb women carried on the practice. During the Renaissance herbal medicine was refined and expanded; however, this knowledge was jealously guarded. Women and nonprofessional healers were forbidden to study and practice, and many were pronounced heretics and burned at the stake. Because of this, even today some people equate herbalism with superstition and quackery.

Today the knowledge is preserved; the art and practice of herbalism persists. The herbs are there for us to use, growing in the woods and along the highways and pushing up through cracks in the pavement. It seems that Mother Nature is determined that we shall never be without her help and comfort.

After World War II, herbalism reached an all-time low. However, in recent decades people became more concerned about the side effects of drugs and wanted to take greater responsibility for their own health care. Herbal medicine is experiencing a remarkable revival.

Like any tool that has strength and power, herbs must be carefully used. Some herbs are harmless and some can damage the system if used carelessly. The Chinese divide herbs into three categories:

1. *Poison herbs.* Very strong. Having very specific benefits. Only for short-term use and allowing no margin for error. (Examples: wormwood, hemlock, and rue.)
2. *Medicinal herbs.* Strong. Having short-term specific benefits with wider margin for error, but cause reversals if used too long or too much. (Examples: golden seal and catnip.)
3. *Food herbs.* Give broader general benefits and can be used copiously and forever with no fear of negative effects and with no reversals. (Examples: parsley, slippery elm, garlic, and psyllium.)

Keep in mind that some herbs work differently on cats than they do on humans. Catnip, for example, is a stimulant and aphrodisiac for a cat, while we humans take the tea as a sedative. *Marijuana, cocoa, and marigold are all poisonous to cats.* Tea tree oil, which is an ingredient in some products for cats, has been found to be extremely toxic and I myself have found it can burn the skin. I would never use it on a cat.

Affirmation and Visualization

Primum est, non nocere: Above all, do no harm.
—Hippocrates

This quotation from Hippocrates, the father of holistic medicine, is my first and guiding rule whenever I consider a therapy for a sick or troubled animal. *Affirmations* (repeating a positive statement) and *visualizations* (mentally seeing and experiencing a situation or thing) are so simple to do that there is virtually no chance of doing any harm with them. In addition, they are free and they require no extra time. You can design them while you're driving, riding on a bus, eating—anytime at all.

They work on the philosophical principle that everything that happens must first be conceived of in the mind. Edgar Cayce, the great psychic, said, "Mind is the builder." So we go to our mind, our own thoughts, and make conscious decisions about what it is we really want to conceive of and have happen. We do this by making up a sentence describing what we want or constructing a picture or scene. We've heard for many years now about "the power of positive thinking." Affirmations are positive thoughts that we've chosen very consciously; visualizations are an extension of positive thinking and involve consciously *visualizing* in our mind's eye the positive outcome we want.

Because animals pick up our attitudes, emotions, and thoughts, it is fairly easy to see the effects of this on cat behavior. In addition, scientific experiments have shown that the effects do go further to influence speed of healing and recovery.

When I first began to practice affirmations and visualizations, my attitude was "It doesn't sound logical to me, but wiser heads than mine have said it works. So, since it won't do any harm and it won't cost anything, I might as well give it a try."

What fun I have had! It's like suddenly having a magic wand. I did make some mistakes at first; you can make mistakes. For example:

1. If you want something to happen now, think and speak in the present tense, not the future tense: "The skin is healing beautifully," *not* "The skin will heal."

2. You must be able to believe what you are saying and visualizing. Repeating the affirmation "The cut is healed; the skin is perfect" while you're looking at a newly sutured incision will definitely not work as well as the more realistic affirmation "Muffy has marvelous recuperative powers; her skin heals fast." That's what I mean when I speak of designing your affirmation. Your sentence must say exactly what you want in a believable way.

3. When designing your affirmations don't concern yourself with *how* a thing will be accomplished: "because we found the right remedy" or "now that he's home with us." Why and how are not important. Focus only on the bottom line: what it is you want.

4. Negatives *do not work*. They only call to mind what you *don't* want and therefore strengthen the possibility of the *wrong* thing happening. For example: "The wound will not become infected." Forget the possibility of infection; forget what you don't want. Concentrate on what you do want: "The wound is healing beautifully."

5. Both affirmations and visualizations work best when you include a strong emotional feeling. This is done most easily by prefacing your statement with a positive phrase such as "I'm so glad that . . . ," "We're so relieved because . . . ," or "We're delighted because . . . ," and really feeling it.

Affirmations can be used alone but work even better when combined with visualizations. The rules for both are the same, but when designing a visualization you involve as many senses as possible.

If I want an incision to be healed, in my mind I

- *See*   Myself stroking my index finger over the healed scar
- *Feel*   The soft new tissue and silky baby hair under my finger
- *Hear*   Muffy purr with comfort and satisfaction as I stroke her there
- *Taste* (Would not apply here but could be included if I were doing an affirmation about Muffy enjoying her new diet)
- *Smell* (Same as taste)

The more I practice affirmations and visualizations the more I enjoy them and the more clearly I realize what a powerful tool they are. Before long I found the rules had become automatic for me and I could design them on the spot as I needed them. Now, whenever I work with a cat, I speak and think in affirmations and visualizations.

When people ask me such questions as "How in the world do you get him to sit there so calmly while you . . ." or "However did you manage to (a) get his temperature down, (b) get his blood count up, or (c) stop the diarrhea," the answer is always the same: in holistic therapy we address problems in many ways at the same time, but one of the ways I always include is affirmation and visualization.

When Do You Need the Veterinarian?

Loving guardians are as choosy about their pet's health needs as they are about their own. You never know when an emergency will come up, so it's important to know the symptoms of illness and to have competent and caring feline health professionals to whom you can turn for expert holistic advice whenever you need it.

"The most common cause of feline death is people bringing the cat to the veterinarian too late." Every veterinarian I know has said these words to me at one time or another. It's not because the guardians are careless; it's just that it is often hard to spot the early symptoms of disease in the cat.

Cats accept pain and discomfort in their bodies just as they accept a rainstorm or a cold day. They assume there's nothing anyone can do about it, so they make the best of it and try to carry on as usual. Because they don't cry or moan or fall down, many guardians are completely in the dark about their friend's deteriorating health until the condition becomes so acute that the cat is weak from dehydration or gasping for breath because the chest is half full of fluid.

The case of Daphne comes to mind. Daphne, a tortoise shell Persian, was a perky little number adopted by a client of mine as a friend for her charming female Persian, Rags. It was I who placed Daphne with this particular lady partly because I hoped that Daphne's jaunty, devil-may-care attitude might serve as a bit of a tranquilizer for her new guardian, Carlota, who was very sweet, but rather high-strung and overprotective. I had had Daphne examined by the veterinarian just before I introduced her to her new home. At the time, Daphne had an intestinal bug, which was medicated and cleared up in less than a week. I groomed her on two occasions during the next four weeks, and my assistant cat-sat while Carlota went out of town for three days, so Daphne did not lack for expert observers. She was flirty and playful and ate like a horse the whole time.

After Carlota came back, I was surprised when she called to tell me that Daphne hadn't passed a stool for two days and asked me if I thought she should take her to the veterinarian. Ordinarily I would have said no and simply had her add ⅛ teaspoon of finely ground psyllium husks and two tablespoons of water to each of Daphne's meals and then call me again the next day. But I remembered Daphne's recent intestinal virus, and I knew that Carlota would continue to worry and pass that tension on to both her cats. So I told her to make an appointment with the veterinarian and take Daphne in right away.

During the course of the examination, Carlota mentioned to the veterinarian that she noticed that Daphne made a funny little noise when she breathed. The veterinarian listened with the stethoscope, and then he listened again—and again. Then he took an X-ray. Sweet, playful, flirty Daphne had pneumonia. Her chest was filling up with fluid, and she had a temperature of 104.5 degrees F (normal cat temperature is about 101 degrees F).

Daphne is feeling fine and healthy now, thanks to the veterinarian's diagnosis and treatment and to Carlota's "overprotective" ways and devoted nursing care. The point of this narrative is that Daphne's pneumonia was discovered almost by accident. If she hadn't had constipation, she might have been allowed to continue to "breathe funny" until her chest was so full of fluid that she couldn't breathe at all. After all, the veterinarian had seen her four weeks before, and both my assistant and I had seen her in the intervening time. Because she didn't act sick, we didn't suspect that she was.

The best advice I can give guardians is this: any change in your cat's usual behavior patterns should be carefully watched. If it persists or if two or three questionable changes occur, call and run it by your holistic health care professional. The first step toward nipping a problem in the bud is reaching out for expert input. Remember, cats don't know that you have the power to make them better, so they are not going to come and tell you if something feels bad. But don't worry and dwell on all the negative possibilities. There is no one better equipped than you, the loving guardian, to spot little changes that could spell trouble and correct them long before they become serious.

Of course, the annual visit to the veterinarian for a physical and dental examination and teeth cleaning is wonderfully reassuring and sometimes uncovers a small trouble long before it becomes serious. Over the years, many guardians have told me stories about taking a beloved animal to the veterinarian for no better reason than "She looked worried to me." In every single case, the guardian was right; illness of one sort or another was discovered in the beginning stages and was diagnosed and treated. Honor your own good instincts.

If you notice a symptom, don't panic; it could be nothing. Observe whether a symptom persists or if there is more than one symptom present. You can go through the checklist below. It will help you gather information that you can make note of and then convey to your holistic professional by phone. He will usually ask questions and the checklist will prepare you to answer them, so that the two of you can decide whether your feline friend needs to go in to the office for hands-on examination.

Checklist of Symptoms

- *Vomiting* is usually not serious unless repeated. It could be that the body is simply trying to rid itself of something. Cats vomit more frequently than humans because of their short intestine. Vomiting hair balls is a good thing; it's what they should do if they swallow too much fur. If the vomited matter looks like a small wet hot dog, it is a hairball. This is *not* a symptom of something wrong; it is normal and natural. Cats can also vomit food if they eat too fast or too much or if the food is too hot or too cold. If none of these reasons apply and if food is vomited repeatedly or if food is vomited hours after it is eaten, that is noteworthy and should be reported. If something other than food or hair balls is vomited, such as mucus or foam, especially if it is yellow or red, then you must note the color, consistency, amount, frequency, and how soon after eating it occurs. Repeated swallowing should also be noted.

- *Loss of appetite* is usually not serious unless prolonged. Cats don't eat the same amount every day. Temperature, stress, a recent snack, a large meal the day before, or leaving food available between meals can ruin the cat's appetite. However, a low-grade infection, nausea, painful gums, dirty or abscessed teeth, constipation, dehydration or any one of several diseases can also cause anorexia. Cats won't eat what they can't smell; a stuffy nose can also cause poor appetite (see "Giving Nose Drops," page 276). Offer a tiny serving so you can see precisely how much your cat is actually eating. You can always give seconds. Keep accurate track of his intake.

- *Claw biting* is a normal part of the cat's grooming procedure, but it could also signal an infection, a split claw with something caught in it, an ingrown claw, or it may be because of dirty cuticles. Check claws, cuticles, and pads. (See "Claw and Cuticle Problems," page 344.)

- *Dirty cuticles* (especially on back claws). A buildup of waxy dirt around the cuticle is a sure sign the cat is scratching at something that itches and is exuding a discharge, usually an ear. The cuticle dirt can infect the toe. Try to find the source of the problem. Check for waxy ears, skin problems, and tooth and gum problems—any of which could lead to dirty cuticles. (See "Soaking Feet and Cleaning Cuticles," page 282.)

- *Excessive sleeping* happens naturally after a big meal or if the cat is bored due to lack of stimulation, or if he's a senior citizen. It also happens during the spring and autumn sheds, but it could also mean the cat's body is fighting off an infection. It could also signal a weak heart, liver, or kidneys. Make note of it and check for other symptoms.

- *Withdrawing or sitting facing the wall* can be signs of depression that indicate stress or inner tension. You need to find out why. It usually means the cat is mourning or in pain or feeling very sick. Hiding, sitting in the litter box, or pressing his forehead against things are also signs of pain. Change of preferred perches and resting places could be caused by a whim or by a change in the weather but also could have a more serious significance, especially if accompanied by a change of temperature preference—such as suddenly seeking warmth (the radiator or under a lamp) or coolness (the bathroom tiles). Kidney and cancer patients seek warmth; hypothyroid patients seek cool spots.

- *Coughing:* if a coughing spell happens while you're petting or grooming around the throat, you may have accidentally touched the cough reflex. In that case, don't worry; it will pass. It could also be due to a temporary irritation, an infection, or something caught in the throat. If it persists there may be a serious obstruction in the throat or windpipe, upper respiratory infection, asthma, pneumonia, roundworms, heart problem, or other serious disease. Note the frequency and duration of coughing spells, when they started and when they happen (for example, after exertion or when he wakes up or after eating, and so on).

- *Sneezing* tells us the cat is trying to discharge something through the nose. The cause can be any sudden sharp smell or sudden temperature change. Environmental causes can be dust, cigarette smoke, room deodorizer, fabric softener, or some of the same things that cause coughing. It might also be caused by an upper respiratory or eye infection or tumor or polyps in the nose or sinuses. Note whether the sneezing produces any discharge and what color it is. Keep the same type of notes as for coughing above.

- *Eyes.* The pupils should both be the same size. They should get small when looking into a light. Face your cat toward a lamp; then cover the cat's eyes with your hand for 10 seconds. When you uncover the eyes, the pupils should be large and then get smaller as you watch. If the pupils are different sizes, alert your veterinarian immediately. Conjunctive tissue around the eyes should be a pleasant pink, not inflamed. Gently draw the skin away from around the eye and note the color of the conjunctive tissue. If it is too light, the cat may be anemic; too red or bloodshot means irritation indicating that an infection, an allergy, or a foreign body is present. Note also if your cat refuses to let you touch the eye.

Discharge collecting in the corner of the eye may be chronic in some cats. Note the color of the discharge: brown is usually not serious; white, mucusy, yellow, greenish, or red discharge should be reported to your veterinarian at once. Copious discharge, whether it is clear or colored, could mean blocked tear ducts, upper respiratory infection, or infected gums. (See also "Eye Problems," page 368.)

- *Scratching mouth with claws or "chewing air" with head tilted.* Something may be caught in the teeth or throat, or there may be painful gum infection, rotten teeth, or an abscess.
- *Scratching head with hind feet* could be due to ear discharge or infection, fleas, mange mites, ear mites, ringworm, an allergic reaction, or a tumor.
- *Shaking head.* See "Scratching head" above. Could also be an inner ear, semicircular canal problem, or brain problem.
- *Stumbling, staggering, or tilting head* could be serious and should be reported double-quick. See "Scratching head" and "Shaking head" above. Also check the pupilary reflex and relative size of both pupils (see "Eyes" above).
- *Licking genitals or "scooting" on rugs,* and the like indicates irritation and/ or itching. Check stool (see below). Have veterinarian check stool sample for parasites or check cat for possible anal gland problems. Also watch urination habits for symptoms of feline urologic syndrome (see "Urine" below and see "Feline Urologic Syndrome (FUS)," page 384).
- *Urine and urinary habits.* The urine output should wet at least a teaspoon of litter each time the cat goes to the box. If your cat voids a smaller amount or nothing at all and runs frequently to the litter, take him immediately to the veterinarian to check for feline urologic syndrome (FUS) and bladder stones. If he voids a normal amount or more than normal and runs frequently to the box this could signal kidney disease or diabetes, especially if the urine is very light yellow or almost colorless and if you also note copious drinking. (Urine should be yellow and have an easily discernible smell.) Take him to the veterinarian immediately. To check color, cover the litter with a white paper towel. If the urine turns it pink there is blood in the urine, which is very serious, and the cat should be taken to the veterinarian at once (even in the middle of the night). Very light yellow or clear with little odor usually means kidney problems as mentioned above. If your cat starts his urination in a squatting posi-

tion but then gradually raises his rear until, sometimes, the stream shoots out over the edge of the box, this could mean arthritic hips, stress in the environment, such as a new cat, or, more seriously, straining because of urinary infection and possible blockage. Report this to your veterinarian. Urination outside the box is almost always caused by a physical problem: early FUS or, in aging cats, weak bladder, general debilitation, or arthritis. (See "Special Litter Box Considerations for the Elder or Ailing Cat," page 110, and "Soiling Outside the Box," page 106.)

- *Stool.* The cat should pass stool once or twice a day. It should be formed (long) in two or three pieces, no more, and it should be softly firm and dark brown. Note any deviation. Diarrhea is sometimes not noticed because the cat covers it and mixes it with the litter. Check the stool once a day, and note the frequency, color, texture, and smell. A too-strong smell can mean intestinal infection or imbalance. Flatulence indicates putrifaction or irritable bowel syndrome (see page 420). Diarrhea can be caused by dairy products in some cats. Many cats get diarrhea when taking antibiotics (see page 242). If stool is not passed every day or is hard or appears in balls, note this and see the section on constipation (page 347). Check for excess shedding (see below), lack of dietary fiber, dehydration, kidney disease, hyperthyroidism, diabetes, or irritable bowel syndrome.

- *Coat.* Except in the shedding seasons (April through June and September and October), shedding should be moderate. Skin should be clean, free of parasites and scabs, hair free of dandruff and oil. Note any deviation and look for further symptoms.

- *Bad smell* can indicate serious problems—find the source of the problem at once. Usually caused by germs and putrefaction, infected or dirty ears, intestinal blockage, impacted anal glands, worms, dirty teeth, licking coat with dirty mouth, soiling on the fur near the anus, or kidney disease.

- *Twitching skin* can be caused by dry skin due to indoor heating during the winter months or from lack of fat in diet or vitamin E deficiency. Examine the cat for scabs and parasites. Twitching skin can also happen because of heart disease or a brain problem.

- *Temperature* should be 100.5 to 101.5 degrees F. The cat's temperature fluctuates more than ours does. Excitement and stress, as well as infection, can cause it to go up. The body may need a high temperature to help destroy invading germs. A low temperature is usually more serious than a high one. (See "Taking the Temperature," on page 290.) If you learn to do this at home, you will be able to give valuable information to your veterinarian.

- *Frequent drinking* always signals dehydration. A normal cat drinks only about twice a week because cats were originally desert animals. More frequent drinking can be caused by too much salt in the diet (most commercial foods). The cat needs to drink more than normal to wash the salt out of the system and avoid dehydration. Frequent drinking is always an attempt to wash too much of something out of the body. Kidney disease, diabetes, and hyperthyroidism all cause excessive drinking because the patient is trying to rid the body of excess creatinine, sugar, or thyroxin, respectively. When these diseases become advanced and the patient can't drink enough to do the job, the body robs its own fluids and the cat becomes dehydrated. There are several signs you can look for such as lack of appetite, constipation, and frequent drinking. Sitting with the head over the water dish, the coat separating into "clumps," a pinched look to the face, or eyes that appear to be sunken are signs of dehydration. This is an indication of serious illness and is often the last stage before collapse. To test the skin, grab a handful of skin at the neck scruff. Grasp it tightly, but don't pull it up; just let it go. It should flatten back into place at once. If it stays in a pinched position or if the cat shakes himself to get it to flatten back into place, he may be dehydrated. Dehydration makes a cat feel nauseated and headachy. The veterinarian can do a blood test to determine the cause. (See "Subcutaneous Hydration," page 297.)
- *Shallow breathing.* Breathing that is shallow and fast often happens when the cat is purring and means nothing. On the other hand, shallow and fast breathing can also be caused by heat, stress, fear, fluid retention, a tumor in the chest or abdomen, pain, or nausea. Breathing with the mouth open is usually a very bad sign.
- *Labored breathing* can be seen by watching the side of the cat's body. The abdomen or the chest should not have to move in or out too deeply or too forcefully. The nostrils should not become larger and then smaller with every breath. Labored breathing is a very serious situation.
- *Pale whitish ears, gums, or tongue* can mean anemia, shock, or a weak heart. The veterinarian will want to see the cat and will probably suggest some tests.

It is hoped that a real emergency situation will never arise for you and your cats. After all, they are eating a high-quality diet, which will keep resistance to disease and stress very high. Their immune response will not have been weakened by steroids or compromised by vaccines. And your annual visit to the veterinarian for teeth cleaning and checkup will help keep you a jump ahead of any challenge to your furry friend's health.

Repeated Infections

If a cat seems to be forever coming down with something—either the same health problems over and over or different problems—this is a sign that the immune response is weak and that there is something very much amiss in the basic body functions. Deeper diagnosis is required. The veterinarian will probably request that you let her run some blood tests or perhaps take X rays, an MRI, or an EKG. At this point the intelligent guardian might begin to question whether the medications he's been giving are treating the cat or just covering up symptoms temporarily and at the expense of the patient's overall health. This is the sort of situation that prompts many guardians to seek out natural and holistic health care or, best of all, a classical veterinary homeopath (see page 213).

This is exactly what happened to sweet-tempered Apollo Kulp. After four successive and random infections, Apollo had lost a lot of weight and he became short-tempered. He began growling at his companions and sulking in corners. Apollo's veterinarian suspected feline leukemia or some other blood disease. Happily, the tests came back negative for leukemia but revealed liver inflammation, which explained Apollo's low resistance to disease as well as his depression. After homeopathic treatment was begun and I upgraded his nutritional program specifically to support liver function and to aid healing, skinny, grumpy Apollo gained weight and became his old easygoing self again.

The Therapeutic Environment in the Veterinary Clinic

Now that you have a better idea of when your cats need medical attention, let's examine where you are taking them and take a look at how you, the guardian, can lend your support to enhance and augment the veterinarian's treatment.

Ask any guardian what his cats do when they are scared, and every time he'll tell you, "They run under the bed, into the closet, behind the bookshelf, or in back of the couch." *Under, into, behind, in back of*—they hide, they find a safe nook. A high-strung cat will hide out of sight for what seems to us to be the flimsiest of reasons. The mere sound of the doorbell is enough to send some purebred types scurrying. Fear of the unknown is the cat's worst fear. To run and hide when frightened is natural to a cat. A declawed cat develops this instinct to an even greater degree.

Nevertheless, most veterinary clinics lump all small animals together as a group. Those clean, airy, open cages that are heaven for dogs are a nightmare for cats. Cats are naturally agoraphobic; open spaces make them nervous. Far from providing the secluded nook they crave, they are trapped in plain sight; everyone can see in and the cats are forced to see out. They are in a constant state of apprehension because of all those new sounds—metal cage doors slamming, dogs barking, cats calling or hissing, and all of them broadcasting panic and distress. There are strange people doing strange things and those frightening, sharp smells. Caged, they cannot run away, and there is no place to hide. Worse still, in the absence of any other alternative, hospitalized cats often seek the limited shelter behind the low sides of their litter box. All day and night they crouch there, tense and ready, expecting to be attacked, adrenalin pumping, vital energy burning away. Some soil themselves, others refuse to pass their urine or stool. Both situations create additional physical problems.

What a shameful waste! After a few hours of this, cats are worn to such a frazzle that any loud noise or unexpected movement is quite enough to cause spontaneous urination or defecation, which immediately adds one more stress to their already wretched state. Think how terrified they must be to hide in the litter box. Then add to that the horror of having to smell excrement or urine on themselves.[1]

1. See also the chapter "Maizey's Story" in *It's a Cat's Life* by Anitra Frazier with Norma Eckroate (New York: Berkley Publishing, 1990).

Some cats are held like that for days. If you were the doctor, how would you like to try anesthetizing a cat in the morning after she had just spent a night like that? How would you like to treat a cat in the clinic over a number of days in this stressful situation? If the cat were ill with some disease, what odds would you give for recovery? If the cat wasn't ill when she came in, she probably would be before long.

Anesthetic is a stress factor that can be isolated—it's a physical thing. Other stresses are no less potent, but unfortunately they are less solid and more difficult for the doctor to isolate, measure, and control. But suppose we could pinpoint and isolate even a few of those additional stresses, then turn them around or simply eliminate them. Think what that would mean in terms of saving the patient's vital energy, calories, and adrenalin and raising the odds in her favor. It would widen the margin of safety and increase the chances for survival on a borderline case.

Although we cannot change the fact that a hospitalized cat is going to be surrounded by many frightening unknowns, it is a relatively simple matter to cushion the shock and soften the harsh realities. To begin with, lay a large brown paper bag (no handles, please) open in the cage, providing the cat with a little cave. If the cage is large enough, a cardboard wine carton lying on its side is even better. In other words, gratify the cat's instinct to hide. Dr. Rowan sometimes draped a towel over the front of the cage to mute the frightening sounds and provide additional privacy for high-strung cats. In his clinic, soft classical music was played and large, healthy plants were hung in every room to add their oxygen to the air. No smoking was allowed, even in the waiting room, and cage doors were opened and shut with care, never slammed.

If the veterinarian treats both dogs and cats, it is not unusual to see them mixed indiscriminately in adjoining cages. But stop and think—the great majority of city cats have never even met a dog. Dogs caged at the veterinarian's clinic usually bark and yap—at least some of the time. This is quite normal for a dog. But just imagine poor, terrified Muffy trapped in her small cage. She cannot see the animals who are making those sharp, loud sounds, but they certainly seem close. She doesn't know why the dogs are barking, but she knows she can't escape and she assumes that they are after her and that any minute they will succeed in breaking into her cage to kill her. She cowers lower into a corner, trembling, ready to fight and die. If Muffy wasn't ill when she arrived, she certainly will be before she leaves. Her resistance will be used up to fight the stress. To help achieve a therapeutic environment, dogs and cats should be housed in separate rooms or, at least, as far away from each other as possible.

In many veterinary clinics and offices, cats are forcibly restrained while medical procedures are performed. The usual method is to hold the cat firmly by the scruff of the neck and the hind feet and stretch the animal out. I know of one veterinarian who was so afraid of being bitten that he insisted that all cats be held like this even for a simple yearly examination. It is a terrifying experience even to watch such a scene. Think of the trauma the cat undergoes. To put it plainly, the cat expects death. "Why else," the cat reasons, "would they hold me this way— stretched vulnerable, unable even to swallow properly?" Again, what a stupid waste of the cat's vital energy. I advise all my clients to insist on being present during all examinations and nonsurgical procedures. Dr. Rowan could do an entire examination, including palpation of the abdomen and anal glands, listening to the heart, clipping the nails, cleaning the ears, cleaning the teeth, taking the temperature—everything—without the cat ever realizing that the exam had even begun. The assistant who held the cat distracted him or her with loving words and expert petting and scratching. Add to this the catnip they always sprinkled on the table at the end of the exam and you can see why cats did not become tense when visiting his office and hospitalized cats rallied quicker and recovered easier even after complex procedures. Their energy wasn't wasted.

Many veterinarians use anesthetics for such routine procedures as taking blood. Besides being a major stress, the anesthetic actually changes the chemistry of the blood that you're trying to analyze. For this reason, more holistically oriented veterinarians avoid tranquilizers whenever possible. They employ veterinary technicians and helpers with the knack of gaining the cat's attention and trust as they hold the cat gently but firmly while the vet does these procedures.

You can spot the holistically aware veterinarian by studying the assistants and technicians in his office. If a therapeutic environment is being maintained, they will be trained to respect the cats' physical bodies even while the cats are under anesthetic. After surgery, anesthetized animals will be carried directly back to the comfort of their quiet cages and the security of their paper bag or cardboard box—never left exposed on the cold table or laid aside on the floor until it is convenient for someone to transport them back. Be sure your veterinarian provides a nice thick pad of newspaper between the patient and the cold metal cage floor or, even better, a towel on top of the newspaper. This prevents hypothermia, a dangerous lowering of the body temperature, which is a serious threat following the use of any anesthetic or tranquilizer.

In a properly run veterinary clinic an animal should never be lifted—awake or asleep—by the scruff of the neck without supporting the hindquarters. Beside the fact that the haunches and pelvis are by far the heaviest part of the animal and therefore must be supported, such action has no part in the attitude of respect we hope to find in a veterinarian and his assistants. Lifting cats by the scruff without supporting the heavier hips may be only a minor trauma to the cat's body, but lifting carefully and with respect is, after all, very easy to do.

In a therapeutic environment cats are made to feel that they have a say in what happens to them. A greeting is given before they are picked up and handled. Reassurance is given before a procedure is done. The cat will pick up the attitude of respect and love and respond with greater cooperation. Dignity will be preserved, and dignity is very important to a cat. If a liquid medication is accidentally spilled or smeared on the furs of the cat's face or ruff, it should be sponged off at once. I have seen fastidious cats distressed by their soiled condition to such an extent that they ripped chunks of fur out by the roots in a desperate attempt to rid themselves of spilled medication that had hardened on the hair. Choose your veterinarian carefully and be alert to the attitude and demeanor of technicians and vet assistants. They often spend as much or more time with the patients than the vet does.

Choosing a Veterinarian

Choosing a veterinarian can be a lot like trying to find a television repairman or a jeweler to fix your watch. You know absolutely nothing about the inner workings of television sets and watches so you feel very much at the mercy of the repairman. Usually all you have to go on is someone else's recommendation. Unfortunately, I have found that most people recommend a veterinarian not because they have any rational method for judging, but simply out of psychological need. Their beloved pet's very life may one day be at stake, and they desperately want reassurance that they have indeed chosen the right veterinarian. So, the more people they can get to agree with them and to use the same veterinarian, the more secure they feel. They go about trying to convince all their friends and neighbors that their veterinarian is the very best and that everyone should use him and no one else. Their judgment of the doctor is actually worth very little as it is based on their own psychological need and not on fact. Your judgment is probably a lot better than theirs, so gather your own evidence and make your own decision.

The time to begin searching for a veterinarian is definitely not during a crisis. Begin making inquiries at your leisure, and when you find a new veterinarian you want to try, take the cat in for an examination.

Over the years I have met many veterinarians. Some were brilliant diagnosticians, some were skilled surgeons, some were gentle and sensitive, some combined many skills. Some were realistically aware of their strong and weak points and were very happy to recommend a talented colleague to perform any procedure if they felt the job could be done better by someone else.

It is important to be consciously aware of what a veterinarian is and what he isn't. Allopathic veterinarians (those who are trained at conventional veterinary schools) do not study health; they study disease. They do not study nutrition. Their training is not focused on prevention but, instead, on treating the problems that occur after the cat's health has already broken down. They are trained to apply that treatment using various drugs, chemicals, and surgical procedures. Unless they elected to specialize in feline nutrition, most vets' training includes only about two hours on that subject during their entire eight years of study. And those two short hours are often taught by a veterinarian who is chosen and paid by one of the big pet food companies. Guess which pet food is then held up as the shining example of good nutrition.

If you are holistically oriented, you are used to building health, for yourself and your animals, through nutrition, supplements, stress management, communication, exercise, and so on. When humans become sick or injured, we have an ever-increasing range of health care professionals at our disposal: chiropractors, homeopaths, acupuncturists, nutritionists, stress management experts, and many others. While many conventionally trained veterinarians used to dismiss these new areas of health and healing, an increasing number are now open to many different healing methods and to using those that feel most comfortable to them.

For people who can't locate a holistic veterinarian nearby, I suggest finding a veterinarian at a distance who practices holistically and will work with you by phone. Dr. Pitcairn and I worked that way for many years. In recent years, I have consulted by telephone with Dr. Dym and Dr. Gil who, like Dr. Pitcairn, are highly skilled classical veterinary homeopaths. Hundreds of my clients have worked with holistic veterinarians on this basis with great success. Then you must secure the services of a local veterinarian to do hands-on examinations, blood tests, diagnosis, and whatever else your holistic vet requests.

After the first six years when I had *no* holistic veterinarian, I finally met Dr. Pitcairn. Fate was kind to me. I had finally found a veterinarian who understood what I was trying to do. The vets I had tried to work with back in the late 1970s—when I began my practice—did not want to hear about nutritional supplements, slippery elm, or psyllium husks. Except for nice Dr. Rowan, they didn't want to hear that stress and fear can make a cat sicker. They didn't care if vitamin C and garlic and saline nose drops would bring a cat safely through an upper respiratory infection without all of the destructive side effects of antibiotics. The nicer vets thought I was a little crazy; the not-so-nice ones called me evil. "You're keeping cats from getting the treatment they need!" was a phrase I heard from several sources. And it took its toll on me. It's very draining to have people you wish you could respect lined up against you.

Your local veterinarian must be a diagnostician and surgeon, a person who likes to handle cats and who demonstrates that he can get along with other veterinarians. The facility should be clean, well-equipped, and well-staffed with loving people. Tell the veterinarian that your cat is the patient of a distant holistic veterinarian and that you would like him to act as your local consulting veterinarian, performing hands-on examinations and tests when your holistic vet requests them, as well as any needed diagnosis. Your holistic vet will be in charge. Any and all treatments or prescriptions will be subject to his approval. Be clear with him that you and your holistic veterinarian may be open to allopathic medicine from time to time, but that you will *always* want to double-check with your holistic veterinarian *before* giving any drugs—even so much as an ear drop—to your cat. If he is open-minded and willing to work as a consulting veterinarian and you feel good about him, you've found your local consultant. If not, persevere until you find someone you and your holistic vet can work with.

If your cat is ever hospitalized, I suggest you make a list of requests as to how your cat is handled, such as (1) doctor and staff announcing their presence before touching the cat, (2) supporting the cat's hindquarters when lifting him, and (3) keeping the cat warm if he is anesthetized by always providing plenty of padding under him and using a heat lamp that you will provide if necessary. (Offer to bring in a lamp.)

Veterinarians are people, too; they have morals and standards. Simply look your veterinarian in the eye and calmly explain that you are aware that certain practices that you are not comfortable with are common in some clinics. Say that, because you have no idea whether any of these things is ever done in his hospital, you need to bring these questions out into the open rather than taking anything for granted. That way you won't be shocked or upset just at a time when you need to be giving calm and reassuring vibrations to your cat. If the veterinarian also looks you in the eye and does not get all touchy and insulted but calmly gives you his word that your cat will be treated as you wish—specifically on all the points just mentioned—chances are it will be done so. You can feel even more secure if you have your requests listed on your cat's cage card and signed by the vet in charge. Everyone who has anything to do with your cat is supposed to consult the cage card. "Always support hindquarters when lifting this patient" becomes like a prescription when it is listed on the cage card. If you visit and your cat seems relaxed, all is probably going well.

To be sure there is no change in the way your cat is handled, I advise owners to double-check and go over these specific requests again each separate time your cat is left at the clinic and certainly if your veterinarian takes on an associate or employs a new helper. I also spring surprise visits to double-check. Remember that different people have different priorities. Your reminder of what your specific priorities are will ensure your cat's comfort and safety and avoid misunderstandings.

See "Holistic Professionals" on page 236 for guidelines on selecting and consulting with a holistic veterinarian and other holistic professionals. The Appendix gives information on organizations that compile lists of holistic veterinarians. However, be aware that even the best of these lists will be extremely broad and will include veterinarians who are not holistic in the literal sense.

Visiting Rights

For me the veterinarian's policy on visiting hospitalized cats is a crucial question—I could never leave my cats in any facility where I could not personally pop in and check on them. When checking out a new veterinarian, find out whether he recognizes the psychological value of moral support by the guardian of a sick cat. Ask if he allows visiting privileges. There may be certain hours on certain days when no visiting is allowed because surgery is going on or some other procedure is in progress, but, other than that, most veterinarians will encourage the guardian to visit.

The Second Opinion

You will also have to ascertain the veterinarian's attitude about getting a second opinion. Whenever there is a question of a disease or any malfunction in the cat's body not responding to treatment, do not accept a verdict of "chronic" or "incurable" without seeking a second opinion from someone outside your own vet's office. The second opinion could be applied also to any case where surgery is suggested as long as the delay would not be considered dangerous to the cat. Especially if your veterinarian is conventional, he may say, "This is an incurable disease" as opposed to "I do not know how to cure this disease." Conventional vets know how to diagnose many conditions and diseases, but their knowledge does not include that vast pool of information known as holistic health care. In the vast majority of cases this is where the cure can be found. The vets in charge of my own cats' health are always classical homeopaths.

Another instance when a second opinion is a good idea would be if you, the guardian, feel that something is not quite right with your cat—perhaps the symptoms are slight and vague. If your own veterinarian can find nothing amiss but your worry persists, seek another opinion. You just might be very glad you did. No one knows your cat better than you and therefore no one is better able to judge when your cat's behavior is abnormal. A holistic vet, especially a classical homeopath, will take very seriously nonphysical symptoms such as:

- Not enjoying meals as much as usual
- Craving warmth or coolness
- Restlessness
- Grouchiness
- Avoiding physical contact

You can't measure such things on a test, but to a classical homeopath they are very important symptoms that point the way toward the appropriate remedy as clearly as do the results of a blood test.

I have several times over the years confronted veterinarians with my intention of taking a cat of mine or one of my clients for a second opinion. Most times the response is the same. The doctor digs out the records of medications given, treatments tried, pulls out any X-rays or test results, slips it all into a big envelope, and, as he hands it to me, he usually says, "Let me know what he says, I'd be interested." Most doctors are always ready to learn something new. I've often heard doctors conferring with other veterinarians by phone.

I can't work with a doctor who harbors a sense of competition or defensiveness over my desire to see if two heads might be better than one. More than once I've brought back to a veterinarian a general confirmation of everything he said but with some little helpful suggestion about possible dietary treatment or therapy to try. Once you have the second opinion, be sure to give your doctor the information so your cat can benefit from the combined knowledge. If there is a difference of opinion, my own choice is always to be guided by my classical homeopath who has the benefit of being knowledgeable in both the conventional and holistic paradigms.

A last word about treatment: if the medicine your veterinarian prescribes doesn't seem to be doing any good, don't hesitate to call him at once and say so. Every living creature is different. There may be allergies and sensitivities to consider, or there may be a second disease lurking behind the primary one. Before you decide to change veterinarians, be sure you have given your present doctor every bit of information you have to help him diagnose accurately. Also, *every* conventional drug has some known side effects. If your cat has an adverse reaction such as diarrhea or excessive sleeping or panting, let the doctor know. The veterinarian is not a psychic; you have to call and tell him. He may just say that your cat's reaction is normal in the circumstances and thus put your mind to rest. After a homeopathic remedy, a reaction that at first seems adverse can often be a sign that the patient is responding beautifully to the remedy, and what you are seeing may be a much-needed discharge of toxins. Temporary worsening of symptoms after a homeopathic remedy is called an aggravation and is usually a very good sign, but always report any change to your homeopath and let him be the judge. The veterinarian is best equipped to judge whether to continue a particular treatment or to change it.

Holistic Professionals

Dr. Richard Pitcairn, my first holistic veterinarian, taught me that the body's natural impulse is toward perfect health. That's why the feline species has survived over the millennia. He explained that, while the conventional veterinarian focuses on the disease symptoms and tries to eliminate them, the homeopath and holistic veterinarian respect the body's own wisdom and try to work with it and support it. Many times, Dr. Pitcairn told me, "Symptoms are the body's logical response to an intolerable situation." Those things that conventional veterinarians call symptoms of disease, holistic veterinarians call symptoms of health. If the body needs to work up a high temperature in order to overcome invading germs, the holistic veterinarian will see it as a very good sign if the patient is strong enough to do so. The conventional veterinarian tries to eliminate the symptoms using antibiotics, steroids, and surgery. The holistic veterinarian encourages the body to sneeze, produce mucus, run a fever, or do whatever it needs to do to defeat the underlying cause of the disease and emerge from the experience stronger than before.

There are as many definitions of "holistic" as there are holistic health care givers. Some of the goals your holistic veterinarian and other holistic professionals strive for are:

1. *Treat the cause, not the symptom.* As I mentioned above, most of what the conventional veterinarians call disease is thought of as a symptom by the holistic professional. For example, tumors are a symptom of (a) the body chemistry being out of balance; (b) an invasion by environmental or food chemicals; (c) congenital predisposition; (d) an immune system weakened by vaccines, steroids, or poor diet; or (e) all or some of the above.

2. *Primum est non nocere: Above all, do no harm.* Drugs such as steroids and antibiotics, and practices like chemotherapy, all do harm to the system. To a holistic practitioner, it makes no sense to use something that harms the patient if you are trying to effect a cure.

3. *Treat the whole animal.* Address body, mind, and spirit using as many complementary therapies as necessary and practical. For example, the *mind* and *spirit* are treated by stress reduction, Bach flower remedies, homeopathy, visualization, and demonstrations of love. The *body* is treated with homeopathy, herbs, acupuncture, exercise, shiatsu, nutrition, orthomolecular therapy, and, on rare occasions, even surgery and antibiotics. (Steroids are almost never used by holistic veterinarians.)

Guardians who practice holistic health care for themselves are usually the ones who seek the same advantages for their feline friends. Increasing numbers of veterinarians are responding, each in his own way and at his own pace. Guardians should keep in mind that we are all on the same team, sharing the same goal of upgrading health care for animals. The aware guardian knows that the modern natural therapies encourage a much greater participation and involvement on the part of the patient or, in this case, the guardian. The responsibility no longer rests exclusively on the shoulders of the veterinarian, nutritionist, or homeopath, but is shared equally by the guardian and whichever health care practitioners he or she is consulting. (I use the word *practitioners* in the plural because I have found that often one of the keys to success is the utilization of more than one source of information.)

This increased involvement of the guardian is as it should be because no one, no matter how skilled, is in a better position than the guardian to build the animal's health and to observe and evaluate the patient's response—physical, emotional, and mental—to any therapy being used. The successful resolution of any problem will depend upon teamwork with much give and take on the part of all team members. This attitude of mutual respect and enthusiasm always results in new knowledge for every member of the team. It's a beneficial side effect cherished by all members of the holistic community.

When a guardian first begins the journey on this particular path, he will encounter new attitudes and find that emphases are differently placed. These attitudes of respect, openness, encouragement, and mutual support are all predispositions that the health-conscious guardian has greatly desired and has long been seeking, but nevertheless, they are unfamiliar and, like the cats, we humans often feel insecure in a situation where there are bound to be many unknowns, puzzles, and surprises. After many years, I still feel insecure, but I have learned that insecurity is not necessarily a negative quality; it keeps me on my toes. However, too much insecurity interferes with efficiency. So, I have found a few ways to cut insecurity down to size.

1. Always request copies of all test results and keep them with the cat. You will need them when you consult a holistic practitioner by phone or if you have to suddenly see a new veterinarian. You will save precious time, money, and stress on the patient if you walk in with all the test results. Most guardians keep them in the carry case.

2. Keep a weekly health log on each cat. If you see what might be a symptom, *log it*. State the time and date. It's easy to forget things when your emotions are involved. Almost all health problems begin long before the guardian realizes that anything is going on. The checklist of symptoms on pages 221–226 will give

you some idea of what to include in your log. If you see three or four deviations from the norm in one week, you can call your veterinarian, homeopath, or other holistic practitioner, and together you will have an excellent chance of nipping a potential health problem in the bud.

3. Minimize the need for crisis intervention by practicing prevention. Follow the suggestions in this book, including a homeopathic evaluation. (See "Homeopathy," page 211.) You can raise the level of your cat's health and learn a lot in the process.

4. Find experienced advisors. "When the student is ready, the teacher will come" is an ancient yoga aphorism. Make an effort to find advisors and teachers (one of whom is a holistic veterinarian) well established in one of the holistic healing arts: homeopathy, herbalism, orthomolecular nutrition, home-nursing care, or acupuncture. Fortunately, like me, many of these experts do phone consultations. We charge for our time, just as if you were making an office visit. (Most cannot take time to answer personal emails or letters.) The standard procedure is to write down your questions until you have several, and then call and request a consultation. You will then be given a time that is mutually convenient when you can call, ask your questions, and receive information and suggestions. Some of these professionals will agree to guide the treatment of your cat by long-distance phone consultation. If the advisor you are calling has written a book, it is both sensible and practical to read the book first.

5. Do away with as many unknowns as possible by increasing your knowledge. There are several ways to do this. I can give you some idea of how I go about collecting information and some guidelines I have discovered along the way, but you must make your own evaluation of my sources and of any other information that comes your way. Only you can tell if it feels right for you and the cats you love.

Sources of Information

1. *Bibliographies.* At the end of most "how to" books like this one, there is a list of source books where the author found useful information. Consult these books and, in turn, check the bibliographies in them. If you see the same book listed in several bibliographies, that should make you especially curious to read it.

2. *Lectures, workshops, seminars, and classes.* Get acquainted with holistic health periodicals and schools. Your health food store probably has one or two

free magazines in which lectures, classes, and books are advertised. Health food stores, herb shops, and bookstores that carry holistic health titles often have bulletin boards. Don't limit yourself to courses and books on animals.

3. *Personal observations*

- New knowledge is never a waste of time; no information is "useless."
- Nobody's perfect. No source of information is perfect. Because someone knows a lot and helps you a lot does not mean that he or she knows everything. Conversely, even if you disagree with or dislike a person or book, you can still learn something from them, even if it's what *not* to do.
- Test and evaluate for yourself and collect other sources of corroboration or disagreement.
- Discover people's strong points. Become aware of the categories in which each of your sources of information is usually the most reliable. For example, ask the surgeon about anesthetics; do not ask the surgeon about nutrition.

A Holistic Perspective on Conventional Veterinary Treatments

Vaccinations and Other Immunizations

A vaccination is made from a live virus or germ that has been weakened or killed. It is injected into the patient purposely to give him that disease but in such a mild form that the body should easily overcome it and build an immunity to that particular virus or germ. Vaccinations are never given if a cat is already sick or if he has only recently recovered from an illness, or within two weeks of being anesthetized.

However, the cat's body has not evolved to handle viruses and germs that are injected under the skin and go directly into the bloodstream. Microorganisms usually enter through the mouth, nose, or intestines. Nevertheless, vaccinations sometimes work if you're willing to take the risks. However, a problem is created when more than one serum is given at the same time. This is the case with the three-in-one shot for cats, which is used all over the country. Most allopathic veterinarians will very conscientiously advise you to have your cat vaccinated for anywhere from three to seven or eight diseases in one day. Dr. Pitcairn, who has a specialty in immunology, warns that this is not practical.

The immune system works like a type of memory. Each disease has a different set of symptoms. Each vaccine "clues in" the immune system in advance to a particular set of symptoms so that if that set shows up in the body again, the immune system will then remember what it did last time and automatically do it again, thus defeating the disease.

Multiple vaccinations given close together (within a few weeks) confuse the immune system's memory and disrupt the immune response at the same time that they are activating it. This frequently results in the immune system's becoming so confused that it turns against its own body, producing autoimmune diseases such as irritable bowel syndrome, where it attacks the body's intestinal lining, or asthma, where it overreacts to something perfectly harmless in the food or air. Skin allergies, hyperthyroidism, pancreatitis, arthritis, warts, tumors, and gum disease are more examples of autoimmune diseases. Such reactions are sometimes referred to as vaccinosis.

Holistic veterinarians caution that a killed virus is safer than a weakened virus and that serums are best used singly, at least six weeks apart. In some states, vaccination for rabies is required by law. Holistic veterinarians and a large number of conventional veterinarians agree that every vaccine on the market, if it works at all, will be effective for the life of the animal. This is not new information. It was published in *Kirk's Current Veterinary Therapy* in the 1980s and remains there to this day. *Kirk's* is a large reference book that every veterinarian keeps handy. The human equivalent is the *Physicians' Desk Reference*. In *Kirk's*, veterinary immunologists Dr. Ronald Schultz and Dr. Tom Phillips stated, "A practice that was started many years ago and that lacks scientific validity or verification is annual revaccinations. Almost without exception there is no immunologic requirement for annual revaccination. Immunity to viruses persists for years or for the life of the animal. . . . Furthermore, revaccination with most viral vaccines fails to stimulate an anamnestic (secondary) response. . . . The practice of annual vaccination in our opinion should be considered of questionable efficacy."[2]

---

2. Schultz, Ronald, and Tom Phillips. "Canine and Feline Vaccines." *Kirk's Current Veterinary Therapy XI: Small Animal Practice.* Ontario: W. B. Saunders Company, 1992, 205.

The "three-in-one" shot, a mixture of panleukopenia, rhinotracheitis, and calicivirus, is cultured on chicken kidneys. Some cats successfully develop anti-bodies against the three diseases in the serum; some do not. Unfortunately, many cats in both of these categories also begin producing antibodies against kidney tissue and the body begins to attack its own kidneys. Kidney disease, a disease of older cats, is now showing up with increased frequency. I am seeing it in cats as young as seven.

An alternative to vaccinations are "nosodes," homeopathic preparations that contain only the energy of the virus or germ but not the microbe itself. They are taken as a series of drops by mouth at prescribed intervals over several weeks or months and serve to bolster gradually the body's immune response to that par-ticular disease. Giving the nosode takes a little more time than a simple injection, but avoids the drawbacks and dangers of allopathic vaccines.

My own preference is to build a cat's general immunity and strengthen the immune response by feeding a well-balanced diet of at least 80 percent raw food (see page 71), as set forth by Dr. Pottenger in his well known studies.[3]

Antibiotics

Antibiotics are used to kill germs and sometimes viruses. If an antibiotic is taken in any form—pill, liquid, injection, on the skin, or as ear or nose drops—it will kill all the germs in the entire alimentary canal, from the mouth right on down to the anus, before it even begins to work on the germs it was sent after. Diarrhea is one of the body's reactions to the absence of all microorganisms in the intestinal tract.

Not all bacteria are bad—a healthy body has lots of friendly bacteria in the intestines. They manufacture some of the B vitamins, help with the absorption of nutrients, and help regulate the acid-alkaline balance in the intestine. When the antibiotic comes into the body, these good bacteria bite the dust with all the rest. The absence of the good bacteria disrupts the acid-alkaline balance, and this causes diarrhea. You can replace the friendly bacteria that were destroyed by add-ing one-quarter teaspoon powdered mixed intestinal flora to each meal for two weeks after the cycle of antibiotics is over. If you give the mixed flora during the

3. Pottenger, Francis Marion. *Pottenger's Cats: A Study in Nutrition.* La Mesa, CA: Price-Pottenger Nutrition Foundation, 1995, 5–14.

course of the antibiotics, most of the friendly bacteria will still be destroyed, but enough may survive to prevent diarrhea. Some antibiotics, such as Keflex, are so harsh and strong that the poor little pussycat will still get diarrhea even though he's getting the mixed flora. Keep it up anyway; he'd be a lot worse off without it. It will help him bounce back faster once the nasty medicine is finished.

To calm a troubled intestine and minimize the diarrhea, I always give a teaspoon of slippery elm syrup (page 319) five minutes before each meal.

Also, remember that diarrhea uses up a lot of fluids and washes many of the water-soluble nutrients out of the cat's body. Now is a good time to add a teaspoon of Kombu broth (page 318) or a pinch of Green Magma powder to each meal to add those vitamins and minerals to the food. Also add $\frac{1}{16}$ teaspoon ascorbic acid crystals to supply 250 units vitamin C, and a piece of a crushed B vitamins complex pill (about 5 mg worth). Check the Appendix for product recommendations.

Remember that if you and the veterinarian decide to use antibiotics you must be sure to follow the directions very carefully. Unlike diuretics and cortisone, antibiotics are not given for the shortest time possible. Once you start, you must give the full course of antibiotics that the doctor prescribes, finishing all the pills. If you're careless and stop too soon, a stray germ or two might survive, slightly injured, to breed an altogether new strain of germ, which is then immune to that particular antibiotic and now a brand-new menace to all the pussycats of the world. (See also "Diarrhea," page 358.)

Diuretics

Diuretics are given to prevent water retention. They help the body drain off the liquid by promoting copious urination. If there is fluid present—in the lungs, abdomen, or around the heart—an herbal or chemical diuretic may be prescribed. Lasix is one type of chemical diuretic. Usually the cat will begin to drink copiously and urinate copiously. And, one hopes, the bad fluid will be drawn to the kidneys and bladder and make its exit with the good fluid. However, with all this washing of fluids through the body, many water-soluble nutrients, vitamins, and minerals will be washed out along with everything else. The biggest loss is potassium. If a cat is given a diuretic get some Nu-Salt or Adolph's Salt Substitute (potassium chloride) and sprinkle a pinch onto the cat's food at each meal. If you're not already doing so, add ½ to 1 teaspoon of Anitra's Vita-Mineral Mix (page 68)

to each meal and also add ⅟₁₆ teaspoon ascorbic acid crystals (or 250 units vitamin C), a B complex vitamin (5 mg level), and a pinch of Green Magma powder.
Chemical diuretics are almost never given over long periods of time. The lower
the sodium (salt) intake, the lower the amount of diuretics that will be needed.
Parsley tea is a natural diuretic used by many modern veterinarians. It is so high
in mineral and vitamin content that it replaces some of the nutrients washed out
by its diuretic action.

Cortisone and Other Steroids

Steroids are sometimes used to reduce inflammation and swelling. They
work by suppressing the body's immune system. (Inflammation and swelling are
a normal part of the body's immune response.) Steroids do not cure anything;
they only suppress the symptoms and drive the problem deeper within the system. They do nothing to address the cause of those problems. For these reasons
most veterinarians dislike using steroids and will do so only in life-threatening
situations, such as when a swelling is blocking an air passage; or at the very end
of a terminal illness, such as cancer or kidney disease, hoping to buy a little time
before the patient is euthanized.

However, my own vet has pointed out to me and I have observed for myself
that death, when it comes for an animal on steroids, is much harder. I counsel the
caregivers of cats who have been treated with steroids to be aware of this and carefully plan in advance to have a veterinarian available twenty-four hours a day for a
quiet euthanasia in case the patient takes a bad turn at any time of the day or night.

Since steroids suppress the immune response, great care must be taken to
avoid all stress and not to expose the patient to any sort of germs, viruses, or
parasites. Any source of infection is potentially lethal to an animal on cortisone or
any other steroid, whether natural or artificial. Now is definitely not the time to
change his environment in any way. No trips and no new additions to the household should be contemplated at this time. Any visitors who have animals of their
own should wash their hands well before touching the patient.

Steroids raise the body's need for vitamins A and C. Add ⅟₁₆ teaspoon ascorbic acid crystals or sodium ascorbate powder (250 units vitamin C) to each meal,
and, for vitamin A, give a dropperful of cod liver oil every day *or* give a capsule
containing 25,000 units vitamin A once a week. Because steroids are usually given

to reduce swelling, you probably are already giving your cat extra vitamin C and cod liver oil to alleviate the condition.

One caution about steroids: never stop them abruptly. Steroids, like diuretics, are always given for as short a time as possible, but unlike diuretics, the dose is always tapered down at the end. Steroids can make cats feel depressed. Coming off the steroids too abruptly depresses them even more. I prefer not to use steroids at all. Modern veterinarians have found alternatives such as various homeopathic remedies, various herbs, and the goldenseal elixir that can eliminate the need for steroids.

Anesthetics, Tranquilizers, and X-rays

I give ¹⁄₁₆ teaspoon of ascorbic acid crystals or sodium ascorbate powder (250 units vitamin C) in the food twice a day for six days before a cat is to be either X-rayed or anesthetized. Vitamin C is manufactured by healthy cats in their intestines. This takes care of the normal requirements. However, "normal" means hunting twice a day, eating raw food, and lounging in the sun—healthy, happy cats. It has been found that any stress can cause vitamin C to be totally depleted—extreme cold, extreme heat, fear, anger, after X-rays, during any illness, after anesthetic, or when chemical preservatives in the food such as ethoxyquin, nitrates, nitrites, and sodium benzoate are ingested. The vitamin C requirement during such situations soars. It is practically impossible to get an overdose of vitamin C, because it cannot be stored. Excess vitamin C is excreted in the urine. I give vitamin C three times a day for three days afterward and then I go back to twice a day for two weeks or longer if the cat is still in the hospital or on any sort of medication. I do this in hopes of keeping the cat's resistance to disease higher. Anesthetization is such a drain on the cat's body that all too often the cat picks up some unrelated infection that becomes evident a couple of days or weeks after he returns home. Adding ¹⁄₁₆ teaspoon Delicious Garlic Condiment (page 318) to the food once a day for three days before and one week after will offer some protection against invading germs and viruses.

I think of vitamin C as a little additional cushion to help the beleaguered body cope with any serious stress. At the risk of belaboring a point, let me say again that the entire nutritional program must be of extra high quality during stress. Anesthetic is one of the worst stresses. Vitamin C is a big help, but vitamin

C can't do it alone. You need the vitamin B family and vitamin E to complete the antistress group. (See "Antistress Supplements," page 305).

Mineral Oil

Mineral oil washes the oil-soluble vitamins A, D, and E out of the system. Fur ball medications and laxatives in a tube contain mineral oils. Holistic veterinarians advise against their use. Most of these products in a tube contain the preservative benzoate of soda (sodium benzoate). If your vet prescribes a mineral oil laxative, use a plain petroleum jelly and follow with a seven-day regimen of replacing those fat-soluble vitamins.

I used to give 400 units vitamin E (alpha tocopherol) and a low potency vitamin A and D pill (10,000 units of vitamin A and 400 units of vitamin D) every week, as a matter of course. Now they are all included in my cats' multivitamin. If a product containing mineral oil must be given for some reason, I follow the veterinarian's directions precisely so I won't have to do it more than once, then I double the above amounts of vitamins A, D, and E for the next two weeks.

If a cat becomes constipated, I seldom use mineral oil. Instead, ⅛ teaspoon of psyllium husk powder from the health food store plus 2 tablespoons water mixed into each meal for a few days usually does the trick. Psyllium is harmless enough to be used on human infants and can be kept up indefinitely as needed. It's great for older cats who tend to produce a dry stool, but be sure to mix extra water in the food: 2 tablespoons to every ⅛ teaspoon of psyllium husks (see "Constipation," page 347).

Surgery and Catheterization

I'll add a word here about nutritional support before and after surgery and catheterization. These procedures present the body with three problems: stress, danger of infection, and scarring. This means that nutrition should emphasize the antistress supplements. Give the antistress supplements found on page 304 three times a day for two weeks before and two weeks after surgery. However, I like to feed three small meals a day instead of the usual two, just so I can mix in the antistress supplements. To speed healing of the incision, spray it twice a day with Irrigation Formula II on page 280. Also, to prevent the healing scar from itching, you can rub vitamin E directly on the scar once the scab is gone. Use a vitamin E capsule punctured with a needle. The vitamin E oil in a bottle expires too quickly.

Hospitalization

If it turns out that your cat must be hospitalized, prepare his cage in the following manner: if the cage is metal, as most of them are, remember that cold metal will rob your cat's body of heat. This is especially debilitating if the patient is elderly; if he has diabetes, kidney disease, liver disease, or cancer; or if he is to be anesthetized. To prevent hypothermia, be sure there is a nice *thick* pad of newspaper, at least six sheets of thickness, under your cat. Put his towel on top of this. Then take a brown paper bag, open it, and turn down a cuff all the way around the top. Do it slowly and carefully so that it doesn't tear. The purpose of the cuff is to hold the bag open. Lay it inside the cage, thus providing a nice little cave of darkness and security the cat can crawl into if he wants to hide. If the cage is large enough, a small cardboard box (like a liquor carton) laid on its side is even better. The object of this is to prevent a frightened cat from cowering inside the litter box. It's nice to lay a small piece of clothing you have recently worn in the bag for your cat to snuggle with. Your scent will provide reassurance in a situation that is new and strange. Put very hot water in a plastic bottle and drop it into a thick sock under the towel. Your object is to cushion a stressful situation in as many ways as possible. You've provided extra warmth with the hot water bottle; an illusion of security and an option of hiding in the paper bag or box; and your dear, familiar scent with your sock.

Take your leave casually. Here is an ideal time to use the ritual phrase that you always use when leaving your own home to signal your cat that this will be a short absence on your part. (See "Communicating 'Good-bye' and 'I'll Be Back,'" in Chapter 1.) For myself, when leaving in the morning for the day's work, my last words are always "See you later, Alligator," as opposed to "Okay, Purr, I'm leaving you in charge," which is what I say if I'm going to be away for the weekend or longer.

If a cat of mine is going to be anesthetized, I always request that the vet order a heating pad or heat lamp until the patient is past the recovery period and fully awake. Set the pad's heat on low and cover the pad with two layers of towel; they all have "hot spots." Anesthetic lowers body temperature and an outside source of heat can mean the difference between a quiet, uneventful recovery and some nasty complications. I advise clients to bring their own heating pad or clip-on light if necessary and to be certain that the vet writes the order for its use on the cage card.

All that is left to do now is to extract an oath signed in blood by the veterinarian and his staff that he will not provide hospital food—which is usually filled with by-products and chemicals—but will use the food that you have provided. Chances are either (1) the cat will not be hungry, or (2) the cat will be required to fast preceding some hospital procedure. You may want to provide some special treats when you visit—such as chicken soup or steamed asparagus tops. You know what your cat loves. Discuss it with the veterinarian. Just make sure that, at this time especially, it is top-quality nutrition. No tortilla chips or rum raisin ice cream!

Euthanasia

This part of the book is about courage. It takes a certain kind of courage to adopt an animal knowing as we do that we live longer than our feline companions and that there will come a time when we will have to say good-bye. It's a fact we all have to deal with.

When first we allow this thought into our conscious mind, it seems a tragedy. But that is only partly true. There is another side to this coin. Tragedy can be turned into a triumph. You may lose your friend, but nature has placed you in a position where you can influence and structure the circumstances surrounding your friend's leaving.

Many guardians are not aware of the options open to them. Although you cannot stop your friend from going, you can greatly influence the manner in which he goes. There are drugs available that make euthanasia a gentle slide into slumber and then out of the body. The homeopathic patient can be helped through the progression of body changes that precede death by careful prescription by his homeopathic veterinarian in conjunction with the conventional euthanasia drugs. However, if corticosteroids have ever been used in the past, a long series of homeopathic remedies must be used to overcome the effect of the steroids and you don't have the time for that now so just depend on the conventional drugs. This is one time when conventional drugs in the hands of a competent veterinarian serve us very well.

Selecting Methods of Treatment and Seeking Professional Help

Many veterinarians will come to the animal's home to perform euthanasia. I am a great believer in prolonging life as long as that life is comfortable. I will use finger feeding, dropper feeding, subcutaneous hydration, and all manner of herbs and remedies to help a guardian extend a cat's life. As long as the patient seems to be enjoying some sort of comfort or satisfaction, be it eating, sleeping, petting, or warmth, I will continue to help the guardian fight for him with everything I know. But when major organs break down there can be pain, inability to breathe, and extreme weakness with accompanying fear. The animal experiences not only the pain but also terror because he cannot control his own body. Then there comes a time when the act of prolonging life turns into the act of prolonging the process of dying.

My aim in each individual case has been to help the guardian judge the time when discomfort begins to outweigh contentment. If the veterinarian and the guardian and I see that a time of fear and pain is fast approaching, then we arrange to help our friend escape from the worn-out body before it can cause him any further distress. The key to success lies in gathering information and planning in advance.

Most veterinarians have been well trained in performing a smooth euthanasia. If you feel that the time has come to help your friend leave his body and you discover that your vet is not available, don't despair. Call around and you will find another veterinarian who will help you. I advise my long-distance clients to find a veterinarian who will give the patient a preliminary intramuscular injection of Telazol before the injection of the euthanasia drug.

Even for the most skilled veterinarian, it is sometimes difficult to find the vein with the needle if the vein is collapsed or very narrow, as can happen with a patient who is very old, very weak, or very dehydrated. A drug was needed that didn't have to be injected into the vein, one that would tranquilize the patient just enough so he would be oblivious to anything the vet was doing, no matter whether it was easily done, or not. Such a drug, Telazol, has become available in recent years.

Telazol is a valium derivative that is used as a light euphoric. It is easy to give because it is injected into the muscle, not the vein. Within five minutes it puts the patient into what is called the "pink cloud state." Many veterinarians use it during teeth cleaning or other simple procedures. The patient feels contentment—he is calm and relaxed. He knows his beloved guardian is there. He focuses on her dear, familiar voice, her scent, and her beloved touch while the veterinarian calmly locates the vein (usually in the inner thigh) and inserts the needle for the final injection. The use of Telazol ensures that finding the vein and inserting the needle will be as smooth and easy as the rest of the procedure.

Facing this challenge, asking the crucial questions, and making the crucial arrangements—all this requires courage. The courage you need can be found in the love you bear for your furry friend. I can assure you that it is much easier to make as many inquiries and plans as possible well in advance, when your cat is active and healthy, rather than waiting until you are already distraught because of his rapidly failing health.

Smoothing the Path: Planning in Advance

1.   Know your veterinarian's euthanasia policies—not every veterinarian has the same procedures. Will he make a house call? Will he allow you or a close friend to be present when the final injection is given? Will he give a preparatory injection of Telazol (intra-muscular) before intravenous injection of the euthanasia drug?

2.   Know your veterinarian's office hours. Discuss with him your preferences and ask his help in finding other veterinarians or animal hospitals that will accommodate your wishes and requirements if he should be unavailable when you need him.

Over the years I have tried to improve my ability to judge the correct time. Knowing what signs to look for gives the guardian a better opportunity to make the right move at the right time. The better informed you are, the better your judgment will be. If your cat already has a serious illness, you can ask your veterinarian what signs to watch for in that particular illness that will help you recognize that the end is near. Although veterinarians seldom volunteer this information, they will always give it to you willingly if you request it. Below are some general signs that appear during the final stages of many illnesses. If one or two or more of the following symptoms appear, you should inform your veterinarian. We always hope that the patient may rally, but it's best to be ready to proceed with the euthanasia at short notice if it is needed.

Here are some of the symptoms that can mean that the body is failing:

- *Confusion.* Inability to locate the litter box or inability to get back to his bed. (This could also indicate blindness, which is not, in itself, a sign that the end is near.)

- *Extreme Weakness.* Staggering while trying to walk. Leaning against things. Collapsing to rest before getting to the litter or back to bed. Lying down and resting halfway through a meal.
- *Sitting or lying in the litter box.*
- *Sitting with head over the water dish.* (Often means extreme dehydration, beyond what can be alleviated by drinking. When subcutaneous hydration is already being given it often means that it is no longer sufficient.)
- *Subcutaneous hydration therapy no longer being absorbed.* Fluids settling in one leg like a thick sock or backing up into the chest or abdomen.
- *Body temperature drops below normal (below 100.5 degrees F).* Cold ears and paws; cold legs.
- *Refusing warmth* even though the temperature is below normal or even though paws are cold.
- *Constant uninterrupted purring for no apparent reason.*
- *Lying or crouching and staring off into space.* Eyes unfocused. Not caring what you do or don't do to care for him.
- *Breathing rapidly through partly open mouth.*
- *Abdomen heaving with each breath.*
- *No more urination.*

One never forgets the circumstances when a beloved friend leaves forever. You are making your memories when you arrange to help your feline companion slip gently out of a body that can no longer serve him. There will be a sadness because of your loss but there will also be peace and pride because of the thoughtful care you gave so steadfastly all the way through to the end.

See also "Ginger's Story" in our book, *It's a Cat's Life* (New York: Berkley Publishing, 1990).

Home Nursing and Health Care

11

The Immune System

The immune system is the body's best friend. The natural state of the body is perfect health. We and our cats, in fact all animals alive today, have evolved successfully because we have all built up a wonderful defense system to withstand the germs and viruses and other microorganisms that have evolved along with us and are always present. That defense system is called the immune response.

Like any really good friend, the immune response will sometimes make us a bit uncomfortable for our own good. If germs invade the body, the immune system will make us uncomfortably warm, raising the body temperature to make an inhospitable environment for those invading germs. The skin protects us from germs. If the skin is punctured, the immune system will send an extra blood flow to the area, carrying white cells and nutrients to fight the invading germs and repair the broken tissue. This extra blood flow causes swelling and redness. If there were no swelling and redness at the site of the wound, invading bacteria would thrive and multiply unchecked. The pus that sometimes forms at the site of a wound is made up of dead white cells and dead bacteria. It is the proof that the body is waging a fierce battle against infection. Fever, swelling, mucus, pus, diarrhea, coughing, vomiting, or any of those things we have been taught to call disease symptoms are actually, to the holistic doctor, symptoms of health. They are proof that the individual's immune response is strong and alert and is reacting as it should to a potentially dangerous condition.

Allopathic medicine, which is practiced by most doctors and veterinarians in first world countries today, tells us that if the cat is coughing up phlegm and sneezing out mucus we should give him an antihistamine or an antibiotic to "stop the disease." A truly holistic veterinarian would explain that what they're really stopping is the cat's healthy response. The immune system is doing exactly what it's supposed to do to expel the germs. He would then prescribe a remedy that would promote the expulsion of toxins. He might also recommend a short fast on chicken broth and some specific supplements to support and enhance the process of detoxification.

Allopathic medicine focuses on the invading germ or virus and tries to kill it with a drug. It is most effective in treating acute conditions, and it can save lives. However, it does nothing to build and strengthen the body's natural immunity; in fact, drugs tend to weaken the immune system while they kill the disease germ so the patient becomes more and more susceptible every time he is treated by a drug.

Holistic medicine, on the other hand, focuses on the many ways of helping the patient's body and mind restore itself to a normal state so the body's own immune system can fight disease as it should. A high-quality diet, herbal preparations, vitamin supplements, acupuncture, chiropractic, and homeopathy are some of the ways to enhance naturally the body's ability to withstand and fight disease.

All allopathic medications have some undesirable side effects. Some are relatively minor while others can be life-threatening. These side effects can range anywhere from destroying bone marrow or the cells of the liver or kidney to depleting or washing out one or more vitamins or minerals from the body.

Remember, when your cat is taking any medication that every cat is different, just as all people are different, and your cat may react badly to one particular type of drug. So if your cat develops some undesirable symptom shortly after beginning a medication, call your veterinarian at once and tell him. It might be a recognized side effect that is not fatal, or it could be a sign that the medication is dangerously toxic to your particular cat. Remember, you are the only one who can monitor your cat's reactions. The veterinarian will appreciate the report of an alert and observant guardian.

Here are some of the changes that can signal a dangerous condition that the veterinarian will want to know about at once:

- *Panting, salivating, or swallowing repeatedly.* Can indicate nausea or poisoning, overload of toxins to the liver or kidneys, or heart problems.

- *Urine changing color, stopping, or becoming copious.* Liver damage or kidney failure.
- *Diarrhea or stool changing color.* Imbalance in intestinal chemistry or liver inflammation.
- *Shallow, rapid breathing.* Pain or internal swelling, possible heart problem.
- *Head tilt, shaking head, stumbling.* Inner ear or kidney problem, or possible complications in brain.

I reason that if a client of mine chooses to use a conventional drug to treat his cat, we can at least try to minimize the side effects. Once we know what the side effects are, we need not accept them as inevitable.

When a cat client of mine is given a medication, I always want to know what it is—what family or category it fits into—antibiotics, diuretics, cortisone or other steroids, anesthetics or tranquilizers, or mineral oil. I then tell the doctor what I intend to do in terms of adjusting the diet and adding nutrients or vitamin supplements. I want to be sure that any changes I make do not in any way aggravate the cat's special problem or interfere with the action of the medication prescribed. I'll give more specific information later, both in this chapter and under the specific health problems in Chapter 12.

Stress: A Cat's Natural Enemy

For a good many years now, the role played by stress in diseases of the human body has been a major concern. In cats, the link between stress and illness is even stronger. Cats have a lower threshold for stress than humans. This means that things not ordinarily stressful to us can sometimes actually be painful to a cat. The cat's sense of smell, for example, is so highly developed as to make ours seem virtually nonexistent by comparison.

Besides the cat's supersensitivity to physical stress such as sharp smells, loud noises, or extremes in temperature, the cat is also extremely sensitive to emotional stress. The loss of a loved one, be it animal or human, often sends the cat's emotions plunging into depression and even beyond, into deep mourning. Such hopeless sadness, if left unchecked, drains the system and leaves the body open to invasion by any germ or virus that happens along.

In the normal course of life, cats can usually handle stress pretty well. But when the cat is faced with multiple stresses, extreme stress, or prolonged stress, the body's reserves of energy are drained to a danger point. Cats faced with too much stress over too long a period of time become tense and nervous and then begin to withdraw. I've noticed that families who habitually hold two or three conversations simultaneously and therefore always speak in a shout often have shy, nervous cats who can usually be found huddled way in the darkest corner of a back bedroom closet. Cats cannot feel at ease in a stress-filled environment. It is obvious to them that they are not safe, and they live in a constant state of readiness for the next assault on their senses.

Cats in such situations are faced with prolonged stress that wears on their nerves and eventually leaves them vulnerable to disease. Stress burns up the body's stores of certain nutrients. A germ, virus, or fungus that other cats would normally throw off can take hold easily when a cat's resistance has been depleted by dealing with stress.

Stress can also be a trigger that activates any latent disease or lurking pathological condition within the body. When the same condition is repeatedly activated by any stressful situation in a cat's life, it is referred to as that cat's "stress target." When confronted with a feline client who tends to get any particular disease again and again, I always question the guardian about what was happening in the household immediately preceding the onset of the disease. Was the family away on a trip and the cat left alone? Was a family member ill or injured; or did someone lose their job? Did the family have visitors—perhaps young and active visitors? Or perhaps the painters came—moving furniture out of place and causing an excruciating smell?

It's a generally accepted fact that feline urologic syndrome, although caused by an alkaline condition in the urine, is emotionally triggered. However, almost any illness, from upper respiratory infection to foot fungus, can become active if too much stress in the environment lowers resistance to the point where a cat's particular weakness can take hold and thrive.

Granted, there will be many times in the life of any cat and its human family when you must knowingly subject your cat to serious stress. So, to avoid having your cat succumb to an illness, simply recognize stress situations for what they are and then make an extra effort to eliminate or at least cushion all other stress in the environment that you can control, and add the following extra antistress nutrients to your cat's meals for one week before and two weeks after:

Antistress Supplements

Nutrient	Dosage	How often
Vitamins A and D	10,000 units A and 400 units D	Once a week
B complex	10 mg	Once daily
Calcium lactate powder	$\frac{1}{16}$ teaspoon	Once daily
Vitamin C complex (ascorbic acid with bioflavonoid, hesperidins, and rutin)	250 units ($\frac{1}{16}$ teaspoon)	Every meal (up to six times a day)

Our first job is to determine what exactly constitutes stress to a cat, especially a sick or nervous cat, and then cushion or eliminate that stress as best we can. Below you'll find a list of some stresses a cat may encounter, along with suggestions about how to cope with them. In a majority of cases, common sense goes a long way.

Stress Factors

- *Any surprise.* Announce your intentions before doing anything—touching the cat, giving medication, and so on.
- *Loud noise.* Caution all visitors to speak in calm and soothing tones. If there is unavoidable noise in another part of the home, put a source of soothing classical music near the cat's resting place. A snug retreat should *always* be available (see page 304).
- *Guardian being upset or unhappy.* If you are dealing with a serious problem in your life, accept the fact that you cannot hide your tension from your feline friend, so don't try. Instead, tell your cat how you feel and assure him you're glad he's always there to help you feel calmer. If your source of worry is his illness, bring into your conscious mind positive

thoughts of love and gratitude that you have found good holistic health care practitioners. Be glad that it is you who will decide what to feed him and how best to support his recovery and discuss with him constructive plans about how you can make him more comfortable and hasten his journey back to health.

- *Change within the cat's environment.* Confine the cat to a small area such as the bathroom where no change is taking place. Or surround your cat with as many familiar things (toys, favorite pillow, a snug retreat [see page 304], one of your sneakers, and so on) as possible.

- *Change to a new environment.* Move the cat into one room that is already furnished with old, familiar furniture. Have the cat's litter box, food and water dishes, and toys already there. Let him get used to that room before introducing the rest of the new territory.

- *Introduction of visitors.* If your cat is shy, any new person should be seated and should first give voice, then eye, contact before touching the cat. Then he or she should extend *one* hand only, palm down, *below* the cat's nose level. Allow the cat to sniff the hand and let the cat reach out and touch the hand rather than the person reaching out to touch the cat. Don't force the issue; let the cat take his own time.

- *Absence of familiar people or being left alone.* See "While You're Away," page 131.

- *Being held down or restrained (during medical procedures such as X-rays or an EKG).* Keep calm and loving thoughts in your mind. Announce your intentions. Try to feel that what you're doing is an extension of petting. Explain "why" before you begin and again during the procedure. The cat will understand your good intentions and that you believe it will be safe. (See "Therapeutic Communication," page 262.)

- *Confinement or caging.* Explain why and tell when you will be back to fetch him. Provide a brown paper bag or small cardboard box in which the cat can hide, as described in Chapter 10, "Selecting Methods of Treatment and Seeking Professional Help."

- *X-rays, anesthetics, and medications.* For a week before until two weeks after, add to each meal the antistress supplements (page 305).

- *Surgery, catheterization, and wounds.* Give antistress supplements (page 305).

- *Preservatives ingested in food, in vitamin preparations, or in hairball remedies.* Preservatives such as sodium benzoate (benzoate of soda), ethoxyquin,

BHA, BHT, nitrites, and nitrates affect both the central nervous system and the autonomic nervous system. Read all labels—even if the product is prescribed or sold by a veterinarian. Their field of expertise does not include a study of chemical preservatives and additives.

- *Inhalation of nerve gas given off by some commercial flea collars.* Buy your flea collars in the health food store. Alert caregivers prefer flea collars made from natural ingredients rather than toxic chemicals. See Appendix, "Product Recommendations."

- *Major trauma or fright,* such as an accident or being attacked. Give Bach Flower Rescue Remedy (see page 215)—three drops every twenty minutes for four doses; then every two hours for three doses; then three times a day for two days.

- *Noise and drafts.* Create a snug retreat (page 304).

- *Extremes of heat and cold.* Use a hot water bottle or an ice pack inside a heavy sock in the carry case (page 31), and use a snug retreat as described on page 304.

- *Litter box problems.* Usually, it's not good to have the litter box near the sleeping area, but in the case of an older or convalescent cat an exception must be made in order to make it easier for the patient. Be extra finicky about keeping it clean—a dirty box is a definite stress. (See Chapter 3, "The Litter Box.")

- *Inactivity.* A sick cat needs rest while recuperating, but the attentive owner will sense the time when a little exercise will not go amiss. The best way to get the circulation going is to encourage the convalescent cat to begin moving about a bit. So, after the patient has gained enough strength, encourage him to walk a bit by carrying him into the next room and letting him walk back to his bed. Easy does it.

- *Sharp smells (tobacco smoke, room deodorizers, or other chemicals).* Try to be aware, and you'll improve your own sense of smell and avoid stress for yourself too.

- *Obesity.* See "Obesity," page 444.

- *Being soiled by excrement, medication, and so on.* Wipe it off at once before it hardens on the cat's fur. See Chapter 8, "Grooming."

- *Any infection or infestation.* Follow your holistic veterinarian's orders. See suggestions under the appropriate health problem in Chapter 12. Also read the appropriate section in *Dr. Pitcairn's Complete Guide to Natural Health for Dogs and Cats.*

- *Tooth tartar or cavities.* Dentistry should be done by the veterinarian as soon as the cat is well enough.
- *Pain.* Minimize salt (sodium) in the diet and add the antistress supplements given on page 305. The vitamin A and D capsule supplies vitamin D, which the body needs to assimilate calcium. If swelling, incision, wound, or redness, is involved, consult your homeopath, but if none is available, give homeopathic remedy arnica 30C twice a day for two days only. (See "Homeopathy," page 211.)
- *Overfilling the stomach.* It's better to feed too little than too much. See "Fasting" and "Force Feeding" in this chapter.
- *Food too hot or cold.* When in doubt, feel the cat's food with your finger. If you like it, he'll like it.
- *Being unneutered.* Have the cat neutered by a competent veterinarian. See Chapter 6, "Neuter and Spay, It's the Kindest Way."

When caring for a cat who is already ill with a disease—in itself a major stress—minimize other stresses as much as possible in order to save the cat's energy, calories, adrenaline, and vital life force, so that they can be used to fight the disease. It is a gratifying experience for the sensitive caregiver to be able to raise the odds in his cat's favor in this way, especially when his cat is ill.

To cushion any stress

- Check environment for *all* of the above.
- Provide a snug retreat (see page 304) in a quiet area and give frequent short contacts of attention and love.
- Bolster the cat's system by including antistress supplements (see page 305) in the cat's diet.

Administering Medications

When doing anything to cats—pilling, force feeding, grooming, and so on—it's best to try to indicate to them *beforehand* what you are trying to do. Don't have any secrets; fear of the unknown is the cat's greatest fear. If you can let him know what you want to do, even though he may not like it or may indicate an objection or try to leave, at least he will not become hysterical. If you keep him from leaving and reassure him as you proceed to gently have your way, chances are the whole thing will be over very quickly. He'll come to regard the experience as one of those bizarre acts that humans indulge in from time to time that are, on the one hand, mildly unpleasant and not to be understood, but, on the other hand, neither painful nor threatening. Because there's nothing a cat can do, he puts up with such acts out of the love he bears in his heart for you. After all, you have not been raised as a cat and therefore cannot be expected to be perfect in every way.

I find I can get away with an awful lot and save a great deal of wear and tear on the cat's nerves by making the cat believe that I am "petting" him. If I have to do any touching with the hands—it doesn't matter what the reason really is—from giving an enema to putting salve in the eyes, if I truly believe in my heart that I am expressing love by doing this thing, then I can convey that feeling to the cat.

Cats do understand that humans are different from cats and have different ways of showing affection. For example, Marshmallow Goodfellow, an abandoned white shorthair, had to take six pills a day during treatment for feline urologic syndrome brought on by bladder stones. Poor Marshmallow had spent his first four years before landing at my place consuming huge quantities of dry food and tuna fish. It would have been surprising if he had *not* developed urinary problems. He was an enormous and fearsome-looking white male whose personality was best described by his name: Marshmallow. His craving for physical affection was so great that he would lift a paw and pat my trousers again and again to get attention and then throw himself on the floor at my feet, roll onto his back, and lick my ankle. When finally picked up and hugged, he liked to wrap his front legs around my neck and hug back, capping the joyful moment by vigorously washing my cheek.

I was very busy during his first weeks with me and never seemed to have enough time to completely fulfill Marshie's need for affection. Because feline urologic syndrome is well-known to be a stress-linked disease, I didn't want him to feel threatened because every time he saw me I started shoving a pill down his throat. I had to condition Marshmallow to believe that petting was petting no matter where he was touched, so I set up a positive association between pilling and petting and love so that he would look forward to the pill rather than fearing it. It wasn't hard. All I did was always assume the kneeling pill-giving position (described later in this chapter) every time I petted him, whether I was giving a pill or not. Then I began to broaden his petting horizons, as it were, by stroking his legs, feet, thighs, and so on, along with all the usual places. Then, because I wanted to give him pills, I even included his teeth, lips, and tongue. He gave me a doubtful look the first time but seemed to accept it philosophically thereafter. When I worked in the actual pilling procedure, that sweet animal accepted it along with all the rest. He looked forward to pilling time with happy anticipation as his own special petting time. And to this day that sweet animal still cherishes the belief that crazy Anitra likes to express affection by petting a pussycat's tongue. You can establish the same petting association with anything you need to do to care for your cat: nail clipping, grooming, and the like. I found it very easy to examine Marshmallow's teeth and flick off tartar with my thumbnail after that.

But first, before you begin any procedures, always remember to wash your hands. And, even more important, rinse them. Remember, the cat's sense of smell is many, many times sharper than yours. If someone wanted to pop a small piece of your favorite candy in your mouth, how would you accept it if, just as the hand approached your face, you caught a whiff of chemical or other unpleasant odor? Good grief! Make sure your hand smells only like a hand.

Therapeutic Communication

Cats easily pick up your intentions, thought pictures, and emotions. So when you're going through all the steps leading up to pilling or wrapping the cat in a towel, or grooming, or whatever, think of each and every step along the way as separate from all the other steps, and fix clearly in your own mind that you are expressing love by doing it. In almost every case, you will be able to find a way to make each separate step feel good to the cat.

As you continue to stroke him, use your own words to convey these ideas:

Tell him the reason for doing the procedure:	"I know how you're feeling . . ." (Describe in detail how his body is feeling.)

and follow with:

Tell him the purpose of what you're doing:	"I'm going to help you feel better . . ." (Describe how you want his body to feel.)

and finally:

Tell him the procedure: "This is what we're going to do to make you feel better. First, . . ." (Describe each step of the procedure. When you're following suggestions from this book, you can read them aloud to your cat.)

Using this method of communicating with your cat accomplishes two goals: First, it conveys to the patient some idea of what you're planning. (Remember, cats hate surprises.) Second, describing the procedure to your cat will actually help you do it better. It's a scientific fact that doing something in your mind before you do it physically improves your technique.

Wrapping the Cat for Medication

As close as my Priscilla and I are, I always have to wrap her to give her remedies by mouth. Otherwise she reaches up her left paw—Priscilla is left-handed—and keeps pushing my hand away so I'm not able to get the remedy beyond the hump in her tongue and down her throat. I know she really wants to cooperate, and she wishes she could, but she simply can't control herself. Cats are like that. Sometimes they just can't cooperate without your help.

Wrapping the cat in a towel gives you much more control. Instead of the cat being almost an equal partner in the project, it puts you totally in command. The towel should not be thick, fluffy, or expensive. The easiest towel to work with for wrapping is a bath towel that is thin and old.

Here is a suggested breakdown of the steps, but you can break any one of these steps down even further if you like (see Figure 12).

1. Set up a chair by the table, place the remedy on the table; put the towel folded in half the long way on the back of the chair.
2. Carry the cat to the chair, sit down with your knees together, and drape the towel across your lap. With the fold toward your knees, stand the cat on the towel facing away from you.
3. Grasp the cat's forelegs up near the chest in your right hand and, with

your left hand on the rump, lift the cat up and lay him on his side on the towel, with feet pointing to the right.

4. Hold the forelegs down flat against the cat's chest, fold the left towel flap, then the right *snugly* over the cat's front legs to pin them down securely. Hold the towel flaps secure with the inside of your knee.

5. Medicate the cat, unwrap him, and then give a treat.

Be sure to wrap the cat firmly. You are not doing the cat a favor by leaving the towel loose. Not only is this totally ineffective, but if there's any room for struggle, rest assured that the cat will struggle and thrash and work himself into a much worse state than if the towel were snug. The whole purpose of wrapping is to immobilize the cat.

It's almost a necessity when you wrap a cat to be able to do it swiftly and smoothly so that your motions are a few beats ahead of what your cat anticipates. That way he can't imagine anything dire or terrible; it's already done before he knows it, and it's not terrible at all—it's only snug and secure.

As always, turn the whole thing into a demonstration of love accompanied by much nuzzling and praise. One of my clients asked her black Persian, Binkey, to help her do "a wonderful new trick." Binkey enjoys performing his towel "trick" for visitors. You might like to practice the wrapping ritual once a week to be sure you have the skill whenever you might need it. Start by practicing only steps 1, 2, and 3 until you are at ease with them. Then add one more step at a time. As long as you're doing a lot of head scratching, and throat stroking, with a treat afterward, your cat will learn to look forward to a pleasant experience when he sees the special towel come out. This is a perfect occasion to end with an Anitra's Natural Cat Treat, PetGuard yeast and garlic tablet, a Purrlicious treat, or a liver tablet, followed by a nice mutual scratch on the post or a chase after a ping-pong ball.

Patience is the watchword. Think of each of the steps as a separate accomplishment. Because during those practice runs you are not under any pressure to actually get medication into the cat, you can spend the first two or three sessions just stroking around the armpits and shoulders, where you will later be grasping to lift and turn him over. That way you'll learn how the leg bones feel, where the underarm tendons are, and how to keep him comfortable.

I feel sorry for people who never stroke beyond a cat's head and back. Cats are very sensual with each other. So, when you learn to enjoy stroking the chest,

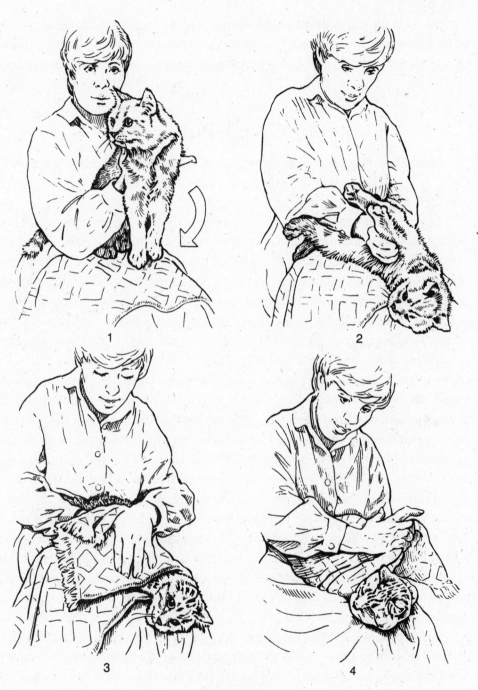

FIGURE 12
Wrapping the cat

armpits, and bloomers and massaging the foreleg muscles and thighs, you are really expressing love in a very cat-like manner. Explore the bone structure and musculature as if you were giving a massage. You and your cat will both love it.

Giving Pills

Note: This information covers giving supplements or medications in pill form EX-CEPT FOR HOMEOPATHIC PILLS. For methods of giving homeopathic pills, see pages 310–312.

Before you begin, file down the nail on the index finger of your pill-giving hand so you won't scratch the cat's throat when you push the pill past the back of the tongue. The easiest way to give a cat a pill is to kneel down with the balls of your feet on the floor, knees apart, feet together behind you, and your seat on your heels. Back the cat in toward you. Have the pill ready on a plate beside you. With your left hand, palm down, gently grasp the cat's cheekbones from above. The heel of your hand will be resting on the back of the head behind the ears. Pressing down with the heel of the hand, lift up the cheekbones. *Slightly* tilt the head back. Pick up the pill and hold it between your right index finger and thumb. *Turn the pill hand palm up*. Then insert the nail of the middle finger between the patient's front teeth and, with the back of the nail, urge the lower jaw downward, opening the mouth. Place or toss the pill into the throat as far back as possible. Don't think of putting the pill into the cat's mouth; you are putting it into his throat. If necessary, you can push it farther back, beyond the hump of the tongue using that index finger with the short nail. Now, suddenly release the mouth and head completely; keeping the cat where he is. The sudden release will make him swallow with surprise. To encourage another swallow put the heel of your left hand just behind the ears and your right hand lightly under the tip of the chin and press the patient's head down and forward, guiding the chin out, away from the body and stretching out the throat again. Release suddenly, guaranteeing a second swallow.

Some people like to massage the sides of the throat down in a swallowing motion. Be sure to stroke down the sides, not down the front over the cough reflex. Don't make the mistake of holding the cat's mouth closed. Cats swallow with their teeth ajar, and the tongue must be able to move out through the front of the lips. In fact, you can tell that the cat has swallowed by watching for the appearance of the little pink tongue flicking out and in. Don't hold the head back once the pill is in the mouth. This, too, prevents the cat from swallowing.

Like so many other things, pilling becomes easier the more you do it. Dr. Rowan preferred to throw the pill down the throat in a lovely little arc. He also had a way of lightly blowing into the cat's nostrils to make the cat open his or her mouth. He had developed "pilling" to a fine art.

I found that my own art developed between my trying to teach the cat how to take a pill and the cat trying to teach me how best to give it. I think with this attitude you will definitely progress. To keep the cats safe, I keep the nail of the right index finger so short it is practically nonexistent. You cannot use this method if you have anything but the shortest of nails. A nail could scrape against the roof of the cat's mouth; the mucous membrane is very delicate back there.

Before you try to pill the cat, find out from your vet if it's all right if he takes the pill with food. Some pills must be given *before* the meal. If it is okay to put the pill in the food, I suggest you use the method I worked out when a pretty little calico named Ruth was boarded with me while she convalesced from a liver infection. I had to make sure she took all of the medication and didn't just eat around it. I delayed the dinner and then took an unusually long time preparing the meal so Ruth smelled the food but couldn't get at it. Her hunger became even sharper. I crushed the pill and divided it into two sections. Then I took a quarter teaspoonful of food and hid a part of the pill inside it. I held the bit of food with the pill inside just out of Ruth's reach, and asked her if she'd like to have it. When she reached for it, I gratified her. I gave it to her with lots of love and encouragement. This way she wolfed that little bit down, never noticing the piece of pill hidden inside.

Now I pretended that that was all I was going to give her. I started making my own salad. When she asked for more to eat, I acted surprised that she was still hungry and repeated the process of holding the tidbit concealing the pill, asking her if she was quite, quite sure she still wanted it. Then again I relented and gave it to her with more gushes of love. Once the pill was consumed, I placed the rest of her dinner in the dish on the floor as usual. I didn't mix the pill in with all of the dinner because that might have been just the day that Ruth decided not to finish it. I had to remain in control of those bits of pill until they passed safely down Ruth's gullet.

If this doesn't work for you, you can try the exact same ritual except that, instead of hiding the pill in quarter-teaspoonfuls of your cat's usual dinner, you can mix it with a small amount of some fabulous treat that your cat is sure to gobble up if he gets the slightest chance—baby food lamb, a quarter teaspoon of soft butter, or perhaps a small piece of sardine if you're desperate—but don't stoop to tuna, that's really beyond the pale. Sometimes even this won't work, and you'll have to pill the cat in the classic manner described earlier, or after wrapping the cat in a towel. Or you can mix the crushed pill with baby food meat and bit by bit wipe it off on the palate just behind the front teeth, as in finger feeding (see page 286).

Giving Liquid Medication

When giving liquid medication, you must be careful not to choke the cat by suddenly shooting a stream down the center of the throat. Don't use a syringe; they sometimes stick and then squirt. This could result in serious choking. Proceed in exactly the same way that you force-feed a liquid (page 288). Insert the dropper at the corner of the mouth, pointing it down the side between the cheek pouch and teeth and releasing the medication in a slow series of gentle drops so the volume of the liquid is small enough each time for the cat to deal with easily. Do not try to give it all at once. Give the cat ample time to swallow whenever she needs to. Patience brings success.

Giving Paste or Gel Medications (the Pâté method)

The pâté method is a technique for getting unpalatable vitamins or other supplements or pills down a sick cat's throat with a minimum of stress. Mix the necessary medication or other supplement into about ½ teaspoon butter or baby food meat, adding water to thin or baby food barley flakes to thicken. Bring it to a pâté consistency that will hold a pea-size shape and stick to the tip of your index finger. Read the section on finger feeding on page 286. Then give the pâté bit by bit the same as when you force-feed.

Cleaning Around the Eyes

This step is only for those cats who have runny eyes or who tend to build up dirt in the corner of the eyes. The area around the eyes should always be cleaned before you administer eyedrops or eye medication to remove any crustiness or discoloration. Because this exudation is caused by debris and discharge from the tear ducts, you will then irrigate the tear ducts to clean and disinfect them.

I have seen eye exudations on cats of all breeds. Dirty residue on the fur around the eyes makes a good home for germs, viruses, and fungus to breed and reinfect the eye. Tear ducts left blocked with dirt or swollen shut will also breed germs and cause more residue to spill out around the eyes. Any herb or medication designed to fight infection in the tear ducts will have little effect if the tear duct is totally blocked or swollen shut so the medication can't get through. If you get liquid medication on the crusty discharge around the eye, you'll turn that crustiness into mud and soil even more of the cat's face.

Runny-eye syndrome often markedly improves and in some cases clears up completely after a holistic regimen is begun. But in cases of eye infection or where careless breeding has rendered the tear ducts all but nonexistent, you do have to clean the cat's eyes every day, and sometimes twice a day.

Wiping away the dried tears and the brown stain will help only temporarily since the cause of the problem persists in the tear ducts. It is the tear ducts and the general health that we must address if we hope to effect real and long-term improvement. Irrigation of the tear ducts is simple, soothing, and remarkably effective. Of course, it would be foolhardy to expect any single therapy alone to result in complete and permanent elimination of the problem. Attention must be given to diet, nutritional supplements, efficiency of the entire waste disposal system, and stress reduction. I see a lot of Persians with runny or crusty eyes, and I am happy to report that regular irrigation of the tear ducts as part of a holistic health program always reduces the problems and often eliminates them altogether. Since the procedure actually feels good to the cat and has no negative side effects, I use it freely.

The purpose of washing the eyes and irrigating the tear ducts is to cleanse and disinfect the ducts and to sooth and shrink swollen tissues so that closed or clogged ducts will open and allow fluid to run freely from the eye into the throat. The procedure given below can also be used in addition to nose drops if your cat is suffering from upper respiratory problems. (See also "Eye Problems," page 368.)

Washing around the eyes is easy, pleasant, and soothing.

1. Start by wiping the discharge lightly with a piece of tissue or paper towel over your index finger. You'll remove any wetness that hasn't dried to a crust yet.

2. Use a fine British comb (see page 163) and carefully begin to comb the crustiness and dirt away. If some of it won't budge, don't worry and don't press the comb harder. The tissue of the skin is very delicate and sensitive around the eyes, so be gentle. Keep cleaning the debris off the comb with your tissue or paper towel.

3. Urge the cat to close his eye by stroking close to and over the eye. Then put two or three drops of saline solution or boric acid solution (see page 271) on the remaining discharge and gently begin to comb it into the dirty area, softening up the crustiness. Again, clean off the comb frequently and blot the softened discharge away with a tissue. This old discharge is not only unsanitary but the skin under this mess is very itchy so your cat may press his face into the teeth of the comb in an effort to scratch the itchy skin. Don't let him get too forceful; the tiny teeth of the flea comb are sharp and could scratch the delicate tissue. Just ask him to be patient as you continue to place the drops and comb and blot a few more times. As you work, remind him that you both want the same thing—clean, comfortable skin, hair, and eyes—and that this is exactly what you are going to be giving him.

If your cat is a Persian, he may have a bone-deep crease between the cheek and nose. Dirt often hides in there. Using the thumb of your stroking hand, you can move the cheek skin out away from the nose, making it easier to get down into the crease with drops, comb, and tissue.

You may not get rid of all the debris on the first day. Don't worry. It's much more important that you teach the cat to *like* the procedure. That's the most important first step. You will get him nice and clean, little by little, and if he likes it, he'll make it easy for the two of you forever after.

Administering Eyedrops and Irrigating Tear Ducts

Eyedrops are used to cleanse and irrigate the tear ducts, soothing and shrinking swollen tissue. Prepare for giving eyedrops by gathering the following equipment:

- Piece of sterile cotton or a tissue or one-eighth of a paper towel
- Paper towel torn in quarters
- Eye drop formula—see formulas below and indications for which formula to use
- Teacup or small cereal dish
- Medium-size bowl or saucepan
- Flea comb

Eye and Nose Drop Formulas

Most human commercial eye or nose drop preparations contain chemicals harmful to cats. Buy unpreserved unbuffered saline solution for contact lens wearers. (Be sure the bottle reads *unpreserved* and does not say *buffered* on the label.) Or, make your own normal saline solution (see directions below). The medical term for saline solution is "normal saline solution."

I. Normal Saline Solution

Use this solution to shrink tissue, open tear ducts, or relieve nose congestion and aid in expulsion of mucus:

½ cup boiled water
⅛ teaspoon salt (sodium chloride or sea salt)

- Dissolve salt in water; *cool* and store in covered container in refrigerator. Keeps for a week or so. Before using, heat to warm bath temperature by standing the container of solution in a bowl or pan of hot water. It should taste less salty than the ocean.

II. Boric Acid Solution

Use this solution to wash out debris in the eyes:

½ cup boiled water that has cooled a bit
¼ teaspoon boric acid

- Combine ingredients in a covered jar. Shake well until powder is dissolved. Cool and store as above with Normal Saline Solution. Strain off any leftover powder.

III. Herbal Solutions

To shrink swollen tissue and disinfect eyes, nostrils, or sinuses:

- Put six drops goldenseal or echinacea extract into a 1 oz dropper bottle and fill to three-quarters with saline solution (or add two drops goldenseal or echinacea to 1 tablespoon saline solution).

To soothe red tissue:

- Add two drops eyebright extract to 1 tablespoon boric acid solution (or six drops into a 1 oz dropper bottle).

Preparation

1. *Practice the technique.* First, put two or three drops of the solution you want to use into your own eye. It will feel fresh and soothing. That is exactly the impression you will convey to your cat. You can put some solution into a one-ounce dropper bottle. If you don't have a dropper bottle, cut a cotton ball in half and saturate it with the solution, or roll up one-eighth of a paper towel and saturate that. If you're using the cotton ball or paper towel, squeeze it out a bit so it doesn't drip. Hold it between the thumb and the *second joint* of the index finger. Point the index finger straight down about a half inch above the sink, and gradually squeeze the cotton so the solution runs down the finger and drops fall off the fingertip one at a time. (See figure 13 on page 274). If you're using a dropper, practice with that until you can count three drops and then stop. Then practice pointing your finger down at a target that represents the inner corner of the cat's eye (the tip of a teaspoon would be a good target). Practice until you are able to make the three drops land where you want them to land. Have your finger only a half inch above the target; otherwise the drops will hit the eye too forcefully.

2. *Warm the solution.* Stand the dropper bottle in a cup of hot water or pour two or three tablespoons of the solution into a cup or shotglass and stand the cup or shotglass in a bowl or pan of hot water. Warm to cat's body temperature (100.5 to 101.5 feels like pleasantly warm bath water).

3. *While the solution is warming, bring the cat to the therapy area.* Take the pilling position (see page 266). Before you give the drops, stroke all around his head, cheeks, forehead, and eyes. As you do this, follow the therapeutic communication technique (page 262). Tell him (a) that you understand his problem (describe how his eyes feel and look); (b) what you're going to do about it (how the drops will cleanse the eyes and/or nasal passages, shrink swollen tissue, and help him breathe more freely so he can enjoy the smells of his friends and his food again); and (c) in detail all the steps in the procedure below. All of this elaborate explaining beforehand has another very important benefit—it improves your technique tremendously.

4. *Follow the procedure below, explaining everything again as you do it.*

Procedure

Note: *Whenever you do anything involving the cat's eyes, never approach directly from the front because this will cause the cat to turn his head away from the oncoming fingers. Instead, keep all motions close to the head and glide in slowly from the back or the top or side of the head to whatever position is required.*

Ask your cat to help you by giving you his cooperation.

1. If using a dropper bottle, draw approximately the correct number of drops into the dropper and hold it, point down, in your right hand. Or, if using the cotton or paper towel, resaturate it with nice warm saline solution, and, holding it between the right thumb and second joint of the index finger, squeeze it out a little so it doesn't drip all over the cat's face.

2. With your left hand grasp the cat's head from above, placing your thumb and middle finger below the cat's cheekbones.

3. Gently tilt the cat's head back until his eyes are facing up toward the ceiling.

4. Stroke the eye closed.

5. Moving the hand holding the eye drops around from behind his head, position the dropper tip about one-half inch above the inner corner of the eye or position your right hand holding the wet cotton or paper towel so the index finger

Figure 13
Administering eye drops

is pointing straight down and the fingertip is about one-half inch away from the inner corner of the cat's closed eye.

6. Squeeze out two or three drops from the dropper or slowly squeeze the cotton or paper towel until three drops roll one at a time down the index finger and drop into the inner corner of the eye. Put the cotton or paper towel down and

urge the eye open a little by gently massaging upward on the skin above the eye, then downward below the eye so the soothing liquid can flow into the eye.

7.   Continue to hold the head back in the tilted position; pick up a dry piece of paper towel; let the eye close; and blot the excess solution with the paper towel before it trickles down the cat's nose or cheek—they greatly appreciate neatness.

8.   Release the head. Pet and praise and thank the cat and watch to see if his tongue tip flicks out at the front of his lips. This tongue action indicates the cat has had to swallow because the solution has run down the tear duct from the eye into the back of the throat. The swallow shows us that the tear duct is open and has been successfully irrigated.

If no tongue appears, indicating that no swallowing was necessary because the tear duct is still blocked, repeat the procedure up to three times. Always irrigate both eyes even if only one eye has a problem.

Applying Salve to the Eyes

Position the cat the same way you do with simple pilling—kneel on the floor and back the cat in between your knees, making sure your feet are together so the cat won't slip out behind you.

Begin stroking the head and the throat—you know your cat's favorite places. Eye medication is usually a salve in a tube. Put a dot of the salve on the tip of your right index finger. (Once again, be sure your nail is short.) Continue stroking the cat's head with your left thumb. Now you want to indicate to the cat that you're going to do something to the right eye. You want him to close his right eye. Stroke ever so lightly near and around the eye until the cat closes it. As soon as he does so, stroke lightly and gently over the closed eye from nose to cheek several times, making loving, murmuring sounds.

Position that right index finger against the lower lid so that the dot of salve can be wiped off on the inside of the lower lid by simply rotating the finger inward. Don't do it yet. The eye is still closed—you are still stroking with your thumb and murmuring. On one of those thumb strokes, stop midway, place the thumb above the upper lid just above the eye slit, pull the lid a little upward and separate it slightly, exposing the eyeball; rotate your right finger inward, and wipe the salve off on the inside of the lower lid. Then immediately release the eye, letting it close, and stroke the forehead a few times. You repeat with the opposite hand for the other eye—put the salve on the left index finger for the left eye. Dr. Camuti, the famous cat doctor, always medicated both eyes. He reasoned that, because cats will always scratch the eye that was treated, you should treat both to create confusion. If the salve is an antibiotic or some other drug, I feel better if I use a dot of plain petroleum jelly on the healthy eye. The fewer drugs in a cat's system, the better.

Keep all your motions very small. Always move in from the back of the head toward the eye. If your cat sees you poking your finger at him from in front, he will naturally try to avoid it by turning his head and wiggling away. It's a reflex action. Humans have the same reflex.

The whole process is really quite pleasant and tranquil. Smearing the dot of salve inside the lower lid is one of those things that cats can place under the catchall heading of bizarre but harmless human behavior that a wise cat learns to accept and forgive.

Giving Nose Drops

Read the section above on giving eyedrops (page 270) and choose plain saline solution, saline solution with goldenseal, or saline solution with echinacea, according to your cat's needs. First, practice the procedure without the cat. Here's the difference in administering nose drops:

To administer nose drops tilt the cat's head so his nostrils are facing up toward the ceiling. Put two or three drops in one nostril; keep the head well back for a count of six so the drops will run into the sinuses before trickling down into the throat. Then let the patient relax and swallow. Now do the other nostril. It feels so good I usually do three rounds. *Be ready with a tissue.* Saline drops break up congestion. If you're lucky, the patient will give a good sneeze. Your cat always appreciates knowing what you're going to do before you do it, so explain the entire procedure to him step by step, making sure to tell him why you do each step and how each step will feel. Explain the results: how the drops will cleanse the nasal passages, shrink swollen tissue, and help him breathe more freely so he can enjoy the smells of his friends and his food again. As I pointed out, all this elaborate explaining beforehand has another very important benefit—it improves your technique tremendously.

Giving Ear Medication

As a general rule, the less you put into the cat's ears, the better. If a cat's ears are clean, pink, and healthy, a careful caregiver can determine on a regular basis that they are indeed staying that way by cleaning only the area that can be seen with the naked eye once a week with a sterile cotton swab moistened with a drop or two of vitamin E oil squeezed from a punctured capsule. Warm olive, almond, or sesame oil will also work. Gently swab all dirt and exudation away from any area you can see; then, holding the swab about one inch from the tip, clean only an inch down into the ear canal. If you see a tiny bit of soft brown wax on the cotton swab, don't panic. All cats—in fact, all creatures, including you—secrete wax in the ears. The wax traps the dust. If you didn't secrete wax, dust could blow in and lodge near the eardrum acting as a sort of mute. So don't worry about a little wax. It's when there's a lot of wax or, worse yet, when there's a great deal of hard, blackish-brown wax, that you are allowed a gasp of dismay and should phone the veterinarian for an appointment. Whatever the diagnosis turns out to be, you will probably be given something—a liquid or salve—to put in the ears. You can also refer to the specific problem in Chapter 12.

Caution: Almost every veterinary ear preparation contains some sort of steroid. I don't use them. If, for some reason, a client of mine decides to use conventional veterinary ear drops, I advise asking the veterinarian if he could give you eye drops that contain the same ingredients but without steroids. Eye medications almost never contain steroids.

Do not put medication or cleaner into a cat's ear immediately after cleaning it out with a cotton swab because the membrane will be irritated and supersensitive. Wait at least a day after using a swab.

You may have to wrap your cat in order to be sure that you get the medication into the ear rather than all over the ruff and whiskers. I usually medicate ears by simply kneeling on the floor and backing the cat in between my legs (as described in "Giving Pills," page 266). Here again, take the opportunity to make each step feel good, and, before you begin, describe to your cat exactly what you are going to do and how it will help him. Remember that the cat's ear canal is itching and/or burning. Have the salve or dropper open and ready on the table beside you and warm all liquids to bath temperature before you use them.

First, make your cat feel a little better by stroking the forehead and behind the ear, thus distracting attention away from the discomfort inside the ear and indicating clearly where you're going to be working so it won't be a surprise. Include the ear itself in your gentle stroking. Next, take hold of the ear shell down near the base. Don't try to hold the tip—but first stroke through that hold position, letting the ear slip through your fingers. Again, it feels good and distracts your cat from the discomfort. While you stroke, look for the hole down which you will drop the salve. Pick up the dropper or tube of salve, and when you have the medicine ready at the tip of the applicator, take a last stroke, and now gently hold the ear still. Insert the tip of the dropper or applicator tube into the hole, pointing it in and down toward the tip of the nose and press out the prescribed amount of the soothing, healing substance. You are making your cat feel better. Now, withdraw the dropper or tube and swiftly press the hole closed by pressing the ear flap over it *from back to front* to hold the healing remedy inside. Be consciously aware of that soothing cream or liquid trickling down the itching, irritated tissue. If you can bring these facts to your consciousness and tell the cat in an honest way what is happening, the cat will focus on the relief experienced rather than on the strangeness of your current mode of expressing love. If you very gently massage the area, you can sometimes hear the medicine gurgling around down in the ear canal, bathing irritated membranes and suffocating the nasty organisms. Tell the cat what you are doing. Loving caregivers have very close relationships with their cats and will derive immense satisfaction from the relief they give during an ear treatment.

Now, a word of caution. If you are dealing with mites, the conventional medications are always quite harsh. Mitox, for example, which is used only once a week or every ten days (but for six or seven weeks), is quite caustic. So skip the massaging part of the ritual. Once any mite medication is in the ear, simply hold the cat's head as still as possible, a little tipped to the side in a position so the liquid can dribble deep into the ear canal and kill the mites. *Don't clean the cat's ears with a cotton swab before or after mite medication—you don't want to irritate the mucous membrane inside the ear in any way.* (See more about ear mites in "Ear Problems," page 363.)

Ear Cleaning and Treatment

When you first begin treatment of an ear problem, you will usually encounter some wax buildup inside the ears. To get the ear medication onto the membrane lining of the ear canal, you'll have to get rid of the wax. If you are going to follow up with medication, it is important not to irritate the membrane by wiping over it with a cotton swab. If the ear membrane is even a little bit irritated, the medication will make it feel like it's on fire! So, clean with a swab *only* if you're not going to put *anything* in the ear afterward. Otherwise, for deep cleaning without irritation, see "Simple Cleaning of the Ears" and "Flushing the Ears" below.

Simple Cleaning of the Ears

Note: Be sure you have not used a swab in the ears for at least twenty-four hours before performing this procedure.

1. *Soften and dissolve wax.* Put a dropperful of warm Wax-O-Sol (see "Product Recommendations" in the Appendix) into the ear. Quickly fold the ear flap forward, from back to front, to close the ear. Hold it closed for 60 seconds. You can gently massage the liquid around while you're holding it in.
2. After 60 seconds, let the ears go. The cat will vigorously shake his head and bits of wax will fly out of the ear. I like to do this procedure in the bathroom where I can easily clean the wax off the wall tiles. You can also hold a dish towel up beside the cat's head, so the wax will fly into the towel.
3. Finish cleaning and leave the ear feeling fresh by repeating the procedure—except this time, use a dropperful of Halo Herbal Ear Wash (see "Product Recommendations" in the Appendix) or use plain witch hazel. If your vet has recommended an ear flush, proceed to "Flushing the Ears" below.

Flushing the Ears

This is an irrigation technique used to wash out debris. Flushing, if done as directed, is safe, gentle, and very effective. Use Irrigation Formula I for cleansing or Irrigation Formula II to soothe and heal.

Irrigation Formula I (for cleansing)

This formula will cleanse, kill germs and fungus, and reduce swelling.

1 cup distilled or spring water
1 teaspoon vegetable rinse *or* **10 drops golden seal extract**
¼ teaspoon sea salt

Irrigation Formula II (to soothe and heal)

This formula will cleanse, soothe, reduce swelling, and promote healing. Do not use this formula on abscesses until the fluid draining out is clear and you are ready to allow the incision to heal over.

1 cup distilled or spring water
¼ teaspoon salt
1 teaspoon tincture of calendula

Irrigation Procedure

For ear flush: Use a rubber ear syringe.

1. Before using, heat the solution to 101 degrees (cat's body temperature) by standing a cup of the solution in a bowl of hot water.

2. Do therapeutic communication (see page 262), explaining to the cat what you intend to do (steps 8 and 9 below) and what you expect to accomplish. Do this even if you've already done the same procedure only moments before. The cats love it.

3. Warm the bathtub by running hot water into it, and let it stand while you go on to step 4.

4. Prepare one of the irrigation formulas given above. Let the cup of formula stand in a bowl of hot water throughout the procedure to maintain a "warm bath" temperature of about 101 degrees.

5. Drain the bathtub, and dry it with a hand towel. A warm tub is more pleasant for the cat to stand in than a cold tub.

6. Get the patient and bring her to the nice warm tub. Get into the warm, dry tub with the cat, take the pill-giving position (page 266), and go through the therapeutic communication procedure again as you proceed step by step.

7. Fill a syringe with the irrigation formula. Stroke the cat's head, neck, and body lovingly; then lightly include the area you will irrigate.

8. Discomfort can occur during an ear flush if the solution is too hot or cold, if the inside of the ear has been irritated during frequent cleanings with a cotton swab, or if the syringe used is not filled completely and emits a hissing or bubbling sound as air is permitted to rush in or out. This squishing sound so close to the eardrum can be painful to a cat, so make sure the syringe is completely full of solution by holding the syringe with the tip upward and slowly squeezing the ball of the syringe until the liquid starts to come out the tip. Then, holding the ball in the depressed position, quickly plunge the tip back into the solution, release the ball, and allow the syringe to fill all the way.

9. Now, communicating as you go, grasp the ear at the wide part near the bottom. Insert the tip of the rubber syringe into the ear, pointing it downward at an angle toward the chin, and express some of the solution forcefully. Only express about half the fluid. Then keep the syringe in the depressed position while you remove it from the ear. This prevents the sucking sound of air going into the syringe from happening close to the cat's eardrum. Release the syringe after it's out of the ear. Refill the syringe before you do the other ear.

10. Rinse out the syringe; fill it with clean, warm water; and repeat step 9 with the clean water. Rinse off any areas where the flush formula has gotten on the furs. Blot the fur dry with a hand towel or paper towel, rinse them off again, and blot the patient nice and dry, including paw pads. Tell her how well she's done and carry her back to the perch where you found her.

Irrigating an Abscess

Use a hypodermic-type syringe, but with a curved tapered plastic tip instead of a needle, or use a baby ear syringe.

1. Follow steps 1–7 under Irrigation Procedure above, using either Irrigation Formula I or II on page 280.

2. Communicating as you go, take hold of the drain (rubber tube) if there is one and gently insert the very tip of the syringe into the rubber tube or into the opening in the abscess, guiding the tip by pressing it against the rubber. *Slowly* express the fluid into the abscess pocket. Then gently press the pocket flat, expressing the fluid. This is much different from the ear flush, which calls for a strong stream of fluid.

3. Repeat this step two or three times. If there are two openings, alternate from one incision hole to the other. Do not move the tip of the syringe around once you start to express the fluid. You'll be more sure of the cat's comfort if you hold the syringe very still with only the liquid moving. Do not let the stream of fluid be too forceful or it might tickle and cause the patient to wiggle.

4. Follow step 10 under Irrigation Procedure.

Soaking Feet and Cleaning Cuticles

A foot soak is a very handy little therapy to have at your disposal. It can be used to cleanse a wound, take down swelling, help heal a cut, and most important, clean away that waxy brown dirt that can build up around the cuticle.

If a cat has dandruff, feline acne, ear mites, head mites, ringworm, or a mouth problem, he will dig at it with his back claws and the dirt and debris are bound to build up around the cuticle. If you neglect to clean the cuticles, you haven't a hope of getting rid of any of the above problems because the cat will reinfect himself every time he scratches with the dirty claws. That waxy, dirty buildup is very difficult to budge and can cause a nasty toe infection if left uncleaned.

I have found a practical solution. However, I must caution you to remember that a cat licks his paws more than any other part of his body. *Always wash off thoroughly anything you put on the feet, legs, or claws.*

Equipment to gather:

2 large heavy ceramic mugs
Appropriate solution (see below)
Terry cloth towel or two to three dry washcloths
Large bowl of clean warm water

Foot-Soaking Solutions

Ringworm Solution

1 cup warm water
10 drops tincture or extract of goldenseal
or
1 cup warm water
1 teaspoon vegetable wash solution

- Soak each foot four to five minutes in one of the above solutions. Do not rinse after goldenseal soak. If you use vegetable wash solution, *rinse well* and then follow with goldenseal soak.

Solution for Puncture Wounds or Dirty Wounds (to draw out infection)

1 cup warm water
1 or 2 teaspoons Epsom salts

- For an open wound, use mildly warm water and only 1 teaspoon Epsom salts. As the wound heals you can use warmer water and 2 teaspoons Epsom salts.
- Soak two to five minutes. *Rinse well* and follow with soak in 1 cup warm water and 10 drops tincture or extract of golden seal.

Solution for Healing Cuts, Punctures, Abrasions, Swelling, and Irritation

1 cup warm water
10 drops tincture or extract of calendula
⅓ teaspoon sea salt

- Soak two to three minutes. Do not rinse.

Solution for Dissolving Cuticle Dirt

(*Note:* Do not use if foot is injured in any way.)

¾ cup warm water
½ teaspoon dishwashing detergent or Murphy's oil soap

• Soak five minutes or more. Rinse extremely well.

Foot-Soaking Procedure

1.   Read through the procedure; then bring equipment to therapy area.
2.   Bring your cat to the therapy area. The kitchen or bathroom is best since you are using a liquid. I like to stand the patient in the dry kitchen sink, but for a very nervous cat I kneel with him in the bathtub. Kneeling in the tub is easiest if you haven't done the procedure a lot. Take the pill-giving position and stroke your cat all over, including the legs and feet. Do the therapeutic communication (page 262), explaining the procedure in detail and what the two of you will accomplish by doing each of the steps. Request his help and cooperation.
3.   Fill one mug one third full of warm soaking solution and place it alongside the foot to be treated.
4.   Gently place the flat of your hand against the same side of the cat as the foot to be treated and press, urging his weight onto the foot on the other side.
5.   Lift the foot to be treated and place it inside the mug but not necessarily down into the warm fluid.
6.   Place the flat of your hand against the cat's opposite side and very gently press, urging him to shift his weight onto the same side as the foot to be soaked. He will naturally lower the foot to support himself and find himself standing in the warm soothing fluid. Tell him he did everything exactly right.
7.   Check to make sure the mug's position allows your cat to stand four square, secure and comfortable. If necessary you can shift the mug a bit or allow the patient to adjust slightly the position of his other three feet.
8.   If you're doing one of the longer soaks and the solution cools, you can have more soaking solution ready in another mug that is standing in a bowl of hot water to keep it warm. Every sixty seconds or so, tip the patient's weight away

from the soaking foot, lift the foot out of the mug, switch the mugs, and replace the foot in the new mug of warm solution. Shift his weight back over the foot so he will again stand down in the mug. The whole time just continue pointing out how warm and good it feels on his pads and between his toes and what the solution is accomplishing. Now is a perfect time for a visualization (see page 217).

Special Cuticle-Cleaning Technique

1. Read through the following procedure and then do the therapeutic communication (page 262), explaining each step to your cat.

2. Extrude each claw and clip the tip (see "Clipping the Claws," page 176).

3. Extrude each claw again and, using your thumbnail, try to gently scrape away some of the dirt. Be aware of the cuticle; it is very sensitive. Don't scrape the cuticle. Don't try to be thorough; this is only the first stage.

4. Now you're going to soften the waxy dirt that's left. Extrude each claw again and massage warm olive oil, almond oil, or Wax-O-Sol for ears into the dirty areas.

5. Wait about three minutes; massage the oil in again; then clean away the softened dirt with cotton swabs or with a tissue over your thumbnail. This may be all you'll need to do.

6. If stubborn, hardened dirt still remains, do the foot soak for dissolving cuticle dirt (see page 284). During the five-minute soak, repeatedly extrude the nails and gently massage the solution around in the dirt. Then, once again, clean away the remaining dirt with cotton swabs or with your thumbnail.

7. *Rinse very well.* You can rinse with a hair rinsing hose attached to your spigot as described on page 190, or you can stand each foot in a succession of two or three mugs of warm water. The rinse mugs should be three quarters full (a higher level than the soaking solution). No soapy solution may be left on the legs and feet. A final rinse in one cup warm water and one-half teaspoon white vinegar will ensure that all soap is gone. Then rinse a last time in clear water. Or, if the cuticles seem irritated, follow with the soothing calendula foot soak given above.

8. Dry with a fluffy towel, washcloths, or soft paper towels. Thank your cat for his help and offer a treat followed by a catnip party.

Fasting

Caution: Do not *fast kittens, immature cats, pregnant or nursing females, and cats with cancer or diabetes. Do fast an ailing cat but not without consulting your holistic veterinarian. Do not fast the cat while you are away. Do it on a day when you are home and can give extra play and love sessions.*

Fasting can be a wonderful tool. Wild animals fast themselves naturally if they become ill. Fasting accomplishes two things. First, it gives the body a chance to "deep clean" itself and pass off some of the old backlog of wastes that have accumulated and that often show up as dandruff, eye discharge, ear wax, or as arthritis when the wastes lodge in the joints as calcification. Second, the energy that would have been used to digest food can now be put to better use by the body to fight germs, viruses, or parasites.

Veterinarians say a fully grown cat in good health can fast three to five days without harm. Personally, unless a cat is under a veterinarian's supervision, I don't like to fast a cat more than three days, but it's a good health-conscious practice to fast your cat for one day per month.

Fasting does not mean taking no nourishment at all and drinking only water. I prefer the gentler approach of a liquid fast on Homemade Chicken Broth (page 308). Twice a day the cat is allowed all the broth he wants.

Fasting can be used to perk up the appetite for cats who won't eat. If you skip one meal or even two—not even offering food (in other words, don't even let them smell food)—then at the following meal, when you finally do offer food, there is a much better chance that they will eat. That trigger mechanism in the brain that is activated by the smell of food has had a rest.

Force Feeding/Finger Feeding or Dropper Feeding

Note: The words "force feeding" are used in this section heading only because that is how most people label the act of helping a cat to eat. I had to use it so that people could find this section. I will not use the term again. "Finger feeding" and "dropper feeding" are terms that describe more accurately both the technique and the mental attitude of the caregiver.

If the cat is very thin and sick it may become necessary to help her to eat, especially if the veterinarian recommends it. Otherwise, don't be in too much of a hurry. Remember, a sick cat just naturally fasts because, during a fast, energy is turned away from digestion and toward healing.

Before resorting to finger feeding, you can try a couple of ploys to try to get the cat to eat on his own. Cats won't eat what they can't smell. You may be offering a delicious snack with a very strong aroma, but if your cat's nose is stopped up, she won't be able to smell it. Try giving the saline nose drops (page 276) five minutes before each meal. You can raise the odds in your favor even more if the food you offer is something absolutely stupendous. I always try juicy broiled chicken. It hasn't failed me yet. But be sure to bake, fry, or broil the chicken—canned chicken or chicken boiled in water are usually not flavorful enough. I've also seen excellent results with the baby food recipe below. Never feed baby food meat alone. The nutritional balance is not suitable for a cat and it can cause constipation.

Understand that these tempting morsels are *not complete nutrition* in themselves. Baby food is low in fat, low in fiber, and low in calcium. It is very overprocessed. The baby food recipe below is a favorite with sick pussycats because it's delicious and with their guardians because it's nicely balanced and easy to finger feed. In fact, it's so well accepted that the patient may become impatient and prefer to lap it up on his own.

Baby Food Recipe

Into a medium-size bowl mix:
1 jar baby food meat
1 tablespoon baby food vegetables
¼ teaspoon soft butter
⅛ teaspoon feline digestive enzymes
⅛ teaspoon psyllium powder
1⁄16 teaspoon fine bran
2 teaspoons water

- Mix well.
- Store in covered glass in refrigerator.
- Warm by standing a portion in a bowl of hot water (never use a microwave).

The main ingredient needed for finger feeding is patience. You must make the experience pleasant for the patient. If the cat is thrashing around or nervous, you can wrap him in a towel first (page 263).

Finger Feeding of Solid Food

Prepare the baby food recipe given above. Or you can substitute broiled chicken for the baby food and purée the entire mixture in a blender. Use just enough water so it will hold together in tiny balls no bigger than a green pea. Pick up a small amount of the food on your right index finger. With your left hand palm down, grasp the cat's cheekbones from above and tilt the nose slightly upward. Then, holding your right hand palm up, insert the nail of your right middle finger between the front teeth. With the back of the nail press the lower jaw down while you quickly wipe the morsel off your index finger onto the palate *right behind the upper front teeth*. In fact, I use the front teeth to scrape the morsel off my finger. The farther forward you leave the morsel, the easier it is for the cat to swallow it. (This is just the opposite of pilling, where you place the pill halfway down the throat.) Then *let go* and allow the cat to swallow several times. You must give ample time for swallowing. As long as the cat continues swallowing and licking, don't try to feed the next morsel. This may be all you need to do to get your furry friend started. Sometimes if she has had trouble smelling the food because of a stuffy nose, she will be able to taste the morsel in the mouth and will take over from there. If not, you can gently continue.

It may take ten to fifteen minutes to get a teaspoonful of food down the cat this way, but a teaspoonful is ample for a feeding because a cat sick enough to be fed in this manner needs tiny amounts every two hours. Frequent small meals are easier for the stomach to handle. Feeding too large an amount may throw the patient into a decline because it takes too much energy to digest a normal or large-size meal—the stomach can't handle it. If the cat vomits it back up, you've lost everything. When your cat starts to eat on her own, you may feed every 3 to 4 hours. But keep each meal moderate. Increase the amount gradually. Slow but sure is the best way. (See also "Weight Loss," page 482, "Starvation," page 470, and "Fasting," page 286.)

Dropper Feeding Liquids

Note: Use a dropper, not a syringe. Syringes are dangerous because the plunger can get sticky, causing the liquid to suddenly squirt out. If the patient happens to be inhaling at the time, a squirt can choke him. I've known it to happen.

1. Assemble these items beside where you're going to work:

large dropper (A dropper that holds ½ teaspoon or 1 teaspoon can be purchased from the baby section in any drugstore.)
¼ cup or so of warm fortified broth in a teacup or shot glass
saucer on which to rest the dropper
paper towel torn in quarters (cats don't like to have their face or ruff wiped with a big floppy full-size paper towel)

2. Become familiar with your dropper. A dropper is always held, carried, and used *tip down, ball up.* If, when you insert the dropper into the cat's mouth, you see that the ball is lower than the tip, STOP. This tells you the cat's head is not tipped back at the correct angle. If you depress the ball now you'll only squirt air into his mouth.

3. Heat the liquid to between room temperature and baby bath temperature by standing the cup or shot glass in a bowl of hot water.

4. Read through the steps below, and while the broth is heating do your therapeutic communication (page 262) with your feline friend, ending by reading the steps below to him and explaining how and why each will be done and asking for his help.

5. Kneel in pill-giving position, with your feet together and knees apart (page 266) and back the cat in between your legs, tucking the tail comfortably around him.

6. With the left hand stroke your cat's head, face, and mouth, explaining again what you're going to do as you do it. Then, with palm down, grasp your cat's face from above, the heel of your hand resting just behind the ears, the thumb and middle fingers hooked under each cheekbone.

7. Pressing down a little on the heel of your hand and gently pulling up on the cheekbones, angle your cat's nose upward but not all the way. If you stretch the throat out too much, he won't be able to swallow.

8.   Insert about a half inch of the dropper just behind the fang pointing it toward the opposite cheek. (*Never point it toward the center of the throat.*)

9.   Using successive gentle drops (not all at once and not suddenly), empty the liquid into the cheek pouch and give ample time between each squirt for the liquid to dribble slowly back and down toward the throat. After you see the kitty swallow, you can give another drop. You and your cat may decide that it's best to let go completely and remove the dropper from the cat's mouth in between each drop. That's fine. Remember, "slow makes neat."

10.   Use the pieces of paper towel the minute any liquid soils the fur anywhere. Your cat will appreciate a fastidious attitude. When you finish, it is considerate to wipe again with a warm, damp washcloth (wiping from back to front, from the corners of the mouth toward the nose, works best).

11.   Carry your friend back to his perch.

12.   Pet and praise as he returns his face, ruff, and paws to his own high standards of cleanliness.

Taking the Temperature

Taking the cat's temperature is a useful skill. If you can do it smoothly, you'll be able to give your veterinarian valuable information by phone. Since a cat's temperature will often fluctuate, getting higher when she is excited or stressed by riding in her carrier or being examined at the vet's, a temperature taken at home will always be more accurate as long as it is taken correctly.

Here is one of those times when your practice of stroking all over your cat's body is going to pay off. Remember how she arches her back and lifts up her tail whenever you stroke strongly down her back from neck to tail. Try giving a few extra scratches at the end of the stroke right before the tail. She'll keep her tail up longer, and you can lean over and reexamine the anal area and locate the opening where you will be inserting the thermometer.

Now is a good time to do your therapeutic communication (page 262) with your cat, explaining in detail all the steps in the procedure below, asking her cooperation and telling her why getting an accurate temperature will be helpful to the two of you and to the veterinarian. Now you're ready to begin.

Here's what you'll need:

- Thermometer—use a rectal or baby thermometer or one of the new digital thermometers. *Never use an oral thermometer on an animal.*
- Petroleum jelly.

Read through the entire procedure before you begin.

It would be nice to have someone else to talk to your cat, encourage her to stand fairly still, and do the back stroking for you, but it's not really necessary. Taking the temperature is done almost exactly the same way you would slide in an enema bottle applicator (see "Giving Enemas," steps 7–11, on page 294).

Here are the steps.

1. Begin, as usual, with therapeutic communication (page 262) and read all the steps below to your cat.

2. Shake the thermometer down—holding the end opposite to the silver tip. For safety, stand on a thick carpet if that's possible and shake the mercury down to the tip. The temperature should read below 95. (This is not necessary with a digital thermometer.)

3. Liberally coat the thermometer with petroleum jelly (and, no, there really is no substitute) from the silver ball at the tip to about one-third of the way up.

4. Have the patient standing sideways to you.

5. Stroke down the neck, continuing down the back and giving a few scratches on the lower back right before the tail. Your cat will probably react by pressing his lower back upward and raising the tail.

6. Continue the stroking and at the same time position the thermometer tip about three-quarters of an inch away from the anal opening. Tell your cat everything you're doing as you do it.

7. Continue stroking and angle the thermometer so it points *slightly* upward toward the spine at the waist. Insert the tip plus about one-third of the thermometer into the anal opening, continuing to angle it slightly upward toward the middle back. If you encounter a block with only the tip inside the anus, take the thermometer out and try again in two or three hours. You don't have to succeed the first time. This is one of those techniques like wrapping the cat for medication that is best learned slowly, one step at a time, until you and your feline friend perfect the trick together.

8. After inserting the thermometer partway, just encourage your cat to stand fairly still and face the same way so you can hold the thermometer in. Don't

press; just loosely hold so the thermometer doesn't come out. Do let her readjust the *angle* for better comfort. Here again, be alert for the lessons she will teach you. After she readjusts her position and stands quietly again, you may be able to gently and steadily push the thermometer in a bit more, still angling upward, until about three-quarters of the thermometer has been inserted.

9. Keep hold of the thermometer end and wait at least one full minute; two is even better. A digital thermometer is faster and will beep when it's time to take it out. Continue stroking her neck and head and telling her how clever she is and how proud you are of her.

10. Slide the thermometer out slowly and steadily, keeping the same angle as when it was inside the patient. Thank your cat for all her help. Wipe off the thermometer with a tissue. Read the temperature and *write it down with the date and time* to be communicated later to the veterinarian. Clean the thermometer first with *cold* water and detergent followed by a wipe with alcohol on a tissue or cotton. Shake the thermometer down again (not necessary with a digital thermometer) and store.

Giving Enemas

People seem so awestruck and impressed by the thought that I would give a cat an enema. Actually it's no big deal. As with any procedure, proper preparation is half the job done. If a cat is badly constipated, there is certainly no safer or gentler way to alleviate the problem than giving an enema. Since dehydration frequently accompanies constipation, especially in older cats, the enema has the bonus effect of allowing the body to absorb needed fluids via the intestinal walls.

So, if your cat is constipated and if you and your vet do not want to use the old tube of habit-forming mineral oil preparations or other laxatives, perhaps you will decide to try the gentle enema.

Here's what you'll need:

- A rubber enema syringe for an infant is about the right size for a cat, or you can use a Fleet enema bottle for a baby. Be sure to *throw away the Fleet enema fluid* and wash the bottle thoroughly. The fluid inside isn't suitable for a cat and can cause kidney damage and death.

- Liquid acidophilus or ¼ teaspoon mixed intestinal flora from the health food store
- Liquid chlorophyll or Green Magma powder
- Distilled or spring water
- Petroleum jelly
- A medium-size bowl
- Towel

Note: Don't hesitate to work on your kitchen counter or grooming table. Enemas are usually not messy. Read through the entire procedure before you begin.

1.   Play with the enema bottle or infant enema syringe and get used to it. Hold it on its side as you would when giving an ear flush, and see how to keep the air bubble in back of the water so you don't squirt air into the cat's rectum (harmless but also totally ineffective). If you're using the plastic bottle, practice rolling it up like a toothpaste tube as the water goes out. Notice how you have to take the cap off when you're finished to allow air in so the bottle will return to its original shape. Get familiar with your equipment.

2.   Into a warm mug or small glass measure one-half cup distilled or spring water. Add ¼ teaspoon mixed intestinal flora (or ⅛ cup fat free plain yogurt) *and* ⅛ teaspoon Green Magma (or 1 teaspoon liquid chlorophyll). This makes what I call a "chlorodophilus solution."

3.   Stand the container with the chlorodophilus in a bowl of hot water until it reaches "warm bath" tempearture (warmer than a baby bath).

4.   Transfer some of the warm chlorodophilus into the clean Fleet enema bottle or baby enema syringe. Be certain the syringe or bottle is completely filled. Hold it upright, tip toward the ceiling, and carefully depress the syringe. When a little chlorodophilus starts to come out, hold it depressed, turn it tip down, and immerse the tip in the chlorodophilus again. Release the depression and allow the syringe to suck up the fluid again and stand the chlorodophilus syringe in the same bowl of hot water. You may need to refresh the hot water in the bowl if it has cooled.

5.   Prepare your cat by doing therapeutic communication with him: (a) assure him you understand how he's feeling (describe his condition in sympathetic terms); (b) describe how you want him to feel; tell him how easily the old stool will slip out, how comfortable his tummy will feel, and that he can take a lovely nap afterward; (c) describe and explain in detail and with love how you are going to accomplish this—

read steps 6–13 in the procedure to him and explain each step carefully. Remember, this not only reassures the patient but also greatly improves your technique.

6.   Bring the cat, the chlorodophilus, and the bowl of hot water to the work area, the bathroom, the kitchen, or a small and pleasant confined space where you can close the door. As you proceed, communicate each step again.

7.   Coat the tip and sides of the enema applicator with petroleum jelly. Tell your cat why.

8.   Place the cat on his side, or, if you have an assistant to stroke the cat and keep him still, you can leave the cat standing up. Obviously he cannot be seated.

9.   Stroke strongly down the cat's back several times from the ears to the tail and give a few nice scratches just before the tail at the base of the spine. This often makes him react by raising his tail and exposing the anal opening.

10.   Continue to scratch the lower back and position the tip of the enema bottle applicator one-quarter inch from the anal opening, ready to go in. Angle the bottle as if you will be sliding the applicator in on a *slightly* upward path, toward the spine and just below the waist.

11.   Continue scratching the lower back and firmly insert and slide in the enema nozzle. Now hold the bottle in place without starting to squeeze in any fluid while you give the cat a chance to readjust his posture if he wishes and settle down again. If you have an assistant, she should assure the cat he's doing beautifully and also direct his attention toward some pleasurable stroking in back of his ears or down the sides of the throat.

12.   Remember, any air inside the syringe will rise to the highest point, so be sure the tip of the applicator is lower than the bulb, or bottle. Then *slowly*, taking a count of at least twenty to do so, begin to squeeze the plastic bottle or syringe. Gradually empty the chlorodophilus fluid into the cat's lower intestine. When using the plastic bottle I always end up by rolling it up like a toothpaste tube from the bottom toward the top.

13.   *Slowly* slide the enema nozzle out. (Your assistant continues to stroke the cat's head.) Encourage the patient to remain where he is, retaining the fluid for sixty seconds or even three minutes. During this time he is free to change positions as much as he likes. I like to tip the patient onto his front legs by lifting his hind quarters a few inches. (It should not look like a handstand.) This allows the enema solution flow deeper into the intestine.

14.   Let the patient walk around near the litter box and wait for desired results.

After the first 13 steps have been completed, any one of the following may occur:

A. The cat will step into the litter box, give a hasty scratch or two, and pass a mixture of chlorodophilus, hard stool, and soft stool. If all of the above happens except that the stool part is hard only, be sure to continue using one-eighth teaspoon psyllium powder and two tablespoons extra water in the food once or twice a day as given in the section on constipation (page 347). A half-teaspoon of chlorodophilus mixture into each meal would also be wise.

B. The cat will walk away, lie down, clean his anal area, and nothing else will happen. No stool or liquid will appear. This usually means that the cat was dehydrated as well as constipated. All the liquid was needed by the system and is being absorbed. Fine. Let him absorb that good chlorodophilus fluid. Wait two or three hours and try again. He may pass the stool later. In addition, remember that your cat was dehydrated and give him one or two servings of Chicken Super Soup (see page 309) between meals every day and ask your veterinarian to take a blood test to check the kidney function, the pancreas, the intestines, or even the thyroid. Periodic subcutaneous hydration (see page 297) will ease the situation considerably even if the kidneys are not the problem.

C. When you insert the nozzle you may encounter a hard mass of stool. *Don't force the nozzle.* Even if you manage to slide by this hard mass and insert half of the nozzle, and begin squeezing the bottle, the liquid may go into the cat only an inch or so and then run out again onto the towel. (Don't worry, chlorodophilus washes out easily.) If this happens, call a veterinarian at once. The stool has probably become impacted. The doctor will want you to bring the cat in at once to be de-obstipated. The veterinarian may have to dig the stool out while the cat is under anesthetic. Don't wait—the condition continues to get worse. After it's corrected, read "Constipation," page 347.

If the cat is put under anesthetic, take advantage of the situation: ask the veterinarian to scale the cat's teeth after he's done the deobstipation if the cat is still anesthetized at that point. At the animal hospital that I use, the veterinarians will, at my request, have one of the interns clean the teeth at the same time that the vet does the deobstipation. If the two procedures are done simultaneously, no additional anesthetic need be given, a definite plus. The less time a cat spends under anesthetic, the safer he is.

In this case, after the cat returns home, continue the psyllium powder and water regimen plus one-fourth teaspoon chlorodophilus in the food, follow the constipation diet, and watch the stool very carefully. If the cat goes more than two days without at least three inches of stool, give another enema before he becomes impacted again. (See also "Constipation," page 347, and "Irritable Bowel Syndrome (IBS)," page 420.)

Compresses

Hot compresses are used to raise the temperature in an area to kill germs, promote drainage, or relax muscles. Cold compresses reduce swelling and pain.

Always begin with a compress that's not too warm or cold. Let the patient's skin get used to the unnatural temperature, then gradually increase the heat or coolness with each succeeding compress. Never allow the temperature to become too extreme. Test the compress on your own wrist if you have a doubt.

Hot Compresses

1. Use Therapeutic Communication (see page 262).

2. Place a nice soft towel on a place that is quiet, pleasant, and a convenient height for you to work on—like a drainboard, counter, table, or a dresser top.

3. Put two washcloths into a large pan half full of hot water or a specific herbal solution.

4. Place the patient on the dry towel and, as you proceed, go through the communication again.

5. Wring out one of the washcloths. If it's not too hot for your hands, it's not too hot for your patient. Fold it in quarters and place it on the desired area.

6. When the washcloth cools, alternate it with the other one. Continue to explain how the nice warm cloth is helping his body feel better.

7. Dry the area; perhaps run a wide-toothed comb through the fur. Compliment and thank the patient and return him to a comfortable spot.

An herbal decoction or infusion (page 321 or 320) can be used to make an herbal hot compress. Simply heat the herbal decoction or infusion and follow the above instructions.

Cold Compresses

Prepare cold herbal compresses the same as hot compresses above, except use cold water. If an herbal decoction is used, let it cool and store it in the refrigerator. Be careful of temperature. If a compress is too cold it will be counterproductive. Test on your own wrist.

Subcutaneous Hydration

Subcutaneous hydration is the injection under the skin of lactated saline solution. This is a simple procedure that corrects the dehydration that occurs in any disease, especially toward the end of a cat's life. Dehydration occurs most frequently in cats with kidney disease, but many other diseases such as irritable bowel syndrome, diabetes, and hyperthyroidism can also produce dehydration, which can then be alleviated by fluids administered subcutaneously.

Subcutaneous hydration augments the kidney's ability to eliminate wastes from the body. Although this therapy is used primarily to add months or years of comfortable high-quality time to the life of cats suffering from kidney disease, it is also used in other situations where dehydration is a factor (see the discussion of dehydration in "Kidney Disease," page 428). None of the organs can work properly when the body is dehydrated. Whenever dehydration occurs, subcutaneous hydration will always raise the odds in favor of recovery simply because a well-hydrated body will fight its way back to health more efficiently. Hydration often makes the difference between death and years of comfortable, happy life.

Subcutaneous hydration is such an efficient and simple therapy that veterinarians wish it were practical for all of God's creatures; but so far cats, (and some breeds of dogs), because of their loose, supple skin, are the only animals whose bodies accept the technique with ease.

The equipment is the same as that used for an intravenous drip. The difference between the procedures is that instead of inserting the needle into the vein, in subcutaneous hydration the needle is slipped under the skin—as with an insulin injection—and left there for a minute or two while a predetermined amount of sterile saline solution drips in and forms a little pocket of fluid in the subcutaneous fat. During the next few hours the patient's own circulatory system disburses the fluid all over the body to hydrate tissues and carry off wastes. Eventually the fluids, now carrying waste materials, are passed off by the kidneys and bladder.

I have helped veterinarians teach hundreds of caregivers to do it themselves at home. No other therapy will so dramatically improve the health and comfort of a dehydrated cat. Knowing how simple it is, I always advise every guardian whose cat has kidney disease to include it in their therapy program. The difference it makes is like night and day, and the caregiver will see this improvement in fewer than twelve hours. Regular hydration and the appropriate diet add months and often years to a cat's life. Indeed, the results must be seen to be believed.

Uses for Subcutaneous Hydration

- *Post Operative:* After surgery or dentistry when no IV is necessary, 100 ml of saline solution given subcutaneously will aid the patient's kidneys in processing out the anesthetic more efficiently. This is especially useful when the patient is elderly or is already showing signs of kidney deterioration.
- *Hyperthyroidism:* Given on a regular schedule, subcutaneous hydration keeps the body normally hydrated, enabling the body to better cope with the excess thyroxin. The dosage of thyroid medication can often be lowered.
- *Diabetes:* Given on a regular schedule, subcutaneous hydration helps the body wash excess sugar out of the blood and reduces the amount of insulin needed. Prevents dehydration.
- *Fever, Anorexia, Diarrhea, Starvation, Vomiting, and Fading Kitten Syndrome:* Greatly improves chances for recovery even for a starved or emaciated animal by enabling the body to assimilate nourishment more efficiently.
- *Kidney Disease:* Given on a regular schedule (weekly to daily), subcutaneous hydration allows even severely compromised kidneys to continue to process wastes with amazing efficiency, returning the quality of life to normal and increasing lifespan by months or years.

One of my first experiences with subcutaneous fluids was with fifteen-year-old Suzi, a little red tabby shorthair. Her story is a good example of what to expect. Suzi had been the hostess with the mostest in her old home. Her guardian was a highly emotional person who loved Suzi very much but could not deal with the extra care Suzi needed. She realized that Suzi's disease was terminal and wanted euthanasia to be carried out at the proper time in a proper way, but she knew she wouldn't have the emotional control to be there with Suzi when the time arrived. So, when Suzi entered the final stages of kidney disease, she was left with me for terminal nursing care.

She arrived dehydrated, anorexic, constipated, stiff in the joints, and so weak she could hardly make it to the litter box. I put her on the kidney diet and began hydration with 100 ml Ringer's lactate once a day. Suzi lived for six more years, eating the raw food diet plus frequent treats of watermelon, cantaloupe, and Chinese broccoli. She continued to receive subcutaneous fluids, but she didn't know she was sick. She felt just fine and took over as hostess at my place. When visitors arrived, they were greeted by fluffy, perky little red-haired Suzi standing tippy-toe on the antique highchair just inside my door, purring and arching her back to be petted and making everyone feel welcome and important.

Setting Up the Subcutaneous Hydration Equipment

Your veterinarian or his helper will show you how to set up and use the subcutaneous hydration equipment. Arrange to have two or three "Sub Q" lessons, ideally with two or three different teachers—for example, the veterinarian, his technician, or another caregiver. That way you can learn everybody's helpful hints.

Here is my method. The equipment comes in three parts: the fluids, the tubing, and the needle. The fluid used is a sterile saline solution, with the same salinity as blood or tears. It comes in a plastic container of 500 or 1000 milliliters. In the United States, it is made by Braun, Baxter, and several other companies. In Great Britain it is made by Aquapharm. The long plastic tubing that runs from the bag of fluids to the patient has an oblong bulb at one end. This is the end that is plugged into the fluid bag. Somewhere along the tubing you will see an open and close valve. Be sure it is in the "closed" position before you plug the tubing in—you don't want the fluids running down the tube and out onto the floor.

Attach the needle to the other end of the tube, and keep it capped until you are ready to use it. I recommend a U.S. one-inch, number 20–size needle, which is very slender. It is larger than the needle used to give insulin but smaller than that used to draw blood from a cat. Veterinarians usually use a number 18, which is wider, because the flow will be faster. You can still have a fast flow with the more comfortable number 20 if the fluid bag is hung high enough so that the bottom of the bag is at least three feet above the cat's body.

To prevent air bubbles from traveling down the tube and into the cat (inefficient but not dangerous), the oblong bulb near the fluids should be kept half full. Hang the bag of fluids on a coat hanger (numbers side out, please) and hang the whole thing over the sink or tub. To bring fluids into the bulb, pinch the very bottom of the bulb, sending air bubbles up into the fluids. Release the pinch and fluids will flow down into the bulb. The bulb is kept only half full because the air space in the top of the bulb is where you can see whether the drops of fluid are proceeding at the correct speed (swiftly dripping, but not running in a steady stream). If the bulb is more than half full, you will not be able to see the drips easily. If you need to empty out a little of the fluids in the bulb, turn the whole thing upside down (with the bulb above the fluids), pinching what is now the uppermost part of the bulb (near where the tubing exits), and sending some of the fluid back into the main fluid container. Release the pinch and a few bubbles of air will enter the bulb.

Last, make sure the tubing between the bag of fluids and needle is full of fluid, not air. Uncap the needle and, holding it lower than the fluids, go back to the open/close valve on the tubing and change it to the "open" position until the fluid runs down the tubing and starts to come out the needle at the other end. Then turn it to "closed" position; the tubing is now full. If no fluid comes out, this probably means your tube has a crimp under the open/close valve. Slide the open/close valve along the tubing; expose the crimp, press open, and proceed as above.

To store the equipment between uses, recap the needle, wind the tubing loosely two or three times around the hanger hook, and hang it in a closet or on a hook in the bathroom. Change the needle as directed by your veterinarian.

The Hydration Procedure

Choose a place to hydrate the patient where you will both feel comfortable and secure. The bag of fluids must be hung above the cat. The little oblong bulb just below the bag should be at least three feet above the patient, otherwise the fluids will drip too slowly and you both may become impatient. Many cats relax better on the floor. If you, too, are comfortable there, the fluids can be hung over a high drawer that's been pulled out or a drawer handle. If you are not comfortable on the floor, try letting the cat crouch on the bed and hang the bag of fluids on a strong picture hook or on top of the closet door or a curtain rod. Many prefer the kitchen counter with the fluids hung over the top of an open cupboard door. Be creative; look all around the house for your preferred place, where the little bulb on the bottom of the bag will be least three feet above the cat.

1.   Before including your feline friend in the project, read through the rest of these instructions and then get familiar with the equipment. Practice opening and closing the flow valve and moving it along the tube so you can pinch out any crimps.

2.   Practice on your clothing with a spare needle. Pull up your slacks away from your thigh and insert the needle into the "tent" you have formed without touching your skin (see step 8 below). Try it a number of times until you are able to push the needle halfway into the tent very swiftly and stop. Learn to slide the rest of it in and to hold fabric (hair) and needle in place with one hand so you can pet the patient with the other.

3.   After you have practiced and are ready to start, heat the fluids to about 102 degrees (warm adult bath temperature; not baby bath). Most veterinarians don't have time to bother with this, but it makes the difference between a cat wiggling to get away from the cold feeling under his skin and a cat purring with contentment, lying on his fluffy towel while the comfortable warm liquid makes him feel better. I heat the fluids by placing the whole thing, tubing and all, in the bathroom sink full of hot water. Test the heat by holding your wrist or cheek against the container for about ten seconds. It should feel so pleasantly warm that you'd like to just dive in and go to sleep.

4.   While the fluids are heating, do your therapeutic communication (page 262) with your feline friend, finishing up by reading all of the steps aloud to her. Explain how and why each step will be done and ask her to help you out.

5.   Veterinarians usually use a number 18 needle, which is large and lets the fluids run through freely. I prefer the number 20, which is thinner but works just as well as long as the small bulb below the fluid bag is suspended at least three feet above the patient. If I want the fluids to run faster, I position the bottle higher above the cat and let momentum and gravity do the rest. Position the open/close valve about three inches above the needle. Leave it in the "closed" position with the needle loosely capped and ready to go.

6.   Now go and get the cat and bring her to the work area. You know how much they love familiar rituals so, as you pick her up, use a special phrase to announce your intentions. The one that works well for me is, "It's feel good time!"

7. Set your feline friend comfortably in place, with her tail wrapped neatly around her haunches so you don't accidently lean on it. Now you are going to do something that will make all the following steps much easier. Pick up the tubing and make a little crimp in it about a foot and a half above the needle. Then hold the crimp firmly between your front teeth. Leave enough slack to allow you to get the needle to the cat without bending forward. Now you can open the valve and check that there is no depression under the valve to crimp the line and prevent a free flow. When you open the valve, fluid will not squirt out of the needle because of the crimp you are holding with your teeth. Keep your teeth closed around it until further notice.

8. The cat's skin is extremely loose. There are a couple of different ways to lift up the skin and insert the needle. The needle will be inserted under the skin, slightly in back of the scruff (in back of and to the side of the shoulder blades). I like to lift the skin by taking hold of a small line of hair and pulling upward until I've lifted the skin into a "tent" about one and a half or two inches high. Practice this a few times. Pull straight up or a little bit toward the tail (toward you), not toward the patient's head. Explore how high a tent your particular cat's skin is going to make. Then later, when you're actually going to give the fluids, touch the tip of the needle to the side of the tent, closer to the top of the tent. Point the needle on a slightly downward angle toward the patient's body. Put your index finger halfway down the needle and *swiftly* push half of the needle in (up to your finger). (If you have an assistant, he should be scratching the patient's head and talking about mice and sparrows while the needle is being inserted.)

9. When the first half of the needle is in, release the crimp by simply opening your mouth. This will allow the fluid to flow. I like to open my mouth to start the flow at the same moment that I put the needle in. Look inside the little bulb under the fluid bottle and double-check to be sure that the drops are now flowing. It's okay if they are flowing fast as long as it's not an unbroken stream; you should see individual drops. It's not necessary to push the entire needle in but if you want to do that, first allow enough drops to create a nice little pocket of fluid inside your tent of skin, then feed the rest of the needle into the bubble of fluid. The nerves are on the underside of the skin (the inner sides of the skin tent). The fluid dripping in is forming a larger and larger bubble of liquid, pushing the inner sides of the tent farther and farther away from the sharp tip of the needle. Keep part of your awareness always on the tip of the needle.

10. Allow the correct amount of fluid to transfer from the bottle, down the

tube, through the needle, and under the patient's skin. (Your vet will tell you how much fluid will benefit your friend.) Many guardians like to use a colored marking pen to mark the numbered lines on the bottle; that way it's easier to measure your progress and see when the correct amount of fluid has been administered.

11. To end the procedure, close the flow valve on the tube or just crimp the tube between your front teeth again; then gently pinch the surface of the skin firmly around the needle and draw the needle straight backward out of the skin. Keep holding the skin gently pinched closed for fifteen seconds. Then pet and praise the kitty and carry her back to the perch where you got her.

12. Store the fluids out of the way. Loop the tubing over the hanger or hook and hang it in a closet or on a hook behind a door that isn't used much.

Be patient with your cat. At first it's best to have a friend help you by stroking the patient's head and encouraging her to lie quietly. Cats catch on by about the third session that this new ritual is making them feel about 300 percent better. They come to expect it and depend on it, and they become quite blasé about giving their quiet cooperation, even if, later on, you need to train a temporary replacement whom you and your cat will then have to encourage and reassure.

Be patient with yourself. Remember when you were first learning to give a pill or eyedrops. Remember you didn't start out perfect; you made mistakes. Human beings make mistakes when they are learning something new. Don't be discouraged if you push the needle in one side and out the other so that the fluids go running down onto the counter. Just stop the flow by crimping the tubing between your front teeth, take the needle out, and try again. Everybody makes that mistake at least once, so don't be surprised when it's your turn. There are a whole bunch of other mistakes a person can make. Your veterinarian made them when he was learning; I made them when I was learning. It's no big deal. Just read the "how to" section again or go back to your teacher, the veterinarian, or his helper, and persevere. That's the kind of guardian everyone admires; the one who won't give up but perseveres for the sake of the cat he loves. Guardians like that always win in the end because love cannot be beaten.

Some Frequently Asked Questions about Subcutaneous Hydration

1. *Should we worry about infection?* Subcutaneous fluids are given the same way as an insulin injection. Many dogs and cats and humans get those injections on a daily basis for years without any problem. Treat your subcutaneous equipment as carefully as you would if you were giving insulin, and all will be well.

2. *Should we be sure to always insert the needle in a slightly different place?* Actually, you can't avoid it, so don't worry.

3. *Which is better: 200 ml every four days or 50 ml every day?* More frequent small amounts are gentler and easier for the body to process and use.

4. *What if my cat's skin won't take as much fluid as the veterinarian wants her to have?* Some cats have skin that needs time to get used to accepting fluids. All cats can do it eventually. You may have to start with only 25 ml once or twice a day at first. After two or three weeks you can gradually increase the amount. One hundred milliliters is an average amount. Larger cats are sometimes given up to 200 milliliters at a time, but I prefer to stay below 125 and repeat the procedure more often if necessary.

5. *Should we always give the same amount of fluid?* If a cat is badly dehydrated, she will need to be hydrated more often in the beginning. After her body is nicely hydrated you and your veterinarian can decide on the best schedule for her. With chronic disease, like kidney disease or hyperthyroidism, hydration continues for the life of the cat and needs to be done more and more frequently as the condition worsens. With an acute situation such as fading kitten syndrome or starvation, one or two treatments may be all that is needed.

Recipes, Formulas, and Extras for Home Nursing

The Snug Retreat

The "snug retreat" is great for cats who are elderly, stressed, ill, recuperating, thin, frightened, or lonely—or for any cat who loves warmth or privacy.

Create a snug retreat out of a cardboard carton placed on its side. A liquor or wine carton is the perfect size. Put it in a quiet, secluded place, back in a closet or behind a chair, and clip a reflector light (with a 60 or 75-watt bulb) onto a pulled-out drawer or table leg and focus it into the box from only two feet away. Place a terry cloth towel or old wool sweater in the box for extra warmth and comfort Use something made of 100 percent natural fibers. Launder the towel or clothing weekly or more often if needed. No fabric softener, please!

Antistress Supplements

- *Vitamin E.* 100 units a day for two weeks; then 400 units once a week. Strengthens the heart, lowers the body's need for oxygen, helps prevent adrenal scarring during stress. Helps heal any damaged tissue and reduces scarring.

- *Vitamin C or vitamin C Complex powder with rutin, hesperidin, and bioflavonoids.* 250 units three to four (or more) times a day. Mix 1/16 teaspoon, or less if the patient insists, into each meal and into every snack. Cushions against all stresses. Vitamin C is used by the body in huge amounts during *any* stress situation. It's almost impossible to overdose; vitamin C is lost in the urine within a few hours of ingestion.

- *B vitamins*—especially B-2, B-6, and pantothenic acid. Empty a 50 mg B complex capsule onto a saucer. Divide the powder into ten parts. (It is not possible to be totally accurate.) Twice a day add one-tenth (5 mg) to each meal. Also, be sure to use Anitra's Vita-Mineral Mix (see page 68) as directed; it is a natural source of these same B vitamins. B vitamins, like C, are lost in the urine.

- *Calcium.* The calcium lactate used in Anitra's Vita-Mineral Mix (page 68) is usually a sufficient amount of calcium in the diet. Calcium calms nerves and raises the threshold for pain and stress. Your veterinarian may prescribe more calcium in times of stress. To absorb calcium the body needs vitamin D.

- *Anitra's Vita-Mineral Mix (page 68).* Be sure to include one or two teaspoons a day mixed into food.

- *Vitamins A and D.* Once a week give one capsule containing 10,000 units vitamin A and 400 units vitamin D. (Organic egg yolk is a good natural source of vitamin A and will help the body use Anitra's Vita-Mineral Mix.) The vitamins A and D and calcium can also be obtained as part of a Nu-Cat or Tabby Tabs multivitamin, taken daily as directed.)

- *Enzymes.* Make sure your cat will digest and use the good food and supplements you are giving him by adding 1/4 teaspoon feline digestive enzymes to each meal. (See Appendix, "Product Recommendations.")

Supplements for Infections and Wounds

The following supplements will help the body fight germs and viruses and promote healing of tissue that is damaged or scarred due to wounds or surgery.

- *Vitamin C.* Give 250 units (1/16 teaspoon) vitamin C complex with bioflavonoids, rutin, and hesperidin, or just use sodium ascorbate powder or ascorbic acid crystals. Mix in the meal or in a small snack four times a day. Vitamin C helps the body process out the invading bacteria and dead white cells.
- *Vitamins A and D.* Give one capsule containing 10,000 units vitamin A and 400 units vitamin D once a day for four to five days; then go back to giving it once a week as usual. Helps the liver detoxify infection and aids in calcium absorption.
- *Vitamin E.* Give 400 units vitamin E twice a week for eight weeks, then go back to giving it once a week as usual—use alpha tocopherol *not* mixed tocopherols. Prevents scarring and helps body build healthy new tissue.

Note: When the crisis is over, you can stop giving vitamins A, D, and E separately and instead use the multivitamin Nu-Cat or Tabby Tabs daily as directed.

- *Anitra's Vita-Mineral Mix.* Make it up yourself (page 68) or purchase at any good pet supply or health food store or online. Mix ½ to 1 teaspoon into each meal. This basic supplement to your cat's daily diet promotes healing by supporting efficient waste disposal. It provides calcium to build strong tissue, calm nerves, and help the body handle pain. It is rich in B complex vitamins, minerals, and the water-soluble nutrients that are needed in larger quantities when the body is fighting infection and healing itself.
- *Snug Retreat (see page 304).* Cushions cat from environmental stress and provides warmth to save the cat's energy and calories. Mutes sounds and gives a feeling of protection and privacy. A snug retreat conserves the patient's vital energy by providing an outside source of heat.

Acid-Alkaline Swing

I have a little trick I use whenever I get a warning that my cat's body might be battling something. I reason that the invading organism has taken hold because the cat's body is either too alkaline (very rare) or too acid. So I proceed to swing the pendulum from acid to alkaline and back again, in an effort to disturb the attacking organism. I do this by feeding supplements that I know have an acid-producing effect for two days and other supplements that tend to alkalize on the next three days. I choose specific supplements that have lots of side effects—all of them beneficial.

On the acid days:

- Give 500 units of vitamin C twice a day, with bioflavonoids, rutin, and hesperidin. (See "Product Recommendations," page 489.) You can use a powder and mix it into the food or choose a tablet that is long and flat-tish, like a lozenge, for easy swallowing (see "Giving Pills," page 266). Ascorbic acid acidifies the urine, getting rid of little bits of crystals and helping to destroy many germs that can breed in the bladder. It also helps build up the body's immune response and enables the system to better deal with stress.
- Once a week on the acid day, squeeze onto the food the contents of a 400-unit vitamin E capsule and a 10,000-unit vitamin A and 400-unit vitamin D capsule.
- Add 2 teaspoons organic tomato sauce to each meal.

On the alkaline days:

- Twice a day mix ⅛ teaspoon Delicious Garlic Condiment into food (page 317). This protects against parasitic invasion and actually contains a natural raw antibiotic.
- Give one-half teaspoon kombu broth (see page 318) mixed into each meal. Kombu is full of minerals and contains very little sodium, so it can be used even for heart patients.
- Give one extra teaspoon of alfalfa sprouts or one teaspoon of finely grated raw zucchini or carrot on the alkaline days and none on the acid days.

An all-raw food diet is the best way to alkalize the system, acidify the urine, and eliminate the need for any other therapy.

Homemade Chicken Broth

This chicken broth is *easy*. For a rich, irresistible flavor and knock-your-socks-off aroma, always begin with chicken that is either baked, broiled, or fried. Never make soup for a cat out of uncooked chicken. When you transfer the cooked chicken into the soup pot, scrape all the burned-on grease and skin into the soup pot with the cooked chicken. That stuff is solid *flavor*!

Put into a large pot:

3–4 lbs cooked chicken (baked, fried, or broiled); I prefer well-done thighs. water

Put the well-cooked chicken into a soup pot large enough so the chicken fills the pot less than halfway. Cover with water until water is one to two inches above the chicken. Cover the pot loosely (tip the lid). Bring to a low simmer. Simmer five to eight hours, occasionally breaking up the chicken and adding more water whenever necessary. (You can do other things while it simmers.) During the last hour, remove the lid and let the water cook down until the chicken is barely covered. Broth is now deliciously strong. Pour off broth and cool to room temperature, leaving the mass of chicken in the pot.

While the broth is cooling, pour enough cold water over the chicken left in the pot to cover. Then let it cool some more until it's cool enough for you to be able to touch. With your hands, knead, squeeze, and stir the chicken around in the water to get all the good out of the meat and into the water. The water will begin to look milky. Finally, leaving the bones behind in the pot, take handfuls of chicken meat, wring out the liquid into the pot, and throw the meat away. (The hours of simmering have succeeded in transferring the usable nutrients from the meat into the broth. What little nutrition is left in the meat at this point would be largely indigestible.) *Now you have the bones and the broth in the pot.*

Pour this broth off and store it with the first batch. Transfer the bones into a smaller pot. Now you have only the bones left in the bottom of the pot. You can stop here; store your fabulous, rich, strong broth and throw the bones away—or you can go one more step and turn it into high-calcium broth.

High Calcium Chicken Broth

Crack the bones up a little if you can so they form a fairly compact mass in the bottom of the pan. Cover the bones with water and add ¼ cup tomato juice (do not use V8 juice). Simmer one-half to one hour. (The acid in the tomato juice will leech the calcium out of the bones.)

Pour off this broth, again combining it with the other broth. You may want to throw away some of the fat on top, but be sure to leave enough so you can include some fat with every serving of soup. Cats need much more fat than humans. Throw the bones away. Store about two cups of the broth in a jar in the refrigerator for immediate use. Store the rest in the freezer in half-pint or pint-size covered freezer containers to be thawed as needed. To thaw, stand the container in a bowl of hot water. *Never* use a microwave.

Chicken Super Soup

Here's how to make your homemade chicken broth even more nutritious. Combine the following ingredients:

¼ **cup Homemade or High-Calcium Chicken Broth (see recipe above)**
¹⁄₁₆ **teaspoon ascorbic acid crystals or C complex (250 units of vitamin C)**
½ **teaspoon nutritional yeast (flaked, brewer's, or tarula)**
¹⁄₁₆ **teaspoon feline digestive enzymes (see Appendix, "Product Recommendations")**

Using Homeopathic Remedies

Because homeopathic remedies work on the level of energies rather than actual susbstances, they must be handled in a manner that is very different from the usual pills and liquids. If not handled correctly, they can easily be accidentally deactivated and neutralized. (See "Homeopathy," page 211.)

Cautions for handling homeopathic remedies:

1. *Do not touch a remedy with your fingers or any part of your body.* The first time a remedy touches a body should be when it goes into the patient's mouth.

2. Remedies can be deactivated by odors. Do not expose your remedies to peppermint, menthol, coffee, or catnip.

3. Keep remedies away from heat, electrical appliances and equipment, hi-fi speakers, and magnets. Don't store near radiators or stoves; do not administer with a hot spoon.

4. Never mix remedies with any food except a little organic milk.

5. Once the remedy is taken, it can be antidoted by extreme stress, or if the patient is treated with acupuncture, or if the patient takes a corticosteroid, peppermint, catnip, or any medicinal herb.

Administering Homeopathic Remedies—Pills

METHOD I

Before beginning, read all directions through once. Then read again, explaining each step to your cat.

1. Tip the correct number of pills from the container into the lid.
2. Take the pill-giving position (see "Giving Pills," page 266).
3. Do therapeutic communication (see page 262).
4. Reaching down from above, grasp the cat's head as for giving a pill (see "Giving Pills," page 266).
5. Tilt head back so that the pill will naturally fall onto the back center of the tongue.
6. With your hand palm up, hold the lid of the bottle with the pill in it between your thumb and index finger, insert the tip of your middle finger or nail between the cat's front teeth, and, using the back of your finger or nail, press the lower jaw down to open the mouth.
7. Double-check the tilt of the head—see step 5 again.
8. Tip the pill from the lid onto the back of the tongue near the center line of the tongue.
9. Let the cat's head and mouth go free. Press down gently on the back of the skull so the head stretches forward and down. Then release and the cat will swallow.
10. Give loving praise and thanks to the patient.

METHOD II
(Spoon Method A)

Before beginning, read all directions through once. Then read again, explaining each step to your cat.

1. Prepare a tablespoon and a teaspoon by standing them in a mug of very hot water for about three minutes.
2. Let them cool and dry on clean paper towels. Don't touch either spoon where it's going to be touching the pill.
3. Measure the pills into the lid of the bottle.
4. Pour the pills onto the tablespoon and crush them to powder with the back of the teaspoon. It is easier if you have the spoon handles sticking out in opposite directions. If the pills roll around, you can wrap them in a layer of paper towel and crush them in that.
5. With the tip of the teaspoon, scrape the powdered pill toward the tip of the tablespoon, and then dump the powder onto the front part of the teaspoon.
6. Take the pill-giving position (see "Giving Pills," page 266).
7. Position the cat's head as in steps 4 and 5 of Method I above.
8. Holding the spoon so the middle finger is free, pry the jaw down as in step 6 of Method I.
9. Toss the powdered pill across the cat's tongue.
10. Let the cat's head go free; stroke the head and throat.
11. Give loving praise and thanks.

METHOD III
(Spoon Method B)

Before beginning, read all directions through once. Then read again, explaining each step to your cat.

Follow steps 1–5 of Methods II above.

6. Add ½ teaspoon of room-temperature milk or cream to powdered pill in the tablespoon and stir carefully with teaspoon tip until nearly dissolved.

7. Offer the mixture on the tablespoon to your cat as a treat or an appetizer before a meal.

Note: Milk or spring or distilled water are the *only* substances with which you may mix a homeopathic remedy. Do not use soup or any food, not even butter.

METHOD IV

Before beginning, read all directions through once. Then read again, explaining each step to your cat.

1. Measure the dosage into the lid of the bottle.
2. Tip the pills onto a piece of clean white writing paper.
3. Roll the paper into a cone.
4. Take the pill-giving position (see "Giving Pills," page 266).
5. Grasp the head as in step 4 of Method I above.
6. Hold the paper cone so your middle finger can pry the cat's lower jaw down.
7. Pour the pills onto the back of the cat's tongue.
8. Let the cat's head and mouth go free. Press down gently on the back of the skull so the head stretches forward and down. Then release and the cat will swallow.
9. Give praise and thanks.

METHOD V

Before beginning, read all directions through once. Then read again, explaining each step to your cat.

1. Follow steps 1–3 of Method II above.

    or

    Place pills between two sheets of clean paper towel and crush by pressing down with the back of a spoon.
4. Then dump powdered pills onto a piece of clean white writing paper, roll into a funnel, and proceed as in method IV, steps 4–9.

Administering Homeopathic Remedies—Drops

Drops should be given according to directions from your homeopathic veterinarian. Some are given straight from the bottle and can be administered as in giving liquid medication by dropper (see page 268). However, you must not touch the dropper from the source bottle to the patient's mouth. Instead use a second dropper that you prepare as follows:

1. Fill a clean, well-rinsed mug half full of very hot spring water.
2. Fill the dropper with the hot water, and let it stand in the hot water three minutes.
3. Flush with cool water. Now the dropper is ready for use. Don't touch the tip with your fingers. Use the dropper as in giving liquid medications (page 268). After using, stand dropper in hot water again; then dry and wrap in clean paper towel so that it's ready for future use.

Using Bach Flower Remedies

Bach flower remedies are prepared homeopathically. When working with them, it is best to treat them as you would any homeopathic remedy (see "Homeopathy," page 211).

How to use Bach flower remedies:

- Choose the Bach flower remedy or remedies you require. Look in Chapter 12 under the appropriate health problem or in Dr. Bach's book, *Bach Flower Remedies.* Another option is one of the commonly-used Bach flower remedy formulas. Rescue Remedy is sold as a ready-made formula of five flower essences: impatiens, star of Bethlehem, cherry plum, rock rose, and clematis. I recommend it whenever the body is in stress. Other frequently used Bach formulas include Formulas II and IV, which are given below.
- Fill a one ounce dropper bottle to three-quarters full with distilled or spring water. Add six drops each of the flower remedies you have cho-

sen. Add 2 drops of brandy. Shake vigorously 108 times. Keeps up to two weeks in the refrigerator.

- Each time you give the remedy, shake seven times.

Bach Flower Remedy Formula II

For inflammation, pain, toxicity, restlessness; helpful for hemorrhoids, feline urologic syndrome, and abscesses.

- Buy these Bach remedies: water violet, crabapple, agrimony, olive, star of Bethlehem.
- To prepare, follow directions above. Give two or three drops four times a day.

Bach Flower Remedy Formula IV

For weakness, exhaustion, long-term illness, or if patient is failing.

- Buy these Bach remedies: water violet, sweet chestnut, olive, clematis, gorse, wild rose.
- To prepare, follow directions above. Give two or three drops every two hours.

Using Herbs

Before trying a new herb on your own, consult a veterinary herbalist to be sure the effect it has on your cat's system will be the one you want. I am not an herbalist, so I limit myself to the few tried-and-true remedies I have always depended on.

The cat's senses of taste, smell, and feeling are much more sensitive than ours. A sharp flavor, such as garlic, can feel like a burn on the delicate tissue inside the cat's mouth and throat. A syrup such as slippery elm, if made too thick, could awaken fears of choking. So first I like to "feel" each remedy on my own tongue or eye or whatever, in case I need to alter it a bit.

If a drop on the tongue tastes too sharp or strong, you can dilute with a little water or chicken broth and add a drop of tamari soy sauce if necessary, or mix it into a flavorful pâté and finger feed it. Use your ingenuity and the refined good taste possessed by all cat lovers.

If an herb is being taken for its concentrated nutrients (such as horsetail tea for silica) or its aromatic oils (such as garlic for flea-repelling properties) or its antimicrobial properties (such as golden seal painted on ringworm), then the actual herbal preparation should be used. However, if the same herb is to be taken for its effect on a condition (golden seal for bladder infection or liver inflammation), then an elixir can be used. This is made in the manner of a homeopathic preparation (see "Elixir," page 322). The healing properties of the herb are enhanced and strengthened while the taste is diluted almost to the level of water.

Herbs must be fresh or they lose their strength. Tightly covered, in a cool, dry, dark place, dried green herbs last six to seven months. Roots, seeds, and bark last two to three years. The very highest medicinal value will be received from fresh-picked herbs growing wild where nature has decreed. The more recently picked, the stronger they will be. However, herb identification is a specialized study. Dried herbs from a store that guarantees freshness and stores them properly will work just fine, but I prefer herbal extracts and tinctures in an alcohol base. They are found in most health food stores these days. They are simple to use and, properly stored, will last for years. Herbs and herbal tinctures are best stored in colored glass containers with screw tops in a cool, dry, dark place.

Here are the herbs I use most often and the indications for use:

- *Arrowroot.* A food herb. The root, ground into a white powder, can be used to thicken liquids. To avoid lumps, it should first be softened in a little cold water before mixing with the hot liquid and stirring at a simmer for two or three minutes. About one teaspoon thickens one cup of liquid.
- *Burdock root.* A food herb. This root is used cooked like a carrot but is also available as an extract. It is high in organic iron and vitamin C; it is alkalizing and soothing to the stomach and intestines. The tea and the cooked root are used as a blood purifier for skin and liver conditions and are often included in diets for cancer, hepatitis, and bowel diseases.
- *Calendula.* A food herb. Used as an external wash, the tea made from this herb promotes incredibly fast healing of cuts, abrasions, and burns. Used as an abscess irrigation, it will close the drainage hole in a matter of hours, so don't use it until the wound has finished draining.

- *Caraway.* A food herb. Caraway seed tea aids digestion and is used as a remedy for flatulence.
- *Carrot.* A food herb. Like burdock root, carrot is considered good for the intestine. Raw grated carrot is sometimes used in the treatment of round-worm. Alkalizing and high in potassium, it is excellent for use in diets for arthritis, heart disease, and other low-salt diets. The seeds made into tea are diuretic and tend to eliminate flatulence.
- *Catnip.* A medicinal herb. The leaves, dried and crumbled, act upon cats as a stimulant and aphrodisiac. Cats will eat them, sniff the dust, or roll in them and lick them off their fur. The effect can be increased if the young plants are transplanted once and then, later, allowed to go almost dry once or twice before harvest. The mature plants are uprooted and hung upside down to dry. The tops will be most potent. The effect on the cat wanes if used more than once a week.
- *Celery seed.* A food herb. The tea made from the celery seed is used as a blood builder and tonic because of its rich mineral content. It is also alkalizing and slightly diuretic. It is soothing to the intestines, stimulates appetite, and prevents flatulence.
- *Comfrey.* A food herb. This herb contains allantoin, which promotes cell production. The tea can be taken internally or used as a wash to aid healing of wounds and broken bones. It is also used as an expectorant and removes mucus from the intestinal tract. It is high in calcium, potassium, phosphorous, and, alas, also in sodium. It is used to quell internal hemorrhaging of lungs, stomach, intestines, and bladder.
- *Dill seed.* A food herb. The tea made from dill seed prevents flatulence, is high in minerals and low in sodium, and stimulates milk flow in nursing mothers.
- *Echinacea.* A medicinal herb. An antiseptic antifungal herb, the extract or tincture can be painted on ringworm to dry it up. The tea, taken internally, reduces fever, purifies the blood, and is widely used in cases of boils, abscesses, and circulatory diseases.
- *Eyebright.* A medicinal herb. The tea is used as an eyewash to soothe red itching eyes.
- *Fennugreek seed.* A medicinal herb. Used as an expectorant. Inhale the steam from the tea to break up mucus in the lungs and bronchial tubes. Promotes discharge of mucus through coughing.

- *Garlic.* A food herb. Called "nature's antibiotic," garlic richly deserves a place in any book on natural health care. This humble and inexpensive herb has been used for centuries for everything from nursing a cold to repelling werewolves. Modern laboratory testing confirms that it does indeed have antibacterial, antiviral, antifungal, antiparasitic, and antithrombotic properties. It also tends to lower blood sugar, strengthen intestinal walls, alkalize the system, aid in the expulsion of intestinal parasites, and render the entire body unappetizing to fleas. I recommend it frequently throughout this book. But the question is always raised: how to give it. Cats' mouths are notoriously sensitive, and raw unadulterated garlic is so strong it can actually feel as if it is burning. Some holistic veterinarians and other natural practitioners have successfully used the mild "deodorized" version of garlic oil in capsules. They tell me these capsules will work for most things. However, purist that I am, I persist in using raw crushed or slivered garlic. I want the patient to get all of the elements nature intended him to ingest along with the oil of the garlic. Science is continually discovering new elements that are indispensable to body function, and those of us who have been eating the *whole* grain, the *whole* fruit, and so on have been gratified to learn that we have been better off all along than those people who were eating only parts of the grain or only the juice of the fruit. And so, when a remedy calls for garlic, I feel more comfortable using a measured portion of fresh raw garlic. Here are my methods for making it delicious when mixed into the food or making it tasteless when given as a pill:

Garlic Given as a Pill

1. Obtain a package of empty gelatin capsules from the health food store. Separate the two halves of the capsule.
2. Carve two or three little pieces off a clove of garlic and insert them into one-half of the capsule.
3. Put the capsule halves back together and give it immediately as a pill (see "Giving Pills," page 266). Don't let it sit around or the capsule will get squishy and break before the patient can swallow it.

Delicious Garlic Condiment

If you're going to take garlic, you might as well enjoy it! Into a teacup or a custard cup measure:

1 tablespoon distilled or spring water
⅛ teaspoon tamari soy sauce
¼ teaspoon raw garlic crushed in a garlic press

Mix ingredients together and let stand three hours. Store in the refrigerator. Keeps three days. Mix ¹⁄₁₆ teaspoon of the garlic into the cat's dinner.

- *Ginseng.* A medicinal herb. An appetite stimulant; the tea made from ginseng is pleasantly sweet and very alkalizing.
- *Goldenseal root.* A medicinal herb. The tea of goldenseal provides a general tonic for all mucous membranes. It is a natural antibiotic, antiseptic, and fungicide. It soothes inflammation and kills germs, viruses, and fungus in eyes, nose, throat, ears, or any mucous membrane and is used to treat yeast infection. The elixir made from goldenseal is used by holistic veterinarians to treat kidney problems. It is also used as an alternative to corticosteroids. The extract or tincture can be painted on ringworm to dry it up. It is extremely alkalizing, has a very bitter taste, and does stain fur a golden color.
- *Horsetail.* A food herb. Taken internally, this tea acts as a tonic because of its high vitamin and mineral content. It is especially high in silica, and therefore it is used to strengthen hair and nails. Slightly diuretic, it is sometimes used for heart and lung problems.
- *Kombu.* A food herb. This seaweed is made into a broth and used in soups. Rich in minerals but low in sodium and very alkalizing, it is excellent in diets for diabetes, arthritis, and kidney disease. Buy dried kombu in the health food store. Break off a square inch and cut, break, or crumble it into tiny pieces. Put it in a small pan and soak it in a cup of water for a half hour. Then cover the pan and simmer it for one hour. Be careful that it doesn't boil dry. Let it cool; refrigerate. Add the kombu and the broth to the cat's food. Don't try to keep it for more than two days. It is extremely perishable; make it up as you need it.

- *Nettle.* A food herb. This tea is slightly diuretic, good for digestion, and rich in minerals.
- *Parsley.* A food herb. Used externally, the leaves make an antiseptic poultice, the root decoction a soothing eyewash. Internally, the plant and the tea are high in minerals, vitamins A, B, and C, and beta carotene. The extremely high potassium content makes this tea a strong diuretic.
- *Pennyroyal.* A medicinal herb. The oil of pennyroyal is used in many herbal flea collars, coat sprays, and flea shampoos. It has insect repellant properties. Cats are not fond of the smell, so I use it very sparingly and always diluted.
- *Plantain.* A medicinal herb. A poultice of the fresh leaves can be used to cover, protect, disinfect, and speed healing of wounds. The tea is used to promote healing after internal injury or surgery.
- *Psyllium seeds.* A food herb. Psyllium seed is used as a stool conditioner. It is a mucoid; that is, it makes the stool slippery so it slides out easily. The husk of the psyllium gives the best result, with finely ground psyllium husks being the most effective. Psyllium husks are mild enough for infants and kittens, but they must be taken with large amounts of water (⅛ teaspoon psyllium husks with 2 teaspoons water) or they can do just the opposite and clog up the intestine.
- *Rosemary.* A food herb. A poultice of leaves or a hot compress of the tea draws blood to the area. It is used for arthritic joints. The tea taken internally is used to aid fat digestion. The tea also makes a nice rinse after shampooing; it leaves the hair shiny and free of soap residue.
- *Rue.* A poison herb. *Used only under veterinary supervision.* Rue is used in herbal worming treatments but always in combination with other ingredients, carefully measured, and for a carefully prescribed period of time.
- *Slippery elm.* A food herb. The powdered bark made into a syrup is very soothing for any inflammation or irritation in the digestive tract. For centuries it has been widely used for diarrhea, ulcers, and vomiting. It contains minerals and some protein and has a pleasant mild taste well accepted by cats. Even sprinkling the powder into food will soothe the stomach and intestines, but that doesn't work nearly as well as the syrup.

Slippery Elm Syrup

Into a small saucepan place ½ cup *cold* water and ¾ teaspoon powdered slippery elm. Whip with a fork until well dissolved. Bring to simmer over low flame, stirring constantly. Simmer 1 or 2 minutes or until slightly thickened. Cool and refrigerate. Usually given by dropper 5 minutes before each meal. Keeps seven or eight days in the refrigerator.

- *Stevia.* A food herb. The leaves or extract can be made into a tea that is extremely sweet-tasting. This can be mixed into food to tempt a cat who is habituated to a commercial food with a high sugar content. Despite its sweet taste, stevia is alkalizing, destroys yeast and fungus, and tends to lower the blood sugar. The refined white stevia has no active therapeutic properties and is widely used in Europe and Asian countries as a natural low-calorie sweetener. The more natural brown stevia extract aids the body in processing and using sugars (see "Diabetes," page 354).
- *Valerian.* A medicinal herb. Valerian is called "nature's tranquilizer." A cold decoction of the powdered root or even the smell of the powder calms the central nervous system. It is used as an antispasmotic and mild tranquilizer. Many cats enjoy the smell; many humans do not.
- *Wormwood.* A poison herb. *Used only under veterinary supervision* in herbal worming preparations. Like rue, it is always carefully measured and used for a very limited time and in combination with other herbs.

Using Herbs

1 teaspoon dried herb = 3 teaspoons fresh herb
1 teaspoon dried herb = 5 drops extract or tincture

Herbal remedies are usually taken three to four times a day; one to two teaspoons of tea for a cat or one-half teaspoon for a kitten. Continue three to four days for minor problems or for several weeks for chronic conditions such as arthritis or diarrhea. If, after long-term treatment, the condition improves, try reducing the dosage gradually.

Herbal Preparations

By far, the easiest way to use medicinal herbs is to buy the tinctures in one-ounce dropper bottles. Always choose the tinctures in an alcohol base, rather than alcohol-free extracts. The action of the herb often requires the alcohol. However, if you prefer to make your own, do not use aluminum, copper, or "no-stick" pans or containers. Do not reuse a storage container for a different herb unless you wash it, sterilize it, and let it stand open for two weeks. Even then, if you still smell the first herb, you have to wash it all over again until there is no odor left. Also, take care not to mix up the lids. Label lids as well as the herb jars. Colored glass containers with nicely fitting lids are best.

INFUSION OR TEA
(for leaves and small stems)

- Into a heatproof container put 1 teaspoon dried or 3 teaspoons fresh herb.
- Add 1 cup boiling water (spring or distilled).
- Let stand, covered, 10 to 30 minutes.
- Strain, refrigerate in covered glass container.
- Keeps three days.

COLD INFUSION

- Soak 6 teaspoons fresh herb (bruised in morter and pestle) or 2 teaspoons dried herb in 1 cup cold water for 8 to 12 hours.
- Strain and store as above.

DECOCTION
(for roots, bark, stems, or seeds)

- Put 1 ounce bruised or crushed herb into small saucepan with 1 pint distilled or spring water.
- Slowly bring to boil; simmer gently 30 minutes. (By this time water should be reduced to one-half or one-fourth. Add more water if it gets lower than this.)
- Turn off heat and let steep, covered, until cool.

- Strain and store as with infusion.
- Lasts three days.

PULVERIZING OR POWDERING
(for use in capsules or to sprinkle on food)

- Grind, bruise, or mash fibers or seeds in blender, mortar and pestle, or clean coffee grinder.

TINCTURE
(Can easily be bought already made—see "Product Recommendations" in the Appendix)

- Put 4 ounces dried or 8 ounces fresh chopped herb into glass jar with tight cover.
- Add 1 pint brandy or vodka that is more than 60 proof. (Do not use ethyl alcohol, rubbing alcohol, or surgical spirits.)
- Stand jar in a warm dark place and shake twice daily for two weeks.
- Strain through double muslin, squeezing herb at the finish.
- Store in covered, dark-colored glass jar. Keeps for years.
- Dosage for cats is 1 to 2 drops. Because of strong taste, always dilute with broth or water or use as an elixir (see below).

ELIXIR
(a homeopathic preparation to increase therapeutic effects while decreasing flavor)

- Fill a clean one-ounce glass dropper bottle to ⅔ full with distilled or spring water and add 3 drops of herbal tincture.
- Cover and shake vigorously 108 times, hitting bottle against a thick rug or padded arm of a chair each time.
- Shake 12 times before each use.
- Dosage is ¼ dropperful 20 minutes before meals.
- Keeps in refrigerator seven days.

POULTICE
(Works like a compress [page 296], but stronger. Actual fresh plant parts are used instead of liquid on a cloth.)

- Mash fresh plant parts, mix with small amount of boiling water, and apply to affected area as hot as can be tolerated (can be contained in a gauze bag). Start with warm and gradually increase the temperature. Test on your wrist.

POULTICE USING DRIED HERB

- Grind dried herb to powder and mix with a few drops boiling water to make paste.
- Follow poultice instructions above.

Old-Fashioned Remedies

In addition to homeopathy, Bach flower remedies, and herbs, I often recommend the following remedies:

- *Intestinal flora.* The practice of using yogurt to promote intestinal health is centuries old. Yogurt contains the friendly bacteria always found in a healthy intestine. Different flora thrive in different parts of the intestine. All must be present for complete intestinal health. If they are killed by antibiotics, worming or flea medications (even those applied to the skin), or some types of infection, they can be replaced by eating yogurt or taking a supplement of mixed intestinal flora. These friendly bacteria manufacture some vitamins inside the intestine and help maintain the proper pH balance to prevent gas, foul odor, and diarrhea. Mixed intestinal flora are available in powder or capsules (see "Product Recommendations," page 489).
- *Chlorophyll.* Chlorophyll inhibits bacterial growth, neutralizes foul odor in all parts of the body, and prevents putrefaction in the intestine. A drop or two can be added to food but no more; it has a very strong flavor. I prefer to use Green Magma. It comes in a convenient powder, and the flavor is not quite as strong as liquid chlorophyll.

- *Charcoal*. Absorbs poisons and is sometimes used as an antidote. It absorbs putrefaction in intestines, prevents flatulence. Will turn the stool black. Charcoal also absorbs digestive enzymes so it should not be used for more than two or three days. It is usually given in capsule form at least one hour after a meal. Give one capsule every twelve hours for three doses. Then stop. (See "Diarrhea" page 358.)
- *Lemon rinse*. A multi-purpose rinse:

> 1 lemon, thinly sliced, including skin
> 1 pint boiling water

Put sliced lemon in a heatproof glass jar. Pour boiling water over it. Cover tightly and let stand at room temperature for twenty-four hours.

- *White vinegar solution*. Used on healthy ears to discourage yeast infections and after other ear treatments to maintain an acid environment in the ear canal.

Combine in a one-ounce dropper bottle:

> 3 drops white vinegar
> Distilled or spring water to fill bottle

Warm to 101 degrees before using by standing bottle in a bowl of hot water. Administer six drops in each ear twice a day. This should feel good. If ear is red or irritated, dilute by half before using. If your cat objects, it probably means the ear tissue is irritated. Until the ear is normal, use a saline wash with calendula (page 280) instead of the white vinegar solution.

- *Soaked oat bran*. Put ¼ cup oat bran in jar; add 1 cup spring or distilled water. Cover loosely and soak at room temperature for twenty-four hours. Store covered container in refrigerator.

Shopping List of Home Nursing Items

Here is a list of most of the items you will need for home nursing and health. To help in finding these items, I've noted those that can commonly be found in the health food store (H), in the drugstore (D), and the pet supply store (P). I have not included those things that one can easily buy in a supermarket as needed.

- Bach Flower Rescue Remedy (H)
- Bathroom and kitchen supplies:

  plastic containers to store in freezer in half-pint and one-pint sizes
  jars to store food, etc., with screw tops in half-pint and one-pint sizes
  measuring spoons (⅛, ¼, ½, and 1 teaspoon and 1 tablespoon sizes)
  paper towels
  2 mugs (for foot and cuticle soaks)
  shampoo bottle, empty plastic bottle to fill as a hot water bottle with
    an old wool sock to use as a cover
  terry cloth towels—never use fabric softener

- Boric acid powder (D)
- Cardboard wine carton (for snug retreat, see page 304)
- Carry case (see page 31 for the type to buy)
- Charcoal tablets or capsules (H or D)
- Chicken broth in freezer (at least one pint or two half pints of Homemade
  Chicken Broth, see page 308)
- Cotton swabs (D)
- Droppers:

  dropper bottle, clean, 1-ounce size (D or some herb shops or a small
    private pharmacy)
  teaspoon-size dropper found in baby supplies (D)

- Enema bottle: infant Fleet brand, emptied and cleaned (D)
- Hair dryer, handheld
- Heating pad (D)
- Herbs—the basic herbs that you'll be glad you have on hand at all times
  are:

  garlic cloves (H)
  psyllium husks in powder form (H)
  slippery elm powder (H)

See also list of herbs on page 315
- Herbal extracts (tinctures in alcohol in 1-ounce dropper bottles)

  calendula (H)
  echinacea (H)

eyebright (H)
golden seal (H)

- Light—clip-on light for snug retreat (see page 304)
- Petroleum jelly (D)
- Salt—buy sea salt (H)
- Syringes: rubber ear syringe (D)
    infant enema syringe (D)
- Thermometer, rectal type for infants or the new digital type is easy to use (D)
- Vegetable rinse (H)
- Vinegar, white
- Vitamins (H):

    vitamins A and D—buy capsules containing 10,000 units vitamin A
        and 400 units vitamin D (refrigerate)
    vitamin C—ascorbic acid crystals, sodium ascorbate powder, or C
        complex with bioflavonoids, rutin and hesperidin
    vitamin E—buy 400-unit alpha tocopherol (refrigerate)

- Water—distilled, filtered, or spring water

A Guide to Common Feline Health Problems 12

Always consult a veterinarian for diagnosis. Remember that each cat will react a bit differently to each disease. It is unusual for one patient to show each and every symptom given. One cat will show one symptomatic picture while another may show some of the same symptoms but some different ones as well. Also remember that every disease will share every one of its symptoms with one or more other diseases. Diagnosis is a high art. If, as I do, you work by telephone with your holistic vet, it is a great help to have a local consultant who is good at diagnosis. Both of my veterinary homeopaths, Dr. Dym and Dr. Gil, are excellent diagnosticians and my local consultant, Dr. Campbell, is too. Her office is well-equipped, and she does hands-on examinations and performs necessary tests knowing that the cats will be treated homeopathically. I always call her after one or two weeks with a progress report to put her mind at ease.

Note: If your cat refuses one of the ingredients suggested in the recommendations for a specific health problem, either (a) start with only the tiniest amount and gradually increase to the recommended amount, or (b) find a different way to give it such as stuffing it into a capsule, mixing it in broth, or giving it by dropper.

Abscesses and Puncture Wounds
(see "Injuries")

Acne
(see "Feline Acne"; see "Skin Problems")

Allergies

An allergic reaction is not a disease in itself; it is a symptom indicating that a weakened or damaged immune system is reacting inappropriately to some harmless substance or to the body itself as in the autoimmune diseases (for example, arthritis, irritable bowel syndrome, allergic dermatitis, asthma).

The immune system is supposed to protect the body by causing vomiting or diarrhea if something irritating or damaging is swallowed. If the immune response is confused and causes vomiting every time something harmless such as wheat or turkey is eaten, that is an allergy. Holistic veterinarians who have specialized in immunology point out that allergies and other autoimmune diseases are caused by a combination of factors:

1. Inbreeding. Dr. Alfred J. Plechner, in his book *Pet Allergies: Remedies for an Epidemic*, states, "The recent history of cosmetic breeding practices among cat and dog breeders is replete with bad news—animals with gross deformities, lost instincts, altered and bizarre behavior, and specific health problems."[1]

2. Use of pet foods containing moldy and rancid meat and grain.

3. Use of foods containing preservatives and colorings.

4. Feeding a diet of all cooked foods. Dr. Richard Pitcairn warns that the immune system will be progressively weakened unless *at least 50 percent of the diet consists of raw food*. Between 1932 and 1942, Dr. Francis M. Pottenger headed a research project that showed that the progeny of cats fed only cooked food would be born with immune deficiencies and that within three generations, if little or no raw food was fed, the immune system deteriorated to virtual uselessness. Many of the kittens were diagnosed with various immune disturbance diseases even before maturity.

5. The use of multiple vaccines. Dr. Pitcairn, who has a specialty in immunology, explains that the use of multiple vaccines, or the giving of frequent or repeated vaccines, can confuse the immune response to the point where it cannot distinguish between harmful and benign substances. Germs and viruses may be allowed to enter the body and thrive while the immune system begins to attack and destroy its own body tissue, as in irritable bowel syndrome.

Allopathic veterinarians will frequently treat allergies as isolated problems, separate from the rest of the cat's system. They attempt to "isolate the offending

1. Plechner and Zucker, p. 7.

substance." The problem with this approach is twofold. First, it is often well nigh impossible to pinpoint which substance or substances are triggering the response. Because a cat is sneezing and has watery eyes does not necessarily mean that "the offending substance" is in the air or entering through the nose. Because a cat has allergic diarrhea does not necessarily mean he is reacting to something in the food. He could be reacting with diarrhea to an inhalant or he could be reacting to his own intestine. Second, even if the allergy-producing culprit is found and eliminated, the problem is not "the offending substance." The problem is the patient's confused and weakened immune response. The cat will most likely develop a reaction to several other things unless the basic problem of a weak immune system is corrected. By all means, eliminate "the offending substance" if you can, but, more important, strengthen the cat's adrenals, pancreas, and liver. Turn him into a healthy animal with a normal immune response (see "The Immune System," page 253).

Symptoms

- Presence of any autoimmune disease: arthritis, asthma, irritable bowel syndrome, allergic dermatitis, feline leukemia, feline AIDS, or feline infectious peritonitis. Cats with any of these diseases will be more allergy-prone.
- Any symptom that persists or is repeated without the usual accompanying symptoms such as runny eyes and nose, with no fever, no depression, no appetite loss.
- Many skin rashes are allergic responses to an insect, a fungus, an ingredient in the food, or they are an autoimmune reaction by the cat to his own skin (see "Vaccinations and Other Immunizations," page 240).

Recommendations

- See your homeopathic veterinarian for diagnosis. Allergies indicate that the underlying cause is deep-seated. This is precisely where homeopathy will have the greatest effect (see "Homeopathy," page 211).
- Avoid use of any corticosteroid drugs, "imitation steroids," or antiinflammatory drugs, which will further damage the immune system (see "Cortisone and Other Steroids," page 244).
- Eliminate from the environment all possible causes of allergy such as in-

secticides, flea preparations, room deodorizers, strong chemical cleaners, fabric softeners, tobacco smoke, and plants.

- Fasting is an important part of allergy treatment. Make a broth by simmering lamb or mutton bones or make High-Calcium Chicken Broth (page 309) but only with organic chicken. (See "Fasting," page 286.) Fast on broth for two consecutive days per week, feeding three or four times a day ¼ cup of broth mixed with ¹⁄₁₆ teaspoon ascorbic acid crystals or sodium ascorbate powder (500 units vitamin C). Vitamin C in high doses has an antihistamine effect.

- Use only spring, filtered, or distilled water for drinking and in preparing broth.

- As quickly as possible, change the cat over to the raw food diet on page 74. Into each meal add:

   10 mg B complex (divide a 50 mg capsule into five parts and use one at a time);

   ¼ teaspoon feline enzymes or ½ digestive enzyme pill (crushed);

   ¹⁄₁₆ teaspoon ascorbic acid crystals or sodium ascorbate powder (250 mg vitamin C).

- Hormones, antibiotics, fungicides, and pesticides that have been sprayed on, injected into, and eaten by food animals may cause allergic reaction when any part of that food animal is eaten by your pet. Until his system is strengthened, try to use only organic foods.

- After one or two months on the above allergy diet, add the following supplements one at a time, trying each one for two weeks to be sure it doesn't cause an allergic response before adding another supplement to the diet. Continue adding an additional supplement to the diet every two weeks until you have included all the listed supplements. *If a supplement causes an allergic reaction, stop its use, move it to the end of the list, and wait two weeks before trying another new supplement.*

   ¼ teaspoon lecithin twice a day;

   ¹⁄₁₆ teaspoon ground psyllium husks twice a day;

   ¹⁄₁₆ teaspoon mixed trace mineral powder or ground kelp twice a day;

   a capsule containing 10,000 units vitamin A and 400 units vitamin

D, given once a week. Try this for four weeks before adding next supplement to the diet or give a multivitamin as directed. (See "Product Recommendations," page 489);

¼ teaspoon fine wheat bran twice a day. When you add wheat bran, stop giving the psyllium husks. If the stool seems hard or dry, use the psyllium as well as the wheat bran;

- After two weeks, if there is still no adverse reaction, you may combine the following, which is a variation of the recipe for Anitra's Vita-Mineral Mix:

Mix together:
  1 cup lecithin granules
  1 cup wheat bran
  ¼ cup mixed trace minerals or ground kelp
  1 cup calcium gluconate powder
  Mix 1 teaspoon of this combination with food morning and evening.

- Try giving once a week one capsule of 400 units vitamin E (alpha tocopherol). Do this for four weeks and continue if there is no adverse reaction.
- Add ⅛ teaspoon nutritional yeast to each meal. If, after two weeks, there is no adverse reaction, add one cup of nutritional yeast to the lecithin, bran, trace mineral, and calcium mixture given above. Use up this mixture and then switch to the usual recipe for Anitra's Vita-Mineral Mix (page 68) or buy the ready-made product at the store.
- Herbal remedy: For a stuffy nose, give three drops in each nostril of warm saline nose drops. If you add 6 drops of golden seal extract to ¼ cup of the solution it will kill germs and viruses and shrink swollen tissue. For red itchy eyes you can use the same solution for eyedrops. Other herbal possibilities are echinacea for viruses, and eyebright for inflamed conjunctive tissue and eye discharge. (See "Administering Eyedrops and Irrigating Tear Ducts," page 270, and "Giving Nose Drops," page 276).
- For itchy skin massage in Lemon Rinse (page 324) or spray the area and massage in Natural Animal Coat Enhancer (see Appendix, "Product Recommendations").
- For diarrhea or vomiting give one teaspoon slippery elm syrup five minutes before each meal. (See "Slippery Elm" page 319, and "Giving Liquid Medication," page 268.) Slippery elm is very soothing.

- For asthma put three drops oil of eucalyptus in a cup of boiling water and let the patient breathe the fumes.
- Bach flower remedy: give Rescue Remedy prepared as given on page 313 to soothe, calm, and cheer. Put three drops in each meal and six drops in water dish.

Arthritis

Arthritis, like asthma, is one of the autoimmune diseases. Usually it builds up for years before it becomes obvious. There are two types of arthritis. *Rheumatoid arthritis* is an inflammation of the membrane that surrounds the ends of the bones at the joints. *Osteoarthritis* causes deposits of calcium to build up within the joints. Bones become very brittle and sometimes wear away at the ends. Modern veterinarians who are holistically oriented now believe that arthritis is caused by a combination of things. As it is an autoimmune disease, we know that it cannot occur unless the immune system has been damaged to the point where the immune response begins attacking the body it is supposed to protect. This confusion can result from corticosteroid therapy or from giving repeated vaccinations or many different vaccines at the same time or very close together (see "Vaccinations and Other Immunizations," page 240). The question is: why does the immune system attack itself in a way that produces arthritis as opposed to asthma or one of the many skin diseases. A partial answer would be that the genes of this particular animal predisposed him with a weakness in that direction. If the animal's body also contains many toxic substances ingested as preservatives and colorings in commercial food or if there is a big backlog of wastes in general due to a slow metabolism caused by the owner's leaving food down for the animal to smell all day long, it's a pretty sure bet that the poisons are going to back up and settle in the joints. Arthritis is the result.

Arthritis is a subtle disease. At first, the little stiffness that creeps into the hips or lower back may not be recognized for what it is. "Well, he's not a kitten anymore" or "We can't expect her to leap up and catch the pipe cleaner the way she did when we first got her" may be all that is said to remark the subtle beginning of a downward spiral in the health of the cat you love.

The disease is made worse by stress and by adrenal exhaustion. Cats living under stress, such as those that are declawed or those forced to live with incompatible humans or animals, or those who are frequently caged, are more prone to the disease. Treatment with cortisone, ACTH, or other drugs can give temporary relief, but at a great cost to the patient (see "Cortisone and Other Steroids" page 244). Larger and larger doses are usually required and, as stated above, the use of corticosteroids further damages the immune system and you soon find out you're caught in a snowball—rolling downhill.

Homeopathy is my choice of treatment for arthritis. A holistic approach could also include exercise, diet, gentle fasting, supplements, herbs, or acupuncture to reduce stress, strengthen the adrenal glands and immune system, and stimulate the organs of elimination to detoxify the body. Improvement usually progresses at a moderate but steady pace and is permanent as long as bad habits are not resumed. Also, with the natural, holistic approach, the side effects are all beneficial.

Herbal remedies have proven very helpful to the arthritis patient. When giving herbal remedies, be alert to the flavors you are asking him to accept into his mouth and throat. You don't want to shock or stress the patient. Taste a drop yourself; if it seems too strong a flavor, too alkaline or too acid, dilute it with water or chicken soup and slowly give however many dropperfuls you need to, depending on how much you have diluted the herbal remedy. Some herbs, such as celery seed tea, may be accepted mixed in the food. Others will have to be given as liquid medication. The action of herbs is slow and gentle. Since arthritis is a disease of long standing, don't expect to see sudden changes. Continue the herbal remedy for three to four weeks before judging its effect.

Arthritis is a painful disease so speed of improvement is important to the concerned guardian. Homeopathic treatment will provide the therapeutic support that will enable the nutrition and other natural therapies to work more quickly. When dealing with arthritis, I always urge the caregiver to consult an experienced homeopathic veterinarian.

When a cat's activity is curtailed by arthritis, he may experience depression, especially if he has enjoyed entertaining the family with acrobatic feats in the past. The Bach flower remedies given below are both simple and effective. Also see "Allergies," page 328.

Symptoms

- Stiffness of movement
- Change of perches: seeking out warmth or, with some cats, seeking out cool spots

- Stiff or ungraceful walk
- Pain during movement of certain joints, when cat is picked up or held in certain positions, or when certain areas are touched or groomed
- Objects to being picked up or held
- Loss of appetite
- Grouchiness with feline friends or humans
- Fatigue; much sleep required
- Swelling around joints
- Constipation
- Skin rashes
- Fever

Recommendations

- Increase the percentage of raw food as soon as possible. Feed the arthritis diet and supplements given below.
- Consult veterinarian for diagnosis.
- Check environment for stresses such as loud radios, careless children, and pollutants (see "Stress: A Cat's Natural Enemy," page 255).
- Provide a snug retreat (see page 304).
- Provide frequent reassurance and love.
- Encourage short gentle play periods chasing a sash or ball two or three times a day.
- Feed three small meals a day; *remove all food between meals.*
- Fast on Homemade Chicken Broth one day a week (see page 308). Under a veterinarian's supervision a longer fast might be used to start the program off. Never fast on plain water alone.
- Guard against weight gain, especially if your cat is less active.
- Folk remedy: have cat wear a copper band collar. Use one that is narrow and has a break or open space (should not be a closed circle of copper).
- Choose one of the herbal remedies below and give one teaspoon three times a day. Can be given as liquid medication (see page 268) or mixed in food.
  To alkalize the system:

Kombu broth (page 318)—use up to ¼ cup per meal;

Celery seed infusion—use 1 teaspoon per meal;

Dandelion root decoction—use ¼ teaspoon per meal (strong flavor).

Against pain:

Chickweed infusion;

Valerian infusion or capsule;

Feverfew—chop one fresh leaf and mix into each meal for pain and swelling.

- Bach flower remedies: Give three drops four times a day of the following mixture prepared as given on page 313.

Crabapple—to promote detoxification;

Hornbeam—to bolster confidence;

Larch—to increase the sense of self-worth.

Arthritis Diet

Use the basic raw food recipe on page 74.

- *Liquid:*

Use High-Calcium Chicken Broth (page 308) mixed with one or more of the herbal remedies (such as kombu broth) listed above. Choose from the herbal remedies depending on (a) what the patient most needs and (b) what flavors the patient will tolerate. In general the measurement should be about one teaspoon of herbal remedy per meal. *Note:* You must not use medicinal herbs or acupuncture if the patient is being treated homeopathically.

- *Into each meal add:*

¼ teaspoon feline digestive enzymes

Anitra's Vita-Mineral Mix—increase to ½ to 1 teaspoon. Add an extra ½ cup of fine bran and an extra ½ cup lecithin to the Vita-Mineral Mix when you first open it or to each 2 cups of mix when you're making it.

A pinch of Green Magma

⅟₁₆ teaspoon ascorbic acid crystals (250 units vitamin C)

⅛ teaspoon Delicious Garlic Condiment (see page 317)

One teaspoonful finely grated carrot or zucchini (if you're not already using raw food recipe).

- *Add to food once a day:*

2 mg zinc tablet (crushed into food)

100 units vitamin E (alpha tocopherol) oil from a punctured capsule—after one month give 400 units once a week as usual

⅛ teaspoon psyllium husks (ground) and two extra tablespoons water

5,000 units vitamin A (the type that is marked fish liver oil). Give this only for the first month, then give 10,000 units vitamin A and 400 units vitamin D once a week as usual or, better yet, use a good feline multivitamin that includes vitamins A and D, see "Product Recommendations," p 489.

- *After one month:*

Discontinue giving Vitamins A, D, and E separately. Instead, use a good multivitamin such as Nu-Cat or Tabby Tabs. (See "Product Recommendations," page 489.)

Autoimmune Diseases

(see "Vaccinations and Other Immunizations")

Bad Breath

(see "Teeth and Gums" and "Kidney Disease")

Bald Patches

(see "Skin Problems")

Blindness

Blindness can be caused by an injury to the eyes or brain, a brain tumor, high blood pressure, extensive cataracts, long-standing infection, kidney malfunction, or a dietary deficiency of the amino acid taurine as in a vegetarian diet. Cats' dietary requirements are different from humans. Nature designed them to be predators. Without an adequate supply of good quality animal protein in the diet, they gradually go blind and then die. A few years back, a pet food company marketed a vegetarian formula for cats. They said it supplied all of the amino acids that cats require from sea vegetables. The idea sounded interesting, but I feel more secure feeding cats a diet that is as close as possible to the food they would naturally eat in the wild! That company is no longer in business.

The cat's senses of hearing and smell are much more acute than ours, so he will be better able to compensate for a loss of sight than we are. Remember that the cat does not know that blindness is not normal; as far as he knows, a loss of sight is simply something to be accepted like a change in the weather. This allows the guardian to eliminate most potential stresses without the cat ever suspecting that it's being done for him. The blind cat can live quite happily if given the additional protection and consideration he requires.

Furniture should always be kept in the same place; care should be taken never to leave packages, toys, or other obstacles lying about. New games can be invented—instead of "catch the mouse," you can play "find the source of the sound." In this game, you make an intriguing sound such as tapping on a lamp base, crinkling paper, or scratching the post. You make the sound every five seconds or so, never moving, until the cat "finds you." You then reward him with lavish praise and petting. Climbing rather than running should be encouraged as an exercise since a running cat might bump into something. Of course, a blind cat must be kept indoors or within a screened enclosure.

To prevent blindness have the cat's vision checked as part of the yearly exam, especially if he is being treated for diabetes. Have eye injuries examined by a veterinarian and treated promptly. And be sure the cat has sufficient taurine from the meat and poultry in his diet. If you are feeding raw meat, the taurine will be both plentiful and highly assimilable.

Symptoms

- Traveling by way of the walls or always brushing up against furniture; seldom cutting across an open space
- Bumping into objects left about
- Falling off the edges of things

- Milky cloud over eye surface
- Red blood spots on the eye
- Pupils do not react to light

Recommendations

- Keep all furniture in the same place.
- Don't leave boxes or children's toys on the floor.
- Give frequent demonstrations of love.
- Make yourself always audible by doing lots of humming or chatting so the cat will know you're around and can enjoy your presence even though he can't see you.
- Always make noise before touching the cat to announce your presence and your intention. (No surprises, please!)
- Invent new sound, touch, and smell games. Be sure the cat "wins" at least two out of three times.
- Install a good quality vertical climbing post or a ramp for climbing exercise.
- Give Bach flower remedies. If blindness comes on suddenly, there may be fear and confusion. Give three drops every two to four hours at first; then gradually reduce the frequency to two to three times a day, and continue until the cat has adjusted to the new lifestyle. Give the following mixture, prepared as given on page 313.

> Mimulus—for fear of darkness, of injury, of being alone;
> Hornbeam—to build confidence in physical ability;
> Walnut—to help accept and handle change.

Body Odors

A body odor indicates that putrefaction and germs are present. There are several possible causes. Dirty teeth mean dirty saliva; a cat who needs his teeth cleaned will spread germs and odor all over his furs and everywhere he licks. Another cause of odor can be germs breeding on dirty skin. If food is left available at all times, the metabolism slows down every time a hint of food odor reaches the cat's brain through the nose. Slow metabolism causes wastes to back up; the body handles the problem by shoving the excess wastes out through the pores as oil and dandruff. This looks and smells terrible. If pores become clogged and/or infected, the smell will be even worse. A low-quality or poorly balanced diet will compound the problem. Soiling is another common cause of body odor. Diarrhea can soil the bloomers on the back legs; long hair can be dirtied by dragging in a badly kept litter box. A discharge from overfull anal glands or infected ears or ear mites will also soil the hair and produce a bad smell. Obesity is almost always accompanied by a bad smell because the cat cannot bend around in the normal way to clean his own genitals. Kidney disease can also produce an odor because the body is forced to overuse the skin as an organ of excretion. The smell of urine all over the fur is a sign of advanced kidney disease. In almost every case this will disappear until close to the end if the cat is hydrated subcutaneously. (See "Kidney Disease," page 426.) Since a smelly cat is always an unhappy cat and inevitably becomes a lonely cat, stress-triggered diseases often follow.

Symptoms

- Bad smell anywhere on body
- Skin irritations
- Oiliness, itching, dandruff
- "Scooting" rear along floor
- Discharge from ears or anal area
- Urine or stool soiling the bloomers
- Shaking the head
- Dirty cuticles

Recommendations

- Have veterinarian diagnose and treat the underlying cause—clean teeth and check for pathological conditions (kidneys, liver, hyperthyroid, respiratory, intestine, ear infection or mites, anal glands, or intestinal virus). Also check on other cats in the household for dirty teeth. Someone else may be grooming him and dirtying his furs.
- Fast on Homemade Chicken Broth (see page 307) one day a week.
- Feed high-quality diet; raw food is best (see Chapter 2, "Diet"). Be sure to include Anitra's Vita-Mineral Mix and other listed supplements to diet.

339

- Feed twice a day; be sure to remove all food between meals, leaving only water available.
- Add to each meal ¹⁄₁₆ teaspoon ascorbic acid crystals or sodium ascorbate powder (250 units vitamin C)—to help body to process out the backup of waste materials.
- Extra ⅛ teaspoon lecithin twice a day (in addition to lecithin already in Anitra's Vita-Mineral Mix)—to emulsify fatty wastes and help eliminate dandruff.
- Reevaluate litter box setup (see page 91).
- Call groomer to remove mats, or, if cat is to be anesthetized for dentistry or other reasons, have mats and soiling removed at that time (see "Anesthetics, Tranquilizers, and X-rays" page 245).
- For longhaired cats, trim hair around the anus to ⅛ inch length and trim a free-fall area under the anus by trimming down the bloomers directly below the anus and between the back legs.
- Reevaluate grooming methods on outer thighs, inner thighs, and bloomers (see pages 171–174).
- Institute regular exercise period each day to speed up metabolism and help anal glands to function normally.
- Bathe cat after underlying cause of odor is diagnosed and successfully treated (see "The Bath," page 189).
- Herbal: A final rinse of one part lemon juice to eleven parts water helps eliminate dandruff, discourages mites, soothes itchiness, and ensures complete rinse-off of any soap residue, or use Natural Animal Coat Enhancer after the bath.

Broken Bones

(see "Injuries")

Burns

(see "Injuries")

Cancer

(see also "Feline Leukemia and Feline AIDS")

Modern research has shown that toxic chemicals in the cat's food and environment are a major factor in producing cancer. However, it is also true that the animal whose health is below par, or the animal living under frequent stress, or the animal whose immune system is not functioning at top efficiency is the most susceptible (see "The Immune System," page 253). Prevention is far easier than curing the disease, but if the disease has not progressed too far, many cats experience remission. Tumors shrink and symptoms disappear when the highest quality diet (see page 66) is fed, supplements are added to build the immune system and detoxify the body of stored pollutants and wastes, and the counsel of an experienced classical homeopath or other holistically oriented veterinarian is sought. Working with my classical veterinary homeopath, I have seen tumors shrink to a persistent tiny smudge on the X-ray that, after months of not changing, both my homeopath and my conventional local consultant agreed must be a bit of scar tissue.

However, if remission does not occur, care should be taken that the animal does not suffer. Arrangements should be made with your veterinarian well in advance for painlessly putting him to sleep if you and the veterinarian and your cat decide that the time has come (see "Euthanasia," page 248).

Symptoms

- Symptoms for all types of cancer are very general. (See symptoms given under "Feline Leukemia and Feline AIDS," page 380).

Recommendations

- Cats diagnosed with any type of cancer can benefit from the diet and treatment given under "Feline Leukemia and Feline AIDS," page 380.
- Folk remedy—if cortisone is being prescribed: As cortisone works only for a limited time, goldenseal elixir (see page 322) can sometimes be substituted for all or part of the cortisone dose. Check with a holistic veterinarian.
- Provide a snug retreat (see page 304) because cancer patients usually need an outside source of warmth.
- If the patient becomes dehydrated, request that your veterinarian administer subcutaneous fluids (Ringer's lactate) to raise the level of comfort and to permit the body to continue to function. Or you and the vet might decide that you should give subcutaneous fluids at home at regular in-

tervals just as you would for a kidney patient or any cat who is having a problem with dehydration. See page 296 for directions.

Cardiomyopathy

Cardiomyopathy is an enlarging and weakening of the heart muscle and is the most frequent cause of heart failure in cats. Cardiomyopathy appears either as a thickening and stiffening of the heart wall or as a thinning and ballooning of the heart wall. In either case, the result is the same: low blood pressure. Blood is not being pumped as quickly or as forcefully as before. Therefore, an insufficient supply of blood reaches the organs. As cardiomyopathy progresses, one or more of the other major organs usually begin to break down. Blood clots frequently occur, causing strokes and thrombosis.

Many cats with cardiomyopathy live long and happy lives if diagnosis is reasonably early, diet is tailored to the patient's special needs, and an experienced homeopathic or holistically oriented veterinarian is consulted. Unfortunately, early symptoms are so unspectacular and general (laziness, easy tiring, difficulty breathing, fast and weak pulse) that most cardiomyopathy cases are not discovered until they are well advanced. Even a veterinarian could overlook a fast pulse, thinking it's the result of nervousness over coming to his office. Cardiomyopathy is the leading cause of sudden death in cats.

If cardiomyopathy is suspected, the veterinarian can employ electrocardiogram and/or X-rays, to get a clearer picture of the condition of the cat's heart. To treat the condition all of the usual nutrients must be supplied in extra large amounts. This is especially necessary to combat the side effects if conventional allopathic medications are used to control the condition. In any case, enormous amount of minerals and B vitamins will be washed out of the cat's system by the copious urination that often occurs or is induced by diuretics. A low-sodium diet helps to correct this condition so that fewer diuretics need to be used.

Symptoms

- Easily tired, pants easily, sleeps more
- Bluish tongue and gums after exercise
- Fast, weak pulse

- Copious drinking and urination (see also "Kidney Disease," page 426, and "Diabetes," page 354)
- Poor appetite
- Prostration or sudden collapse
- If left side of heart is affected: dry cough, difficulty breathing, wheezing, and worsening symptoms during exercise or activity
- If right side of heart is affected: fluid retention in legs and or abdomen (pot belly)
- Hind legs cold, bluish, and then paralyzed. *This is an emergency situation.* Cat can be saved by a veterinarian only if treated immediately—in less than one day.

Recommendations

- At first, if the disease is not too far advanced, frequent short, gentle activity periods. Walking or strolling—not running.
- Administer oxygen if tongue becomes blue.
- Eliminate all toxins and pollutants from environment, especially cigarette smoke, which immediately aggravates symptoms.
- Use spring water—no chlorine or fluoride in water, no softened water (softened water has a high sodium content).
- If cat is heavy, reduce weight (see "Obesity," page 444).
- Provide a snug retreat (see page 304), both to reduce stress and as a source of warmth.
- Feed three or four smaller meals a day so heart is not taxed by large meals.
- Feed raw food diet (page 74), but change proportions to 70 percent meat and 30 percent vegetables. Diet should be low sodium, high vitamin and mineral content.
- Add kombu broth (page 318) as liquid portion of food recipe. This provides minerals and alkalizes the system.
- Use store-bought Anitra's Vita-Mineral Mix or, if you make it yourself using the recipe on page 68, use mixed trace minerals rather than kelp.
- Give 1/16 teaspoon ascorbic acid crystals or calcium ascorbate mixed in each meal (250 units vitamin C)—do not use sodium ascorbate.
- Increase vitamin E (alpha tocopherol) to 100 units a day for one month to

strengthen heart muscle and minimize body's need for oxygen. After one month, decrease to 400 units once a week.

- In each meal give:

> Vitamin B complex 10 mg (divide a 50 mg capsule into 5 parts)
> ½ of a multimineral pill (crushed)—should be low potency and must include selenium and chromium (no sodium); see "Product Recommendations" in the Appendix.
> Give 2 to 3 mg zinc each day if not included in above multimineral pill.

- Herbal remedies:

> Parsley Tea—if veterinarian prescribes a diuretic (such as Lasix), the parsley tea will promote copious urination. Add it as part of the liquid portion of the food. Perhaps the vet will be able to lower the dosage of the diuretic drug or even eliminate it as a low-sodium diet is now being given;
> Dill seed tea or horsetail tea is rich in minerals. A teaspoon can be added to meals if your cat enjoys the flavor.

- Bach flower remedies: Give three drops four times a day of the following mixture prepared as given on page 313:

> Oak—to encourage patience with self when the patient is too tired to keep up with what he used to do;
> Hornbeam—to build self confidence.

Cataracts

(see "Eye Problems")

Claw and Cuticle Problems

There are three types of claw and cuticle problems:

1. *Nail loss,* either from declawing or through an accident, affects the cat physically by weakening the corresponding leg and shoulder muscles. Scratching serves to tone those muscles, and cats who cannot scratch have poor balance. Loss of claws affects the cat psychologically as well because the claws (not the teeth) are the cat's first line of defense. Cats without claws are more tense, careful, and suspicious, as a person would be if he had no fingers.

2.   *Nail abnormality* can be either breaking, chipping, or overgrowth of claws or crooked regrowth of claws on a declawed cat. Nails break and chip because of a dietary lack of calcium, silica, or other minerals, vitamins C and D, protein or oils, or because the cat is not assimilating these nutrients even though they are present. This is a common problem in older cats. Nail overgrowth means the nails are too long. As they grow around and under in a curve, they can grow up into the cat's paw pad, embedding themselves deeper and deeper if they are not clipped. Old, sick, or injured cats who cannot wear the claws down with use or by scratching the post sometimes end up with ingrown nails.

The growth of deformed nails on declawed cats occurs because declawing is a delicate and difficult operation and is frequently done poorly. Instead of cutting the claw out of the joint and severing the tendons with a scalpel, an instrument resembling a miniature guillotine is frequently used and the toe joints are simply lopped off. Under these circumstances it is not unusual for one or more of the claws to grow back; however they never grow in a normal way. Usually the claw grows backward or sideward and into the paw. Often the cat does not limp but simply lives with the pain of having a claw through her foot, accepting the situation as normal because she has known no other life. Such cats are usually defensive about being picked up because they know it always hurts to land on their paws when you put them down again. The only hope they have that the condition will be discovered is if one of the deformed claws finally becomes infected and a veterinarian—hopefully not the one who caused the problem—is consulted.

If you should adopt a cat who has been declawed, be sure to have your veterinarian carefully examine the cat's toes to be sure the amputations were done carefully.

3.   *Cuticle infection* occurs when dirt gets caught between claw and cuticle and neither the cat nor the guardian cleans it out. A poorly kept litter box can cause such a problem either because it is dirty or because a spray or powder containing irritating chemicals was used (see page 91). But more often dirt under the cuticle is the result of a cat using the back claws to dig at waxy ears. Ear wax is too thick for the cat to lick off his claws thoroughly, so it builds up under the cuticle and causes swelling and redness. Ringworm often develops as well. If left untreated, infection can spread to the toe and foot.

Symptoms

- Limping or refusing to walk
- Not wanting to be picked up; hissing with distress when put down; not wanting to jump down from high places
- Frequent biting or licking at nails
- Pieces of thread or fabric caught on claw, claws catching on clothing and rugs
- Claws clicking on hard floors
- Claw tip embedded in pad
- Redness, swelling of cuticle or pad
- Discharge (wetness) around cuticle or pad

Recommendations

- Have veterinarian examine toes for abnormalities.
- Gently remove any wax or dirt with your thumbnail and clean cat's claws with almond oil, olive oil, or use "Solution for Dissolving Cuticle Dirt (page 284).
- Feed a high-quality diet with as much raw food as possible (page 66). Be sure to include Anitra's Vita-Mineral Mix and other listed supplements to diet.
- Add to each meal:

  ¼ teaspoon feline digestive enzymes to insure assimilation of all nutrients;

  ¹⁄₁₆ teaspoon ascorbic acid crystals or sodium ascorbate powder (250 units vitamin C) if there is an infection present.

  ½ to 1 teaspoon kombu broth (page 318) or horsetail tea (page 318) for extra silica and other minerals.

- Provide suitable scratching post (See "Product Recommendations" page 491), or cover any other scratching post with carpet backside out; be sure scratching post is stable.
- Practice greeting ritual to reinforce use of scratching post (see page 114).
- Fondle feet and claws and examine them every day (see page 176).
- Clip tips of claws every two to three weeks (see page 177).
- Reevaluate litter box setup to check for sanitation (see page 91).

- Do not use cleaning compounds such as Lysol, kitty box deodorant sprays, or baking soda. They can irritate cats' feet.
- For ingrown claws, seek help of veterinarian or groomer at once.
- Have veterinarian check for fungus or parasites in ears or on body.
- If dirt around cuticles has built up from scratching ringworm or ear mites, follow directions for cleaning cuticles (see page 282), and then soak feet in goldenseal or echinacea infusion as part of the general treatment (see page 282).
- If there is a wound and healing is desired, soak foot in calendula infusion. See "Soaking Feet and Cleaning Cuticles," page 282.
- If, instead of a clean wound, infection is present or if an ingrown claw has been extracted, draw out the poison with a foot soak of one cup warm water with two teaspoons Epsom salts twice a day until infection has drained. Always follow the Epsom salt with a *thorough* rinse of clear water. The cat should not lick the Epsom salt solution. Epsom salt has a laxative effect.

Coccidia

(see "Parasites")

Colitis

(see "Irritable Bowel Syndrome (IBS)")

Concussion

(see "Injuries")

Constipation

(see also "Irritable Bowel Syndrome (IBS)")

Constipation, straining at stool or passing hard dry stools, has become so prevalent among domestic cats as to be virtually universal. Commercial foods, all-meat diets, and fish are all low in fiber and result in a hard stool that passes slowly and with difficulty through the intestine. Constipation can also be a symptom of hair impaction or dehydration due to kidney disease, diabetes, pancreatitis, hyperthyroidism, cardiomyopathy, or irritable bowel syndrome.

Frequently when cats are sick, guardians call to ask me what to do about the additional problems of constipation. Because a sick cat often stops eating, the desperate caregiver tries to get the cat to eat by offering baby food meat. This usually gets the cat to eat all right, but baby food meat is very incomplete nutrition and so low in fiber that it forms into hard little balls inside the cat's intestine and causes constipation because there is no roughage whatsoever for the intestine to "grab onto."

If constipation is not treated, the intestinal walls will stretch and pockets will form as in diverticulosis. This will cause the cat to strain even more. In extreme cases the cat will be forced to take an unusual posture to pass stools, sometimes even standing with a paw up on the side of the litter box. Because a hard stool is held inside the body longer, some of the wastes will be reabsorbed and a coating of old stool will build up on the intestinal walls.

Both constipation and diarrhea are symptoms; they are not diseases in themselves but a sign that something else could be very wrong deeper in the body. If the intestinal tract is very badly obstructed, chances are that even the vet's laxative won't help. So don't wait more than three days, and make sure the vet knows it has already been three days since the cat passed a stool. The vet will have to wait an additional day after administering a laxative to see if it works before deciding whether to do an X-ray, give an enema, or even resort to surgery. If the cat's diet is high quality and rich in fiber and the cat is groomed every day, such a situation almost never arises.

A healthy cat passes a stool once or twice a day. The stool color can range from medium to dark brown, and it should be in long pieces and soft enough to be easily flattened when pressed. It is natural for the stool to have a strong odor.

Good health can best be maintained and recovery from any disease can be speeded up to a great extent if attention is given to strengthening the intestine, balancing the friendly bacteria, and promoting an easy, normal stool.

Symptoms

- Hard stool, often very dark, almost black in color
- Stool formed of several small hard pieces or even balls
- Straining while passing stool
- Remaining in squatting position for a long time before and/or after stool is passed

- Blood in stool
- Crying out while passing stool
- Failure to pass stool daily
- Copious drinking (shows dehydration). Ask your vet to check for kidney disease, diabetes, or hyperthyroidism.

Prevention:

- Groom cat at least thirty seconds a day to prevent hair impaction.
- Reevaluate grooming tool (see Chapter 7, "Grooming").
- Feed a high-quality diet with as much raw food as possible (see page 66), being sure to include Anitra's Vita-Mineral Mix (see page 68) which contains bran to condition the stool.
- Three times a week add an additional one teaspoon grated carrot per meal to help clean intestinal walls.
- Include 1/16 teaspoon fine bran in every meal, along with an extra tablespoon of water.
- Once a day, add 1/8 teaspoon psyllium husk powder and 2 teaspoons water to food.

Recommendations

After one day of not passing a stool:

- Follow suggestions above.
- Prepare the following Stool Softener Treat and serve once or twice a day, sprinkled with brewer's or nutritional or flaked yeast if your cat is a yeast lover. It can also be finger fed as a pâté or mixed into the meal.

Stool Softener Treat

1 tablespoon baby food vegetables and meat mixture
½ teaspoon melted butter
⅛ teaspoon *ground* psyllium husks
⅛ teaspoon powdered or fine bran
2 tablespoons water (or more—use your judgment)

349

- Mix ½ teaspoon powdered bran with ½ teaspoon butter and serve as a treat.
- Add to food three times a week: ⅛ teaspoon Delicious Garlic Condiment (page 317). It will strengthen intestinal muscles.
- Add to one meal a day ⅛ teaspoon *ground* psyllium husks and 2 tablespoons water (first choice) *or* plain, unflavored Siblin or Metamucil (whole psyllium) and 2 tablespoons water.

For serious constipation (no stool for two or three days)

- Follow suggestions above.
- Ask veterinarian to check for hair balls or disease.
- If laxative gel in a tube is prescribed, be sure to give the medication at least two hours before or after meals, never mixing with food. Never use a brand that is preserved with sodium benzoate or benzoate of soda. Cats are particularly sensitive to this particular poison. You can also use plain petroleum jelly as I do. (See "Giving Paste or Gel Medications," page 268.)
- If the veterinarian suggests it, give an enema (see page 292).
- Ask your vet if your cat seems dehydrated. If he says yes and if your cat has no heart problems, request that he hydrate the cat subcutaneously with 100 ml or so of Ringer's lactate solution. This therapy is simple and very valuable and always serves to give the patient's body a wonderful head start toward perfect health. (See "Subcutaneous Hydration," page 297.)
- Herbal remedies: I do not use laxatives, herbal or otherwise. However, psyllium husks, especially when finely ground, are an efficient stool conditioner and mucoid. They help the stool slip out easily and are not habit-forming. They are classified as a food herb. Be sure to add plenty of extra water when you use them.
- Bach flower remedies: Constipated cats tend to hold tension in their bodies and secret worries in their minds. Give three drops four times a day of the following mixture prepared as given on page 313:

> Crabapple—to help expel toxins;
> Vine—to help relax;
> Aspen—to dispel vague fears.

Corneal Ulcer

(see "Eye Problems")

Cuts

(see "Injuries")

Cystitis

(see "Feline Urologic Syndrome (FUS)")

Dandruff

Dandruff is a waste product. As Chapter 2 discusses, when the smell of food triggers the brain to prepare the body for digestion, waste disposal is slowed down tremendously, along with the rest of the metabolism. So, if the guardian leaves food available between meals, the cat constantly smells food and the metabolism is constantly slow. The result is that wastes build up and back up. Disposing of wastes and toxins is just as important as taking in food. When the primary avenues of excretion—the kidneys and the intestines—are not able to handle these large amounts of wastes, they are rerouted through the secondary organs of excretion: the lungs, as carbon dioxide, and the pores of the skin, as grease and dandruff. Cats who smell food all day are prone to dandruff. Germs then build up on the dirty skin, which becomes a home for funguses, parasites, and infections. The coat mats easily because it is oily and dirty.

Dandruff can also be caused by any of several deficiencies, disorders, or imbalances. Its appearance signals that one or more of the other organs of excretion or detoxification have become too weak to do their own job. Also, the cat might be ingesting a large amount of toxins (as found in semimoist food) or an excess of proteins (as in an all-meat diet). Dandruff or oiliness is also one of the first signs that the body's metabolism has become too slow. Ninety percent of all cats with dandruff have guardians who allow their cats to smell food all day long by leaving some sort of food or a dirty food bowl on the floor between meals and by giving frequent snacks or treats. Dry food is the usual culprit here. Dandruff almost always disappears when caregivers begin removing all food between meals. The lecithin granules contained in Anitra's Vita-Mineral Mix help emulsify the fatty wastes so the blood and urine can carry them away and send them out through the urine and stool.

Cats with dandruff are not inviting to snuggle and pet. The rejection that results leads to depression—which is a stress. This lowers the cat's resistance and makes him more vulnerable to disease and parasites—a classic snowball situation. Matted hair prevents the cat's tongue from reaching his dirty skin to clean it, and, in areas where he can lick and clean himself, he will only be recycling his own wastes—a "can't win" situation.

Symptoms

- White or brown dandruff flakes on cat's coat, on floors, furniture, and your clothing
- Oily fur, tendency to mat
- Frequent throwing up of hair balls
- Excess shedding of hair
- Tendency to pick up fleas, mange mites, or ringworm
- Constant licking and/or scratching
- Body odor

Recommendations

- Have veterinarian check for illness—especially in kidneys, intestines, liver, and thyroid.
- Increase metabolic efficiency by feeding only twice a day, unless your veterinarian suggests otherwise, and removing food between meals, leaving water always available (see page 56).
- Eliminate impurities in the diet by avoiding commercial cat foods that contain chemicals and by-products; feed a high-quality diet with as much raw food as possible (see "Diet," page 66). Be sure to include Anitra's Vita-Mineral Mix and other listed supplements in the diet.
- Add to each meal:

   Extra ⅛ teaspoon lecithin (in addition to lecithin in Vita-Mineral Mix) to help body dispose of fatty wastes;

Extra ⅛ teaspoon bran (in addition to bran in Vita-Mineral Mix) to aid the intestines.

- Use finely grated carrot or zucchini as the fresh vegetable in the meal at least once a day.
- Encourage energetic play before meals once or twice a day to help speed metabolism and facilitate normal waste disposal.
- Bathe every two or four weeks until condition is corrected to prevent re-cycling of wastes (see "The Bath," page 189). Finish the bath with an acid rinse: one part lemon juice to eleven parts water *or* one part cider vinegar to twenty parts water.
- Bach flower remedies: give three drops of crabapple prepared as given on page 313 four times a day to encourage cleansing.

Deafness

(see also "Ear Problems")

Deafness can be caused by wax impacted against the ear drum; an infection causing swelling around the ear drum; wax or swelling and/or injury due to ear mites; rupture of the ear drum due to infection or injury; or congenital deafness as found in some but not all blue-eyed white cats and odd-eyed white cats. Deaf cats should never be allowed to wander free. They are missing a major sense, the one that gives them early warning of danger. Deaf cats are vulnerable to attack by dogs, wandering toms, coyotes, mountain lions, and other predators, and they are incapable of detecting an oncoming motor vehicle until it is too late.

Symptoms

- Cat does not react when others are responding to a sound stimulus
- Cat does not react to another cat's communication by sound, such as a hiss or warning growl
- Cat is easily startled by touch unless he has seen you coming or felt your vibration on the floor.

Recommendations

- Ask veterinarian to determine cause.
- Treat any infection.
- Check for dirty teeth, which can cause infection that then spreads to the ear.
- Use veterinary wax-dissolving oil followed by an ear flush (see page 279).
- If veterinarian is anesthetizing cat for another procedure, such as teeth cleaning, ask him to do an ear flush as well.
- Feed a high-quality diet with as much raw food as possible, including Anitra's Vita-Mineral Mix and other supplements to the diet (see page 66).

If deafness is incurable

- Be sure *always* to signal before you touch the cat either by sight or by tapping on the floor or on the surface where the cat is sitting.
- Continue to talk to cat when you hold him or whenever you have his attention. He can still pick up on your mental attitudes and pictures. You convey these best when you verbalize them.
- Be alert to help the deaf cat avoid impending social difficulties that may arise with other cats because of his inability to hear a warning or challenge.
- Protect the deaf cat by confining indoors or to a screened-in area. Never allow cat to roam or be in the yard unsupervised.
- Devise vibration and sight signals to communicate. Here are a few examples:

  1. To say "come" flick the lights off and on or stomp a particular number of times in a particular clear pattern;
  2. To indicate "May I pick you up?" extend your hands palms up where he can see them.

Diabetes

Diabetes is a disease of the pancreas, whose job it is to produce insulin. Insulin combines with the tissue cells making it possible for (a) sugar to enter the cells to be used, or (b) sugar to be changed into fat or starch for storage, or (c) stored fat to be burned up and used for energy. If the pancreas is not manufacturing sufficient insulin, the sugar remains in the blood until, with the help of copious drinking, it is passed off in the urine. Sugar in the urine is a sign of diabetes. Without sufficient insulin little fat is available for storage, and stored fat cannot be converted to energy. Because of copious drinking and frequent urination, most of the water soluble vitamins and minerals will be washed out of the system. Every time the insulin level falls, a stress situation results and *all* the antistress nutrients (vitamins E, C, B complex, and potassium) are rapidly depleted. Both extreme stress and cortisone therapy have been known to produce a diabetic like reaction.

The typical diabetes-related diseases and complications, such as fatty liver, clogged arteries, gangrene, obesity, retinitis, and cataracts, have all been prevented when the high nutritional needs are met. When a nutritional program is instituted that supplies all the nutrients the cat's body needs to build up the pancreas, heal pancreatic scarring, replace water soluble nutrients and those nutrients used up by stress, stimulate insulin production by the pancreas, and, at the same time, lower the body's need for insulin, then the dose of insulin the animal needs to take is always dramatically lowered. Often, the dosage can be completely discontinued except if a stress situation again occurs. It is essential to work closely with the veterinarian while you are building up your cat's health and his ability to produce his own insulin again. You are walking a very fine line between insulin shock and diabetic coma.

Insulin shock means that too much insulin has been given to the cat. The need for insulin will always be reduced if the diet is improved and stress reduced, so again, be sure to work closely with your veterinarian. If you are using an experienced classical homeopath, success will come more quickly, so be vigilant. Diabetic coma means that the body still needs more insulin therapy; perhaps a reduction can be made later if the pancreas can be built up more or stress further reduced. I repeat: I have always worked very closely with the veterinarian, who constantly adjusts the insulin level as the cat improves. It does take time and attention for a while, but you usually end up with a cat who is healthier than he ever was before the trouble began, because all sorts of small problems will automatically be corrected along with the diabetes.

Several years ago an herbal sweetener, called stevia, containing almost no calories, appeared in health food stores. It is made from the sap of a Central American bush. Stevia is widely used all over the world now as a sweetener. The more natural form of stevia is brown and it has an interesting side effect. It causes the system to handle sugars more efficiently and allows diabetics to reduce their insulin intake. (The more refined white stevia has almost no effect.) The first cat I tried it on was a pretty little calico named Daisy. Using stevia as described in the recommendations section below, I was able to reduce her insulin dose from twelve units to one unit per day.

Diabetes often produces copious urination as the body tries to wash the excess sugar out of the system. Copious urination is a sign that more insulin may be needed. If the patient becomes dehydrated, ask the veterinarian to hydrate your cat with Ringer's Lactate solution given subcutaneously. Because I have the Ringer's lactate at home to hydrate the kidney patients, my own vet has asked that I give Daisy, my diabetes patient, 50 ml of fluid subcutaneously every day to help wash the sugar out of the blood and prevent constipation. We first made sure Daisy's heart was strong and her blood pressure normal so we knew there was no danger of a build-up of fluids anywhere in the body. (See "Subcutaneous Hydration," page 297.)

Diabetes patients crave warmth, so it is wise to provide an outside source of heat such as a snug retreat, which also serves to cushion stress.

Symptoms

- Copious drinking and copious urination (*note:* this can also signal kidney disease or other problems; see page 426)
- Good appetite but loss of weight or sudden weight gain or intractable weight gain
- Repeated infections: feline urologic syndrome, respiratory problems, cysts, feline acne, and so on
- Wounds not healing
- Tendency to cataracts
- Urine tests high in sugar
- Urine tests high in xanthic acid (shows vitamin B-6 deficiency, which causes damage to pancreas)

Recommendations

- Consult veterinarian for a firm diagnosis and to set beginning insulin level.
- Feed diabetes diet given below.

- Groom and eliminate mats, fleas, ringworm, and the like to reduce stress.
- Be sure teeth are clean and anal glands normal.
- Provide a snug retreat (see page 304).
- Provide *regular* play and exercise—be sure it's regular or insulin needs will fluctuate.
- Hydrate the patient *regularly* to lower the amount of sugar in the blood. Let your holistic vet guide you as to the amount of subcutaneous fluids to give. (See "Subcutaneous Hydration," page 297.)
- Give Bach flower remedy to reduce stress. (Stress raises the body's need for insulin.) Give 3 drops twice a day of the following mixture prepared as given on page 313:

  > Hornbeam—to bolster self confidence;
  > Mimulus—to reduce fear.

- Herbal remedy—give a teaspoon to a tablespoon of herbal tea added to all food. Ask your cat which he prefers: dill tea (increases appetite and provides minerals) or horsetail (gives strength and provides minerals).
- Stevia: If you want to reduce insulin need by giving brown stevia, work closely with your veterinarian and do it gradually. The less insulin you need to give, the better off the patient will be. I like to put 1 drop of stevia into a teaspoon of water and begin by just putting 1 drop of this mixture into each meal. (Your veterinarian may tell you to use more because he knows your particular cat.) I then increase the amount every day, being careful to always test the urine for sugar before each insulin dose. *Slowly is safely.* It may take many days to discover how much to give your cat, but this method is tried and true; it will lower insulin needs. I say again, be sure to keep your veterinarian informed.

Diabetes Diet

Note: the goal of this diet is to strengthen the pancreas, reduce scarring, reduce insulin needs, stimulate insulin production, replace nutrients lost in urine or because of stress, and prevent the main complications associated with diabetes.

- Feed the raw food diet on page 74. It's good to feed three to five smaller meals a day, but it's important to stick to the same schedule every day.

Raw ground chicken is the best choice for the meat portion for a diabetic, but be sure the chicken is organic and be sure it is *not* lowfat; 85 percent lean is good. If you can only get low fat, add 1 raw organic egg yolk and ½ teaspoon butter to each half-pound of ground chicken. When adding liquid in the raw food diet, choose kombu broth (page 318), parsley tea (page 318), a vegetable broth, or ½ cup chicken broth with $\frac{1}{16}$ teaspoon of Green Magma powder.

- *Add to each meal before serving:*

    ½ teaspoon Anitra's Vita-Mineral Mix (see page 68);
    a pinch of Green Magma (not too much; the meal must be delicious);
    $\frac{1}{16}$ teaspoon ascorbic acid crystals or sodium ascorbate powder (250 units vitamin C);
    a pinch of potassium chloride (salt substitute);
    Stevia in whatever amount you and your vet have decided upon.

- *Once a day (after breakfast) give:*

    100 units vitamin E (alpha tocopherol) capsule. After two weeks, reduce to 400 units once a week.

- *Once a week add to meal:*

    10,000 units vitamin A and 400 units vitamin D from an A and D capsule that you have punctured.
    Or, better yet, use a feline multivitamin containing A and D. (See "Product Recommendations" in the Appendix.)

Note: If you must use canned food, avoid fish and add to each meal one-half of a raw, organic egg yolk and the supplements as with the homemade diet above. (Review "The High-Quality Diet: Fluff City in Thirty Days" on page 66.)

Diarrhea

(see also "Irritable Bowel Syndrome (IBS)")

Note: Diarrhea in kittens under three months old can be very serious. If a young kitten gets diarrhea, *do not wait* more than half a day; take him straight to a veterinarian. Dehydration from diarrhea can kill a tiny kitten in one day.

Diarrhea, the passing of frequent soft or watery stool, is usually a sign that the body is trying to rid itself of some unusually toxic waste material by passing it out through the intestine. This is as it should be, and if diarrhea in an adult cat does not continue for more than one or two days, it is not serious and often clears up naturally when the backlog of toxic wastes have all been excreted. If there are no other negative symptoms present, don't be too quick to run to the medicine chest and grab something that will stop it right away. Instead, help the body to handle the problems by smoothing the path and minimizing the discomfort and the negative side effects.

If soft or runny stool persists for more than two days, it may mean that the intestinal wall is irritated or that parasites are present. The veterinarian should be consulted because diarrhea can be a symptom of poisoning or of any number of diseases such as hepatitis, colitis, pancreatitis, or irritable bowel syndrome. Many adult cats cannot digest milk products and will get diarrhea if milk, cheese, or yogurt are included in the diet. The early stages of hair ball impaction can also produce diarrhea as can intestinal parasites. Oddly enough, extreme dehydration can also produce diarrhea, which clears up after the cat is hydrated (see "Subcutaneous Hydration," page 297).

Symptoms

Note: If diarrhea is violent or accompanied by vomiting, withhold food and consult veterinarian at once. This is an emergency situation.

- Passing stool frequently, three or more times a day
- Passing of loose, unformed, soft, or watery stool
- Unusually foul odor to stool
- Stool mixed with mucus
- Straw-colored or yellow soft stool
- Passing gas with stool
- Lethargy or depression
- Hiding
- Refusal to eat or eating voraciously and not gaining weight
- Soil on bloomers

Recommendations

Diarrhea for one day

- At the first sign of diarrhea withhold all solid food and put the cat on a fast of Homemade Chicken Broth (see "Fasting," page 286, and broth recipe, page 308). The patient may have as much as he likes three to five times a day, but remove the leftovers between feedings as you would with any food.
- Alkalize the system (diarrhea almost always indicates a hyper-acid system). Add one tablespoon of kombu seaweed broth to the chicken broth each time you feed.
- Soothe the intestine by giving one teaspoon slippery elm syrup five minutes before each meal (see page 319). Slippery elm is soothing, alkalizing, and full of minerals.
- Restore the balance of friendly bacteria in the intestine by adding ¼ teaspoon mixed intestinal flora to the chicken broth. (Ask your health food store for vegetarian mixed intestinal flora that contains no milk or lactose.) (See "Product Recommendations" in the Appendix.)
- Alkalize and purify the entire intestinal tract by giving a pinch of Green Magma three times a day—either in the chicken broth or mixed with a teaspoon of the broth and given as a liquid medication. (See "Giving Liquid Medication," page 268.)
- Herbal remedy: if there is irritation in the intestine, golden seal infusion will soothe and provide a tonic for the entire digestive tract. Put five drops golden seal extract into ½ cup water. Give one to two teaspoons twice a day between meals (at least two hours before or after food). Or give ¼ dropperful golden seal elixir twenty minutes before meals. Discontinue after five days. (See "Giving Liquid Medication," page 268, and "Using Herbs," page 314.)

Diarrhea for two days

- Follow suggestions above.
- Consult veterinarian by phone.
- Watch for any other symptoms.

- If stool has a strong smell or if there is flatulence, give a charcoal capsule or tablet after the slippery elm syrup (see above) twice a day or empty the capsule into the teaspoon of slippery elm and give both together by dropper. Charcoal absorbs the poisons that cause gas.
- Continue to withhold solid food and fast on chicken broth.

Diarrhea persisting on third day

- Follow suggestions above; *and*
- *Consult veterinarian by phone or visit.*
- Continue chicken broth fast.
- Be sure cat is drinking water or broth (at last 30 cc daily) to prevent dehydration.

Diarrhea continuing unabated on fourth day

- *Take cat to veterinarian for diagnosis.*
- Dehydration can sometimes cause diarrhea to persist. Ask veterinarian if your cat seems dehydrated. As long as your cat has no heart problems, you can request that he administer fluids subcutaneously (see page 297). This always gives the patient a nice head start toward recovery.

Dry Coat
(see also "Skin Problems")

An extremely dry coat is not as common as an oily coat. An oily coat that has collected large amounts of dust and dirt or one in which the oils have hardened and clogged the pores is often mistaken for dry coat. In true dry coat, the hair is almost always sparse, and the skin easily seen through the hair. The hair is characterized by a coarse feeling and will sometimes break off at varying lengths and is easily matted. The skin will be sensitive to grooming or touch because of damaged capillaries that are not adequately feeding the skin nerves and hair follicles. Poor circulation or a lack of vitamin A, vitamin C, bioflavonoids, minerals, or B vitamins can result in weak or damaged capillaries. Another possible cause of dry coat is a lack of usable fats in the diet, often the result of feeding too lean a diet, or the failure of the liver or gall bladder to process the fats present in the food. Malabsorption, anorexia, and dehydration can all produce the same effect (see "Weight Loss," page 482). Dry coat can also be a result of hyperthyroidism (see page 399).

Any skin or coat problem is a sign that the cat's system is not functioning properly. It is out of balance. Classical homeopathy as practiced by an experienced veterinarian is the fastest, most thorough way to balance the system and allow all of your other efforts to give maximum benefit (see "Homeopathy," page 211).

Symptoms

- Thin, sparse hair; skin easily seen through hair
- Dry skin easily sunburned
- Sensitivity to grooming and to being touched
- Coarse hair, sometimes brittle and breaking
- Sensitivity to heat and cold
- Dandruff (sometimes)
- Ringworm or other fungus; mange mites or fleas (see "Ringworm," "Parasites," "Mange Mites," and "Fleas")

Recommendations

- Have veterinarian examine and run tests to diagnose for illness and/or parasites (intestinal or skin) and/or dehydration.
- Treat for any illness or deficiency diagnosed by vet.
- Feed a high-quality diet with as much raw food as possible (see page 66). Be sure to include Anitra's Vita-Mineral Mix and other listed supplements in diet.
- Add to food twice a day:

  ¼ teaspoon feline digestive enzymes to ensure digestion of food and supplements;
  ¼ teaspoon skin and coat oil supplement from PetGuard or fish oil supplement.

- Remove food between meals, leaving only water available.
- Groom lightly and frequently to stimulate skin capillaries. Use a soft

brush at first until condition improves; then work up to wire slicker brush after cat is well. Use wide-toothed metal comb for longhaired cats. (See Chapter 8, "Grooming.")

- Be careful to protect cat from heat, cold, and sun.
- Have a regular daily play period to stimulate circulation.
- Give homeopathic treatments prescribed by a classical homeopathic veterinarian.

Ear Mites

(see "Ear Problems")

Ear Problems

(see also "Deafness")

Just as a cat's sense of smell is so many times greater than ours, so are the ears much more sensitive. The sign of something wrong with the cat's ears is not always wax or discharge, although those are the most common. Any sort of irritation inside the ear canal, any kind of swelling down there, will cause an itch. The very first sign of trouble is a cat trying to relieve that unreachable itch by rapidly shaking his head or trying to dig into the ear with a hind claw. (Dirt buildup around the cuticles of the hind claws is frequently a sign of either ear problems or skin problems.) Sometimes sores on the forehead or around the ear are a sign not of trouble where the sores are but of the cat's desperate scratching in an attempt to reach a maddening itch deep inside the ear canal.

Wax in the ears—or any kind of discharge—can be caused by any one of a number of things. Ear mites produce a dry, dark brown wax; swelling and redness due to allergies or infection are often accompanied by a softer light brown or yellow wax. Untreated infections and wounds will produce pus and/or blood. *The only course is to take the cat to the veterinarian and let the veterinarian determine the cause.*

Ear problems are easier to treat if they are caught and diagnosed early—even before a discharge begins to form. Head shaking, head tilting, or digging with the back claw in and around the ear and above the eye are all signs of ear trouble. If left untreated, ear infection can spread to throat, eyes, gums, or even into the brain. Ear pain and itching are high-stress situations that weaken the body, rendering it easy prey to germs or viruses.

Earwax but No Mites

If your veterinarian determines that your cat's earwax is not caused by mites, the other possibilities are germs, some sort of waste discharge or eruption inside the ear canal, an allergic reaction, or a yeast infection of already damaged tissue. First make sure that the problem is only in the outer ear canal and does not include the inner ear. If that is the case, my own veterinarian recommends a cleansing flush (see page 279) with vegetable wash and water solution followed by the mild white vinegar solution (see page 324), which leaves the ear canal with a desirable acid balance. Then for the next week or so, use Halo Herbal Ear Wash ("Simple Cleaning of the Ears," see page 279). I have found that it takes about three weeks to completely clear up the problem.

I have found it important to clean the back claws and cuticles once or twice a week. You can't look very far into the ear canal to see how well you're succeeding, but you will be able to monitor your progress by noting how much dirt has collected around the back cuticles. By the third week there should be almost nothing for you to clean off. Cleaning the cuticles also prevents reinfection of the ear when the cat scratches with the dirty claws.

- Day 1—flush ears with vegetable rinse solution ("Irrigation Formula I," page 280) followed by vinegar solution (page 324)
- Days 2–7—twice a day put one dropperful of warm Halo Herbal Ear Wash into each ear. Repeat for three rounds. (See "Simple Cleaning of the Ears," page 279.)

Ear Mites

Ear mites are nearly microscopic sluglike creatures. They burrow into the delicate tissue inside the ear canal and lay their eggs there under the skin. Ear mites cause wounds and scarring of the membrane. Therefore, when treating for mites, attention must be given to healing the tissue and treating the cat for stress (see "Antistress Supplements," page 305) as well as destroying the mites.

Dr. Pitcairn's herbal prescription for treatment addresses these problems very nicely. This is the method I employ to eliminate ear mites:

- Follow diet recommendations below.
- Flush ears and clean back cuticles as above for ear wax. Also use the vegetable wash solution to shampoo around the ears, head, and the end of the tail, which rests near the ears when the cat sleeps. Mites and eggs are sometimes found there.

Dr. Pitcairn's Ear Mite Treatment

- Days 1, 2, and 3—heal the membrane inside the ear canal and smother some of the mites by using one dropperful of Dr. Pitcairn's healing ear oil (see below) in each ear once a day. Hold the ear flap closed over the oil and massage the oil around. Then let the cat go ahead and shake the excess oil out. Blot the fur dry with a paper towel. (See "Giving Ear Medication," page 277).
- Days 4, 5, and 6—rest. Do nothing.
- Days 7, 8, and 9—kill the mites. Put one dropperful of Dr. Pitcairn's Herbal Ear Mite Solution (see below) into each ear once a day the same as you did with the healing oil.
- Days 10–18—do nothing.
- Day 19—put one dropper of Wax-O-Sol in each ear to break up any wax, then flush the ears with a warm vegetable wash solution. (See "Flushing the Ears," page 279.)
- Days 20–28—to catch any mites that have hatched since the first treatment, repeat the whole process, following directions for days 1–9 above.

Dr. Pitcairn's Healing Ear Oil

Into a one-ounce dropper bottle put:

¾ oz almond oil
¼ oz olive oil
**400 units vitamin E oil (from punctured capsules), to preserve oil and
      heal tissue**

Refrigerate. Warm before using by setting bottle in bowl of warm water.

Dr. Pitcairn's Herbal Ear Mite Solution

2 teaspoons ground dried rue
5 teaspoons witch hazel extract
1 cup boiling water

Steep rue in boiling water for fifteen minutes. Strain. Add witch hazel to liquid. Refrigerate. Warm before using by standing container in bowl of hot water.

If you decide to use a veterinary preparation for mites instead of the more gentle herbal method outlined above, here's a word of caution: when dealing with ear mites, be very sure to follow strictly the veterinarian's orders as to how often and how long to repeat the treatment. Mites are like fleas in that you can't kill the eggs. The veterinarian knows the life cycle of the organism and will gear the treatment so that you catch and kill the little horrors shortly after they hatch and before they can reproduce. When the prescribed time is over, before you heave a sigh of relief, a second test must be made by the veterinarian to see that all signs of the infestation are truly gone. It's a good idea to shampoo around the ears and tail tip as you would when doing the herbal treatment. Eggs clinging there could reinfest the ears. Many veterinary mite preparations contain steroids (see page 244), plus a very caustic chemical poison to kill the mites. If you decide to use one of these, *do not use a cotton swab to clean the ear first.* Rubbing against the very delicate ear membrane with the swab sensitizes the tissue. The mite medication may then feel like it's burning the inside of the ear.

However, beginning the treatment with a warm, gentle ear flush (see page 279) will give the patient relief and help the medicine to work faster (see "Giving Ear Medication," page 277). Here, too, it is wise to clean the cuticles as given above to prevent reinfestation.

Symptoms

- Ear exudation of hard dark brown wax, or flaky brown wax
- Head shaking after being touched anywhere near the ears
- Head tilt, stumbling, or falling
- Digging into ear or over eye or on upper throat with back claws

- Wax under cuticle (which can cause toe infection or reinfest the ears)
- Bald patch or redness anywhere around ear or below ear on neck

Recommendations

- Determine the cause of the problem. Have veterinarian check for fleas; mites; bacterial, viral, or yeast infection; and so on. *Do not clean the ears before the examination.*
- Feed a high-quality diet (see Chapter 2, "Diet"). Be sure to include Anitra's Vita-Mineral Mix and other listed additions to diet.
- Raise the cat's resistance by feeding as much raw food as possible (see page 66) and by removing all food between meals.
- Add an extra $\frac{1}{16}$ teaspoon sodium ascorbate or ascorbic acid crystals (250 units vitamin C) to each meal to help the body process out the toxic ear mite medication.
- Add the antistress supplements (page 305) to food. Ear mites are extremely uncomfortable.
- Add an extra ¼ teaspoon lecithin to each meal (in addition to lecithin in Anitra's Vita-Mineral Mix).
- Add ⅛ teaspoon Delicious Garlic Condiment (page 317) to each meal once a day.
- During any exudation, fast the cat for one day a week on Homemade Chicken Broth (see page 308; see "Fasting," page 286).
- Carefully follow veterinarian's directions for ear medication. This is especially important when treating mites. Do not clean ears with cotton swab before administering medication—you don't want to irritate the inner membrane (see "Giving Ear Medication," page 277). However, you may want to precede the treatment with a nice cleansing ear flush (see page 279).
- Clean wax off back claws and from under back cuticles with peroxide, almond oil, or sesame oil on cotton swabs, scrape your own thumbnail, or, better yet, soak the feet and clean the nails and cuticles (see page 282).
- Herbal remedy: after cleaning the claws thoroughly, if the cuticles are red, swollen, or injured, add a final soak in warm calendula solution to soothe and heal. Mix 2 cups warm water, 1 teaspoon salt, and 20 drops calendula extract or tincture of calendula.

- Bach flower remedies: give three drops four times a day of the following mixture prepared as given on page 313.

> Crabapple—to help expel impurities;
> Impatiens—to calm.

Emergencies
(see "Injuries")

Entropion
(see "Eye Problems")

Eye Problems
(see also "Blindness")

Eye discharge may appear temporarily if there is an eye wound or if a foreign body is lodged there. The eye will then automatically secrete an unusually large amount of tears in an attempt to cleanse itself. However, if the discharge is constant, this indicates an abnormal condition. A backup of wastes in the body may cause the eyes and/or ears to run as the system tries to rid itself of toxins through any door it can find. A diet high in chemicals (preservatives and other food additives) or a poorly balanced diet, such as an all-meat diet, can be the cause, as can leaving food available between meals, which slows the metabolism and causes wastes to back up. An infection in an eye can spread from dirty teeth or from upper respiratory problems. Conversely, infected tear ducts can spread infection into the mouth, nose, ears, or upper respiratory tract.

By far the most common cause of chronic eye discharge is blocked or malformed tear ducts. Persian cats especially are plagued with eye problems because of inbreeding to purposely produce the congenital deformity of a very flat face (called the "peke-face"). The flat, straight nose of the very inbred Siamese can also produce the same problem because, as with the Persian's face, there is not enough room for normal tear ducts in the deformed skull structure. Many cats with eye problems come out of catteries where they are inbred to produce this specific facial structure because it is considered desirable and is necessary for winning ribbons in the show ring. Cats who win ribbons and their offspring are worth more money. In other words, it is done without regard for the health or the comfort of the animal.

A cat who has spent time under the care of an insensitive human may have had several uncomfortable or frightening experiences in life to deal with before coming to you, the guardian who loves him and cares more for his comfort, health, and happiness than for the shape of his nose. The Bach flower remedies given below will help the cat put such negative emotional memories behind him.

(See below for specific eye problems: cataracts, corneal ulcer, and entropion.)

Symptoms

- Swollen, red, conjunctive tissue
- Frequent squinting or blinking
- Running eyes
- Brown-stained fur around eyes and nose
- White or yellow discharge from eyes
- Snuffling or sneezing, repeated respiratory infections
- Bad breath, red gums
- Bloody spot on the eye

Recommendations

- Remove brown stain and encrustation from fur around the eyes (see "Cleaning Around the Eyes," page 269).
- Have veterinarian check for infections, foreign objects, entropion, or wounds in eyes.
- Clip nails of all animals in the household to prevent accidental injury during play or scuffles.
- Give ½ teaspoon cod liver oil six days a week. On the seventh day, give a capsule containing 10,000 units of vitamin A and 400 units of vitamin D, *or* give a feline multivitamin containing A and D (see "Product Recommendations," "Giving Liquid Medication," page 268, or "Giving Pills," page 266).
- Remove all food between meals, leaving only water available.

- Feed a high-quality diet with as much raw food as possible (see page 66). Be sure to include Anitra's Vita-Mineral Mix and other listed supplements to diet.
- Fast the cat on Homemade Chicken Broth one day a week until discharge clears up (if you're not already doing a regular weekly fast) (see page 308).
- Add 1/16 teaspoon ascorbic acid crystals or sodium ascorbate powder to each meal to help the body fight infection.
- Wash eyes with goldenseal and saline solution (see "herbal remedies" below and also see "Administering Eyedrops and Irrigating Tear Ducts," page 270).
- Bach flower remedies: give three to four drops four times a day of the following mixture prepared as given on page 313:

> Willow—to break away from old patterns, memories, and ties;
> Crabapple—for cleansing;
> Walnut—to welcome change.

- Herbal remedy: make a normal saline solution of 1/2 cup water and 1/8 teaspoon salt. Add 5 drops of one of the herbal extracts given below. Choose according to what you and your veterinarian decide and what makes your cat feel good.

> Calendula—to speed healing of wounds in or around eye; also soothes soreness and inflammation;
> Chamomile—to reduce inflammation and soothe;
> Golden seal—is antifungal and antiseptic; it also reduces inflammation and swelling;
> Eyebright—to reduce inflammation;
> Echinacea—is antifungal and also reduces inflammation.

Cataracts

A cataract is a white cloudiness occurring in the clear lens of the eye where light and images are transmitted and focused. Cataract is most frequently found in old or diabetic animals, but it is sometimes seen in younger cats as well. It is often difficult to trace the cause. A congenital predisposition is sometimes a factor, but any one of several dietary deficiencies have produced cataracts in laboratory animals. A vitamin B-2 deficiency can produce oily skin and eyelashes as well as cataracts. A cholesterol problem will clog all of the blood vessels, including the small capillaries feeding the eye, and cataracts can result. A diet lacking the amino acids histidine, phenylalanine, or any one of several others has produced cataracts. A cat forced to survive on a vegetarian diet will always go blind from lack of taurine, an amino acid found only in animal flesh; cats cannot manufacture their own taurine as humans can. Certain types of cataracts have been produced when vitamin C was lacking; the problem then improved when vitamin C was supplied.

Symptoms

- Cloudiness inside the eye behind the pupil
- Chewing and licking nonfood items such as glue, wires, plastic, bricks, and cat litter
- Symptoms of blindness (see "Blindness," page 336)

Recommendations

- See veterinarian for diagnosis.
- Feed a high-quality diet with as much raw food as possible (see page 66). Be sure to include Anitra's Vita-Mineral Mix and other listed supplements to diet.
- Give $\frac{1}{16}$ teaspoon ascorbic acid crystals or sodium ascorbate powder in each meal (250 units vitamin C).
- Increase vitamin E to 100 units a day for two weeks; then return to a maintenance dose of 400 units once a week or use a high-quality feline multivitamin.
- Wash eyes and tear ducts three or four times a day with one of the herbal eye wash solutions (see "Administering Eyedrops and Irrigating Tear Ducts," page 270).

Corneal Ulcer
(scratch on the eye)

A corneal ulcer is a minor or deep wound on the surface of the eye itself. The scratch is usually difficult to see, but it causes a runny eye for a day or two, then heals over if the animal is in a state of normal health. *If there is any blood in the eye discharge—any at all—the cat should be rushed to the veterinarian for treatment.* Blood in an eye wound is always serious and indicates that the very delicate inner eye has been injured and that the wound is very deep.

Symptoms

- Watery eye or brown or yellow eye discharge
- Closing eye or squinting
- Bloody discharge—*see veterinarian at once*
- A bloody spot on the eye from a corneal ulcer looks fresh as opposed to a reddish-brown spot that remains unchanged. (This latter often signals high blood pressure.)

Recommendations

- See veterinarian if discharge is bloody or if symptoms do not disappear after three or four days.
- Give a capsule that contains 10,000 units vitamin A and 400 units vitamin D twice a week until healed; then reduce dosage to once a week. Puncture capsule and empty contents into food, or see "Giving Pills," page 266. Or give a feline multivitamin containing vitamins A and D (see "Product Recommendations," in the Appendix).
- Increase vitamin E to 100 units a day until healed.
- Place one drop cod liver oil into eye or inside lower lid four times a day.
- Wash eyes three or four times a day with calendula saline eyewash solution (see "Administering Eyedrops and Irrigating Tear Ducts," page 270).

Entropion
(lower eyelid turned inward)

When a cat's lower eyelid rolls permanently inward—*entropion*—the lower lashes will rub against the cornea and produce an ulcer that is sometimes visible as a white line from healed "old" ulcers or a crater in the cornea. In some cats, entropion is a congenital deformity. In others, it can develop slowly because of repeated inflammation or swelling caused by infections or injuries, washing while teeth are dirty, germ growth in blocked tear ducts, or infections spreading from the nose. When the lower lid swells and shrinks again and again, the tissues become abnormal in shape and can shrivel inward, producing entropion. This condition is easily corrected by surgery but will recur if the underlying cause is not cleared up.

Symptoms

- Constant tearing and eye discharge of colorless, brown, or white material
- Frequent blinking and squinting
- Sometimes a white line visible just under lower lid
- Lower lashes touching eye

Recommendations

- Clean away crusty, brown discharge from fur around the eyes (see "Cleaning Around the Eyes," page 269).
- Ask veterinarian to diagnose, then perhaps correct the condition with surgery. Unlike tearduct problems, entropion can nearly always be corrected by surgery.
- Eliminate cause by treating any infections, cleaning teeth, and so on.
- Give 100 units per day vitamin E for two weeks; then return to maintenance dose of 400 units once a week or give a feline multivitamin containing vitamin E to help normalize lower lid tissue.
- Wash eyes three or four times a day with an herbal eyewash solution (see "Administering Eyedrops and Irrigating Tear Ducts," page 270).

Feline Acne

(see also "Skin Problems")

Feline acne appears under the chin as one or more small lumps or black debris or pimples. I have noticed during the shedding seasons in spring and autumn that there always seems to be an increase of feline acne cases. During the sheds the body processes shift into a sort of "clean-out" gear. Besides getting rid of the old hair, old body wastes are excreted through the pores. When the sebaceous glands under the chin oversecrete, filling the pores with sebaceous fluid, the pores can become clogged and feline acne results.

It is not a serious problem, it is simply a little warning signal to alert you that (a) there are too many wastes building up in your friend's body, and (b) the organs of excretion are not functioning at top efficiency and are not handling the wastes as they should. The problem always improves when you upgrade the diet, remove all food between meals, nurture all of the organs of excretion, and keep the area of eruption clean.

If the acne persists, let your veterinarian examine the area just to be sure it really is acne. If he confirms that it is indeed acne, persevere with the treatments below, especially the weekly fasting day and the improved diet. The added vitamins A and D will help the liver detoxify the old wastes; the vitamin C will help the lymph ducts carry off the old wastes; zinc and vitamin E will strengthen the skin and aid in its repair. As a general rule I always like to help the body get rid of wastes during the spring and autumn sheds by fasting the cats on broth one day a week. My chicken broth is very strong and delicious so the cats think of the fast day as a treat day.

My own vets caution against the use of antibiotics or other drug therapy for feline acne. I heartily agree. Homeopathic treatment administered by a classical homeopathic vet has been very effective in speeding a complete cure.

Symptoms

- One or more small lumps or black debris or pimples under the chin

Recommendations

- Change to the raw food diet. If this is not possible, upgrade the diet by eliminating all poisons, chemicals, and meat by-products from the diet by double-checking ingredients listed on the food you feed your cat. Do not feed any by-products (found even in some so-called "health food" and veterinary brands of food), preservatives, colorings, or sugar (see page 59). Include Anitra's Vita-Mineral Mix and other listed supplements.

- Help the body build resistance to disease by feeding as much raw food as possible (see page 66). Reread the section "Changing over to the New Diet," page 82.
- Use a feline multivitamin (see "Product Recommendations," page 489) containing the supplements below or give them separately:

> $\frac{1}{16}$ teaspoon ascorbic acid crystals (250 units vitamin C) to each meal;
> 10,000 units vitamin A and 400 units vitamin D once a week;
> 5 mg zinc to each meal;
> 400 units vitamin E from a punctured capsule once a week.

- Follow the feeding rules on page 56, by feeding only twice a day, removing all leftovers after one-half hour, and leaving only water available between meals.
- Fast the cat one day a week on Homemade Chicken Broth (see page 308) and see "Fasting," page 286.
- Add to each meal (in addition to the usual supplements):

> ¼ teaspoon bran (in addition to bran in Anitra's Vita-Mineral Mix);
> 1 teaspoon finely grated carrot or zucchini;
> ½ raw organic egg yolk (or 1 yolk per 5.5 oz can of food)—to support the kidneys by keeping the urine acid to prevent the growth of germs.

- If the stool is quite smelly or if the cat has gas, give one charcoal capsule twice a day before meals for two days only.
- If the stool seems dry or hard or if it comes out in more than two pieces, add $\frac{1}{16}$ teaspoon psyllium husks and 2 tablespoons water to each meal.
- If any antibiotics have been given in the last year, add ¼ teaspoon mixed intestinal flora powder to each meal (see "Product Recommendations" in the Appendix).
- Keep the area of infection clean. Follow these steps twice a day:

    1. Clean away any old dried exudation by first using a hot compress (see page 296), then gently scraping away loose debris

with your fingernail, or combing outward toward the chin with a small flea comb. Do not press hard.

2. Apply peroxide with a cotton ball (it will foam on contact).
3. Rinse thoroughly.
4. Apply solution of ½ cup water and ⅛ teaspoon white vinegar generously with cotton ball.

- Herbal remedy: a poultice of mashed dandelion or watercress leaves is cleansing and purifying.
- Bach flower remedy: prepare as given on page 313 and give three drops four times a day of crabapple to assist the cleansing process.

Feline AIDS

(see "Feline Leukemia and Feline AIDS")

Feline Infectious Peritonitis (FIP)

Feline Infectious Peritonitis, or FIP, is an immunological disease. The FIP virus itself is very fragile and cannot survive long outside of the warm moist body fluids. It can be destroyed in the environment with a simple solution of one part chlorine bleach to thirty-two parts water. And yet FIP is considered a deadly disease, nearly always fatal once symptoms develop.

The reason is that the virus all alone does not produce the symptoms. The virus enters the body via intimate contact: washing, playing, biting, or being sprayed with infected mucus when a sick cat sneezes. The well cat's immune system then sends antibodies to combine with the invading viruses and destroy them. This is the normal immune system response, and this is what has always worked in the past. Unfortunately, this time the invader is an FIP virus. Instead of the antibodies combining with it and destroying it, the viruses and the antibodies bind together to form a whole new entity: a virus-antibody complex. These immune complexes, as they are called, attach to the walls of small veins, damaging the walls so that fluid leaks out into the body cavities.

Any veterinarian will tell you that FIP is difficult to diagnose. That is because the early symptoms, lethargy and a mild upper respiratory infection, look like the early symptoms of about twenty other diseases and are often so mild they are overlooked. The later symptoms, which can appear anywhere from weeks to years later, vary according to where in the victim's body the virus-antibody complex has taken hold. If the virus has settled in one of the abdominal organs, fluids will leak out and fill the abdomen. You will have a very skinny cat with a big belly. If the virus is in the pleural cavity around the lungs, there will be fluid in the chest cavity producing breathing difficulties. This is called the "wet" form of FIP. There is a dry form where fluid does not leak. Some veterinarians say the dry form is more common than the wet form; others say the reverse is true. The dry form is even harder to diagnose than the wet form, since there is no telltale excess fluid present. Symptoms will show up according to which organ has been attacked. If the liver is affected, you may see jaundice with personality changes; if the kidneys are being damaged, copious drinking and urination. FIP in the brain would produce seizures or paralysis. In the ear it would produce a head tilt and staggering. I have a theory that many cats have died of undiagnosed FIP, especially the dry form. They were probably treated for the secondary diseases produced when the virus attacked one organ or another.

Any diagnosis is like putting together the pieces of a jigsaw puzzle. In FIP one important clue is a persistent high temperature. FIP is found mostly in cats under two or over thirteen and in cats who already have an immune system disease, such as feline leukemia, asthma, or arthritis. My own theory here is that the first autoimmune disease was a signal that the immune system was weak and needed serious attention. If poor diet continued or, worse yet, if the primary disease was treated with steroids or other strong drugs, this would weaken the immune system further so that a more serious illness could take hold. Cats under two have usually undergone a series of vaccinations, sometimes being vaccinated for three, four, or even seven diseases in the same week. The more modern and holistic veterinarians have warned us that this weakens and *confuses* the immune response. I put this information together with what we know about FIP and I became even more determined to limit or eliminate my own cats' vaccines and to build a strong immune response by feeding the raw food diet (page 71).

The blood test for FIP is not conclusive. FIP is one of several corona viruses. A positive result only means that the cat has one of the many corona viruses; the test is not specific. As for what to do if a cat of yours is diagnosed with this supposedly fatal disease, my advice is to pull out all the stops. I've done it; I've fought and lost, but I've also fought and won! But never alone. Every successful treatment of FIP (or feline leukemia) with which I've been involved has always been treated by what I call the winning team: the captain is my classical homeopathic veterinarian (who lives far away); we consult by phone daily if necessary. Supporting him is my local veterinarian doing the hands-on examinations, running the tests, and dispensing whatever my homeopath decides is right. Then there's me, coordinating the efforts, designing the raw food diet and supplements, and making sure the cat's guardian understands what to do and how to do it and, most important, why. The guardian is the key member of the team. It takes time and effort, patience, and lots of determination, courage, and most of all love.

Remember when you start out that your chances of achieving a cure are fifty-fifty or less. The bottom line is that you want to keep your furry friend as comfortable as possible for as long as possible. I like to help the guardians turn this into a win-win situation. We work very hard and if our efforts help to achieve a cure, fine—we've won. On the other hand, if it becomes apparent that the patient's body is no longer able to sustain life without great discomfort, the guardian and the rest of the team may decide that euthanasia (page 248) is the kindest and the most unselfish choice. As this means that you are still controlling the situation and you are still achieving your desire to prevent suffering, I call this another "win." You choose to prolong life; you refuse to prolong the process of dying. May the spirit of the Cat Goddess be with you.

Also see "Allergies," page 328.

Symptoms

- Begins with minor upper respiratory infection; then weeks or years later, it shows up disguised as some other disease, depending upon where in the cat's body the virus has settled
- High fever that persists despite all efforts to lower it
- Presence of another immune system disease: feline leukemia, cancer, arthritis, allergies, dermatitis, granular skin growths, severe gum disease, or asthma
- Presence of fluid in abdomen, distended abdomen
- Presence of fluid in chest, breathing difficulties

Recommendations

- Consult veterinarian for diagnosis.
- Consult a classical homeopathic veterinarian for diagnosis and treatment (see "Homeopathy," page 211).

- If FIP is producing symptoms of another disease, read the appropriate section for help in alleviating those symptoms.
- If diuretic is prescribed (Lasix), read "Diuretics," page 243.
- Keep the patient warm; provide a snug retreat (page 304).
- If patient is eating, use all or as much raw food as possible in diet. Purée everything to aid digestion. Feed four to six small meals a day.
- Add to each meal:

    ¼ teaspoon feline digestive enzymes;
    ¹⁄₁₆ teaspoon ascorbic acid crystals (250 units vitamin C)—do not use sodium ascorbate;
    up to ¹⁄₁₆ teaspoon Green Magma;
    ¼ teaspoon mixed intestinal flora (see "Product Recommendations," in the Appendix);
    ⅛ teaspoon Delicious Garlic Condiment (see page 317);
    10 mg CoEnzyme Q10.

- If force feeding is necessary, see page 286.
- If only liquids are tolerated or if the patient refuses any of the above supplements, make Chicken Super Soup (page 309), using only spring or filtered water. Mix the above supplements into ⅛ cup of the soup and give by dropperful every two to four hours (see "Dropper-Feeding Liquids," page 289).
- Provide spring or filtered water to drink, and remove all chemicals from food and environment, including fabric softener on towels, room deodorizer, and so on.
- Keep stress low. Before giving any remedy or preparation, read the appropriate section in this book. Always explain to your cat everything you're going to do before you do it.
- Bach flower remedies: give three drops four times a day of the following mixture prepared as given on page 313:

    Mimulus—to quell fears concerning bodily functions;
    Olive—to bolster energy;
    Gorse—to banish despair.

Feline Leukemia and Feline AIDS

Note: Because my recommendations for feline AIDS are the same as those for feline leukemia, I am covering them together. Both feline leukemia and feline AIDS (feline immunodeficiency virus) are contracted and spread in exactly the same manner, and both depress the cat's immune system. Feline leukemia may lead to lymphosarcoma. Lymphosarcoma is a cancer of the cells found in the lymph nodes and tissue, thymus gland, or blood and bone marrow. Other internal organs can also be affected, but this is less frequent. Leukemia affects blood cells and is often associated with anemia.

There are several blood tests for feline leukemia virus. *This is not a test for cancer.* It simply tells whether the cat is *carrying* the virus. The results can be inconclusive, and no test is infallible. A positive result does not mean the cat has cancer; it means that the cat is carrying the virus that can sometimes cause leukemia and cancer and that he can shed that virus in the urine and saliva and this may infect other cats. A carrier should be kept separate from other cats, especially the old, the very young, or the sick.

When a positive cat—one carrying the virus—comes into contact with a negative cat—one not carrying the virus—the negative, but exposed cat may:

- not become affected in any way;
- become infected (positive), develop immunity, and revert again to being negative;
- become positive, but not become ill and remain positive—thus becoming a new carrier of the virus;
- become positive and develop AIDS, lymphosarcoma, leukemia, or other cancer;
- become positive and be ill from the virus infection, much like flu; and then recover and remain positive or become negative.; *or*
- become positive and be very ill and not recover.

A positive cat who has not developed cancer symptoms can be tested again in three months. If he has been treated by an experienced holistic veterinarian, preferably one who practices classical homeopathy, and put on a high-quality raw food diet (page 71) designed to build general health and strengthen the immune system, chances are good that he will have reverted to negative.

A negative blood test result means that the cat is not carrying the virus in his blood at that particular time. Yet it does not mean that he is immune. Furthermore, if the cat is in the very early stages of infection, presence of the virus may not show up on the test. A second test taken three to six months later that still shows negative results would be more conclusive. Other types of cancer may be present, but will not show up on the test.

The virus is not transferable to humans and is very perishable. It cannot live more than a few hours outside the cat and then only in a warm, moist environment. It is easily destroyed with chlorine bleach in water (use thirty parts water to one part bleach). However, if a cat has died of feline AIDS or leukemia-related cancer, veterinarians recommend waiting thirty days before getting another cat just to be absolutely certain all the virus is gone from the environment.

The most recent cancer research has amassed a wealth of evidence linking a large percentage of all forms of feline AIDS and leukemia to environmental pollution. Many chemicals in the air, water, and food; garden and household cleaners; and insecticides are carcinogens. Chemicals used directly on the cat, such as flea sprays and collars, can be even stronger factors. Modern veterinary immunologists warn that giving repeated vaccinations or several vaccinations together can depress and confuse the immune response (see "Vaccinations and Other Immunizations," page 240) as can any sort of steroid, whether used in an ear drop or given systemically as a pill (see "Cortisone and Other Steroids," page 244). The presence of other disease, viruses, or stress increases susceptibility. All of the above weaken the immune system.

One of the latest theories to come out of cancer research is called the "surveillance theory." In an article for *Prevention* magazine, Dr. Richard Pitcairn explains: "Cancer cells may be arising all the time in the body, but normally they are killed off by certain white blood cells which have the function of recognizing these deviants." He suggests, "If the immune system is healthy and strong, then it will do its job of eliminating any mutant cancer cells that arise." As with any disease, prevention is easier than curing, but in either case, the recommendations of Dr. Pitcairn and other holistically oriented veterinarians are the same: assist the body to protect itself and heal itself by (1) strengthening the immune system and (2) eliminating anything that depresses the immune system such as stress, chemicals, food colors, preservatives, concentrated hormones (found in meat meal, dry food, meat by-products), and cortisone and other steroids.

I have worked with a number of feline leukemia–positive cats who became feline leukemia–negative and lived long and happy lives. Each case was different and took between six months and fifteen months before the patient tested negative. The treatment protocol was the same in every case. A classical veterinary homeopath was in charge overall. The caregiver fed the raw food diet and used all suggested supplements. The local consulting veterinarian did hands-on examinations and tests but absolutely no drugs or vaccines were ever given and the only tests performed were those specifically ordered by the homeopath in charge.

Leukemia and AIDS patients may have to travel to the veterinarian more frequently than other cats, and they will probably pick up your emotional tones. You will likely be experiencing worry and concern. These stresses can be minimized and cushioned a bit. Focus your mind on the positive aspects of what is being done. For example: remember that the veterinarian will help your cat feel better. Also try to emphasize short-term pleasures, such as the warm snug retreat and delicious homemade food. Do not dwell on negative possibilities and fears of the future.

Also see "Allergies," page 328.

Symptoms

Note: Early symptoms are general and similar to a number of other, unrelated diseases.

- Weight loss
- Depression
- Repeated persistent infections
- Failure of wounds to heal
- Persistent anemia
- Tumors revealed by palpation or X-ray
- Fluid accumulation in chest or abdomen

Recommendations

- Consult a holistic veterinarian, preferably one who practices classical homeopathy, for diagnosis and treatment.
- Isolate the cat; provide separate litter box and water and food bowls.
- Maintain a relaxed, supportive attitude. Give frequent eye and voice contact, petting, and snuggle sessions. These can be as short as 60 seconds but should be often.

- Groom daily (see page 159).
- Many leukemia patients crave warmth; if your cat is one of these, provide a snug retreat (see page 304).
- Protect the immune system by eliminating cortisone and all other steroids and antiinflammatory drugs; all chemicals, which are found in commercial foods (especially dry and semimoist food); household cleaners; insecticides; air fresheners; fabric softeners; and cat litter treated with chemical deodorizers. Use only herbal flea products. (See Appendix, "Product Recommendations.")
- Feed only organic meat, fish, eggs, poultry, and dairy products. Meat is at the top of the food chain and therefore has higher concentrations of agricultural chemicals. Nonorganic meat also contains antibiotics and steroids. Use only filtered or spring water.
- Feed the raw food diet given on page 71. Use only organic meat. For the vegetable portion, carrot, string beans, and zucchini are best because they are alkalizing. However, the first requirement is that the patient enjoy the food and continue to eat. Try baked carrot (see recipe on page 81).
- Add to each meal:

  > A feline multivitamin (see "Product Recommendations," in the Appendix);
  > ½ teaspoon Anitra's Vita-Mineral Mix (see page 68);
  > 1 tablet bioplasma, crushed into food;
  > ¼ teaspoon feline digestive enzymes to aid assimilation;
  > 10 mg CoEnzyme Q10;
  > 10,000 units vitamin A or ½ teaspoon cod liver oil (has been found to retard tumor growth in mice);
  > 2 to 3 mg zinc—to detoxify the body of heavy metals and helps body utilize vitamin A;
  > a pinch of Green Magma.

- Give a total of four doses of 250 units vitamin C each day (use ¹⁄₁₆ teaspoon ascorbic acid crystals or sodium ascorbate powder). Vitamin C is not stored in the body well so is most effective given in several doses throughout the day. Always mix vitamin C with a little Homemade Chicken Broth (page 308) or a teaspoon of a food the cat loves. Never give vitamin C without a little food.

- Once a week, with food or after meal, give 400 units vitamin E (alpha tocopherol) to help aid assimilation of vitamin A and protect body from the effects of some pollutants.
- Herbal remedies:

  1. Korean white ginseng increases resistance. When mixed half-and-half with caraway seeds in a tea, it tends to stimulate the appetite and provides extra minerals. Ginseng has a mild sweet taste. Try adding one teaspoon of this tea to each meal.
  2. Give daily one drop goldenseal elixir diluted in one teaspoon chicken broth (see page 322). Never give goldenseal undiluted. Discontinue if symptoms worsen (poor appetite, and the like); then resume dosage when cat's condition is stabilized. This is a powerful alkalizing agent and has been found to shrink swellings.

- Offer ¼ teaspoon coconut oil as a treat or mix it into the food. Coconut oil boosts immunity. Some cats will lick a dollop of coconut oil like a popsicle.
- Bach flower remedies:

  1. Give three or four drops. Rescue Remedy (prepared as given on page 313) two hours before going to the vet and every two hours after that until you return home.
  2. On normal days (with no break in the routine such as trips to the vet) give three drops four times a day of the following mixture prepared as given on page 313:

     Mimulus—for fear of illness and of being alone;
     Aspen—for fear of the unknown;
     Crabapple—for cleansing;
     Hornbeam—for strength.

Feline Urologic Syndrome (FUS)

(see also "Kidney and Bladder Stones")

There are many misconceptions about feline urologic syndrome (FUS), sometimes referred to as cystitis. In FUS, crystals that irritate the bladder and urethra are formed in the urine. These crystals are sometimes called sand or gravel. They are made mostly of magnesium and phosphorus that have been ingested in the diet as ash. Dry food and fish bones and scales contain high amounts of ash; they should be avoided. Other factors that can contribute to FUS include an alkaline urine. The cat's urine should be acidic; the crystals will dissolve in an acid urine. However, when owners leave food available all day long the mere *smell* of the food causes the body chemistry to turn the urine alkaline. Another cause of alkaline urine is a lack of digestible high-quality protein in the diet. Methionine, one of the amino acids that make up protein, acidifies the urine. However, when protein is overcooked, overprocessed, or of poor quality, the cat cannot digest or assimilate it, so the methionine never gets into the cat's system but is passed off as a waste product. Raw food guarantees an acidic urine.

The irritation from the crystals in the bladder and urethra causes redness, swelling, itching, and burning, and, finally, bleeding. It is first uncomfortable and then painful. In the beginning, the itching, and burning make the cat think he needs to urinate all the time. He will run to the litter box three or four times in ten minutes and then squat and perhaps strain. He may pass up to a tablespoonful of urine, or only enough to moisten three pieces of litter—or there may be no urine at all. Often the urine is bloody. If you lay white paper towels over the litter you'll soon be able to tell.

FUS is easiest to treat and cure if it is caught early. So if your cat runs to the litter box two or three times in one hour, call your holistic veterinarian, and take the cat to your local consulting veterinarian that very day. Here is one situation where I would use an emergency facility if my vet's office is closed. Better safe than sorry. At this early stage of the disease, when the veterinarian examines the cat, he will find that the bladder is small and hard because the urethra is not yet swollen shut and the cat is successfully voiding every drop of moisture as soon as it enters the bladder. If the disease is left untreated, the urethra will swell shut, and the veterinarian will discover a distended, full bladder.

There is a popular misconception that FUS is only a disease of male cats. This is not true. When female cats get FUS, they too run frequently to the litter box and sometimes have blood in their urine. But females usually don't get urinary blockages and surgery isn't necessary. Nevertheless, I've met many people who know that dry food in the diet can bring on an attack of FUS but still feed dry food to their female cat. They think that because she is female she is therefore immune.

If your cat should begin the frequent litter box syndrome (more than two or three times a day), be it male or female, move fast and get the cat treated. FUS can end in horrible death, and it happens all too frequently because it is such a quiet disease. There is no vomiting, no fits, no foaming at the mouth until the very end. There can be blood in the urine, but this is usually not noticed in the litter box. Usually that pitiful running back and forth to the litter box is the only apparent symptom. If you suspect blood in the urine, lay a white paper towel over the litter so any blood will show up clearly.

Sometimes the cat starts random wetting during the early stage of FUS. Several times guardians have called to ask me what to do because their cat has suddenly begun wetting all over the house. They often tell me that, in their opinion, their cat is trying to punish them for being away from home an unusual amount of time or for changing the brand of food or because they had a baby. I always advise them to have their veterinarian check for FUS. Then I explain that there is a fine distinction here. Cats do *not* use urination to express anger or dismay. Although it may appear that way to us humans, wetting outside the box is probably more distressing to the cat than it is to you. Here's what really happens: a stress situation results from your being away, or having a baby, or whatever. The stress target area in this particular cat is the urinary tract. The irritation and itching in the urethra force the cat to squat and urinate wherever he happens to be. The stress situation caused the problem that led to the urination outside the box, but your cat certainly didn't plan it. Random wetting is so against the cat's nature that I always insist that there is some cause that has nothing to do with the cat's making a conscious statement. The ancient prohibition against drawing predators to the area because of the urine smell is far too strong. (See Chapter 3, "The Litter Box.")

There are two other reasons why the cat may wet outside the box. If the urethra has begun to swell closed, the cat may have to strain to pass urine. While straining he may straighten his hind legs, lifting the genital area up while he is still wetting, and spray over the side of the box, or onto the wall or floor. Finally, if the cat experiences discomfort, itching, or burning in the genital area while urinating in the box, he may, in his little cat mind, decide to try to find a "safer" place, that is, a place that will not cause his genitals to itch or burn. He doesn't know why he's itching and burning; he just knows that it happens every time he goes into that litter box, so he goes looking for a safer place.

As a precaution and, more important, as a convenience to your pussycat during a dreadful and painful disease, put at least one litter box in each and every room he frequents. Your cat will bless you for it. I like to give a choice of one or two boxes lined with folded newspaper or a wee-wee pad just as a precaution.

Another consideration with this disease is warmth. I always provide a snug retreat warmed by a clip-on light for an FUS cat (see page 304).

If this disease is left untreated and blockage occurs, the bladder swells with urine. The cat will crouch again and again in the litter box, straining to empty the badly swollen bladder, unable to pass one single drop of urine through the urethra, which is now swollen shut. If you call the veterinarian at this stage, he will undoubtedly tell you to drop everything and come *now*. My own veterinarian will come charging over to the clinic even in the middle of the night. The cat must be catheterized at once. The backup of poisons caused by the retention of the urine can kill the cat in a matter of hours.

Catheterization is painful and must be done under anesthetic, which is not only dangerous but also a drain on the cat's system. Catheterization poses a danger of bladder infection. It is a potential side effect, and veterinarians know they have to watch for it. Antibiotics are usually given, and many a holistic veterinarian has agreed that, in this instance, antibiotics must be used. I remember Dr. Pitcairn saying, "We'll deal with the after-effects of the antibiotics later."

Because FUS is affected by emotions, hospital visits by the guardian are of paramount importance. And once the cat is treated, the bladder emptied, antibiotics administered, and the disease controlled, the diet must be tailored to promote an acidic urine and the emotional environment altered to prevent a recurrence. Repeated attacks can be a sign of bladder stones.

If the diet is not improved, or if the cat remains distressed, insecure, or unhappy and attacks recur, there comes a time when further catheterization is no longer possible. Too much scarring has occurred already. At this point, many cats are euthanized (put to sleep) rather than left to suffer while the poisons build up and permeate their entire body, bringing a horribly slow and painful death. The alternative at this stage is an operation called a *urethrostomy*, which some vets perform and some vets do not. It is major surgery and involves removing the penis with the urethra and widening the opening from the bladder. I have known several cats who had this surgery and did very well afterward. Of course, all of them were maintained on a very high-quality raw food diet and were given a lot of conscious physical affection.

Symptoms

- Wetting outside the litter box or urinating all over the house
- Wetting on the wall or floor around the litter box
- Frequent trips to litter box, passing a small amount of urine, or none at all
- Blood in urine
- Crying out in litter box
- Frequently licking the genital area
- Seeking warmth
- Loss of appetite
- Depression

Recommendations

- Contact your holistic veterinarian at once and describe the symptoms. He will help you stabilize the patient and decide whether your cat needs immediate, hands-on treatment.
- Cover the litter with a layer of white paper towel so you will be able to tell if your cat is passing (a) no urine, (b) only a tiny amount of urine, or (c) bloody urine.
- Give three drops of Bach Flower Rescue Remedy (prepared as given on page 313) every four hours for three days, then twice a day until disease is controlled.
- If your cat goes to the litter box more than twice in one hour and passes no urine, *do not wait; rush to the veterinarian.*
- At first sign of urinary problem, withhold *all* solid food and acidify the urine by giving 500 units of ascorbic acid (vitamin C) or ⅛ teaspoon ascorbic acid crystals mixed with 1 or 2 teaspoons chicken broth. Use only ascorbic acid. Other forms of vitamin C will *not* acidify the urine. Also give 100 units vitamin E.
- Fast on Homemade Chicken Broth until crisis is past.

During attack and convalescence (in addition to veterinarian's treatment):

1. Fast on Homemade Chicken Broth (see page 308) three or four times a day for two days and give ¹⁄₁₆ teaspoon ascorbic acid crystals (250 units vitamin C) mixed each time into the broth (see "Fasting," page 286).

2. Withhold all solid food, including baby food and milk.

3. If antibiotic is a part of treatment, add ¼ teaspoon mixed intestinal flora (see "Product Recommendations" in the Appendix) from health food store to food and continue for two weeks after attack. Treat for temporary diarrhea by giving 1 teaspoon slippery elm syrup five minutes before each meal. (See "Antibiotics," page 242, and "Diarrhea," page 358.)

4. Eliminate all stress in cat's environment (see "Stress: A Cat's Natural Enemy," page 255).

5. Provide a snug retreat (see page 304).

6. Keep a quiet, cheerful attitude when you're around the cat.

7. Feed a high-quality diet including as much raw food as possible (see Chapter 2, "Diet"). From listed choices use carrots, green beans, organic tomato sauce, or zucchini as the vegetable; use Homemade Chicken Broth (see page 308) as liquid; choose organic raw ground chicken for the meat portion.

8. Eliminate yeast from the diet for the next month. Make your own Anitra's Vita-Mineral Mix without the yeast (see recipe on page 68) and use the same amount as always. Give about 10 mg of vitamin B complex twice a day (divide a 50 mg capsule into five parts).

9. Eliminate all organ meats (liver, kidney, and the like) from the diet.

10. Add to diet:

    250 units vitamin C (ascorbic acid) to each meal;

    1 raw organic egg yolk each day;

    a feline multivitamin (see "Product Recommendations," in the Appendix).

After attack:

1. Continue to feed a raw food diet; be sure never again to feed dry food or low quality canned food.

2. Organ meats may be used occasionally again a month after the attack is over.

3. Go back to regular Anitra's Vita-Mineral Mix formula a month after the attack is over, but only if your cat is on raw food or is getting at least four raw organic egg yolks a week.

4. To keep urine acid and resistance high, feed only two meals a day and be sure to clean away dirty dish and all crumbs after a half hour. Continue adding to diet:

> 1 organic egg yolk three times a week;
> A feline multivitamin into each meal;
> $\frac{1}{16}$ teaspoon ascorbic acid crystals (250 units vitamin C) to each meal.

5. Continue to keep litter box very clean.
6. Be sure your cat's posture is normal during urination and be sure he's not running frequently to the box.

Fleas

(see also "Skin Problems" and "Parasites")

One scratch doth not a flea problem make. Many skin problems can cause itching. If you suspect fleas, groom your cat, save the hair in a pile, then spread it out and hold it up to the light. If you see debris—little black dots as if someone had sprinkled pepper on the hairs—this may be flea excrement. To be certain it's not just a bit of dust from the bottom of the closet or a little dirt from the potted palm where your cat occasionally lounges, you'd better do:

The White Towel Flea Test

Lay two white paper towels on the kitchen counter, one on top of the other. Moisten with water. Take a bunch of your cat's hair that has some debris mixed in and spread it out on the wet towels. Fold the towels over the hair, press them flat, and wait one or two minutes. Unfold the towels; if the black specks look like they're bleeding rust, your furry friend has fleas. The rust is your cat's blood, digested by the fleas and then excreted as those black specks.

Unless the infestation is very bad, you probably will not see fleas themselves as only 10 percent of the total flea population is on the cat at any one time. Ninety percent remain hidden in the environment, mostly where the cat sleeps, as eggs, larvae, and adults. Those few that are on the cat like to stay close to the skin. Under the chin and at the base of the tail are two favorite places.

Since fleas, like all parasites, are known to prefer sick, old, and weak animals, the presence of fleas is a sign that your cat's health is below par. A cat who is not in the best of health or one whose metabolism is slow because the caregiver forgets to remove food between meals will usually have oily, dandruffy skin. The fleas will love it, especially if there are a few convenient mats in the fur to hide under.

Fleas jump onto your pet because they need a drink of blood before they can lay their eggs. They lay the eggs on the cat and many eggs fall off into cracks in the floor and the spaces under and around large appliances and furniture. The places under or near where your cat usually rests will have the largest number of eggs and larvae. In one to five days the eggs hatch into larvae, tiny white worms with large toothy mouths. They feed on the debris existing in these dark crevices: dandruff, dust, mold, hair, and flea excrement (which is mostly your cat's digested blood). They will gobble up practically anything short of the missing pens and small coins that are also found there. The babies remain in the larval stage from ten to two hundred days depending upon the conditions. Then they spin a cocoon around themselves and in another ten to two hundred days they emerge as full-grown fleas ready to hop on your friend, chomp into his skin, drink his blood, and start the cycle all over again.

Using sprays, dips, powders, and collars may kill the fleas present on the animal, but they won't in any way inconvenience that large segment of the flea population lounging about, hatching, eating, and maturing all over your home. Furthermore, the commercial flea preparations contain chemicals that are debilitating and harmful to the cat and the humans he lives with. Labels warn us not to breathe the fumes, not to allow the product to remain long on our hands, or to get it anywhere near our eyes or mouth. In the next sentence, they tell us to "soak the animal's coat thoroughly" and to leave the flea preparation on our beloved pet's skin for an indefinite period of time! Many commercial flea collars use various forms of military nerve gas. Organophosphates are nerve paralyzers. Carbomates can cause vomiting, convulsions, and respiratory arrest.

Laboratory experiments assure us that use of these chemicals even in tiny amounts increases the chances of the animal developing cancer, allergies, nerve damage, reproductive problems, and breathing difficulties. Subjecting the cat's body to these toxic chemicals will even further damage the animal's state of health, weakening him and making him an even more attractive breeding ground for fleas. Thus, more of these toxic treatments will then be required and at more and more frequent intervals, causing the cat's health to deteriorate at an ever increasing speed and his immune system to become weaker and weaker. He will finally be laid low, not by the fleas themselves but by the treatments or by some "unrelated" disease that his badly weakened immune system hasn't the strength to fight off. An unhealthy cat will always attract more fleas. Here, again, we see the classic snowball situation. It's rather like trying to rid your kitchen of flies by shooting them off the wall with a bazooka. You'll certainly kill the flies, but the holes left behind will only let in more flies. The best you can say for that method is that soon you'll have no kitchen left to worry about.

Happily for all of us, cats and humans alike, during the last few years several highly effective natural products have appeared on the market, and new methods of attack have been developed. Some of the products, like Natural Animal Coat Enhancer, are actually beneficial to the cat; others, such as the pyrethrin-based Premise Spray, can be relatively harmless but only if used carefully as I mentioned above, because most of these pyrethrins are synthetic and more toxic than natural pyrethrins. I have tested these natural products, and all work as well as—if not better than—the poisonous chemical products.

To ensure your success in evicting all fleas from both pet and premises, you must follow three ground rules:

1. Cover all the bases. Leave no weak link in the chain. No one product or method will work well if used alone. Attack the fleas on the cat, in the house, and in the yard, and follow the suggestions given under each of these categories.

2. Thoroughness is very important. Do each step of your program as if it is the one and only method at your disposal. Vacuum as if you had no carpet spray; then spray the carpet as if you had no vacuum. Flea comb the cat's coat as if you cannot bathe; then bathe as if you had no flea comb.

3. Make the cat's body an unappetizing morsel for a flea by improving your pet's health and including in the diet those supplements having flea-repelling properties (see below).

When it comes to fleas and the use of chemicals, each case presents different challenges and requirements. If the cat is being treated homeopathically, all chemicals must be avoided. Years ago, I was working with a very elderly lady whose Siamese cat, Pandora, was seventeen years old and suffering from kidney problems, liver problems, and fleas. Cat and guardian were devoted to each other. Homeopathy and excellent nutrition were keeping Pandora alive and comfortable. Her loving human elected not to disturb this very successful treatment by introducing any chemicals into the environment. She would rather have the fleas than rock the boat. Her Scottish housekeeper, also quite elderly, could not accept the idea of fleas in the apartment and most certainly not in "her kitchen." She began a rigorous campaign using vacuum cleaner and flea comb as her only weapons. She vacuumed daily, immediately threw the bag out of the apartment each time, and went through Pandora's coat with a fine-tooth flea comb three or four times a day, drowning any fleas she caught in a bowl of warm water. That was all she was allowed to do, but she carried out her attack with typical Scottish thoroughness and perseverance. Six weeks later, when I returned, I was delighted to tell her that I could find no signs of fleas on Pandora. "Weel, no," she replied, frowning fiercely, "We could na' have that now, could we."

Sometimes even the most careful caregivers will use pyrethrin-based Premise Spray but only in totally inaccessible areas such as under the refrigerator and stove. Each person will make his own decisions and do the best he can.

Symptoms

- Scratching and biting, especially under chin, behind ears, and at the base of the spine
- Pulling out hair
- Shedding and bald spots, sometimes scabs
- Presence of small black dots, like black pepper, in hair
- Presence of fleas

Recommendations

Note: It is imperative that you incorporate treatments from each of the categories below to assure success in getting rid of fleas.

Diet

This is a must. Without this, nothing else will do much good.

- Raise the cat's resistance to parasites by feeding a raw food diet (page 71). Remove all food after a half hour and leave *only* water available between meals.
- Make your cat an unappetizing morsel for a flea. From three weeks before flea season until after the first hard freeze (or all year round in warm climates), include the following supplements in the food:

  1. Once a day add to the food ⅛ teaspoon of Delicious Garlic Condiment (page 317).
  2. Into ten teaspoons brewer's yeast, crush and add 10 mg thiamine (a B vitamin). Give ½ teaspoon of this yeast mixture twice a day in the food. If you are making your own Anitra's Vita-Mineral Mix (page 68), this yeast mixture can be used as your yeast portion.
  3. Use PetGuard yeast and garlic wafers. They make a great snack or treat and help the body to repel fleas. (See Appendix, "Product Recommendations.")

  If you plan to use a room fogger or carpet spray (listed below), add ⅟₁₆ teaspoon ascorbic acid crystals or sodium ascorbate powder (250 units vitamin C) to each meal.

A Cautionary Word about Flea Control Products

I am often asked to comment on the flea control products that are applied as drops, available in pet supply shops and from conventional veterinarians. I will not use them, nor do I recommend them. The packaging directs you to put a few drops on the top of the shoulders. They work much like chemotherapy in that the poison then spreads throughout the body and kills any flea that bites the cat, both those on the body and those in the environment when they jump on to get their blood meal.

I don't believe I have the right to turn any individual's body into a walking poison pellet, much less a cat for whom I am a "caregiver." The question that springs to mind is this: which is more dangerous—the disease or the remedy?

Grooming and Bathing

- Remove mats and loose hair and stimulate circulation to the skin by daily grooming and massage.
- Buy a flea comb at a pet store or by mail (see Appendix, "Product Recommendations"). It is only about an inch-and-a-half long and has fine teeth that are very close together. Comb out fleas and debris with the flea comb, giving special attention to the top of the head, chin and neck, lower spine, and skirts near the thigh. (See Chapter 8, "Grooming.") Submerge all hair and fleas in a bowl of hot water with *only* one or two drops of dish detergent to keep the fleas from crawling out. Put the detergent in after the water so you don't create foam where fleas can hide and breathe from the bubbles.
- Kill all fleas remaining on the cat by spraying the coat liberally with Natural Animal Coat Enhancer. Massage it in and wait ten minutes before bathing.
- Bathe (see page 189). Fleas drown easily, but you must be sure to get the shampoo and water all the way down to the skin where they will be hiding. The best way to do this is to do the first soaping with 1 part dishwashing detergent and 8 parts water. This will cut through the cat's natural oils and get down to the roots of the hair and the skin. Use it generously, work up a good suds, and massage it in well. Rinse and follow with an herbal flea shampoo for cats or Dr. Bronner's liquid castile soap from the health food store. Leave second soaping on the coat for five to ten minutes before rinsing thoroughly.
- If cat's skin is damaged by flea bites or if he has scratched himself red and raw, Natural Animal Coat Enhancer will soothe the skin. If you can't get that, use lemon rinse (page 324) after the bath to soothe and heal skin and repel fleas. *Or* add a few drops of citronella or eucalyptus to the final rinse to scent the fur. These herbs are flea repellants.
- When cat is thoroughly dry, prevent further infestation by doing one or all of the following:

    1. Spray coat with Natural Animal Coat Enhancer three times a week during flea season.

2. Use an herbal flea collar (see Appendix, "Product Recommen-dations"), or use citronella, or eucalyptus to scent a cloth flea collar.

3. If you can't get Natural Animal Coat Enhancer:

   A. use the lemon rinse (page 324); *or*
   B. dust the coat with PetGuard yeast and garlic powder; *or*
   C. dust the coat with an herbal flea powder; *or*
   D. dust the coat with a combination of diatomaceous earth powder and one of the other powders mentioned above.

On the Premises

Note: An ounce of prevention—if you adopt a cat off the street or from a shel-ter or if your cats have been outside or boarding at a place where you suspect they may have picked up fleas, confine the cats to a bathroom or the kitchen (or any room without a rug) until you determine conclusively that they have not brought back any unwelcome guests in their furs. Then, if you, the groomer, or the vet do find fleas, you won't have to treat your whole house for larvae and eggs, only the one room where the cats have been.

- *Treat every room where the cats have been for eggs, larvae, and adult fleas.*
- Vacuum both carpets and floors thoroughly. Use the vacuum nozzle to clean every crack and crevice because eggs and larvae will be found there. Throw the vacuum cleaner bag away (out of the house) after each vacuuming *or* suck some flea-killing powder into the vacuum bag *or* burn the bag.
- Suffocate developing larvae and eggs by waxing the floors.
- Cut the protective shell of fleas and larvae so they dehydrate and die by (a) sprinkling diatomaceous powder in all cracks and/or (b) sprinkling the carpet liberally with salt or diatomaceous powder. Leave overnight and vacuum up the next day. Choose a *dry* day to do this.
- Kill the fleas, larvae, and eggs by:

  1. Steam-cleaning carpet or steam-ironing carpet, sofas, and so on;
  2. Putting pillows, pet bedding, comforters, and the like in clothes dryer on hot temperature for fifteen to twenty minutes;

3. Laying old terry cloth towels on all the cat's perches and sleeping places to catch the larvae and eggs that drop off the cat. Wash all the towels twice a week and dry on *hot* cycle.

- Spray floors, furniture, and bedding with a 5 percent solution of Safers Insecticidal Soap. Do this every five days. (Do not do this while diatomaceous powder is on the carpet.)

Several flea products use pyrethrins (made from crysanthemum) as the active ingredient. Products that contain synthetic pyrethrins or pyrethrins modified to be more toxic are acceptable but less safe than the natural pyrethrins. Some premise sprays and room foggers also use methoprene, a growth inhibitor, which keeps larvae from maturing. They live and die in their dark crevices and never develop to biting age. These products are only relatively safe. They are certainly better than those containing more toxic chemicals but I keep their use to a minimum. To make doubly sure of safety, I suggest that all people, animals, birds, fish, and plants vacate the premises for more than the length of time recommended on the can. My own vet suggests twelve hours. In addition, you and your cat should take extra vitamin C for two to three weeks after spraying—250 units twice a day will aid the body in processing out any residues.

Fractures
(see "Injuries")

Gastrointestinal Upset
(see "Vomiting")

Gums
(see "Teeth and Gums")

Hair Balls

It is natural for cats to vomit up hair balls from time to time because they groom themselves with the tongue and swallow the hair. Some hair will be passed out with the stool if shedding is not too copious and the diet is adequate, with enough fiber, fats, and oils. However, during the shedding seasons when a cat swallows a lot of hair, he should from time to time vomit up a hair ball that looks like a small wet sausage. If he cannot vomit it successfully, the body will try to pass it through the intestines. If intestinal action is weak because of poor nutrition or frequent snacking and smelling of food, the hair ball may stop somewhere along the way and form an impaction like a cork. The body may first pass a very runny diarrhea around the impaction; then complete constipation will set in. The cat will become lethargic and refuse food. Wastes will build up and, finally, serious infection will overcome the entire system.

Symptoms

Note: Vomiting hair balls is not a symptom; it is normal if it happens less than twice a week and only during the spring and autumn shedding seasons.

- Vomiting foam, vomiting many hair balls, vomiting hair balls all year round
- Diarrhea or constipation
- Bad breath
- Excess shedding (other than in spring and autumn)
- Unsuccessful vomiting attempts
- Lethargy, loss of appetite

Recommendations

Stage 1: To help cat successfully vomit hair balls

- Groom more often—once or twice a day (see page 159).
- Reevaluate grooming tool (see page 162).
- Feed a high-quality diet with as much raw food as possible (see page 71). Be sure to include Anitra's Vita-Mineral Mix and other listed supplements.
- Remove all food between meals; leave only water available.
- Include ⅛ teaspoon Delicious Garlic Condiment (see page 317) in food three times a week for four weeks to strengthen intestinal muscles.

Stage 2: If cat is vomiting unsuccessfully and diarrhea and/or constipation are present

- Follow Stage 1 treatments above.
- Ask veterinarian if you should give cat an oral hair ball lubricant. This is always given two to three hours before food. If it comes in a tube, administer approximately three inches. Choose a product that does not contain benzoate of soda (sodium benzoate) *or* use plain petroleum jelly and give about ½ teaspoon.

Stage 3: If the cat has had no stool for three days, has no appetite, and is lethargic

- Don't wait—take the cat to the veterinarian immediately for treatment (enema or surgery may be required).
- After the veterinarian's treatment, when the cat comes home, give one charcoal capsule (wet the tip before pilling) one time to absorb any putrefaction left behind. (See "Giving Pills," page 266.)
- For two weeks add to food ¼ teaspoon fine bran and ¼ teaspoon mixed intestinal flora powder.
- Continue to groom a minimum of thirty seconds every day all year.
- Follow all Stage 1 treatments above.

Hookworm

(see "Parasites")

Hyperthyroidism

Hyperthyroidism is a disease of middle-aged to older cats. "Hyper" means high or over. In hyperthyroidism the thyroid is overproducing the hormones thyroxin and/or, less commonly, tri-iodothyronine. Thyroxin regulates the speed at which all body functions proceed (the metabolism or metabolic rate). If there is too much thyroxin, the metabolism speeds up: the heart races, blood pressure and temperature go up, digestion speeds up, and cells die and are replaced more quickly.

Because many of the symptoms—skinniness, oily coat, copious drinking and urination—can be signs of other diseases (kidney disease and diabetes), the veterinarian will want to do complete blood tests that will reflect liver function and kidney and pancreatic function, as well as the extra test, called a T3–T4 test, for the thyroid. There are two thyroid blood tests currently in use. The T3-T4 is the one most often done, but it sometimes gives a false negative if the patient also has other physical problems such as kidney disease or some sort of infection. The other thyroid test is called a Free T4 test and is more dependable but also more expensive. I usually opt for the Free T4 because it leaves no doubt and I need the accuracy. Frequently the doctor will be able to feel the enlargement of the thyroid in the throat, but more evidence than this is needed to make a firm diagnosis.

As with most physical problems, the cause is attributable to a combination of things. If there is insufficient iodine in the diet, the thyroid may become enlarged and overactive to compensate for the deficiency. Since vitamin E is needed before the body can absorb iodine, a vitamin E deficiency can sometimes provoke the same response. If there is not enough iodine in the food, the thyroid will absorb any radioactive iodine that is present in the environment and this will do further damage. Liver damage can also produce symptoms of hyperthyroidism because the liver supplies an enzyme that deactivates excess thyroxin. If that liver enzyme is absent or underproduced, too much thyroxin will remain in the blood.

The practices of inbreeding and of feeding a diet of heat-processed food that also contains chemicals and diseased tissue will weaken any animal as well as its progeny. If there is a predisposition to thyroid problems in the genes, which is then exaggerated by inbreeding, a low-quality diet will then be enough to cause thyroid problems by the cat's middle years.

There are four orthodox treatments for hyperthyroidism:

1. *Surgery.* All or part of the thyroid gland is removed and the cat is maintained for the remainder of his life on thyroid hormones given orally. I have seen many hyperthyroid patients do quite well after thyroid surgery. The thyroid has two lobes and if only one is abnormal, that one lobe can be removed alone. If your holistic veterinarian feels the cat is too sick to be able to wait for homeopathy or other holistic modalities to work, surgery may be an option. Many cats survive for years after thyroid surgery, but only when the basic diet has been totally changed to the highest quality, mostly raw food diet, with all supplements present. Also, the patient must be carefully monitored by the veterinarian to be certain the thyroxin level is properly balanced with the cat's ever-changing chemistry and metabolism.

2.   *Thyroid-inhibiting drugs.* Drugs such as Tapazol (methmazole) inhibit the synthesis of hormones by the thyroid gland. They work only while the drug is being taken. There are possible side effects: anorexia, vomiting, lethargy, rashes, and facial swelling. If a drug must be used lest the excess thyroxin cause a heart attack or other life-threatening situation, every effort should be made to permanently correct the condition through homeopathy and nutrition in hopes of diminishing and then stopping the drug. Cats on thyroid medication should be monitored at least every six months; every three months is better.

3.   *Iodine and propranalol.* This treatment, which decreases the heart rate and output, is seldom used because cats must be constantly monitored.

4.   *Radioactive iodine therapy.* This treatment is seldom used because the cat must be quarantined for days or weeks after the treatment, and the radioactive urine and stool must be disposed of according to government regulations. I have never recommended it. I have known several cats who were treated with radioactive iodine. Two of them seemed to come through it all right. The rest were never the same afterward. One sweet pair of domestic shorthairs came home gravely altered. I had known them from kittenhood. Their jolly demeanor never returned. They began getting upper respiratory infections again and again. They had little appetite. We lost them both within two years of the radioactive iodine treatment. They were eight years old. Radioactive iodine treatment is also very expensive.

My preference, whenever possible, is a regimen of diet and classical homeopathy, guided by a homeopathic veterinarian.

Hyperthyroid cats will have super-high nutritional requirements because the racing metabolism causes the body to use up nutrients very quickly. They often have oily coats because they tend to dispose of wastes through the pores and to produce excess oil. Also, the increased drinking and urination common to hyperthyroid cats washes the water-soluble nutrients out of the body. Besides supplying nutrients in large amounts, food should be easily digestible and extra digestive enzymes should be included to ensure that all the nutrients in the food will be assimilated, not just swallowed and passed swiftly through the digestive system and out the other end.

Symptoms

- Dull coat, sometimes very dry, sometimes very oily
- Skinniness despite large appetite
- Copious drinking and urination (as in diabetes or kidney disease)
- Slightly high temperature, seeks cool places
- Nervous energy, hyperactivity
- Hypersensitivity to sounds, movement, touch; jumpy
- Easily angered
- Hiding out of the way
- Fast pulse, high blood pressure
- Vomiting
- Diarrhea or an excessively large amount of stool
- Muscle weakness
- Veterinarian can sometimes feel enlarged gland in the throat

Recommendations

- Consult a classical homeopathic veterinarian or your local consulting vet for diagnosis and treatment.
- Feed three or four meals a day of a high-quality diet with as much raw food as possible (see page 66). Be sure to include Anitra's Vita-Mineral Mix and all other listed supplements in diet.
- Add to each meal:

  ¼ teaspoon feline enzymes or ½ digestive enzyme pill;

  ⅛ teaspoon ascorbic acid crystals or sodium ascorbate powder (500 units vitamin C);

  1/16 teaspoon granular kelp (in addition to both the kelp in Anitra's Vita-Mineral Mix and your veterinarian's iodine pill);

  10 mg of vitamin B complex (open a 50 mg capsule and divide into five parts).

- Once a day give:

  100 units vitamin E (alpha tocopherol) for four weeks, then reduce dose to 400 units once a week;

> 10,000 units vitamin A in fish liver oil. Once a week substitute a capsule containing 10,000 units vitamin A and 400 units vitamin D. After one month, reduce dose to capsule containing 10,000 units vitamin A and 400 units vitamin D once a week. Or use a feline multivitamin (see "Product Recommendations" in the Appendix).

- Herbal remedies: because minerals are being used up and lost in the urine, a teaspoonful of any of the following added to meals will be helpful:

  > Kombu broth (page 318);
  > Horsetail grass infusion (page 321);
  > If diarrhea is a problem, give one teaspoon slippery elm syrup five minutes before each meal.

- Provide a snug retreat (page 304) but without the heating light.
- Ask your vet if you can hydrate the patient subcutaneously. This will help wash the excess thyroxin out of the body and lowers the need for Tapazol. It makes the patient feel more normal and reduces all symptoms.
- Bach flower remedies: hyperthyroid cats are "hyper" everything—oversensitive, overactive, overhungry. They need to be calmed and protected. Give three drops three times a day of the following mixture prepared as given on page 313:

  > Mimulus—to calm fear of noise, lights, motion, and the like;
  > Impatiens—to soothe anxiety;
  > Elm—to help cope with too many stimuli.

Hypoglycemia

Hypoglycemia used to be practically nonexistent in cats. Today, however, almost every product in the grocery store pet section contains some form of sugar: corn sweeteners, corn syrup, fructose, sucrose, and barley malt syrup are all high in sugars. The semimoist foods and semimoist treats are usually the worst.

Hypoglycemia (low blood sugar) can be caused by a malfunction of the pancreas or the liver. One of the jobs of the pancreas is to produce insulin, which neutralizes excess sugar in the blood. If large amounts of sugar or carbohydrates are eaten frequently (as in a diet of semimoist food), the pancreas is overstimulated. It becomes trigger-happy, as it were, and begins producing too much insulin—neutralizing all of the sugar instead of just the excess—and hypoglycemia results. Low blood sugar produces a big appetite so the cat reacts by overeating. This overstimulates the insulin trigger again, and the pancreas overproduces again, and a vicious circle results.

Another cause of hypoglycemia is liver damage. One of the liver's duties is to produce an enzyme that deactivates excess insulin. If the liver is damaged and does not produce the enzyme, excess insulin remains active to neutralize too much sugar and store it as fat instead of burning it for energy. Here again hypoglycemia will result. Hypoglycemia is a warning that diabetes is on the way.

Fortunately, hypoglycemia is simple to treat by natural methods once it is diagnosed. Frequent small high-protein meals that are easily digested and nicely balanced, along with the elimination of sugar of any kind from the diet, will begin to put things right. Progress will continue as long as the new regimen is maintained. If the condition has progressed so far that water retention has become a problem, parsley tea used in the food will act as a gentle diuretic. If obesity has developed, do not attempt to fast the cat or put him on a reducing diet. The weight will melt away gradually as one of the many beneficial side effects of your furry friend's improved lifestyle.

Symptoms

- Depression, anxiety, or irritability
- Obesity with voracious appetite
- Laziness
- Leg cramps
- Arthritis
- Vertigo, dizziness, stumbling
- Trembling
- Indigestion
- Asthma
- Blood test may show low liver values and/or high pancreas values

Recommendations

- Consult veterinarian for diagnosis. Have blood tested for sugar level, liver function, and pancreatic function.

- Feed *four* small high-quality meals each day.
- Eliminate all sugars from the diet—*no semimoist food or treats. Read labels.* Feed a high-quality diet. If you use canned foods, choose only those that are natural and contain no by-products, sugars, or chemical additives (see Chapter 2, "Diet"). You'll always be safe with PetGuard but a home-made raw diet is best of all.
- Be sure to include Anitra's Vita-Mineral Mix and other supplements to diet (see page 68).
- Add to each meal:

  $\frac{1}{16}$ teaspoon ascorbic acid crystals or sodium ascorbate powder (250 units vitamin C);

  $\frac{1}{4}$ teaspoon feline digestive enzymes—to ensure normal digestion and assimilation;

  A few grains of salt substitute (for a week or two)—to replace potassium lost in urine.

- *Regular* exercise periods each day.
- Have another blood test done in three to six months.
- Consult an experienced classical homeopathic veterinarian (see "Homeopathy," page 211) to ensure speedy results.
- Herbal remedies:

  1. Parsley tea can be mixed in food if water retention or obesity is a problem. Use about 1 teaspoon of the tea per meal.
  2. Use 1 drop brown stevia extract or 1 teaspoon stevia infusion added to the food to help stabilize blood sugar and give a sweeter taste to food.

- Bach flower remedies: hypoglycemic cats will feel tired and lack energy. They will experience periods of depression, especially while the excess ounces are melting away and the old toxins stored in the fat are being processed out by their system. The following is a good general formula of Bach flower remedies for a hypoglycemic cat. Give three drops four times a day of the following mixture prepared as given on page 313.

  Crabapple—for those who need to lose weight;
  Larch—for those who expect failure and do not try;
  Hornbeam—for those who need to be strengthened and encouraged.

- *Two months after symptoms disappear:*

  1. Cut number of meals down to three each day; then a week later, to two meals a day;
  2. Maintain high-quality raw food diet with no sugar.

Hypothyroidism

"Hypo" means "under," as in hypodermic—under the skin. The thyroid gland produces the hormone thyroxin, which regulates metabolism—the speed at which all the other glands and all the body processes function. Hypothyroidism means that the thyroid gland is not producing enough thyroxin, so the metabolism is slow. This is the opposite of *hyper*thyroidism. The cause is usually a lack of iodine in the diet or an inability to assimilate the iodine that is present, because of a lack of vitamins E, C, B-6, or choline. The presence of radiation from color television, microwave ovens, nearby atomic energy plants, and so on will increase your cat's need for iodine.

Supposedly cats are not subject to hypothyroidism and yet, in recent years, again and again, I see cases that look exactly like it. It is difficult to diagnose it in humans. I reason that it probably would be in cats as well. Therefore, I use food, food supplements, and food herbs while my veterinary homeopath treats the whole cat as always.

Symptoms

- Fatigue, lethargy
- Cold ears, paws; seeking a warm place
- Slow pulse, low blood pressure
- Gains weight easily even though appetite is normal or poor
- High cholesterol level
- Chipping claws
- Oily coat

Recommendations

- Have your veterinarian take a blood test to rule out other problems.
- Feed a high-quality diet with as much raw food as possible (see Chapter

2, "Diet"). Be sure to include Anitra's Vita-Mineral Mix and other listed supplements.

- Remove all food between meals to help speed up metabolism.
- Have a short play period twice a day. Use your ingenuity to tempt your friend into activity. Try a peacock feather or a Cat Dancer or a Feline Flyer.
- Add to each meal:

    ¼ teaspoon lecithin (in addition to lecithin in Anitra's Vita-Mineral Mix) to help rid the body of cholesterol buildup;

    ⅟₁₆ teaspoon ascorbic acid crystals or sodium ascorbate powder (250 units vitamin C);

    ¼ teaspoon feline digestive enzymes—to ensure proper digestion and assimilation of nutrients.

- Three to five times a week add to food a raw organic egg yolk (as a source of choline)—to help body assimilate iodine efficiently.
- Once a week give 400 units vitamin E (alpha tocopherol) from a punctured capsule.
- Provide a snug retreat (page 304). Hypothyroid cats will feel cold even on a warm day.
- Herbal remedies:

    1. Kombu seaweed (page 318) is an excellent source of iodine and other minerals. Give 1 teaspoon to ¼ cup mixed into meals, depending on how well your cat likes the taste, *or*
    2. Mix ⅟₁₆ teaspoon powdered kelp into food.

- Bach flower remedies: hypothyroid cats will lack energy and enthusiasm. They will seek out the warm spots and sleep most of the time. Also, since the metabolism is slow, there is bound to be some backlog of wastes. Give three drops three times a day of the following mixture prepared as given on page 313:

    Wild rose—for those without enthusiasm;
    Crabapple—for cleansing.

Injuries

(including Abscesses and Puncture Wounds, Cuts, Burns, Concussions, and Fractures)

In any emergency situation you should aim to get the patient to the veterinarian as fast as you can, keeping him as comfortable, calm, clean, dry, warm, and still as possible while you do so. There is no question of opting for home care: *a veterinarian must be consulted.* You must be able to act quickly and put aside your own feelings. Now is not the time to give in to your emotions; you can do that after your cat is safely in the hands of the veterinarian. Here are the steps to handling an emergency:

1. Always be prepared in advance. Keep copies of all veterinary records and test results in the carry case. These are invaluable if you have to see a veterinarian who doesn't know your cat. Know where the nearest twenty-four hour veterinary clinic is and keep the telephone number along with other emergency numbers with you at all times. Keep at least one carry case easily accessible.
2. Reassure your pet that you understand that he is frightened and in pain. Tell him that you are going to help him feel better.
3. Call the veterinarian or ask someone else to call for you to warn him that you are on your way with an emergency situation.
4. Ask for the assistance of others in obtaining any necessary items such as the carry case, towels, wee wee pads, and so on.
5. Give your cat three drops of Bach Flower Rescue Remedy, prepared as explained on page 313 and take three drops yourself. Repeat every thirty minutes.
6. See appropriate heading below for the type of emergency—"Abscesses and Puncture Wounds," "Cuts," "Burns," "Concussions," and "Fractures."

Abscesses and Puncture Wounds

The most common sort of wound in cats is a puncture wound, because both the teeth and claws of other animals produce the typical puncture shape: a deep wound with a very small opening. Most punctures don't bleed much, and without that mildly antiseptic wash of the saline blood, puncture wounds become infected unless the cat is very healthy with a good strong immune response. If the cat is only moderately healthy, he may still be protected against serious harm because the body will usually form an abscess around the infection to seal it off and prevent infection from spreading.

My first experience with an abscess was atop the head of a sweet little blue cream shorthair named Tammy. Tammy had spent fifteen contented years quietly caring for an elderly invalid lady. I inherited Tammy when the lady passed away. During her introduction into my household of seven cats, someone (I'm naming no names) gave Tammy a ritual bop on the head. It was just a mittenbop with sheathed claws; nevertheless one claw, sharper and longer than the others, pierced Tammy's scalp. An infection began and Tammy had a lump the size of a marble on the top of her head the next morning. Tammy's immune system was swinging into action; the body's defenses were being mobilized; an abscess was forming to protect Tammy's system from the spread of that infection. Millions of white cells were being carried to the area by the blood to battle the invading microbes and kill them. The dead white cells and germs formed the white pus that the abscess contained in a sort of flexible bubble. The longer the battle raged, the more cells and microbes would die and the bigger the abscess would become. By afternoon the lump on Tammy's head was the size of a ping-pong ball. It looked grotesque. Tammy's temperature was 102—another good sign. The immune system was making the body uncomfortably warm for the invading microbes.

I called my veterinarian, Dr. Pitcairn, who prescribed a homeopathic remedy. He also told me to raise the temperature in the abscess area further by applying hot compresses four times a day (see "Hot Compresses," page 296). Tammy was a model of quiet cooperation; the compresses felt good.

When the body is fighting any infection, it is always helpful to put the patient on a light healing fast of chicken broth with supplements added. I also offered Tammy a snug retreat (see page 304), where she spent most of her time for the next three weeks.

There are three ways that an abscess can be resolved:

1.   If the abscess is not very large the body can absorb the pocket of pus and carry the poisons away in the blood and send them out in the stool or urine.

2.   The abscess can burst, discharging the pus, and then heal as any wound would. Often the patient will encourage this by frequent licking. When the abscess is ready to burst, it begins to itch; thus nature encourages the animal to lick. If this happens to your pet and he swallows a bit of the fluid, don't worry; the germs will take a direct route to the stool and urine and be disposed of there. Just keep giving the supplements for infections and wounds (see page 306) and follow your holistic veterinarian's instructions.

3.   If the abscess is very large, if you want to ensure that it will drain neatly, or if the abscess has burst but then closes up and again fills with pus, you can have your veterinarian shave the whole area, lance the abscess, and tie in a drain to keep the abscess from closing up before the pus is all gone. To do this the cat may or may not have to be tranquilized or lightly anesthetized (as for teeth cleaning). The vet will make two clean incisions, one on each side of the abscess. A small rubber tube with several holes cut in it is then looped in one side and out the other and fastened together on the outside. This holds the incision open so the abscess can continue to drain and be irrigated easily.

In Tammy's case the abscess was resolved on the fourth day in spectacular fashion. As we were finishing our morning compress ritual, Tammy's abscess suddenly started to itch. She reacted by giving her head a good shake, and with that the abscess burst and a stream of bloody pus shot straight across the room and hit the wall on the other side. Tammy just sat there, calmly waiting for me to finish doing whatever it was I wanted to do to her today. The pressure was relieved and the itch was gone.

After I cleaned the smelly mess off Tammy's neck, off the wall, and off my sleeve, I called Dr. Pitcairn to report the latest development. He gave me the formulas for irrigation (see page 280), and I immediately began squirting Irrigation Formula I into the newly opened abscess hole, filling up the pocket that the abscess left behind, and then gently pressing it flat to empty it out. By evening, when I went to repeat the treatment, the hole was healed closed. "Good," I thought. But Tammy's body was not finished dealing with the invading germs. She was older, had just come out of a stressful situation, and had never had the advantage of a high-quality diet. Her immune response was working slowly. The abscess filled up again. I know now that I could have just waited for it to burst again, but after seeing all that nasty pus come out I couldn't stand the thought of leaving all that filth on Tammy's head. I was impatient; I did not let nature take its course. Instead, I called my local conventional veterinarian and got an appointment to bring Tammy over. The veterinarian shaved the area and put in a nice drain, as described above. He didn't even have to anesthetize her because the skin flap where he needed to make the incision was dead tissue that had no feeling. Now I could syringe out the abscess pocket twice a day without fear of it healing closed prematurely. This all happened quite early in my career. I was still learning. Since then I always let the body heal an abscess naturally while I support the effort with less intrusion—either way is "right."

There is a marvelous hypodermic syringe that has a tapered curved plastic tip instead of a needle. It is perfect for abscess irrigation. Twice a day I would fill it with Irrigation Formula I (see page 280), insert the tip into one of the vet's incision holes in the rubber tube, and inject the solution gently into the abscess cavity (see "Irrigating an Abscess," page 281). I would then carefully press the abscess flat, expelling the solution and any pus from the abscess pocket.

Tammy always knew that whatever I did would be completely comfortable. I always kept paper towels handy to sop up any dead white cells that had been washed out onto her fur by the irrigation solution. Then I'd dry her with a nice absorbent towel (paper towels work best).

We want the abscess to heal from the inside out, so it is important to keep the abscess pocket open and draining until no more pus is being formed inside. Leave the drain in place until the irrigation fluid comes out of the pocket clear or with only a little blood mixed in. You are then ready to switch to Irrigation Formula II (see page 280) with the added calendula. Calendula causes raw tissue to knit together and heal very fast. If you use Formula II with calendula too soon, the incisions will close up before the infection is gone inside and you'll end up with another abscess on your hands and have to start all over again.

After the abscess pocket is clean, irrigate with Formula II twice a day for two days. On the third day irrigate in the morning and then remove the drain. In the evening irrigate again only if you can easily insert the tip of the syringe into one of the openings. If the openings are healed shut, leave it alone and continue the supplements and remedies listed below. Here is a wonderful opportunity to do visualization (see page 217) and watch it come true as the old skin dries up and drops off and the body sloughs the old dead skin and manufactures perfect new skin with lovely silky hair growing out of it. Miracles do happen every single day.

Symptoms

- A deep wound with a very small opening
- Balloon-like swelling around the wound which is filled with pus

Recommendations

- Inform your holistic veterinarian of the situation and discuss what you are doing about it.
- Irrigate the abscess as described in paragraphs above, or be patient and let the body take care of the problem at its own pace while you support the effort with nutrition and homeopathy.
- Treat with homeopathy. It's always better to consult a veterinary homeopath rather than self-prescribe. If that is quite impossible, give homeopathic remedies as follows:

  1. Silica 30C—give one tablet one time and wait three days; *then*
  2. Sulfur 30C—give one tablet one time only.

  Be sure to read the section on "Homeopathy," page 211, especially on how to administer homeopathic remedies.

- Apply hot compresses (see page 296) four times a day.
- Instead of regular meals:

  1. For two days fast the cat on Homemade Chicken Broth (see page 308). Give three to six meals a day of ¼ to ½ cup, adding a feline multivitamin (see "Product Recommendations," in the Appendix), 10 mg B complex a day (divide a 50 mg capsule into five parts), *and* ¹⁄₁₆ teaspoon ascorbic acid crystals or sodium ascorbate powder into each meal to provide 250 units of vitamin C, which will help the body process out of the toxins.
  2. *Then* gradually introduce a high-quality diet with as much raw food as possible (see page 71), adding to each meal the supplements for infections and wounds (see page 306).

- Provide a snug retreat (see page 304).
- Herbal remedies:

1. Add five drops of golden seal to ½ cup of the first irrigation formula—it has antiseptic properties.

2. Add five drops of calendula to the final irrigation formula to promote quick healing and closing of ruptured tissue.

- Give Bach Flower Remedy Formula II, prepared as explained on page 313. In Tammy's case I also added two drops of Bach Flower Walnut to help her break the old ties to her former home.

Cuts

A deep cut bleeding profusely can be frightening to anyone. But remember, blood is a cleansing and healing substance. It is better if a wound bleeds a little. When the skin is broken by a wound, the body reacts at once, sending blood to wash the area and carry healing antibodies to the site. After the first shock (and by the next day), the tiny cells of the skin begin to contract, pulling the wound as much toward a closed position as possible. White cells in the blood fight invading germs, lymph carries away dead germs and white cells, and the skin begins manufacturing a quick protective covering—a scab. Scar tissue, if needed, will be forming slowly inside the tissue. To aid and support this process we need to:

1. Stop any copious bleeding by applying direct pressure on the wound with a clean cloth folded into a square. In an emergency, two folded paper towels, a kitchen towel, or a wash cloth can be used. If quick action is needed and you don't have anything else available, a piece of cloth can be torn from an article of your clothing or you can even use your fingers to apply pressure to the cut. If the wound is on a foot or lower leg and direct pressure is not working, make a tourniquet by looping a twisted dishtowel around the leg above the wound and twisting it rather tight in a wringing motion. This should slow the bleeding. *Do not stop it completely.* Loosen the towel or cloth every ten or fifteen minutes for five or ten seconds and then tighten it again. After a half hour or so try using direct pressure again as it is safer.

2. Call the veterinarian (or ask someone else to call) to tell him that you are coming in immediately with an emergency.

3. If for some reason you must wait a matter of hours to see the veterinarian, carefully clip away any hair that is getting into the wound. Hair carries germs that will contaminate the wound. Then cleanse away any debris, dirt, and germs by

squirting saline solution (page 271) or hydrogen peroxide onto the wound using an ear syringe, an empty clean shampoo bottle, or a hypodermic syringe without the needle. The solution should be body temperature. *Do not* use any solution containing alcohol or soap. If the wound is old, clots may have formed. Unless you see pus or obvious infection, don't disturb the clots to clean the wound because you might start major bleeding. Just get the cat to the veterinarian quickly.

The veterinarian may shave the area clean and then use either butterfly adhesive clamps or sutures (stitches). Sutures require that the cat be anesthetized. The veterinarian will try to avoid bandaging the cut because it's best to let the air circulate around the wound. He may shave the hair away all around the wound. A clean dry wound heals fastest.

Do not put any oil, salve, or ointments on an open wound or scab. They collect debris and germs. Do not wash a wound that has been closed with adhesive butterfly sutures.

Recommendations

- To keep a wound clean and promote healing, wash twice a day with normal saline solution (see page 271), warmed to body temperature, squirted on with a syringe. You can add the following herbs to the solution:

  1. If there is pus (indicating infection), add five drops golden seal extract to each ¼ cup saline solution.
  2. To promote quick healing of a clean wound, add five drops calendula extract to each ¼ cup saline solution. Keep the leftover solution in the refrigerator and, before use, reheat to body temperature by standing the container in a bowl of hot water.

- Once the scab falls off and the scar is formed, you can rub in a drop of vitamin E oil (from a vitamin E capsule that you've punctured) once a day for a week to encourage normal tissue growth.
- Add to your usual high-quality diet (page 66):

  400 units vitamin E (alpha tocopherol) twice a week for one month; then reduce to once a week as usual.

  Minerals aid healing. Add 1 teaspoon horsetail grass tea (page 321) to each meal.

Vitamin C helps fight infection and garlic is a natural antibiotic. Once a day add 1/16 teaspoon Delicious Garlic Condiment (page 317) and 1/16 teaspoon ascorbic acid crystals or sodium ascorbate powder (250 units vitamin C) to food.

Burns

Burns are usually caused by a cat walking on a hot surface, by a hot fluid being spilled on the cat, by the cat biting an electric cord, or by his ingesting a caustic chemical. Burns cause extreme pain; the patient should be treated for shock as well as for the wound. The burn area should be kept clean and moist while the cat is rushed to the veterinarian. Try not to touch the burn, even if you see that hair is getting on it—it is too painful. If the burn covers more than an inch or two, dehydration may occur and the veterinarian may want to hospitalize the patient and hook up an IV to give him fluids (page 297) for a day or two.

Because burns cover a wider expanse than a cut or puncture, the skin cells will not be able to close the wound by contracting. Burns take a long time to heal and must be kept scrupulously clean while they do so. Your veterinarian will undoubtedly clip or shave the hair away all around the burn site.

Recommendations

- Call the veterinarian (or ask someone else to call) as soon as possible and let him know you're on your way with a very serious emergency. Tell him it's a burn case.
- Give three drops Bach Flower Rescue Remedy (prepared as given on page 313) every thirty minutes. Take it yourself as well.
- Assure your cat that you know he is in pain and that you are going to help him feel better.
- If for some reason you have to wait hours before seeing the vet, use a rubber ear syringe or a clean squirt bottle to *very gently* wash the burn area with either:

    1/2 cup saline solution (page 271) and five drops urtica urens tincture;
    or

½ cup saline solution (page 271) and five drops Bach Flower Rescue Remedy.

- *Do not use salves or ointments on burns.* Keep the wound moist while traveling to the veterinarian by squirting a little solution on the wound every three to five minutes. Be sure the patient is lying on several layers of towel. Don't touch the wound. The veterinarian will probably give a tranquilizer before he attempts to clean it. (If the emergency veterinarian doesn't know your cat, those old veterinary records you brought with you will be invaluable and hopefully may allow the vet more leeway to use a stronger anesthetic or analgesic to control the pain.)

- If the skin over the burn becomes hard and stiff, this means that the skin has died. It is best to leave it in place to serve as a natural protective bandage. You should irrigate all around the edges at least twice a day with one of the following solutions:

  1. If pus or infection is present, use ½ cup saline solution (page 271) with five drops golden seal extract or tincture;
  2. If no pus is present and any discharge looks clean and clear, use ½ cup saline solution (page 271) with five drops calendula extract or tincture.

- Add to the food once a day for three weeks:

  An extra ¹⁄₁₆ teaspoon bone meal, calcium lactate, or calcium glutonate (in addition to that in Anitra's Vita-Mineral Mix);
  10,000 units vitamin A (except once a week give a capsule containing 10,000 units vitamin A and 400 units vitamin D instead);
  100 units vitamin E.

After three weeks, either change to a feline multivitamin (see Product Recommendations page 489) or reduce above supplements to the following, given once a week:

  400 units vitamin E;
  10,000 units vitamin A and 400 units vitamin D.

- Feed a high-quality diet with as much raw food as possible (see page 71). Be sure to include Anitra's Vita-Mineral Mix and other listed supplements in diet.

Concussions

A sudden, violent bump on any part of the head can cause a concussion. The most common cause is the "high rise" syndrome—falling from a window or balcony. Being hit by a car or something heavy falling on the cat are other possible causes of a concussion. If the blow injures an area of the brain, causing swelling, then brain function will be partially impaired. It is to be hoped that the effects will be temporary. With rest, quiet, and gentle nursing, the swelling will subside and the whole episode can be relegated to the category of unpleasant memory. Homeopathy can do a lot to speed recovery.

A veterinarian should always be consulted as quickly as possible whenever any of the symptoms below appear, since they can also indicate other very serious conditions, feline infectious peritonitis and rabies among them.

Prevention

- Screen all windows.
- Never allow cat to sit out on balcony or windowsill.
- Provide protected, screened run for outdoor exercise.

Symptoms

- Dizziness; falling to the side, circling, or staggering
- Tipping head to one side
- Uneven size of pupils
- Vomiting
- Inability to lap food

Recommendations

- Confine cat to carry case and take straight to veterinarian.
- Give Bach Flower Rescue Remedy—three drops in mouth every thirty minutes until there is some improvement; then give three drops three times a day.
- After returning home confine to large cage or small room with dim light and quiet.

- Play soft classical music.
- Eliminate possibility of climbing until dizziness passes and balance returns.
- Finger-feed if necessary until balance returns (see page 286). If dropper feeding is necessary, go slowly and carefully (see page 286).
- Provide snug retreat (page 304).
- Herbal remedy: if there are tremors or spasms or restlessness give a teaspoon of valerian root decoction (page 321) or ½ valerian capsule every three hours. *Note:* Your holistic veterinarian should be consulted before giving any medicinal herbs. If you have a homeopath, stick with homeopathy and use no medicinal herbs unless your homeopath agrees.
- For one day (or longer if veterinarian advises) fast on Homemade Chicken Broth given three to four times a day (page 308). To each ¼-cup serving of broth add the following:

  ¹⁄₁₆ teaspoon ascorbic acid crystals or sodium ascorbate powder (250 units vitamin C);
  10 mg vitamin B complex (divide a 50 mg capsule into five doses);
  ¹⁄₁₆ teaspoon mixed trace mineral powder or ¼ mixed mineral pill.

- Once a day give 100 units vitamin E (alpha tocopherol); after one week reduce to 400 units once a week as usual.

Fractures

A fracture (a break in the bone) can be caused by the cat falling, by something falling on him, being struck by a car, by the cat being crushed or caught in a slamming door, or by a bite from a larger animal. An actual break is less likely to occur when bones are kept strong by regular exercise and a high-quality diet rich in calcium, vitamin D, and trace minerals. The types of fractures are (a) hairline—the bone is cracked; (b) simple fracture—the broken is broken; or (c) compound fracture—the bone is broken and part of the bone is protruding out through the skin.

Broken bones are extremely painful. The injury can be made worse merely by allowing the cat to move about. If not tended by a veterinarian, infection can set in and the animal can be permanently crippled, lose the limb, or die from the infection.

Prevention

- Screen all windows. Do not allow a cat to sit on a balcony or unscreened windowsill.
- Look before you slam any door behind you.
- Provide a screened, protected run for outdoor exercise.

Recommendations

- Tell the cat you understand he hurts and that you are going to help him feel better.
- Give Bach Flower Rescue Remedy (prepared as given on page 313)—three drops into the mouth every thirty minutes and take some yourself.
- Confine the cat to the bathroom or carry case while you call the veterinarian and tell him you're coming with an emergency.
- If the cat cannot walk or if you are doubtful about the extent of his injuries, keep him lying in whatever position you found him and slide him onto a tray or board *covered by a towel.* (A serving tray or the drip tray from under the broiler in the oven may be the right size.)
- If front leg is broken, very gently and carefully slide the inside roll from a toilet paper or paper towel roll over the leg to protect it. Do this only if the cat does not object.
- Keep the cat warm—cover with a towel or blanket.
- Add to food during recuperation:

  an extra ⅛ teaspoon bone meal, calcium lactate, or calcium glutonate (in addition to that in Anitra's Vita-Mineral Mix);
  antistress supplements (page 305);
  1 teaspoon comfrey tea.

- Give one capsule containing 10,000 units vitamin A and 400 units vitamin D twice a week for three weeks; then reduce to once a week or use a good multivitamin (see "Product Recommendations" in the Appendix).
- While healing is taking place, devise ways of exercising that do not include the injured part. Use your ingenuity.

Irritable Bowel Syndrome (IBS)

Irritable Bowel Syndrome (IBS) is an autoimmune disease. The body's immune system has become confused and is attacking the body itself—in this case, the inner walls of the intestine. Because the membranes lining the intestine are raw and sensitive, the body tries to rid itself of anything in the intestine as quickly as possible by increasing the force and frequency of peristaltic action and secreting copious amounts of mucus into the intestine. This results in frequent runny and/or gaseous stools. Sometimes the body will try to correct the situation by stopping peristalsis, causing the stool to remain in the intestine, dry out, and become hard—and then constipation will alternate with diarrhea. This always happens if the veterinarian resorts to an antispasmotic drug. All of the holistic veterinarians I use counsel against the use of antispasmotic drugs for IBS. Because of the irritation and scarring, the intestinal walls become thickened. Nutrients cannot pass from the intestine into the bloodstream, and malabsorption results. IBS was once thought to be incurable, but it is now known that IBS "responds beautifully to a high-fibre diet" (*British Lancet,* April 25, 1987). I have seen complete success so often that I always expect an eventual cure when nutritional therapy and classical homeopathy are combined.

Any autoimmune disease is a signal that the immune system is weak and confused. Therefore, we must nurture and strengthen the failing immune system as well as the inflamed, swollen, and ulcerated intestinal walls. Modern veterinarians point out that autoimmune diseases appear most frequently in cats who have been treated at some time in their lives with corticosteroids or in cats who have been vaccinated frequently with vaccines combining several viruses (see "Vaccinations and Other Immunizations," page 240). Cortisone, Prednizone, and other corticosteroids suppress the body's immune response (see "Cortisone and Other Steroids," page 244). Negative side effects of steroids sometimes show up as IBS many months or even years after treatment has been stopped. Giving more steroids in an attempt to control the symptoms of IBS may give short-term improvement but this is always followed by return of symptoms—this time, much worse.

IBS is *not* always incurable. I've seen it disappear time after time (but only when the patient's guardian insisted that *no* drugs be used). Some veterinarians try steroids or an antibiotic preparation called tylan that was developed for pigs. Here again, the drug will suppress the symptoms for a little while, but then they usually return, worse than ever. It's easier to effect a permanent and true cure with classical homeopathy when no drugs at all have been used beforehand. Homeopathic treatment, guided by a classical homeopathic vet, always enhances any other natural treatment and speeds the recovery. If drugs have ever been used in the past, homeopathy is indispensable, but after drugs it will take longer to achieve a cure (see "Homeopathy," page 211).

During IBS the body sometimes becomes dehydrated to a degree, especially if there has been much diarrhea and even vomiting. Hydration with Ringer's lactate solution given subcutaneously will give the patient immediate relief and ensure that the body takes a giant step toward healing itself. I personally have never seen it fail in this. You can have the vet or his assistant do this procedure, or, like many of my clients, you can learn to give subcutaneous fluids yourself at home. All it takes is a desire to do it and patience with yourself while you learn (see "Subcutaneous Hydration," page 297. Also see "Allergies," page 328).

Symptoms

- Constipation or diarrhea or both alternating
- Diarrhea consisting of thin, liquid, offensive stools that "sputter" when passed
- Much mucus with stool; sometimes blood in stool
- Constantly demanding food
- Voracious appetite
- Steady weight loss despite large appetite
- Vet will feel thickening of intestinal wall and lack of flexibility

Recommendations

- Nurture and strengthen the immune system:

    1. Change as quickly as possible to an all raw food diet (see page 70). The immune system gradually fails without the enzymes that are present only in raw foods.
    2. Add ¼ teaspoon powdered feline digestive enzymes to all meals.
    3. Be sure to give Anitra's Vita-Mineral Mix (page 68) and all additional supplements recommended in Chapter 2, "Diet"—especially vitamins A, C, D, and E.

4. Encourage a rapid and efficient metabolism by removing *all* food between meals. Leaving snacks lying around will *not* help the cat gain weight—just the opposite. It's helpful to feed three or even four meals a day, but don't leave food around for more than one-half hour.

- Have vet or his assistant give subcutaneous fluids one, two, or more times a week, *or* ask him to teach you how to do it yourself at home (see page 297).
- Give 1 teaspoon slippery elm syrup (see page 319) by dropper five to ten minutes before each meal to soothe and calm the intestinal walls (see "Giving Liquid Medication," page 268).
- To absorb putrefaction, give one charcoal tablet morning and evening for two days, then stop. This will eliminate flatulence and foul smell (stool will look black) (see "Giving Pills," page 266).
- To minimize putrefaction and encourage friendly bacteria in the intestine, add to each meal:

    $\frac{1}{16}$ teaspoon Green Magma; *and*
    $\frac{1}{4}$ teaspoon mixed intestinal flora;
    or try mixing the Green Magma and acidophilus with 1 or 2 teaspoons Homemade Chicken Broth (see page 308) and give as a liquid medication (see page 268).

- Bach flower remedies: cats with IBS tend to be rather nervous and fearful. They are easily upset by other animals or by people. Give three drops three or four times a day of the following mixture prepared as given on page 313:

    Gentian—to give courage;
    Aspen—to dispel undefined fears;
    Mimulus—to quiet fear of bodily discomfort.

- *If constipation is a problem:*

    1. Do all of the above.
    2. Add $\frac{1}{8}$ teaspoon ground psyllium husks and 2 teaspoons water to food twice a day until stool is normal. It's okay to continue indefinitely. Psyllium is a food herb and quite harmless as long as the added water is included.

3. Add an extra ⅛ teaspoon fine wheat bran to each meal.

4. See also "Constipation."

- *If diarrhea is a problem:*

    1. Whenever diarrhea appears, immediately stop feeding solid foods.

        A. Give the patient all of the Homemade Chicken Broth (see page 308) he wants three to four times a day;

        B. Give one charcoal tablet twice a day for two days (see "Giving Pills," page 266).

        C. Give by dropper one teaspoon slippery elm syrup (see page 319) five minutes before each meal (see "Dropper Feeding," page 286).

    2. Then gradually go back to solid food and:

        A. Do all of the above (except the steps under constipation and diarrhea), especially Green Magma and acidophilus mixture;

        B. Add to food once a day ⅛ teaspoon Delicious Garlic Condiment (see page 317);

    3. See also "Diarrhea."

Kidney and Bladder Stones

(see also "Feline Urologic Syndrome (FUS)")

Stones and gravel are really crystals that form in the kidneys and, more often, in the bladder. The razor-sharp edges slice and tear at the bladder or kidney walls, providing an ideal breeding ground for germs. If tiny pieces of the stones break off and pass out through the urethra, the scraping and tearing continue all the way, causing great pain and blood in the urine. Scarring of the urethra walls usually results, thickening the walls and narrowing the passage, making it even more difficult to pass the rest of the crystals. If a crystal blocks the urethra, or if the urethra swells shut, no urine or blood can get through. Then the wastes back up and a serious toxic condition quickly builds in the body. Repeated bouts of FUS (feline urologic syndrome), with its accompanying swelling and infection in the urethra, recurring despite all dietary and veterinary treatment, can sometimes be explained by the presence of bladder stones and gravel. (See "Feline Urologic Syndrome (FUS).")

One reason for the formation of these mineral crystals is the presence of large amounts of insoluble mineral salts in the diet, such as those found in tuna and fish bones and scales. Stones and gravel can also be caused by an alkaline condition in the urine. The *smell* of food triggers metabolic changes that produce an alkaline urine, so if you're not already doing so, feed only twice a day and remove all food, including the dirty food plate, after a half hour. To help keep the urine acidic, allow no smell of food between meals. An acidic urine will dissolve mineral crystals and pass them out of the body as liquid waste. Urine also becomes alkaline if there is a dietary lack of vitamins A, B-6, or C, or if the diet does not contain enough of the protein methionine, or if the protein in the diet, no matter how copious, has been over-processed and cannot be assimilated efficiently by the cat's system. The meat by-products and meat meal found in most commercial foods are so highly processed that they cannot easily be digested and it is questionable how much of the protein actually finds its way into the cat's system.

A nutritional imbalance producing stones can also result from stress as in cases of immobilization due to a cast or confinement in a cage, since stress uses up nutrients very quickly. Stones and gravel create a condition where pain is great, stress levels are high, and toxicity leading to death can build up quickly. If you see blood in the cat's urine, don't wait; get the cat to the veterinarian at once. A homeopathic veterinarian may be able to treat your cat successfully with homeopathy and diet (see "Homeopathy," page 211). However, if large stones are present that do not respond to treatment and your vet counsels that surgery is unavoidable, discuss the pros and cons of consulting a surgical specialist experienced in this particular operation. It is a bit tricky since the bladder has to be cut open and it must be sewn together again so that it will hold liquid. I've known many cats who have had bladder stone surgery, and all have done fine afterward. You can ease the stress and help with a rapid recovery using diet, supplements, homeopathy, and the Bach flower remedies. (See "Surgery and Catheterization," page 246.)

Symptoms

- Crying out while at the litter box
- Repeated bouts of FUS or other urinary infection despite care and medication
- Blood in urine

Recommendations

- Ask veterinarian to test for stones (urine test, X-rays, and blood test).
- Acidify the urine by giving veterinarian's medication, removing *all* food between meals, and carefully balancing the high-quality proteins in the diet. Methionine, the acidifying protein, is plentiful in egg yolk. Give ½ organic raw yolk in each meal.
- Stress level is very high because of pain—give extra demonstrations of love and provide a snug retreat (page 304).
- Eliminate all dry and semimoist food, organ meats, tuna, and other fish from diet.
- The best way to keep urine acidic is to feed your cat the raw food diet. Do it as soon as possible. Failing that, feed a high-quality diet with as much raw food as possible (see Chapter 2, "Diet"). *Note: If FUS is present, along with the stone and gravel, it's best to eliminate liver and other organ meats and also the yeast from Anitra's Vita-Mineral Mix recipe until the crisis is past.* So, for the time being, make your own without yeast using the recipe on page 68 rather than buying it in the store. You can supply the B complex vitamins by giving 10 mg (divide a 50 mg pill into five pieces of B complex). Do not use dolomite when making Anitra's Vita-Mineral Mix; instead, use bone meal, calcium lactate, or calcium glutonate.
- Add to each meal:

    Anti-stress supplements (see page 305);
    ¼ teaspoon feline digestive enzyme powder to ensure assimilation of all food;
    ¹⁄₁₆ teaspoon bone meal, calcium lactate, or calcium glutonate (in addition to that in Anitra's Vita-Mineral Mix);
    ¹⁄₁₆ teaspoon ascorbic acid crystals (250 units vitamin C) to help acidify urine and fight infection.

- Once a day add to food ¹⁄₁₆ teaspoon Delicious Garlic Condiment (see page 317) to guard against the complication of infection.
- Add to food once a week for two months or until crisis is past:

    Contents of a 400-unit vitamin E capsule to help heal scarring;
    Contents of a capsule containing 10,000 units vitamin A and 400 units vitamin D to help assimilate the calcium.

- Continue to use a feline multivitamin as always (see "Product Recommendations" in Appendix).
- Bach flower remedies: bladder stone cats are frightened cats. They don't know why they're having this terrible pain or when it may strike again. They feel confused, helpless, and afraid. Stress level is very high; depression and loss of will to live are a constant threat.

    1. Give three drops Rescue Remedy (prepared as given on page 313) every two to four hours until the stones are gone.
    2. After stones are gone give three drops four times a day of the following mixture prepared as given on page 313:

    Star of Bethlehem—for comfort after shock;
    Elm—to cope with a bad situation;
    Gorse—to banish hopelessness;
    Mimulus—to dispel old fears.

Kidney Disease

Kidney disease is distressingly common in cats. Kidney damage can take the form of fatty kidneys, scarred kidneys, and/or dead tissue. Symptoms are listed below, but the first to appear and the easiest to spot are frequent, copious drinking with copious urination and obvious weight loss, often despite a good appetite.

To correct the problem, it is best if you understand the kidneys, how they work, and what they do. The kidney's job is to filter wastes, drugs, chemicals, poisons, and unused proteins out of the blood and send them to the bladder to be excreted in the urine. The kidneys of a cat filter hundreds of pints of blood every day. These hardworking organs will keep on functioning well into extreme old age if the diet is balanced and digestible and if no extreme stress is put on them. Stresses that destroy kidney tissue include exposure to toxins such as pesticides; chemical or drug treatments for fleas, worms, or other parasites; anesthetics; tobacco smoke; and many prescription drugs and vaccines.

Some vaccines, for example the "three in one" vaccine for calicivirus, rhinotracheitis virus, and parvovirus, are cultured on chicken kidneys. Kidney disease, usually found in older cats, is now showing up in much younger cats who have been vaccinated with serums cultured on kidney tissue. Since a vaccine prompts the body to develop antibodies against a particular disease, holistic veterinarians are researching the possibility that the vaccinated cats are developing antibodies not only against the diseases they are being vaccinated for but also against kidney tissue in general, including their own.

A chemical called phenol—found in many bathroom, tub, and tile cleaners and deodorizers such as Lysol and Pine-Sol—can damage the kidneys beyond repair. If a cat walks across a surface where a phenol residue remains and then licks his paws, the result is usually swift and fatal. Antifreeze is another swift killer of both cats and dogs, who are attracted by its sweet taste.

By far, the most common and relentless cause of kidney failure is commercial cat food made of low-quality proteins that are overprocessed, overcooked, and largely indigestible. Proteins are made up of twenty-two different amino acids. In the same way that the alphabet's twenty-six letters can be combined in different ways to make thousands of words, nature has created thousands of different proteins by combining these twenty-two amino acids in different ways. To be used by the body, the amino acids in a meal must be present in a certain ratio. If there is too much of any one amino acid, the kidneys must process out the extra as waste. Protein is called "high quality" if the amino acids that it contains are nicely balanced so that a large percentage of it can be used by the body. For a cat, muscle meats and fish filets are high-quality proteins. Chicken feet, beef intestines, ears, and leather are not.

Over the millennia, cats have evolved into creatures who require a diet extremely high in protein. Their protein requirements are much higher than those of dogs or humans, which is why commercial cat food is made up mostly of proteins. If these proteins were of high quality and were completely digestible when they finally got to the cat, all would be well.

Unfortunately processed commercial pet foods have introduced some serious problems. That high protein diet the wild cats are thriving on is entirely unprocessed and raw. Cats in the wild do not put their sparrows and mice on the end of sticks and toast them like little marshmallows over a campfire. The more meat is cooked, the less digestible and usable the proteins become. The government requires that canned pet food be cooked at a certain temperature and for a definite length of time. Dry food is cooked and processed even more than canned food.

Another problem is the *protein source*. When we read the words chicken, beef, or fish on a label, most of us assume that they refer to the same sort of meat that would be served on the average kitchen table. Many people don't understand that on a pet food label the word *fish* can and often does include fish heads, tails, bones, and scales. *Chicken* often includes heads, feet, and even tumors. *Beef* can mean eyes, ears, intestines, and leather. While they are technically "proteins," these body parts all require extensive processing to render them even minimally digestible. And then even the digestible protein is of very low quality, with unnaturally large quantities of out-of-balance amino acids left over to be processed out day after day, year after year, by the already exhausted kidneys. It seems a major miracle that they continue to perform as long as they do.

When the kidneys begin to fail they become less and less efficient at filtering out wastes, so the cat drinks more and more water to compensate for the decline in kidney function. The urine looks more and more watery and pale, has little odor, and is less acid. A cat can compensate for the loss of up to 75 percent of both kidneys just by copious drinking. So at this stage, no hint of a kidney problem may appear in a blood test, despite the fact that the kidneys are damaged beyond repair. When more than 75 percent of both kidneys becomes useless, the cat will not be able to drink enough water to compensate and will begin to urinate a great deal more than he can possibly replace by drinking. To aid vital waste disposal, the body will draw moisture out of its own tissues to try to get the water it needs to detoxify itself, and the cat will become dehydrated.

Dehydration makes a cat feel and look terrible. The face gets a pinched look; the coat seems rough and sheds easily. Now some of the wastes that should have been filtered out by the kidneys will recirculate in the body, because there is just not enough water to do the job. These wastes build up and soon begin to affect other organs. The body will try to dispose of these wastes in any way it can: through the pores as dandruff or via the intestine as diarrhea (which soon becomes constipation). Sometimes an aroma very like urine can be detected in the fur. The cat will feel nauseated and ache in every joint.

Dehydration is the most serious symptom of kidney disease. It is, in fact, the cause of all the other symptoms because none of the body's processes can work well when an animal is dehydrated. The cat cannot eat, swallow, digest food, or pass wastes.

Luckily, this grim scenario can be avoided. Dehydration can be completely reversed and the patient spared all of the painful and destructive symptoms if the human caregiver (a) takes firm control of what is offered in the cat's food bowl and (b) learns to administer fluids subcutaneously to prevent dehydration. (See "Subcutaneous Hydration," page 297).

Cats are desert animals and a normal cat drinks water only about twice a week. More frequent drinking is a sign of dehydration. As more kidney tissue is damaged, the patient must drink more and more water. For example, if half the kidney tissue has been destroyed, the cat will need to drink twice as much water as before and the remaining kidney tissue will have to work twice as hard as before. The kidneys compensate so beautifully in this way that no indication will show up in the blood or on the blood tests to show that the kidneys are failing until more than 75 percent of both kidneys are destroyed.

A number of times a cat's guardian has said to me, "My vet told me not to worry because the kidney values on the blood test were only a little bit high." Translation: A little bit more than three-quarters of both kidneys have already been destroyed. Perhaps the kindly veterinarian doesn't want to worry the cat's guardian because in conventional veterinary practice there is little or nothing that can be done about it anyway. Fortunately, the holistic paradigm offers a great deal more that can be done.

When treating a cat with failing kidneys, it is important to work closely with a holistic veterinarian who is experienced in homeopathy and can teach you how to hydrate subcutaneously. Because the copious drinking and urinating washes all the water-soluble nutrients out of the body, they should be replenished at least twice and preferably three or four times a day by supplementation in the food. Because the urine will be dilute and therefore less acid, extra ascorbic acid, methionine (found in egg yolk), and raw meat should be added to the food to help acidify the urine and prevent the growth of germs or the formation of crystals in the bladder. Use only spring or filtered water for drinking, and eliminate all chemicals from the cat's environment.

Symptoms

Kidney disease always causes dehydration; therefore, almost all symptoms of kidney disease are also symptoms of dehydration. However, dehydration also occurs in diabetes, irritable bowel syndrome, and hyperthyroidism. A blood test will differentiate among these health problems.

- Frequent and copious drinking
- Frequent and copious urination
- Sitting with head over the water bowl

- Urine dilute with little odor or color
- Body odor; fur smells like urine
- Anorexia (no appetite)
- Constipation; hard stool
- Pinched look around the eyes
- Asking to be fed, then not eating
- Weight loss, sometimes while appetite is still very good
- Achy joints; sits hunched; withdraws to closet or under bed
- Seeking out warm places
- Copious dandruff

Recommendations

- Ask vet to do a blood test.
- Provide warmth and a snug retreat (see page 304).
- Provide plenty of spring or filtered water.
- Eliminate all chemicals from the environment including room deodorizer and fabric softeners.
- If dandruff is copious, consider bathing if your cat accepts it well so he won't lick off and swallow the dandruff and recycle his own wastes. Use a mild castile shampoo or soap such as Dr. Bronner's diluted in water on a one-to-five ratio.
- Ask your vet to teach you how to administer sterile saline solution subcutaneously at home. (See "Subcutaneous Hydration," page 297.) This will add many months of comfort to your cat's life and eliminate most of the other symptoms. Your veterinarian or holistic health care practitioner will guide you as to how much fluid to give and how often to perform this simple procedure.
- The urine will tend to be too dilute. Acidify the urine by:

  1. Adding 250 units of vitamin C ($\frac{1}{16}$ teaspoonful) in the form of ascorbic acid into each meal;
  2. Adding one raw organic egg yolk to food each day;
  3. Feeding the raw food diet (see page 71). If this is not possible, include as much raw meat in the food as possible (see recipe below).

- Include Anitra's Vita-Mineral Mix in the diet (see page 68). The yeast is a rich source of B vitamins. However, use the store-bought version of the recipe as given on page 68 *only if* you are acidifying the urine by (a) feeding a raw food diet, and/or (b) implementing the above suggestions to acidify the urine. If you are not taking these steps, mix up your own batch of Anitra's Vita-Mineral Mix and eliminate the yeast from the recipe.
- Include 10 mg vitamin B complex in the food daily (crush a 50 mg pill and divide it into five doses).
- Include a good multivitamin in each meal. (I use Nu-Cat or Tabby Tabs.)
- Provide extra B vitamins and minerals by adding a sprinkle of Green Magma powder to all meals. (Available in health food stores.)
- Sprinkle all food with Nu-Salt or any salt substitute made entirely of potassium chloride.
- Encourage gentle exercise.

Diet for the Cat with Kidney Problems

Purpose: To acidify the urine and provide high-quality proteins that are easy to digest.

75 percent (or ¾ cup) of full fat, not lean, *raw meat*. Use ground beef or organic chicken or turkey.
25 percent (or ¼ cup) vegetable. Choose those your cat likes best:
  Baked carrot or winter squash
  Steamed asparagus or broccoli
  Finely grated carrot or zucchini
  Finely cut sprouts (alfalfa or clover)
  Organic canned tomato sauce or pumpkin
One organic egg yolk
Water or leftover vegetable broth. Use enough to make a nice soft consistency.

Mix all ingredients together and store in a glass container in the refrigerator. Feed three or four small meals a day. Serve warm to room temperature or slightly above.

At mealtime, add the following to each portion:

- 1 multivitamin crushed and mixed in well. I prefer Nu-Cats or Tabby Tabs.
- Pinch of Green Magma.
- Scant 1/16 teaspoon ascorbic acid.
- 10 mg vitamin B complex. Crush a 50 mg pill and divide into five doses.
- A sprinkle of potassium chloride (salt substitute). I use Nu-Salt.
- Bach flower remedy: give 3 drops three times daily of the following mixture prepared as instructed on page 313:

  Hornbeam—to strengthen;
  Aspen—to banish vague fears;
  Crabapple—to encourage expulsion of poisons from the system.

Liver Disease and Liver Damage

The liver has many jobs. It detoxifies poisons in the system, such as drugs and chemicals; it detoxifies excess hormones, such as insulin and the male-female hormones; and it produces bile to digest fats, store them, and convert them to starch. Liver breakdown can be caused by a diet deficient in choline or magnesium. It can also occur when the amount of outside poisons entering the body— such as antibiotics; toxic chemicals in household cleaners, food preservatives, and colorings; insecticides; or moth ball fumes—becomes too great for the liver to handle, and too many liver cells are destroyed too quickly. Inflamed swollen liver (hepatitis) or fatty or scarred liver (cirrhosis) then occurs. When liver cells die, the liver swells and becomes inflamed and sore. In this stage the condition is called hepatitis. When liver tissue is replaced by scar tissue that cannot do the liver's work of detoxifying, further damage occurs more easily and then more scarring occurs. This snowball effect is called cirrhosis. A lack of bile in the system causes digestion to break down, resulting in malabsorption of fats. Tissues become waterlogged and/or hypoglycemia develops because of the inability of the liver to deactivate excess insulin. An imbalance of the male or female hormones can also occur, resulting in bad temper or fearfulness. Hepatic lipidosis or fatty liver can be caused by prolonged fasting or starvation.

The liver has a miraculous ability to regenerate itself if given adequate nutritional support and help from a homeopathic veterinarian (see "Homeopathy," page 211). But liver disease is seldom diagnosed early because the symptoms are so general that they could be confused with any number of other difficulties from hair balls to urinary disease.

Symptoms

- Personality changes; lethargy or aggression
- Weight loss
- Random wetting or spraying, milky urine, diarrhea, light-colored (fatty) stool
- Digestive upsets, vomiting foam or yellow liquid, distended abdomen
- Yellow eye whites (often does not occur until late in the disease)
- Recurrent allergic reactions
- Tendency to pick up fleas and ringworm

Recommendations

- Ask veterinarian to do a blood test that includes a specific liver enzyme evaluation (e.g., SGPT).
- Seek the help of a holistic veterinarian experienced in classical homeopathy and nutrition.
- Follow veterinarian's treatment carefully.
- Together with veterinarian, try to determine the cause of liver trouble by examining:

    dietary deficiencies or possibility of recent prolonged fasting;
    presence of toxic substances in environment such as household cleaners; basin, tub, and tile cleaners; room deodorizers; litter deodorizers; moth ball fumes; paint fumes; flea chemicals;
    chemical preservatives and colors in food such as BHA, BHT, propylgallate, nitrates, nitrites, sodium benzoate, and so on.

- Provide a snug retreat (see page 304) to eliminate stress.
- Feed raw food diet (page 71) or a high-quality diet with as much raw food as possible. (See Chapter 2, "Diet.")
- Feed three or four small meals a day.

- Make Anitra's Vita-Mineral Mix yourself rather than buying it in the store, and alter the recipe (page 68) as follows:

    1½ cups yeast;
    2 cups lecithin;
    1½ cups bran;
    ½ cup kelp or mixed trace mineral powder;
    2 cups bone meal, calcium lactate, or calcium glutonate.

- Add to each meal:

    ½ teaspoon of special Anitra's Vita-Mineral Mix recipe above;
    ¼ teaspoon cod liver oil;
    ⅟₁₆ teaspoon ascorbic acid crystals or sodium ascorbate powder (250 units vitamin C);
    ¼ teaspoon feline digestive enzyme powder;
    10 mg vitamin B complex once a day (divide a 50 mg capsule into five doses);
    ¼ teaspoon mixed intestinal flora.

- Add to food three times a week:

    200 units vitamin E (alpha tocopherol);
    1 raw organic egg (not necessary if you are feeding the raw food diet)
    a good feline multi-vitamin that contains vitamins A and D (see "Product Recommendations," in the Appendix).

- Bach flower remedies: liver patients feel tired and despondent, and all are subject to extremes of emotion, and some experience mood swings. Give them quiet cheerfulness and frequent gentle affection. Don't let their extreme or inappropriate mood influence yours. You must be the Rock of Gilbraltar providing the emotional stability they desperately need. Four times a day give three drops of the following mixture prepared as given on page 313:

    Larch—to promote feelings of self worth;
    Hornbeam—to give strength and courage;
    Cherry plum—for fear of losing control;

plus one of the following:

> Impatiens—for those who are easily angered (touchy) or seem to go
> looking for an argument;
> Aspen—for those who are fearful, seemingly without good reason.

Mange Mites

(for ear mites, see "Ear Problems")

Mange is a skin condition caused by one or two types of mites: *sarcoptic* mites, which burrow under the skin; or *demodectic* mites, which live on the hair follicles. Sarcoptic mites cause especially terrible itching and can be transferred to humans who have low resistance. Some people, including me, are sensitive to mites. If you discover you have itchy red bumps like mosquito bites in straight lines, widely spaced, then you know your cat has mites. The mites follow the lines of blood vessels; that's why they appear in straight lines. You usually find them in places against which your cat has been resting, such as your inner arm or the side of your body. Besides treating the cat, you will want to treat yourself and stop the itching. First of all, don't panic. Remember that cat and dog mites cannot reproduce on a human, so, unless you have the human variety, or unless you reinfest yourself from your pet or someone else's or from a piece of clothing where the mites have been lying dormant and waiting for you, the mites will gradually die out and the bites will disappear. Personally that's not fast enough for me.

I've tried many different preparations and techniques, and I've found that the quickest, easiest, and safest way to get rid of a mite bite on humans and stop the itching at once is to brush the bite with a dry natural bristle bath brush. The reason this helps is that it aids the lymph ducts to carry away the toxic, itchy residue the pesky little critters leave behind. Always brush in one direction: toward your solar plexus. Brush in toward your body on the limbs, brush up on the buttocks.[2] After the brushing, you can deaden the itching even longer if you chill each bite. Ice is drippy and unpleasant; it's better to half-fill a container made of glass or metal and keep it in the freezer. After brushing, press it on each bite for thirty seconds. Yes, this will also work for mosquito bites or any itchy bite. This works even after you've had the bites for a day or two, but you'll have to do it

2. Airola, Paavo, PhD, ND. *How to Get Well.* Sherwood, OR: Health Plus Publishers, 1984, 225–229.

every few hours. If you do it when you first feel the bite, even before much of a bump has formed, you probably won't have any more trouble with it.

Mites proliferate on cats who are very old or sick. If I'm doing nursing care for such a cat, I protect myself by wearing a closely woven heavy blouse or smock. Mites will seek heat, so if they can't perceive your body heat, they'll stay on the cat. If it's too hot for a smock I put some citronella oil or Natural Animal Coat Enhancer on my arms.

My veterinarian showed me a young kitten infested with mange mites. The bizarre feature of this particular case was that the kitten was perfectly comfortable and maintained a normal coat of hair through it all. The infestation was discovered only because the guardian was going through a positive agony of itching. The man's dermatologist uncovered the cause and suggested that the man's cat be treated as the source of the problem. Any veterinarian I've ever talked to seems to agree that skin problems are by far the hardest to diagnose.

Demodectic mites are mites that live in the hair follicles. Symptoms appear as a bald patch above the eyes, around the ears, or on the chin, and therefore they are sometimes called head mites. They are usually transferred from one animal to another, or they can be carried by an unsuspecting human.

Mange is supposed to be very rare in cats, but, being a groomer, I have seen it with increasing frequency. Every year conventional veterinarians recommend that you let them give your cat more and more different vaccines. Is there a connection? Holistic veterinarians say yes. Multiple vaccines weaken and confuse the immune system (see "Vaccinations and Other Immunizations," page 240), and they have found that mange mites take hold on animals with weak immune systems. As the liver is a key organ in the immune system, any cats with liver disease are prime targets for mange mites, as are any cats who are ill, on medication, or genetically weak because of inbreeding. If mange is diagnosed, the orthodox treatment has always been to apply a highly poisonous liquid to the skin. The solution is so toxic that only a part of the animal can be treated at one time. The liquid is specifically designed to be absorbed through the skin, killing the mites on the way. Unfortunately, being highly toxic, it also destroys many liver cells, doing further damage to the immune system. This is why cats once infested with mange seem to get it again and again.

Mange is difficult to diagnose and was once believed to be practically nonexistent in cats, therefore, it is often mistaken for some other condition or simply called an "allergy." Cortisone is frequently used to "stop the itching, at least" (see "Cortisone and Other Steroids," page 244). This is simply treating a symptom and not getting rid of the mites. The swelling and itching is a normal immune response. Cortisone is a drug specifically designed to weaken the immune response. It doesn't cure anything; that's not what it's for. The itching will return the minute the cortisone treatment is stopped. Also, it is well known that cortisone depresses the immune system even more than the mange medicine. Once cortisone has been used, recovery from mites becomes very difficult. Since mange, like any parasite, is a sign that health is poor and resistance is low, a more effective solution is to build general health, with special attention to the liver to ensure strong resistance levels, and to treat the mites topically with natural preparations. Homeopathy can be invaluable in building up the immune system again (see "Homeopathy," page 211).

Symptoms

- Hairless patches around eyes, ears, or chin
- Hairless patches in long narrow lines on body
- Itching and scratching
- Pinhead-size scars on neck, chest, or back, enlarging to large open sore after much scratching
- Red itching welts appearing in straight lines on guardian's inner arm or body

Recommendations

- Immediately begin a change over to the raw food diet (page 71).
- Consult veterinarian for a definite diagnosis of the condition. Mites are extremely hard to diagnose, even with a scraping examined under the microscope.
- Fast two or three days on Homemade Chicken Broth (see page 308 and see "Fasting," page 286).
- Feed diet and supplements given in section on "Liver Disease and Liver Damage," page 432, except include 10,000 units a day of vitamin A (for three weeks), which tends to inhibit the spread of mange.
- Feed twice a day and remove all food between meals, leaving only water available.
- Add to food once a day:

½ raw organic egg yolk;

5 mg zinc;

¹⁄₁₆ to ⅛ teaspoon Delicious Garlic Condiment (page 317) or put 2 or 3 slivers of garlic into a capsule and give as a pill (see "Giving Pills" page 266).

- Eliminate all dairy products from diet.
- Eliminate fatty treats such as butter.
- Bathe cat in natural flea shampoo daily (see Appendix, "Product Recommendations").
- After shampoo, sponge on Lemon Rinse (see page 324) or spray with Natural Animal Coat Enhancer.
- Herbal remedy: make Lemon Rinse with herb tea as the liquid instead of water. I use golden seal, but plaintain or lavender also tends to kill mites. Massage it into the skin once a day.
- Bach flower remedies: itchy mites make a cat feel out of sorts. If it goes on very long, they become nervous and depressed. Four times a day give three drops of the following mixture prepared as given on page 313:

Elm—to help cope with an uncomfortable situation;

Aspen—for those who are nervous;

Gorse—to banish hopelessness.

Matting Fur

Matting occurs when the body sheds hair, but the hair is not groomed out—by either the cat or the owner. The loose hair will eventually build up from the skin to halfway up the hair follicle, forming first soft and then hard mats. Matting is more common in longhaired cats because the cat's tongue cannot reach all the way down to the roots of the hair. Only a wide-toothed metal comb can groom a longhaired cat thoroughly. First, you may need to have the cat shaved by the veterinarian or dematted by a groomer (see Chapter 8). During spring and autumn, when heavy shedding occurs, any cat can mat, especially if a poor-quality diet has produced a poor-quality coat; or if frequent snacking has produced an oily coat; or if any spray, powder, or "cream rinse" has coated the hair follicles, making them sticky. Also, fleas encourage matting by leaving eggs and debris on the skin and coat. Finally, mats can form around dirt, debris, or soiling on the fur.

Soft mats are often not noticed by the guardian. A comb with teeth too close together will simply slip through the top half-inch of the hair and not reveal the trouble building up at the roots. If the partially matted coat is then bathed or treated with a flea preparation, the soft mats immediately become hard mats. Never bathe, spray, or powder a matted cat; instead remove the mats first, then comb through (see page 178). Hard mats can inhibit free movement of limbs and are favorite places for fleas and ringworm. No air can reach the skin under the mat, and the cat cannot wash himself there, so he always suffers from itching, irritation, redness, and dandruff in those areas. Mats are unsanitary, uncomfortable, and a constant source of stress. Never try to comb through a mat. They must be removed by a veterinarian or groomer with a shaver or scissors.

Review Chapter 8, "Grooming," especially "Step 4: Getting Rid of the Mats," page 178.

Symptoms

- Lumps near skin in the armpit or on the chest, inner thighs, outer thighs, lower back, around the ears and neck, or around and under the anus
- Comb snags during grooming; cat objects to grooming
- Scratching with hind foot
- Pulling on hair with teeth
- Bald spots where cat has torn the mat out
- Impaired motion at joints, inability to jump or land properly
- Unpleasant odor
- Demoralization and depression

Prevention

- Feed a high-quality diet with as much raw food as possible (see Chapter 2, "Diet"). Be sure to include Anitra's Vita-Mineral Mix and other listed supplements to diet.
- Remove food between meals, leaving only water available.
- Use proper grooming tool and methods (see Chapter 8, "Grooming").

- Establish a regular grooming schedule:

    For longhaired cats: at least sixty seconds a day;
    For shorthaired cats: at least thirty seconds three times a week.

- Keep hair clean. If you bathe, never use a cream rinse.

Recommendations

- Give a lot of love and affection, but don't pet on or around the mats; they're very uncomfortable and itchy.
- To remove mats, see page 178, or use the services of a cat groomer or veterinarian. Try to find one who will let you stay and watch. Don't hesitate to call a halt if your feline friend becomes upset or if you see any roughness or carelessness.
- After the mats are removed, begin prevention program as outlined above and have veterinarian check for cause of any diarrhea. If necessary, treat for fleas, parasites, or fungus, in a safe natural way.
- Herbal remedy: to keep hair from matting again after a shampoo and make it easier to comb out, rinse with one cup of a decoction (see page 321) made with rosemary. Make the tea doubly strong.
- Add to diet:

    one teaspoon horsetail infusion into each meal;
    ½ egg yolk a day to food;
    ½ teaspoon Anitra's Vita-Mineral Mix into each meal.

- Bach flower remedies: because mats make it uncomfortable to be picked up, a matted cat will be feeling a little lonely and his self-esteem will be low. Start before the grooming and continue for two weeks after he is clean and silky again by giving three drops four times a day of the following mixture prepared as given on page 313:

    Walnut—to forget old thought patterns and troubles;
    Larch—to encourage feelings of self-worth.

Mites

(see "Mange Mites")

Mites, Ear

(see "Ear Problems")

Nervousness, Hiding, and Ill Temper

Nervousness, hiding, and ill temper are all warning signals that the cat is either afraid or ill or both. Nervousness is nearly always caused by a combination of things: environmental stress, a congenital predisposition, chemicals in the diet or environment, and/or a physical disease. The most ubiquitous cause of feline tension and nervousness (sometimes referred to as hypersensitivity to stimuli) is the presence of chemicals in *all* of the cat foods on the supermarket shelves—and even in those sold by most veterinarians. These preservatives, colorings, and flavor enhancers actually abrade the cat's nerve endings. When you change over to one of the pure foods that have no chemicals, you will always see a change for the better in your cat's temperament. There are no exceptions to this rule. Even cats who already seem perfectly fine and happy will become more mellow or jocular or playful. You should also eliminate the possibility of chemical residues such as air fresheners, moth ball odors (which destroy liver cells), and floor or bathroom cleansers containing phenol (which destroys kidney cells). Vaccinosis, which can be caused by frequent vaccination, multiple vaccines, or even a single vaccine, is also a frequent cause of nervousness.

Causes of a nervous temperament nearly always include some discomfort, pain, or weakness. If a cat is not feeling up to par, he knows he cannot escape as easily if need should arise. What if someone picks him up carelessly or puts him down wrong and he is accidentally hurt? What if he is squeezed too hard or held in a position where breathing is difficult or his skeletal structure is unsupported? All these circumstances take on greatly increased importance to a cat with an undiagnosed illness. Cardiac disease, lung disease, arthritis, and liver problems all require very special handling of the cat's body. Ingrown claws that are puncturing one or more of the cat's pads make being put down a torture. A nervous cat, or one who "doesn't like to be picked up," should have a very thorough physical examination to determine whether or not disease is a part of the problem. Check each claw carefully and have the teeth and gums examined and have them treated and cleaned if necessary.

Now check out the following list of possible environmental causes, looking at them from the cat's point of view. Remember that a cat's acute hearing and sense of smell render him much more sensitive to noises and odors than you are, and yes, a cat can be afraid of an odor. A noise level that is normal to you may be loud and startling to a cat; a noise that is loud and startling to you is probably downright painful to the cat's ears. The smell of a dirty litter box is a source of great tension to a cat. In the wild the smell of urine or stool attracts predators, so over the millennia cats have developed an instinctive fear that makes them bury their wastes. This instinct continues to operate in the cat's subconscious even when he lives in a city apartment where, we would assume, there is a total absence of predators. The smell of a dirty litter box can still make a cat tense and afraid.

Also, remember that a cat is ten to fifteen times smaller than you. Imagine how you would feel if you were living with a family of elephants. Even if they all loved you dearly, wouldn't you be afraid of their feet—especially if there were several elephants in the same room with you, or if they were moving about too quickly? What if there were young elephants who picked you up suddenly and put you down carelessly? Prolonged exposure to stresses like this will make any animal nervous and irritable, and finally weaken him to the point where he becomes an easy target for disease. Also, nervous animals are not a pleasure to handle, therefore the nervous cat usually lacks the physical affection he badly needs and so becomes even more withdrawn.

Symptoms

- Hiding, trembling, or hiding for specific reasons—from strangers, from thunder, from the vacuum cleaner, etc.
- Scratching and/or biting others with little or no obvious provocation
- Defensive behavior, hissing
- Unwillingness to be held or to be touched in one or more places

Causes

- Guardian experiencing high stress or sadness and ignoring their feline friend's attempts to give comfort

- Dirty litter box
- Disease or pain
- Declawing, or ingrowing claws (see page 115; see also "Claw and Cuticle Problems," page 344)
- Improper diet, chemicals in the food or in over-the-counter medications for hair balls, etc. (see page 55)
- Possible liver damage, arthritis, or heart or lung problem
- Excess or prolonged stress (noisy household, unusual household activity, children, or adults who don't handle cat properly)
- Congenitally weak nerves and/or congenitally low intelligence due to careless breeding (inbreeding)
- Previous negative life experiences: early separation from mother, lack of human contact, careless or brutal handling
- Fear of other animals, members of household, objects such as vacuum cleaner, strangers, or anything else new and unknown
- Cat being deaf or blind without owner being aware
- Hyperthyroidism (see page 399)

Recommendations

- Have veterinarian examine carefully for any painful or diseased conditions such as ingrown claw (especially on declawed cats), dirty teeth, swollen anal glands, and constipation, or have blood test to reveal any more serious disease, especially hyperthyroidism.
- Homeopathy has the most immediate and powerful effects of any therapy used in cases of emotional problems.
- Eliminate all commercial pet food, even food from health food store or from veterinarian. Feed a high-quality diet with as much raw food as possible (see Chapter 2, "Diet"). Be sure to include Anitra's Vita-Mineral Mix and other listed supplements.
- Add antistress supplements (page 305) to diet.
- Reevaluate litter box position and condition (see page 91).
- Reevaluate stress level in cat's environment (see page 255).
- Reevaluate items used to clean your home and eliminate any containing phenol.
- Begin practicing good cat etiquette: no surprises, give warnings; approach

with hand below cat's nose level; control children; allow cat to sniff before you touch him; instruct all humans to speak softly and move slowly. Re-evaluate the way you pick up and put down the cat (see page 27).

- Provide a snug retreat (see page 304).
- Try to structure as much sameness and repetition as possible into the cat's life.
- Herbal remedy: This is a stopgap measure; use only until you discover the real cause and as *part* of total program. Include all of the above suggestions as well. Give one teaspoon valerian tea for nine days only. Can be mixed half-and-half with Homemade Chicken Broth (see page 308) and given as liquid medication (see page 268) *or* can be mixed in food. The dry herb can also be sprinkled around a resting place.
- Bach flower remedies: nervous cats, whether they attack or hide, will always benefit from a program of detoxification to expel irritants from the system. Give three drops four times a day of the following mixture prepared as given on page 313:

  Elm—to help cope with the situation;
  White chestnut—to banish unfounded worries;
  Aspen—to cushion hypersensitivity;
  Mimulus—to quell fears.

- Also add any appropriate remedies listed under any disease that is diagnosed by your veterinarian.
- Consult your holistic veterinarian or classical homeopath. Homeopathy is very often the answer in cases of both vaccinosis and/or mental problems.
- Also see "Emotions and Well-being," page 13, "Dealing with Abused or Neglected Animals," page 26 and "Fear Biting," page 20. For more detailed instructions on calming and repatterning "attack cats" or scaredy-cats, see "Maizey's Story" in our book *It's a Cat's Life.*

Obesity

Obesity is another problem that can be caused by leaving food available between meals. If cats are on a low-quality diet, their bodies will be craving nutrients that are missing or non–digestible. They will eat and eat the low-quality food that is in the dish in an attempt to get those nutrients. The low-quality diet has an overabundance of unbalanced cheaper proteins, some of which the body converts and stores as fat while the rest must be processed out by the kidneys.

Cats may also become obese if their diet is too rich in fats, sugars, or salt. Almost all commercial cat foods contain large amounts of sugar or salt, or both, often hidden under such pseudonyms as sodium chloride or very salty cheese (for salt) and sucrose, dextrose, corn sweetener, corn syrup, molasses, fructose, or malt syrup (for sugar). Also, the processed foods available in grocery stores are usually deficient in any number of trace elements that the cat requires and would normally ingest if she were hunting in the wild. Furthermore, the alarming percentages of chemical colorings, toxic preservatives, and high hormone by-products in these foods create an unusually high need for these missing nutrients because they are required by the body to help detoxify, process, and dispose of these chemical nonfood items. The cat tries to supply her body with those missing nutrients by eating more and more of the only food available, the poor diet. Thus, she gets enormous amounts of some elements, and almost none of the others, creating an ever greater imbalance.

Cats fed on all organ meat are usually not only fat but also greasy. It's such a sad thing to see an overweight cat. It is not only the drain on the cat's laboring heart that saddens one but also the fact that the cat can't play and therefore the circulation is slower. And what really tears at my heart is to see a cat so overweight that he cannot bend enough to wash and clean himself properly. This is a frequent cause of mats in the bloomers and around the genitals of even shorthair cats. The suppleness of the cat is as legendary as his cleanliness. It is criminal to allow the cat's body to get into a condition where he cannot reach his own anus to clean it. I cry inside every time the guardian of an obese cat says to me, "Oh, well, she's been spayed, that's why" or "He's old and fat, there's nothing we can do." A cat that is properly cared for keeps a beautiful figure his whole life through. It's never too late to correct the problem. A loving caregiver will jump at the chance the minute he or she finds out what to do.

I do not believe in crash diets. When confronted with an obese cat and contrite guardians, I explain to the guardians that changing to the recommended diet will automatically begin to slim the cat down, albeit very slowly. This will happen because after a few days he won't *want* to eat as much; those missing nutrients he was reaching for will now be generously supplied. Also, the high-quality protein and fat in the new diet have a stick-to-the-ribs effect, which is another reason

445

he will not feel hungry. Coming at the problem from another angle, the fact that you are removing food between meals means that the metabolism will speed up again. The cat will have more energy to play, exercise, and burn up calories.

Once they are aware of the dangers and discomfort that come with obesity most caregivers are eager to do little special things to speed up the weight loss and to make it easier on their cats.

I recommend feeding any one of the diets given in the diet chapter. Let me caution again: DO *NOT* try to reduce the *quantity* of food right off the bat. When the nutrients he needs are first made available to him, he may gobble them up and ask for more. It's okay to feed a third meal during the first two weeks on the new regimen. Just don't leave the food available for more than a half hour at each mealtime. When your cat's body has had a chance to absorb all the nutrients it has been missing, he won't need to eat as much and will taper off of his own accord. In fact, at this stage some guardians get worried and call me to complain that "He's not eating." I then ask, "How are his spirits? Is he using his litter box as usual?" "Yes," they reply, "but he's not eating." Then I have to ask, "Do you mean that he's eating nothing or that he's eating much less?" "Well," they usually reply, "he's eating but it's a lot less." Then I have to tell them not to worry. He won't need to eat as much now that you're giving him food rich in high-quality nutrients. He's eating quality as opposed to quantity. Now you can begin to watch the ounces gradually melt away.

If your veterinarian has advised you to set about the weight loss program with all possible speed because of danger to the heart or pancreas, then *do it*. However, one word of caution: no veterinarian would want you to take a cat's weight down too quickly. The cat's body (and ours, too) stores toxins in the fat. It's the body's way of keeping poisons away from the major organs. When the fat starts to melt away, those toxins are released into the bloodstream and carried to the liver to be processed and then sent to the kidneys to be excreted as waste. If the fat melts away too fast, too many toxins will be released and the liver and the kidneys won't be able to handle the backup of wastes, which can cause toxicity—both physical and emotional.

I caution the guardians to provide extra attention at this time, not only petting and cuddling but also frequent casual eye and voice contact. If, without realizing it, you have been teaching your cat that "food is love," you must now introduce him to some of the other delightful ways that love can be expressed. Attention is love, too, you know, and so is grooming.

Often a lonely pussycat comes to his guardian for attention, and, without thinking, the person assumes that the cat is asking for food. If your cat is overweight, you may have trained him to do just that. So when he comes to you and cries, distract him with an alternate pleasure. Get out a brown paper bag and throw it on the floor—or roll a ping-pong ball. Or pick him up and hug him. Be sure, too, that you approach him with petting and praise at times when he's *not* expecting it. The more secure and relaxed he feels, the easier it will be to change the undesirable pattern of his eating habits.

As the weight goes down, everything else will improve. The eyes will be brighter, the fur silkier, the skin pink and clean. It's easier to pick up a lighter cat. When you do, and you snuggle your nose into the ruff, take a good sniff and enjoy the delicate aroma exuded by the furs of a healthy cat. Don't be surprised at the change in temperament. Your cat may well become more gregarious and alert, yet at the same time more mellow—relaxed but not lethargic.

Guardians are always surprised when a correction in the diet produces an improvement in temperament. To me, it's only logical. A fat, uncomfortable cat who can't clean his own anus is bound to be nervous, grouchy, and lethargic. I frequently remark that they're wasting their cat. They don't know what a beautiful animal they really have. It's not a matter of creating anything new. You're simply uncovering the reality that's already there.

Symptoms

- Looks overweight; thick waist; head and legs appear to be too small for the large body
- Inactivity
- Inability to bend enough to clean himself, causing dirty bloomers and unpleasant smell
- Anal gland impaction
- Dandruff and/or oiliness
- Bad disposition—due to discomfort and feelings of rejection
- Heart disease
- Diabetes
- Digestive problems
- Constipation
- Overeating—as the cat attempts to supply missing or non-digestible nutrients in poor-quality food

Recommendations

- Have a veterinarian check for illness.
- Feed a high-quality diet with as much raw food as possible (see Chapter 2, "Diet," page 66). Be sure to include Anitra's Vita-Mineral Mix and other listed supplements.
- Remove *all* food between meals; leave food out only one-half hour.
- Add to each meal:

  extra ⅛ teaspoon bran;
  1 extra teaspoon finely grated carrot or zucchini;
  2 tablespoons water;
  1/16 teaspoon sodium ascorbate or ascorbic acid (250 units vitamin C).

  The added carrot, zucchini, and bran are low-calorie ingredients that will expand the portion and fill up the tummy. They also give a beneficial side effect of conditioning the stool. And the vitamin C will help the body handle the extra wastes released when the fat melts away.
- Spread food on an extra large plate so it takes longer to eat. The increased area will make it seem like a bigger meal. Remember that the cat is a small animal so he needs only ¼ to ½ cup of food, twice a day.
- Express your love with petting, hugging, play, and kisses instead of snacks.
- Build a feeling of security by giving honest compliments while physical appearance improves (beautiful eyes; sumptuous whiskers).
- Schedule regular play periods to make sure your cat is active each day, or, better yet, get an energetic kitten for your cat to romp with.
- *For kittens:* feed smaller meals more often so kitten's stomach is not stretched—six meals a day up to three months; four meals a day up to six months; three meals a day up to eight or nine months; two meals a day thereafter.

Oily Coat

(see also "Skin Problems")

"The skin is a mirror of the health of the intestines."[3] Skin, functioning as an organ of excretion, normally discharges small amounts of oily wastes through the pores. Oily coat indicates that, for some reason, the skin is eliminating much larger amounts of oily wastes. Either the body is attempting to lubricate an irritation or infection on the skin, such as eczema, or the oil is being used to carry an overload of toxins out of the body. These toxins usually result from a backup of wastes due to failure of an organ, such as the kidney or liver; ingestion of an unusual amount of toxic wastes; a dietary imbalance; a lack of minerals or fatty acids; a diet that is too rich, such as an all-meat regimen; or a slowed metabolism caused by leaving food available between meals. The expelled grease coats the hair and clogs the pores. The oily hair then collects dirt and germs like a dust mop; matting can occur. When the cat tries to clean himself, he recycles his own wastes. Resistance is lowered and disease can result.

Symptoms

- Dandruff, excess shedding
- Greasy fur, fur holding dust and dirt ("dust mop" effect)
- Mats in fur
- Frequent vomiting of hair balls
- Tendency to attract fleas and parasites
- Tendency to skin conditions such as hair loss, itching, redness, rashes, fleas, mange, and ringworm
- Constipation from impacted hair balls or lack of fiber

Recommendations

- Have veterinarian check for problems in kidneys, lungs, intestines, liver, thyroid, and all major organs.
- Especially when diagnosis is vague or inconclusive, homeopathic treatment often succeeds where all else fails. Consult with a classical homeopathic veterinarian.

3. Airola, Paavo, PhD, ND. *Every Woman's Book.* Sherwood, OR: Health Plus Publishers, 1979.

- Remove food between meals to aid in establishing normal metabolic tempo.
- Feed a high-quality diet with as much raw food as possible (see Chapter 2, "Diet").
- Add to each meal to help intestinal efficiency:

    ¼ teaspoon feline digestive enzymes to aid in assimilation of nutrients;

    Extra ½ teaspoon raw grated carrot;

    ½ teaspoon Anitra's Vita-Mineral Mix;

    ½ raw organic egg yolk;

    Extra ⅛ teaspoon bran and ⅛ teaspoon lecithin (in addition to bran and lecithin in Anitra's Vita-Mineral Mix);

    ¹⁄₁₆ teaspoon Green Magma and ¼ teaspoon mixed intestinal flora—continue with these until bottles are finished; then stop.

    The Green Magma and mixed flora can be mixed with 1 tablespoon Homemade Chicken Broth (page 308) and given as liquid medication (page 268).

- Eliminate low-quality and highly chemical foods such as dry food, semi-moist food, and other commercial cat food.
- Increase exercise and schedule two regular play periods a day.
- Encourage circulation by grooming and massaging at least thirty to sixty seconds a day.
- Always thoroughly groom out any mats or loose hair before bathing cat (see Chapter 8, "Grooming").
- If extreme oiliness or very thick waxy oil is present on tail, lower back, or armpits, use a dry shampoo before bath with corn starch or herbal combination given below, then follow with a regular bath.
- Bathe weekly to prevent recycling of wastes as cat washes himself.
- If dandruff is present, rinse with a mixture of 1 quart water and ½ teaspoon white vinegar or lemon juice, and massage into skin.
- Herbal remedies:

    1. Dry shampoo between baths or before a bath with a mixture of 4 tablespoons each of powdered orris root and powdered arrowroot. Leave on ten minutes and then brush or comb out. (Cornstarch also works, but not quite as well.)

2. Calm overactive sweat and oil glands and reduce irritation with a rinse of calendula tea (see page 321).

3. Horsetail tea strengthens sparse, damaged hair. Give 1 teaspoon twice a day in food or mix 1 teaspoon tea with 1 teaspoon chicken broth or water and give as liquid medication (page 268).

4. Lemon Rinse (page 324) or lemon balm tea are mild disinfectants and fungicides. Use as a rinse after bathing.

- Bach flower remedies: cats with oily coats are usually nervous because of a backup of irritating toxins in the system. Give three drops four times a day of the following mixture prepared as given on page 313:

Larch—to encourage self-confidence.

Pancreatitis

The pancreas has two functions: to produce digestive enzymes, which are sent to the stomach through the pancreatic duct, and to produce insulin, which neutralizes excess sugar and makes it possible for the body to burn and use sugar, to change it into starch or fat, or to burn stored fat for use. Literally *pancreatitis* means inflammation of the pancreas; however, the term is also used to refer to a swollen, fatty, or scarred pancreas. Damage to the pancreas can occur in several ways. Long-term poor nutrition will cause the cat to overeat as he attempts to supply the missing nutrients. The consumption of excess fats, sugar, or carbohydrates will overwork the pancreas, and the pancreatic duct may become inflamed and swollen shut. The cat will continue to overeat even though no digestive juices are getting through to the stomach. As inflammation worsens, the pancreas cannot produce the digestive enzymes at all. Gas is then formed in the stomach, and fat is excreted in the stool. Hemorrhaging can occur in the pancreas, followed by scarring and calcification, impairing insulin production and potentially causing diabetes. Cortisone, ACTH, or radiation therapy can damage the pancreas, as can a vitamin B-6 deficiency. Stress, which automatically leads to the release of large amounts of cortisone into the system, is also very hard on the pancreas. Finally, because digestion is poor in pancreatitis patients, the nutrients needed to rebuild the pancreas and reduce scarring are not assimilated from the food, and recovery is often pitifully slow.

Symptoms

- Bits of undigested food in stool; gas
- Vomiting
- Fat, blood, or mucus in stool
- Constipation or diarrhea
- Depression or grouchiness
- Pain
- Poor appetite
- Poor coat quality
- Weakness or coma
- Diabetes or hypoglycemia

Recommendations

- Contact your holistic veterinarian for diagnosis and treatment.
- Keep stomach's workload low by feeding four small meals a day.
- Feed Pancreatitis Diet given below (best choice) or feed a high-quality diet with as much raw food as possible (see Chapter 2, "Diet," page 66). Be sure to include Anitra's Vita-Mineral Mix and other listed supplements.
- If you mix up your own Anitra's Vita-Mineral Mix, double the lecithin in the recipe to help with digestion of fats. If you purchase it in the store, simply add an extra 1½ tablespoons of lecithin to the jar.
- Add to each meal:

    1 feline multivitamin (see "Product Recommendations," in the Appendix);

    ¼ teaspoon feline digestive enzyme powder to aid in digestion;

    ¹⁄₁₆ teaspoon ascorbic acid crystals or sodium ascorbate powder (250 units vitamin C);

    ¼ crushed bioflavonoid pill;

    ¼ teaspoon Delicious Garlic Condiment (see page 317);

    1 drop stevia extract or 1 teaspoon stevia infusion (see page 320).

- Add to food twice a day 10 mg vitamin B complex (divide 50 mg capsule into five parts).
- Keep fat intake low (that is, butter, oils, and the like).

- If necessary, reduce gas by giving:

  1 charcoal tablet one hour before dinner (see "Giving Pills," page 266); continue for three days only. Charcoal turns the stool black but don't worry;

  ¼ teaspoon mixed intestinal flora (see "Product Recommendations," in the Appendix).

- If diarrhea (page 358) or constipation (page 347) are present, follow suggestions given in those sections.
- Reduce scarring by giving contents of a punctured 100-unit vitamin E (alpha tocopherol) capsule in food once a day for two weeks; then reduce to 400 units a week.
- Exercise gently to stimulate metabolism and lower stress.
- Bach flower remedies: pancreatitis cats are sometimes out of sorts because of discomfort. Give three drops four times a day of the following mixture prepared as given on page 313:

  Aspen—for anxiety over feeling sick;
  Mustard—for those who feel gloomy.

Pancreatitis Diet

Use the raw food diet given on page 74, but choose low fat chicken or turkey or ground beef that is 85 percent to 90 percent fat free. For the vegetable portion, choose steamed peas or asparagus. Use Homemade Chicken Broth (page 308) for the liquid.

Parasites

(Roundworm and Tapeworm, Hookworm and Coccidia)

The four most common intestinal parasites are roundworm, hookworm, tapeworm, and coccidia. It's sometimes hard to tell which kind of worms a cat has. You have to take the cat to the veterinarian and let him collect a swab of stool and examine it.

If worms are diagnosed, there are three ways that you can handle the problem.

453

1. You can let the doctor give you the medication to administer, with specific instructions about fasting a number of hours beforehand and further instructions about what the first full meals should consist of. He may also prescribe a laxative.

2. Under certain circumstances, the doctor may advise that the cat be hospitalized because worming medicine is caustic and toxic and the cat may vomit. The veterinarian may want to be sure that the medication stays in the cat to do the job.

3. Call your holistic vet and follow his instructions.

Do not buy any kind of worming preparations over the counter. Worming preparations are all poisons, and you must be very careful how you use them. *Worming should always be supervised by a veterinarian.*

Here are specific details on these intestinal parasites.

Roundworm and Tapeworm

If the cat has roundworms or tapeworms, you have the choice of using the herbal worming procedure formulated by herbalist Juliette de Bairacli Levy, which is given in *Dr. Pitcairn's Complete Guide to Natural Health for Dogs and Cats* (Rodale Press). I did this with my Big Purr, who had tapeworms. I had been horrified to see those awful wiggly, maggoty things in his stool. So I made an appointment to take Purr to the vet to have a stool sample taken and examined under the microscope. Purr seemed healthy as a horse, pert and chipper as ever, so I knew that this was not an emergency situation. I dropped off the stool sample at the veterinarian's, saying that I suspected it was tapeworm.

Tapeworms are carried by fleas, but Purr has no fleas; I asked the doctor where in the world Purr could have picked up tapeworms. He said that they could have been lying dormant in the intestine for years. As the standard worming medication is so toxic, my local veterinarian agreed that I should first try the natural herbal remedy along with the fasting and herbal laxatives that Dr. Pitcairn recommends. He was enthusiastic and curious to see if the natural method would work, and both he and Dr. Pitcairn agreed that if it didn't work we could always give the standard chemical treatment afterward.

The herbal worming procedure took about a week (see "Treatments," below).

The hard part was not so much stuffing powdered herbs and wet, gooey, crushed garlic into empty gelatin capsules or even tracking down a source of such esoteric ingredients as wormwood and powdered rue (see Appendix, "Product Recommendations"). The hardest part was keeping myself from feeding Purr during the fast days as required. Purr was several ounces overweight, and I knew it. That fast did him a world of good, and he took it very well. But even though I knew that what I was doing was really great for him in every way, still I found it very, very hard not to feed him. It certainly made me understand the "food is love" syndrome that many guardians fall victim to.

I waited a couple of weeks after it was over, examining Purr's stool every morning for signs of wiggly, maggoty things. When everything still remained normal-looking, I told my veterinarian that the herbal worming seemed to have worked. Like all holistic treatments, it benefitted Purr's general health as well.

The herbal remedy is more trouble, but the big plus is that it is safe and the side effects are all beneficial. A fast of a couple of days renews the cat's youth. The backlog of wastes and toxins in the system is cleaned and flushed out. Purr was much more playful and jaunty after the experience. I would recommend the herbal worming to any guardians who are able to give pills to their cat (see "Giving Pills," page 266). If we can avoid giving poisonous chemicals simply by spending some extra time, I feel that it is a very small price to pay and results in huge dividends in health for the cat.

Symptoms

- Weight gain or loss; loss of appetite or voracious appetite; a big, fat distended abdomen or a bony appearance
- Dull coat or hair loss
- Egg sacs in the stool or around the anus—about the size of a sesame seed or a grain of rice, they are white, and they sometimes move in a maggot-like fashion
- Dragging the anus along the carpet (this could also be a sign of impacted anal gland)
- Constant licking of anal area
- Vomiting—sometimes worms can be seen in the vomitus

Recommendations

- Have veterinarian check the cat and run tests on stool sample.
- Administer medication according to veterinarian's instructions *or* follow the herbal worming procedure below:

Herbal Worming Procedure

Note: Keep your holistic veterinarian informed as you proceed. These herbs are less toxic than the conventional worming medications, but rue and worm-wood are still poison herbs.

What you need:

Rolled oats—soak 1 cup oats in water 24 hours; repeat every day

Herbal deworming capsules *or* make your own. Buy large gelatin capsules at your health food store or pharmacy. Open the capsules and fill with:

       1 part raw garlic sliver

       1 part wormwood (ground)

       1 part rue (powder)

Capsules containing ¼ teaspoon senna and a pinch of ginger

Castor oil

Charcoal tablets or capsules

Deworming Slurry

Into a small pan mix:

1 cup raw milk or skim milk

1 teaspoon slippery elm powder

Bring to a simmer and stir until thickened.

Add ¼ teaspoon honey and 3 tablespoons soaked oats.

Cool and refrigerate.

Fish and Oat Food

**2 tablespoons cod, haddock, or halibut simmered in small amount of
water on a low flame for one minute**
½ cup soaked oats
1½ teaspoons Anitra's Vita-Mineral Mix (see page 68)
Garlic, raw crushed—a piece the size of a pea

Allow fish to cool and then mix with other ingredients.

Here's the plan:

Days 1, 2, and 3	Feed morning and evening meals of fish and oat food
Day 4	Fast on water (see "Fasting," page 286)
	Before bed give 1 teaspoon castor oil (see "Giving Liquid Medication," page 268)
Day 5	Fast on water
	Early evening—give 4 deworming capsules (see "Giving Pills," page 266)
	30 minutes later give 1 teaspoon castor oil
	45 minutes after that give ½ cup deworming slurry
Days 6, 7, and 8	Give 3 meals a day of deworming slurry
	In morning, 30 minutes before meal, give 2 deworming capsules
	Before bed give ¼ teaspoon senna with a pinch of ginger (in capsules)

Days 9, 10, 11, and 12	Feed fish and oat food twice a day
After 12th day	Feed normal high-quality diet; the raw food diet is best. Be sure to include at least some raw food at each meal and ⅛ teaspoon Delicious Garlic Condiment (page 317) daily for 1 month, then 3 times a week
	Give 1 charcoal tablet or capsule in the morning at least a half hour before breakfast 3 times a week for 2 weeks
	Add ¼ teaspoon mixed intestinal flora (see "Product Recommendations," page 489) to all meals. Continue until container is used up.

Hookworm

Hookworms are found mostly in hot humid areas of the country. They enter the cat through the mouth if he eats something that is contaminated with hookworm larvae such as prey or partially rotten meat. Kittens can become infected from the mother's milk. Larvae can also penetrate the skin, usually around the toes. They then migrate to the small intestine, where they chew into the intestinal wall and suck blood and tissue, leaving small ulcers that bleed and become infected. Large numbers of eggs are laid, most of which pass out in the feces.

Hookworms are a serious matter. They cause anemia, dehydration, and, finally, death. If your vet diagnoses hookworms in your cat, follow his directions to the letter and have your cat retested every three or four months because now you know you are living in a hookworm area. Be sure to keep his resistance high by feeding a high-quality raw food diet.

Symptoms

- Weakness; listlessness
- Dehydration
- Weight loss, eating voraciously but not gaining weight
- Diarrhea or loose stool, dark red or black stool

- Rash between toes
- "Scooting" on floor

Prevention

- Feed as much raw food as possible in regular high-quality diet or, better still, feed the all-raw-food diet (see page 71).
- Add ⅛ teaspoon Delicious Garlic Condiment (page 317) to food every day.
- Give PetGuard yeast and garlic wafers as treats.

Recommendations

- See veterinarian for a firm diagnosis and proper treatment.
- After treatment follow suggestions for prevention above.
- For a few weeks after treatment add to each meal:

    ⅟₁₆ teaspoon ascorbic acid crystals (250 units vitamin C);
    ¼ teaspoon mixed intestinal flora powder.

Coccidia

Coccidia are microscopic intestinal parasites. Consequently, they are the most difficult of the parasites to diagnose. Like all parasites they are a sign of a weak immune system. If you acquire a skinny stray or a cat with a bloated abdomen, he has probably been eating a poor-quality diet. Ask the vet to do a general physical exam and to include a fecal smear under the microscope for coccidia.

Follow the vet's directions to the letter. Recheck the cat a few weeks after the treatment to be certain no coccidia remain. Your vet will tell you when the best time would be for this follow-up exam.

Symptoms

- Voracious appetite but skinny cat
- Distended abdomen
- Persistent soft stools or diarrhea

Recommendations

- See the veterinarian for firm diagnosis and treatment.
- Follow additional treatment suggestions under "Hookworm" above.

Poisoning

(see "vomiting")

Respiratory Infections

Respiratory infections can range anywhere from a sniffle and a sneeze to bronchial congestion or the lungs filling up with fluid. Often the first symptom is the appearance of eye discharge or runny eyes. If the lungs are filling up with fluid, the cat cannot breathe, and you will need to have the veterinarian relieve this condition by tapping the lungs. A high temperature is a good sign. It means that the immune system is responding as it should. Germs and viruses will not thrive if the body temperature is higher than normal.

Respiratory infections can be frightening because they do tend to spread to other cats, especially in households where no raw food is fed. As with all ailments, an ounce of prevention is worth a pound of cure. If any cat in the house exhibits respiratory symptoms, isolate the patient, keep him warm and snug, and then dose all of your cats with garlic and vitamin C (ascorbic acid) and commence the acid-alkaline swing (see page 307) for six to eight days. Repeated respiratory infections indicate that the immune system is weak; germs and viruses are finding it easy to take hold and multiply. Like any other disease in the feline, the earlier you catch it, the easier it is to cure.

Symptoms

- Sniffle, sneeze, or cough
- Runny eyes
- Spraying mucus from nose that is either clear, white, or yellow
- Change in stool
- Elevated temperature

- Appetite loss
- Listlessness
- Rattling when breathing
- Coughing up phlegm
- Breathing with mouth open

Recommendations

- Have veterinarian make a diagnosis to make sure the problem really is an infection and not a tumor or asthma.
- For all cats in the household add ⅛ teaspoon Delicious Garlic Condiment (page 317) to all meals until infection is cleared up and/or use PetGuard yeast and garlic wafers as treats.
- For all cats in the household commence the acid-alkaline swing (see page 307) for six to eight days. Include vitamin C at 250 units per cat per meal on the acid days.
- If possible, isolate the patient.
- Provide a snug retreat (see page 304).
- Give eye and nose drops before each meal, using normal saline solution (see page 270). Because the tear ducts run from the inner corner of the eyes into the back of the throat, by giving eyedrops you also treat the throat. Nose drops, if done well, treat the nose, the sinuses, and also the throat. Also, because some cats refuse to eat when they can't smell their food, giving nose drops before the meal can help the cat who has a stuffy nose smell his broth.
- For two to three days stop all solid food and put patient on Homemade Chicken Broth (page 308) three to four times a day. If the patient refuses the broth, let him fast for one day. Then on the second day you may flavor the chicken broth with ½ teaspoon PetGuard Savory Seafood or a one-inch piece of sardine in tomato sauce so he can smell the broth even with his stuffy nose.
- Give ¹⁄₁₆ teaspoon ascorbic acid crystals mixed with chicken broth or 250 units vitamin C as a pill (see "Giving Pills," page 266) four to six times a day.
- Mix ¹⁄₁₆ teaspoon Delicious Garlic Condiment (page 317) with ½ teaspoon butter. Give morning and evening. Most cats lap it off your finger. If not, give it as a pâté (see "Force Feeding," page 286).
- Check the teeth. Tarter and filth in the mouth create an excellent breed-

ing ground for germs that can spread disease to the nose, throat, and bronchial tubes.

- If the infection persists for more than a week, or if it seems to be spreading into the lungs, you should consult a classical veterinary homeopath if you have not already done so (see "Homeopathy," page 211), or you may need to resort to antibiotics (see "Antibiotics," page 242).
- Herbal Remedies—add to your saline solution for eye and nose drops:

    1. If the patient has a stuffy nose and a nasal discharge, goldenseal will kill germs and help shrink tissues and echinacea will kill viruses. Give three drops herbal nose drop solution in each nostril and each eye twice a day. See "Administering Eyedrops and Irrigating Tear Ducts," page 270, and "Giving Nose Drops," page 276, and follow directions for herbal solution with golden seal or echinacea.

    2. If the veterinarian says the patient's throat is red and sore, use five drops chamomile extract or tincture instead of goldenseal in the nose drop solution and give as both nose and eyedrops (page 271) since the tear ducts run into the back of the throat.

    3. For bronchial or lung congestion Dr. Pitcairn has recommended goldenseal elixir (page 322) taken ¼ dropperful twice a day twenty minutes before meals. Also, the patient can inhale the vapors of strong fenugreek tea or eucalyptus oil in hot water.

- Bach flower remedies: cats with respiratory problems feel gloomy and tired and can become depressed. Give three drops four times a day of the following mixture prepared as given on page 313:

    Mustard—to dispel gloom;
    Crabapple—to help cleanse;
    Hornbeam—to strengthen.

Ringworm

(see also "Parasites")

Ringworm is not a worm; it is a fungus like athlete's foot. Once it infects an area it usually grows outward, spreading in a circle and then starting other new little circles. I have seen ringworm as a tiny little spot on a healthy cat's nose or as extensive areas of baldness all over the body of an old or sick cat. Ringworm patches may be hairless or the hair may break off to a stubble. The skin may become thickened and gray or pink to red in color and sometimes will be scabbed from scratching. It may itch but often it does not. Ringworm is mildly contagious and can spread to other animals or to humans whose resistance is low.

I always deal with any fungus or parasitic infestation in three ways: topically, with an application on the skin; systemically, by alkalizing the system and making sure the overall quality of health is improved; and environmentally, by throwing everything possible into the clothes dryer, including the bed pillows and cushions, and running it on the hottest cycle for twenty minutes.

Ringworm is around us all the time. You and I probably have ringworm spores on our skin right this moment. So why don't you and I have ringworm lesions? For the same reason that we don't have a virus cold even though we are frequently breathing viruses into our nose and lungs. We are healthy, our resistance is high, and our acid-alkaline balance is such that our bodies do not make a good home for viruses, germs, or parasitic infestations. If I see ringworm on a cat, my main concern is not the ringworm. Ringworm can be cured. My main concern is to discover what has caused the cat's immune system to become weak and allow the fungus to take hold. Has the cat perhaps been eating foods with preservatives or a protein source where the amino acids are over processed and indigestable? Commercial semimoist and dry foods are good examples of that. Cats who eat commercial dry or semimoist food seem much more prone to pick up fungus and parasitic infestations. Or perhaps someone new was taking care of the cat, and food was left available between meals several days in a row. The resultant slowing of the metabolism causes a backlog of wastes. The pores then need to expel these wastes and this changes the pH (acid-alkaline) balance of the skin, allowing the ringworm to thrive. All of these things are easy to correct.

The other possibility is that the cat is under some sort of stress or the cat's system is currently fighting some other infection somewhere in the body. Perhaps the cat's system will win out in the end, but in the meantime the battle is depleting it and giving the ringworm a chance to take hold. The thing to do, along with your topical application at the site of the ringworm, is to mobilize and arm your cat's body with extra vitamins in addition to the raw food diet. Now is the time for all those additional supplements you occasionally add to the food.

Fulvacin (gresiofulvin) is a drug in pill form that stops growth of ringworm

463

fungus. It works like chemotherapy in that it poisons the whole system in order to kill the ringworm on the skin. It passes through the digestive system into the blood, and some of it is deposited in the keratin layer under the skin. From there it is incorporated into the hair follicle. Some of the Fulvacin will be excreted in the urine and some in the stool.

In some cases conventional veterinarians will shave the cat, treat the ringworm topically, and then give the cat Fulvacin for several weeks. This always gets rid of the ringworm but, as you can imagine, it takes a big toll on the cat's general health, thus making him even more susceptible to repeated infestations not only of ringworm from spores still in the environment but also of fleas, mites, viruses, germs, or anything else that might come along. There is a long list of possible complications that can result from the use of Fulvacin: loss of protein through the kidneys, skin rashes and hives, diarrhea, lowered white cell count, lethargy, brain and nerve damage, mental confusion, vertigo, vomiting, or foaming at the mouth, or painful tongue. I have never used Fulvacin on a cat under my care.

Symptoms

- Bald patches spreading outward in a ring—usually starts on forehead and around ears and muzzle but can appear on toes or anywhere
- Skin is gray or red or scabbed
- Sometimes itching and scratching (but not usually)
- Usually (but not always) shows up fluorescent under veterinarian's ultraviolet light (but so do petroleum jelly and golden seal)
- Always shows up purple after five days in veterinarian's test tube culture.

Recommendations

- Fast one day a week on Homemade Chicken Broth (see page 308).
- Change immediately to the raw food diet (page 70) or to a high-quality canned food with as much added raw food as possible (see Chapter 2, "Diet," page 66). Be sure to include Anitra's Vita-Mineral Mix and other listed supplements. If preparing homemade diet, use grated carrot or zucchini or baked carrot (see baked carrot recipe, page 81) as the vegetable portion.

- Add ¹⁄₁₆ teaspoon Delicious Garlic Condiment to morning meal to help alkalize system (see page 317).
- Add to each meal:

  Feline multivitamin;
  ¼ teaspoon mixed intestinal flora powder;
  Extra ¼ teaspoon yeast (in addition to yeast in Anitra's Vita-Mineral Mix) or give two or three PetGuard yeast and garlic treats a day (see Appendix, "Product Recommendations").

- Once a day give 5 mg zinc (crush pill and divide into 5 mg portions and add to meal).
- Once a week give 400 units vitamin E capsule (alpha tocopherol) and a vitamin A and D capsule (10,000 units A and 400 units D).
- An all-raw-food diet is best of all (page 71), but at the minimum feed one tablespoon raw liver or raw organic egg yolk three or four times a week.
- Feed twice a day; remove all food between meals, leaving only water available.
- Bach flower remedies: cats who contract ringworm are often oversensitive, reticent types. This can manifest itself either as withdrawal to secluded nooks or as an overreadiness to strike out for little apparent reason. Give three drops four times a day of the following mixture prepared as given on page 313:

  Elm—to help cope with the situation;
  Mimulus—to allay fears;
  Aspen—for those who retreat and hide;
  Holly—for those who sometimes lash out.

Treating the Skin

- Clip hair away on *and around* affected areas.
- Bathe the cat (see page 189), soaping twice using 1 part dishwashing detergent and 8 parts water for first soaping. Then, for the second soaping, use Betadyne surgical scrub. Allow the second soaping to remain on the cat for five to ten minutes before rinsing thoroughly. While you're waiting, thoroughly clean the claws and cuticles (see page 282). The ring-

worm spores will be concentrated in the dirt around the cuticles and can reinfect the cat whenever he scratches. You can finish with a rinse of one quart water and 18 drops of goldenseal extract.

When the cat is dry, paint each ringworm patch with golden seal extract in alcohol. (Do not use alcohol-free extract.) Paint the ringworm once a day for five days then every other day until you see fuzz growing back where the ringworm used to be.

Treating the Environment

- Chlorine bleach kills ringworm spores. Wash bedding (yours and the cat's), adding ⅛ cup chlorine bleach to the wash. Dry bedding and pillows in the dryer on hot temperature.
- Wash windowsills and floors with one part chlorine bleach to 30 parts water.
- Continue adding chlorine bleach to all cleaning water for a few weeks *after* all signs of ringworm are gone from the cat.

Roundworm

(see "Parasites")

Skinniness

(see "Weight Loss")

Skin Problems

(see also "Allergies," "Dandruff," "Feline Acne," "Fleas," "Mange Mites," "Parasites," "Ringworm")

Bald patches can be caused by any number of things. Sometimes a cat will try to scratch a mat out of his fur, pull too violently, and end up with a bald patch where some of the hair was torn away. This is not serious, and eventually it grows back in. However, most skin conditions, including some cases of bald patches, are symptoms of more serious underlying problems. Poor circulation to the skin due to a heart condition or clogged capillaries can cause thinning hair or bald patches. Many medications can also cause hair loss, especially on cats eating low-quality diets. When dealing with skin problems, the holistically-oriented caregiver does well to remember what Dr. Pitcairn teaches, "A symptom is the body's logical response to an intolerable situation." Rather than suppressing the problem with steroids, the holistic approach allows the skin to do its work while focusing on building up the general health and finding and eliminating the underlying problem. In other words, better out than in.

Skin problems are notoriously difficult to diagnose. The term "skin allergy" has become a catchall phrase used whenever the cause of a skin problem cannot be readily diagnosed. The cat is usually treated with one of many cortisone preparations that cause the symptoms to disappear immediately. This can feel very satisfying to all concerned—the doctor, the cat, and the guardian—until the medicine is used up and the same old problem comes back, always worse than ever. It then becomes apparent that the cortisone has merely suppressed the symptoms. It has done nothing to cure the cause of the problem. The cause—and therefore the problem—is still there. Furthermore, cortisone suppresses not only the symptoms but the entire immune system, leaving the patient very vulnerable to both infection by germs and viruses and infestations by parasites and fungus. In other words, it's a quick fix that does much harm and no lasting good. This covering up of the symptoms also tends to make the problem more and more difficult to treat and cure. I do not recommend it.

Many conventional veterinarians like to use steroids (cortisone) because of its impressive quick-fix effect. Because it has acquired a bad reputation among informed and health-oriented caregivers, conventional veterinarians will sometimes call them something else such as corticosteroid, artificial steroid, antiinflammatory, anti-itch, desensitizer, allergy shot, and the like. So always ask the veterinarian if the ointment, shot, or pill is a corticosteroid or cortisone derivative (see "Cortisone and Other Steroids," page 244).

As the skin is the largest organ of excretion, the body will attempt to eliminate excess wastes or poisons through the pores if there is too much for the kidneys, intestines, and so on to handle or if one of these other organs weakens or breaks down. For example, kidney disease patients usually have terribly oily, dandruffy skin and coat. Alter the diet to "cushion" the kidneys, and the skin will improve. The skin will do its best to pass the poisons out of the body until the load becomes too much for the pores to handle and clogging occurs. Then dirty skin becomes inflamed and parasites and germs can infest the buildup of oil and dirt lodged at the base of each hair, causing redness, itchiness, or bald spots. Nervousness, frustration, and loneliness are the leading causes of stress-triggered skin problems; so single cats and unneutered cats are more prone to problems in this area. Cats on poor diets will always have large amounts of wastes for the body to dispose of because of the nutritional imbalances. An all-meat diet is another possible cause: protein imbalance overwhelms the kidneys, while the absence of sufficient bulk and roughage clogs the intestines. Here again, excess wastes are pushed out of the pores. The chemicals in commercial foods will overload the organs of excretion as well as the liver and, here again, the skin will bear the brunt. The use of aluminum utensils or fluoridated water can compound the problem. The sugar in many commercial foods promotes an acid system where funguses and parasites can thrive. The groomer's use of powders, compounds, sprays, ointments, creams, or rinses adds to the burden of wastes the overworked skin must try to slough off, and the condition worsens.

But take heart—the skin renews itself rapidly. So once the quality of the diet is improved, toxins are eliminated, stress is reduced, and regular exercise is begun, you should see a definite improvement in just three to six weeks (unless cortisone treatment was used; in that case a change for the better will be more gradual).

Treatment by an experienced holistic veterinarian, preferably a classical homeopath, will always speed up the cat's healing. Homeopathy works very fast on skin problems (see "Homeopathy," page 211).

Symptoms

- Scratching or biting at the skin
- Bald patches
- Pus, scabs, or inflammation
- Excess ear or eye discharge
- White or brown dandruff
- Stud tail (see "Stud Tail" page 474)
- Oiliness
- Bad odor
- Redness, thickened skin, grayness
- Nervousness
- Waxy build-up around cuticles

Recommendations

- Have veterinarian check for parasites, fungus, or problems with liver, kidneys, intestines, glands, or other internal organs.
- Upgrade diet and begin internal cleansing to decrease wastes in system and take the burden of waste disposal off the skin:

    1. Fast on Homemade Chicken Broth (see page 308) for one to three days; then one day every week thereafter, until general health improves;
    2. Feed high-quality diet with as much raw food included as possible (see Chapter 2, "Diet," page 66). Be sure to include Anitra's Vita-Mineral Mix and other listed supplements;
    3. Remove all food between meals, leaving only water always available;
    4. If you mix up your own Anitra's Vita-Mineral Mix, add extra ½ cup of fine wheat bran to the recipe (see page 68); if you purchase it at the store, add 2 tablespoons of fine wheat bran to the jar. Temporarily increase the amount of Anitra's Vita-Mineral Mix in each meal to 1¼ teaspoons;
    5. Add antistress supplements (see page 305) to diet;
    6. Add to each meal ¼ teaspoon PetGuard skin and coat oil supplement (see "Product Recommendations" in the Appendix);
    7. Eliminate all preservatives and other chemical additives and coloring from diet (check labels carefully—even on brands purchased from the health food store or from the veterinarian);
    8. Never store food in can; aluminum molecules and lead sealers can "bleed" into food once can has been opened;
    9. Give 5 mg zinc once a day for two weeks; then decrease to 2–3 mg a day to strengthen skin and help body process out toxins.

- Feed raw homemade food whenever possible. Use alkalizing vegetables such as garlic, kelp, kombu seaweed, carrots, zucchini, and string beans.
- Neuter or spay, and eliminate other stresses in the environment.
- Bathe every one to four weeks—use only natural preparations on the skin. (See "The Bath," page 189.)
- Stimulate the flow of blood in the small capillaries that feed the skin

by grooming and massaging vigorously once a day (see Chapter 8, "Grooming").

- Keep grooming tools nice and clean.
- Encourage exercise. Have a play time at least once a day. (See "Game Time and Encouraging Exercise," page 48.)

Starvation

(see also "Weight Loss")

Starvation goes beyond skinniness. Cats with little or no fat are thin or emaciated; cats whose fat is all used up and who are burning their own muscle mass to stay alive are starving. Starvation occurs if a cat cannot eat because of a mouth infection, tumor, or injury. Mouth injuries happen when cats fall out of windows or from balconies. Starvation can also happen if a cat is trapped somewhere and cannot escape—such as in a garage or deserted apartment—or when they are thrown out to survive on their own by humans who rationalize that, "cats can take care of themselves." Strays and feral cats will starve if they are injured and cannot hunt or get to a food source. A nursing mother can starve if she fails to find enough food to feed both herself and her kittens. Heavy snows over a long period of time will cause starvation among the wild population. When all the fat and most of the muscle mass have been burned up, the cat becomes too weak to stand, too weak to lift her head, and finally too weak to draw a breath. Toward the end, liver tissue becomes fatty. Hepatic lipidosis sets in and the cat dies.

Rescuing a starving cat and bringing her back from the brink of death is one of the most emotionally rewarding experiences a human can have, but it takes a lot of work and heroic patience and, above all, restraint. You can kill a starving cat very quickly by feeding too much at once. You must tread a delicate balance between nourishing the patient and over-feeding. Starvation shrinks the stomach to the size of a nickel; it won't stretch back to normal overnight. Starving cats are *always* dehydrated, so there will be little or no digestive juices in the stomach.

The ideal course of action is to take the cat to a veterinarian where she can be put on intravenous fluids for hydration and nourishment. At the same time, she can be fed tiny amounts by mouth every two hours. The IV fluids will greatly help her body to digest and assimilate the food taken by mouth. CAUTION: The veterinarian must have patience too. A well-meaning vet can kill a starving cat by giving even one vaccine. Vaccines challenge the immune system. This cat does not have enough strength to meet the challenge and would surely be overcome. Likewise, she must not be given a poison such as worming medication, ear mite medication, or a flea preparation. Not even a tiny bit. She would never survive it. Instead, call your holistic veterinarian, follow her guidance, and read the appropriate sections in this book for safe alternatives. (*Note*: Even the herbal worming given on page 456 would be too strong for such a cat.)

This was the dilemma faced by my friend Emma who is the caregiver and manager of a feral cat colony in Riverside Park. She found a female gray tabby whom she had never seen before collapsed next to a footpath lying on her side, a filthy bag of bones, her eyes staring, her lips drawn back from her teeth. She was gasping and hissing as she struggled for every breath. Emma rushed her to a vet who determined that she had hepatic lipidosis brought on by starvation and was too far gone to save. Rather than put her to sleep, Emma brought her over to me.

Three years later, as I write this, I can reach out and stroke the silky fur between her ears. She's just finished dinner, and she lies stretched out in her usual place at the foot of the bed, relaxed and content. Her name is Linda. It suits her; Linda means "pretty" in Spanish.

Symptoms

- Emaciation: the thigh muscle that should be thick and wide is thin and can be easily circled with your index finger and thumb
- All bones are prominent; spine, ribs, and hips can be easily felt
- Coat is dry, dull, and clumping
- Eyes are dry; cat has difficulty blinking; sometimes cannot close them
- Eye and/or nose discharge
- Weakness, staggering, collapsing, inability to rise
- Inability to support head with neck. Head and neck dangle when cat is lifted
- Cold ears and extremities
- Gasping for breath; breathing with mouth open
- Hepatic lipidosis (fatty liver; last stage before death)

Recommendations

Day One: The Rescue

- Wrap cat in blanket, towel, or jacket to conserve heat.
- Provide outside source of heat. The snug retreat (page 304) is, by far, the best. Until you assemble it, you can use: (1) heating pad turned on low, under two layers of towel; (2) clip-on light with 60 or 75 watt bulb within one foot above the patient; or (3) plastic bottle of hot water dropped into a very thick sock under one layer of towel. If you use the hot water bottle, remove when it has cooled; otherwise it will rob heat from the cat's body.
- Support head and neck when carrying.
- Buy a dropper that holds one teaspoonful from the baby section in the drugstore.
- Read "Giving Liquid Medications" (page 268) and "Dropper Feeding Liquids" (page 289).
- Give Bach Flower Rescue Remedy, prepared as given on page 313. Give three drops six times a day. Put the drops on the inside of the lip or on the gums, teeth, or tongue.
- Try to get veterinary assistance. Intravenous or subcutaneous fluids would be invaluable now (see "Subcutaneous Fluids," page 297). Do *not* permit the use of vaccines, ear mite medications, worming medications, or flea preparations. If antibiotics are used, be sure there is a specific reason and that it is not done simply as a matter of policy.
- If cat is staying at the vet's:

  1. Request (a) a heat lamp or (b) a heating pad on low under two layers of towel;
  2. Bring some of your own supply of fortified soup because veterinary dropper feeding formulas are usually high in sugar and should be avoided.

- Whether or not the patient is getting IV or subcutaneous fluids, feed ½ teaspoon fortified chicken broth (see recipe below) every two hours. Remember to feed *very slowly*, one drop at a time. If the cat can swallow successfully, she has a chance.

Fortified Chicken Broth

You will really increase your odds for success if you have a pint or so of homemade chicken soup stashed in your freezer. If not, buy some organic chicken thighs and make some as soon as you can (see page 308). In the meantime, buy some plain chicken broth in the health food store, one made without onions. Into a shot glass, measure:

One tablespoon chicken broth (include a drop or two of fat or butter);
Few grains or a pinch of mixed intestinal flora powder;
One drop organic raw honey;
⅛ feline multivitamin, crushed;
Few grains vitamin C complex.

Store covered in refrigerator. Heat to a little above room temperature by standing in a bowl of hot water. *Never use a microwave.* Give ½ teaspoon every two hours by dropper very slowly, drop by drop. After two or three feedings, empty out the shot glass and start fresh. The shot glass is small enough to make it easy to (a) heat up the broth, (b) suck the soup into the dropper, and (c) mix up the very small amount you need.

Moving Onward

After the third or fourth feeding, if the cat seems more comfortable or if, heaven be praised, she seems to be asking for more, try giving ¾ to 1 teaspoon for each two-hour feeding—but be sure to go slowly, drop by drop. When Linda was brought to me, she could only handle ½ teaspoon at a time for the first two days. I continued feeding her throughout the first night and gave three feedings during the second and third nights.

Day by day, you can gradually increase the amount to 2 or 2½ teaspoons or even a tablespoon per feeding and feed only every three or four hours and only once at night. After a day of this, you can start mixing a tiny bit of canned PetGuard chicken into the soup, but continue the supplements and keep the food runny enough to be fed by dropper.

When the cat is able to eat on her own, gradually increase the proportion of solid food. Go at the cat's pace and be patient! The stomach needs time to stretch back to a normal size. Don't give more than two tablespoons at a time. (Measure accurately!) Feed every four hours for the first two weeks. During this time, change over to the raw food recipe on page 74.

Stud Tail

Stud tail is caused by overactive sebaceous glands found along the top of the tail and up the base of the spine. It happens when these glands oversecrete sebaceous fluid and the pores become clogged. The excess fluid becomes hardened into a substance closely resembling half-dried ear wax. It is waxy rather than oily and usually dark brown or black.

Stud tail, as the name implies, is found on almost all unneutered males, but unfortunately it is not limited to them. I've seen it on neutered males and females, too, when food is left available between meals and the diet is not up to par. Neutering or spaying almost always helps to clear up the condition provided the diet is adequate and food is removed between meals. A cat with stud tail will be supersensitive in that area. If left untreated, the pores and glands of the tail become inflamed, clogged, and infected. Pain and itching result, and the cat may bite the tail until it bleeds, so be extremely gentle. The fur over the area usually becomes matted and sometimes falls out because hair roots are clogged by wax and lack nourishment.

I have noticed that every year at the cat show someone comes up with what he claims is a surefire cure for stud tail. These cures always involve spraying, powdering, or dipping the tail into something. The reason why there is always a new cure every year is that none of them ever work. Many breeders who show cats have their own private "secrets" that they hold to despite their inefficiency and the possible health hazards involved in implementing some of the more bizarre solutions. I have been made privy to secrets involving kitchen cleanser, kerosene, and Windex. Forget it. Stud tail is a result of what is happening inside the cat's body because of a backup of wastes. It is caused by poor feeding and a slowdown of the metabolism combined with overactive sebaceous glands. You can't cure stud tail from the outside alone; you must also neuter the cat and rethink the diet.

However, I too have a secret remedy, temporary though it may be. This is

474

the best method I have found to date and is to be used in the beginning while you are waiting to get an appointment to have the cat neutered and while the new, improved diet is slowly doing its work to permanently eradicate the condition. That hard, waxy grease cannot be washed off by any kind of detergent, soap, alcohol, or you-name-it. It's impossible. So don't try to wash it off. Instead, powder the area heavily with finely ground cornmeal and cornstarch and let it set for five minutes while it absorbs the greasy exudation. Then comb, shake, and jiggle the greasy cornmeal out. Do it again a few more times; you can use cornstarch alone for the last round for a more thorough cleaning. Then wash just the tail and lower back with a solution of one part dishwashing detergent and five parts water. Rinse and follow with a complete shampooing with a shampoo for oily hair from the health food store. This cornmeal and cornstarch trick can also be used around the ears after an oily ear medication. Cornmeal and cornstarch are harmless—because they have no perfumes or conditioners. Here's another case where the cheapest and easiest also turns out to be the best.

Symptoms

- Copious oily or black waxy exudations from lower back to halfway down tail.
- Discolored, oily, waxy tail hair that is prone to clumping and matting
- "Dust mop" effect—hair on tail attracts dirt and dust
- Skin on top of tail and on lower spine is red and very sensitive
- Sebaceous glands are inflamed and swollen
- Cat gnaws tail with teeth

Recommendations

Temporary

- Gently comb out loose hair and split any mats and remove them. (See "Splitting the Mats," page 180.)
- Powder liberally with a mixture of half fine corn meal and half cornstarch and wait five minutes; then comb out (as described above).
- Wash tail with a 1 to 5 solution of dishwashing liquid and water. Repeat two times.

- Shampoo the whole cat with a castile shampoo for oily hair or Dr. Bronner's liquid soap.
- Rinse with water and then with Lemon Rinse (see page 324).

Permanent

- Have cat neutered or spayed.
- Feed high-quality diet with as much raw food included as possible (see Chapter 2, "Diet"). Be sure to include Anitra's Vita-Mineral Mix and other listed supplements.
- Add to each meal:

  ⅛ teaspoon lecithin (in addition to lecithin in Anitra's Vita-Mineral Mix);

  ¼ teaspoon cod liver oil *or* once a week give the contents of one capsule containing 10,000 units vitamin A and 400 units vitamin D;

  a feline multivitamin (can be mixed in a meal or given as an appetizer).

- Fast on Homemade Chicken Broth (see page 308) one day a week until condition is completely normal.
- Increase exercise. (See "Game Time and Encouraging Exercise," page 48.)
- Shampoo, and rinse with Lemon Rinse (as given in "Temporary" treatments above).
- Herbal remedies:

  1. Instead of cornstarch, you can powder the tail with a mixture of 4 tablespoons each orris root and arrowroot;
  2. Instead of using the Lemon Rinse after bathing, use a strong tea of witchhazel and burdock root *or* use calendula tea if there are sores and scabbing.

- Bach flower remedies: stud-tail cats are usually tense from not being neutered, from irritating chemicals in the diet, or from itchy, burning skin. Give three drops four times a day of the following mixture prepared as given on page 313:

  Crabapple—to aid in cleansing the system;
  Impatiens—to calm anxiety;
  Elm—to help cope with itching and discomfort.

Tapeworm

(see "Parasites")

Teeth and Gums

Cats develop tartar on their teeth just as you and I do. And, like humans, some produce more tartar than others; some produce tartar that is soft and can be flicked off with a fingernail, while others, like my Priscilla, produce tartar that resembles granite. It amazes me how often I find tartar-covered teeth on the cats I groom. I always check the teeth and gums at the end of the grooming, especially on new clients. What really surprises me is when I find tartar coating the teeth of a cat who has just been to the veterinarian for a yearly exam. Either the veterinarian's examination leaves something to be desired, or, if he indeed saw the tartar on the teeth of an otherwise healthy cat and didn't suggest doing anything about it, that veterinarian's standards for feline oral health are a lot different from mine.

While my cats are healthy I always take the opportunity to keep their teeth beautifully clean. It's much more difficult to clean the teeth of a cat who is already elderly or sick because no veterinarian wants to chance the use of anesthetic on a cat whose health is already compromised. All too often, I have seen distraught guardians caught between a rock and a hard place when they are told that, on the one hand, their beloved feline companion cannot get well unless his abscessed teeth and germ-laden tartar are removed. On the other hand, the vet is afraid to put the patient under anesthetic to do the necessary dentistry because the cat is too ill and might not make it through. It's easier to *keep* the teeth clean than to be faced with a monumental problem that compromises the prognosis of a sick cat.

Tartar leads to inflamed, infected gums because it is full of germs. Germs make the mouth smell bad. (I've often seen my own veterinarian, Dr. Gil, open a cat's mouth, put his nose up to it, and sniff. Then he does the same with the ears.) Germs and infection in the mouth can lead to infection in the nose, throat, and upper respiratory tract, or, at the other end, in the anal glands—in fact anywhere the cat licks to wash himself.

When I see tartar on the teeth, I always try to scrape off a nice big piece with my thumbnail and show it to the guardian. I then invite him to examine the cat's gums while I open the mouth and lift the lip. I point out the inflammation at the gum line, and I explain that this hurts. Mouth pain can make a cat nervous and ir-

477

ritable. Because eating hurts, this is a possible reason why a cat is off his food and getting thin. New clients often respond that they have been giving dry food every day, so they can't understand why the teeth are not in perfect condition. *Dry food does not clean the teeth.* It never has, and it never will. Even the dry food companies have never claimed that dry food cleans the teeth. Cats fed an exclusive dry food diet for years frequently have the worst tartar of all. Dry food can exercise the teeth and jaw muscles, which is also important. But because commercial dry food has so many drawbacks—indigestibility, low protein quality, and abundance of poisonous chemicals—it is much more rational to provide other substances for teeth and jaw exercise that have only beneficial side effects and no drawbacks. As discussed in Chapter 2, in the section "Delicious Treats and Crunchies" (page 78), I prefer such things as PetGuard Purrlicious treats or PetGuard yeast and garlic wafers, raw or broiled chicken neck vertebrae, and many wholesome treats packaged by reputable natural pet food companies.

Whether or not I am able to get some of the tartar off the cat's tooth with my thumbnail, I always recommend a visit to a veterinarian who will make a really thorough and complete examination. If the condition of the mouth was passed over during the previous visit, one wonders what else might have been passed over as insignificant. Several vets I know will scale (clean) the teeth during the yearly office visit without using anesthetic. If a cavity is discovered or if the teeth have deteriorated to such a state that an extraction is necessary, then the patient can be admitted to the hospital for dental cleaning and extraction under anesthetic. Follow the usual procedure for caring for the cat in the hospital and after arriving home (see Chapter 10, "Selecting Methods of Treatment and Seeking Professional Help").

If I find that the red gums persist, as often happens with cats who have been for many months on a low-quality diet, I have had good results using the acid-alkaline swing, and rubbing teeth and gums with a cheddar cheese paste. The first time I tried this on a cat with inflamed gums, I figured it couldn't hurt, because all the side effects are beneficial anyway.

I have seen red and swollen gums respond immediately to treatment with cortisone (see "Cortisone and Other Steroids," page 244). However, the response lasts only as long as the cortisone is being taken. In other words, cortisone does not cure but only masks the symptoms. Cortisone, as everyone agrees, is death on the immune system. It's like killing a fly with a bazooka. I wouldn't allow it.

The persistent swollen gum problem is prevalent today. My own feeling had always been that this is simply a weakness a particular cat has that bubbles to the surface and explodes when the diet is overprocessed, low in quality, and laced with too many artificial colors, artificial flavors, artificial scents, and poisonous chemicals used as preservatives. However, Dr. Pitcairn, who has a specialty in immunology, has pointed out to me that although the diet is certainly extremely important, the real underlying cause is vaccinosis: a chronic disease state caused by repeated vaccinations. This causes the immune response to become confused and begin attacking some part of its own body—in this case, the gums. A combination of diet, homeopathy, and topical therapy is the only way I know to gradually correct the problem.

Perfect health is a body's natural state. It is a rule of nature that the body will proceed toward perfect health when we eliminate all poisons and other destructive elements and give it all the support we can to build the robust health that is its birthright.

Symptoms

- Inflamed, infected, swollen, and/or bleeding gums
- Bad breath
- Brown or yellow deposits of tartar on teeth, particularly on back teeth
- Bad smell on fur or on fur of cat friends
- Loss of appetite or weight loss
- Can lead to infection in the nose, throat, upper respiratory tract, or in the anal glands—anywhere the cat licks to wash himself
- Sensitive mouth; doesn't want teeth to be examined or touched.

Recommendations

- Visit vet to have teeth cleaned. Try to find a vet who has high standards and who will try to clean the teeth without anesthetic during the exam. If he then finds reason for use of anesthetic, give extra supplements (see "Anesthetics, Tranquilizers, and X-rays," page 245).
- Add to each meal:

  1/16 teaspoon ascorbic acid crystals or sodium ascorbate (250 units vitamin C);

  1/4 teaspoon Delicious Garlic Condiment (see page 317).

- Put cat on acid-alkaline swing (see page 307) using kombu seaweed (page 318) on the alkaline days and vitamin C given twice as frequently on the acid days.
- Inflamed gums are usually a sign of a weakened immune system. To help build up the immune system switch to a raw food diet (see page 71).
- To prevent serious immune deficiency diseases, consult an experienced holistic veterinarian, preferably one who practices classical homeopathy (see Homeopathy," page 211).
- Clean your cat's teeth. Be sure to read the sections on communication (page 262) and administering medications (page 260) before you begin. Then choose one of the following options:

  1. Make a paste of mild cheddar cheese and water. Wipe it on the teeth and gums. It tastes good; it's harmless; the salt content soothes and shrinks red swollen gums; and the enzyme that changes milk into cheddar also dissolves tartar. I don't suggest that it will remove serious, thick tartar, but it makes a pleasant maintenance treatment when used four or five times a week.

  2. Leba III dental spray by LebaLab, Inc. This product is made from derivatives of a special kind of rose and mint. It is harmless and will eventually rid the teeth of even serious tartar buildup. Do not feed for twenty minutes before and after treatment, and don't permit the cat to groom himself for twenty minutes after or you'll have tartar-free fur but no effect on the teeth. All you do is spray a tiny bit of Leba III into the space between the cat's cheek and the teeth, twice a day for one month. The spray mixes naturally with the saliva, changes the chemistry in the mouth, and gradually dissolves the tartar. It also kills bacteria under the gums. It's easy to use because you don't have to spray it on the teeth. After the tartar is gone, you can maintain oral health by spraying only three times a week—or sometimes using the cheddar cheese paste instead. *Note: If your cat is being treated homeopathically, check with your homeopath before using. Mint can antidote some homeopathic remedies.*

- Every day give three or four PetGuard Purrlicious treats.
- Herbal remedies: to soothe and heal sore and bleeding gums, add ¼ tea-

spoon salt to ½ cup strong lukewarm calendula infusion (page 320) and pat on gums with a cotton ball to cleanse teeth and gums daily.

Upper Respiratory Infections

(see "Respiratory Infections")

Urination, Random Wetting

(see "Feline Urologic Syndrome (FUS)")

Vomiting

A cat's alimentary canal is relatively short, so vomiting is fairly common. If it does not frequently recur, it is usually not serious. Cats often vomit hair balls in spring and autumn when shedding is copious (see "Hair Balls," page 397). Overeating, eating food that is too hot or too cold, or wolfing too much food at once can all cause vomiting. These things are very easy to check out and to correct.

Vomiting becomes serious if it is prolonged or repeated, because fluids and minerals are lost. The resulting dehydration, if it is prolonged, can result in coma and death. Repeated, persistent vomiting is always a symptom of a serious problem within the body. Adverse drug reaction or poisoning by toxic plants or chemicals such as bathroom cleaners, sprays, or flea treatments will all provoke violent vomiting. Vomiting is often a symptom of disease, intestinal parasites, or inflammation of certain organs, such as in hepatitis, gall bladder inflammation, and pancreatitis.

In the case of repeated or prolonged vomiting, telephone a veterinarian immediately. Before you call, make a list of pertinent facts to tell him: (1) any other symptoms, such as lethargy, diarrhea, constipation, or bad temper; (2) what the vomit consists of—food, white foam, hair balls; (3) if the vomiting was unsuccessful; and (4) when it occurred (before or after meal), time of day, and how often.

Symptoms

- Vomiting unsuccessfully (dry heaves)
- Vomiting of foam, food, mucus, hair balls, plant leaves or pieces of plastic
- House plant's leaves have been nibbled and torn

Recommendations

- Be sure cat did not swallow a string, thread, foreign object, or toxic plant leaves
- Have your vet check for intestinal parasites
- Check to be sure food is not too hot or too cold.
- Be sure food is not spoiled.
- Be sure cat isn't eating too fast—spread the food around on a large platter.
- Be sure cat is passing a normal stool daily.
- Withhold food for three hours and if no vomiting recurs, give ¼ cup clear broth (chicken or vegetable) with 1 teaspoon slippery elm syrup (see page 319). Continue to fast the cat on the chicken broth and slippery elm for one to two days; then gradually reintroduce regular food (see "Fasting," page 286).
- If vomiting recurs, call veterinarian and describe symptoms as suggested above.

Weight Loss

(see also "Starvation")

Weight loss, especially sudden weight loss, is always a sign that something is wrong. The wise guardian will immediately begin to look for any other symptoms such as copious drinking, frequent urination, soft stool, restlessness, voracious appetite, lack of appetite, craving heat, seclusion, or any change of normal behavior. If one or more additional symptoms are present, make a note of them to tell your vet when you go for the appointment. If a cat displays two or three of these symptoms, I always recommend asking for a complete blood test including thyroid values. Weight loss can be an early symptom of kidney disease, liver disease, hyperthyroidism, or irritable bowel syndrome. Intestinal parasites can also cause weight loss. In all cases, diagnosis is made twice as easy with a blood test. If your cat is diagnosed as having any of the above diseases, look that disease up in the contents or in the Index. There is much you can do to smooth the path toward recovery.

If skinniness is not a result of obvious starvation or of a large litter draining nutrients from the mother cat and if there is no tumor or other disease, then it is a symptom of *anorexia*—refusal to eat—or *malabsorption*—inability to utilize food even though large quantities are being eaten.

Anorexia

Anorexia, or refusal to eat, can have a physical cause, such as bad teeth or gums, intestinal blockage by hair or tumor, nasal congestion that prevents the cat from smelling his food (see "Respiratory Infections," page 460), or pain anywhere in the body (as in postoperative anorexia). Several antibiotics can cause anorexia.

If your feline friend seems fairly normal in all other ways, another possibility is that he may be suffering from what I refer to as the "finicky eater syndrome." Because the smell of food triggers the brain, if the cat is smelling food every time he passes the food dish or a vagrant breeze wafts the odor his way, sooner or later that trigger mechanism wears out and the cat begins to eat less. Ninety percent of all finicky eaters have guardians who leave food available between meals or give frequent snacks. Often finicky eaters also have dandruff. Add to this a slowed metabolism, which results in inefficient digestion, and you have a skinny, undernourished cat surrounded by food. Because circulation and respiration also are slower when food is left available, less blood and oxygen are reaching the organs. Less blood pumping through the organs means the cat will age earlier. A cat who smells food all day long cannot live as long as he could have if his guardian cleared away all food between meals.

Anorexia can occur if a cat is dehydrated, making it uncomfortable to swallow. Kidney disease, hyperthyroidism, diabetes, and irritable bowel syndrome nearly always cause dehydration. A blood test will tell which one, if any, are present. Finally, anorexia can result from a psychological shock, most often the loss of a playmate or beloved guardian. The cat decides that life is finished and begins to move toward death.

Malabsorption

Malabsorption is the inability of the body to process and extract nutrients from food consumed, even though the diet may be of high quality and large amounts are eaten. Possible causes include a lack or imbalance of digestive enzymes or hy-drochloric acid in the stomach due to disease or old age; overstuffing the stomach so digestion is inefficient; overactive peristaltic action, which passes food through the stomach and intestine too quickly, as in irritable bowel syndrome; coating and clogging of the intestinal walls resulting from lack of roughage in the diet or from the use of bentonite or silica based clumping litter; or a slowed metabolism caused by leaving food available all day long. Poor circulation due to heart dis-ease can also cause malabsorption, as can the failure of a major digestive organ such as the pancreas or the liver. Then the cat's resistance to heat, cold, stress, and disease becomes dangerously low, and the undernourished system is easy prey to any disease, germ, or virus that happens along.

If a cat is not eating because he is suffering from a disease or recovering from illness (some antibiotics tend to suppress appetite), a very good way to tempt him is with Chicken Super Soup (see page 309). I used to bring this soup along with me when I was working night duty at Dr. Rowan's Cat Practice. Very often cats who could not be tempted even with baby food would break their fast for Chicken Super Soup. The liquid will help keep a sick cat from dehydrating. Also, it is high in protein, calcium, phosphorus, the B vitamins, and vitamin C.

When trying for weight gain in elderly cats or cats depleted from sickness, give three or four moderate-size meals a day. Don't feed large meals, because they are too hard to digest and assimilation will not proceed efficiently. Always leave at least four hours between meals for the same reasons.

A word about the finicky eater syndrome: if you acquire a cat who refuses your delicious high-quality food, you have probably inherited a finicky eater ad-dicted to the taste of sugar, salt, and the rotten taste of sterilized spoiled meat or MSG or any of the other items commonly found in supermarket cat food, which we do not use for obvious reasons. Do not despair; just be patient and read the section in Chapter 2, "Diet," on making the change to a new diet (page 82). Don't be afraid to add one or two of the bribe foods for a week or so.

No matter what the cause—or even if the cause is undiagnosed—a classical homeopathic veterinarian will be a great help in remedying the situation.

Symptoms

- Skinniness, boniness
- Nervousness, easy startling, trembling

- Copious drinking or inability to drink
- Refusing all food—even favorite treats—or eating only a lick or two
- Recurrent health problems (eye, ear, respiratory, and so on), ringworm, or repeated infections
- Porous bones that break easily, hip dysplasia
- Lethargy, oversleeping, lack of stamina
- Seeking warmth and seclusion, easy chilling
- Excess shedding and/or dandruff
- Tooth and gum problems

Additional symptoms of anorexia

- Inability to drink
- Refusal to eat or only eating small amounts
- Urination and defecation slow almost to a stop

Additional symptoms of malabsorption

- Voracious appetite but skinny body
- Diarrhea or constipation

Recommendations

Note: Anorexia and malabsorption are always symptoms of a serious underlying problem. Consult a veterinarian to determine and correct the underlying cause, such as tooth problems, pancreatitis, hairball impaction, and so on; otherwise any treatment will merely be a stopgap measure.

- Provide warmth and security so cat will burn up fewer calories (see "Snug Retreat," page 304).
- Feed high-quality diet with as much raw food as possible (see Chapter 2, "Diet"). Be sure to include Anitra's Vita-Mineral Mix and other listed supplements.
- Feed three or four smaller meals a day for easier digestion.
- Don't be afraid to use bribe foods (see page 75).
- Never leave food available between meals.

- Add ¼ teaspoon feline digestive enzymes to all meals.
- Add antistress supplements to each meal (see page 304).
- Eliminate stress in cat's environment; provide calm reassurance and love (see "Stress: A Cat's Natural Enemy," page 255).
- Massage the cat's body lightly all over, especially on the sides of the spine, thighs, throat, and shoulders to stimulate blood flow and speed up metabolism.
- Invite cat to gentle play two or four times a day to speed metabolism. Before the meal is the best time for play.

Additional treatments for anorexia

- Give ginseng royal jelly mixture (found in health food stores, some pharmacies, Chinese stores). Serve two to three drops twice a day (can be mixed into one teaspoon Homemade Chicken Broth [page 308] and given as liquid medication [page 268]).
- Force-feed four to five times a day until appetite returns (see page 286).
- Feed ¼ cup or less at a time; *do not overfeed* (see "Force Feeding," page 286).
- Be sure cat gets plenty of liquid. Serve Fortified Chicken Broth once or twice a day two hours away from meals. (See page 473.)
- Bach flower remedies: if anorexia occurs because of sadness due to the loss of a friend, give three drops three times a day of the following mixture prepared as given on page 313:

> Walnut—to help break old bonds and encourage a smooth transition;
> Honeysuckle—to help move on after past despair.

Additional treatments for malabsorption

- Fast for one day on Fortified Chicken Broth (see page 473) to help cleanse the system.
- Add ¼ teaspoon feline digestive enzymes to each meal (see "Product Recommendations," in the Appendix).
- Add extra ¼ teaspoon bran (powdered or flaked) to all meals to help clean intestinal walls.

- Be sure there is some fat in the diet to slow emptying of stomach. Add ¼ teaspoon butter (not margarine) to food if in doubt.

Worms

(see "Ringworm"; see "Parasites")

Wounds

(see "Injuries")

APPENDIX

Product Recommendations

I recommend the products below because, over many years, these are the ones I rely on totally. There may be other products in each category that are dependable and good—but I have learned, after 35 years of experience, that the products below are the ones I can recommend without reservation because they have maintained the same high quality from the first day I tried them. These products are available in health food stores, quality pet stores, or online. Contact information is given for those companies whose products may be a bit difficult to find. Any product found in a pet store can be ordered from Pet Stop by calling 212-580-2400. They also carry hard-to-find items such as calcium lactate powder and Resco professional grooming combs.

Grooming and Flea Products

- *Anitra's Herbal Eye Wash*, from PetGuard.
- *Flea Comb*, from PetGuard.
- *Herbal Collar*, from PetGuard.
- *Natural Herbal Ear Wash*, from Halo, Purely for Pets.
- *Natural Animal Coat Enhancer*, from Natural Animal, Inc.
- *Wax-O-Sol*, from Life Science Products.

Supplements, Foods, and Treats

COMMERCIAL FOOD:

- *PetGuard.* My preferred brand of commercial food is PetGuard's canned food in all flavors. (*Note:* I don't use the dry food as a food, but rather as a treat, five or six pieces at a time; see PetGuard dry food in Treat section below.) Website: www.PetGuard.com; Phone: 904-264-8500.

FELINE DIGESTIVE ENZYMES:

- *Feline Digestive Enzymes (powder; also contains high-quality probiotics),*from PetGuard. Website: www.PetGuard.com; Phone: 904-264-8500.
- *Feline Formula Digestive Enzymes,* from Dr. Goodpet. Website: www.Good-Pet.com; Phone: 800-222-9932.

FELINE MULTIVITAMINS:

- *Nu-Cat,* from Vetri-Science Laboratories. Website: www.VetriScience.com; Phone 800-882-9993 or 802-878-5508, ext. 3195.
- *Tabby Tabs,* from U.S. Animal Nutritionals. Website: www.USAnimalNu-tritionals.com; Phone: 800-526-5227.

HERBS:

- *Angelica Herbs.* Any hard-to-find herbs, such as wormwood and rue, which are needed for herbal deworming, can be purchased from this little herb shop in New York City. Phone orders: 212-677-1549.

MIXED INTESTINAL FLORA:

- *Jaro-Dophilus + FOS Powder,* from Jarrow Formulas. Website: www.Jar-row.com; Phone: 310-204-6936.

NUTRITONAL SUPPLEMENTS:

- *Anitra's Vita-Mineral Mix,*from PetGuard, Inc. Website: www.PetGuard.com; Phone: 904-264-8500.
- *Calcium Lactate Powder,* from WowBow Distributors Ltd.
- *Green Magma,* from Green Foods Corporation. A freeze-dried powdered barley grass juice supplement.

- *Nu-Salt* (salt substitute), from Cumberland Packing Corp.
- *Yeast and Garlic Powder,* from PetGuard.
- *Yerba Prima Psyllium Husk Powder,* from Yerba Prima. A natural dietary fiber and mucoid.

Scratching Posts and Supplies

- *Karate Kat,* from Pet Stop. Website: www.PetStopNYC.com; Phone: 212-580-2400.
- *Felix Katnip Tree,* from Felix Katnip Tree Company. Website: www.FelixKatnipTreeCompany.com; Phone: 206-547-0042.
- *Top Cat,* from Top Cat Products. Website: www.TopCatProducts.com; Phone: 866-874-1221.
- *Disposable corrogated cardboard scratching pad.* Various brands.
- *Sticky Paws,* Felines, Inc., Website: www.StickyPaws.com. Transparent, medical-grade, double-sided adhesive strips that deter scratching.

Treats

- *Anitra's Natural Cat Treat,* from PetGuard. A whey and yeast treat; irresistably delicious, they are rich in the B complex vitamins and easily digested protein.
- *Purrlicious,* from PetGuard. Low fat organic chicken treat that helps to keep teeth clean.
- *Liv-A-Littles,*from Halo, Purely for Pets. Freeze-dried treats; I prefer the chicken, salmon, or cod.
- *PetGuard Dry Food (all flavors).* Give five or six a day as a treat.
- *Dinner Party,* from Halo, Purely for Pets. Powdered meat, vegetable, and herb treat to sprinkle on your cat's meal.
- *Yeast and Garlic Wafers,* from PetGuard. Given as a treat, adds protein and essential B complex vitamins.
- *Kitty Kaviar,* from Kitty Kaviar. An all-natural fish treat made from dried Bonito filets, shaved paper thin. Bonito is a schooling fish of the mackerel family.
- *Organically Grown Catnip,* from PetGuard.
- *Nori Seaweed.* Various brands; sold in health food stores.

Recommended Books and Periodicals

Bach Flower Therapy, by Mechthild Scheffer; HarperCollins Publishers Ltd., 1998.

Dr. Pitcairn's Complete Guide to Natural Health for Dogs and Cats, by Richard H. Pitcairn, DVM, PhD, and Susan Hubble Pitcairn; Rodale Press, 1982 and 2005 (revised edition).

Food Pets Die For: Shocking Facts about Pet Food, by Ann N. Martin; NewSage Press, 2002.

Health and Healing Wisdom (Journal), Price-Pottenger Nutrition Foundation, P.O. Box 2614, La Mesa, CA 91943-2614; Website: www.ppnf.org; Phone: 800-366-3748 or 619-462-7600.

Homeopathy: Beyond Flat Earth Medicine, by Timothy Dooley, MD, ND; Timing Publications, 2002.

How to Get Well: Dr. Airola's Handbook of Natural Healing, by Paavo Airola, ND, PhD; Health Plus Publications, 1984.

Implementing a Community Trap-Neuter-Return Program, by Bryan Kortis; The Humane Society of the United States, 2007.

It's a Cat's Life, by Anitra Frazier with Norma Eckroate; Berkley Books, 1990.

King Solomon's Ring, by Konrad Lorenz; Crowell, 1952.

On Aggression, by Konrad Lorenz; Harcourt Brace Jovanovich, 1974.

Stop the Shots: Are Vaccinations Killing Our Pets? by John Clifton; Foley Square Books, 2007.

The Abandoned, by Paul Gallico; Knopf, 1950, 1987.

The Neighborhood Cats TNR Handbook: A Guide to Trap-Neuter-Return for the Feral Cat Caretaker, by Bryan Kortis: Neighborhood Cats, Inc., 2576 Broadway, Suite 555, New York, NY 10025; Website: www.NeighborhoodCats.org; Phone: 212-662-5761; published 2004.

The Wild Life of the Domestic Cat, by Roger Tabor; Arrow Books, 1983.

Holistic Veterinarians

Listed below are organizations that promote holistic veterinary care. Some veterinarians are entirely holistic and devote their practice to one or more of the holistic modalities. Others combine holistic treatments and allopathic medicine; this is usually referred to as an integrative practice. My recommendation is to find a veterinarian who has a completely holistic practice. Even better would be to find a veterinarian who is a specialist in the particular modality you need and who studies and practices only that. Obviously, I am not familiar with all of the many doctors who appear on the referral lists of the organizations below. I simply present them here as a place for you to start your search. For more information on how to determine if a vet is holistic or is a classical homeopath, see Chapter 10, "Selecting Methods of Treatment and Seeking Professional Help," page 211.

Animal Natural Health Center. Website: www.drpitcairn.com. This website provides a referral list of veterinarians who have taken professional-level training in veterinary homeopathy in Dr. Richard Pitcairn's year long *Professional Course in Veterinary Homeopathy*, a classically based, tested approach to homeopathy.

International Veterinary Acupuncture Society, P.O. Box 271395, Ft. Collins, CO 80527-1395; Website: www.ivas.org; Phone: 970-266-0666. A nonprofit organization dedicated to promoting excellence in the practice of veterinary acupuncture as an integral part of the total veterinary health care delivery system. The Society endeavors to establish uniformly high standards of veterinary acupuncture through its educational programs and accreditation examination. The organization seeks to integrate veterinary acupuncture and the practice of western (conventional) veterinary science.

The Academy of Veterinary Homeopathy, P.O. Box 9280, Wilmington, DE 19809; Website: www.theavh.org; Phone: 866-652-1590. This professional association was founded in 1995 by Drs. Richard Pitcairn, Christina Chambreau, and Jana Rygas. It is for licensed veterinarians who use homeopathy in their practices. Many members have been trained by Dr. Pitcairn. The Academy provides information on training, an annual conference, a mentor program for veterinarians presently in training, and a journal for members. The website lists member veterinarians.

The American Holistic Veterinarian Medical Association, c/o Dr. Carvel G. Tiekert, Executive Director, 2218 Old Emmorton Road, Bel Air, MD 21015; Website: www.ahvma.org; Phone: 410-569-0795. This organization functions as a forum for the exploration of alternative and complementary areas of health care in veterinary medicine. The website lists member veterinarians.

The American Veterinary Chiropractic Association, 442154 E. 140 Road, Bluejacket, OK 74333; Website: www.animalchiropractic.org; Phone: 918-784-2231. Formed in 1989, this organization furthers the profession of animal chiropractic. The AVCA has a threefold mission: to function as a professional membership group, to promote animal chiropractic to professionals and the public, and to act as the certifying agency for doctors who have undergone animal chiropractic training. One of the major goals of the AVCA is to provide the public with unhampered access to ethical doctors trained in animal chiropractic.

The National Vaccine Information Center, 204 Mill St., Suite B1, Vienna, VA 22180; Website: www.nvic.org; Phone: 703-938-0342. The National Vaccine Information Center is a national nonprofit organization dedicated to preventing vaccine injuries and deaths through public education and defending the right to informed consent to vaccination.

BIBLIOGRAPHY

Airola, Paavo, PhD, ND. *Every Woman's Book.* Sherwood, OR: Health Plus Publishers, 1979.

———. *How to Get Well: Dr. Airola's Handbook of Natural Healing.* Sherwood, OR: Health Plus Publishers, 1984.

Bach, Edward, MD, and F. J. Wheeler, MD. *Bach Flower Remedies.* New Canaan, CT: Keats Publishing, Inc., 1952, 1979.

Ballard, Juliet Brooke. *Treasures from Earth's Storehouse.* Virginia Beach, VA: A.R.E. Press, 1980.

Black, Dean, PhD. *Health at the Crossroads: Exploring the Conflict between Natural Healing and Conventional Medicine.* Springville, UT: Tapestry Press, 1988.

———. *Regeneration: China's Ancient Gift to the Modern Quest for Health.* Springville, UT: Tapestry Press, 1988.

Boone, J. Allen. *Kinship with All Life.* New York: Harper & Row, Publishers, 1954, 1976.

———. *The Language of Silence.* New York: Harper & Row, Publishers, 1970.

Bragg, Paul C., ND, PhD, and Patricia Bragg, PhD. *The Miracle of Fasting.* Santa Barbara, CA: Health Sciences, 1983.

Bremness, Lesley. *The Complete Book of Herbs: A Practical Guide to Growing and Using Herbs.* New York: Viking, 1988.

Clifton, John. *Stop the Shots: Are Vaccinations Killing Our Pets?* New York: Foley Square Books, 2007.

Davis, Adelle. *Let's Eat Right to Keep Fit.* New York: Harcourt Brace Jovanovich, 1970.

———. *Let's Get Well.* New York: Harcourt Brace Jovanovich, 1965.

de Bairacli Levy, Juliette. *The Complete Herbal Handbook for the Dog and Cat.* New York: Arco, 1986.

Dooley, Timothy, MD, ND. *Homeopathy: Beyond Flat Earth Medicine.* San Diego, CA: Timing Publications, 2002.

Elkins, Rita. *Stevia: Nature's Sweetener.* North Orem, UT: Woodland Publishing, 1997.

Frazier, Anitra, and Norma Eckroate. *It's a Cat's Life.* Rev. ed. New York: Berkley Books, 1990.

Gallico, Paul. *The Abandoned.* New York: Knopf, 1950, 1987.

Bibliography

Gawain, Shakti. *Creative Visualization*. New York: Bantam, 1978, 1982.

Gray, Robert. *The Colon Health Handbook*. Oakland, CA: Rockridge Publishing Company, 1983.

Healing Currents Newsletter: Trends in the Art of Health. Tapestry Press, P.O. Box 653, Springville, UT 84663. 800-333-4290 or 801-489-3265.

Home Research Projects. Membership service of Association of Research and Enlightenment, P.O. Box 595, Virginia Beach, VA 23451.

Integral Yoga magazine. Satchidananda Ashram, Yogaville, Rt. 1, Box 172, Buckingham, VA 23921.

Kloss, Jethro. *Back to Eden*. Twin Lakes, WI: Lotus Press, 1997.

Kortis, Bryan. *Implementing a Community Trap-Neuter-Return Program*. Washington, D.C.: The Humane Society of the United States, 2007.

———.*The Neighborhood Cats' TNR Handbook: A Guide to Trap-Neuter-Return for the Feral Cat Caretaker*. New York: Neighborhood Cats, Inc., 2004.

Lappé, Frances Moore, *Diet for a Small Planet*. New York: Ballantine, 1971, 1982.

Lazarus, Pat. *Keep Your Pet Healthy the Natural Way*. Indianapolis/New York: Bobbs-Merrill Company, 1983.

Lorenz, Konrad. *King Solomon's Ring*. New York: Crowell, 1952.

———. *On Aggression*. New York: Harcourt Brace Jovanovich, 1974.

Maltz, Maxwell. *Psycho-Cybernetics*. Englewood Cliffs, NJ: Prentice-Hall, 1960.

Martin, Ann N. *Food Pets Die For: Shocking Facts about Pet Food*. Troutdale, OR: NewSage Press, 2002.

Milani, Myrna M., DVM. *The Body Language and Emotion of Cats*. New York: William Morrow, 1987.

Muramoto, Naboru. *Healing Ourselves*. St. Louis: Formur International, 1973.

Ohsawa, George. *Macrobiotics: An Invitation to Health and Happiness*. Oshawa Foundation, 1434 Corson, Los Angeles, CA, 1971.

Pitcairn, Richard H., DVM, and Susan Hubble Pitcairn. *Dr. Pitcairn's Complete Guide to Natural Health for Dogs and Cats*. Emmaus, PA: Rodale Press, 1982 and 2005.

Plechner, Alfred J., DVM, and Martin Zucker. *Pet Allergies: Remedies for an Epidemic*. Very Healthy Enterprises, P.O. Box 4728, Inglewood, CA 90309, 1986.

Plummer, George Winslow. *Consciously Creating Circumstances*. Kingston, NY: Society of Rosicrucians, 1939.

Prevention Magazine. 33 East Minor St., Emmaus, PA 18049.

Richard, David. *Stevia Rebaudiana: Nature's Sweet Secret*. Ridgefield, CT: Vital Health Publishing, 1999.

Scheffer, Mechthild. *Bach Flower Therapy*. New York: HarperCollins Publishers Ltd., 1998.

Sivananda, Swami Paramahansa. *Yoga, Health, and Diet*. Rishikesh, India: Yoga-Vedanta, Forest Academy, 1958.

Tabor, Roger. *The Wild Life of the Domestic Cat*. London: Arrow Books, 1983.

Venture Inward magazine. Association for Research and Enlightenment, P.O. Box 595, Virginia Beach, VA 23451.

Wilbourn, Carole C. *The Inner Cat*. Briarcliff Manor, NY: Stein and Day, 1978.

INDEX

Abrasions, 315
  soaking solution for, 283
Abscesses, 222, 224, 315, 316, 409–11
  irrigating, 281–82, 410–11
Abused animals, dealing with, 26–27. *See also*
  Communication with cat; Nervousness
Accidents. *See* Injuries
Acid-alkaline diet swing, 57, 307–8, 460
Acidophilus, 293
Acne, feline. *See* Feline acne
ACTH, 333, 451
Acupressure, 214
Acupuncture, 211, 213, 214, 310
Adolph's Salt Substitute, 243
Adrenal glands, 332, 333
Affirmation, 217–19
Aggression. *See* Anger; Fear; Nervousness
Aging cat, 225, 247
  feeding, 89–90
  litter box considerations, 110
AIDS, feline. *See* Feline AIDS (feline immu-
  nodeficiency virus)
Airplane travel, 126–29
Allantoin, 316
Allergic dermatitis, 329
Allergies, cat, 71, 223, 328
  recommendations, 329–32
  symptoms of, 329
Allergies, human, 123–25
Allopathic medicine, 213, 232, 233, 253–54,
  328–29
Alpha tocopherol. *See* Vitamin E
Altering your cat. *See* Neutering; Spaying
American Society for the Prevention of Cru-
  elty to Animals (ASPCA), 45, 87, 116, 143
Ammonia, 109

Anal glands, 224, 225, 339, 455
Anemia, 223, 226, 380, 458
Anesthesia, 258
  declawing and, 116
  for grooming, 158, 159, 161, 182
  impacted stool and, 295
  juvenile neutering and, 139
  for routine procedures, 230
  stress of, 229
  for teeth cleaning, 187, 477
  vitamin C supplements and, 245
Anger, 22–23, 245. *See also* Fear
  biting and, 22–23
Animal Poison Control Center, 45, 46
Anorexia, 222, 298, 362, 483, 485–86
Antibiotics, 225, 237, 242–43, 323, 330, 374
  feline urologic syndrome (FUS) and, 387
  injected in meats and poultry, 70, 77
  natural, 307
Antifreeze, 47, 427
Antispasmodics, 420
Antistress supplements, 129, 132, 245–46, 257,
  305, 367
Appetite, 82, 83–84, 222, 226, 286, 318. *See also*
  Anorexia; Diet
Arnica, 260
Arrowroot, 315
Arthritis, 71, 214, 241, 286, 328
  diet for, 318, 335–36
  herbs and, 318–20, 333–35
  litter box and, 107, 225
  recommendations, 334–35
  symptoms of, 225, 333–34
  types of, 332
Artificial colors, 59, 61, 66, 332, 441, 445
Artificial flavors, 59, 61, 441

Index

Ash. *See* Feline urologic syndrome (FUS)

Aspen, 23

Assimilability of cat foods, 62–63. *See also* Malabsorption

Asthma, 223, 241, 328

Autoimmune diseases, 139, 241, 328, 420. *See also individual diseases*

Autonomic nervous system, 259

Babies, new, 119–21

Baby foods, 66, 268, 348
recipes, 287

Bach, Edward, 215, 216, 313

Bach flower remedies, 6, 23, 129, 215–16, 259, 313–14, 325. *See also* Feline health problems, guide to common

Baked Carrot or Winter Squash Recipe, 81

Baking soda, 97, 347

Balcony, falling off, 43

Bathing your cat, 151, 189–97, 353
flea treatment, 197, 395

Beef by-products, 61–62

Behavior modification, 211

Behavior of cats, changing patterns of, 16–19, 223

Benzoate of soda, 61

Beta-carotene, 319

BHA, 61, 259, 433

BHT, 61, 259, 433

Bibliographies, 239

Bile, 432

Birth of kittens, problems related to, 137

Biting:
anger, 22–23
of claws, 222
dealing with bite, 25–26
dealing with cat, 24–25
by declawed cats, 116–17, 121
fear, 20–22, 26
"hugging," 13
during play with cat, 17–19
preventing, 23

Bizzy-Kitty Scratching Pad, 112

Bladder, weak, 385. *See also* Feline urologic syndrome (FUS)

Bladder stones, 63, 64, 224, 387, 423–26

Blindness, 250
causes of, 336–37
recommendations, 338
symptoms of, 337–38

Blood, sugar in. *See* Hypoglycemia

Blood pressure, 155, 356

Blood tests:
for feline infectious peritonitis (FIP), 377
for feline leukemia and AIDS, 380–81
for hyperthyroidism, 400
for liver disease, 433

Boarding your cat, 131

Body language of cats, 11–12. *See also* Communication with cat

Body odors, 352
causes of, 338–39
recommendations, 339–40
symptoms of, 339

Bonemeal, 68

Boric acid solution, 270, 271–72, 325

Brain problem, 255

Bran, 55, 67, 124, 198, 331, 349, 350, 353
soaked oat bran, 324

Break-away collars, 29

Breathing:
labored, 226
shallow and rapid, 226, 251, 255

Breeding, 136–37

Brewer's yeast. *See* Yeast

Bribe foods, 75–76, 83, 84

Broken bones, 418–19

Brushes, 162, 163, 183–85

Burdock root, 315

Burns, 315, 415–16

B vitamins. *See* Vitamin B complex

Calcium, 68, 73, 137, 257, 260, 305, 306, 316, 331, 345. *See also* Chicken Broth, High-Calcium

Calendula, 246, 280, 283, 315, 325, 411

Calicivirus, 242, 426

Campbell, Dr., 327

Camuti, Dr., 276

Cancer, 59, 84, 95, 136, 223, 315, 340. *See also* Feline AIDS; Feline leukemia
recommendations, 341–42

Cape Cod Clip, 197, 200–201

Caraway, 316

Carbohydrates, 403

Carbomates, 391

Cardiomyopathy:
recommendations, 343–44
symptoms of, 342–43

Carrot, 316, 349

Carry case, 31–34, 126–28

Cataracts, 355, 356. *See also* Blindness; Diabetes
causes of, 370–71
recommendations, 371
symptoms of, 371

Catch and Kill game, 18, 19, 49–50, 115
Cat Dancer toy, 51
Catheterization, 258
    feline urologic syndrome (FUS) and, 387
    nutritional support after, 246–47
"Cat Kiss," 10–11
Catnip, 52–53, 113, 115, 133–34, 188, 217, 310
    described, 316
Cayce, Edgar, 218
Cedar, 44
Celery seed, 316, 333, 335
Cellophane balls, 47, 52
Central nervous system, 259
Cesarean section births, 137
Chamomile, 370
Charcoal, 324, 325, 361
Chasing between cats, 41
Chemicals. See Poisonous substances
Chemotherapy, 237, 464
Cherry plum, 216, 313
Chicken Broth:
    High-Calcium, 309, 330, 335
    Homemade, 286, 308, 325
Chicken neck vertebrae, 79–80
Chicken Super Soup, 295, 309, 379, 484
Chickweed, 335
Children, 121–22
Chinese herbs, 213
Chiropractic, 211, 215
Chlorine bleach, 101, 102, 466
"Chlorodophilus solution," 293–96
Chlorophyll, 293, 323
Choline, 432
Choosing new cat, 37–38
Chromium, 344
Cigarette smoke, 223, 259, 343
Cirrhosis, 432
Citronella, 395
Claws and cuticles:
    biting, 222
    cleaning, 178, 284, 285, 364
    clipping, 176–78
    cuticle infection, 345
    declawed cats, 116–18, 228
    declawing procedure, 115–16, 345
    dirty cuticles, 176, 178, 222, 284, 285, 364
    nail abnormality, 344–45
    nail loss, 344–45
    play with cat and use of, 17–19
    recommendations, 346–47
    symptoms of problems, 346
    types of problems, 344–45
Clay litter, 94, 96–98

Cleaning compounds, 44, 433
    for litter box, 44, 102
Clematis, 216, 313, 314
Clumping litter, 94–96, 98, 101, 106
Coat, 225
    dry, 361–63
    matting of. See Matting fur
    oily, 156, 189, 351, 361, 449–51
    as reflection of diet, 55–56, 69, 156–58
Coccidia, 459–60
Cocoa, 217
Cod liver oil, 76, 90, 244, 245, 369, 372
Cold, extreme, 245, 259
Cold compresses, 297
Cold infusion, herb, 321
Collars, 29–30
Combing:
    after bathing, 195
    angle of comb, 169–70
    before bathing, 190
    "egg-beater technique," 169–70
    light, 166–76, 183
    order of, 167–76
Combs, 162–64, 439
    flea, 163, 270, 395
Comfrey, 316
Communication with cat, 9–13
    behavior patterns and, 16–19
    with deaf cat, 354
    Good-bye-I'll-be-back ritual, 34–36, 247
    introducing new cat, 38
    therapeutic. See Therapeutic communication
Compresses, 296–97, 409
Concussions, 417–18
Confusion, 250
Constipation, 222, 225, 226, 398. See also Irritable bowel syndrome (IBS)
    causes of, 347–48
    giving enemas, 292, 295–96
    prevention of, 349
    recommendations, 349–50
    symptoms of, 348–49
    treatment of, 246, 349–50
Copper band collar, 334
Corn-based litter, 94–97, 101, 106, 107
Corneal ulcer, 372
Cornmeal and cornstarch, 475
Cortisone and corticosteroids, 243, 244–45, 248, 333, 341, 381, 383, 420, 436–37, 451, 467, 478
Coughing, 223, 253, 254, 316, 343
Creatine, 226

Cuticles. *See* Claws and cuticles
Cuts, 315, 413–15
    soaking solution for healing, 283
Cystic ovaries, 136
Cystitis. *See* Feline urologic syndrome (FUS)

Dandelion root, 335
Dander. *See* Dandruff
Dandruff, 57, 124, 156, 189, 193, 282, 339
    causes of, 351
    recommendations, 352–53
    symptoms of, 352
Dangers in the home, 42–48
Deafness:
    causes of, 353
    recommendations, 354
    symptoms of, 353
de Bairacli Levy, Juliette, 454
Declawing, 18, 111, 121
    physical and emotional effects of, 115-118.
        See also Claws
    procedure, 115–16, 345
Decoction, herb, 296, 297, 321–22
Dehydration, 222, 225, 226, 251, 297–98, 303,
        341–42, 349, 359, 361, 428–29, 458, 470,
        481
Delicious Garlic Condiment, 307, 336, 350,
        367, 394
    recipe for, 318
Demodectic mites, 435, 436
Dental care. *See* Gums; Teeth
Deobstipation, 295
Deodorant sprays, for litter box, 102, 347, 433
Deodorizers, 45, 97, 223, 259, 383, 427, 433
Depression, 46, 222–23, 227, 245, 255, 333, 352
Detoxification, 254, 306, 351
Deworming slurry, 456
Diabetes, 84, 224–26, 297
    cataracts and, 370
    diet for, 318, 357–58
    insulin shock, 355
    recommendations, 356–57
    subcutaneous hydration and, 298, 356, 357
    symptoms of, 356
Diabetic coma, 355
Diarrhea, 46, 225, 253, 255, 348. *See also* Ir-
        ritable bowel syndrome (IBS)
    antibiotics and, 242–43
    herbs for, 319, 320
    kittens and, 358
    recommendations, 360–61
    subcutaneous hydration after, 298
    symptoms of, 359

Diet, 55–90. *See also specific ailments. See also*
        Feline health problems, guide to common
    acid-alkaline diet swing, 57, 307–8, 460
    additional acceptable foods, 80–82
    for aging cat, 89–90
    allergies and, 123–24
    amount to feed, 58, 82
    beneficial side effects of a high-quality,
        55–56, 85–86
    bribe foods, 75–76, 83, 84
    changing over to the new diet, 82–85
    chicken neck vertebrae, 79–80
    coat as reflection of, 55–56, 86
    dry cat food, 63–64, 351, 463, 478
    finicky eater syndrome, 57, 483
    foods to avoid, 59–66
    ham and pork, 65–66
    high-quality, 66–70, 156–58, 445–46
    while hospitalized, 248
    human, allergies and, 124, 125
    I'll-Do-Anything-for-My-Cat Diet, 70–76
    for kittens, 66, 86–89
    raw-food, 71–75, 328, 330, 339, 343
    reducing, 404, 446
    removing food between meals, 55, 56–59,
        69–70, 84, 156, 351
    semimoist food in packets, 64, 351, 383, 463
    supplements. *See* Supplements
    treats. *See* Treats
    tuna and other fish, 62, 64–65, 85
    variety in, 80–81
    vegetarian, 337, 371
Digestive enzymes, 76, 89–90, 451
Digestive process, 57
    herbs that help, 316, 319
    malabsorption of, 362, 432, 483–86
Digital thermometers, 291, 292, 326
Dill seed, 316
Dill seed tea, 344, 357
Diuretics, 243–44, 319, 342, 344
Diverticulosis, 348
Diveticulosis. *See also* Irritable bowel syn-
        drome (IBS)
Dr. Bronner's liquid castile soap, 190, 395
*Dr. Pitcairn's Complete Guide to Natural Health
    for Dogs and Cats* (Pitcairn), 259, 454
Dr. Pitcairn's Healing Ear Oil, 365
Dr. Pitcairn's Herbal Ear Mite Solution, 366
Dogs, 69, 95, 229
Drinking, copious, 224, 226, 243, 343, 349,
        355, 428
Dropper feeding. *See* Finger and dropper
        feeding

Droppers, 289–90, 325
Drugs. *See* Medications
Dry cat food, 35, 63–64, 463, 478
Dry coat, 361–63
    causes of, 361–62
    recommendations, 362–63
    symptoms of, 362
Dryers, 190–91, 194–96
Dry shampoo, 197
Dym, Dr. Michael, 140, 212, 232, 327

Ears:
    cleaning, 187–88, 278–82
    discharge from, 222, 363
    flushing, 159, 279–81, 354, 364, 366
    hearing, sense of, 42, 337
    infection, 324, 339
    inner ear problem, 364
    medications for, giving, 277–78
    mites, 224, 282, 339, 364–67
    pale, 226
    recommendations, 367–68
    symptoms of problems, 366–67
    wax buildup, 278–79, 345, 363
Echinacea, 272, 276, 316, 325, 331, 347, 370
Eco-friendly litters, 92, 97
Edema. *See* Fluid retention
Electrocardiogram, 227, 342
Elixirs, 315, 322
Elm, 23
Emergencies, 343, 358, 359, 408–19
Emotions, cat's sensitivity to human, 13–16,
        257–58. *See also* Stress
Endorphins, 214
Enemas, 156, 350
    giving, 292–96
Entropion, 373
Enzymatic cleaners, 109
Enzymes, feline digestive, 76, 305, 330, 335,
        346, 362
Epsom salts, 25, 283, 347
Ethoxyquin, 59–60, 61, 245, 258
Eucalyptus, oil of, 332, 395
Euthanasia, 137, 139, 244, 248–51, 298–99,
        341, 378, 387
Exercise, 48–50, 357. *See also* Play
    convalescing cat and, 259
    before meals, 49
Eyebright, 316, 326, 331, 370
Eyes:
    blindness. *See* Blindness
    cataracts. *See* Cataracts
    cleaning, 185–86, 269–70

conjunctive tissue, 223, 331
corneal ulcer, 372
discharge from, 224, 331, 368
entropion, 373
examining, 223–24
eye drops, giving, 270–75
eye medication (salve), giving, 275–76
infection, 223
protecting, when bathing, 191
taurine deficiency, 337, 371
tear ducts, 185, 269, 270–75, 368
washing, 269–70, 371–73

Fabric softener, 44–45, 223, 304
Fading kitten syndrome, 298
Fasting, 56, 84, 286, 287, 330, 334, 360, 370,
        388, 454, 455
Fats, in food, 65–66, 73, 86, 361–62, 445, 446
Fear, 16, 193, 196, 215–16, 226, 228, 245, 249
    biting and, 20–22, 26
Feeding. *See* Diet
Feet. *See* Claws and cuticles
Feline acne, 282, 356
    recommendations, 375–76
    symptoms of, 374
Feline AIDS (feline immunodeficiency virus),
        329
    diagnosis of, 380–81
    recommendations, 382–84
    symptoms of, 382
Feline digestive enzymes, 76, 305, 330, 335,
        346, 362
Feline health problems, guide to common,
        327–487
    allergies, 328–32
    arthritis, 332–36
    blindness, 336–38
    body odors, 338–40
    cancer, 340–42
    cardiomyopathy, 342–44
    claw and cuticle problems, 344–47
    constipation, 347–50
    dandruff, 351–53
    deafness, 353–54
    diabetes, 354–58
    diarrhea, 358–61
    dry coat, 361–63
    ear problems, 363–68
    eye problems, 368–73
    feline acne, 374–76
    feline infectious peritonitis (FIP), 376–80
    feline leukemia and feline AIDS, 380–84
    feline urologic syndrome (FUS), 384–90

Feline health problems (*cont.*)
  fleas, 390–97
  hair balls, 397–98
  hyperthyroidism, 399–403
  hypoglycemia, 403–6
  hypothyroidism, 406–7
  injuries, 408–19
  irritable bowel syndrome (IBS), 420–23
  kidney disease, 426–32
  liver disease and damage, 432–35
  mange mites, 435–38
  matting fur, 438–40
  nervousness, hiding, and ill temper, 441–44
  obesity, 444–48
  oily coat, 449–51
  pancreatitis, 452–53
  parasites, 453–60
  respiratory infections, 460–62
  ringworm, 462–66
  skin problems, 466–70
  starvation, 470–74
  stud tail, 474–76
  teeth and gums, 477–81
  vomiting, 481–82
  weight loss, 482–86
Feline infectious peritonitis (FIP), 329
  diagnosis of, 376–77
  dry and wet form of, 377
  recommendations, 378–79
  symptoms of, 377, 378
Feline leukemia, 38, 329
  diagnosis of, 380–81
  recommendations, 382–84
  symptoms of, 382
Feline urologic syndrome (FUS), 5, 57, 71, 384, 423
  dry cat food and, 63
  recommendations, 388–90
  stress and, 14–15, 256
  symptoms of, 224, 385–86, 388
  yeast and, 76
Feliway, 108
Felix Fine Ground Catnip, 52
Felix Katnip Tree, 51, 112
Fennugreek seed, 316
Feral cats, 10, 107, 143–54
  colonies, 145–45
  difference between strays and ferals, 144–46
  kittens, 150–53
  TNR (Trap-Neuter-Return) movement, 142, 143, 146
Fertilizers, chemical, 77
Fever, 253, 298, 377, 378

Feverfew, 335
Fiber, dietary, 225
"Fight and win" games, 18
Fighting, by unneutered males, 136, 147
Find Toto, 30
Finger and dropper feeding, 268, 286
  baby food recipe, 287
  of liquid food, 289–90
  of solid food, 288
Finger grooming, 164–65
Finicky eater syndrome, 57, 483
Fish, 64–65, 85
  and Oat Food, 457
  tuna, 62, 65, 85, 268
Flatulence, 225, 316, 361
Flea collars, 5, 259, 319, 381, 396
Fleas, 224, 352, 362, 438–39, 454
  garlic and, 317, 394
  how to check for, 390
  treatment of, 323, 391–97
Flea sprays, 381, 391–92
Fleet enema, 292
Flower essences. *See* Bach flower remedies
Flowers, poisonous, 45–46
Fluid retention, 226, 243–44, 343
Fluids, subcutaneous. *See* Hydration, subcutaneous
Food. *See* Diet
Food herbs, 217
Foods, toxic, 46–47
Foot-soaking procedure and solutions, 283–85, 347
Force feeding. *See* Finger feeding
Fractures, 418–19
Freeze-dried cat food, 66, 67
Frozen cat food, 66, 67
Fulvacin (gresiofulvin), 463–64
Fungicides, 330
Fungus, 280, 329, 347, 362, 462–66

Game playing. *See* Play
Gangrene, 355
Garlic, 217, 233, 315, 325, 460
  benefits of, 317
  Delicious Garlic Condiment, 307, 318, 336, 350, 367, 394
  given as a pill, 317
Gas. *See* Flatulence
Genitals, licking, 224
Gil, Dr. Alberto, 212, 232, 327
Ginseng, 318
Goldenseal, 217, 272, 276, 280, 283, 315, 318, 326

Good-bye-I'll-be-back ritual, 34–36, 247
Gorse, 216
Green Magma, 76, 90, 124, 243, 244, 293, 323, 335, 358, 360
Green tea litter, 98
Gresiofulvin, 463–64
Grooming, 4, 155–203, 363–64. *See also* Matting fur
  area set aside for, 160
  the bath, 189–97
  Cape Cod Clip, 197, 200–201
  by cats, 155–56
  cleaning ears, 187–88
  cleaning eyes, 185–86
  clipping claws, 176–78
  conditioning cat to, 160–61
  daily, 159, 161, 188
  diet and coat, 156–58
  examining teeth and gums, 186–87
  final comb-out for longhaired cats, 183
  finding a groomer, 158–59
  finger grooming, 164–65
  flea problem and, 395–96
  light combing, 166–76, 183
  location for, 160
  music for, 161
  procedure for, 164–88
  in seasonal and stress situations, 155–56, 197–203
  shavers, 158, 161–62
  slicker brush for shorthaired cats, 183–85
  Teddy Clip, 197, 199, 201–3
  tools for, 160, 162–64
Growling and screaming, 40
Gums, 241
  bluish, 342
  examining teeth and, 186–87
  painful, 187, 222
  pale, 226

Hahnemann, Dr. Samuel, 211–12
Hair. *See* Coat
Hair balls, 156, 221–22, 246, 350, 352, 359, 397
  recommendations, 398–99
  symptoms of, 398
Halo Herbal Ear Wash, 279, 364
Ham, 65–66
Head:
  mites, 282
  scratching, with hind feet, 224, 363, 366
  shaking, 224, 255, 363, 366
  tilting, 255, 363, 366
Healing touch, 211

Health-food brands of cat food, 66–67, 83
Health log, 238
Health problems. *See* Feline health problems, guide to common
Hearing:. *See also* Ears
  sense of, 42, 337
Heart:
  cardiomyopathy. *See* Cardiomyopathy
  lesions, 71
  problems, 223, 226, 254
Heat, 226, 245
  extreme, 259
  providing, 233, 247–48, 306
  seeking, 223
Heather, 216
Hemlock, 217
Hepatitis, 71, 315, 432
Herbs, 211, 213, 214, 216–17, 314–23, 3325–26. *See also* Feline health problems, guide to common; *specific herbs and illnesses*
Hiding, 223, 228, 441–44
High-Calcium Chicken Broth, 309, 330, 335
High-quality diet, 66–70, 156–58
Hippocrates, 217
Hissing, 11, 20, 40, 41
Histidine, 371
Holistic professionals, 232–34, 236–47, 492–94. *See also* Home nursing and health care
Holly, 216
Homemade cat food, 67
Homemade Chicken Broth, 286, 308, 325
Home nursing and health care, 253–326
  administering eyedrops and irrigating tear ducts, 269, 270–75
  administering medications, 260–62
  applying salve to eyes, 275–76
  Bach flower remedies, 313–14
  cleaning around eyes, 269–70
  compresses, 296–97
  ear cleaning and treatment, 278–82
  fasting, 286
  finger/dropper feeding, 286–90
  giving ear medication, 277–78
  giving enemas, 292–96
  giving liquid medication, 268
  giving nose drops, 276
  giving paste or gel medication, 268
  giving pills, 266–68
  herbs, 314–23
  homeopathic remedies, 309–13
  immune system, 253–55
  recipes, formulas, and extras for, 304–9

Home nursing and health care (*cont.*)
  shopping list for, 324–26
  soaking feet and cleaning cuticles, 282–85
  stress, 255–60
  subcutaneous hydration, 297–304
  taking temperature, 290–92
  therapeutic communication, 262–63
  wrapping cat for medication, 263–66
Homeopathy, 188, 211–14. *See also specific*
  ailments
  administering drops, 313
  administering pills, 310–12
  cautions for handling homeopathic rem-
    edies, 309–10
Hookworm, 458–59
Hormones, injected in meat and poultry, 70
Horsetail, 315, 318
Hospitalization, 6, 228, 233, 247–48
Hot compresses, 296, 409
Hotels, staying at, 130
"Hugging," 13
Humane Society of the United States, 116,
  143
Hydration, subcutaneous, 207–9, 251, 295,
  297, 341–42, 350, 356, 361, 421, 428–29
  procedure, 300–303
  questions about, 303–4
  setting up equipment, 299–300
  uses for, 298–99
Hydrogen peroxide, 25, 414
Hyperthyroidism, 23, 84, 225, 226, 241, 297,
  298, 362
  diagnosis of, 400
  recommendations, 402–3
  symptoms of, 400, 402
  treatments for, 400–401
Hypoglycemia:
  diet and, 403–4
  recommendations, 404–5
  symptoms of, 404
Hypothermia, 230–31, 247
Hypothyroidism:
  recommendations, 406–7
  symptoms of, 406

Identification tags, 29–30
I'll-Do-Anything-for-My-Cat Diet, 70–74
  recipe for, 74–75
Immune system, 95. *See also* Autoimmune
  diseases; Cortisone
  allergies and, 328–29
  dangerous conditions, 254–55
  homeopathy and, 211–12, 254

steroids' suppression of, 227, 244
  tranquilizers and, 129
  vaccinations and, 139, 241, 328, 377, 381,
    436, 479
Immunization. *See* Vaccinations
Impatiens, 216, 313
Inbreeding, 328, 368
Incision, healing, 246–47
Infections, 222, 259, 303, 347. *See also location*
  of specific infections
  repeated, 227, 356
  supplements for, 306
Information sources, on holistic medicine,
  239–40
Infusion, herb, 296, 321
Ingrown nails, 345, 347, 441
Injuries, 408–19
Insulin, 303, 354–57, 403–4, 451
Insulin shock, 355
Interspecies communications, 6, 13, 205–9,
  211
Intestines, 124, 315, 316, 319, 323, 351, 360. *See*
  also Irritable bowel syndrome (IBS)
  blockage of, 94–95, 156
Introducing new cat, 37–42
Iodine, 400, 401, 406
Irrigating ears and abscesses, 280–82, 410–11
  formulas for, 280
Irrigating tear ducts, 269, 270–75, 371
Irritable bowel syndrome (IBS), 71, 77, 94,
  124, 225, 241, 297, 329. *See also* Diarrhea
  recommendations, 421–23
  symptoms of, 421
Irritations, soaking solution for, 283
It's a Cat's Life (Frazier and Eckroate), 105,
  106, 251

Jekyll and Hyde biting, 20–21, 22
Juvenile neutering, 138–41, 149

Karate Kat Ultimate Scratching Post, 112
Keflex, 243
Kelp, 68, 83, 330
Khury, Samantha, 206–7
Kidney problems, 47, 60, 77, 223–26, 242, 254,
  297, 298, 318, 339, 351
  diet and, 299, 427–28, 431–32
  failure, 255
  herbs for, 318
  recommendations, 430–31
  symptoms of, 426, 429–30
  vaccinations and, 426–27
Kidneys, function of, 426

Kidney stones, 423–26. *See also* Feline urologic syndrome (FUS)
Kirk's Current Veterinary Therapy, 241
Kittens, 37
　diarrhea and, 358
　diet for, 66, 86–89
　feral, 150–53
　litter box training, 104–6
　nursing formula, 88
　play of, 18, 19
　problems in birth of, 137
　unwanted, 137–38
　waste of, 104–5
　weaning of, 89
Kitty Go Crazy Interactive Cat Toy, 51
Kitty grass, 78–79
Kombu broth, 243, 307, 318
KoogaTAG, 29–30
Kortis, Bryan, 144

Laboratory use, cats for, 137
Larch, 23
Lasix, 243, 344
Laxatives, 77, 156, 246, 292, 348, 350
Leave-taking ritual, 34–36, 247
Leba III dental spray, 480
Lecithin, 67, 68, 124, 198, 330, 331, 340, 352, 367
Lemon juice, 340, 353
Lemon rinse, 324, 331, 395, 438
Leukemia, feline. *See* Feline leukemia
Licking, as sign of affection, 12, 261
Liquid medications, administering, 268
　homeopathic, 313
Litter box, 91–110
　checking stool, 99, 102–3
　cleaning, 101–2
　easy, convenient, and effective system,
　　99–101
　feline urologic syndrome (FUS) and,
　　386–87
　nervousness and condition of, 259, 442
　older or ailing cat and, 107, 110
　overview of popular, 97–99
　as problem, 91–93
　requirements for, 93
　soiling outside, 104, 106–8, 386
　solution for cleaning, 44, 102
　training kittens to use, 104–6
　types of litter, 94–99
　when visiting new place, 130
Liver, function of, 432
Liver disease and damage, 44, 227, 254, 255,
　400, 404

　recommendations, 433–35
　symptoms of, 433
Liver tablets, 264
Loneliness, 77, 132, 133
Low blood sugar. *See* Hypoglycemia
Lungs, problems of, 316, 460, 462
Lysol, 44, 347, 427

Magnesium, 85, 385, 432
Malabsorption, 362, 432, 483–86
Mammary glands, 136
Mange mites, 224, 352, 362, 435–38
Marigold, 217
Marijuana, 217
Mating, 135–37, 147
Mat splitter, 162
Matting fur, 340. *See also* Grooming
　breaking up soft mats, 182–83
　cutting out mat, 159, 178–79, 181–82,
　　197–98
　recommendations, 439–40
　shaving mats, 159, 182
　splitting mats, 180–81
　symptoms of, 439
　technique for getting rid of, 178–83
McGargle, Dr. P.F., 61
Meat by-products, 61–62, 424, 445
Meats, for raw food diet, 71–73
Medications:
　administering, 260–62
　ear, giving, 277–78
　eye, giving, 275–76
　irrigating ears or abscesses, 280–82, 410–11
　liquid, giving, 268
　paste or gel (the Pâté method), giving, 268
　pills, giving, 266–68
　side effects of, 254
　thyroid-inhibiting, 401
　wrapping cat to give, 263–65
Medicinal herbs, 217
Melamine, 59, 60
Mercury, 65, 85, 291
Meridian lines, 214
Metabolism:
　fast, 86, 399, 401
　slow, 57, 156, 189, 332, 338, 351, 391, 406
Metamucil, 350
Methionine, 385, 424, 429
Methmazole, 401, 403
Methoprene, 397
Methylmercury, 65
Microwave ovens, 74, 473
Mimulus, 23, 216

Mineral oil, 65, 77–78, 188, 246, 292
Minerals, 330, 344, 360. *See also* Feline health
    problems, guide to common; *specific
    minerals*; Supplements
    trace, 331
Miscarriage, 119
Mites:
    ear, 224, 282, 339, 364–67
    head, 283
    mange, 224, 352, 362, 435–38
Moth balls, 44, 433, 441
Mouth, scratching, with claws, 224. *See also*
    Gums; Teeth
Moving to new home, 130–31, 258. *See also*
    Travel
Moxibustion, 214
MRI (magnetic resonance imaging), 227
Mucus, 253, 254, 271, 316
Mugwort, 214
Multivitamins, 67, 68, 75–77, 86, 246, 305, 336,
    358
Music, for calming, 161, 229

Nail clippers, 176–77
Nails. *See* Claws and cuticles
National Feral Cat Summit, 146
Natural Animal Coat Enhancer, 197, 331, 340,
    392, 395, 396, 438
Natural Cat Treat, Anitra's, 75, 264
Nausea, 222, 226, 254
Needle, for subcutaneous hydration, 297,
    299, 301, 302
Neighborhood Cats, 143, 144, 149, 153
Nervousness, 117, 129, 161, 441–44. *See also*
    Fear
Nettle, 319
Neutering, 135–42, 260
    juvenile, 138–41, 149
    procedure, 141–42
    proper time for, 138–41
    undesirable behavior of unneutered male,
        107, 135–36, 147
New cat:
    choosing, 37–38
    introducing, 37–42
New places, visiting, 129–31
Newspaper-based litter, 98–99
Nitrates and nitrites, 61, 66, 245, 259, 433
Noise, loud, 77, 255, 257, 259
Normal Saline Solution, 271, 272
Nose:
    polyps, 223
    stuffy, 331
    tumor, 223
Nose drops, 233, 287
    administering, 276
    formulas for, 276
Nosodes, 242
Nu-Cat, 67, 75, 305, 306, 336
Nursing formula for kittens, 88
Nu-Salt, 243
Nutraceuticals, 211
Nutrition, 211, 214, 231. *See also* Diet

Oak, 344
Obesity, 57, 84, 339, 355
    causes of, 444–45
    diet and, 445–47
    recommendations, 448
    symptoms of, 447
Odors. *See* Body odors; Smells
Oil-soluble nutrients, 77
Oily coat, 156, 189, 351, 361, 449–51
Old cat. *See* Aging cat
Opiates, 214
Organophosphates, 391
Osteoarthritis, 332

Pain, 226, 249, 260
Pancreas, 355, 356, 403–4. *See also* Diabetes
    functions of, 451
Pancreatitis, 241, 451
    diet for, 453
    recommendations, 452–53
    symptoms of, 452
Panleukopenia, 242
Panting, 254
Pantothenic, 305
Parasites, 38, 71, 95, 224, 225, 307, 347, 359,
    453–60. *See also specific parasites*
Parsley, 217, 319
Parsley tea, 76, 344, 358
Pâté method, 268
Pennyroyal, 319
Peppermint, 310
Peritonitis, feline infectious. *See* Feline infec-
    tious peritonitis (FIP)
Persian cats, 55, 93, 97, 137, 138, 164, 194,
    198–203, 269, 270, 368
Pesticides, 70, 330
Pet Allergies: Remedies for an Epidemic (Plech-
    ner), 64, 328
Petco Foundation, 143
PetGuard, 52, 61, 63–65, 72, 75, 78, 143, 188,
    264
Petroleum jelly, 291, 293, 294, 326, 350

PetSmart Charities, 143
Phenol, 44, 427, 441
Phenylalanine, 371
Phillips, Dr. Tom, 241
Phosphorus, 73, 316, 385
Picking up a cat, 27–28
    by veterinarian, 231, 233, 234
Pick up Put down game, 28, 34, 152
Pills:
    garlic given as, 317
    giving homeopathic remedies, 310–12
    giving medications, 266–68
Pitcairn, Dr. Richard, 60, 80, 212, 213, 232,
        233, 236–37, 241, 328, 364–66, 381, 387,
        409, 410, 467, 479
Plank game, 48–49
Plantain, 319
Plants, poisonous, 45–46
Play, 48–50. See also Exercise
    ritual in, 28, 52
    rough, 17–19
    sexual, 142
Plechner, Dr. Alfred, 61, 64, 328
Pliny the Elder, 216
Pneumonia, 220–21, 223
Poison herbs, 217
Poisoning, 255, 359
Poisonous substances, 44–47. See also Artifi-
    cial colors; Artificial flavors
Pork, 65–66
Potassium, 243, 316, 319
Potassium chloride (salt substitute), 83, 358
Pottenger, Dr. Francis M., 71, 242, 328
Poultice, herb, 319, 323
Prednizone, 420
Pregnant women, toxoplasmosis and, 120
Premise Spray, 393
Preservatives, 59, 64, 66, 71, 77, 258–59, 332,
        433, 441, 445
Product recommendations, 489–91
Propranalol, 401
Propylgallate, 61, 433
Protein, 71, 90, 385
    quality of, in cat food, 62, 427–28
Psyllium, 213, 217, 220, 246, 295, 319, 325,
        330, 331, 336, 349, 350
Puncture wounds, 136, 408–9
    soaking solution for, 283
Purring, constant, 251
Pus, 41, 253, 409–11, 414
Pyrethrins, 393, 397

Queen's milk, powdered, 87, 88

Rabies vaccine, 23, 241
Radioactive iodine therapy, 401
Random wetting, 106–8, 386
Rashes. See Skin problems
Raw-food diet, 71–74. See also Feline health
        problems, guide to common
    recipe for, 74–76
Reiki, 211
Repellant sprays, 108
Resco combs, 163–64, 313
Rescue Remedy, 216, 259, 325, 332
Respiratory infections, 223, 233, 356
    recommendations, 461–62
    symptoms of, 460–61
Retinitis, 355
Rheumatoid arthritis, 332
Rhinotracheitis, 242, 426
Ringer's lactate solution, 299, 341, 350, 356,
        421
Ringworm, 224, 282, 315, 316, 318, 345, 347,
        352, 362
    recommendations, 464–66
    soaking solution for, 283
    symptoms of, 464
Roach traps, 45
Rock rose, 216, 313
Rosemary, 319
Roundworms, 223, 316, 454–58
Rowan, Dr. Paul, 4, 5, 53, 55, 79, 92, 141, 229,
        230, 267
Rue, 217, 319, 366, 455, 456
Runny-eye syndrome, 269, 460

Safers Insecticidal Soap, 397
Salivating, 254
Salt (sodium), 97, 226, 243, 244, 260, 316, 326,
        445
    diet low in, 83
    saline solution, 25, 271, 276
    substitute, 83, 358
Sarcoptic mites, 435
Scabs, 225, 246, 413
Scanner-microchip systems, 30
Schultz, Dr. Ronald, 241
Scissors, 162
    to get rid of mats, 179–82
"Scooting" on rugs, 224
Scratching. See Claws and cuticles; Scratching
        post
Scratching post, 111–18, 346
    encouraging use of, 17, 114–15
    positioning of, 114
    selection of, 111–13

Screens, window, 44
Sea salt, 326
Seasonal grooming. *See* Grooming
Second cat. *See* New cat
Second opinion, 235–36
Selenium, 344
Semimoist food in packets, 64, 351, 383
Sex hormones, 139
Sexual maturity, 138–41
Shampoo, 190, 191, 319
    dry, 197
    flea, 197
Shavers, 158, 161–62
Shedding. *See* Grooming
Shiatsu, 214
Shock. *See* Stress
Shopping list, of home-nursing remedies,
    324–26
Siamese, 368
Siblin, 350
Sick cats. *See specific ailments*
Silica, 318, 345
Silica clay litter, 94–96, 98
Silica gel litter, 99
Sitters, 132–34, 198
Skinniness, 57
Skin problems, 329. *See also* Coat; *specific skin
    problems*
    causes of, 466–68
    recommendations, 469–70
    symptoms of, 468
    twitching, 225
Sleeping, excessive, 222
Slicker brush, 183–85
Slippery elm, 213, 217, 319, 325
    syrup recipe, 320
Smart Cat's Ultimate Scratching Post, 112
Smell, sense of, 42, 57, 255, 262, 337, 442
Smells:. *See also* Body odors
    bad, from cat, 187, 225
    sharp, 259
Sneezing, 223
Snug retreat, 106, 130, 133, 257, 259, 306, 325,
    326, 341, 343, 356, 383, 387
    how to assemble, 304
Sodium. *See* Salt (sodium)
Sodium ascorbate. *See* Vitamin C
Sodium bentonite, 94–96, 98
Sodium benzoate, 77, 245, 246, 258, 433
Spaying, 135
    proper time for, 138–41
    undesirable behavior of unspayed female,
        136–37

Spraying, by unaltered males, 135–36
Spring water, 343, 379, 383, 428
Star of Bethlehem, 216, 313
Starvation:
    recommendations, 472–74
    subcutaneous hydration and, 298
    symptoms of, 471
Steatitis, 65
Steroids, 77, 227, 237, 244–45, 248, 310, 329,
        366, 381, 383, 420, 467
Stevia, 320, 355–56, 357
Stomach, 316, 319
Stool:. *See also* Constipation; Diarrhea; Litter
        box
    changing color, 255
    checking, 99, 102–3, 225
    conditioner, 319
    enemas, 292–96
    health problems indicated by, 225
    impacted, 295
    normal, 225, 348
    soiling coat, 259, 339
    toxoplasmosis transmitted by, 119–20
Stool Softener Treat, 349
Strays, difference between ferals and, 144–46
Stress, 14–15, 108, 130, 226
    absence of humans and, 132–33
    antistress supplements, 129, 132, 245–46,
        257, 305, 367
    arthritis and, 332
    declawing and, 116
    diabetes and, 355
    disease and, 14–15, 255–56
    factors in, 257–60
    hospitalization and, 228–29
    skin problems and, 468
    stress target, 256
Stress reduction techniques, 211
Stroking, 9–10, 167–69
Stud tail, 474–76
Stumbling, 224, 255, 366
Subcutaneous hydration. *See* Hydration,
        subcutaneous
Subluxations, 215
Sugar, 226, 320, 403–4, 445
    in urine, 355, 356
Supplements:. *See also* Feline health problems,
        guide to common; *specific supplements*
    antistress, 129, 132, 245–46, 257, 305, 367
    for infections and wounds, 306
    reasons for needing, 76–77
Surgery, 213–14, 237, 258
    for entropion, 373

herbs and, 319
for hyperthyroidism, 400–401
nutritional support after, 246–47
subcutaneous hydration after, 298
urethrostomy, 5, 387
Surveillance theory, 381
Swallowing, repeatedly, 222, 254
Sweet chestnut, 314
Swelling, 244, 245, 253, 255
soaking solution for, 283
Symptoms checklist, 221–26, 238–39
Syringes, 289, 326

Tabby Tabs, 67, 75, 305, 306, 336
Tail:
body language of, 12
grooming and, 172, 176
stud tail, 474–76
Tapazol (methmazole), 401, 403
Tapeworm, 454–58
Tartar, on teeth, 63, 159, 186–87, 260, 477
Taurine, 59, 60, 337, 371
Tear ducts, 185, 269, 270–75, 368, 371
Tea tree oil, 217
Teddy Clip, 197, 199, 201–3
Teeth, 224, 477–81
cleaning of, 187, 339, 480
dirty, smell from, 187, 225, 338
dry food and, 63, 478
examining gums and, 186–87
tartar, 63, 159, 186–87, 260, 474
Telazol, 249–50
Tellington TTouch, 211
Temperament, 85–86
Temperature of cat, 225–26, 231, 251
fever, 253, 298, 377, 378
taking, 290–92
Therapeutic communication, 258, 262–63,
273, 280, 285, 290, 293, 296, 301, 310
Thermometers, 291–92, 326
Thyroid, 399–400, 406. See also Hyperthyroid-
ism; Hypothyroidism
Thyroxin, 226, 399, 400, 406
Tinctures, herb, 321, 322
TNR (Trap-Neuter-Return) movement, 142,
143, 146
Tongue:
bluish, 342, 343
pale, 226
Touching your cat, 9–10
Toxoplasmosis, 119–20
Toys:
dangerous, 47, 52

play with, 21, 23
safe, 48, 51–52
Trace minerals, 331
Traditional Chinese Medicine (TCM), 214
Training, 16
abused and nervous cats, 26
kittens, 18, 19, 104–6
Train travel, 127
Tranquilizers, 129, 230
for grooming, 158
natural, 320
Travel:. See also Carry case
air, 126–29
care for your cat, 131–34
leave-taking ritual, 36
train and bus, 127
with your cat, 126–29
Treats, 58–59, 78–80
Tree House Animal Foundation, 48
Tri-iodothyroxine, 399
Tumors, 223, 226, 237, 241, 341. See also Can-
cer; specific parts of the body
Tuna, 62, 65, 85, 268
Twinco slicker brush, 185
Twitching skin, 225
Tylan, 420

Ulcers, 319, 373
Urethrostomy, 5, 387
Urinary infection, 110
Urine and urinary habits:. See also Feline urologic syndrome (FUS); Kidney problems;
Litter box
acidic, 63, 97, 385, 424, 425, 430
alkaline, 63, 97, 385, 424
blood in urine, 224, 385, 386, 423
changes in, 255
diabetes, 355, 356
problems indicated by, 224–25
random wetting problem, 106–8, 386
removing odor, 106, 109
spraying by unaltered males, 135–36
Uterus, 136

Vacations:
care for your cat, 131–34, 198–99
leave-taking ritual for, 36
taking cat along, 126–29
Vaccinations, 23, 139. See also Immune system
booster shots, 140, 241, 332, 381
kidney problems and, 426–27
multiple, 241, 242, 328, 377, 381, 420, 436,
441, 479

Index

Vaccinations (*cont.*)
  rabies, 23, 241
  starvation and, 471
  vaccinosis, 241, 441, 479
Valerian, 129, 320, 418
Vegetable oil, 65, 73
Vegetables, 73–75, 80–81, 90, 353
Vegetarian diet, 337, 371
Veterinarian:
  annual examination by, 230
  checklist of symptoms, 221–26, 238–39
  choosing, 231–34
  euthanasia, 244, 248–51
  holistic, 236–40
  holistic perspective on conventional treatments, 240–47
  hospitalization, 228, 233, 247–48
  repeated infections, 227
  second opinion, 235–36
  therapeutic environment, 228–31
  visiting rights policy, 234
  when to seek help of, 219–27
Veterinary homeopaths, 212–14, 232–34, 236–47
Veterinary prescription foods, 66
Vine, 350
Vinegar, 109
Vinegar solution, white, 324
Visiting new place, 129–31
Visiting rights policy of veterinarian, 234
Visitors in home, 122–23, 258
Visualization, 6, 35–36, 217–19, 285, 411
Vitamin A, 67, 68, 76, 77, 89, 244, 246, 257, 260, 305, 306, 319, 326
Vitamin B-2, 305
Vitamin B-6, 356, 451
Vitamin B-complex, 76, 77, 90, 132, 243, 244, 257, 319
Vitamin C, 77, 90, 132, 233, 243–45, 257, 305–7, 319, 326, 460
Vitamin D, 67, 68, 76, 77, 89, 137, 246, 257, 260, 305–7, 326
Vitamin E, 67, 68, 77, 89, 188, 246–47, 305–7, 326
  deficiency, 65, 225, 400
Vita-Mineral Mix, 69, 75, 90, 132, 156, 157, 198, 243, 305, 306. *See also* Feline health problems, guide to common
  recipe for, 68
Vitamin supplements. *See* Feline health problems, guide to common; Supplements; *specific vitamins*

Vomiting, 46, 78, 156, 221–22, 253, 288, 319, 359. *See also* Hair balls
  recommendations, 482
  symptoms of, 481

Wall, sitting facing, 222–23
Warmth, providing, 304, 341, 343, 356, 383, 387, 472. *See also* Heat; Snug retreat
Warts, 241
Water, 326, 330, 343, 379, 383, 428. *See also* Fluid retention; Hydration, subcutaneous
Water-soluble nutrients, 77, 243, 246, 306, 355
Water violet, 314
Wax-O-Sol, 279, 285, 365
Weaning, 86
  recipe, 89
Weight gain, 334, 356. *See also* Obesity
Weight loss, from illness, 356, 482–86
Weight reduction, 343
Wheat-based litter, 97
Wheat grass, 78
White vinegar solution, 324, 364
Windows, 43–44, 122, 123, 417
Witch hazel, 279, 366
Withdrawing, 222–23
Wood-based litter, 98
World's Best Cat Litter, 94, 96
Worming, 319, 323
  herbal procedure, 456
Worms, 225. *See also* Parasites; *specific types of worms*
Wormwood, 217, 320, 455, 456
Wounds, 258
  herbs for, 319
  puncture, 136, 408–9
  soaking solution for, 25, 283
  supplements for, 306
Wrapping cat, for medical care, 263–65

Xanthic acid, 356
X rays, 77, 227, 245, 258, 342

Yarn, dangers of, 47
Yeast, 55, 67, 68, 76, 83, 157
Yeast infections, 95, 324
Yogurt, 323

Zinc, 336, 344